PLACE NAMES OF ATLANTIC CANADA

Windows on the history and culture of the region, the toponyms of Atlantic Canada have attracted attention and interest for centuries. Almost a millennium has passed since the Norse first landed in Vinland, but even earlier the Amerindian and Inuit people bestowed their own place names on Atlantic Canada. Many of these have survived not only the centuries and a variety of translations but also several attempts at cultural assimilation. There followed names from Basque, Portuguese, French, British, and other sources.

Information about the evolution of place names is never static; new archaeological, historical, and linguistic sources are always being discovered. In *Place Names of Atlantic Canada*, William B. Hamilton provides a wide-ranging overview of the origin and meaning of hundreds of regional place names to reveal the colourful history of the area.

Some element of selectivity was needed in the compilation of the book; there are currently 62,880 officially approved Atlantic Canadian place names recorded by the Canadian Permanent Committee on Geographical Names. In Newfoundland alone more than 200 distinct features incorporate the word 'Green.' Hamilton concentrates on three broad categories; size – the major centres of population and most important physical features; history – those locations that have had an impact on the evolution of the Atlantic region; and human interest – those place names most likely to provoke the question 'Where did they get *that* name?'

Based on archival research supplemented by field studies, *Place Names of Atlantic Canada* is the first volume to approach this topic from a regional perspective. Hundreds of cross references lead the reader to related information in all four provinces. The book also breaks new ground in tracing the evolution of names of important undersea features on the Grand Banks and off the Nova Scotia coastline.

An ideal reference book with more than 2,000 entries arranged alphabetically by province and aided by five maps, *Place Names of Atlantic Canada* will appeal to anyone interested in place naming in general and in the culture and social history of Atlantic Canada.

WILLIAM B. HAMILTON is professor emeritus in the Faculty of Social Sciences at Mount Allison University. A former chair of the Toponymic Research Committee of the Canadian Permanent Committee on Geographical Names, he has written extensively on place names. His books include *Local History in Atlantic Canada* and *The Macmillan Book of Canadian Place Names*.

WILLIAM B. HAMILTON

Place Names
of Atlantic Canada

UNIVERSITY OF TORONTO PRESS
Toronto Buffalo London

© University of Toronto Press Incorporated 1996
Toronto Buffalo London

Printed in Canada

ISBN 0-8020-0471-7 (cloth)
ISBN 0-8020-7570-3 (paper)

∞

Printed on acid-free paper

Canadian Cataloguing in Publication Data

Hamilton, William B. (William Baillie), 1930–
  Place names of Atlantic Canada

  Includes bibliographical references.
  ISBN 0-8020-0471-7 (bound)   ISBN 0-8020-7570-3 (pbk.)

  1. Names, Geographical – Atlantic Provinces.
  I. Title.

  FC2002.H35 1996   917.15′003   C96-930845-0
  F1035.8.H35 1996

University of Toronto Press acknowledges the financial assistance to its publishing program of the Canada Council and the Ontario Arts Council.

Contents

Maps appear on pages 14, 42, 152–3, 280, and 424.

Preface

In 1794–5 an able seaman in the Royal Navy, Aaron Thomas, spent several months cruising Newfoundland waters aboard the frigate HMS *Boston*. He kept a detailed journal of his travels, which remains, after the passage of two centuries, a vivid portrayal of local life and lore. In an age when most ranks 'below decks' were illiterate, Thomas displayed evidence of a good education, and a keen eye for the off-beat incident and for what he described as the 'whimsical.' High on the list of the latter were place names. This interest led him to search out unusual examples and to speculate on their meaning and origin. Thus, in a very real sense, the *Newfoundland Journal* of Aaron Thomas was the first in a long line of books to touch on the toponymy of the region.

Since Thomas, numerous others have mined the place-name lode of Atlantic Canada. Individuals such as Howley and Seary, in Newfoundland; Brown and Fergusson, in Nova Scotia; Ganong and Rayburn, in New Brunswick; and Douglas and Rayburn (again), in Prince Edward Island, are among those who have made noteworthy contributions to the understanding of regional place names. However, each generation, while benefiting from what has gone before, must recognize that information concerning the evolution of place names is ever changing. New archaeological, historical, and linguistic discoveries are constantly being made, and previously lost documents, maps, and records being uncovered; revised interpretations inevitably result. Perhaps the most significant example may be the recent research relating to the sixteenth-century Basque presence in Atlantic Canada. Thanks to the work of Selma de Lothbinière Barkham, we are now able to pinpoint with some accuracy the not inconsiderable Basque contribution to the toponymy of Atlantic Canada.

It is inevitable that the process of compiling any work of this kind must be brutally selective. To put the matter in context, it is worth recording that, at the time of writing, there were 62,880 officially approved Atlantic Canadian place names on the computer list maintained by the Canadian Permanent Committee on Geographical Names (CPCGN). The vast majority of these names are descriptive in nature, and many are repetitious. To illustrate: in Newfoundland and Labrador there are more than 200 distinct features that incorporate 'Green,' including 20 with the name Green Cove. Nova Scotia is not far behind. It boasts some 130 variants of 'Green,' numbered among them 25 locations known as 'Green Island.' With this aspect of place names in mind, three broad categories were used as selection criteria in determining whether an entry would be included. (1) *Size*: The major centres of population and the most important physical features – rivers, mountains, lakes, and so on – qualified. (2) *History*: Those places that have had some significant bearing on the historical evolution of Atlantic Canada also appear, for example, Cape Dégrat, Newfoundland; Port Royal, Nova Scotia; Maugerville, New Brunswick; and Abells Cape, Prince Edward Island. (3) *Human Interest*: This category includes place names that are most likely to provoke the question: What is the origin or meaning or significance of that name? Naked Man Hill, Newfoundland; Musquodoboit Harbour, Nova Scotia; Barony, New Brunswick; and Duvar, Prince Edward Island, are examples. In some cases the human interest may stem from the name itself; in others it may be based on the life of a famous person or event associated with the location. Whatever the focus, there has been no shortage of such entries in all four provinces.

Throughout *Place Names of Atlantic Canada*, the spelling adopted in the most recent of the provincial gazetteers issued by the CPCGN has been followed. A few of the place names included are found locally but not sanctioned by the CPCGN or the provincial naming authorities. In these instances, the accepted community spelling has been used. The reader is forewarned that the spelling of some place names in this book may conflict with that used in other sources. Some examples: In Newfoundland, 'Meelpaeg Lake' and not 'Moelpoeg Lake' is the authorized spelling; 'Torbay' denotes the community, although 'Tor Bay' is still officially prescribed for the bay. In Nova Scotia, 'Caribou,' rather than 'Cariboo,' is the accepted version for the ferry terminal near Pictou. One important exception is found in chapter 2. The reasons, historical and otherwise, for using the form 'St. John River' instead of 'Saint John River' are indicated in the entry for the former. Generally, New Brunswick French/

Acadian place names include the hyphen, as in 'Saint-François-de-Kent,' while Newfoundland place names normally do not, as in 'Isle aux Morts.' However, there are some exceptions in Labrador, where 'L'Anse-au-Diable' and 'L'Anse-au-Loup' may be found. Both forms are also used in Nova Scotia; thus, the hyphen is included in 'Petit-de-Grat' but not in 'Ste. Anne du Ruisseau.' It should be noted that there are only two recognized dual bilingual place names in Atlantic Canada – Grand Falls/Grand Sault and Caissie Cape/Cap de Caissie, both in New Brunswick. The period after 'St.' and 'Ste.' appears in all officially approved Canadian place names and is used throughout this text. The apostrophe has fared less well; although still commonly retained in Newfoundland, it is authorized in only a few place names elsewhere in the region. Examples in Nova Scotia include St. Mary's Municipality, St. Peter's, and Clark's Harbour.

Throughout the text, small caps are used to indicate that additional information will be found in entries for these toponyms. The maps are intended to assist readers, especially those unfamiliar with the region. The county or regional divisions are noted here; precise locations can then be found in a provincial atlas. Maps of the three Maritime provinces show their respective county divisions. In Newfoundland and Labrador, where there are no county divisions, the five regional sectors used by the provincial government – Avalon, Eastern, Central, Western, and Labrador – are shown. Another map shows the major fishing banks off the Atlantic Canadian coastline. For those who live near the sea, locations such as Banquereau Bank and Georges Bank are as important as their inland counterparts. Numbered among the former are some of the oldest toponyms within the region.

Place Names of Atlantic Canada approaches toponymy from the historical, cultural, and regional perspective. It reveals that, through the evolution of place names, important links of commonality may be found within Atlantic Canada. Chapter 1, 'Windows on History and Culture,' sets the stage for what follows by pointing to some of these connections, and by summarizing the many insights revealed by toponymy. It also provides an opportunity to discuss place names found in more than one part of the region. For the sake of convenience, entries are arranged alphabetically by province; however, frequent cross-references will lead the reader to additional interprovincial associations. Readers with an appetite for more historical detail are directed to the appropriate sections of the Bibliographical Essay.

My gratitude to those who have previously written on the subject and related themes is expressed in the Bibliographical Essay. Further, I am indebted to Jacynth Hope-Simpson, Sherborne, Dorset, literary executor of the Sir John Hope Simpson papers, for permission to use the quotations on pages 231, 263, and 268. (A selection of the Hope Simpson correspondence, edited by Peter Neary, was published in 1996 by the University of Toronto Press under the title *White Tie and Decorations*.) Appreciation is also extended to Thom Peppard for his assistance in drafting the maps. I have relied heavily on primary source material, and a special note of appreciation must go to the personnel at the National Archives of Canada, the National Map Library, and the Canadian Permanent Committee on Geographical Names, all in Ottawa; the four provincial archives, in Fredericton, Halifax, Charlottetown, and St. John's; Mount Allison University Archives; Acadia University Archives; the Maritime Conference Archives, United Church of Canada; Parks Canada; the New Brunswick Museum, Saint John; the Prince Edward Island Museum and Heritage Foundation; the Institute of Island Studies, at the University of Prince Edward Island; and the Centre for Newfoundland Studies, at Memorial University. In addition many librarians and museum personnel in all corners of Atlantic Canada were helpful in responding to specific enquiries. One side-benefit of my research was the necessity to travel extensively throughout the region. During these field trips many people contributed insight and information.

Throughout this entire enterprise, Gerald Hallowell, University of Toronto Press, has been both supportive and helpful, offering editorial advice and assistance. A full measure of gratitude must be extended to my copy-editor, Beverley Beetham Endersby, who fulfilled the arduous task of reviewing and editing a complex text with thoroughness and sensitivity. As time goes on, new information on the place names of Atlantic Canada will inevitably surface. I would be pleased to hear from readers with comments to share. These may be forwarded to me in care of the publisher.

It is appropriate that this preface is being written on Queen Victoria's birthday. A search of the record reveals that no other monarch is more firmly etched on the place-name canvas, not only of Atlantic Canada, but of her 'other realms and territories' around the world.

24 May 1996

PLACE NAMES OF ATLANTIC CANADA

1

Windows on History and Culture

The Far Horizon, 1000–1700

To examine the place names of Atlantic Canada is to recognize that they encompass, in the broadest of outlines, a history of the region. It is also to conclude that they shed valuable light on the cultural evolution of the people who, during the far, middle, and nearer horizons of history, wrested a living from a sometimes inhospitable landscape. As windows reflect the passing scene, so, too, do the place names assigned by those who once inhabited these shores.

The first place names on the far horizon were bestowed by the original inhabitants, the Amerindian and Inuit peoples. It is a testimonial to the innate knowledge of geography of Canada's aboriginal peoples that many of these names have survived, not only time and a variety of translations, but also more than one attempt at cultural assimilation. Even the comparative absence of such place names, as on the island of Newfoundland, is a telling commentary on one of the most tragic chapters in our past: the extinction of the Beothuk people. While variants of many Mi'kmaq/Maliseet names are still in use, it is important to recognize that others have become lost. The Mi'kmaq name for the region today described as the Maritime provinces was *Megamaage* or *Megamage*, translated by the Reverend Silas T. Rand (1804–1889) as 'land of the Mi'kmaq.' It is possible that *Megamage* is the 'ancestor' of MIRAMICHI, and, if so, the latter may well be one of the oldest place names in Atlantic Canada. The Mi'kmaq territory was divided into seven distinct districts, each with a chief and its own local government. The chiefs met annually with other representatives in a form of a 'Grand Council' to discuss matters of mutual interest. Rand, who served among them as a missionary, may be credited with virtually saving the language. Besides translating much of the Bible into Mi'kmaq, he compiled both a grammar and a dictionary of the language, as well as writing extensively on many aspects of the culture.[1]

History has not recorded the name of the first European to visit Atlantic Canadian shores. Could it have been the sixth-century Irish monk St. Brendan; or perhaps the legendary Prince Henry Sinclair, who reputedly sailed from the Orkney Islands to reach what is present-day Nova Scotia in 1398? More familiar are the legends and the supporting archaeological evidence that the Norse not only explored the eastern seaboard, but established a settlement on the northern tip of Newfoundland, at L'ANSE AUX MEADOWS. Discovered by the Norwegian explorer Helge Ingstad and his archaeologist wife, Anne Stine, in 1960–1, this location has been designated a World Heritage Site by UNESCO. For Atlantic Canada, it provides irrefutable evidence that the Norse settled on the coast of Newfoundland nearly five hundred years before Columbus. Down the centuries there has always been conjecture concerning the original sites of Helluland, Markland, and Vinland, all mentioned as landfalls in the Norse sagas. For obvious reasons, their exact locations will probably never be known, although the weight of evidence would suggest that Helluland, the land of stone slabs, was contemporary Baffin Island; Markland, the wooded land, the coast of Labrador; and Vinland, their name for Newfoundland.

A review of the literature concerning possible Norse sites is of little help in the quest for their specific locations. A classic example of the problems surrounding original Norse sources is found in the story of the Vinland Map, discovered in 1957 and the subject of a book published by Yale University in 1965. If genuine, it would have filled many gaps in Canadian cartography.[2] Over time, Vinland has been attached to portions of the North American coastline ranging all the way from Newfoundland to Florida. The most reasonable explanation is provided by Ingstad, who theorizes that Vinland was probably a more northerly site than previously thought, and that it referred to present-day Newfoundland. There was an inclination among the Norse to select attractive names for new locations, for example, *Green* land. It is Ingstad's conclusion that Vinland falls into this category. He also points out that 'nowhere in the sagas or in other Icelandic sources is it said that the name Vinland has any connection with grapes ... the Norse voyageurs probably made wine from wild berries, of which there abound many kinds along the [Newfoundland] coast.' Ingstad also quotes the opinion

of Swedish philologist Sven Soderberg to the effect that the *vin* in Vinland does not refer to grapes but is the old Norse word for 'grazing
land' or 'meadow,' as it exists in Norway today in names such as Vinas
and Vinje.[3] Despite a lack of specificity as to location, and the fact that
the names Helluland, Markland, and Vinland have vanished, they lurk
in the background of European nomenclature in Atlantic Canada.

What, then, is the oldest surviving place name of European origin in
Atlantic Canada? In seeking an answer it is necessary to move to a study
of early maps and the documentary evidence provided by the first
explorers. Yet, once again, a note of caution must be struck, as the ongo-
ing scholarly dispute concerning the exact 1497 landfall of John Cabot
verifies. Predictably the anniversaries of Cabot's voyage have given rise
to reruns of the debate, as Cape Breton, Prince Edward Island, and
Newfoundland advance rival claims. Such was the case nearly a century
ago, in 1897, and a renewal of the controversy may be anticipated in
1997.[4] As a prelude to the disputes that were to follow, the Newfoundland government was successful in 1886, with the concurrence of the
governor general of Canada, the Marquess of Lansdowne, to have the
strait separating Newfoundland and Cape Breton styled on the Admiralty charts as Cabot Strait. The name was subsequently approved by
the Geographic Board of Canada. It achieved general acceptance and
remains in use. Later, to mark the four-hundredth anniversary of
Cabot's arrival in 1897, Newfoundland issued a set of postage stamps
with the dual purpose of commemorating both this event and the con-
current Diamond Jubilee of Queen Victoria.[5] In the 1930s and 1940s, the
government of Nova Scotia managed to alienate Newfoundlanders by
erecting a monument near CAPE NORTH, on Cape Breton Island, to mark
Cabot's landfall, designating the magnificent 300-kilometre highway
that circles the northern portion of the island as the Cabot Trail and
establishing Cabot Landing Provincial Park. Not to be outdone, the government of Prince Edward Island named a tract of land, fronting on
MALPEQUE BAY, Cabot Provincial Park. Controversy and legislative
decrees aside, it is apparent that the claim put forward by Newfoundland is historically much stronger than those of its rivals. Following
exhaustive documentary and cartographic research, and an aerial and
sea reconnaissance of the Atlantic Canadian coastline, American naval
historian Samuel Eliot Morison (1887–1976) concluded that Cabot's
landfall was at CAPE DÉGRAT, on the northern peninsula of Newfoundland.[6]

Regrettably, although Cabot made both a globe and a map depicting his discoveries, neither has survived. As William Francis Ganong (1864–1941), perhaps the leading authority on Atlantic Canadian nomenclature, once observed: 'How wonderfully would the not impossible discovery of a Cabot map illuminate these matters!'[7] Meanwhile, Morison's careful research of all extant evidence, plus his reasoned rebuttal of competing theories, lends credence to the Cape Dégrat landfall. Morison bases his case, in part, on information contained in an important letter by John Day, a West Country entrepreneur and wine importer who resided in Seville. Discovered in the Spanish archives at Simancas, in 1956, the letter was undoubtedly written by Day to Christopher Columbus.[8] The importance of the Day letter, in Morison's view, lies in its navigational data. He uses this information, along with an unrivalled knowledge of the sea and fifteenth-century seamanship, to buttress the argument in favour of a Newfoundland landfall. If Morison's thesis is accepted, then the entry dated 10 August 1497, in the Privy Purse expenses of King Henry VII – 'to hym [Cabot] that founde the new isle £10' – and the 30 September 1502 item in the Daybook of King's Payments – 'to the merchauntes of bristolle that have bene in the newe founde launde £20'[9] – achieve great significance. Both references lend proof that the *Newe founde lande*, and its later linguistic variations *Terra Nova* (Portuguese), *Tierra Nueva* (Spanish), and *Terre Neuve* (French), is the oldest existing place name of European origin in Atlantic Canada.

In the evolution of regional place names, three of the earliest, Labrador, Acadia, and Cape Breton, make an appearance on the far horizon. Most authorities credit the origin of the name Labrador to João Fernandes, a Portuguese explorer and *llavrador*, 'land holder,' from the Azores. At first, the name Labrador was applied to what was then thought to be a continuous mainland from Greenland to Newfoundland. Later, when it became clear that Greenland was separated from the North American coast by Baffin Bay and Davis Strait, the name Labrador 'shifted' to indicate the neighbouring mainland coast. Historians acknowledge one Jean Alphonse de Saintonge, whose actual name was Jean Fonteneau, as the discoverer of (or first to document), in the mid-sixteenth century, 'that part of the Atlantic between Labrador and Greenland, and as the first to recognize that [the two] were not continuous.'[10]

A further transfer of the name Labrador has been noted. Writing in 1829, the Nova Scotia historian and author Thomas Chandler Haliburton pointed to a connection between this place name and BRAS D'OR LAKE in Cape Breton. The Lazaro Luis map of 1563, which reflected the voyages of João Alvares Fagundes in the 1520s, 'applied the name *La Terra doo Laurador* to Cape Breton Island and mainland Nova Scotia. The name reappeared in 1672 in the form *Lac de Labrador*, given to the great salt water lake of Cape Breton ... which survives as the present Bras d'Or lake.'[11] Earlier, Nicolas Denys used the same name when describing the neighbourhood of his fort at ST. PETER'S, on Cape Breton Island: 'That which is called Labrador is a stretch of the sea, cutting in half the island of Cape Breton, with the exception of eight hundred paces or thereabouts of land which remain between the Fort of Saint Pierre and the extremity of this Sea of Labrador.'[12] As is often the case in Atlantic Canadian nomenclature, the appearance this far to the south of the name Labrador may, in all probability, be credited to mapping errors. Happily, the mistake resulted in the euphonious place name BRAS D'OR LAKE.

Another early regional shift name, Archadia or Arcadia (later l'Acadie or Acadia), was first applied in 1524, by Giovanni da Verrazzano, to the present-day U.S. mid-Atlantic coastline. According to the *Dictionary of Canadian Biography*, Verrazzano was the first European to sail the coast of North America from Florida to Newfoundland. Alan Rayburn has cited the source of Verrazzano's 'name [as] a popular book of the time by Jacopo Sannazzaro, entitled *Arcadia*.'[13] The name itself refers to the mountainous region of ancient Greece, traditionally presented in literature as a haven of pastoral peace and contentment. Over the years a second theory has emerged, suggesting that Acadia may be traced to the suffix *cadie* common in Mi'kmaq place names. The Mi'kmaq word *quoddy* or *cady* meant 'a piece of land or territory.' In the final analysis, there seems little evidence to substantiate this explanation, and the similiarity of *cadie* to *Acadia* is probably coincidental. Several maps, beginning with that of Gastaldi (1548), use the name Larcadia and, by 1585, the name had moved northward and was being used as a designation for today's peninsular Nova Scotia. As time went on, the French version, l'Acadie, prevailed to eventually become Acadia, the name of the easternmost French colony in the New World.

A few kilometres northeast of the French fortress at Louisbourg lies CAPE BRETON, the most easterly point on the island of the same name. Low lying and exposed to the full force of the north Atlantic, this landmark was long known to fishermen from western Europe. The first hint of the name is found on an anonymous Portuguese map of 1516–20. The entrance to the Gulf of St. Lawrence was also indicated on this map, and opposite was placed the inscription 'the land which was discovered by the Bretons.' *C. Dos Bretoes* appears for the first time as a place name on the Miller map of approximately 1521. By the end of the sixteenth century, there was cartographic agreement that Cape Breton was the name not only for the cape, but also for the island.

On the far horizon, names of western European origin start to appear by the end of the fifteenth and early sixteenth centuries. Soon the bold promontories and dangerous shoals, and the safe harbours, bays, and inlets, became known and named, as was necessary in order to stake out territorial claims and to create landmarks for the developing fishery. Numbered among these early 'name makers' were the Portuguese, Spanish, Basque, West Country English, and French. Among the last, the Normans and Bretons were especially prominent. Many of the first maps of the north Atlantic were the result of Portuguese cartography, giving clear indication of a Portuguese presence on the northeastern seaboard. Names such as CAPE SPEAR, the most easterly point on the continent, CAPE RACE, and CAPE FOGO are illustrative of this influence.[14] The Spanish impact on local place names was less pronounced. Two probable examples in Newfoundland are SPANIARD'S BAY and SPANISH ROOM. PLACENTIA and CARBONEAR have also been cited by some authorities as of possible Spanish origin; however, both may stem from other sources.

It is apparent that the contribution of the Portuguese and Spanish, while initially important, fades with the decline of their colonial ambitions in the north Atlantic. Since it was the lot of France and England to settle the ultimate fate of the northeastern section of the continent, their imprint on place names was inevitably greater. However, such was the inaccuracy of early maps that it would be rash to equate some of these early names with exact locations. Until comparatively recent times cartography was an inexact science. Thus, for nearly the whole of the sixteenth century, it was thought that Newfoundland was an archipelago! Of special significance is the fact that Jacques Cartier, on his 1534 voyage, already knew the names for several prominent features on the Newfoundland and Labrador coast. Also, on this first voyage, while exploring the STRAIT OF BELLE ISLE, near Bonne Espérance in contemporary Québec, he encountered 'a large ship from La Rochelle that in the night had run past the harbour where she intended to go and fish ... we went onboard with our longboats and brought her into another harbour one league further west.'[15] What is particularly noteworthy about this account is that Cartier did not regard such a chance meeting as anything unusual. Obviously, many sixteenth-century visitors had a vested interest in both transatlantic travel and remaining anonymous.

Archaeological research has revealed a strong Basque presence on the south coast of Labrador. The location known to the English as RED BAY, to the French as *Havre des Buttes*, and to the Basques as *el puerto de Buytres* had a thriving Basque whaling station by the 1540s.[16] Despite this early beginning, an understanding of the extent and importance of the Basque fishery is a recent historiographical development. Thanks to studies conducted by linguists, historians, and archaeologists, there is now a more complete picture of this early chapter in the history of eastern Canada. Labrador, Newfoundland, and Nova Scotia bear traces of Basque place names. Thus, Samedet on the Labrador coast evolved into EAST and WEST ST. MODESTE. Cape Dégrat, PORT AU PORT, and INGORNA-CHOIX BAY on Newfoundland are of Basque origin, as are PETIT-DE-GRAT, ASPY BAY, and SCATERIE ISLAND in Nova Scotia. In addition, *Baccalieu*, derived from the Basque *bakailua*, for 'codfish,' was sometimes used as a designation for Newfoundland itself.[17] It still survives in BACCALIEU ISLAND, off the east coast of Newfoundland, and in BACCARO, Nova Scotia.

It was the contention of economic historian Harold Innis (1894–1952) 'that the French arrived on the [north Atlantic] fishing grounds at about the same time as the Portuguese ... possibly as early as 1504.'[18] Thus, longevity and the three strategic voyages of Jacques Cartier helped embed an early French imprint on Atlantic Canadian place names. During his first voyage in 1534, Cartier explored the eastern coastline of Newfoundland and Labrador from the *Cap de Bonne Vista* (BONAVISTA) to the *Baie des Châteaux* (CHATEAU BAY). From there he reconnoitred the present-day Gulf of St. Lawrence, assigning names as he went along. The river was discovered on 10 August 1535, St. Lawrence Day, and the name was eventually to be applied to both the gulf and the river. Although many of Cartier's place names have disappeared, those that survive underscore the importance of the French presence. Contemporary place names in this category include CAPE ROUGE, GRAND QUIRPON, and Chateau Bay (Newfoundland and Labrador); Île Brion and Cap St. Pierre (Magdalen Islands); and BAIE DES CHALEURS (New Brunswick).

Another prominent coastal name, of probable French origin, but not associated with Cartier, is the Bay of Fundy. Undoubtedly the bay was visited by western European fishermen from the early 1500s onward. The name was formerly thought to be of Portuguese origin, from *fondo*, meaning 'deep.' However, *Fundy* is more likely an English corruption of the French *fendu*, applied first by the French to the modern Cape Split at the tip of the Blomidon peninsula. For a time during the early seventeenth century, the location was known as *La Baye Française*. In 1604 Lescarbot noted upon leaving Port Mouton, on the south shore of Nova Scotia, 'we ... weighed anchor in order to explore the interior of a bay some forty leagues in length and fourteen, or at most, eighteen in breadth, which was called French Bay.'[19] Following the capture of Port Royal in 1614 by the English, under Sir Samuel Argall, it was known briefly as Argall's Bay. However, this name did not achieve wide currency and soon disappeared. Throughout the late seventeenth and early eighteenth centuries, various spellings appear: *Baye Foundy* (Thornton map 1688) and *Fundi Bay* (Moll 1720). By the middle of the eighteenth century, the contemporary spelling, 'Bay of Fundy,' was in common usage.

The earliest place names of English origin in Atlantic Canada, with the exception of the 1497 naming of Newfoundland, were all translations of earlier designations by the Portuguese and French. It is the opinion of Dr. E.R. Seary that 'the first original English name, unique in a nomenclature otherwise seemingly Portuguese, is Bay of Bulls' (now known as BAY BULLS).[20] This place name dates from the Hood manuscript map of 1598. Only after 1610 and the establishment of the colony at CUPIDS did English place names such as the AVALON PENINSULA, CALVERT, and BRISTOL'S HOPE begin to dot the map of Newfoundland. In other parts of Atlantic Canada, it was not until after the watershed Treaty of Utrecht in 1713 that the assignment of English toponyms becomes commonplace. One place name on the far horizon marks Scotland's first venture in colonization. It began on 29 September 1621, when Sir William Alexander (1570–1640) received a grant of 'the lands lying between New England and Newfoundland ... to be known as New Scotland or Nova Scotia.' Three years later, in 1624, the Knights Baronet of Nova Scotia were created, largely as a scheme to raise money for the proposed colony. The prospective baronets, on paying for their title, were spared the inconvenience and expense of crossing the Atlantic to claim their lands; a portion of the Edinburgh Castle esplanade was officially designated 'Nova Scotia.' Standing on this plot of ground, which is marked today by a nearby plaque, the baronets were enabled to take their oaths.

Alexander issued a prospectus extolling the virtues of New Scotland and included a map of the new colony, liberally sprinkled with Scottish place names. Present-day Nova Scotia was to be the province of Caledonia; contemporary New Brunswick and the Gaspé Peninsula, the province of Alexandria. The ST. CROIX RIVER was renamed the Tweed, and the ST. JOHN RIVER was to be the Clyde. With the exception of Nova Scotia, to be revived following the Treaty of Utrecht, all of Alexander's place names have disappeared. By 1632 the territory was ceded back to France, and the Scottish colonial dream was over. Today, the coats of arms of the Knights Baronet decorate the walls of the Nova Scotia Commemorative Room in Menstrie Castle, birthplace and ancestral seat of Sir William. The name Nova Scotia, and the armorial bearings granted by King Charles I in 1626, forming the basis for the distinctive Nova Scotian flag and coat of arms, are the only permanent legacies of this early effort at Scottish colonization. (See the entries for PORT ROYAL and BALEINE in chapter 4.)

The far horizon is also marked by the appearance of a number of early names that are 'held in common' by more than one part of Atlantic Canada. The most ancient is Atlantic, for the ocean that touches the shoreline of the region. The word may be traced to the sixth century B.C., to the Greek historian Herodotus, who wrote of a sea called 'Atlantis' that reputedly lay beyond the Pillars of Hercules, now the Strait of Gibraltar. A number of other early Atlantic Canadian names delineate sea features rather than land locations. The famous north Atlantic fishing banks extend in a rough line from Newfoundland to the waters off Nantucket Island and Cape Cod, Massachusetts. One of the oldest and the most important is the Grand Bank, to the southeast of Newfoundland. This vast continental shelf is equal in area to that of France and has been at the centre of international controversy down to the present day. There can be no question but that 'anonymous' western European fishermen had discovered these rich fishing grounds before Cabot's first voyage in 1497. However, it was Cabot who reported fish so plentiful that they could be scooped out of the water in baskets. Knowledge quickly spread of what was, until recent times, the world's largest and most productive fishing grounds. Because of the passage of time and lack of documentation, it is virtually impossible to pinpoint the origin of this descriptive name. It appears in various translations on sixteenth-century maps and was well established by the 1580s. This is confirmed in the writings of, among others, the English geographer Richard Hakluyt. Marc Lescarbot recorded in his *Histoire de la Nouvelle France* the pleasure of the Poutrincourt expedition upon reaching *le grand banc aux morues* on 22 June 1606. He provided the following description:

The Grand Bank is a chain of mountains seated in the deepest ocean, and lifting their tops to within thirty, thirty-six or forty fathoms of the surface. Once past it there is no bottom on either side until the land is reached. When the ships reached the Grand Bank, the sails were furled, and the crews fished for cod ... with infinite joy and contentment because of the fresh meat, of which we had our fill, after being so long in want of it. [Some crew members] passed their time in gathering the hearts, tripes, and the most delicate portions of the innards of the said codfish, which they hashed small with bacon, spice, and the flesh of the cod, whereof they made as good a white pudding as could be made in Paris and we ate of them with right good will.[21]

The Grand Bank, because of its size, sometimes overshadows three nearby banks – Burgeo Bank, due south of the Burgeo Islands; St. Pierre Bank, to the south of St. Pierre and Miquelon; and the Green Bank, off Placentia Bay. The first two take their names from locations on land; Green Bank, originally known as *banc aux vers* or *verde* (Levasseur 1601), was named by Breton or Norman fishermen. A century later its economic potential was still being stressed by William Taverner (1680–1768) in his 1713–14 survey of the south coast of Newfoundland. He commented: 'Banc Verte and the other banks lyeing about the coast of Chapeauxrouge should be surveyed ... severall of the French inform'd me that Banc Verte was the finest bank for codfish in the world, and a great many of their ships loaded fish yearly upon it.'[22]

Within the centre of the Grand Bank, there is an area known as the Virgin Rocks. It is a series of rocky ridges only 3.6 metres, or 2 fathoms, deep. In all probability this name does not have religious connotations, as it was a common designation for isolated rocks or shoals off the Newfoundland coast. It is also an older name, being clearly marked on the Augustine Fitzhugh chart of 1693. In 1964 an expedition from Memorial University and the College of Fisheries in St. John's undertook an underwater exploration of the Virgin Rocks. During the course of their investigations, three divers, Hugh Lilly, John Snow, and Calvin Trickett, made history as the first men to walk on the floor of the Grand Bank. On 23 June 1964, at 46° 28' latitude, 50° 48' longitude, they fastened a plaque on an underwater rock to mark the event.

By the 1970s and 1980s Canada began to awaken to the realization that the once plentiful north Atlantic fish stocks were being depleted. For many years the French, English, Spanish, Portuguese, Atlantic Canadian, and U.S. fleets had fished these waters. Following the Second World War, other nations, large and small, most notably Japan and the former USSR, began serious fishing on the banks off Newfoundland and Nova Scotia. Reasons for the decline in fish stocks are many, and although there is no single explanation for the phenomenon, there is agreement that major contributing factors were the technological advances which led to overfishing and the presence of the so-called factory ships on the Banks. On 1 January 1977, Canada declared a 200-mile fishing zone and established quotas for the amount of fish that could be taken. A particular problem has centred around jurisdiction of the 'straddling stock' on the Nose and Tail of the Grand Bank, and on the Flemish Cap off the eastern edge of the Grand Bank. The situation was made more difficult since all three areas lie outside Canadian territorial waters. The Nose and Tail are descriptive names that denote projections in the boundaries of the Grand Bank. Tail of the Bank was officially approved as a designation in 1970; while Nose of the Bank, although in common usage, awaits official sanction. The Flemish Cap is a reminder that fishermen from Flanders were once active in this area. In 1607 Marc Lescarbot reported sighting in the mid-Atlantic as many as '13 Flemish ships bound for Spain' and, closer to the Grand Bank, of 'falling in with a Spanish ship well manned with Englishmen and Flemings.'[23] Jurisdiction over the straddling fish stocks of the the Nose and Tail of the Grand Bank became the focal point for an international dispute between Canada and Spain in 1995. It should be noted that 'Grand Banks' is sometimes used as a collective term for all fishing banks located southeast of Newfoundland.

Another group of fishing banks are found in the Labrador Sea. Unlike those just described and others to the south of Nova Scotia, these are extensions of the mainland and not separated from the coastline. All are named for adjacent land features, and their origins may be found in chapter 3. From north to south these are: SAGLEK, NAIN, MAKKOVIK, HARRISON, HAMILTON, and BELLE ISLE BANKS. The Nova Scotia banks are separated from those of Newfoundland by the 97-kilometre-wide Laurentian Channel. This name is an adaptation of the Latin *Laurentia*, applied to features associated with the St. Lawrence River and Gulf. There are also four smaller fishing banks situated within the Gulf of St. Lawrence. The largest and most important encircles the Magdalen Islands.

The banks directly off the Nova Scotia coast were grouped together in the Paul Ollivier chart of 1624 as *bancq d'accadie*; however, this name did not survive. Instead, the names of nearby land features were applied, as in: CANSO, SABLE, SAMBRO, BACCARO, ROSEWAY, and LAHAVE. Banquereau

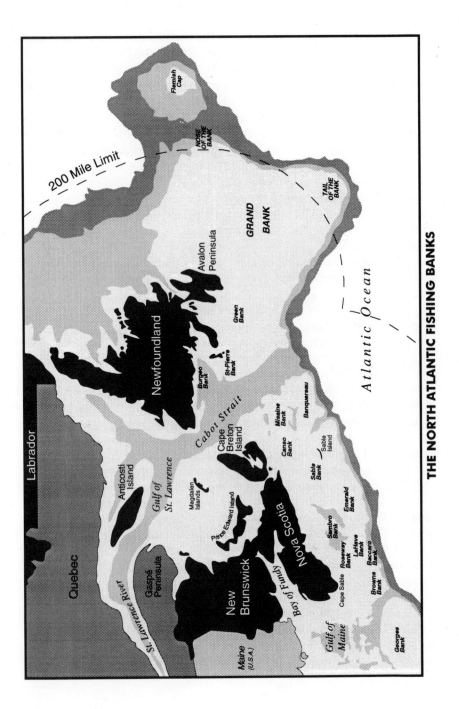

THE NORTH ATLANTIC FISHING BANKS

Bank, to the southeast of Canso Bank, is probably a variation of the French *banc* or *banque*. Banquereau Bank appears as *Banquereaux* on the Champlain map of 1632, and from the late seventeenth century onward the contemporary spelling is consistent. Banquereau is separated from St. Pierre Bank by a deep channel. Also of French origin is Misaine Bank, situated northwest of Banquereau. This name is derived from an old French word which meant 'foresail.' Sable Bank takes its name from the island (see Nova Scotia entry for origin). Emerald Bank, west-southwest of Sable Island, is undoubtedly a descriptive name. The precise origin of Browns Bank, at the western end of the Nova Scotia banks, is not known. It is listed on the Charles Morris 1755 Chart of the Peninsula of Nova Scotia; however, it is probably much older.

Georges Bank, off the southwestern tip of Nova Scotia, is a shared jurisdiction with the United States. First known as Gorges Bank, the origin of the name may be traced to Sir Ferdinando Gorges (*ca* 1566–1647). A military commander and colonizer, Gorges was a native of Somerset, England. Confidant and associate of Sir Humphrey Gilbert, Sir Walter Raleigh, and Sir Francis Drake, Gorges was a fascinating character who deserves to be better known. An active member of the Plymouth Company and the promoter of the 1607 Popham colony, he is sometimes referred to as 'the father of Maine.' Although he never crossed the Atlantic, Gorges became an enthusiastic supporter of the settlement and development of New England. Shortly before his death in 1647, he published his *Briefe Narration of the Originall Undertakings of the Advancement of Plantations into Parts of America*. His enthusiastic description of the economic potential of the fishing bank extending from Cape Cod to the Bay of Fundy caused it to be known as Gorges Bank. Over time this name was first corrupted to St. Georges Bank, and later shortened to Georges Bank.

The Middle Horizon, 1700–1815

The opening years of the eighteenth century mark a shift in the perspective provided by the windows of history and culture as the far horizon recedes to permit a focus on the middle horizon. The early 1700s also signal a turning-point in the fortunes of France in eastern North America. Although the colony of Acadia dated from the Gua de Monts expedition in 1604–5 and the subsequent founding of PORT ROYAL, serious colonization did not begin until the 1630s and 1640s. By the time of the 1671 census, there were some 70 distinct families in a population of about 500. Thereafter, there was little emigration from France; thus, the majority of Acadians, even today, are direct descendants of these founding families. A high birth rate and low infant mortality soon contributed to a rapid rise in population. By 1707 their numbers had grown to 1,400 and were to reach approximately 13,000 by 1755.[24]

In reality there were two Acadias, one the area settled and developed by the Acadians, the other much larger and claimed as French territory. Gradually the Acadians moved up the Rivière au Dauphin (ANNAPOLIS RIVER) through to the Bassin des Mines (MINAS BASIN), where they established one of their largest and best-known settlements at GRAND PRÉ. Soon their villages ringed the basin, from Pisiquid (WINDSOR) to NOEL, to Cobeguit (TRURO), and stretched on beyond Havre à l'Avocat (ADVOCATE HARBOUR) around Cap Doré (CAPE D'OR) to Beauséjour and the Tintamarre (TANTRAMAR) Marshes. From here settlement proceeded eastward along the coast to BAIE VERTE, Remsheg (WALLACE), and TATAMAGOUCHE.

This settlement pattern evolved from the Acadian preference for locations where, through the building of dykes, they might farm the fertile marshlands that follow the coastline. For many, their homeland was the west coast of France, where the estuaries, marshes, and tidal waters were similar to those of Acadia. The place names cited in this expansion mark an important trend in the toponymy of the middle horizon. Acadian place names were a mixture of distinctively French names with others of Mi'kmaq origin. It is worth noting that, in almost every instance, the latter indicated important topographical features. The Mi'kmaq, in common with the Maliseet and Passamaquoddy, were good geographers. They possessed an inherent respect both for features of the landscape and for the total physical environment. In addition, a close bond developed between the Mi'kmaq and Acadians. Dating from the days of the great chief Membertou (?–1611), the Mi'kmaq became not only Acadian allies in war, but also their guides in peacetime exploration. It was no accident that, during the darkest days of their expulsion in 1755, numbers of Acadians found a safe haven among the friendly Mi'kmaq.

Although the relationship between later settlers of British origin and the Mi'kmaq and Maliseet was never close, the practice of utilizing existing Amerindian place names continued unabated. Thus, the vast majority of important rivers in the region, such as the MIRAMICHI, RESTIGOUCHE, and MADAWASKA, to cite but three examples, have retained their original names. Later, James DeMille (1833–1880), poet and novel-

ist, waxed eloquent concerning the retention of Amerindian names in
his poem 'Sweet Maiden of Quoddy':

MEDUXNAKAEG's waters are bluer;
NEPISIQUIT's pools are more black;
More green is the bright OROMOCTO,
And browner the bright PETITCODIAC;
But colours more radiant in autumn
I see when I am casting my hook
In the waves of the Skoodowabskoosis
Or perhaps the SKOODOOWABSKOOK.[25]

In 1710, Port Royal, which had passed from French to British hands and
back again on many occasions, surrendered for the last time, and France
gave up its claim to Acadia by the Treaty of Utrecht, signed in 1713. In
the words of the treaty: 'All Nova Scotia or Acadia with its ancient
boundaries as also the city of Port Royal, and all other things in these
parts which depend on the said lands and islands ... are yielded and
made over to the Queen of Great Britain and to her crown forever.' It
soon became clear that the phrase 'ancient boundaries' would be given
widely different interpretations. The British reverted to Sir William
Alexander's claim of 'the land between New England and Newfoundland'; the French, not surprisingly, were unwilling to accept such a
sweeping definition of territory. From their standpoint Acadia meant
the southerly portion of peninsular Nova Scotia and no more. In the
end, although they were forced to give up mainland Nova Scotia, they
retained Île-Saint-Jean (Prince Edward Island) and Cape Breton Island,
which they renamed Île-Royale. Almost immediately the French began
the erection of a massive fortress at LOUISBOURG, to be named the capital
of the colony of Île-Royale in 1719.

A further indication of the impact of France on the nomenclature of
the region can be found in the designation French Shore, once applied to
a large portion of the coast of Newfoundland. In the late seventeenth
century, the French settlement at Plaisance (PLACENTIA) was fortified to
strengthen a claim to a portion of the Newfoundland coastline, and to
provide shelter for France's fishing fleets. The English countered by
erecting fortifications to protect the harbour at ST. JOHN'S, by this time a
well-established rendezvous for their fishermen. The wars of 1689–97
and 1702–13 saw a number of raids on rival settlements, with the French
occupying St. John's for a time in 1708. By the Treaty of Utrecht in 1713,

France ceded Newfoundland to Britain and, notwithstanding a later attempt at capture during the Seven Years War (1756–63), it was to remain in British hands. After 1713, many of the resident and migratory French fishermen located on the south coast of Newfoundland moved to Île-Royale.

Briefly stated, the French Shore[26] referred to the section of the coast where the French were granted fishing and curing rights from 1713 through to the Anglo-French Convention of 1904. The territory was first defined as north from CAPE BONAVISTA, on the east coast, to POINT RICHE, on the west. This was confirmed by the Treaty of Paris in 1763, the same treaty which ceded St. Pierre and Miquelon to France. A further adjustment took place by the Treaty of Paris in 1783 through its redefinition of the boundary from CAPE ST. JOHN to CAPE RAY. Following the 1783 treaty, the Americans were given the right to land and dry fish on the coast of Labrador, a right that was reaffirmed in 1818. Taken together, the French and American fishing rights proved to be a serious handicap to the development of Newfoundland. Although France lacked the right to make permanent settlements on the French Shore, the migrant fishermen left behind an impressive list of place names. Examples of contemporary names which may be traced to this period include CAPE NORMAN, CASTORS RIVER, CONCHE, CROQUE, FALAISE POINT, FLEUR DE LYS, GROAIS ISLAND, and LA SCIE. During the heyday of the French migratory fishery, the Northern Peninsula was known as the 'Petit Nord.'

Following 1713, in the new British colony of Nova Scotia, little was to change beyond the substitution of flags. The renaming of Port Royal as ANNAPOLIS ROYAL was the only outward sign of the new order. Few efforts were made to encourage colonization, with the result that the Acadians became a clear majority by mid-century. Sporadic attempts were made to extract an oath of allegiance from the Acadians; however, they strongly resisted. Their sole concession was a promise of neutrality and a pledge not to bear arms against either France or England. Only a small number accepted French enticements to vacate their fertile lands and move to Île-Royale, Île-Saint-Jean, or the area around FORT BEAUSÉ-JOUR, erected in 1750 to guard the Isthmus of CHIGNECTO. Meanwhile the supposedly impregnable fortress of Louisbourg fell to a force of New Englanders, only to be restored by the Treaty of Aix-la-Chappelle in 1748. Ironically, the fortress was designed to withstand an attack from the sea; however, on this occasion, and again in 1758, it was to be captured by land, where its defences were weakest.[27]

The middle of the eighteenth century witnessed an awakening of interest in Nova Scotia by Britain. In 1749, HALIFAX was founded as a counterbalance to Louisbourg, and the capital was moved there from Annapolis Royal. Immediately on the heels of this action, some 2,700 German- and French-speaking 'Foreign Protestants' were encouraged to settle in Nova Scotia. In 1753 the majority were eventually to locate in and around LUNENBURG. Some of these settlers and their descendants eventually scattered to many parts of the region, but it is here that their distinctive accents and customs are still to be found. Beyond the Lunenburg area, two communities in northern Nova Scotia, TATAMAGOUCHE and RIVER JOHN, were resettled by the 'Foreign Protestants.' Originally a people of the land, they were transformed in a few generations into some of the most successful sailors and fishermen of the Atlantic coast.[28]

With the outbreak of hostilities in the mid-1750s, Fort Beauséjour was captured by the British on 16 June 1755. Simultaneously, FORT GAS-PEREAU, a French supply depot on BAIE VERTE, fell. Six weeks later, on 25 July 1755, the governor and council of Nova Scotia reached a decision to expel the Acadians from the province and to disperse them 'in such a manner as may best answer our design in preventing their reunion.' From the historical standpoint not only was the 'design' unsuccessful, but many pre-expulsion Acadian place names have survived to mark the lands they once occupied. LAHAVE, PORT JOLI, PORT LATOUR, BEAR RIVER, Port Royal, PARADISE, PEREAU, CANARD, NEW MINAS, Grand Pré, NOEL, DEBERT, MASSTOWN, ADVOCATE HARBOUR, CAPE D'OR, and AULAC are but a random sample of locations that are now occupied by the descendants of others, but remain as toponymic sentinels of old Acadia.[29]

In the late 1750s and the 1760s, lands vacated by the Acadians were immediatedly snapped up by emigrants from New England. Two groups were involved in this migration. The first group was attracted by the rich Acadian dykelands at Annapolis, Minas, and Cobequid, and on the Isthmus of Chignecto. The *Oxford English Dictionary* defines 'Planter' in its eighteenth-century context as simply one who 'planted' or founded a colony. There were also New England Planter settlements in the St. John River valley, especially in the MAUGERVILLE area. Still another group, composed largely of fishermen, took up lands on the south shore of Nova Scotia, mainly in communities such as YARMOUTH, BARRINGTON, and LIVERPOOL. This relocation placed them closer to the lucrative fishing banks off the coast of Nova Scotia and Newfoundland. All too frequently the influence of the New England Planters has been overlooked or obscured by the later and more numerous Loyalist migration.[30] In common with other emigrant groups, especially the Loyalists, they did revive a few New England place names such as Yarmouth, CAMBRIDGE, and CHESTER. More pronounced was their inclination to incorporate Planter surnames in new community names, for example, ATWOODS BROOK, COFFIN ISLAND, LOCKEPORT, SHEFFIELD MILLS, STARRS POINT, TUPPERVILLE, and WALTON.

The importance of the Planter migration from New England goes beyond numbers and place names. They came during a formative period in the history of Nova Scotia and took effective possession, imparting to their new homeland many distinctive characteristics. Steeped in the tradition of self-government in church and state, they and their descendants were to help end religious, political, and educational privilege in the province and, by example, elsewhere. Finally, the New Englanders had not experienced the bitter uprooting of the Loyalists. Their parting with their homeland was by choice; as a result, they were to exert a moderating influence on the anti-Americanism characteristic of many Loyalists.

Following the Seven Years War (1756–63), the two remaining French colonies in the region, Île-Royale and Île-Saint-Jean, were ceded to Britain. Six years later, the latter was designated as the separate colony of St. John's Island. Subsequently, in 1799 its name was to be changed to Prince Edward Island in honour of Prince Edward, Duke of Kent. Meanwhile, the Acadians began the long and painful process of resettlement. On 11 July 1764 an order-in-council was passed, making it legal for Acadians to return to British territories, provided they were willing to take an unqualified oath of allegiance. Many had endured exile in the Thirteen Colonies, to the south, or overseas, in France and England. Still others were prisoners of war at Halifax, Annapolis Royal, Windsor, and Fort Beauséjour; a smaller number, who had escaped deportation by living with the Mi'kmaq, now reappeared on the scene.

One group took up lands in the ST. MARY'S BAY region, soon to be named the district of CLARE. Acadians who had lived in the PUBNICOS, where their lands had not been resettled, returned home. This area was later known as the district of ARGYLE. The eastern and northern coast of contemporary New Brunswick and the upper St. John River valley attracted the largest number of Acadian settlers. In another area, the MEMRAMCOOK VALLEY, a number of Acadians had escaped deportation, and thus retained their old lands. There was also a general return of Acadians to St. John's Island, ISLE MADAME, and the CHETICAMP region of Cape Breton. The territorial limits of the new Acadia, particularly north of the Isthmus of Chignecto, can be traced through the names of their communities, such as GRAND-SAULT, SAINT-FRANÇOIS-DE-MADAWASKA, RIVIÈRE-VERTE, SAINT-LÉONARD, GRANDE-ANSE, BAIE-SAINTE-ANNE, SAINT-ANTOINE, and BARACHOIS. Interspersed were a large number of older and distinctly Mi'kmaq place names: CARAQUET, SHIP-PAGAN, TRACADIE, RICHIBUCTO, BOUCTOUCHE, and SHEDIAC. Very quickly these locations, and others nearby, took on the character of their new inhabitants to become, in the public mind, identifiably Acadian.

A direct result of the British victory in the Seven Years War was the impetus given to the cartography of eastern North America. If Britain was to successfully administer her newly won territories, accurate maps and charts were essential. In turn, three famous surveyors – J.F.W. Des-Barres (1721?–1824), Samuel Holland (1728–1801), and James Cook (1728–1779) – were destined to play key roles in the mapping of much of the coastline of Atlantic Canada.[31] Details of their careers may be gleaned from entries for locations named in their honour: DESBARRES POINT and HOLLAND COVE, in Prince Edward Island, and COOKS HARBOUR, in Newfoundland. In 1764 DesBarres was responsible for naming the stretch of water that separates Prince Edward Island from mainland Nova Scotia and New Brunswick. He called it Northumberland Strait, after HMS *Northumberland*, the flagship of Rear Admiral Lord Colvill (1717–1770), the commander-in-chief of British naval forces in the North Atlantic from 1767 to 1770. Originally, the strait had been named Baie de Lunario by Jacques Cartier, who entered its northern end on 1 July 1534, the day of St. Lunarius. For a time it was also known by the descriptive 'Red Sea.' Holland reported 'the sea is frequently of a red hue ... by many people called the Red Sea.' On the occasion of the four-hundredth anniversary of Cartier's first voyage, in 1934, a campaign was launched by the Ligue des Intérêts Nationaux to rename the strait in honour of its discoverer. Following a lengthy debate and extensive archival research, it was revealed that Cartier had not sailed through the strait and, further, that he had mistaken it for a 'bay.' This point, combined with lack of local support for any change, caused the Canadian Board on Geographic Names to affirm the name Northumberland Strait.

If for no other reason than geography, the outbreak of the American Revolution was bound to have a profound impact on Atlantic Canada. Economic ties with New England were close; both regions formed part of a natural north Atlantic trading unit, and more than half the population of Nova Scotia was of New England stock. For a time it appeared that Nova Scotia might well be the fourteenth colony to rebel. In the end, a combination of circumstances prevailed to keep the province apart from the revolutionary cause. As yet a scattered and comparatively new population, Nova Scotians were deterred by the British presence in Halifax, and more so by British naval superiority. No help was forthcoming from the other thirteen colonies, and the majority of New England Planters, labelled 'His Majesty's Yankees,' attempted to remain neutral. The only serious pro-revolutionary outbreak occurred on the Isthmus of Chignecto and was led by Jonathan Eddy (1726/7–1804), a onetime MLA for CUMBERLAND. It ended in failure, and the Eddy Road that still crosses the AMHERST MARSH serves as a reminder of what might have been. Subsequently, Eddy returned to New England, where he received a grant of land near Bangor, Maine. It was named Eddington in his honour. As the revolution wore on, few ports along the Atlantic Canadian coast were spared raids by American privateers, so that any lingering support for the revolutionary cause was swept away. Examples of such incidents may be found in the entries for Liverpool and Lockeport, in Nova Scotia, and WRIGHTS CREEK, on Prince Edward Island. Even locations farther away, such as ANTELOPE HARBOUR on the Labrador coast, reveal an association with this war.

Following the American Revolution the region received a major increase in population through the migration of some 30,000 Loyalists. Most coastal communities in Nova Scotia, Cape Breton, and St. John's Island gained settlers; however, the numbers reaching Newfoundland were small by comparison. The chief areas of settlement were, temporarily, at SHELBURNE, Nova Scotia; north of the Bay of Fundy; and along the St. John River Valley. Between May and November 1783, approximately 14,000 to 15,000 people came to the river valley. The next year, the new province of New Brunswick was created. The official partition took place on 10 September 1784, and the name was chosen as a compliment to King George III, who was descended from the House of Brunswick. Earlier proposals for naming the new province were New Ireland, suggested by William Knox, then under-secretary of state, but rejected because Ireland was out of royal favour, and Pittsylvania, for William Pitt, then prime minister. In the same year, Cape Breton was created a separate colony, remaining apart from Nova Scotia until 1820.

As with other emigrant groups the Loyalists left their imprint on the nomenclature of the region. Sometimes this is evident in transplanted place names such as HAMPSTEAD, KINGSTON, LINCOLN, and WESTFIELD, in New Brunswick; ALBANY CROSS and WESTCHESTER, in Nova Scotia; and

BUNBURY, on Prince Edward Island. By virtue of the Loyalists' status as prominent landholders, their patronymics were frequently incorporated in community names. This explains, by way of example, BLISSFIELD, GIBERSON SETTLEMENT, and SHAMPERS BLUFF, in New Brunswick; BARTON, in Nova Scotia; and LINKLETTER and HASZARD POINT, on Prince Edward Island. The settlement patterns of Loyalists may also be traced in other, less obvious ways. CHARLOTTE COUNTY, New Brunswick, settled principally by Loyalists, was named in 1785 for Queen Charlotte, consort of King George III. In 1784 some 190 Quaker Loyalists founded a community they called Bellevue, now Beaver Harbour, on the Fundy coast. Lack of fertile soil and a disastrous forest fire forced them to move to the plateau behind the settlement, which they named Penn's Fields, later PENNFIELD RIDGE, for William Penn, the famous English Quaker.[32]

Many Loyalists had strong ties with the military, and a number of grants were made for meritorious service during the revolutionary war. Although first founded by New England Planters, the largely Loyalist settlement of WEYMOUTH, Nova Scotia, became associated with the remarkable military career of Lieutenant-Colonel James Moody (1744–1809), who saw service on the British side during the war. In like fashion, the many place names associated with Sir Guy Carleton, Lord Dorchester (1724–1808), who played a pivotal role during the revolution, and his brother, Thomas Carleton (1735–1817), the first lieutenant-governor of New Brunswick, are important historical signposts on the middle horizon of Atlantic Canadian toponymy. Other military ties may be seen in names associated directly or indirectly with regiments or ships that saw service during the revolution. Thus, PRINCE WILLIAM, New Brunswick, although it honours the future King William IV (1765–1837), was named for him because he was patron of the Kings American Dragoons, a prominent regiment in the war, whose disbanded members received land grants in the area. Similarly, DIGBY, Nova Scotia, was named for Admiral Robert Digby (1732–1815), commander of HMS *Atlanta*, flagship of the convoy which brought Loyalist settlers to the Digby area.

BIRCHTOWN, adjacent to the important Loyalist settlement of Shelburne, points to yet another important facet of the Loyalist migration. During the American Revolution an offer of freedom was made to any slaves who might flee their masters, cross to the British lines, and fight for the British king. As a result, in the summer of 1784 a brigade of some 1,500 arrived to take up lands on the northwest arm of Shelburne harbour. The settlement was named Birchtown in honour of Brigadier-

General Samuel Birch, the British commandant at New York, their port of embarkation. Other black Loyalists were settled at Digby, Annapolis, PRESTON, and GUYSBOROUGH COUNTY, all in Nova Scotia. Time and historical neglect have obscured the role of these Loyalists; however, recent research has drawn attention to their role on the British side in the revolutionary war.[33]

Although the Loyalists had a considerable impact on the nomenclature of the middle horizon, their other more intangible contributions are also worthy of note. Particularly in New Brunswick, they provided the nucleus of a ruling élite and quickly assumed positions of leadership in church and state. Esther Clark Wright has summarized their overall impact:

... loyalty to the British crown meant respect for law and order and for orderly procedure. it meant unwillingness to resort to violence, and willingness to wait for years rather than to jeopardize ultimate victory by depending on [revolutionary] methods ... As the Loyalist developed into New Brunswicker this was the most valuable contribution he made to the new province and the nation of which it ultimately became a part.[34]

Meanwhile, Newfoundland was being gradually transformed from 'an island moored for the convenience of the fishery' to the status of a colony. Although for some time anti-colonization policies had been in effect, these were singularly unsuccessful in preventing permanent settlement. One illustration of these regulations is found in the terms of the Palliser Act of 1775, which sought to force the annual return to Britain of fishermen, sailors, and others at the end of each fishing season. It was named for Sir Hugh Palliser, who acted as adviser to the government upon his return to England from service as governor of Newfoundland from 1764 to 1769 (see PALLISER POINT). Since no effective provision was made to enforce the laws forbidding settlement, fishermen went ahead and established year-round residence. Thus, as early as the 1760s, the word *Newfoundlander*, as a descriptor for permanent residents, began to appear in print.[35] Thirty years later, in 1793, Chief Justice John Reeves (1752?–1829) could say with assurance to the British government: 'The consequence of [your policies] has been that Newfoundland has been peopled behind your back ... you have abandoned it to be inhabited by anyone who chooses.'[36]

Although this admonition rings true, by the middle horizon, a distinctive pattern of colonization was beginning to develop in Newfoundland. For the English, settlement was confined largely to the coastal area from CAPE BONAVISTA to CAPE RACE. By the mid-eighteenth century, in addition to ST. JOHN'S, the following locations had a substantial year-round population: BAY BULLS, WITLESS BAY, RENEWS, FERMEUSE, FERRYLAND, OLD PERLICAN, TRINITY, CARBONEAR, and BAY DE VERDE. It is estimated that the summer population of St. John's and immediate vicinity, including QUIDI VIDI, TORBAY, and PETTY HARBOUR, was about 3,000 in the 1750s. By the time of the American Revolution, this figure had doubled; however, the permanent winter population was still slightly fewer than half of the total. Farther afield, and northward from GREENSPOND, FOGO ISLAND, and TWILLINGATE, English settlers were being attracted, and some became full-time residents. Following the Treaty of Utrecht, a permanent English presence was beginning to emerge on the south Newfoundland coast, particularly in the area of PLACENTIA BAY. From FORTUNE BAY westward, prior to the American Revolution, numbers dwindled to approximately 600 in the winter months.

Who were these people who were willing to brave the elements and extreme isolation to live year-round in Newfoundland? The permanent population during the years 1713 to 1815 was largely drawn from two basic strands: West Country English and Irish, with the latter mainly from Ireland's southern counties. By 1730 many fishing ships *en route* to Newfoundland called at ports such as Waterford and Cork, providing opportunity for the recruitment of Irish emigrants. Inevitably immigration and settlement were tied to the mercantile and commercial interests then active in Newfoundland. It has been shown by Handcock and others that the territorial expansion of this period was dominated by West Country merchants, especially from Poole, in Dorset. Other contributing factors were the growth of the seal and salmon fisheries and the desire to pursue the inshore cod fishery.[37] Another group to have a demographic impact during this period came from the Channel Islands. By the eighteenth century Channel Islanders, especially from Jersey, were active along the south coast of BURIN PENINSULA, which became known as the 'Coast of Chapeau Rouge,' and at Carbonear, HARBOUR GRACE, and CONCEPTION BAY. Their presence can also be pinpointed in place names on the southern coast such as HERMITAGE BAY, JERSEYMANS HARBOUR, JERSEYSIDE, and RENCONTRE BAY. During the same period, Channel Island mercantile interests were also active in Nova Scotia (see entries for ARICHAT, ISLE MADAME, JANVRIN ISLAND, and POINT TUPPER).[38]

One final category of place names requires mention before we leave the middle horizon of Atlantic Canadian toponymy. By an order-in-council dated 17 August 1759, the colony of Nova Scotia was divided into five counties, ANNAPOLIS, CUMBERLAND, HALIFAX, KINGS, and LUNENBURG. All were larger than the contemporary divisions of the same name, and all were destined to be further subdivided. For example, by the proclamation of 7 October 1763, Cape Breton Island was formally annexed to Nova Scotia and became part of Halifax County. Two years later, the island was set apart as a separate county. Following a brief existence as a colony (1783–1820) and subsequent reannexation to Nova Scotia, it was again named CAPE BRETON COUNTY. Still later, three additional counties – RICHMOND, INVERNESS, and VICTORIA – were to evolve on the island. In 1765, surveyor Samuel Holland was responsible for the allocation of the three counties – KINGS, QUEENS, and PRINCE – created on St. Johns Island (later Prince Edward Island). Within New Brunswick, eight counties were established by legislation in 1786: CHARLOTTE, KINGS, NORTHUMBERLAND, QUEENS, SAINT JOHN, WESTMORLAND, and YORK. The seven new counties created after 1786 were to be carved from the original eight. Details surrounding the origin of county names are provided in the individual entries for each. In the chapters dealing with New Brunswick, Nova Scotia, and Prince Edward Island, county divisions have been included with the entries as a guide to geographical location (see maps on pages 42, 280, and 424). In lieu of county divisions in Newfoundland, the five regional sectors – Avalon, Eastern, Central, Western, and Labrador – established by the provincial government have been substituted as a locational aid (see maps on pages 152 and 153).

The Nearer Horizon, 1815–Present

While posterity may not agree with the opinion of *The Times* of London that 'nothing in ancient or modern history equals the effect of the victory at Waterloo,'[39] there is agreement that it was a major historical landmark. The decisive defeat of the French under Napoleon on 18 June 1815, and the victory of the British and their allies, led by the Duke of Wellington, had repercussions far beyond the boundaries of Europe. So complete was the triumph that even today the very word *Waterloo* has not lost its meaning as a synonym for the most crushing defeat. Predictably the battle and the name of the 'Iron Duke' found a firm niche in the toponymy of Atlantic Canada. Both Newfoundland/Labrador and Prince Edward Island have a WELLINGTON and a WATERLOO POINT. In New Brunswick there is a WATERLOO CREEK, LAKE, and STATION, plus two WELLINGTONs, two WELLINGTON BROOKs, and a LAKE WELLINGTON.

Nova Scotia claims three WELLINGTONs, a WATERLOO LAKE, and a WATER-LOO RIVER.

The peace that followed Waterloo ushered in a tide of emigration from the British Isles, particularly to the three Maritime provinces. In Nova Scotia, recently disbanded soldiers, including some who served in the War of 1812 between Britain and the United States, received land grants in several parts of the province (for examples, see entries such as ALDERSVILLE and NEW ROSS). During the 1820s and 1830s, successive waves of Scots, Irish, and to a lesser extent English and Welsh emigrants came to Nova Scotia. In 1815 the population stood at approximately 75,000; by 1827 this figure had grown to more than 150,000 and was to reach 200,000 a decade later. The largest proportion of the new settlers came from Scotland. In a five-year interval between 1815 and 1820, 1,674 immigrants entered through the port of PICTOU alone.[40] This Scottish migration had begun in the previous century with the arrival of the ship *Hector* from Loch Broom, Scotland, on 15 September 1773. The flood-tide of emigration reached its peak in the early decades of the nineteenth century when thousands of Scottish Highlanders were forced to seek refuge overseas. The dream of Sir William Alexander was being fulfilled in an unexpected manner as Nova Scotia became New Scotland in fact as well as in name (see entry for BRORA LAKE, Nova Scotia).

The course of this nineteenth-century Scottish settlement of northern Nova Scotia is easily traced through place names: SCOTSBURN, LOCH BROOM, NEW GLASGOW, GAIRLOCH, SUNNY BRAE, GLENGARRY, GLENCOE, GLENELG, KNOYDART, ARISAIG, DUNMAGLASS, LOCHABER, and LOCH KATRINE tell their own story. The Scottish immigrants, whether because of homesickness, innate clannishness, or a sense of history, were more prone than any other group to impose names reminiscent of their homeland. A glance at the map of Cape Breton bears eloquent testimony to this point. Here may be found BARRA GLEN and BARRA MENS COVE; BEN EOIN and BEINN BREAGH; LOCH BAN and LOCH LOMOND; PIPERS COVE and PIPERS GLEN; INVERNESS and IONA; SKIR DHU and SKYE GLEN; ULVA and USIGNE BAN FALLS.

In 1815 the Loyalists and their descendants still constituted the core of New Brunswick's population. However, they were rapidly being out-numbered by new immigrants, chiefly Irish and Scots, many of whom entered the province on timber ships returning from Britain. As a result, SAINT JOHN and sections of the Miramichi Valley began to acquire a decidedly Celtic cast. By 1815 the Irish in Saint John were sufficiently numerous to petition the legislature for aid in building a church.

Although fewer Scots emigrated to New Brunswick than did to Nova Scotia, they left their imprint on the map of the province, as one cluster of Scottish place names in Restigouche County will verify: ATHOLVILLE, BLAIR ATHOL, GLENCOE, GLENLIVET, BALMORAL, and DUNDEE. The population of New Brunswick continued to increase in the early years of the nearer horizon. From 25,000 in 1805, it grew to 74,000 in 1824. Ten years later, it was just under 120,000, and by mid-century was close to the 200,000 mark. Much of this increase can be accounted for by emigration from the British Isles.

By the 1820s society on the Miramichi which 'had always been voluble and explosive' was augmented by 'a powerful Irish ingredient which appreciably increased these qualities.'[41] The Irish settlement of this region is epitomized in the legendary DUNGARVON RIVER and the fact that an Irish Festival is held annually to remember an extraordinarily storied past. Elsewhere the Irish presence is indicated by scattered place names, such as LONDONDERRY, WATERFORD, SHANNON, SHANNON VALE, INNISHANNON BROOK, IRISHTOWN, and IRISH SETTLEMENT. A number of former soldiers, including members of the New Brunswick Fencibles, fresh from service in the War of 1812, received land grants in what was to become Victoria County. The Royal West India Rangers gave their name to RANGER SETTLEMENT, located south of Grand Falls/Grand Sault. The New Brunswick and Nova Scotia Land Company, organized in London in 1832, was responsible for placing a number of British immigrants in York County. Communities such as STANLEY and TEMPERANCE VALE date from this period.

From its institution in 1767, the settlement of Prince Edward Island was dominated by the tortuous debate that surrounded the 'land question.' A final resolution to the problem was not reached until 1878 (see entries for EGMONT BAY, CENTRAL LOT 16, ABELLS CAPE, and HAY RIVER). In 1800 the total population was under 5,000; by 1827 it had risen to 23,226. Thereafter there was a slow but steady rise, from 32,392 in 1832 to 94,021 in 1871, just prior to the province's entry into Confederation in 1873. As was the case in northern Nova Scotia and Cape Breton Island, the majority of new immigrants to Prince Edward Island came from Scotland. Place names of Scottish origin are to be found in all three counties; however, Queens, which attracted the majority of Scottish settlers, has the largest number. Thus we find place names such as MONTROSE and ELLERSLIE in Prince County; BREADALBANE, STRATHGARTNEY, CLYDE RIVER, DUNSTAFFNAGE, ARGYLE SHORE, KEPPOCH, and UIGG in Queens; and ANNANDALE, ROCK BARRA, and DUNDEE in Kings. One example of the Scottish sense of nostalgia and history may be found in the proliferation of place names flowing from from the Jacobite Rebellion of 1745 and the attempt by Prince Charles Edward Stuart to claim the British crown. Prince Edward Island alone has a GLENFINNAN, CULLODEN, GLENCORRADALE, SCOTCHFORT, KINGSBORO, and MILTON, all names with strong Stuart associations. Remarkably, these names and many others, throughout Atlantic Canada and beyond, were bestowed long after the death, both of the prince and of his cause.[42] During the nineteenth century the Irish ranked next to the Scots in the demographic mix that was Prince Edward Island. Arriving later than the Scots, they settled in the interior of Prince and Queens counties and along the border of Queens and Kings counties. Their toponymic footprints may be traced in such place names as EMERALD JUNCTION, EMYVALE, KELLYS CROSS, and KINKORA.

It is not surprising to find that place names of English origin constitute the largest classification of names assigned in the nearer horizon, from 1815 to the present. During the first half of the nineteenth century, place-naming was largely the prerogative of the colonial governor and council. The majority of governors and other administrative officials either were English or were educated in England. Most had seen service in the British army or navy, and this was to colour their recommendations concerning place names. By way of illustration, the first two lieutenant-governors of Nova Scotia following 1815, Dalhousie and Kempt, were both veterans of Waterloo. As new settlement took place during the nineteenth century, names of English origin and of the governors themselves were assigned with amazing frequency.

Among the many governors who managed to enshrine their names or have them enshrined were: (Newfoundland) Sir Charles Hamilton, Sir Anthony Musgrave, Sir John Glover, Sir Alexander Bannerman, Sir Cavendish Boyle, and Sir Ralph Campney Williams; (New Brunswick) Thomas Carleton, Sir Howard Douglas, Sir Archibald Harvey, and Sir Edmund Head; (Nova Scotia) Sir John Wentworth, Sir John Sherbrooke, Earl of Dalhousie, Sir John Kempt, and Sir Peregrine Maitland; (Prince Edward Island) J.F.W. DesBarres and Sir Henry Vere Huntley. Usually the surname was used; however, in some instances, as with Sir Edmund Head and Sir Cavendish Boyle, the baptismal name became the place name. The award for bestowing the largest number of names in the shortest span of time must go to the Earl of Dalhousie, who served as lieutenant-governor of Nova Scotia from 1816 to 1819. Within this short period nine locations and a university were to be assigned his name, including DALHOUSIE, EARLTOWN, and LAKE RAMSAY. Later, when he became governor-in-chief of Canada (1819–28), he did not lose interest in place-naming. The parish of DALHOUSIE in New Brunswick, along with the town and two other nearby features (by association), bear his name, as does Dalhousie Station in the Soulanges district of Québec. To round out the honours, there is a Dalhousie Township; two Dalhousie Lakes, and a Dalhousie Mills in eastern Ontario, plus a Port Dalhousie that is now part of St. Catharines, Ontario.

During the mid-nineteenth century, the Crimean War (1853–6), fought by Britain and France against Russia, was to inspire a number of place names. INKERMAN, HAVELOCK, MALAKOFF, FLORENCEVILLE, and ALMA, in New Brunswick, and KARSDALE, PORT WILLIAMS, FENWICK, WIL-LIAMSDALE, and ALMA (again), in Nova Scotia, all have Crimean associations. Following Confederation in 1867, the expansion of the railway system and postal service led to a widespread assignment of new names or the replacing of names frequently duplicated elsewhere. Dozens of place names in all parts of Atlantic Canada mark the name of the first postmaster (see EVERETT, HATFIELD POINT, LAGRACEVILLE, and THOMAS-TON CORNER, in New Brunswick). Provincially, the adoption of free school legislation began in Nova Scotia in 1864–5 and soon expanded to the other two Maritime provinces. The definition of school-section boundaries, especially in rural areas, led to the adoption of new names, many of which were destined to become community names. Often the latter were selected by popular vote and sometimes commemorated a local person or incident. Prince Edward Island examples include FARM-INGTON, HARMONY, KILMUIR, and NEW ACADIA.

Towards the end of the nineteenth century, governments began to recognize that a formalized procedure was necessary in order to bring direction and consistency to the field of nomenclature. On 18 September 1897 an order-in-council was passed establishing the Canadian Board on Geographic Names. Its lineal descendant, the Canadian Permanent Committee on Geographical Names, dates from 1961. Membership on the committee is drawn from all federal authorities with an interest in nomenclature, along with representatives from the provinces and terri-tories, and the academic community. Its responsibilities and functions are broadly defined as relating to 'all questions of geographical nomen-clature dealing with Canada,' and the undertaking of 'research into the origin and usage of geographical names.'[43]

In 1904, Newfoundland created a Nomenclature Board with the power 'to recommend ... the name or renaming of any town, village or settlement or any geographical feature in Newfoundland.'[44] In the evolution of Newfoundland place names there had been a great deal of repetition, often resulting in identical or similar names. Thus, Broad Cove, Conception Bay, became ST. PHILLIPS; Broad Cove, Trinity Bay, SOMERSET; and Broad Cove, south of Ferryland, CAPPAHAYDEN. PORTUGAL COVE, Trepassey Bay, was renamed PORTUGAL COVE SOUTH to distinguish it from the other PORTUGAL COVE, on Conception Bay. Many of the 'Seal Coves,' or variants thereof, were replaced; for example, Seal Cove, Bonavista Bay, became PRINCETON. Similarly, several Tickle Harbours were changed, as in Tickle Harbour, Trinity Bay, which became BELLEVUE.

In addition to these necessary changes, there were others of a more controversial nature. The late Victorian–Edwardian era of the nearer horizon was a time of place-name reform remarkably akin to the 'politically correct' linguistic campaigns of the 1990s. Examples of place names that fell by action of the Newfoundland Nomenclature Board were Cuckolds Cove, which became DUNFIELD; Turks Gut, MARYSVALE; Grand River Gut, SEARSTON; Famish Gut, FAIR HAVEN; Pipers Hole, SWIFT CURRENT; and Scilly Cove, WINTERTON. Not all of the edicts of the board were accepted. SIBLEYS COVE was renamed Prowsetown in honour of historian D.W. Prowse, only to revert to its original name. However, the name Prowsetown is still used occasionally for this village southwest of Bay de Verde.[45] It is worth noting that, while Famish Gut was to disappear, nearby PINCHGUT POINT survived place-name reform, as did TURKS GUT LONG POND. Likewise, DILDO was successful in overcoming several attempts at expurgation. The ghosts of surveyors James Cook and Michael Lane, responsible for some of these unusual and 'whimsical' names, would approve.

Place-naming in the most recent part of the near horizon, the twentieth century, followed patterns already well established over time. Descriptive names, evocative of some aspect of the land or sea, continued to dominate place-naming. Surprisingly, the First World War, with its epic battles in which Newfoundlanders and Canadians played significant roles, inspired few Atlantic Canadian place names. One exception was the Battle of Saint Quentin, an important Allied victory in the last year of the war. In 1919 the name of Andersons Siding, New Brunswick, was changed to SAINT-QUENTIN in recognition of this battle. In 1931, Passchendaele, scene of a major engagement by the Canadian army in 1917, was adopted as a post-office name in Glace Bay, Nova Scotia. This area is still called Passchendaele by older residents. Perhaps as a substitute for community names, many streets throughout Atlantic Canada commemorate First World War battles. Thus there is scarcely a town or city, large or small, that does not have a Vimy Street or Avenue. The Second World War battle of DIEPPE, 19 August 1942, is remembered in the town adjacent to Moncton, New Brunswick. Two Newfoundland locations have direct links with this war: BANTING LAKE and the HOGAN TRAIL. While their names stem from other sources, GOOSE BAY, Labrador, and GANDER, Newfoundland, became internationally recognized during the Second World War for their role in the aerial defence of the north Atlantic.

The names of the famous, and sometimes the not so famous, have always inspired place names. CHURCHILL, Prince Edward Island, named for Winston Spencer Churchill (1874–1965), was assigned as early as 1900 for his exploits as a correspondent in the Boer War. More controversial was the decision by Newfoundland premier J.R. Smallwood to rename Hamilton Falls and River for the revered Second World War British prime minister (note the entry for CHURCHILL FALLS). Sir John Hope Simpson (1868–1961), a member of the Newfoundland Commission of Government in the early 1930s is remembered in PORT HOPE SIMPSON, Labrador. One major interest of Simpson's, a land-resettlement scheme for the unemployed, reached back to the Norse MARKLAND as a name for its most successful project. LUMSDEN DAM and MOUNT McCURDY, both in Nova Scotia, and SEARY PEAK, in Newfoundland and Labrador, continued the trend of naming features for individuals.

New Brunswick has honoured a wide variety of people, both from the historical and more contemporary fields. This is particularly notable in the names of peaks in the Geologists, Historians, and Missionaries ranges, and the Naturalists Mountains. In 1964 a unique approach to mountain-naming was put forward by Arthur F. Wightman, the New Brunswick representative on the CPCGN. Adjacent to North Pole Stream was NORTH POLE MOUNTAIN. This inspired Wightman to recommend the names of St. Nicholas's reindeer, drawn from the poem by Clement Moore, for the surrounding peaks. The range is now generally known as the CHRISTMAS MOUNTAINS, a name first used by David Folster, a New Brunswick journalist. In 1964 an unsuccessful attempt was made to rename SEVOGLE, New Brunswick, 'Mount Kennedy,' for U.S. president John F. Kennedy, assassinated on 22 November 1963. It is now the official policy of the CPCGN not to bestow place names for non-Canadians, thus closing a once popular source of names.

Upon occasion names from the historical past have been utilized in later place-naming. In 1962 the stretch of water between Prince Edward Island and New Brunswick was designated Abegweit Passage, after the MV *Abegweit,* one of the Marine Atlantic ferries traversing this route. Rand suggests that the name is derived from the Mi'kmaq *Abahquit,* 'lying parallel with the land,' or *Epegweit,* 'lying in the water.' The word is also 'freely' translated as 'cradled on the waves.' It was once applied to the entire island, one of the seven Mi'kmaq districts of the Maritimes. In recent years a concerted effort has been made to restore original Inuit names for features in Labrador (see KAUMAJET MOUNTAINS, KILLINIQ ISLAND, and KIKKERTASOAK ISLAND). The naming of MOUNT CAUBVICK in 1981 is an illustration of the appropriate use of historical names. At the very least, indigenous place names are seldom repeated elsewhere!

An important category of contemporary names has resulted from municipal amalgamations. If the number of units to be combined is small, original names are frequently joined, as in PERTH–ANDOVER, New Brunswick, or CHANNEL–PORT AUX BASQUES, Newfoundland. Sometimes this becomes impossible, as in 1980 when nine Newfoundland communities were combined to form CONCEPTION BAY SOUTH. For the same reason MIRAMICHI became the name, in 1995, of the newly amalgamated city on the Miramichi River in New Brunswick. In other instances new names are sometimes selected by voters in a special plebiscite. STRATFORD, Prince Edward Island, came into being 1 April 1995, when a group of communities on the eastern edge of Charlottetown united to form a new town. In the late twentieth century, many suburban areas were systematically amalgamated or annexed to adjacent towns and cities. Despite the passage of years, a number of these 'absorbed' place names are still in common use. Thus, ROCKINGHAM, ARMDALE, and SPRYFIELD remain as widely used local names within the city of HALIFAX. By reason of their longevity and current usage, many such names have been included in this book. At the time of writing, Cape Breton Regional Municipality is the designation for the 1995 union of all municipal units in Cape Breton County. In like fashion, Halifax Regional Municipality is the 'working title' for Halifax, DARTMOUTH, BEDFORD, and adjacent areas amalgamated in 1996. Within the enabling legislation, there is a provision for changing this name, at the discretion of the new council elected 2 December 1995.

Why do place names, such as many of those cited in this chapter, endure? Can the claim be made that they are windows on the history and culture of Atlantic Canada? One answer is provided by New Brunswick scientist and historian William Francis Ganong, who wrote: 'Place names form a permanent register or index of the events or course of a country's history; they are fossils exposed in the cross section of that history, marking its successive periods; and so lasting are they that records in stone or brass are not to be compared with them for endurance.'[46] It is a long way back to the place names first implanted on Atlantic Canadian shores. Almost a millennium has passed since the Norse first discovered Vinland; but even before that time the Amerindian and Inuit people were here, as their toponymic traces testify. By the late fifteenth century, place-naming as a territorial landmark by west Europeans had became an accepted practice in the New World. There then followed nearly two centuries of conflict, largely between France and England, for supremacy on the sea and control of the land. When the dust of battle had settled, many of the place names first noted on the far horizon remained, demonstrating that endurance so eloquently inferred by Ganong. Not even cataclysmic events, such as *le grand dérangement*, the expulsion of the Acadians in 1755, was sufficient to erase the record.

The late eighteenth and nineteenth centuries saw a succession of migrations to various sections of Atlantic Canada, and with each wave of people scores of new place names were added to the map. In the transition from the middle to the nearer horizon, a succession of people pass before our eyes: New England Planters and exiled Acadians drawn back to their homeland; the 'Foreign Protestants' from central Europe, and Loyalist refugees from the Thirteen Colonies to the south; famine-weary Irish and displaced Scottish Highlanders; disbanded English soldiers and Lowland Scot and Welsh adventurers; West Country merchants and Channel Island entrepreneurs – to name but a cross-section. Through their place names, all were to join other settlers in enriching the heritage of the region. While it is not being suggested that every aspect of the past of Atlantic Canada may be interpreted through toponymy, it is fair to advance the claim that place names provide a series of illuminating windows on the history and culture of the region.

NOTES

1 Rand was also responsible for compiling a list of Mi'kmaq place names with appropriate translations. See Silas T. Rand, *Micmac Place Names in the Atlantic Provinces* (Ottawa: Queen's Printer 1919). The Mi'kmaq form of government is discussed in Daniel N. Paul, *We Were Not Savages: A Micmac*

Perspective on the Collision of European and Micmac Civilization (Halifax: Nimbus Publishing 1993); note particularly chs. 1 and 2.

2 See R.A. Skelton, Thomas E. Marston, and George D. Painter, *The Vinland Map and the Tartar Relation* (New Haven: Yale University Press 1965) and R.A. Skelton, 'The Vinland Map and the Tartar Relation,' *Geographical Magazine* 38/9 (1965–6), 662–8. Canadian cartographer T.E. Layng has placed the question of possible Norse maps in perspective: 'It is very unlikely that the rugged Vikings of the generations that frequented our shores ever produced anything on durable material which we would recognize as a map. Considering that the earliest extant chart of the Mediterranean world dates from the 14th century, it surely would be a matter of wonder if the Norsemen, without a compass and without any fixed idea of orderly exploration, had left a pattern of their voyages': T.E. Layng, ed., *Sixteenth Century Maps Relating to Canada* (Ottawa: National Archives of Canada 1956), vii. A new and expanded edition of *The Vinland Map and the Tartar Relation* was issued by Yale University Press in 1996. Recent scientific evidence shows that the ink used on the map, previously thought to be of the twentieth century, is fifteenth century in origin. Whether the map, drawn by an unknown cartographer, was actually based on records or traditions of the Norse explorers will, however, continue to be a matter for scholarly debate. Fortunately, since the first edition in 1965, we now have archaeological proof of the Norse presence in Newfoundland. See also Brian Cuthbertson, 'Voyages to North America before John Cabot: Separating Fact from Fiction,' paper read before the Royal Nova Scotia Historical Society, 15 November 1994.

3 Helge Ingstad, *Westward to Vinland* (Toronto: Macmillan of Canada 1969), 75

4 At the time of writing, planning for the 1997 anniversary of the Cabot voyage is well under way on both sides of the Atlantic. The Newfoundland Department of Tourism has already targeted the potential of this historic event with advance advertising. Overseas, at Redcliffe Quay in Bristol, a replica of Cabot's ship, the *Matthew*, is under construction, at a cost of $2 million Canadian. It is scheduled to sail to Newfoundland in June 1997. In view of the uncertainty surrounding Cabot's precise landfall, it is hoped that *Matthew II* will also visit Cape Breton and Prince Edward Island.

5 The stamps issued by Newfoundland were a two-cent rose stamp, bearing a portrait of Cabot (or, rather, a suggested likeness, since no known portrait exists); a ten-cent brown stamp, with a sketch of the *Matthew*; and a sixty-cent black stamp, depicting Henry VII. In 1949, when Newfoundland entered Confederation, Canada issued a four-cent stamp, also showing a picture of the *Matthew*. The depiction of Cabot's ship used on both stamps was a reprint of an American issue of 1893, when the same sketch appeared on the

three-cent stamp as the 'flagship of Columbus.' For more on the controversy see Alan Rayburn, 'The Use of Names to Retrofit History: The Naming of Features for John Cabot,' paper read at the conference of the Canadian Society for the Study of Names, University of Prince Edward Island, 28 May 1992.

6 Samuel Eliot Morison, *The European Discovery of America: The Northern Voyages, A.D. 500–1600* (New York: Oxford University Press 1971), 161–209

7 William Francis Ganong, *Crucial Maps in the Early Cartography of Atlantic Canada* (Toronto: University of Toronto Press 1964), 39

8 For the text of the John Day letter see *Canadian Historical Review* 38 (1957), 211–14. See also Morison, *European Discovery of America*, 192–209.

9 Quoted in James A. Williamson, *The Cabot Voyages and Bristol Discovery* (London: Hakluyt Society 1962), 214–16

10 Bernard G. Hoffman, *Cabot to Cartier* (Toronto: University of Toronto Press 1961), 168–71, 213–14

11 Ganong, *Crucial Maps*, 204

12 Nicolas Denys, *Description and Natural History of the Coasts of North America* (Toronto: The Champlain Society 1908), 178–9

13 Alan Rayburn, *Acadia: The Origin of the Name* (Ottawa: Department of Energy, Mines and Resources 1973), 26

14 E.R. Seary, *Place Names of the Avalon Peninsula of the Island of Newfoundland* (Toronto: University of Toronto Press 1971), 28–9

15 Ramsay Cook, ed., *The Voyages of Jacques Cartier* (Toronto: University of Toronto Press 1993), 9

16 Much credit for our present knowledge of the Basque contribution to Canadian history must go to Selma de Lothbinière Barkham. For her ground-breaking research she was awarded the Royal Canadian Geographical Society's Gold Medal in 1980. See the following: Selma Barkham, 'The Identification of Labrador Ports in Spanish 16th Century Documents,' *The Canadian Cartographer* 14/1 (June 1977), 1–9; 'First Will and Testament on the Labrador Coast,' *The Geographical Magazine* 49/9 (June 1977), 574–81 ; [with Robert Grenier], 'Filling a Gap in our History between Jacques Cartier and Champlain,' *Canadian Geographic* 96/1 (February–March 1978), 8–19: 'Divers Find Sunken Basque Galleon in Labrador,' *Canadian Geographic* 97/3 (December 1978–January 1979), 60–3; 'Finding Sources of Canadian History in Spain,' *Canadian Geographic* 100/3 (June–July 1980), 66–73; 'Documentary Evidence for 16th Century Basque Sailing Ships in the Strait of Belle Isle,' *European Settlement and Exploitation in Atlantic Canada* (St. John's: Memorial University 1982), 87–99; and *The Basque Coast of Newfoundland* (Plum Point, NF: Great North-

ern Peninsula Development Corporation 1989), 1–22. See also Michael M. Barkham, 'Aspects of Life Aboard Basque Ships ...,' *Parks Canada Report* 1981, and 'French Basque Newfoundland Entrepreneurs ...,' *Newfoundland Studies* 10/1 (Spring 1994), 1–43.

17 Miren Egaña Goya, 'Basque Toponymy in Canada,' *Onomastica Canadiana* 74/2 (December 1992), 55; see also 53–74

18 Harold A. Innis, *The Cod Fisheries* (Toronto: University of Toronto Press 1954), 15

19 Marc Lescarbot, *The History of New France* (Toronto: The Champlain Society 1911), 233

20 Seary, *Place Names of the Avalon Peninsula*, 56

21 Lescarbot, *History of New France*, 30

22 Robert Cuff, 'Robert Taverner's Second Survey,' *Newfoundland Quarterly* 89/3 (Spring-Summer 1995). I am indebted to Dr. W. Gordon Handcock for drawing this reference to my attention.

23 Lescarbot, *History of New France*, 296

24 The definitive study of Acadian demography is to be found in Andrew Hill Clark, *Acadia: The Geography of Early Nova Scotia to 1700* (Madison: University of Wisconsin Press 1968). As well, see Andrew Hill Clark, *Three Centuries and The Island* (Toronto: University of Toronto Press 1959). See also references to Naomi E.S. Griffith in the Bibliographical Essay.

25 James DeMille, 'Sweet Maiden of Passamaquoddy,' *New Dominion: True Humorist*, 16 April 1870, 171

26 See Frederic F. Thompson, *The French Shore Problem in Newfoundland* (Toronto: University of Toronto Press 1961).

27 Some of the basic historical and demographic information in this chapter is drawn, in part, from William B. Hamilton, *Local History in Atlantic Canada* (Toronto: Macmillan of Canada 1974).

28 See Winthrop Pickard Bell, *The Foreign Protestants and the Settlement of Nova Scotia* (Toronto: University of Toronto Press 1961).

29 The historical analysis of the Acadian expulsion is very extensive. Readers interested in more detail are directed to the Bibliographical Essay. See also Stephen White, *Patronymes Acadiens* (Moncton: Les Editions d'Acadie 1972), and the National Film Board documentary *The Acadian Connection*. The latter highlights the heritage of a prominent Acadian family, the LeBlancs. Genealogists estimate that there are more than 250,000 descendants of Daniel LeBlanc and Françoise Gaudet, who were married at Port Royal in 1650 (see entry for Cormier Cove, New Brunswick).

30 For more detail see R.S. Longley, 'The Coming of the New England Planters to the Annapolis Valley,' *Collections of the Royal Nova Scotia Historical Society*

33 (1961), 81–101, and W.O. Raymond, *The River St. John* (Sackville: Tribune Press 1950), 130–87.

31 See references listed in the Bibliographical Essay. DesBarres was also a notable artist. In 1982 the Dalhousie University Art Gallery held a major exhibition entitled 'J.F.W. DesBarres: Views and Profiles.' The exhibition catalogue contains an overview of DesBarres's role as an artist. In 1992 the Prince Edward Island Museum and Heritage Foundation opened a major exhibition, 'Prince Edward Island in the Age of Discovery,' at the Confederation Centre Art Gallery. The maps and engravings (including one by DesBarres) were from the collection of James W. McNutt. The catalogue that accompanied the exhibition contains an essay that summarizes important trends in Atlantic Canadian cartography.

32 The New Brunswick settlement was named for the Quaker leader William Penn II (1644–1718); however, the state was earlier designated by King Charles II for his father, Sir William Penn I (1621–1670). It has been erroneously claimed that the state of Pennsylvania was named for the son rather than the father.

33 For further detail see Marion Robertson, *King's Bounty: A History of Early Shelburne, Nova Scotia* (Halifax: Nova Scotia Museum 1983). An update on Black Studies research will be found in C. Mark Davis, 'Recent Black Maritime Studies,' *Acadiensis* 23/2 (Spring 1994), 148–52.

34 Esther Clark Wright, *The Loyalists of New Brunswick* (Moncton: Moncton Publishing Company 1972), 241

35 Peter Neary and Patrick O'Flaherty, *Part of the Main: An Illustrated History of Newfoundland and Labrador* (St. John's: Breakwater Books 1983), 53

36 John Reeves, *History of the Government of the Island of Newfoundland* (London: J. Sewell 1793), 21

37 See John Mannion, ed., *The Peopling of Newfoundland: Essays in Historical Geography* (St. John's: Memorial University 1977); C. Grant Head, *Eighteenth-Century Newfoundland* (Toronto: McClelland and Stewart 1976); and W. Gordon Handcock, *So longe as there comes noe women: Origins of English Settlement in Newfoundland* (St. John's: Breakwater Press 1989).

38 Recent research by Guernsey historian John Sarre provides detailed information on the Channel Island connection with Cape Breton. See John Sarre and Lorena Forbrigger, 'Some Guernsey Connections with Cape Breton Island,' *Nova Scotia Historical Review* 14/1 (1994), 66–78; Rosemary E. Ommer, *From Outpost to Outport: A Structural Analysis of the Jersey–Gaspé Cod Fishery, 1767–1886* (Montreal: McGill–Queen's University Press 1991); and Stephen J. Hornby, *Nineteenth Century Cape Breton: A Historical Geography* (Montreal: McGill–Queen's University Press 1992).

39 *The Times*, 28 June 1815

40 For detail concerning emigration to Atlantic Canada see Helen I. Cowan, *British Emigration to British North America* (Toronto: University of Toronto Press 1961); Winthrop Pickard Bell, *The Foreign Protestants and the Settlement of Nova Scotia* (Toronto: University of Toronto Press 1961); Gillian T. Cell, *English Enterprise in Newfoundland, 1577–1660* (Toronto: University of Toronto Press 1960); Graeme Wynn, *Timber Colony: A Historical Geography of Early Nineteenth-Century New Brunswick* (Toronto: University of Toronto Press 1981); J.M. Bumstead, *The Peoples Clearances: Highland Emigration to British North America, 1770–1815* (Edinburgh: Edinburgh University Press 1982); Handcock, *So long as there comes noe women*. See also Mannion, *The Peopling of Newfoundland*, and Head, *Eighteenth-Century Newfoundland*.

41 W.S. McNutt, *New Brunswick, A History: 1784–1867* (Toronto: Macmillan of Canada 1963), 179–80

42 William B. Hamilton, 'Place Names Over the Water ... The Impact of Prince Charles Edward Stuart on Atlantic Canadian Nomenclature,' paper read at the Conference of the Canadian Society for the Study of Names, Université du Québec à Montréal, 2 June 1995. For the romantically inclined, it should be noted that, although the direct male Stuart line 'died out,' there is still a Stuart claimant to the British throne. Prince Michael Stuart, a direct descendant on the maternal side, lives in Paris. 'He is well informed on modern Scottish affairs and speaks eloquently, with a trace of Scottish accent, of his plans should [the House of Stuart] ever be restored': *In Britain*, July 1995, 15.

43 From Principles and Procedures adopted by the Canadian Permanent Committee on Geographical Names (CPCGN). It should be pointed out that the provincial and territorial governments are the ultimate naming authorities. The CPCGN acts in an advisory and coordinating role.

44 The Newfoundland Nomenclature Board was created in 1904 and continued under the Commission of Government (1934–49). The act establishing the board was amended on 28 May 1938 and proclaimed again following confederation with Canada: *Statutes of Newfoundland*, 1959, no. 13. The present Newfoundland and Labrador Names Board dates from 1979.

45 Prowestown was so used by Patrick O'Flaherty in *Come Near at Your Peril* (St. John's: Breakwater Books 1994), 53.

46 William Francis Ganong, 'A Monograph on the Place Nomenclature of the Province of New Brunswick,' *Transactions of the Royal Society of Canada*, 2d ser., 1896, 176

2

New Brunswick

Aboujagane River (Westmorland)   Flows into the NORTHUMBERLAND STRAIT, east of SHEDIAC. William Francis Ganong attributes the name to unknown Mi'kmaq sources; it appears as *Naboujagan* in the 1812 journal of Bishop Joseph-Octave Plessis (1763–1825). Highway 930, which roughly parallels the lower section of the river, is known locally as 'the Aboujagane Trail.' Haute-Aboujagane and Basse-Aboujagane, on the east and west sides of the river, respectively, were adopted as post-office names in 1953. See also BEAUBASSIN EAST.

Acadians Range (Northumberland)   South of the NEPISIGUIT RIVER. The name was first put forward in 1899 by William Francis Ganong as a means of honouring Acadians prominent in the history of the province. See also MOUNT DENYS.

Acadieville (Kent)   On Highway 130, south of ROGERSVILLE. The name may be traced to Acadie, or Acadia, the name of the French colony which, at various times, included the present Maritime provinces and adjacent parts of Québec and Maine. For derivation see chapter 1, page 7.

Acton (York)   Northeast of HARVEY. Probably named for John Dalberg Acton (1834–1902), who, as Lord Acton, achieved fame as a historian and advocate of home rule for Ireland. He is also remembered for coining the oft-quoted maxim: 'Power tends to corrupt and absolute power corrupts absolutely.' The area was settled in 1842 by Irish immigrants. The post office dates from 1865.

Adamsville (Kent)   On Highway 126, south of HARCOURT. The name was bestowed in honour of

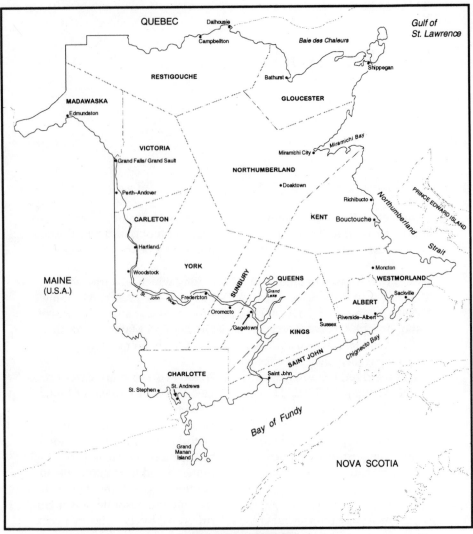

QUEBEC

Dalhousie
Campbellton

Baie des Chaleurs

Gulf of
St. Lawrence

RESTIGOUCHE

Bathurst

Shippegan

GLOUCESTER

MADAWASKA

Edmundston

VICTORIA
Grand Falls/ Grand Sault

Miramichi City

Miramichi Bay

NORTHUMBERLAND

Doaktown

Richibucto

Northumberland

PRINCE EDWARD ISLAND

Perth–Andover

CARLETON

KENT

Bouctouche

Strait

Hartland

YORK

SUNBURY

QUEENS

Moncton

WESTMORLAND

MAINE
(U.S.A.)

St. John River

Fredericton

Oromocto

Grand
Lake

Gagetown

KINGS

ALBERT

Sackville

Riverside–Albert

Sussex

SAINT JOHN

Chignecto Bay

Woodstock

CHARLOTTE

St. Stephen

St. Andrews

Saint John

Bay of Fundy

Grand
Manan
Island

NOVA SCOTIA

NEW BRUNSWICK

Michael Adams (1845–1899), MLA for Northumberland–Miramichi. Adams served as surveyor general under Premier John J. Fraser (1829–1896), who held office from 1878 to 1882.

Albert County; Albert Mines
The county fronts on CHIGNECTO BAY. It was created in 1845 and named for Prince Albert (1819–1861), consort of Queen Victoria. Albert Mines, southeast of HILLS-BOROUGH, was the site of the discovery in 1849 of the mineral albertite, a bituminous, jet-black hydrocarbon that yields oil and gas. The communities of Riverside and Albert were incorporated as the village of RIVERSIDE–ALBERT in 1966.

Albert Mines   *See* Albert County.

Aldouane (Kent)   *See* Grande-Aldouane.

Allardville (Gloucester)   Southeast of BATHURST. The village takes its name from the parish, which, in turn, was named for Monsignor Jean Joseph-Auguste Allard (1884–1971). During the Depression of the 1930s, Allard encouraged a group of the unemployed to settle on lands provided by the provincial government. The Allardville community was the result.

Alma (Albert)   On CHIGNECTO BAY, near the entrance to FUNDY NATIONAL PARK. It was established in 1856 and named for the Battle of Alma River, 20 September 1855, one of the major engagements of the Crimean War (1853–6). See also ALMA, Nova Scotia.

Anagance; Anagance River
(Kings)   Southwest of PETITCO-DIAC. The name was applied first to the river and is derived from the Maliseet *Olnegansek*, which has been translated by William Francis Ganong as 'little portage stream.' The post office dates from 1875.

Anagance River   *See* Anagance.

Andover   *See* Perth–Andover.

Anse-Bleue (Gloucester)   *Anse* is an Acadian topographical term for 'cove' or 'bay' and is a part of many place names in New Brunswick, Nova Scotia, and Newfoundland. The French spelling for this community was officially adopted in 1968. See also nearby GRANDE-ANSE, and GRANDE ANSE, Nova Scotia.

Apohaqui (Kings)   First known as 'Mouth of Millstream' for its location in relation to this feature. William Francis Ganong suggests that the name, of Maliseet origin, is 'probably their name for Millstream, but possibly it may mean the junction of two streams.' The post office was opened in 1869. It is the birthplace of the Honourable Frank McKenna, premier of New Brunswick (1987–).

Aroostook; Aroostook River
(Victoria)   A tributary of the ST. JOHN RIVER. The name originates with the river and is of uncertain Maliseet origin. It may be derived from *Woolastook*, the Maliseet designation for the St. John River. It appears first on DeRozier's map of 1699 as *Arassatuk* and has been translated as 'good river for everything.' The contemporary spelling dates from 1854, with the establishment of the post office. As a result of imprecise wording in the Treaty of Paris (1783), the Aroostook River valley became the centre of a boundary dispute between New Brunswick and Maine during the 1830s and early 1840s. By 1839 a series of incidents resulted in the amassing of troops on both sides of the border. Although outright war was averted, the skirmishes are remembered in local folklore as the 'Aroostook' or 'Lumberman's' war. The matter was not settled until the Webster–Ashburton Treaty of 1842. See also ASHBURTON HEAD.

Aroostook River   *See* Aroostook.

Arthurette (Victoria)   Southwest of PLASTER ROCK. The name was bestowed by Sir Arthur Hamilton Gordon (1819–1912), lieutenant-governor of New Brunswick from 1861 to 1866. In his book *Wilderness Journeys in New Brunswick,* he noted: 'I ... named it for the little border village [Arthuret, south of Carlisle] where Sir James Graham (1792–1861) lies buried.' Graham served as first lord of the Admiralty (1852–5) and was, for a time, a member of the British Parliament for Carlisle.

Ashburton Head (Charlotte)   On GRAND MANAN ISLAND. The name commemorates a marine tragedy that took place off this headland on 19 January 1857, when the *Lord Ashburton* sank, leaving only eight survivors from a crew of twenty-nine. The ship, built in ST. ANDREWS, was named for Lord Ashburton (1799–1864), one of the negotiators of the Webster–Ashburton Treaty of 1842. This treaty defined the present boundary between New Brunswick and Maine. See also AROOSTOOK and BAKER BROOK.

Astle (York)   Southwest of BOIESTOWN. Lieutenant-Colonel Joseph Gubbinson, during a tour of militia units in New Brunswick in 1811–13, noted: 'I halted at an inn kept by Captain John Astle. The whole house consisted of one large room but he partitioned off a corner of it with a curtain for my accommodation. Militia titles do not convey great ideas of rank or respectability in this quarter of the world.' The locality is named for the innkeeper.

Atholville (Restigouche)   West of CAMPELLTON. One of several Scottish-inspired place names in the northern section of the county. Robert Ferguson (1768–1851), a native of Logierait, Scotland, emigrated to this area in 1796. He quickly established himself as a leading merchant and shipbuilder. By the 1840s Ferguson was known in some circles as 'the father and founder of the Restigouche.' Atholville, the site of his shipbuilding enterprise, was named for his home, which he called 'Athol House,' undoubtedly inspired by Blair Atholl, situated near Ferguson's birthplace in Scotland. A nearby community, southeast of Atholville, is named for Blair Atholl. See also FERGUSON POINT.

Aulac (Westmorland)   On the Franquet map of 1754, the village of *Le Lac* is placed at the head of the Rivière-du-Lac. Over time this location became known as 'Au Lac,' or 'at the lake.' The French descriptive has survived as Aulac, a border-crossing point between New Brunswick and Nova Scotia.

Baie de Caraquet   *See* Caraquet.

Baie des Lamèque   *See* Lamèque.

Baie des Chaleurs (Restigouche and Gloucester)   During Jacques Cartier's first voyage to the New World, in early July 1534, he entered and subsequently explored a bay and surrounding territory which he described as being 'more temperate than Spain and the finest it is possible to see. There is not the smallest plot of ground bare of wood, but is full of wild wheat, as well as pease, as thick as if they had been sown and hoed; of white and red currant bushes, of strawberries, of raspberries, of white and red roses and of other plants of a strong, pleasant odour. Likewise there are many fine meadows with useful herbs, and a pond where there are many salmon ... We named this bay Chaleur Bay [the 'Bay of Heat,' 10 July 1534].' Over the years Baie des Chaleurs has been noted for numerous sightings of a phantom ship. An artistic interpretation of the ship has been incorporated in the logo for the Chaleur region tourist authority.

Baie-Sainte-Anne (Northumberland)   Southwest of ESCUMINAC, on the south shore of MIRAMICHI BAY. Settled in 1760 by Acadians, who had returned following the expulsion five years earlier, and named for Sainte Anne, mother of the Blessed Virgin Mary and patroness of the Mi'kmaq.

Baie Verte (Westmorland)   The village in on Baie Verte, near the border with Nova Scotia. A descriptive, the name was inspired by the salt-water grasses, which in summer give it the appearance a great meadow. In 1832 Thomas Baillie, the province's surveyor general, noted: 'Bay Vert gets its name from the quantity of salt water grass which grows in the mud and floats on the surface.' It appeared on the Franquelin map of 1701 as *B. Verte* and on a chart dated 1749 by Jean-Baptiste de Couagne (1687–1740) as *Baye Verte*. (The latter was earlier involved in making a map of the seigneuries of New France and Acadia.) The land surrounding the bay was within a seigneury granted to Alexandre Leneuf de La Vallière et de Beaubassin (1666–1712) on 24 October 1676. As part of the defence of the ISTHMUS OF CHIGNECTO, the French built Fort Gaspereau, east of Baie Verte village.

Baillie (Charlotte)   East of Canoose Lake. Named for Thomas Baillie (1796–1863), who was appointed by the British government to serve as surveyor general of the province (1824–51). In a classic use of understatement, historian James Hannay (1842–1910) suggested that Baillie 'was not a general favourite in New Brunswick.' In fulfilling his mandate the surveyor general managed to alienate most New Brunswickers by his dictatorial methods, ostentatious lifestyle, and 'unnecessary display of wealth.' On the positive side he earnestly sought to improve the administration of crown lands, to increase provincial revenues, and to encourage the investment of capital. His *An Account of the Province of New Brunswick*, published in 1832, is a valuable portrait of the province. Today, the small community of Baillie remains as his memorial. See also BAIE VERTE.

Baker Brook (Madawaska) Flows southeast into the ST. JOHN RIVER, southwest of Edmundston. This area was the setting for one of the many boundary disputes between New Brunswick and Maine. In 1827 John Baker (1796–1868), for whom the feature is named, proclaimed the area to be American territory, 'the republic of Madawaska.' When ordered to remove the American flag, Baker refused, and was arrested and sent to FREDERICTON for trial. He was subsequently found guilty and sentenced to two months in jail. The boundary question was not finally settled until 1842. See also AROOSTOOK, ASHBURTON HEAD, and EDMUND-STON.

Bald Peak (Victoria)   Southeast of NICTAU, in the northern section of the county. The name is descriptive of this 640-metre-high mountain.

Balmoral (Restigouche)   Southwest of DALHOUSIE. Named in 1856 for Balmoral Castle, near Braemar, Scotland. The castle became a royal residence in 1852, when it was purchased by Prince Albert. The name is Gaelic in origin and may be translated as 'homestead in a clearing,' or more freely as 'majestic dwelling.' See also BALMORAL, Nova Scotia.

Barachois (Westmorland)   A place name common to Newfoundland, Nova Scotia, and New Brunswick. For derivation see BARACHOIS, Nova Scotia.

Barnaby; Barnaby River (Northumberland)   The river is a tributary of the MIRAMICHI, roughly paralleling Highway 126. William Francis Ganong suggests that it was named for a Maliseet chief. The community takes its name from the river. The post office was established in 1871.

Barnaby River   *See* Barnaby.

Barony (York)   Near the mouth of the POKIOK STREAM, which flows into the ST. JOHN RIVER. The name originates with the estate of a prominent Loyalist, John Saunders (1745–1834). A native of Virginia, he attempted to emulate in New Brunswick his previous lifestyle as a major landholder, and eventually succeeded in amassing more than 2,000 hectares. 'The Barony,' built in 1795, was identical to his home in Virginia except that wood was used in its construction rather than brick. Following the death of his son, John Simcoe Saunders (1795–1878), the estate was sold. According to author and naturalist Moses Henry Perley (1804–1872), the estate was 'a waste howling wilderness ... "a barren eh" rather than a Barony.' The place name has proved to be more enduring than either the house or the estate.

Bartibog; Bartibog River (Northumberland)   The river flows into the MIRAMICHI, at Bartibog Bridge. This place name is of uncertain origin. It may be a corruption of a Mi'kmaq descriptive, or more likely an adaptation of a person's name. According to William Francis Ganong, 'tradition derives it from the name of an Indian, Bartholomew LaBogue or Barthélemi Labauve.' Alan Rayburn suggests that this individual was called 'Balt Bogue by the Indians and Bartabogue by the French and English.' The town was settled in 1812 by emigrants from Scotland. In 1815, on a point of land where the Bartibog River joins the Miramichi, one of these settlers, Alexander Mac-Donald, built a stately Georgian-style two-storey house of local sandstone. Beautifully sited, it has been a landmark for generations. The house was restored in the 1970s and is now open to the public as a historic site and working farm.

Bartibog River   *See* Bartibog.

Bartlett's Mills (Charlotte)   On GOLDSMITHS STREAM, which flows into the WAWEIG RIVER. In 1808 Leonard Bartlett (1779–1854) emigrated with his family from Alna, Maine, to this section of New Brunswick. Determined to capitalize on the economic potential of the location, Bartlett erected a dam across the stream, enabling a carding mill and sawmill to be established. Later a grist mill and finishing mill for lumber products were added. Thus, it was inevitable that the community would become known as 'Bartlett's Mills.' When the post office was established in 1877, it was located in the mill, with Jesse Bartlett (1815–1902) as the first postmaster. Nearly two centuries later, the family is still in the lumber business. Marvin Bartlett, a direct descendant, manufactures cedar fencing for export; his nephew Hugh Bartlett operates a sawmill on the nearby Waweig River. See also ST. STEPHEN.

Bas-Caraquet   *See* Caraquet.

Basse-Aboujagane   *See* Aboujagane River.

Bass River (Kent)   Flows into the RICHIBUCTO RIVER, southwest of REXTON. The name is descriptive and is indicative of the quantities of bass once caught here. The post office dates from 1867. There is a second Bass River in GLOUCESTER COUNTY.

Basswood Ridge (Charlotte)   North of ST. STEPHEN, in an area settled by emigrants from Sutherlandshire, Scotland, in 1803. The name derives from a stand of basswood trees encountered by these first settlers. Nearby SCOTCH RIDGE was founded at the same time.

Bath (Carleton)   North of BRISTOL, on Highway 105. Formerly known as 'Munquart,' or 'Monquart,' for the river which flows through the village. The name is a Maliseet descriptive and is derived from *Abmutqualtuk*, variously translated as 'clearwater river' or 'in a line with the main river.' In 1875 the name was changed to Bath for the city and spa near Bristol, England. See also BRISTOL.

Bathurst (Gloucester)   On NEPISI-GUIT BAY, an arm of BAIE DES CHALEURS. First known as 'Nepisiguit,' and later 'St. Peters,' it was renamed in 1826 by Lieu-tenant-Governor Howard Doug-las (1776–1861) for the colonial secretary, Henry, third Earl of Bathurst (1762–1834). Nepisiguit was the site of a post established in 1652 by Nicolas Denys (1598–1688), where he completed his most lasting contribution, the writing of the monumental *Description géographique et his-torique des costes de l'Amérique sep-tentrionale*. In Denys's words: 'Here I was obliged to retire after the burning of my Fort of Saint Pierre in the Island of Cape Bre-ton [during the winter of 1668–9]. My house is flanked by four little bastions with a palisade with six pieces of cannon in batteries. The lands are not of the best: there are rocks in some places. I have a large garden in which the land is good for vegetables, which come on in a marvellous way. I have sown the seeds of Pears and Apples, which have come up and are well established, although this is the coldest place that I have lived, and the one where

there is the most snow. The Peas and Wheat come on passably well; the Raspberries and the Strawberries are abundant every-where.' Denys died at Nepisiguit and lies buried near the site of his 'beloved house and garden,' now part of the Gowan Brae golf course. As expressed in the *Dic-tionary of Canadian Biography*: 'His is the distinction of being the first Acadian author and lumber-man, an arresting figure whose remarkable ability and force made him one of the principals in this new land during its infancy.' Bathurst was incorporated as a town in 1912 and as a city in 1966. See also ST. PETER'S, Nova Scotia.

Bay du Vin; Bay du Vin Island; Bay du Vin River (Northumber-land)   The bay is an extension of MIRAMICHI BAY. A number of the-ories exist to explain this place name. The most logical is that given by Alan Rayburn, who sug-gests that it is 'probably corrupted from *baie des ventes* meaning "*bay of winds*" ... not in reference to wine.' Site of an Acadian refu-gee camp after the fall of FORT BEAUSÉJOUR and the expulsion of the Acadians in 1755. Bay du Vin River and Bay du Vin Island are in the same general area.

Bay du Vin Island   *See* Bay du Vin.

Bay du Vin River   *See* Bay du Vin.

Bayfield (Westmorland)   West of CAPE TORMENTINE. The name marks the career of Henry Wolsey Bayfield (1795–1885), who was responsible for surveying much of the coastline of New Brunswick, Prince Edward Island, and Nova Scotia during the 1840s and 1850s. The name is fitting since, during the summers of 1842 and 1843, Bayfield charted this coastline and adjacent waters. It is possible that members of the survey crew landed near the community which bears his name; certainly he sailed within sight of the location on several occasions. See also BAYFIELD, Nova Scotia and Prince Edward Island.

Bay of Fundy   *See* chapter 1, pages 9–10.

Beaubassin East (Westmorland) On 8 May 1995, New Brunswick's first officially designated 'Rural Community' came into being. The former local service districts of Botsford, Boudreau West, Grand Barachois, HAUTE-ABOUJAGANE, CORMIER-VILLAGE, and St. Andre LeBlanc were amalgamated to form the community of Beaubassin East. The name is historic and dates back to the seigneury of Michel Leneuf de La Vallière et de Beaubassin (1640–

1705), commandant and governor of Acadia from 1678 to 1684. On 24 October 1676, Louis de Buade, Comte de Frontenac (1622–1698), governor of New France, granted Beaubassin a seigneury of 10 square leagues on the ISTHMUS OF CHIGNECTO.

Beaubears Island (Northumberland)   The name serves as a reminder of the military career of Charles Deschamps de Boishébert et de Raffetot (1727–1797). Following the 1755 expulsion of the Acadians, some 3,500 survivors gathered in the MIRAMICHI area. Boishébert, a career army officer, was placed in charge of these refugees, who subsequently established camps on both sides of Miramichi Bay and farther inland, on an island and point near the confluence of the Southwest and Northwest Miramichi rivers. Both the island and point were named for Boishébert; however, the former was later renamed for a New Jersey Loyalist, John Wilson. 'Beaubears Island,' a corrupted version of the commandant's name, survives. See also THE ENCLOSURE.

Beauséjour   *See* Fort Beauséjour.

Beaver Brook Station (Northumberland)   Northeast of Newcastle. Famous as the inspiration for the title Lord Beaverbrook, assumed in 1917 by Max Aitken (1879–1964). See also NEWCASTLE.

Becaguimec Island; Becaguimec Lake; Becaguimec Stream
(Carleton)   The stream enters the ST. JOHN RIVER at HARTLAND. The name stems from *Abekaguimek*, the word used by the Maliseet to describe the place where salmon may be found. The stream rises in the centre of YORK COUNTY, near the sources of the KESWICK RIVER and NACKAWIC STREAM. Becaguimec Island and Becaguimec Lake take their name from the stream.

Becaguimec Lake   *See* Becaguimec Island.

Becaguimec Stream   *See* Becaguimec Island.

Beechwood (Carleton)   Northwest of BATH; site of a major hydro-electric development. Bumfrow Brook flows into the ST. JOHN RIVER at this point. Bumfrow may be traced to *Bumfrau*, a corruption of the French *bois franc*, for 'hardwood.' It was descriptive of the beech and other hardwood trees found nearby.

Belledune (Gloucester)   A descriptive for the excellent beaches, with characteristic sand-dunes, that may be found along much of the coastline of BAIE DES CHALEURS. At Belledune a deep-water harbour and accompanying industrial complex dominate the landscape; however, 'beautiful dunes' may still be found.

Belleisle; Belleisle Bay; Belleisle River (Kings)   The bay is an inlet of the ST. JOHN RIVER, between WASHADEMOAK LAKE and the KENNEBECASIS. Esther Clark Wright has described Belleisle Bay: 'It is less formidable than the Kennebecasis, more homelike than the Long Reach, more varied than the Washademoak. It is for those who live beside it and for those who love to linger along it.' One of the first settlers who 'chose to live beside it' was the Alexandre Le Borgne de Belle-Isle II, who moved here from Annapolis in 1656. Son of the one-time acting governor and seigneur of Port-Royal, Alexandre Le Borgne de Belle-Isle I (1643–1693), Belle-Isle gave his name to the community, the bay, and the river.

Belleisle Bay   *See* Belleisle.

Belleisle River   *See* Belleisle.

Ben Lomond   *See* Loch Lomond.

Beresford (Gloucester)   On the western outskirts of BATHURST. The town takes its name from the parish named for William Carr Beresford, first Viscount Beresford (1768–1854), a prominent

English general who achieved fame during the struggle for the Iberian peninsula (1808–14). Incorporated as a town in 1984.

Bertrand (Gloucester)   West of CARAQUET. Incorporated as a village in 1968. Named for the first settlers, the Bertrands, one of the 'original' Acadian families.

Big Bald Mountain (Northumberland)   East of the South Branch NEPISIGUIT RIVER. This mountain, 762 metres high, was named by nature. Little Bald Mountain, 658 metres high, lies some 15 kilometres northeast 'as the crow flies.' It is also a descriptive.

Big Sevogle River   *See* Sevogle.

Big Tracadie River   *See* Tracadie.

Billy Island (York)   A small island in GRAND LAKE, on the New Brunswick–Maine border. A local legend, possibly apocryphal, relates that a couple named Billy and Nan were canoeing across the lake, *en route* to their wedding. When night fell and they had not reached their destination, Nan took refuge on one island, while Billy paddled on to the next one – thus observing Victorian proprieties. In any event, the two adjacent islands still bear the names Billy and Nan.

Blacks Harbour (Charlotte)   Southeast of ST. GEORGE. Renowned as a centre for the sardine- and herring-canning industry. The precise origin of the name is unknown; however, it was probably named for an early settler.

Blackville (Northumberland)   On the MIRAMICHI RIVER, south of RENOUS. The name marks the career of William Black (1771–1866), a native of Aberdeen, Scotland, who emigrated to SAINT JOHN in 1798 to join his brother John in the timber trade. When the latter moved to HALIFAX in 1808, William Black assumed control of the Saint John branch of the firm. By 1812 it had become one of the largest business enterprises in British North America. He later served as member of the executive council and administrator of the province (1829–31).

Blair Athol   See Atholville.

Blissfield (Northumberland); **Blissville** (Sunbury)   Blissfield is on the MIRAMICHI, northeast of DOAKTOWN. Soon after their arrival in New Brunswick, following the American Revolution, the Bliss family became part of the New Brunswick Loyalist establishment. A characteristic of this group was their attempt to reserve official appointments for members of select families. While administrator of the province, in 1824 John Murray Bliss (1771–1834) took the opportunity to name his son, George Pidgeon Bliss, to the combined offices of surveyor general, receiver general, and auditor general. Following the arrival of Lieutenant-Governor Sir Howard Douglas (1776–1861), two of these appointments were revoked, and the younger Bliss had to be content with the post of receiver general. Blissville, southeast of Fredericton Junction, is also named for John Murray Bliss.

Blissville   *See* Blissfield.

Bocabec; Bocabec Cove; Bocabec River (Charlotte)   The river flows into PASSAMAQUODDY BAY. The name is derived from the Passamaquoddy *Pokabek*, of unknown meaning. The community and cove take their name from the river. The place name has given rise to a folk expression in the form of a curse: 'Woe onto you ye Bocabecers!' Although today the expression is repeated only in jest by older residents, it is deeply rooted in the folklore of the area. The curse refers to an early-nineteenth-century incident involving two of the founding families, the Hansons and Turners. The younger men of these families were working in a winter lumber camp, miles from Bocabec. One of their 'patriarchs,' a Hanson, died in his home at Bocabec. During the funeral service the officiating clergyman, the Reverend William Mullen (?–1888), condemned the non-attendance of the younger generation with the words: 'Woe unto you ye Bocabecers, ye Hansons and ye Turners, that ye would not come out of the woods to bury your father.' Although probably embellished over the years, the mere survival of the 'curse' is an indication of the strength of folk tradition: *Collections of the New Brunswick Historical Society* 19 (1966), 96–104.

Bocabec Cove   *See* Bocabec.

Bocabec River   *See* Bocabec.

Boiestown (Northumberland) On the Southwest Miramichi River, near the YORK COUNTY boundary. In 1832 Robert Cooney wrote: 'Mr Thomas Boies, an active and enterprising American, lately established a village, popularly called Boiestown after its founder.' Established as a company town, it included, in addition to the Boies sawmill, a theatre, a non-denominational church, and workmen's houses. Boies sold his interest in the company in 1835. The post office dates from 1840.

Boishébert (Gloucester)   Northwest of TRACADIE. Named for Charles Deschamps de Boishébert et de Raffetot (1727–1797), a native of Québec City and officer with the French colonial troops. His career became entwined with the survival of the Acadians following the expulsion. See also BEAUBEARS ISLAND.

Brantville (Northumberland) Near the NORTHUMBERLAND–GLOUCESTER county border. The district is a migratory sanctuary for the Brant goose (*Branta bernicla*).

Bouctouche (Kent)   The name may be traced to the Mi'kmaq descriptive *Chebuktoosk*, usually translated as 'big bay.' Although the name is of much earlier origin, the area was first settled by Acadians who returned following the expulsion. Bouctouche is the home of noted Acadian author Antonine Maillet. Of her work Janice Kulyk Keefer has written: 'There is an overwhelming sense of particular time and local place in her writing, an impassioned commitment to [Acadia] as a social and political entity.' The title character of her best-known work, *La Sagouine*, with its Rabelaisian humour and satire, is 'not an individual but a collective being, the memory of the Acadian people.' The plays and novels of Maillet are featured each summer at the theme park Le Pays de La Sagouine in Bouctouche. On 24 July 1985, Buctouche village had its status changed to a town and its spelling altered to 'Bouctouche.' Other nearby features carrying the name, such as Buctouche River, were not affected by this change.

Bristol (Carleton)   Formerly known as 'Shikatehawk,' for the stream that flows into the ST. JOHN RIVER at this point. Because the English spelling and pronunciation of the original Maliseet 'was sometimes less than refined,' a decision was reached to change the name. It was renamed for Bristol in England, inspired, no doubt, by its proximity to Bath, farther up the St. John River. See also SHIKATEHAWK STREAM.

Broad Arrow Brook (York) Flows into the KESWICK RIVER. The name is derived from the eighteenth- and early-nineteenth-century practice of marking pine trees 30 centimetres in diameter and upward with the 'Broad Arrow' symbol. The trees thus marked were reserved to supply masts for the Royal Navy. See also KINGSCLEAR.

Buctouche River   *See* Bouctouche.

Bumfrow Brook   *See* Beechwood.

Burnt Church; Burnt Church Point; Burnt Church River
(Northumberland)   On MIRAMICHI BAY. Following the capture of Louisbourg in July 1758, Colonel James Murray (1721–1794) was sent to destroy the Acadian settlements in the MIRAMICHI area. He reached Miramichi Bay on 15 September 1758, and later reported: 'On the evening of the 17th in obedience to instructions embarked the troops, having two days hunted all around us for the Indians and Acadians to no purpose, we destroyed their provisions, wigwams and houses. The church, a very handsome one built with stone, did not escape.' It was this incident that resulted in the English place name Burnt Church for the Mi'kmaq village of *Eskinwobudich*, the latter name a descriptive for 'lookout place.'

Burnt Church Point   *See* Burnt Church.

Burnt Church River   *See* Burnt Church.

Burton (Sunbury)   Originally assigned to the township and parish, and later to the village northeast of OROMOCTO. Named for Brigadier Ralph Burton (?–1768), who served at the capture of Louisbourg in 1758, and of Québec in 1759. He was later military governor of the Trois-Rivières district (1760–2).

Burtts Corner (York)   Northwest of FREDERICTON, on the KESWICK RIVER. Named in 1893 after Elwood Burtt, the first postmaster. The community is known locally as 'BC.'

Butternut Ridge   *See* Havelock.

Caissie Cape/Cap de Caissie
(Kent)   On the NORTHUMBERLAND STRAIT, near the boundary with WESTMORLAND COUNTY. As befits an officially bilingual province, an effort has been made to have New Brunswick place names reflect the predominant language of the local population. Thus, in 1983, Cassie Cape became Cap de Caissie, and changes to this effect were made on highway signs. This prompted an outcry from both francophone and anglophone elements in the population, and a petition protesting the change was circulated. Eventually a compromise was reached: the name was officially changed to Caissie Cape/Cap de Caissie. Thus, the community became one of two populated places in the province with a name approved in both official languages (see also GRAND FALLS/GRAND-SAULT). The name

may be traced through the records to an Irish family named Casey, who were early settlers in the area. Over the years it has evolved through various spellings – from 'Kuessey' to 'Caissy' and the contemporary 'Caissie.'

Cambridge Narrows (Queens) On WASHADEMOAK LAKE. Honours Prince Adolphus Frederick, Duke of Cambridge (1774–1850), uncle of Queen Victoria.

Campbell Settlement (York) East of NACKAWIC. Settled in 1835 during the tenure of Sir Archibald Campbell as lieutenant-governor of New Brunswick (1831–7). Although he was an unpopular official (see CAMPBELLTON), this did not prevent him from exercising his gubernatorial authority in the assignment of place names.

Campbellton (Restigouche)   On BAIE DES CHALEURS. Sir Archibald Campbell (1769–1843) served most of his life in the British army, and, like so many other officers, received his reward in the form of the lieutenant-governorship of New Brunswick (1831–7). Although historian James Hannay's indictment of Campbell – 'no governor of New Brunswick has ever been less in sympathy with its inhabitants' – is overly harsh, Campbell's arbi-

trary rule and stubborn resistance to the transfer of crown-land control to the province help explain his unpopularity. One of his supporters, the merchant baron of the RESTIGOUCHE, Robert Ferguson (1768–1851), suggested that Martins Point be renamed Campbellton for the lieutenant-governor (see also ATHOLVILLE). It had been the site of the Acadian refugee village of Petit Rochelle, which was destroyed by the British sweep of all such settlements in the MIRAMICHI–Restigouche region. The battle of the Restigouche, the last naval engagement between France and Britain for the possession of Canada, was fought on the river above the present site of the city on 8 July 1760. Incorporated as a town in 1888 and as a city in 1958. See also SUGARLOAF MOUNTAIN.

Camp Gagetown   *See* Gagetown.

Campobello Island (Charlotte) In the BAY OF FUNDY, northwest of GRAND MANAN. The island was first known by the Passamaquoddy name Ebaghuit, translated by F.H. Eckstrom as 'lying parallel with the land.' It was later called Great Island of Passamaquoddy by Captain Cyprian Southack in 1733. A grant of the island was made in 1770 to Captain William Owen (1737–1778), of the Royal Navy. He later wrote: 'I renamed the island Campobello, the latter partly complimentary and punning on the name of the governor of the province [then Nova Scotia] Lord William Campbell, and partly as applicable to the nature of the soil and fine appearance of the island, Campobello in Spanish and Italian being, I presume, synonymous to the French Beau-Champ.' In 1835 his illegitimate son, William Fitz-William Owen (1774–1857), became the sole proprietor of Campobello. The younger Owen inherited his father's flair for the unconventional, and had earlier achieved fame as a surveyor and hydrographer. His work in Canada included systematic surveys of the St. Lawrence River and lower Great Lakes. Henry Wolsey Bayfield was among those who learned surveying under Owen's direction (see BAYFIELD). In his second career Owen was elected to the New Brunswick Assembly, and later accepted an appointment to the legislative council. Historian Paul Cornell has assessed his later years: 'An exotic figure who became an admiral, Owen looms larger than life in the island's oral tradition. An authoritative, aging man who was essentially benevolent in his intentions, he was not like many of his peers, addicted to alcohol, but rather to women.' Despite their eccentricities the Owen family may be credited with leaving an important imprint on New Brunswick nomenclature. During the twentieth century Campobello was to achieve fame as the summer home of President Franklin Delano Roosevelt (1882–1945). The Roosevelt Memorial Bridge, spanning Lubec Narrows and linking the island with Maine, was completed in 1962. Two years later the Roosevelt Campobello International Park, surrounding the Dutch-gabled Roosevelt summer cottage, was opened.

Canaan River   *See* New Canaan.

Canterbury (York)   South of MEDUCTIC, at the junction of Highways 122 and 630. Named for Thomas Manners-Sutton (1814–1877), later third Viscount Canterbury, who served as lieutenant-governor of New Brunswick from 1854 to 1861. Although a time of political turmoil, an important watershed was reached early in his term of office. On 27 October 1853, by a vote of twenty-seven to twelve, the government led by John Ambrose Street (1795–1865) was defeated, and Manners-Sutton called on the leader of the opposition, Charles Fisher (1808–1880), to form a new administration. Responsible government had come to New Brunswick.

Cap-Brûlé (Westmorland)
Extends into the NORTHUMBER-
LAND STRAIT, east of SHEDIAC. A
French descriptive for 'burnt
cape.' Appears as 'cap' or 'pointe'
in several locations in New Bruns-
swick and Nova Scotia, indicating
that the discoverers found the
land ravished by forest fires.

Cape Enragé (Albert)   Extends
into SHEPODY BAY. One of the old-
est names on New Brunswick's
BAY OF FUNDY coast, it is an early
French descriptive, 'cape of rage,'
indicating that stormy conditions
are often encountered in the area.
Appears as *C. aragé* (Franquelin–
DeMeulles 1686) and as *Cape
Enraged* (DesBarres 1779).

**Cape Jourimain; Jourimain
Island** (Westmorland)   West of
CAPE TORMENTINE. The name was
first applied to the island, and
later to the cape. Possibly named
for an early French settler. There is
no verification for the suggestion
that the first settler on the island
was a German, and that the name
became corrupted to its present
form. The Fixed Link from BOR-
DEN, Prince Edward Island,
reaches the New Brunswick coastline at this point. A significant
spin-off from the building of the
Fixed Link is the development of a
protected national wildlife area at
Cape Jourimain. Estimated to cost
$2.9 million, it will be, when com-

pleted, one of the most important
ecological sites in Atlantic Canada. Within its 640 hectares, the
visitor will find sand-dunes, salt-
and still-water marshes, beaches,
and forested upland. The area is
also a natural sanctuary for many
species of migratory birds and
rare plants.

Cape Maringouin (Westmorland)
The southern tip of the county
that projects into CHIGNECTO BAY.
The unwelcome presence of mosquitoes was a common complaint
of many early European visitors
to the BAY OF FUNDY region. Two
eighteenth-century examples:
'There is an abundance of Mus-
kettoes [*sic*] here so that on a calm
hot day, 'tis almost impossible to
live especially among the Trees'
(Hale 1731), and 'The mosquitoes
are a terrible plague in this country. They grow worse every year
and they bite the English the
worst' (Harrison 1774). National-
istic intent aside, the French were
the first to enshrine the lowly
insect in a place name. 'Maringouin' is a corruption of the
Acadian word for small mos-
quito-like insects. Appears as *C.
des maringouins* (Franquelin–
DeMeulles 1686), *Mosquito Point*
(Benjamin Church 1704), and *Cape
Marangouin* (DesBarres 1779).

Cape Tormentine (Westmorland)   At the eastern tip of the

county and bounded by the NORTHUMBERLAND STRAIT and BAIE VERTE. The name was already known to Nicolas Denys (1598–1688): 'Following the coast one comes upon *Cap Tourmentin*. It is a great point which advances into the sea, and is only two leagues and a half from *Isle Saint Jean* [Prince Edward Island]. This is the narrowest place in all this strait.' The name is undoubtedly a variation of the French Cap du Torment, or 'cape of storms.' The modern spelling dates from the Frederick Holland survey of 1791. It is known locally as 'The Cape.'

Cap-Lumière (Kent)   On the NORTHUMBERLAND coast, south of RICHIBUCTO. Named for the lighthouse on the cape.

Cap-Pélé (Westmorland)   East of SHEDIAC, on the NORTHUMBER-LAND coast. A descriptive. The post-office name was changed from Cape Bald to Cap-Pelé by petition of local residents in 1949. The name was approved by the CPCGN on 2 March 1950.

Caraquet; Baie de Caraquet; Bas-Caraquet; Haut-Caraquet; Île de Caraquet (Gloucester)   The town fronts on Baie de Caraquet. The precise origin and meaning are in doubt. It may be the French version of an earlier Mi'kmaq place name, possibly Ka-la-gue, trans-lated as 'the junction of two rivers' (Ganong). In 1811, Bishop Joseph-Octave Plessis (1763–1825) described the locality: 'The settlement of Caraquet does not date further back than the conquest of Canada. The first colonists were Acadians ... [Here] the advantage of the fishery makes up for the scarcity of meat, as the scarcity of bread is made up for by potatoes which grow in abundance. The codfish, salmon, herring, macquerel [*sic*], perch, eel, trout, flatfish, sturgeon, lobster, are abundant in the entire bay.' Each August, the town of Caraquet is host to an Acadian Festival that includes music, displays, theatrical presentations, and parades. The name of Upper and Lower Caraquet was changed 11 December 1952 to Haut-Caraquet and Bas-Caraquet. The Village Historique Acadien is located nearby. It is a 'living' museum, where artisans, such as the blacksmith, cobbler, and wheelwright, ply their trade. Women card wool, weave cloth, make soap, and dry fish, all in the manner of the eighteenth century.

Cardigan (York)   South of STANLEY. First known as 'Cardigan Settlement.' As the name implies, the area was settled by Welsh from Cardiganshire in 1819–20. They formed part of of a group who sailed 'on the fast sailing brig

called the *Albion* of Cardigan.'
The voyage of the *Albion* and the
founding of the first Welsh settle-
ments in Canada have been elo-
quently described by historian
Peter Thomas in *Strangers from a
Secret Land*. See also WELSHTOWN,
Nova Scotia.

Carleton Brook   *See* Carleton
County.

Carleton County   In western
New Brunswick and adjacent to
the state of Maine. Originally
included within YORK COUNTY, it
was created a separate entity in
1832. The name commemorates
the career of Thomas Carleton
(1735–1817), appointed first governor of the newly created province of New Brunswick on 16
August 1784. In 1786, with the
appointment of his brother, Sir
Guy Carleton, as governor-in-
chief of British North America,
the position was renamed lieutenant-governor. Overshadowed by
his brother's career and harshly
treated by nineteenth-century historians such as James Hannay,
Thomas Carleton has been dealt
with more kindly by posterity.
Although he returned to England
in 1803, retaining the governorship until his death in 1817, he
may, in retrospect, be called 'the
founder of a province.' Carleton
Parish (Kent), Carleton Brook
(Carleton), and Carleton Lake

(York) were named for the lieutenant-governor. See also FREDER-
ICTON and MOUNT CARLETON.

Carleton Lake   *See* Carleton
County.

Carleton Parish   *See* Carleton
County.

Casco Bay Island (Charlotte)
Between CAMPOBELLO and DEER
ISLAND, in PASSAMAQUODDY BAY.
Probably named for Casco Bay,
near Portland, on the Maine coast.
According to F.H. Eckstrom,
Casco is derived from the
Abenaki *kasqu'*, which means 'the
great blue heron,' a familiar bird
along the shoreline of New
England and Atlantic Canada.

Catons Island (Kings)   Within
LONG REACH, a section of the ST.
JOHN RIVER. The meaning of the
Maliseet name for the island,
Ahmennenik, has become lost. It
was here, in 1610, that Robert
Gravé Du Pont (*ca* 1585–1621),
along with a party of traders and
fishermen from St. Malo, estab-
lished the first European settle-
ment in present-day New
Brunswick. Here also, on 3 Octo-
ber 1611, the Jesuit priest Pierre
Biard (1567–1622) celebrated
Mass, probably the first such ser-
vice in New Brunswick. The
French rendering of the Maliseet
name was Emenenic; following

the British occupation it was listed by Colonel Robert Monckton (1726–1782) as *Isle au Garce*. Still later it became part of a pre-Loyalist grant to Isaac and James Caton of Philadelphia, thus explaining its present name.

Centreville (Carleton)   Northwest of WOODSTOCK. A common descriptive found throughout Atlantic Canada and, in this instance, indicative of its location equidistant from nearby villages. The post office dates from 1862.

Chaleur Bay   *See* Baie des Chaleurs.

Chamcook; Chamcook Bay; Chamcook Creek; Chamcook Lake; Chamcook Mountain (Charlotte)   From the Passamaquoddy *K'tchumcook*. Of this place name William Francis Ganong has written: 'Many meanings have been given, but none are certain.' The community lies northeast of ST. ANDREWS, on Highway 127. Since 1988 the Atlantic Salmon Federation has operated an Information and Visitor Centre on Chamcook Creek, which flows into PASSAMAQUODDY BAY. The bay has become the location of an important Atlantic salmon-aquaculture industry. The creek, lake, and mountain were named for the community.

Chamcook Bay   *See* Chamcook.

Chamcook Creek   *See* Chamcook.

Chamcook Lake   *See* Chamcook.

Chamcook Mountain   *See* Chamcook.

Chance Harbour (Saint John)   Southwest of SAINT JOHN. Settled by Loyalists in 1784. First known as 'Harbour by Chance,' indicative of the navigational hazards that mark the harbour entrance. Even today *The Bay of Fundy Pilot* warns mariners by listing the reefs and ledges, concluding: 'Small vessels with local knowledge can anchor in the inner part of Chance Harbour.'

Chapmans Corner (Westmorland)   North of PORT ELGIN, on CAPE TORMENTINE. Settled by Frederick and Bowden Chapman in 1855. They were descendants of the Yorkshire immigrants to the boundary area between New Brunswick and Nova Scotia in the 1770s.

Charlo; River Charlo (Restigouche)   On BAIE DES CHALEURS, east of DALHOUSIE. A local legend attributes the names of the adjacent rivers Charlo, Benjamin, and Jacquet to three trappers from Québec who came to this region and lined out their separate trap lines. The community was first known as 'Charlo Station'; the post office dates from 1882.

Charlotte County   Situated in the southwest corner of the province. The county was established in 1785. It was named for Queen Charlotte Sophia (1744–1818), consort of King George III.

Chatham; Chatham Head (Northumberland)   On the south side of the MIRAMICHI RIVER. Chatham was founded in 1800 by Francis Peabody, a New England Planter who moved from MAUGERVILLE, on the ST. JOHN RIVER. He suggested the name in honour of William Pitt, first Earl of Chatham (1708–1778). Chatham's son, William Pitt 'the Younger' (1759–1806), was British prime minister at the time of the first settlement. In 1820 Joseph Cunard (1799–1865), who later was associated with the founding of the Cunard steamship line, came here from Halifax to establish a branch of the family's banking, shipping, and export business. Chatham was also the home of John Mercer Johnson (1818–1868), one of the New Brunswick Fathers of Confederation. It was incorporated in 1896. Chatham Head takes its name from the town and is located 8 kilometres southeast; it is now part of the city of Miramichi. The Celtic heritage of the region is heralded each year with the Irish Festival. It has become a major tourist attraction on the Miramichi. See also MIRIMACHI.

Chatham Head   *See* Chatham.

Chiefs Plateau (Northumberland)   East of the South Branch NEPISIGUIT RIVER. Names for the mountains rising from the plateau were suggested by William Francis Ganong in 1899 to honour some of the principal Mi'kmaq and Maliseet leaders. Examples include Mount Halion, Mount Membertou, and Mount Scudon (sometimes spelled 'Chkoudon'), named for prominent seventeenth-century tribal leaders. Mount Francis and Mount Julian honour eighteenth-century chiefs from the MIRAMICHI area.

Chignecto Bay; Isthmus of Chignecto   Located at the head of the BAY OF FUNDY. The name is probably of Mi'kmaq origin and was first applied to CAPE CHIGNECTO, on the Nova Scotia mainland. It has been traced by Silas T. Rand to the Mi'kmaq *Sigunitk*, meaning 'foot cloth, alluding to some legend.' Early spellings were *Chinictou* (Biard 1611) and *Chignitou* (LaValière 1676). A French map of 1755 has *'Beaubassin – en anglais, Segnekto,'* providing evidence that the name was also applied, at an early date, to the isthmus linking present-day New Brunswick and Nova Scotia.

Chipman (Queens)   Northeast of GRAND LAKE. Named for Ward Chipman, Jr. (1787–1851), who served as chief justice of New Brunswick from 1834 to 1851. Previously he was elected MLA for SAINT JOHN, and named Speaker in 1823. A year later he followed his father, Ward Chipman, Sr. (1754–1824), a prominent Loyalist, to the Supreme Court by appointment.

Chiputneticook Lakes (York) On the New Brunswick–Maine border. From the Passamaquoddy *Chiputneticook*, 'great fork river,' a possible reference to the ST. CROIX RIVER. The meaning of the word is unknown.

Christmas Mountains (Northumberland)   'On Tuesday the 17th of September, our party left Fredericton for the purpose of making a survey on the North West Miramichi river, whose waters take their rise from the sides and base of a range of ten hills near the head of the Tobique and Nepisiguit, and which separate the streams tributary to the River St. John from those that flow into the Bay of Chaleur. This country is covered by the original forest ...' This description of a section of north-central New Brunswick was written by crown-lands surveyor Edward Jack in 1883. The 'range of ten hills' was so remote that they were not named until 1964. The name North Pole Mountain was undoubtedly suggested by its proximity to North Pole Stream. The latter was so designated because of its distance from any settlement. Inspired by the Clement Moore (1779–1863) poem, written in 1823, "Twas the Night before Christmas,' A.F. Wightman, of the Department of Lands and Mines, and provincial representative on the CPCGN, assigned eight additional names in the area of North Pole Mountain: Mounts Dasher, Dancer, Vixen, Prancer, Comet, Cupid, Donder, and Blitzen. It was his intent to name the final peak Mount Rudolph, after the reindeer immortalized in the 1949 hit tune 'Rudolph the Red-Nosed Reindeer' by Johnny Marks (1909–1985). The latter was deemed 'too commercial' by the CPCGN; thereupon Wightman substituted the name Mount St. Nicholas, which was subsequently accepted. The name Christmas Mountains, by which the peaks are known collectively, was coined shortly afterward by David Folster, a New Brunswick journalist. Although not an officially approved name, it has widespread usage, both within the province and beyond. More recently, the area has become the centre of a major environmental controversy. Satellite photography has revealed that the Christmas Mountains are surrounded by the largest expanse of virgin forest in New Brunswick. The photographs also indicated the encroachment of clear-cut lumbering operations on this last stand of original forest. The campaign to 'save' the area as a protected wilderness park has united the visions, more than a century apart, of Jack in 1833 and Wightman in 1964.

Clifton (Gloucester); **Clifton Royal** (Kings)   Clifton Royal is on the KENNEBECASIS RIVER, opposite GONDOLA POINT. The name Clifton was adopted by public vote in 1852 and was probably suggested by the many communities of the same name in England. The literal meaning is a settlement upon a hill. 'Royal' was added later to distinguish it from Clifton in GLOUCESTER COUNTY. Clifton, the settlement on NEPISIGUIT BAY, is sometimes referred to as 'Clifton–Gloucester.'

Clifton Royal   *See* Clifton.

Cocagne Island; Cocagne River (Kent)   In the seventeenth century Nicolas Denys (1598–1688) travelled the east coast of New Brunswick and described the setting: 'Having passed a little island [Cocagne Island], one is well under shelter, and finds water enough. The anchorage is in front of a large meadow. I have named this place the *River of Cocagne*, because I found so much with which to make good cheer during the eight days which bad weather obliged me to remain there.' Denys then goes on to enumerate the abundance of birds, fish, and shellfish characteristic of this coast. *Cockaigne* is the French equivalent of Utopia, 'a land of fabled abundance, with food and drink for the asking.' The present spelling is consistent from the DesBarres survey of 1799 onward.

Cocagne River   *See* Cocagne Island.

Codys (Queens)   This area northwest of SUSSEX was settled in 1819 by William Cody, an emigrant from Ireland. A descendant, Charles Cody, the first postmaster, gave the family name to the community in 1885. A member of the same family, and a native of Codys, Archdeacon H.A. Cody (1872–1948), achieved fame as the author of a long series of novels that focus on life in rural New Brunswick.

Coles Island (Queens; West-morland)   The first Coles Island is situated where WASHADEMOAK LAKE narrows and becomes the CANAAN RIVER. Named for David Cole, an early Loyalist settler. The second is within the confines of the TANTRAMAR MARSHES and takes its name from Jonathan Cole, a native of Rhode Island, who was part of the New England Planter migration to this area in the 1760s.

College Bridge (Westmorland) Northwest of SACKVILLE, on High-way 106. Named for the adjacent Collège Saint-Joseph. See SAINT-JOSEPH and MEMRAMCOOK VAL-LEY.

Cork   *See* Temperance Vale.

Cormier Cove (Westmorland) A small village located on the MEM-RAMCOOK RIVER, south of SAINT-JOSEPH; referred to locally as 'L'Anse-aux-Cormier.' Notable as the birthplace of the Right Honourable Roméo A. LeBlanc, installed as the twenty-fifth gov-ernor general of Canada on 10 February 1995 – the first Atlantic Canadian and first Acadian to fill this post. On an inaugural vice-regal visit to his native Memram-cook Valley, the new governor general quipped 'that Rideau Hall has more rooms than there are houses in L'Anse-aux-Cormier.' The village became part of the

new town of MEMRAMCOOK VAL-LEY in 1995.

Cormier-Village (Westmorland) Southeast of SHEDIAC. Named for Jacques Cormier, a late-eigh-teenth-century settler. The vil-lage became part of the rural community of BEAUBASSIN EAST in 1995.

Cornhill (Kings)   West of PETIT-CODIAC. This area was settled in 1810 by emigrants from Cornhill in Cumbria, England. It is the site of a 52-hectare nursery that spe-cializes in varieties of perennials, shrubs, and fruit trees adapted for growth in the New Brunswick climate.

Coronary Lake (Charlotte)   West of the LEPREAU RIVER. Obvious origins to the contrary, this lake was named for Coraneary Lake in Ireland. Over time the spelling was simplified to fit the pronunciation.

Courtenay Bay (Saint John) Forms part of SAINT JOHN har-bour. The name was assigned by J.F.W. DesBarres (1721?–1824) for John Courtenay (1741–1816), who served as the surveyor gen-eral of ordinance in the British government.

Coverdale   *See* Riverview.

Covered Bridge (York)   South-east of STANLEY. Once the site of a covered bridge; however, the structure was replaced in 1940. Although the community name is now Nashwaak Bridge, the older place name is still used locally and serves as a reminder of the covered bridges that remain a characteristic of the New Brunswick landscape.

Crabbe Mountain (York) Named for the Crabbe family, who were early landholders in nearby Lower Hainesville, off Route 104, 56 kilometres north of FREDERICTON. Now a major ski resort, with New Brunswick's highest vertical at 269 metres.

Crocks Point (York)   West of FREDERICTON, and the farthermost reach of the tide on the ST. JOHN RIVER. The name may be traced to the nickname of an early settler, Jean Cyr. Noted for the production of maple-sugar products, he was reputed to always ask visitors: 'Voulez-vous avoir quelque chose à croquer?' Over time 'croquer' became anglicized to 'crock.' Cyr later moved to an area southwest of EDMUNDSTON, where he gave his name to Rivière-des-Crocs.

Crystal Beach (Kings)   On the KINGSTON PENINSULA, northwest of SAINT JOHN. The place name dates from 1910, when it was selected by a developer for a summer-cottage colony. Today many residents commute daily to Saint John.

Cumberland Basin (Westmorland)   Between the ROCKPORT peninsula in New Brunswick and the MINUDIE marsh area of Nova Scotia. Takes its name from CUMBERLAND COUNTY, Nova Scotia, replacing the earlier French name Beau Bassin. For derivation see Cumberland County, Nova Scotia.

Dalhousie (Restigouche)   On the north shore of New Brunswick, at the mouth of the RESTIGOUCHE RIVER. Name chosen by Sir Howard Douglas (1776–1861) for George Ramsay, ninth Earl of Dalhousie (1770–1838), lieutenant-governor of Nova Scotia from 1816 to 1819 and governor-in-chief of Canada from 1819 to 1828. The area was settled in the late 1820s by Scottish emigrants who laid the foundation for the local shipbuilding and lumbering industries. One of these settlers, Captain John Hamilton (?–1848), a native of Kingscross, on the Isle of Arran, became Dalhousie's first merchant. The town was incorporated in 1905. See INCH ARRAN POINT, below, and also DALHOUSIE, Nova Scotia.

Daly Point (Gloucester)   Northeast of BATHURST harbour. First known as 'Enaud Point' for Phillipe Enaud, an early settler. In the early 1800s it was renamed Daly Point, after a later landowner and sea captain, Timothy Daly. It is now a nature reserve of salt marsh and wooded areas. During the summer the rare Maritime ringlet butterfly, found in only three other salt marshes in the world, may be seen. Each autumn thousands of Canada geese arrive, as the reserve is on their migratory flight path.

Dark Harbour (Charlotte)   On the western shore of GRAND MANAN. The name is descriptive of the fact that the inlet is surrounded on three sides by high basalt cliffs. It is in reality a saltwater lagoon linked to the open sea by a narrow channel. The nineteenth-century naturalist Moses Perley (1804–1862) described the harbour thus: 'Once within the sea wall vessels are completely landlocked, and may ride in perfect safety, as if in an inland lake, however violently the tempest may rage without.' The unusual topography of Dark Harbour provides another benefit: the same cliffs that gave the location its name have had a positive impact on the famed local dulse. This dark red marine algae, found in many places along the Atlantic seaboard, is shaded from the sun at Dark Harbour, thus enhancing its quality.

Darlings Island (Kings)   In the KENNEBECASIS RIVER. Honours an early New England Planter and trader, Benjamin Darling, a native of Marblehead, Massachusetts. Esther Clark Wright notes that he reputedly purchased the island in the 1770s for 'two bushels of corn, one barrel of flour, a grindstone, some powder and shot and sundry knives, hatchets and other implements.'

Dawsonville (Restigouche) Southwest of CAMPBELLTON. Known first as 'Dawsonvale,' for three Dawson brothers who were early grantees in the area. With the establishment of the post office in 1885, the name was changed to Dawsonville.

Debec (Carleton)   Southwest of WOODSTOCK. Named for George Debeck, who opened a local lumber mill in 1835. The earlier name, 'Debeck Station,' was shortened *ca 1875*.

Deer Island (Charlotte)   Northwest of CAMPOBELLO ISLAND, in PASSAMAQUODDY BAY. According to F.H. Eckstrom the name is a translation of the Passamaquoddy descriptive *Eduki m'niku*, or 'Deer Island.' See also THE WOLVES.

Demoiselle Creek (Albert) Flows into SHEPODY BAY, near

HOPEWELL CAPE. This section of ALBERT COUNTY was originally settled by the French; however, the only contemporary traces are place names such as this one. Hopewell Cape was known during the French period as 'Cap-des-Demoiselles,' and the nearby watercourse as 'Cap-de-Moiselle-anse.' The precise origin of the name has been lost.

Derby (Northumberland) Southwest of NEWCASTLE, on the MIRAMICHI RIVER. The name was first bestowed on the parish created in 1859. It honours Edward George Geoffrey Smith Stanley, fourteenth Earl of Derby (1799–1869), British prime minister of the day. According to John A. Macdonald, the earl (serving his last stint as prime minister in 1866–8) contributed a footnote to Canadian history by insisting that 'the title of the country be changed from Kingdom to Dominion [so as not to] wound the sensibilities of the Yankees.'

Devils Back (Kings)   A cliff some 130 metres high fronting on LONG REACH. The name is probably a translation of a descriptive from the French colonial period. It is shown as *Cap Diable* on early maps; the Morris survey of 1775 has *Cape Devil*. Nearby, Devils Back Brook flows into Long Reach.

Devils Back Brook   *See* Devils Back.

Dieppe (Westmorland) Adjacent to the eastern boundary of MONCTON. First known as 'Leger Corner,' for an early settler, then renamed in 1946 in honour of the Canadian servicemen who fell in the Battle of Dieppe, 19 August 1942, one of the more controversial incidents of the Second World War. Of the 5,000 Canadians involved, more than 900 were killed and 1,874 taken prisoner. While some military strategists have labelled the raid 'a failure,' it is clear that it did provide valuable experience for the later successful amphibious assault on Normandy, 6 June 1944. Incorporated as a town in 1952.

Digdeguash Lake; Digdeguash River (Charlotte)   The river flows into Digdeguash harbour. William Francis Ganong attributes the name to the Passamaquoddy *Dik-te-quesk*, of unknown meaning.

Digdeguash River   *See* Digdeguash Lake.

Dipper Harbour (Saint John) Near the boundary with CHARLOTTE COUNTY. Named for a species of duck known as the 'bufflehead' or 'dipper' duck. On some early maps it appears as *Duck Cove.* The Dipper Harbour post office dates from 1852.

Doaktown (Northumberland) On the south side of the MIRAMI-CHI RIVER, northeast of BOIES-TOWN. Until the 1850s this settlement 'remained nameless.' In 1853, with the establishment of a post office, the name was selected to honour Robert Doak (1785–1857). A native of Ochiltree, Scotland, Doak settled here in 1825, and not long after was operating a carding mill, grist mill, and kiln, along with a sawmill. The Doak House has been restored by the Central Miramichi Historical Society and is open to the public. As befits a region known internationally for its salmon fishery, the Miramichi Salmon Museum is also located in Doaktown.

Dochets Island   *See* St. Croix River.

Dorchester; Dorchester Island (Westmorland)   Dorchester Island and the area that is now the village of Dorchester, northwest of SACKVILLE, were settled by Loyalists in the 1780s. The parish was established in 1787 and named in honour of Sir Guy Carleton, first Baron Dorchester (1724–1808), who served as lieutenant-governor, then governor,

of Québec (1766–8) and governor-in-chief of British North America (1782–3, 1786–96). *The Macmillan Dictionary of Canadian Biography* concludes that he was 'a sort of pro-consul who was required to guide the destinies of Canada during difficult and dangerous times.' He also left a legacy of place names in all three Maritime provinces. Stone-quarrying and shipbuilding led to nineteenth-century prosperity, and in 1801 Dorchester became the shiretown of WESTMORLAND COUNTY. By mid-century the community was eclipsed by nearby MONCTON and, with the demise of the 'Age of Sail,' its fate was sealed. The domestic architecture of this earlier era is a reminder of former prosperity. Three examples, built from local stone, are Keillor House Museum, in early Regency style; 'Rocklyn,' the home of Edward Barron Chandler (1800–1880), one of New Brunswick's Fathers of Confederation; and the Bell Inn, built around 1811 and believed to be the oldest stone building in the province.

Dorchester Island   *See* Dorchester.

Douglastown (Northumberland) On the north side of the MIRAMI-CHI RIVER. This community was originally known as 'Gretna

Green,' for the town of the same name in Scotland. In 1812 Alexander Rankin (1788–1852) and James Gilmour came to the Miramichi to open a branch of the famous Scottish mercantile firm of Pollok, Gilmour and Company. Their firm (Gilmour, Rankin and Company) soon constructed wharves, stores, and a sawmill and shipyard. Other branches were set up at BATHURST, DALHOUSIE, and SAINT JOHN. During the summer of 1825, prior to the Miramichi fire, which devastated the community, its name was changed to Douglastown to mark an official visit by Sir Howard Douglas (1776–1861), lieutenant-governor of New Brunswick (1823–32). Several other locations were also named for Sir Howard: Douglas Parish (York); Douglas Harbour (Queens); Douglas Island (Charlotte); Mount Douglas (Queens); and Douglasfield (Northumberland).

Drummond (Victoria)   The parish of Drummond was established in 1872; the community takes its name from this source. William Francis Ganong suggests that its origin may be traced to Sir Gordon Drummond (1772–1854), British commander on the Niagara frontier during the War of 1812, and later administrator of Canada (1815–16). Drummond is the home of the jockey Ron Turcotte. He holds the distinction of being a Triple Crown champion in horse-racing, riding the famous horse Secretariat (1970–1989).

Dumbarton (Charlotte)   On Highway 127, in the northwest section of the county. First known as 'Dumbarton Station,' and named for Dumbarton, near Glasgow, Scotland.

Dumfries (York)   West of FREDERICTON. Named after Dumfries in Scotland, the home of Adam Allen, an early settler.

Dundee (Restigouche)   Southwest of DALHOUSIE. Named for Dundee in Scotland by early Scottish settlers.

Dungarvon River (Northumberland)   Flows into the RENOUS RIVER, a tributary of the MIRAMICHI. It was named for Dungarvan River, Ireland. A local tradition, quoted by William Francis Ganong, attributes the naming to Michael Murphy, a native of Dungarvan, Ireland. His favourite shout during a dance was: 'I'll make Dungarvan shake.' The river is celebrated in Miramichi folklore as the reputed haunt of a famous ghost, known locally as 'the Dungarvon Whooper.' Whooper Spring, adjacent to the river, is the supposed site of a murder and the supposed setting for a strange whooping noise after sundown.

Eagles Nest (Kings) Strategically located on the east side of the ST. JOHN river, where it narrows above the opening of BELLISLE BAY. The name *Nid d'Aigle,* or 'Eagle's Nest,' was applied to this locality on the Bellin map of 1744 and the Couagne chart of 1749. The D'Anville map of 1755 renders it as *Establissement François,* or 'French Settlement.' It was the site of an earthwork fort built by the French commander Charles Deschamps de Boishébert et de Raffetot (1727–1797). During the War of 1812 the British erected a battery and blockhouse at this location. According to W.O. Raymond the narrowness of the river 'rendered it well nigh impossible for an enemy to creep past either by day or night, without escaping detection.'

Eastern Wolf Island *See* The Wolves.

East Riverside–Kingshurst (Kings) South of ROTHESAY. The two communities were amalgamated to form the village of East Riverside–Kingshurst in 1966. Both names were coined, and probably inspired by their location. East Riverside is situated on the KENNEBECASIS RIVER; 'Kings'

was derived from the county, and 'hurst' is a common ending for many English place names, and means 'wooded hill.'

Edgetts Landing (Albert) South of HILLSBOROUGH, on the PETITCODIAC RIVER. Named for Joel Edgett (1760–1841), an early New York Loyalist settler.

Edmundston (Madawaska) The city is built about the junction of the MADAWASKA and ST. JOHN rivers. It was first named Petit-Sault, for the falls at the mouth of the Madawaska. It was renamed in 1850 for Sir Edmund Head (1805–1868), who served as lieutenant-governor of the province (1848–54). It fell to Head to introduce the concept of responsible government to the then colony. By gradually initiating his ministers and the general public in the principles of parliamentary procedure, he was able to achieve this objective without many of the problems experienced elsewhere. In 1854 he went on to succeed Lord Elgin (see ELGIN) as governor-in-chief of Canada. This region of New Brunswick is sometimes referred to as the 'Republic of Madawaska' (see also BAKER BROOK). In keeping with this concept, a flag and coat of arms were designed, and each year the incumbent mayor of Edmundston is given the role of 'president.' The highlight of the year is a midsummer festival known as the 'Foire Brayonne' (Brayon Fair). Inhabitants of the 'republic' refer to themselves as 'Brayons,' a name that may be traced back to seventeenth-century France. Many of the first settlers came from Bray, a region of France bordering on the old provinces of Picardy and Normandy. In France such people were known as 'Brayants,' 'Braytois,' or 'Brayons.' A less likely theory attributes the name to a corruption of *broyer*, an old French verb meaning 'to pulverize' or 'to flay,' in reference to the 'flaying of flax' for the linen industry, once prominent in Picardy. The Madawaska region also lays claim to the legendary lumberjack Paul Bunyan. Folk-tales surrounding Bunyan were carried by lumbermen into Maine, and as far west as Wisconsin. Displays in the Madawaska Museum elaborate on the rich and colourful heritage of the region. Edmundston was incorporated as a city in 1952.

Eel River; Eel River Crossing (Restigouche)   Flows into BAIE DES CHALEURS, southeast of DAL-HOUSIE. The name is a translation of the French designation Anguille. The Eel River sandbar provides a unique swimming opportunity – having fresh water on one side and the salt water of Baie des Chaleurs on the other. Eel River Crossing was incorporated as a village in 1966.

Eel River Crossing   *See* Eel River.

Elgin (Albert)   On Highway 905, in the southwestern section of the county. Named for James Bruce, eighth Earl of Elgin and twelfth Earl of Kincardine (1811–1863), governor-general of British North America from 1847 to 1854. He is remembered for his commitment to responsible government, which was achieved in the United Province of the Canadas in 1849. Of his career, historian W.L. Morton has written: 'Elgin's conduct defined responsible government and he was to expand it into a major anticipation of the Canadian nationhood which was yet in embryo.'

Elmtree River (Gloucester) Flows into BAIE DES CHALEURS. This place name may be a direct translation from Mi'kmaq to French, and then to English. The original name, Wikpeyaktcheebo-geecht, has been translated as 'where elm trees grow' (Rayburn). In 1832 it was rendered both as *R. aux Ormes* and *Elm Tree River*.

Ennishone (Victoria)   Southeast of GRAND FALLS/GRAND-SAULT.

The community name is sometimes given as Ennishore and is
probably a corrupted version of
'Innishowen,' in County Donegal,
Ireland. The post office was established in 1882 as Ennishore.

Enniskillen (Queens)   Since this
area in the southwestern corner of
the county was settled by immigrants from Ireland, there can be
no doubting its origin – for Enniskillen, a town southwest of
Omagh in Ireland. The name may
be traced to the Irish *Inis Ceith-
leann*, meaning 'Cethlenn's
Island.'

Escuminac; Point Escuminac
(Northumberland)   Juts into the
NORTHUMBERLAND STRAIT, at the
southern entrance to MIRAMICHI
BAY. Originates with a local
Mi'kmaq descriptive *Eskumu-
naak*, translated as 'outlook place.'
In 1959, as a result of a sudden
storm, thirty-five fishermen from
Escuminac and BAIE-SAINTE-
ANNE were lost at sea. An
inspired work of sculpture, *Fishermen's Memorial*, by Acadian artist Claude Roussel, marks this
tragedy. The name of nearby
Mocauque d'Escuminac refers to
'an area of swampy ground, characterized by abundant mosses
and few trees' (CPCGN Files).

Evandale (Kings)   On the west
side of the ST. JOHN RIVER, oppo-

site EAGLES NEST. Following the
American Revolution, the community was named Wordens, for
New York Loyalist Jarvis Worden
(*ca* 1756–1842). The contemporary
name dates from the establishment of the post office in 1886.
Lord Evandale, a character in Sir
Walter Scott's *Old Mortality*, may
well have provided the inspiration.

Evangeline (Westmorland;
Gloucester)   Both communities
were named for the fictional
'Evangeline' created by American
poet Henry Wadsworth Longfellow (1807–1882). The community
names date from the establishment of their respective post
offices: Evangeline, northeast of
MONCTON, in 1910, and Evangeline, north of INKERMAN, in
1949.

Everett (Victoria)   Northeast of
PLASTER ROCK. Originally known
as 'Dows Flats,' for an early settler. The name was changed with
the arrival of the post office in
1885, in honour of George Everett, the first postmaster.

Fairville (Saint John)   Part of
SAINT JOHN. The name was
bestowed by the Reverend Robert
Wilson, a Methodist clergyman,
for Robert Fair (1824–1901), a
local merchant. Wilson wrote: 'As
Lancaster was too indefinite a

designation ... without consulting anyone, I called the village Fairville, in honour of Mr Fair.' The name was changed to Lancaster in the 1940s.

Fanning Brook (Queens)   Flows into the ST. JOHN RIVER, south of HAMPSTEAD. The name serves as a reminder of the career of Loyalist David Fanning (1755–1825). A leader of the pro-British forces in South Carolina, Fanning emigrated to New Brunswick in 1784. Settling first in KINGS COUNTY, he moved, in the 1790s, to the mouth of the brook that bears his name. From 1791 until January 1801, Fanning was a member of the New Brunswick House of Assembly. In the latter month he earned the dubious distinction of being the first member 'expelled for a felony conviction.' Earlier, in July 1800, he was accused of attempting to rape a young girl, who was described in the press as 'fifteen and stout ... but unimpeachable on the article of chastity.' Fanning was subsequently convicted, sentenced to death, and expelled from the House. He was able to evade the death penalty by successfully appealing to the lieutenant-governor, Thomas Carleton, for clemency. Thereafter, he was forced 'to live in exile' in DIGBY, Nova Scotia!

Fawcett Hill (Westmorland) North of PETITCODIAC. Named

for Thomas Fawcett (*ca* 1775–1855). An emigrant from England, he settled first on Prince Edward Island, later moving to SACKVILLE, and from there to Birch Hill, which was renamed in his honour in 1832 (Rayburn).

Ferguson Point (Restigouche) Projects into the RESTIGOUCHE RIVER at ATHOLVILLE. Named for Robert Ferguson (1768–1851), the 'father and founder of the Restigouche.' There are also two Ferguson Points in GLOUCESTER COUNTY. The first, south of TRACADIE, was named for William Ferguson, a Pennsylvania Loyalist. The second, which juts into BATHURST harbour, honours Francis Ferguson, an early settler.

Five Finger Brook; Five Fingers (Restigouche)   The settlement is east of Saint-Quentin, on the Five Finger Brook. It takes its name from the brook's, which William Francis Ganong identifies as a 'descriptive of its branching just above its mouth.' See also SAINT-QUENTIN.

Five Fingers   *See* Five Finger Brook.

Flaglor Brook (Kings)   Flows into LONG REACH, east of Central Greenwich. The name commemorates Simon Flaglor (*ca* 1744–1816), a Dutchess County, New

York, Loyalist who settled here in 1783. In 1790 Simon and Elizabeth Flaglor deeded part of their grant to the school trustees for one shilling.

Flat Wolf Island   *See* The Wolves.

Flemming (Madawaska)   Northeast of SAINT-LÉONARD. First known as 'Flemming Siding.' Named for James Kidd Flemming (1868–1927), prominent lumberman and politican who served as premier of New Brunswick (1911–14) and later as federal member of Parliament for Victoria–Carleton (1925–7). His career was to be emulated by his son, Hugh John Flemming (1899–1982), who was premier of New Brunswick (1952–60) and elected to the House of Commons for Royal in 1962, switching to Victoria–Carleton (1962–72). During his tenure in federal politics, Hugh John Flemming was minister of Forestry and National Revenue in the Diefenbaker cabinet.

Florenceville (Carleton)   On the ST. JOHN RIVER, north of HARTLAND. First known by the prosaic name 'Buttermilk Creek,' the community was renamed in 1855 during the Crimean War (1853–6) to mark the contribution of Florence Nightingale (1820–1910),

the founder of modern nursing. Since 1957 it has been the home of McCain Foods Limited, one of the largest food-processing plants in the world and parent company of the McCain Group, with operations in the United States, Europe, Australia, New Zealand, and South America.

Foley Brook (Victoria)   Located 6 kilometres northeast of NEW DENMARK. Named for an early settler. The post office was established in 1892. This area is noted for the spectacular view obtained from the Foley Brook Road. The city of GRAND FALLS/GRAND-SAULT is clearly discernible, with the state of Maine in the background. Nearer at hand is the CNR trestle bridge built in 1910; it is 64 metres high and more than 1,200 metres long.

Fort Beauséjour (Westmorland) Designated a national historic park in 1926, the location is significant as the site of a fort built by the French between 1751 and 1755. It was captured by the British, under Colonel Robert Monckton (1726–1882), in June 1755. Renamed Fort Cumberland, the fort withstood an attack during the American Revolution by New England settlers under command of Jonathan Eddy (1726?–1804). The name may be traced to Pointe à Beauséjour, the French designation for the southernmost end of the ridge and eventual site of the fort. It, in turn, took its name from a local landowner, Laurent Chatillon, Sieur de Beauséjour.

Fort Folly Point (Westmorland) Projects into SHEPODY BAY, at the mouth of the MEMRAMCOOK and PETITCODIAC rivers. The precise origin of the name has been lost. Alan Rayburn lists two plausible theories: that it was the site of a supply depot for Jonathan Eddy's rebel force in the American Revolution (see FORT BEAUSÉJOUR), or a name given by sailors 'because the area was dangerous to navigation.'

Franquelin Hill (Victoria) Southwest of NICTAU LAKE. It was suggested by William Francis Ganong that it was named for Jean-Baptiste-Louis Franquelin (*ca* 1651–1712), cartographer and king's hydrographer. In 1688 Franquelin presented to the French court 'a most beautiful map of all then known North America ... showing the boundary lines between New France and New England.' His maps were frequently consulted in the research for this book.

Fredericton (York)   New Brunswick's capital is a city of stately elms, historic buildings, and a striking location, on the ST. JOHN RIVER. In 1817, while serving as lieutenant-governor of Nova Scotia, the Earl of Dalhousie recorded some first impressions, many of which still apply: 'Fredericton is laid out very well in broad streets. The Assembly, the Legislature, the Courts of Justice and the Headquarters of the Militia, have gathered here a very respectable community, and their dwellings give to Fredericton an appearance of superiority and prosperity. It stands on a flat on the river; a range of hills on both sides forms a fine valley. But it is insufferably hot in summer, and intensely cold in winter.' Settlement began with the Acadian village of Sainte-Anne in 1731; it was later renamed Saint Anne's Point by New England Planters. A new name was enacted by order-in-council on 22 February 1785: '... a town at Saint Anne's Point on the River St. John, to be called Fredericktown after His Royal Highness Prince Frederick Augustus, Duke of York [1763–1827] and second son of King George III.' The 'k' and 'w' were dropped shortly thereafter. In 1845 Anglican bishop John Medley (1804–1892) selected the community as the site for the architecturally magnificent Christ Church Cathedral, an act which led to the elevation of the town to city status in 1848. King's

College, which evolved from the Provincial Academy of Arts and Sciences, founded in 1785, became the secular University of New Brunswick in 1859. One noteworthy Fredericton institution is the Beaverbrook Art Gallery. Originally funded in 1959 by Max Aitken, Lord Beaverbrook (1879–1964), the gallery has undergone three major additions and is today one of the few art galleries in the country to be built, maintained, and endowed largely by the private sector. Classified as a 'Canadian national treasure,' its permanent collection boasts, in addition to a large representation of Canadian art, and particularly Atlantic Canadian art, a wide selection of European works. These range from a study of the now destroyed portrait of Sir Winston Churchill by Graham Sutherland (1903–1980) to a magnificent Salvador Dali (1904–1989), *Santiago el Grande*, a gift of the Sir James Dunn Foundation.

French Fort Cove (Northumberland)   Adjacent to Nordin and now part of the city of MIRAMICHI. Site of a French fort and encampment of Acadian refugees following the 1755 expulsion. There is a firmly held local belief that this community is the setting for the folk legend of the 'Headless Nun.' Reputedly, the nun, returning from 'an act of mercy,' was attacked by a mad trapper and beheaded. He immediately buried the head, and the body was returned to France for burial. According to local lore, 'each year on a night when the moon is full, the shrouded figure of the headless nun reappears.' The legend became the subject of a ballad composed by folk-singer Shayla Steeves.

Friars Head (Charlotte)   On CAMPOBELLO ISLAND. The name is descriptive for an outcropping of rock said to resemble the head of a friar.

Frosty Hollow (Westmorland) Southwest of SACKVILLE, on Highway 106. Descriptive for a low-lying area reputed to have the first frost in the immediate area.

Fundy National Park (Albert) For origin of the name Fundy see chapter 1, pages 9–10. Established in 1947 the park stretches for 17 kilometres along the shoreline of the Bay of Fundy. Indented by many coves and inlets, it extends inland to include a 335-metre-high plateau cut by deep valleys and streams. During the nineteenth century the area was logged, and colourful names were bestowed by the lumbermen for the more dangerous sections of the waterways used for transporting logs.

Thus, The Keyhole, on the Point Wolfe River, and Hells Gate, at the confluence of the same river and its East Branch, received their names. The Kinnie Brook Nature Trail, one of several hiking trails in the park, provides a dramatic illustration of the impact of glaciation as the brook disappears under glacial till, only to reappear several hundred metres away. The park is also an ideal habitat for many species of plants, birds, and animals.

Gagetown; Gagetown Creek (Queens)   The town is on Gagetown Creek, adjacent to the ST. JOHN RIVER. Named in 1765 for General Thomas Gage (1721–1787), one of its original grantees. Following service in the Seven Years War (1756–63), Gage became military governor of Montreal, and later, on the outbreak of the American Revolution, was appointed governor of Massachusetts. Earlier, on 17 May 1767, he had divested himself of his vast holdings on the west bank of the St. John River. As quoted by W.O. Raymond: 'For ten pounds current money of the province of New York his 20,000 acre grant was transferred to Stephen Kemble,' and the area was thereafter known for a time as 'Kemble Manor.' Gagetown was the birthplace of Sir Leonard Tilley (1818–1896), one of the

New Brunswick Fathers of Confederation. The Tilley homestead, with its many reminders of his long and illustrious career as premier, federal cabinet minister, and lieutenant-governor, is open to the public. The Canadian Forces Base, Gagetown, comprising sections of both QUEENS and SUNBURY counties, was established in 1952. See also GRIMROSS ISLAND and TILLEY RIDGE.

Gagetown Creek   *See* Gagetown.

Gannet Rock (Charlotte)   An isolated windswept rock in the southern section of the BAY OF FUNDY. Long a navigational hazard, a lighthouse was erected on 'the rock' in 1831. It was named for the northern gannet (*Sula bassanus*), a large white seabird with black-tipped wings and a pointed white tail. Gannet Rock has the distinction of being home to one of the oldest wooden lighthouses in Canada, and one of a dwindling number with a resident lightkeeper.

Gaspereau River (Westmorland) Flows into BAIE VERTE, east of the Baie Verte River. Near its mouth the French built a fortified post named Fort Gaspereau. It was captured in 1755 and renamed Fort Monckton, for Lieutenant-General Robert Monckton (1726–1782). There is also a Gaspereau River in

QUEENS and KENT counties. All take their name from a species of herring common to the Maritime provinces, a fish called by the Acadians *gasperot* or *gaspareau*.

Geary (Sunbury)   South of ORO-MOCTO, near the boundary of CAMP GAGETOWN. William Francis Ganong attributes the name to Admiral Sir Francis Geary (1710–1796); however, Alan Rayburn points out that the first settlers were from Niagara, in Upper Canada, and that its first name was New Niagara. The contemporary pronunciation of Niagara was 'Ni-a-ga-ree,' from which 'Geary' evolved.

Geologists Range (Restigouche and Northumberland)   The name for this range southwest of NICTAU LAKE was suggested by William Francis Ganong in 1899 to honour Canadian geologists. For example: Mount Bailey (Loring Bailey, 1839–1925); Mount Dawson (George Mercer Dawson, 1849–1901); Mount Ells (Robert W. Ells, 1845–1911); Mount Chalmers (Robert Chalmers, 1833–1908); Mount Hartt (Charles F. Hartt, 1840–1878); Mount Matthew (George F. Matthew, 1837–1923).

Giberson Settlement (Carleton) Northeast of BATH. This community was first settled by Gilbert, John, and William Giberson, New Jersey Loyalists of Dutch descent. They had served in the King's American Dragoons. Direct descendants are still to be found throughout CARLETON COUNTY.

Gin Creek (Gloucester)   Flows into the KEDGWICK RIVER, near the Québec–New Brunswick boundary. Probably a descriptive for the colour of the water.

Gin Hill (Victoria)   Near Nason Brook, in the northern sector of the county. Named for a nineteenth-century incident in which 'two workers had their load of logs upset on this hill and a case of Geneva gin ... was partly destroyed; [later] the horses returned without the men, and a search party found them drinking gin at the foot of the hill' (CPCGN Files).

Glassville (Carleton)   East of BRISTOL, on Highway 580. Founded in 1861 and named for the Reverend Charles Gordon Glass, a minister of the Free Church of Scotland. He was instrumental in securing the first land grant and encouraged Scottish immigrants to settle in the area.

Glencoe (Restigouche; York); **Glenelg** (Northumberland);

Glenlivet (Restigouche); **Glen-vale** (Westmorland); **Glenwood** (Kings; Restigouche)   The two Glencoes commemorate the 1692 massacre (see also GLENCOE, Nova Scotia). Glenelg was named for Charles Grant, Lord Glenelg (1788–1866), secretary of state for the colonies in the British cabinet. Glenlivet was named for Glenlivet in Banffshire, Scotland, home of the famous malt-whisky distillery. Glenvale and the two Glenwoods are coined names.

Glenelg   *See* Glencoe.

Glenlivet   *See* Glencoe.

Glensevern Lake (Charlotte) On Campobello Island. The name was bestowed by William Fitz-william Owen (1774–1857) for the ancestral home of the Owen family in Wales. See also CAMPO-BELLO ISLAND.

Glenvale   *See* Glencoe.

Glenwood   *See* Glencoe.

Glooscap Reach (York)   Part of the lake created by the construc-tion of the Mactaquac Dam. The headpond covered two small snowshoe-shaped islands, reput-edly once belonging to Glooscap, the legendary deity of the Mi'kmaq and Maliseet.

Gloucester County   The county was carved from NORTHUMBER-LAND COUNTY in 1827. It was named in honour of Princess Mary, Duchess of Gloucester (1776–1857), daughter of King George III and wife of the Duke of Gloucester (1776–1834).

Goldsmiths Lake; Goldsmiths Stream (Charlotte)   The lake is adjacent to Highway 1; the stream flows into the WAWEIG RIVER. Both features were named for Loyalist Henry Goldsmith, who settled here in 1784. He was a nephew of the Anglo-Irish poet, novelist, and playwright Oliver Goldsmith (1728–1774). In 1796 the family moved to Halifax. Henry's son, named Oliver Goldsmith (1794–1861) for his grand-uncle, also aspired to be a poet, but had lim-ited success. Fred Cogswell has noted that Goldsmith's *The Rising Village* was 'the first volume of verse by a native-born Canadian to receive serious attention at the hands of critics.' Unfortunately his work thereafter was 'undistin-guished and makes the reader view Goldsmith's retirement from versemaking without regret.' See also AUBURN, Nova Scotia.

Goldsmiths Stream   *See* Gold-smiths Lake.

Gondola Point (Kings)   Extends into the KENNEBECASIS RIVER,

north of Fairvale. In the nineteenth century, 'gondola' referred to a 'small dugout canoe or
scow used as a ferry' (Ganong
and Rayburn). The Gondola Point
Ferry is the oldest in the province,
its service dating from 1825.

Goshen (Albert)   South of PETIT-
CODIAC. The community was
named in the early nineteenth
century after the biblical designation for Egypt, east of the Nile. It
was described as: 'Goshen ... a
land of plenty and of light.'

Grafton (Carleton)   Situated
opposite WOODSTOCK, on the east
side of the ST. JOHN RIVER. William Francis Ganong suggests
that this is a 'made up place
name.' In the late nineteenth century, 'a local firm, Sharp and
Shea, had an extensive nursery
and grafting operation,' giving
rise to the place name. The post
office dates from 1875.

Grand Bay (Kings and Saint
John)   In the ST. JOHN RIVER on
the KINGS–SAINT JOHN county
boundary. The name is descriptive and may be traced to Le
Grande Baye, a name assigned
during the French colonial
period.

Grande-Aldouane (Kent)
Northwest of RICHIBUCTO. The
name was applied first to the

river, and is of unknown
Mi'kmaq origin. William Francis
Ganong notes that 'a map of 1793,
in the Crown lands office has
"Northwest River" by the
Mi'kmaqs [sic] Aldouane.'

Grande-Anse (Gloucester)   A
common place name repeated
several times throughout New
Brunswick and other parts of
Atlantic Canada. It is an Acadian
descriptive and refers to an
'indentation or cove in the line of
a coast or shore, rounded in form
and small in size' (CPCGN Files).
See also GRANDE ANSE, Nova
Scotia.

Grande-Digue (Kent)   Fronting
on SHEDIAC BAY. Formerly spelled
'Grandigue,' the name was officially changed on 31 March 1944
to Grande-Digue. The name is
descriptive and is from the
French *digue*, for 'dyke.' The dyke
earthwork was still visible in the
early twentieth century.

Grand Falls/Grand-Sault (Victoria)   This descriptive name for
the 23-metre cataract on the ST.
JOHN RIVER dates from at least
1686. In that year the Bishop of
Québec, Jean-Baptiste La Croix de
Chevrières de Saint-Vallier (1653–
1727), visited the area. He wrote:
'On 16 May we arrived at the
place called *le Grand Sault Saint
Jean-Baptiste*, where the river falls

from a height over lofty rocks into the abyss making a wonderful cascade: the rising mist hides the water from sight, and the uproar of the fall warns from afar the navigators descending in their canoes.' Celebrated in legend from the time of the Maliseet onward, Grand Falls saw a small French settlement develop in the mid-eighteenth century; by 1790 a military post was established by Lieutenant-Governor Thomas Carleton. With the development of sawmills in the 1830s the population began to expand. The town was incorporated in 1890. From Grand Falls onward, the St. John River is entirely within Canadian territory. See also *Caissie Cape/Cap de Caissie.*

Grand Lake (Queens; York) Grand Lake in QUEENS COUNTY is more than 30 kilometres in length and the largest lake in the province. The name is descriptive and may have originated with the Morris survey in the mid-eighteenth century. The name of Grand Lake in YORK COUNTY, on the international boundary with Maine, is of English origin and was applied by analogy with other Grand Lakes.

Grand Manan Island (Charlotte) In the BAY OF FUNDY, southeast of CAMPBELLO ISLAND. The name is derived from a combination of Amerindian and French sources – in particular, the Maliseet–Passamaquoddy word *Munanook*, meaning 'island,' to which the French added the prefix *Grand* to distinguish it from Petit Manan, in present-day Maine. The original French name assigned by Champlain was *Menane*. It appears on the Franquelin–DeMeulles map of 1686 as *La Grand Menane*. The contemporary name, Grand Manan Island, is consistent from the late eighteenth century onward. In local conversation 'Island' is usually dropped in favour of simply 'Grand Manan.'

Grimross Island (Queens)   In the ST. JOHN RIVER, north of GAGETOWN. William Francis Ganong suggests that the name is 'probably derived from the Maliseet through the French.' As a result its original meaning has become lost. On the Monckton map of 1758, *Grimrosse* was applied to the French settlement on the site of present-day Gagetown.

Gyles Cove (York)   South of WOODSTOCK. Named for John Gyles (*ca* 1680–1755). In 1689 the nine-year-old Gyles was captured by a Maliseet raiding party near his home in Pemaquid, in present-day Maine. Held as a hostage for six years, he was 'sold' in 1696 to Louis Damours de

Chauffours (*ca* 1655–1708), who had a seigneury at Jemseg. Eventually, Gyles was delivered to the captain of an English vessel and sailed to Boston in 1698. Later he wrote a vivid and compelling account of his experiences, providing a firsthand look at seventeenth-century Maliseet life. See also JEMSEG.

Hammond; Hammond River; Hammondvale (Kings)   The river flows into the KENNEBECASIS RIVER and is named for Sir Andrew Snape Hamond (1738–1828), who served as lieutenant-governor of Nova Scotia from 1780 to 1782. He was an early landholder in the area. The contemporary spelling has always been in use. Sometimes the feature is referred to as the 'Little Kennebecasis River.' Hammond and Hammondvale take their name from the river. See also NAUWIGEWAUK.

Hammond River   *See* Hammond.

Hammondvale   *See* Hammond.

Hampstead (Queens)   On the west side of the ST. JOHN RIVER. This area was settled by Loyalists from New York in 1786 'Named by Richard Hewlett after Hempstead, Long Island, New York' (Rayburn).

Hampton (Kings)   On the KENNEBECASIS RIVER. There is some evidence that this place name may be of New England origin. In all probability it was named for one of the several Hamptons in the Thirteen Colonies, for example, in New Hampshire, New Jersey, or New York. The post office was established in 1845.

Hanwell (York)   Southwest of FREDERICTON, on Highway 640. Listed first in Thomas Baillie's *An Account of the Province of New Brunswick*, published in 1832. Hanwell, now a part of Ealing in West London, England, was his birthplace. See also BAILLIE.

Harcourt (Kent)   On Highway 126, between Kent Junction and ADAMSVILLE. Named in 1826 by Lieutenant-Governor Sir Howard Douglas for William Harcourt, third Earl of Harcourt (1743–1830). The latter saw service in the American Revolution as commander of the 16th Light Dragoon Regiment.

Hartland (Carleton)   North of WOODSTOCK, on the ST. JOHN RIVER. Name bestowed in 1874 to honour James R. Hartley (1833–1868), a surveyor who served as MLA for CARLETON COUNTY (1867-8). Site of the longest (339 metres) covered bridge in the world. Hartland was the home town of the Honourable Richard Hatfield (1931–1991), premier of New Brunswick from 1970 to 1987 (the longest term in office to date). See also NEWTOWN and SUSSEX.

Harvey (York; Albert); **Harvey Lake; Harvey Mountain** (York) Established in 1837 in YORK COUNTY, on the road between FREDERICTON and ST. ANDREWS and, according to the press, 'very properly named after its founder, Sir John Harvey (1777–1852),' lieutenant-governor from 1837 to 1841. Nearby Harvey Lake and Harvey Mountain take their name from the settlement. The name also appears in ALBERT COUNTY as Harvey, and Harvey Bank on the SHEPODY RIVER. Although there is no documentary evidence to connect these names with Sir John Harvey, in all probability they were named after him.

Harvey Lake   *See* Harvey.

Harvey Mountain   *See* Harvey.

Hatfield Point (Kings)   On BELLEISLE BAY. Originally known as 'Spragues Point,' for the first settler, Thomas Sprague. In 1880, with the establishment of the post office, the name was changed to honour the four Hatfield families then resident in the area.

Haut-Caraquet   *See* Caraquet.

Haute-Aboujagane   *See* Aboujagane River.

Havelock (Kings)   Northeast of PETITCODIAC. The community was first called Butternut Ridge, for the butternut tree (*Juglans cinera*), a species of the walnut family found here. The name was officially changed in 1858 to honour Sir Henry Havelock (1795–1857), a hero of the Crimean War (1853–6), who died in India following the relief of Lucknow in 1857. Despite the change, the older name was still in use locally in the late twentieth century.

Hawkshaw (York)   Juts into the ST. JOHN RIVER, opposite NACKAWIC. Named for Howard 'Hawk' Shaw, who established a tannery here in the late nineteenth century. The post office dates from 1897.

Head Harbour (Charlotte) Descriptive for its location at the head of Campobello Island. First named by Samuel de Champlain as Port aux Coquilles (Shell Harbour). Captain William Owen (1737–1778) of the Royal Navy attempted to rename it Conway, for Conway in Wales; however, both earlier names were supplanted by local preference for Head Harbour. See also CAMPOBELLO ISLAND.

Heath Steele (Northumberland) In the northeastern section of the county, on Highway 430. The community takes its name from Heath Steele Mines Limited, which opened a mine here in 1957. It produces concentrates of lead, zinc, and copper.

Henderson Settlement (Queens) Northwest of HATFIELD POINT, on Highway 710. Named for its first settlers. The post office dates from 1874.

Hillsborough (Albert)   On 31 October 1765 the township, South of MONCTON, was created and named for Wills Hill, Earl of Hillsborough (1718–1793), then the lord commissioner of trade and plantations. The declaration also attempted to rename the PETITCODIAC RIVER, noting that the township was to extend to 'the Fall of Petitcoudiack now called Hillsborough River.' Fortunately, the attempt was unsuccessful, and the euphonious Petitcodiac prevailed as the name for the river. For a time the settlement was known as 'Dutch Village,' having been settled by immigrants of German origin from Pennsylvania in 1766. Included in their number were Heinrich Stief (later Steeves) and his seven sons. They were to found a dynasty now said to number in excess of 150,000

worldwide. William Henry Steeves (1814–1873), one of the New Brunswick Fathers of Confederation, was a native of Hillsborough. His home still stands and is open to the public.

Historians Range (Northumberland)   Between the South Branch NEPISIGUIT and the Northwest MIRAMICHI rivers. Named for prominent New Brunswick historians. For example: Mount Hannay (James Hannay, 1842–1910); Mount Fisher (Peter Fisher, 1782–1848); Mount Raymond (William Raymond, 1853–1923); Mount Manny (Louise Manny, *ca* 1891–1970); and Mount Webster (John Clarence Webster, 1863–1950).

Hopewell; Hopewell Cape; Hopewell Hill (Albert)   Adjacent to HILLSBOROUGH. Established as a township in 1765. In common with its neighbour, it was first settled by German immigrants from Pennsylvania. Although the settlement was sometimes referred to as 'German Town' in contemporary documents, the name Hopewell became fixed wth the establishment of the parish in 1785. The name is a reminder of Hopewell, Pennsylvania, home of some of the first settlers. Hopewell Cape and Hopewell Hill take their name from the township. The second wave of settlers came

from across the BAY OF FUNDY.
As fertile land in the Cornwallis–
Horton areas became scarce, a
number of New England Planters moved to Hopewell, among
them a second-generation New
England Planter, Benjamin Bennett. His grandson, Richard Bedford Bennett (1870–1947), was
born at Hopewell Hill, later moving to Calgary, where he established a law practice and entered
politics. Bennett served as prime
minister of Canada from 1930 to
1935. Following retirement he
lived in England, and was created Viscount Bennett of
Hopewell and Calgary by King
George VI in 1941. The Bennett
coat of arms shows, at the left, a
buffalo, indicative of Alberta,
and, on the right, a moose, representing New Brunswick – sym-
bols that, along with maple
leaves, encompass the sweep of
Canada. See also THE ROCKS.

Hopewell Cape   *See* Hopewell.

Hopewell Hill   *See* Hopewell.

Hoyt (Sunbury)   South of Canadian Forces Base GAGETOWN.
Named for an early landholder,
William Hoyt. The post office was
established in 1878.

Île de Caraquet   *See* Caraquet.

Île Lamèque   *See* Lamèque.

Inch Arran Point (Restigouche)
On BAIE DES CHALEURS, near DAL-
HOUSIE. Named in 1831 by John
Hamilton, a native of Arran, an
island in the Firth of Clyde, Scot-
land. The word *Inch* is also of
Scottish origin and is sometimes
used as part of the name for small
physical features. It is also a well-
known New Brunswick surname.
See also DALHOUSIE and INCHBY
RIDGE.

Inchby Ridge (Queens)   Within
the confines of Canadian Forces
Base GAGETOWN. The name originated with Nathaniel Inch, who
emigrated from Ireland to this
area in 1825. With the disappear-
ance of the community of Inchby,
a nearby ridge was so named by
the CPCGN in 1970.

Inches Ridge (York)   Northwest
of CANTERBURY. Named for
Andrew Inches, chief clerk of the
Crown Lands Office during the
1860s. Inches became involved in
controversy over irregularities in
the allocation of Crown lands.
During the course of a legislative-
committee investigation, his testimony inplicated the then premier
and attorney general, Charles
Fisher, who was eventually
forced to resign because of the
scandal.

Indian Island (Charlotte)   Between CAMPOBELLO and DEER

ISLAND. Site of a Passamaquoddy burial ground that gave rise to the name.

Inkerman; Inkerman Ferry; Inkerman Lake (Gloucester)   The town is on Highway 113, west of Pokemouche Beach. Named for a ridge near Sebastopol, the location of an important battle in the Crimean War (1853–6). On 5 November 1854, the Russian army was repulsed by the Anglo-French forces.

Inkerman Ferry   *See* Inkerman.

Inkerman Lake   *See* Inkerman.

Innishannon Brook (Gloucester) South of NEW BANDON. Named for Innishannon, on the River Bandon in Ireland.

Irish Settlement (Kings) Northwest of SUSSEX. The name of the community reflects the local demography. There is a second Irish Settlement, with the same name origin, west of WOODSTOCK.

Irishtown (Westmorland) North of MONCTON, on Highway 115. Descriptive of the fact that the area was settled by Irish emigrants about 1821.

Isthmus of Chignecto   *See* Chignecto Bay.

Jacks Lake (Northumberland) North of Tuadook Lake. Named for Edward Jack (1826–1895), a surveyor with the Department of Crown Lands. See CHRISTMAS MOUNTAINS.

Jacquet River (Restigouche) West of BELLEDUNE, on the BAIE DES CHALEURS. Possibly a variation of the French *Jacques*, which over time became *Jacquet* (see CHARLO). Alan Rayburn suggests that it may have been named for James Doyle, an early settler in the area.

Jeanne-Mance (Gloucester) South of BATHURST. Named in honour of Jeanne Mance (1606–1673), the founder of Hôtel-Dieu de Montréal hospital in 1642.

Jemseg; Jemseg River (Queens) The settlement is east of Grand Lake Meadows at the southern end of GRAND LAKE; the river flows south into the ST. JOHN RIVER, at Lower Jemseg. The name is from the Maliseet *Ah-jim-sek*, variously translated as 'picking-up place' or 'depot,' since the Maliseet used to cache supplies at this location. William Francis Ganong credits derivation to the Maliseet *Kadjimusek*, or 'jumping-off place,' in reference to 'the narrow part of Grand Lake at the head of the Jemseg River.' Jemseg has had a place in history for over three hundred years. In 1659, during one of the periods when Acadia was under British rule, Thomas Temple (1613/14–1674), an associate of Charles de Saint-Étienne de La Tour, built a trading post beside the Jemseg River. After Acadia was returned to the French, the post was captured by Dutch forces during one of the many seventeenth-century wars. Later it passed into the possession of Louis Damours de Chauffours (*ca* 1655–1708). By 1695 he had 25 hectares under cultivation; however, as a result of the flooding of the St. John River in 1701 and the French decision to abandon forts along the St. John, Damours moved to Port-Royal. Later in the century the area was resettled by Loyalists. See also GYLES COVE.

Jemseg River   *See* Jemseg.

Jolicure; Jolicure Lake (Westmorland)   Northeast of POINT DE BUTE, on the edge of the TANTRAMAR MARSHES. Named for an early French family. Other spellings were 'Jollycoeur' and 'Jolicoeur'; the contemporary spelling dates from the establishment of a post office in 1838.

Jolicure Lake   *See* Jolicure.

Jourimain Island   *See* Cape Jourimain.

Juniper (Carleton)   On the South Branch Southwest MIRAMICHI RIVER. For *Juniperus L.*, a tree common to the area. Juniper is a twentieth-century settlement, founded in 1914, when two lumbermen, George Gilmore and George Foster, built a sawmill on the north bank of the river.

Kars (Kings)   Overlooking BELLE-ISLE BAY. Named, following the end of the Crimean War (1853–6), for the relief of Kars by Sir William Fenwick Williams (1800–1883). See also PORT WILLIAMS, Nova Scotia.

Kedgwick; Kedgwick River (Restigouche)   The river flows into the RESTIGOUCHE. A variation of the original Mi'kmaq Madawamkedjwik, the name was 'shortened by the river men to Tom Kedgwick or Kedgwick' (Ganong). Of uncertain meaning. Appears as *Grande Fourche*, 'Big Fork,' on some maps; however, the older variant has prevailed.

Kedgwick River   *See* Kedgwick.

Kennebecasis River (Kings) Flows into Kennebecasis Bay, an arm of the ST. JOHN RIVER, north of SAINT JOHN. Esther Clark Wright has written: 'The Kennebecasis is a bay, a lake, an island and a river. It is aloof and majestic, a river system in itself, with its own tributaries, its own far reaching water shed.' Derived from *Kenepekachichk*, a Maliseet descriptive translated as 'little long bay place' (Rayburn). It is not, as some claim, a diminutive of Kennebec River in Maine. The latter may be traced to Kinibiki, a French rendering of an Algonquin place name. The evolution of the name may be traced on period maps: *R. Casibecquechiche* (Franquelin–DeMeulles 1686); *Rivière Quinibequi* (Franquelin 1701); *R. de Canibeckis* (Couagne 1748); and *Kenebekawskoi* (DesBarres 1779). From the early nineteenth century onward, the contemporary spelling is consistent.

Kennedy Lakes (Northumberland)   Northeast of Highway 108. Lower, Main, and Upper Kennedy lakes were named for an early-nineteenth-century lumberman, John Kennedy. In January 1994, 6,800 hectares around the lakes were proclaimed by the provincial government as 'a wilderness area ... to protect a rugged and secluded chain of waterways.'

Kent County   Originally part of NORTHUMBERLAND COUNTY, it was separated in 1827 and named in memory of Prince Edward, Duke of Kent (1767–1820), father of Queen Victoria. Kent Junction and Kent Lake (Kent) take their name from the county.

Kent Junction   *See* Kent County.

Kent Lake   *See* Kent County.

Keswick; Keswick Ridge; Keswick River (York)   The river flows into the ST. JOHN, west of the NASHWAAK. There is no evidence for the claim that the name is traceable to the town of Keswick in northern England. According to William Francis Ganong, it is a shortened and altered form of the Maliseet *Noo-kum-keech-wuk*, meaning 'gravelly river.' The name was first corrupted to Madame Kisaway, then Kisaway, and finally Keswick. The river is still referred to occasionally by the older generation as the 'Kisaway.'

Keswick Ridge   *See* Keswick.

Keswick River   *See* Keswick.

Kilburn (Victoria)   On Highway 105. First known as 'Kilburns Landing,' for William H. Kilburn, an early settler. Name shortened to Kilburn in 1887.

Killoween (Carleton)   North of BATH, near the VICTORIA COUNTY border. The community was named for Charles Russell, first baron Russell of Killowen (1832–1900). He was named Lord Chief

Justice of England at the time of the settling of the community in 1894.

Kilmarnock (Carleton)   Southeast of WOODSTOCK. Named in 1843 by an early settler, William Gibson, for his home in Kilmarnock, Scotland.

Kincardine (Victoria)   East of KILBURN. Named for Kincardine, Scotland. In 1873 a group of Scottish emigrants were settled in this area, described as 'a wilderness much less attractive than that which they had been led to expect' (Ganong).

Kingsclear (York)   West of FREDERICTON. In 1722 the British Parliament passed an act prohibiting the cutting of white pine trees in the king's woods in North America. When the first land grants were made in New Brunswick, the stipulation 'Saving and reserving nevertheless to us, our heirs and successors, all pine trees' was always incorporated. However, it was the custom, from time to time, for the surveyor of woods to grant licences to cut and take away such timber as was 'unfit for His Majesty's service,' but only after inspection and the marking with the Broad Arrow any trees fit for use as masts. Kingsclear was named for one

such clearing in 1786. See also BROAD ARROW BROOK.

Kings County   One of the original eight counties established by legislation passed in 1786. The name was selected as an expression of loyalty to the crown. (Note also QUEENS COUNTY.) Because of the large number of covered bridges within its boundaries, it is sometimes referred to as 'the covered bridge capital of Atlantic Canada.' See also SUSSEX.

Kingshurst   See EAST RIVERSIDE–KINGSHURST.

Kings Landing (York)   On the ST. JOHN RIVER, at PRINCE WILLIAM. Name selected in 1969 for the historical village established by the New Brunswick government to depict a riverside community of the central St. John River valley during the period 1780–1870. There are more than seventy restored buildings, including a farm, two mills, a store, a blacksmith shop, and a variety of historic homes. The St. John River provides a dramatic backdrop for this carefully restored village. In common with the Village Historique Acadien (see CARAQUET), Kings Landing features more than 100 'costumed residents,' who, along with the architecture and artefacts, lend an air of authenticity to the site. See also MACTAQUAC.

Kingston; Kingston Peninsula
(Kings)   Kingston, on Route 845,
is 10 kilometres west of HAMP-
TON. The first settlers were Loyalists, a number of whom came
from the Dutchess County region
of New York state. The name of
the parish, established in 1786,
and later transferred to the village, might have been suggested
by Kingston, on the Hudson
River. It may also have been an
attempt on the part of the Loyalists to underscore their allegiance
to the crown, or perhaps the naming is attributable to a combination of both theories. Until 1871,
Kingston was the shiretown of
the county. The peninsula,
bounded by the KENNEBECASIS
RIVER and LONG REACH, takes its
name from the village.

Kingston Peninsula *See* Kingston.

Klokledahl Hill (Victoria)
Within New Denmark. The derivation is possibly a Danish surname. See also NEW DENMARK.

Klondike Settlement (Sunbury)
West of Fredericton Junction, on
Highway 645. Named for the
Klondike district and river in the
Yukon, where the discovery of
gold in 1896 led to the gold rush
of 1897–8.

Knapp Lake (Kings)   West of
HAMPTON. Named for the first settler, Lieutenant Jonathan Knapp,
a Loyalist and member of the
Connecticut Company regiment.

**Kouchibouguac Bay; Kouchi-
bouguac National Park; Kouchibouguac River** (Kent)   The
river flows into Kouchibouguac
Bay, an indentation of the
NORTHUMBERLAND STRAIT. The
park fronts on the strait. The
name is a corruption, partially
through the French, of the
Mi'kmaq *Pijeboogwek*, meaning 'a
river of long tides,' a descriptive
for the length of the river's tidal
estuary. The national park, established in 1969, capitalizes on this
location, Nestled behind a 25-
kilometre curve of sandspits and
islands lie estuaries and lagoons,
salt marshes and bogs, ponds
and brooks, plus a river, all of
which provide distinct habitats
for a varied assortment of plant,
animal, and bird life. It has been
estimated that there are more
than 600 types of plants and
more than 200 species of birds to
be found within the park. One of
the most popular areas is the
South Kouchibouguac Dune, site
of Kellys Beach, reached by a
boardwalk. Seldom 'overpopu-
lated' by people, even during
the tourist season, Kouchibouguac is the perfect location for a
swim or beach hike. The name
was officially adopted for the
national park in 1971.

Kouchibouguac National Park   *See* Kouchibouguac Bay.

Kouchibouguac River   *See* Kouchibouguac Bay.

Lac-Baker (Madawaska)   North of the ST. JOHN RIVER, near the Québec boundary. Named for James Baker (1796–1868), who was involved in the boundary dispute between New Brunswick and Maine in 1827. See also BAKER BROOK.

Lagracéville (Northumberland) Northwest of CHATHAM. First known as 'Lagracé Settlement,' after the Reverend W. Lagracé, who served as local parish priest and postmaster. The name Lagracéville has been in common usage since 1913.

La Hetrière (Westmorland) West of MEMRAMCOOK, on Highway 106. A descriptive denoting that beech (*hetre*) trees were once prevalent in the district. Sometimes referred to as 'Memramcook West.' In 1995 the area became part of the town of MEMRAMCOOK VALLEY.

Lake Edward (Victoria)   East of the ST. JOHN RIVER. The district was settled in the early years of the twentieth century and named for the reigning monarch, King Edward VII (1841–1910).

Lake George (York)   Southwest of KINGS LANDING, on Highway 635. Settled by Loyalists and named for George McGeorge, one of the first grantees.

Lake Utopia (Charlotte)   Northeast of ST. GEORGE. The name is a facetious reference to the granting of lands that ran directly underwater to Captain Peter Clinch on 20 February 1784. Alan Rayburn quotes an 1829 plan of Clinch's land that showed 'a reserve to make good the deficiency caused by the Lake Eutopia.' Clinch was later to serve (1785–95) as MLA for CHARLOTTE COUNTY. Lake Utopia has two claims to fame. In 1826 a red granite medallion with a carving of a man's head was unearthed near the western end of the lake. Of unknown origin, it may be the first example of European sculpture found in North America. The lake is also the reputed home of a sea serpent rivalling the Loch Ness monster.

Lamèque; Baie de Lamèque; Île Lamèque (Gloucester)   The name is of Amerindian rather than French origin. From the Mi'kmaq *Elmugwadasik*, a descriptive reference to the fact that 'the head of the tidal river is turned to one side.' The name of the island was approved in 1974, the result of a local petition, replacing the earlier name Shippigan Island.

North of Lamèque is the descriptively named Petite-Rivière-de-l'Ile. Here, St. Cecile Roman Catholic Church plays host annually to an International Baroque Music Festival. Celebrated artists from around the world gather each summer to sing and play the music of the post-Renaissance period, 1600–1750.

Lansdowne (Carleton)   North of HARTLAND. The name was changed in 1887 from Alexandria to honour the then governor general, Henry Charles Petty Fitzmaurice, fifth Marquis of Lansdowne (1845–1927). His term of office was from 1883 to 1888.

Légereville (Kent)   Southwest of BOUCTOUCHE. Named for the first settlers, Charles and Samuel Légere. The post office dates from 1883.

Le Goulet (Gloucester)   South of SHIPPAGAN, and overlooking the Gulf of St. Lawrence. The name is a common Acadian descriptive for 'a body of standing water, often a saltwater harbour, with a narrow entrance' (CPCGN Files).

Lepreau Harbour; Lepreau River; Point Lepreau (Charlotte)   The river empties into the BAY OF FUNDY, southwest of SAINT JOHN.

While the name is of uncertain origin, the headland was named first. It is almost certainly a corruption of an earlier French designation, *la pereau,* for 'little rabbit,' or *le proe.* It appears on early maps as *Pte aux Napraux* (Franquelin–DeMeulles 1686); *Point La Pro* (Southack 1733); and Point Lapreau (Holland 1798). The contemporary spelling has prevailed since the mid-nineteenth century. The Point Lepreau Nuclear Generating Station, operated by NB Power, supplies 30 per cent of New Brunswick's electricity needs.

Lepreau River   *See* Lepreau Harbour.

Letang; Letete; Letete Passage (Charlotte)   South of ST. GEORGE. A French descriptive for *l'étang,* or 'the pond.' It usually denotes a calm, shallow body of water and was frequently used as a place name in areas explored or colonized by the French. Letete is also of French origin and is derived from *la tête,* for 'the head,' a possible reference to adjacent headlands at Greens Point or on Macs Island, at either end of the passage. See also GRAND ETANG, Nova Scotia.

Letete   *See* Letang.

Letete Passage   *See* Letang.

Lincoln (Sunbury)   On the boundary between SUNBURY and YORK counties. Settled by Loyalists, and probably named by them for Lincoln, Massachusetts. The post office was established in 1867.

Little Bald Mountain   *See* Big Bald Mountain.

Little Sevogle River   *See* Sevogle.

Little Shemogue   See Shemogue.

Little Tracadie River   *See* Tracadie.

Loch Lomond; (Saint John) Near the boundaries of SAINT JOHN and SUNBURY counties. The loch and adjacent mountain, Ben Lomond, were named by Lauchlin Donaldson 'in remembrance of these places in Scotland' (Ganong). A native Scot, Donaldson held a grant at the western end of the loch. Donaldsons Point, a promontory in the loch, was also named by him. See also LOCH LOMOND, Nova Scotia.

Loggieville (Northumberland) At the mouth of the MIRAMICHI RIVER. First known as 'Black Brook,' for John Black, who settled there about 1780. A decade later the Logie or Loggie family arrived from Scotland and began the economic transformation of the community. Over time the Loggie brothers, Andrew, Robert, and Frank, became the area's best-known and most successful entrepreneurs. Beginning as door-to-door salesmen, they soon branched out to merchandising, lumbering, and the fishery, expanding their operations throughout northern New Brunswick, Maine, and Nova Scotia. By the turn of the nineteenth century, A. & R. Loggie and Company was a major mercantile operation. Andrew Loggie, one of the founders, was also postmaster, and in 1895 the name was changed from Black Brook to Loggieville.

Londonderry (Kings)   Southeast of SUSSEX. Named in the 1850s by Irish immigrants for Londonderry, in Ulster.

Long Reach (Kings)   An arm of the ST. JOHN RIVER. The name is descriptive and may be traced back through the English, French, and Maliseet languages. One of the meanings of 'reach' in English is 'an arm of the sea or a sound.' On French colonial maps and documents the name appears as *Longues Veues*, translated as 'long view' or 'reach.' Two Maliseet names have been given for this location: Sasagipakek, 'straight bay place,' and Peecha-wamgek, 'long reach.' There is also a Long Reach on the Kennebec River in Maine.

Longs Creek (York)   Flows into MACTAQUAC LAKE, below KINGS-CLEAR. First settled by Loyalists, and named for Abraham Long, who served with the New Jersey Volunteers during the American Revolution. The Maliseet name for the area was Eskootawopskek, meaning 'the fire rock' or 'red hot rock.' Over time, and a filtering through French and English, the Maliseet place name became Skoodowabskoosis, immortalized in James DeMille's poem 'Sweet Maiden of Quoddy' (see chapter 1, page 17).

Lorne (Restigouche); **Lorneville** (Saint John)   Lorne is southwest of the JACQUET RIVER; Lorneville is southwest of SAINT JOHN. Both names mark the career of Sir John Douglas Sutherland Campbell, ninth Duke of Argyll, Marquis of Lorne (1845–1914), who served as governor general of Canada from 1878 to 1883. Lorneville replaced Pisarinco, a Maliseet name of uncertain origin and unfortunate English pronunciation.

Lorneville   See Lorne.

Lower Kennedy Lakes   See Kennedy Lakes.

Lower North Branch Little Southwest Miramichi River (Northumberland)   Flows southeast into Little Southwest Miramichi River. This descriptive has been cited as 'the longest place name in Canada' and may be one of the most confusing names in the country!

Ludlow (Northumberland) Northeast of BOIESTOWN, on the MIRAMICHI RIVER. Named for the Honourable George Duncan Ludlow (1734–1808), who served as the first chief justice of New Brunswick, from 1784 to 1808. Prior to the American Revolution, Ludlow was a judge of the Supreme Court of New York, master of the rolls, and chief superintendent of police on Long Island. His brother Gabriel George Ludlow (1736–1808) was the first mayor of SAINT JOHN.

Lutes Mountain; Lutesville (Westmorland)   Northwest of MONCTON. Settled in the early nineteenth century by members of the Lutz (Lutes) family, part of the 1765 Pennsylvania German migration to the PETITCODIAC region. The present spelling dates from the establishment of the Lutes Mountain post office in 1859.

Lutesville   See Lutes Mountain.

McAdam (York)   On Highway 2, east of the U.S. border. Named for politician and lumberman John McAdam (1807–1893) who served as MLA for Charlotte in 1854–66 and 1882–6. He served briefly (1872–4) as the federal MP for Charlotte. The name was officially changed from McAdam Junction to McAdam on 16 December 1941.

Maces Bay (Charlotte)   Fronts on the BAY OF FUNDY, between POCOLOGAN and POINT LEPREAU. The origin is uncertain; however, it may have been named for Benjamin Mace, a surgeon with the 22nd Regiment (Rayburn). There were various spellings on early maps and records: *Mesh's Bay*, *Maise's Bay*, and *Mae's Bay*. The settlement, near Point Lepreau, has been consistently known as 'Maces Bay' since 1854.

Machias Seal Island (Charlotte) Near the mouth of the BAY OF FUNDY, claimed by both Canada and the United States. The Canadian case is based partly upon occupancy. Since 1832 the island lighthouse has been maintained, first by the British, and later, after 1867, by the Canadian federal government. In 1944 the island was designated by the Canadian Wildlife Service as an official bird sanctuary. The sovereignty question may be traced to imprecise word-

ing in the Treaty of Ghent of 1814, when a number of Bay of Fundy islands, including DEER, GRAND MANAN, and CAMPOBELLO, were ceded to the British. As with many other islands, Machias Seal Island takes its name from a feature on the mainland. The word *Machias* is of Maliseet origin and is probably derived from *Mecheyisk*, a reference to the 'little falls' on the Machias River in Maine (Eckstrom). Since the area was once noted for seals, early maps render the name as *Seal Island* (Moll 1715) and *Western Seal Island* (Holland 1798).

Mactaquac Lake; Mactaquac Provincial Park; Mactaquac Stream (York)   From the Maliseet *Maktequek*, or 'big branch,' a possible reference to the ST. JOHN RIVER above tide. The artificial lake created by the New Brunswick Power Commission in 1967 stretches about 65 kilometres upstream, from Mactaquac Provincial Park to Woodstock. The park features a large campground and an eighteen-hole championship golf course. Some of the buildings at KINGS LANDING were relocated as a result of flooding caused by the Mactaquac Dam.

Mactaquac Provincial Park   *See* Mactaquac Lake.

Mactaquac Stream   *See* Mactaquac Lake.

Madawaska County   The county, established in 1873, takes its name from the river which flows into the ST. JOHN at EDMUNDSTON. For name's origin see MADAWASKA RIVER. See also EDMUNDSTON.

Madawaska River (Madawaska) Flows southeast into the ST. JOHN RIVER, at EDMUNDSTON. The name may be traced to the Maliseet *Medaweskak*, reputedly for 'porcupine place.' Of the other suggested translations, that given by Silas T. Rand, 'where one river enters another,' appears most logical. The name first surfaces in the granting of the seigneury of Madouesca in 1683. It was rendered *Madawascook* by Gyles (1686) and *Madaousca* by Delisle (1703). The modern spelling has been in use since 1791. William Francis Ganong points out that 'Madawaska appears elsewhere; as a branch of the Aroostook in Maine, as a river in eastern Ontario and as a lake in the Adirondaks, all examples of familiarization, the alteration of names to make them sound like familiar ones.'

Magaguadavic Lake (York); **Magaguadavic River** (York and Charlotte)   The name of the river is derived from the Maliseet and Passamaquoddy *Mageecaatawik*, which has been translated as 'river of big eels.' Early spellings include: *Magaguaguadavick* (1786), *Maacadavic* (1842), and *Magaguadavic* (1859). According to William Francis Ganong, 'the name has the distinction of retaining a cumbersome spelling for a simple pronunciation, which is always "Mac-a-day-vy."' The settlement is noteworthy as the home of Sarah Edmonds (1841–1898). As a young woman she moved to the United States, where she developed a talent for subterfuge. Disguising herself as a man, she joined the Union Army in the American Civil War. As part of her career as a 'soldier,' she became a spy and infiltrated the Southern lines, posing variously as a pedlar, a cavalryman, and a clerk. Following the war she married a SAINT JOHN lumberman, Linus Seelye, settled down, and had a family of three children. In 1884 she applied for and was awarded an American Army pension of $12 per month. Thus, this New Brunswicker was the first woman to receive a pension from the United States army.

Magaguadavic River   *See* Magaguadavic Lake.

Magnetic Hill (Westmorland) On the northern outskirts of MONCTON. Descriptive for an optical illusion: the formation of the surrounding countryside makes the slope appear to run in the opposite direction from that which it actually does. Named in the 1930s by Muriel Lutes Sikorski and promoted relentlessly as a tourist attraction ever since.

Main Kennedy Lakes   *See* Kennedy Lakes.

Maisonnette (Westmorland) On BAIE DE CARAQUET. Probably a descriptive reference to the existence of a 'little house' there during the French colonial period. Appears as *Maisonette* or *Mizzenette Point* in some eighteenth-century records. For a brief period (1920–36), the community was known as Ste. Jeanne d'Arc. The name Maisonnette was officially adopted on 1 October 1936.

Malakoff (Westmorland)   East of DIEPPE. Also named for a battle, but in an earlier war. On 8 September 1855, during the Crimean War (1853–6), Malakov or Malakoff Tower was captured, giving rise to this place name. Another Malakoff may be found in eastern Ontario.

Manawagonish Cove; Manawagonish Island (Saint John)   The cove is part of LORNEVILLE harbour; Manawagonish Island lies adjacent, in the BAY OF FUNDY. Derived from the Maliseet *Ma-na-wag-on-eesk*, which has been translated as 'a place for clams.'

Manawagonish Island   *See* Manawagonish Cove.

Maryland Hill   *See* New Maryland.

Marys Point (Albert)   At the mouth of SHEPODY BAY. The name is of uncertain origin. William Francis Ganong suggests that it was originally named St. Marys Point, while Alan Rayburn credits 'a part Indian Marie Bidoque' as the origin of the name. A local waterfowl sanctuary is a prime location to watch, in midsummer, the aerobatic displays provided by thousands of piping plovers. Known as the Hemispheric Shorebird Reserve, the sanctuary is the creation of noted naturalist Mary Majda.

Maugerville (Sunbury)   A New England Planter settlement on the east bank of the ST. JOHN RIVER, below FREDERICTON. It was first known as 'Peabody,' for Francis Peabody, an early grantee. The name was changed to honour Joshua Mauger (1725–1788), a native of Jersey who established himself as a merchant in HALIFAX during the period 1749–61. Later he became the agent for Nova Scotia in London. In 1763 he was successful in securing for the New

Englanders along this stretch of the river formal title to their lands. Thus the community was re-named Maugerville in his honour. Its importance in the evolution of New Brunswick has been out-lined by Esther Clark Wright: 'The New England pattern of living would have been only a minor factor in New Brunswick but for the Maugerville settlers and their diffusion throughout the prov-ince. The Maugerville settlement was successful because it was formed by a closely knit group, with religious ties, and experience in a not dissimilar environment. The Maugerville settlers came because they wanted to come. They succeeded because they wanted to succeed.'

Mechanic Settlement (Kings) East of SUSSEX. In 1843 a group of mechanics and labourers from SAINT JOHN established a new set-tlement, which gave rise to the name.

Medea Rock (Westmorland)   In SHEDIAC BAY. The name marks the location where, on 17 September 1838, an incident involving HMS *Medea* was reported in the press: 'In approaching [without a pilot] the ship struck a ledge and remained there until the 18th, when she most fortunately floated off without the slightest injury.'

Medford   *See* Ranger Settlement.

Meductic (York)   On the west bank of the ST. JOHN RIVER, near the CARLETON COUNTY boundary. Derived from the Maliseet *Medoc-tic*. Alan Rayburn gives its mean-ing as 'the end, in reference to the portage from Eel River.' The area was visited in May 1686 by Bishop Jean-Baptiste de La Croix de Chevrières de Saint-Vallier (1653–1727) *en route* to Port-Royal on a pastoral visit. He wrote: '*Megogtek* is the first fort in Aca-dia.' The present spelling has been in use since the mid-nine-teenth century. Sabian Symbals Limited, located in this small community, has achieved fame within the international music scene. It is the supplier of finely crafted cymbals to musicians in more than eighty countries.

Meduxnekeag River (Carleton) Flows into the ST. JOHN RIVER at WOODSTOCK. Traceable to the Maliseet *Meduxnakeag*, translated as 'rough or rocky at its mouth.'

Melrose (Westmorland)   West of CAPE TORMENTINE. First known as 'Savagetown,' for an early family in the area. Name was changed to Melrose, for Melrose, Scotland, with the establishment of the post office in 1890.

Memramcook; Memramcook River; Memramcook Valley (Westmorland)   Between MONCTON and DORCHESTER, on Highway 106; the river flows south into the PETITCODIAC. Silas T. Rand suggests that this place name is derived from the Mi'kmaq *Amlamcook*, meaning 'variegated.' Alan Rayburn points out that it may have been first applied to a cove near CAPE MARINGOUIN, 'where the rock has variegated colours.' The present spelling has been consistent since 1800. In 1995 eight communities were amalgamated to form the new town of Memramcook Valley. In addition to Memramcook and Memramcook East, Breau Creek, CORMIER COVE, LA HETRIÈRE–McGinley–La Montagne, PRÉ-D'EN-HAUT, Old Shediac Road, and SAINT-JOSEPH were included in the merger.

Memramcook River   *See* Memramcook.

Memramcook Valley   *See* Memramcook.

Menneval (Restigouche)   Northeast of Saint-Jean-Baptiste-de-Restigouche, on Highway 17. Named for Louis-Alexandre Des Friches de Meneval (?–1709), who served as governor of Acadia from 1687 to 1690. He had the misfortune to be in command at Port-Royal during its 1690 capture by Sir William Phips (1651–1695). Menneval was taken prisoner to Boston and did not return to Acadia. He was succeeded as governor by Joseph Robinau de Villbon (1655–1700).

Metepenagiag (Northumberland) Adjacent to RED BANK, on the Northwest MIRAMICHI RIVER. For nearly 3,000 years this area has been the site of an important Mi'kmaq village. The name is derived from the descriptive *Metdeppnnakeyaka*, which may be translated as 'red bank.' Since 1975 more than 100 Mi'kmaq sites have been identified at Metepenagiag. Two of these, the Augustine Mound discovered by Elder Joseph Augustine and the adjacent Oxbow location, have been officially designated National Historic Sites by the federal government. The archaeological excavations, combined with careful study of the hundreds of artefacts, have provided a clear picture of the sophistication of Mi'kmaq culture prior to the arrival of the Europeans. The site has been called 'New Brunswick's oldest village' by archaeologist Patricia Allen, who has devoted a decade to unravelling its story.

Midgic (Westmorland); **Midgic Bluff** (Charlotte)   Midgic was once known as 'Midgic Station' on the now abandoned CNR rail line from SACKVILLE to CAPE TORMENTINE. The name is of Mi'kmaq origin; however, the precise meaning has become lost. William Francis Ganong surmises that it may be a Mi'kmaq descriptive for 'a point of highland into a marsh [the Tantramar].' Midgic Bluff is at the mouth of the MAGAGUADAVIC RIVER in CHARLOTTE COUNTY.

Midgic Bluff   *See* Midgic.

Millerton (Northumberland)
On the Southwest MIRAMICHI RIVER. The community, once called Miramichi, developed into a major lumber-mill town in the mid-nineteenth century. The boom began with the arrival, in 1869, of John C. Miller (1818–1902) from Picton, Ontario. He established a tanning-extract operation using the bark of hemlock trees. By the 1890s, there were five sawmills, a pulp-and-paper mill, barrel factory, plank mill, grist mill, wool-carding mill, shingle mill, and lath mill in the community. Over the years the place name evolved as a tribute to John C. Miller and as an industrial descriptive for the abundance of mills once located there. The Millerton post office dates from 1881.

Millidgeville (Saint John)
Within the city of SAINT JOHN. The Millidge family became part of the Loyalist establishment in both Nova Scotia and New Brunswick. Thomas Millidge I (*ca* 1735–1816), a native of Hanover, New Jersey, settled at Granville, in the Annapolis Valley, and was a long-time (1785–1806) member of the Nova Scotia Assembly. His son Thomas Millidge II (1776–1838), for whom Millidgeville is named, was born 12 August 1776. As a young man he moved across the BAY OF FUNDY to Saint John, where he established himself as a merchant and shipbuilder. Following in his father's footsteps, Thomas Millidge II entered politics and was elected a member of the New Brunswick Assembly for the constituency of Saint John city and county, serving from 1816 to 1820. Upon his death, on 21 August 1838, his son, Thomas Millidge III (1814–1894), carried on the family business. See also ALBANY CROSS, Nova Scotia.

Milltown   *See* St. Stephen.

Ministers Island (Charlotte)   In CHAMCOOK harbour, north of ST. ANDREWS. This 200-hectare island is accessible by land only during low tide; the rest of the time the Bar Road to the mainland lies under 5 metres of water. First known as 'Chamcook Island,' it was renamed Ministers Island, for the Reverend Samuel Andrews (1737–1818), the first rector of the local Anglican parish. A native of Wallingford, Connecticut, and an ardent and active Loyalist, Andrews purchased the island in 1791 and resided there for the rest of his life. Later, the island was purchased by Sir William Van Horne (1843–1915), the first president of the Canadian Pacific Railway. On the island, which he acquired in sections over a five-year period (1891–6), Van Horne built a large summer home, which he named 'Covenhaven.' The island was acquired by the province in 1977 and placed under the Historic Sites Protection Act. The mansion and grounds are open to the public during the tourist season, subject always to the whims of the tide.

Minto (Sunbury)   On the border of SUNBURY and QUEENS counties. The community was named for the Earl of Minto (1845–1914), who served as governor general of Canada from 1898 to 1904. Coal mining has been carried on in this area since the 1760s, when Joseph Garrison discovered significant outcroppings of coal along the shore of GRAND LAKE and farther inland. Today a surface coal mine is operated by NB Coal.

Miramichi; Miramichi Bay; Miramichi Lake (York)**; Miramichi** (Northumberland) **Miramichi River**   The precise origin of this prominent place name is unknown. The area was described by Jacques Cartier on his first voyage in 1534: 'We went in our long-boats to [Blackland Point] and found the water so shallow that there was a depth of only one fathom. Some seven or eight leagues to the northeast of this cape lay another cape [Escuminac] and between the two there is a bay, in the form of a triangle, which ran back a long way.' Miramichi is probably from the Mi'kmaq Megamaage or Megamage, translated by Silas T. Rand as 'the land of the Micmacs.' William Francis Ganong agrees, and suggests that it may well be 'a greatly altered European form of an aboriginal place name.' In any event, the name was important to the Mi'kmaq, as this was the headquarters for one of the seven regions into which they had divided the Maritimes. Miramichy was applied to the river by Nicolas Denys in 1672. Miramichi Lake, northeast of NAPADOGAN, near the head of the Southwest Miramichi River in YORK COUNTY, takes its name from the river. There is also a settlement known to many local residents as 'Miramichi' on BAY DU VIN; however, it is now part of the service district of Black River-Hardwicke. On 1 January 1995, the new city of Miramichi came into being. It consists of an amalgamation of the towns of CHATHAM and NEWCASTLE; the villages of DOUGLASTOWN, LOGGIEVILLE, and

NELSON–MIRAMICHI; and the communities of Chatham Head, Douglasfield, Moorefield, and Nordin, and their adjacent areas.

Miramichi Bay   *See* Miramichi.

Miramichi Lake   *See* Miramichi.

Miramichi River   *See* Miramichi.

Miscou; Miscou Island (Gloucester)   North of ÎLE LA-MÈQUE. The name is from the Mi'kmaq *Susqu*, meaning 'low land' or 'boggy marsh.' 'It forms an admirable descriptive name, for the most striking fact about the physical geography of Miscou is the prevalence of open bogs' (Ganong).

Miscou Island   *See* Miscou.

Mispec Bay; Mispec River (Saint John)   The river flows into Mispec Bay, an arm of the BAY OF FUNDY, east of SAINT JOHN. The name may be traced to the Mi'kmaq *Mespak*, for 'overflow,' an undoubted reference to the high tide at the mouth of the river.

Mispec River   *See* Mispec Bay.

Missaguash River (Westmorland)   The river forms part of the boundary between New Brunswick and Nova Scotia. Its origin

may be traced to a Mi'kmaq word, usually translated as 'muskrat.' It appears as *Musaguash* (Morris survey of 1750), *Mesiguash* (DesBarres survey of 1781), and *Missaguash* from at least the 1880s onward.

Missionaries Range (Northumberland)   Northwest of Popple Depot, near the RESTIGOUCHE–NORTHUMBERLAND boundary. Mount Biard was named for Père Pierre Biard (1567–1622), an early-seventeenth-century Jesuit missionary in Acadia, and Mount LeClercq for Père Chrestien LeClercq (1641–1700), a Recollet missionary among the Mi'kmaq of northern New Brunswick and the Gaspé peninsula during the later years of the seventeenth century. LeClercq's experiences formed the basis for two important books which shed much light on the early life of the Mi'kmaq people. In 1691 he published *Nouvelle Relation de la Gaspésie* and *Premier établissement de la foy dans la Nouvelle-France*. LeClercq also devised a form of hieroglyphic writing subsequently used by the Mi'kmaq. Names for the mountains were first suggested by William Francis Ganong in 1899 and officially approved by the CPCGN in 1969.

Mistake Cove (Kings)   Northeast of OAK POINT, on LONG

REACH. The cove, a narrow indentation, is 5 kilometres long. Accordingly, it could easily be mistaken for a channel in Long Reach. This was what happened in 1763, when a New Englander, Captain Edward McCoy, an early grantee in the area, drew the wrong conclusion. For a time it was called Coy's Mistake, and later Mistake Cove.

Mocauque d'Escuminac   *See* Escuminac.

Moncton (Westmorland)   On a bend in the PETITCODIAC RIVER. The area, first settled by the Acadians, was variously known by descriptive names such as 'La Chappelle' (the chapel), 'Le Coude' (the elbow), and 'Terre-Rouge' (for the red banks of the river). Following the expulsion of the Acadians, the lands were resettled in 1765 by Pennsylvania German emigrants, and family names such as Stief (Steeves), Trietz (Trites), and Lutz (Lutes) remain common in the district (see HILLSBOROUGH). The new settlers landed at a location called by the French Panacadie, but renamed Halls Creek for John Hall, captain of the sloop which brought them from Pennsylvania. Known also for a time as 'The Bend,' it was renamed for Robert Monckton (1726–1782), commander of the British expedition against FORT BEAUSÉJOUR in 1755, and for a number of years was so spelled. In 1786, the 'k' was omitted by clerical oversight in official documentation, and thereafter the name Moncton prevailed. A campaign was mounted in 1930 to replace the missing letter, and for a period of thirty-six days the city was, officially, 'Monckton.' On 10 March 1930 the local press reported that, 'in a burst of sentimental enthusiasm,' the city council passed a resolution outlining the spelling change. Unfortunately for the council, the people were not on their side. Following a 'public outcry' the resolution was rescinded on 25 April 1930 (*Times Transcript*, March–April 1930). In the nineteenth century shipbuilding was a major industry, while Moncton's importance as a railway centre dominated the economy for a century following Confederation. In recent years, the city, capitalizing on its central location within the three Maritime provinces and a bilingual workforce, has been transformed into a major telecommunications centre. It is home to Université de Moncton, a French-language university established in 1963.

Mount Acquin (Northumberland)   Near LITTLE BALD MOUNTAIN, in the northern section of the county. Named for Gabriel Acquin (1811–1902), a Maliseet guide. Acquin became a celebrity through acting as guide for Edward, Prince of Wales, on his 1860 trip to New Brunswick.

Mount Bailey   *See* Geologists Range.

Mount Biard   *See* Missionaries Range.

Mount Carleton (Northumberland)   South of NICTAU LAKE, near the RESTIGOUCHE COUNTY boundary. Marks the career of Thomas Carleton (1736–1817), the first lieutenant-governor of New Brunswick. At 817 metres, it is the highest point in the Maritime provinces. In 1969, 17,000 hectares surrounding Mount Carleton were set aside for a provincial wilderness park. Trails covering 62 kilometres lead the visitor to old forests, woodland meadows, waterfalls, and finally to spectacular vistas from the mountain. There are also groomed trails for cross-country skiing in winter. See also CARLETON COUNTY.

Mount Chalmers   *See* Geologists Range.

Mount Chamberlain   *See* Naturalists Range.

Mount Cooney (Northumberland)   East of the NEPISIGUIT

LAKES, and within the bounds of Mount Carleton Provincial Park. It calls attention to the remarkable career of Robert Cooney (1800–1870), clergyman, journalist, and author. A native of Dublin, Cooney studied for the Roman Catholic priesthood, emigrating in 1824 to New Brunswick. Against the wishes of Bishop Angus MacEachern (1759–1835), he helped 'deliver' the Irish Catholic vote to Joseph Cunard in the election of 1828. In retaliation, the bishop had Cooney 'read from the altar.' Partly as a result of this action Cooney joined the Methodist church and was ordained in 1837. After serving several pastorates in the Maritimes, he moved to serve Methodist churches in Lower and Upper Canada. Along the way he managed to write two important books: *A Compendious History of the Northern Part of the Province of New Brunswick and of the District of Gaspé, in Lower Canada* (Halifax 1832) and *The Autobiography of a Wesleyan Methodist Missionary ...* (Montreal 1856).

Mount Cox   *See* Naturalists Range.

Mount Dawson   *See* Geologists Range.

Mount Denys (Northumberland) South of Indian Falls Depot, on

the NEPISIGUIT RIVER; in the ACA-
DIANS RANGE. A tribute to Nicolas
Denys (1598–1688), explorer,
trader, author, and governor. For
forty years, from 1632 until 1672,
he was one of the leading figures
in Acadia. In 1654 Denys was
appointed governor of the coasts
and islands of the St. Lawrence
from Canso to Gaspé, as well as
Newfoundland. See also
BATHURST and ST. PETER'S, Nova
Scotia.

Mount DesBarres (Northumberland)   South of Sixty Nine Mile
Brook, a tributary of the NEPISI-
GUIT RIVER. Named for J.F.W. Des-
Barres (1721?–1824), one of the
most colourful personalities in
Atlantic Canadian history. At
various points in his long career,
he was an army officer, military
engineer, surveyor, artist,
hydrographer, colonizer, lieutenant-governor of Cape Breton
(1784–7) and governor of Prince
Edward Island (1804–12). Among
his vast lanholdings was a tract of
land at PETITCODIAC, New Brunswick. See also DESBARRES POINT,
Prince Edward Island; and TATA-
MAGOUCHE, FALMOUTH, and SYD-
NEY, Nova Scotia.

Mount Elizabeth (Northumberland)   Some 5 kilometres to the
east of MOUNT DESBARRES. The
name recalls the life of Louise-
Elisabeth de Joybert de Soulanges

et de Marson (1673–1740). Born at
JEMSEG, in the then French colony
of Acadia, she became the Marquise de Vaudreuil following her
marriage to Philippe de Rigaud,
Marquis de Vaudreuil (*ca* 1643–
1725), who served as governor of
New France from 1703 to 1725.
Their son, Pierre, was destined to
be the first native-born governor
general of New France. He served
from 1755 to 1760.

Mount Ells   *See* Geologists
Range.

Mount Fisher   *See* Historians
Range.

Mount Francis   *See* Chiefs Plateau.

Mount Frederic Clark (Carleton)
East of Knowlesville, near the
YORK COUNTY boundary, and
named for Dr. George Frederic
Clarke (1883–1974), noted archaeologist, historian, and author. For
many years Dr. Clarke was a den-
tal surgeon in WOODSTOCK; however, it was his all-consuming
interest in archaeological research
and writing relating to the Maliseet that brought him lasting
fame. Many of his archaeological
finds are on display in the New
Brunswick Museum and in the
Woodstock library. Of his fourteen books, the two best known
are *Too Small a World: The Story of
Acadia* (Fredericton 1958) and

Someone before Us: Our Maritime Indians (Fredericton 1968). In the latter he unequivocally sets out his position regarding the Maliseet: 'We took from the Indian his rightful heritage, uprooted him from a way of life that had been his for untold centuries. We cajoled him with special promises, broke solemn treaties. He was assured that he would be allowed to take fish from the rivers, game from the forests, birchbark for his canoes, black ash for his basketry ... Of late years, in New Brunswick, there has been much talk of equal opportunity for all. I cannot help wondering whether this is meant to include the Indian!'

Mount Ganong (Northumberland)   Part of the NATURALISTS RANGE. Named for Dr. William Francis Ganong (1864–1941), internationally recognized botanist, historian, and cartographer, and the leading authority on the place names of Atlantic Canada. His ground-breaking *A Monograph of the Place-Nomenclature of the Province of New Brunswick* remains a classic in the field of toponymy. The best tribute to his research is to record that, more than a half-century after his death, his work remains authoritative. The number of times the citation 'Ganong' appears in this book bears witness to this fact.

Mount Halion   *See* Chiefs Plateau.

Mount Hannay   *See* Historians Range.

Mount Hartt   *See* Geologists Range.

Mount Julian   *See* Chiefs Plateau.

Mount LeClerc   *See* Missionaries Range.

Mount MacIntosh   *See* Naturalists Mountains.

Mount McNair (Victoria)   East of SERPENTINE RIVER. Bestowed in honour of John Babbit McNair (1889–1968), who served as premier from 1940 to 1952; chief justice from 1952 to 1956, and lieutenant-governor of the province from 1956 to 1968. He was a native of ANDOVER, in VICTORIA COUNTY.

Mount Manny   *See* Historians Range.

Mount Matthew   *See* Geologists Range.

Mount Membertou   *See* Chiefs Plateau.

Mount Moses   *See* Naturalists Mountains.

Mount Raymond   *See* Historians Range.

Mount St. Nicholas   *See* Christmas Mountains.

Mount Scudon   *See* Chiefs Plateau.

Mount Webster   *See* Historians Range.

Mount Whatley (Westmorland) An elevated area between AULAC and POINT DE BUTE, overlooking the Missaguash Marsh. It was known during the French colonial period as 'Butte à Mirande,' for a Portuguese settler named Mirande who married a French woman and had a farm there. Later, during the siege of FORT BEAUSÉJOUR in 1755, the British established their main encampment on the site and it became known as 'Camp Hill.' In the 1790s the area was resettled by Robert Whatley, for whom it was later renamed.

Murray Corner (Westmorland) West of CAPE TORMENTINE, on Highway 955. The settlement was named for members of the Murray family who emigrated to the area from Scotland in the 1820s.

Musquash Cove; Musquash Harbour; Musquash River (Saint John)   West of SAINT JOHN and

adjacent to the BAY OF FUNDY. According to William Francis Ganong, the origin is 'uncertain, it is either a descriptive or a corruption of a Maliseet name.' One of the earliest references is to *Mushaguash Cove*, in a 1696 account by Benjamin Church.

Musquash Harbour   *See* Musquash Cove.

Musquash River   *See* Musquash Cove.

Nackawic; Nackawic Stream (York)   The stream flows into the section of the ST. JOHN RIVER known as MACTAQUAC LAKE. The name is of Maliseet origin and is 'derived from *Nelgwaweegek*, possibly meaning "straight stream," in reference to the fact that its lower part, prior to flooding by Mactaquac Lake, was in line with the Saint John River' (Rayburn). The town, built around a pulp-and-paper mill, claims 'the world's largest axe.' It is constructed of steel and looms over the waterfront. Nearby is an international garden containing trees from around the world.

Nackawic Stream   *See* Nackawic.

Nan Island   *See* Billy Island.

Nantucket Island (Charlotte)   A small island located to the east of

GRAND MANAN. Named for Nantucket Island off the southeast coast of Massachusetts. Whalers from Nantucket and Cape Cod once frequented this area.

Napadogan; Napadogan Brook; Napadogan Lake (York)   The settlement is on Highway 107, in the northwest section of the county. The brook was named first, and was spelled 'Napudogan.' William Francis Ganong attributes the word to the Maliseet *Napudaagun*, possibly meaning 'brook to be followed' in travelling to nearby MIRAMICHI LAKE.

Napadogan Brook   *See* Napadogan.

Napadogan Lake   *See* Napadogan.

Nashwaak Bridge   *See* Covered Bridge.

Nashwaak Lake   *See* Nashwaak River.

Nashwaak Mountain   *See* Nashwaak River.

Nashwaak River (York)   Flows into the ST. JOHN RIVER, opposite FREDERICTON. The name is derived from the Maliseet *Nahwijewauk*, of uncertain meaning. Of this river, Esther Clark Wright has written:

'The beautiful river Nashwaak was one of the advantages Edward Winslow claimed for the choice of St. Anne's [Fredericton] as the capital of the province. By opening up a considerable area for settlement, and by furnishing a route to the Miramichi and thus to the North Shore, the Nashwaak was of very great value. Although Saint John never ceased to hope that the capital might be moved [there], Fredericton's position was strengthened by accessibility to the northern part of the province.' Nashwaak Lake and Nashwaak Mountain are at the head of the river.

Nashwaaksis; Nashwaaksis Stream (York)   The stream flows into the ST. JOHN RIVER, at Nashwaaksis, a surburban community now part of FREDERICTON. Derived, as well, from the Maliseet, and in translation means 'little Nashwaak.'

Nashwaaksis Stream   *See* Nashwaaksis.

Naturalists Mountains (Northumberland)   Located southeast of UPSALQUITCH LAKE and named for a group of important New Brunswick naturalists. For example, Mount Chamberlain, for Montague Chamberlain (1844–1924), ornithologist; Mount Cox, for Philip Cox (1847–1939), zoologist; MOUNT GANONG, for William Francis Ganong (1864–1941), botanist; Mount MacIntosh, for William MacIntosh (1867–1950), first director of the New Brunswick Museum (1934–40); Mount Moses, for Allan Moses (*ca* 1885–1955), ornithologist.

Nauwigewauk (Kings)   On the HAMMOND RIVER, a tributary of the KENNEBACASIS. The village name, of unknown meaning, is of Maliseet origin (see NASHWAAK). Originally it was the Maliseet name for what is now the Hammond River.

Neguac; Neguac Island (Northumberland)   The island is located at the entrance to MIRAMICHI BAY. The name is of uncertain Mi'kmaq origin and may well be traced to *Negwek*, for 'springs out of the ground' (Rand).

Nelson–Miramichi (Northumber-land)   Once known as South Nelson, and now part of the city of MIRAMICHI, it was named for Admiral Horatio Nelson (1785–1805). In 1805 he claimed his greatest victory against the combined French and Spanish fleet, at the Battle of Trafalgar. The name Nelson–Miramichi was adopted on 26 April 1968.

Nepisiguit Bay; Nepisiguit Falls; Nepisiguit Lakes; Nepisiguit River (Northumberland and Gloucester)   The Nepisiguit River, the fourth-largest in New Brunswick, flows north and east 128 kilometres from the interior of NORTHUMBERLAND COUNTY, to empty into Nepisiguit Bay, an arm of BAIE DES CHALEURS. The name is traceable to the Mi'kmaq *Winpegijawik*, which has been translated as 'rough water,' an apt description of the river. It appears in the *Jesuit Relations* (1643) as *Nepeguit*, a corruption of the Mi'kmaq through the French language. Nepisiguit Lakes is a collective term for three small lakes (Bathurst, Camp, and Teneriffe) located within Mount Carleton Provincial Park. The lakes, bay, and falls take their name from the river.

Nepisiguit Falls   *See* Nepisguit Bay.

Nepisiguit Lakes   *See* Nepisguit Bay.

Nepisiguit River   *See* Nepisguit Bay.

New Bandon (Northumberland; Gloucester)   New Bandon in NORTHUMBERLAND COUNTY lies northeast of BOIESTOWN; the same place name may also be found northeast of BATHURST. Both communities were settled by the Irish and named for Bandon in County Cork, Ireland.

New Canaan; New Canaan River
(Queens)   The river flows southwest into Washademoak Lake
and takes its name from the settlement of New Canaan, which
was named after the biblical designation for Israel prior to its conquest by the Hebrews. See also
WASHADEMOAK LAKE.

New Canaan River   *See* New
Canaan.

Newcastle (Northumberland)
On the north bank of the MIRAMI-
CHI RIVER; became part of the city
of MIRAMICHI in 1995. Ironically,
'Miramichi' was the first name
suggested for the new town
established in 1790. However, the
sheriff, Benjamin Marston,
decided that it was 'too difficult
to pronounce and spell' and put
forward 'Newcastle' as an alternative. It honoured Thomas Pel-
ham Holles, Duke of Newcastle
(1693–1768), who served as British prime minister from 1754 to
1762. The 'Great Miramichi Fire'
of 7 October 1825, which claimed
almost 200 lives, laid waste to
Newcastle and the surrounding
areas. However, such was the
resilience of the people that a new
town soon arose, based upon
shipbuilding and the export of
lumber. The town was incorporated in 1899. The most famous
sons of the town were Peter
Mitchell (1824–1899) and Max

Aitken, Lord Beaverbrook (1879–
1964). Mitchell was a member of
the Legislative Assembly, premier, a Father of Confederation,
Canada's first minister of Fisheries, a senator, and a member of
Parliament. Max Aitken lived in
Newcastle from the age of ten
months to eighteen years. Later in
life, when he achieved fame and
fortune as a financier, newspaper
baron, and member of the British
wartime cabinet, he never forgot
his home town. Among his many
gifts were the town hall, rink,
library (his boyhood home, now a
museum), and church organs,
chimes, and bells. Other significant gifts were two parks. One he
named THE ENCLOSURE and the
second became Newcastle's
'The Square.' Here he erected
memorials to Peter Mitchell and
the Miramichi lumbermen. On
9 June 1964, his ashes were interred in a monument in The
Square. It is surmounted by an
Oscar Nemon bronze bust of
Beaverbrook. Newcastle has been
the traditional home of the internationally famous Miramichi Folk
Festival. The town is now part of
the city of Miramichi. See also
FREDERICTON.

New Denmark (Victoria)   On
Route 108, 25 kilometres from
PLASTER ROCK. Founded 19 June
1872 by six Danish families. Each
year, on the anniversary of this

date, residents celebrate their heritage with a Founders Day. St. Ansgar's Anglican Church bears the name of the patron saint of Denmark. Known as the 'apostle of the north,' St. Ansgar brought Christianity to the Danish homeland in A.D. 825. New Denmark has prospered over the years and is now one of the largest Danish communities in North America. See also KLOKLEDAHL HILL.

New Maryland (York)   South of FREDERICTON. First known as 'Maryland,' after the American state. On 2 October 1821, the community was the scene of a duel between George Ludlow Wetmore (1795–1821) and George Frederick Street (1787–1855). Both were lawyers, members of the Fredericton establishment, and bitter opponents in the courts. Following an acrimonious trial in which they predictably represented opposite sides, the two almost came to blows outside the courtroom. Subsequently, Wetmore challenged Street to a duel, and the two men 'along with their seconds repaired to Maryland Hill' to settle matters. In the second round of shots, Wetmore was killed; since duelling was illegal, Street and his seconds fled to Maine. Later he returned to stand trial and was acquitted, as 'foul play' could not be proved. The decision did little to improve relations between the two families. Wetmore's widow, who lived to be ninety-four, reputedly never spoke to a Street for the remainder of her life.

New River Beach (Charlotte) On MACES BAY. According to William Francis Ganong, it 'was so called when newly found.' Site of New River Beach Provincial Park, with a magnificent crescent-shaped white sand beach.

Newtown (Kings)   Northeast of SUSSEX. Originally known as 'Newton,' for an early grantee, it has been spelled 'Newtown' since 1892. Noted as the location of the Oldfield Covered Bridge, named for the family on whose property it was erected in 1910. A sketch of this bridge was selected for a 25-cent coin issued in January 1992 to mark the 125th anniversary of Confederation. There are some seventy covered bridges in New Brunswick, and they are a distinct part of the provincial heritage. There was a practical reason for their construction: to protect wooden flooring from the impact of snow, rain, and sun. Uncovered bridges might last a decade, but the covered ones could be expected to survive for at least seventy-five to eighty years. See also COVERED BRIDGE, HARTLAND, and SUSSEX.

Nicholas Denys (Gloucester) Northwest of BATHURST. Named for Nicolas Denys (1598–1688). For information on Denys see BATHURST and MOUNT DENYS.

Nictau; Nictau Lake (Victoria) The settlement is located at the forks of the TOBIQUE RIVER and traceable to the Maliseet descriptive *Niktawk*, for 'forks.' The lake, within Mount Carleton Provincial Park, was named for the settlement.

Nictau Lake   *See* Nictau.

Nigadoo; Nigadoo River (Gloucester)   The river flows into BAIE DES CHALEURS, northwest of BATHURST. The meaning of this Mi'kmaq place name has been lost. Nigadoo was incorporated as a village in 1967.

Nigadoo River   *See* Nigadoo.

Northesk Boom (Northumberland)   On the Northwest MIRAMICHI RIVER. The community name stems from the township of Northesk, named for William Carnegie, Earl of Northesk (1758–1831), who served with Admiral Horatio Nelson at the Battle of Trafalgar. 'Boom' is a lumbering term for a structure of logs strung all or partway across a river to restrain floating timber.

North Pole Mountain *See* Christmas Mountains.

North Pole Stream   See Christmas Mountains.

Northumberland County   One of the eight counties established by legislation in 1786. It was then much larger and included the present RESTIGOUCHE, GLOUCESTER, and KENT counties. Since a considerable portion of the original county fronted on NORTHUMBERLAND STRAIT (previously designated in 1764 by J.F.W. DesBarres), it was so named. An additional reason was the fact that it then adjoined WESTMORLAND COUNTY. (Kent County was not created until 1827.) At that time two counties so named were located in close proximity in northern England.

Northumberland Strait   See chapter 1, page 21.

Norton (Kings)   Southwest of SUSSEX. The village takes its name from the parish established in 1795. Since many early settlers were natives of New England, it was probably named for Norton in southern Massachusetts.

Notre-Dame (Kent)   On Highway 115. Formerly known as 'Scovil's Mills,' the name was changed with the establishment of the post office in 1887. It takes its name from the parish.

Notre-Dame-de-Lourdes (Madawaska)   Northeast of STE. ANNE-DE-MADAWASKA. Named after the parish founded in 1943.

Oak Bay (Charlotte)   East of ST. STEPHEN and adjacent to the ST. CROIX RIVER. The name may be traced to a Passamaquoddy descriptive, *Wahquaoek*, for 'head of the bay.' On the Owen map of 1798, it is given as *Aouk Bay*, a corruption of the latter part of the original name. Over time this became Oak Bay.

Oak Point (Kings)   A descriptive for a point of land that extends into LONG REACH. Provincial parks are located at both OAK BAY and OAK POINT.

Odell River (Victoria)   Flows into the TOBIQUE RIVER, northeast of ARTHURETTE. This place name marks the contribution of the Odell family to the history of New Brunswick. The dynasty was established by Loyalist Jonathan Odell (1737–1818), clergyman, physician, author, and provincial secretary of New Brunswick (1784–1818). His son, William Franklin Odell (1774–1844), succeeded him in 1812 as provincial secretary, and served until his death in 1844. The latter's son, William Hunter Odell (1811–

1891), was deputy provincial secretary 1838 to 1848, when he became a judge of the Court of Common Pleas. In 1867 he was appointed to the first Senate of Canada.

Old Mission Point (Restigouche) Juts into the RESTIGOUCHE RIVER at ATHOLVILLE. Once the site of a Mi'kmaq mission, that was later moved across the river to Québec, it appears as *Old Church Point* in some nineteenth-century documents.

Old Sow (Charlotte)   A whirlpool located south of DEER ISLAND, in PASSAMAQUODDY BAY. The name of this navigational hazard is descriptive and refers to the roaring sound caused by the spinning of the tidal currents, said to resemble 'the roar of a sow.'

Oromocto; Oromocto Island; Oromocto Lake; Oromocto River (Sunbury)   The settlement is opposite MAUGERVILLE, on the ST. JOHN RIVER. The name originates with the river and is derived from the Maliseet *Welamooktook*, meaning 'good river for easy canoe navigation.' Earlier spellings were 'Ramouctu' and 'La Rivière Kamouctu' (Freneuse seigneurial grant, 1684). 'Oromocto' was given by Charles Morris in 1775 and has been the spelling from the early nineteenth century onward. The island and lake take their name from the river. The town of Oromocto, incorporated in 1956, is the headquarters for Canadian Forces Base GAGETOWN.

Oromocto Island   *See* Oromocto.

Oromocto Lake   *See* Oromocto.

Oromocto River   *See* Oromocto.

Otnabog Lake; Otnabog Stream (Queens)   The lake is separated from the ST. JOHN RIVER by a narrow strip of land on which the railway passes precariously. The stream empties into the lake. The name Otnabog is of Maliseet origin and was attributed to the word *Wednebak* by William Francis Ganong. The meaning is uncertain.

Otnabog Stream   *See* Otnabog Lake.

Oven Head (Charlotte)   On PASSAMAQUODDY BAY, west of ST. GEORGE. A descriptive for the shape of the headland. Internationally known for its high-quality smoked salmon.

Owen Head (Charlotte)   On Campobello Island. Serves as a reminder of the career of Captain William Owen (1735–1778), who lived there from 1770 to 1771. See also CAMPOBELLO ISLAND.

Pabineau River (Gloucester) Flows into the NEPISIGUIT RIVER 11 kilometres east of BATHURST. The name may be traced through the French back to original Mi'kmaq sources. It refers to a type of low bush fruit or cranberry called by the Mi'kmaq *wosabaygul* and by the French *pabina*. The Pabineau Falls area is well known to salmon anglers.

Paquetville (Gloucester)   South of CARAQUET, on Highway 350. The village was named for Père Joseph-Marie Paquet (1804–1869), who served a number of parishes on the east coast of New Brunswick, including nearby Caraquet. Paquetville achieved international fame as the title of a hit song by Edith Butler, well-known Acadian singer–composer. Born here on 27 July 1942, she has sometimes been referred to as a 'paquet' of dynamite. Through Butler's many stage appearances both in Canada and in Europe, she has contributed to the advancement of Acadian culture and heritage.

Parlee Beach   *See* Pointe-du-Chêne.

Partridge Island (Saint John)   At the mouth of SAINT JOHN harbour. It was known to the French as 'Île

Perdrix'; thus the present name is the English translation of the original. Although largely abandoned and neglected today, Partridge Island played an important role in the history of Saint John. Once the location of a quarantine station for immigrants, today the ruins of fortifications erected to defend the city in time of war, a lighthouse, and a Celtic cross are the only reminders of its storied past. In 1927 the citizens of Saint John erected the cross as a memorial to their Irish ancestors, many of whom lie buried on the island. See also REVERSING FALLS.

Passamaquoddy Bay (Charlotte) Traceable to the Passamaquoddy *Peeskutam-akadi* or *Peskutu-maquadik*, meaning 'the place where pollock leap entirely out of the water.' The name was originally applied to the waters separating CAMPOBELLO, DEER, and Moose islands, and was later transferred to the entire bay. One of the earliest references, *Pesemou-quote*, is found in the *Jesuit Relations* (1675). It appears as *Pesmonquady* on the Franquelin–DeMeulles map of 1686, and as *Pesmoucadie* on the Couagne chart of 1749. By the end of the eighteenth century, the contemporary spelling is verified by the George Sproule chart of New Brunswick (1799). Of Passamaquoddy, Esther Clark Wright has written: 'The bay

is an extraordinary maze of channels and tide rips [see OLD SOW], which alone would make it a unique and fascinating area. But in addition ... it is a location where the past is always present in the place names bestowed so long ago, in the international boundary line, not seen but ever protruding.'

Peekaboo Corner (Kings)   North of the village of NORTON. The local explanation for the name is that it refers to the fact that a house once obscured the visibility of travellers at the crossroad in the community.

Pennfield Ridge (Charlotte)   On Highway 1, between POCOLOGAN and Upper Etang. First known as 'Penn's Field,' in memory of William Penn II (1644–1718), an English Quaker leader. The first settlers were Quaker Loyalists from Pennsylvania. The modern spelling dates from the mid-nineteenth century. See also chapter 1, page 23.

Penniac Stream (York)   Flows into the NASHWAAK RIVER. Derived from the Maliseet *Pan-weook*, translated as 'opening out land' by William Francis Ganong. Appears as *Pamouak* as early as 1783. When the post office was established in 1879, the spelling was 'Peniac'; by 1900 it had become 'Penniac.'

Penobsquis (Kings)   Northeast of SUSSEX, off Highway 2. A coined name developed during the construction of the European and North American Railway line in the 1850s. The name may be traced to the Maliseet *Penobsq'*, for 'stone,' and *sips*, meaning a 'brook,' thus replacing the earlier 'Stone Brook.' Alan Rayburn contends that this, and adjacent railway names, 'were made up by surveyors' and, as a result, they are 'translations into bad Maliseet.' See also PLUMWESEEP and QUISPAMSIS.

Perth–Andover (Victoria)   On Highway 105. Dating from 1833, the parish name stems from Andover in Hampshire, England, and means literally 'ash tree stream.' Since 1966 the community has been part of the village of Perth–Andover. The twin communities were originally named for locations in the United Kingdom – Perth for the Scottish city; Andover for a town in Hampshire, England. The joint name was approved on 6 July 1970.

Petitcodiac; Petitcodiac River (Westmorland)   The river flows southeast into SHEPODY BAY. A Mi'kmaq descriptive, the name is a corruption of *Pet-koot-koy-ek*, which has been translated as 'the river that bends around back.' One of the earliest references is the Franquelin–DeMeulles map of 1686, which gives *Petcoucoyek*. It is listed as *Petitcodiak* in the Morris survey of 1760. In 1774 John Robinson and Thomas Rispin, in their *Journey through Nova Scotia*, rendered the name phonetically as *Petticoat Jack*. The present spelling did not become common until the mid-nineteenth century. The community was first known as 'Head of Petitcodiac' and the name was shortened to Petitcodiac in 1865.

Petitcodiac River   *See* Petitcodiac.

Petite-Rivière-de-l'Ile   *See* Lamèque.

Petit-Rocher (Gloucester) Northwest of BATHURST, on Highway 134. The name is a descriptive for 'little rock.' In early July, Petit-Rocher hosts the annual Festival de Rameurs, the Dory Boat Festival.

Plaster Rock (Victoria)   On the TOBIQUE RIVER. Named after the reddish gypsum rock prevalent in the region. It is an entry point for the high plateau area of northern New Brunswick and Mount Carleton Provincial Park.

Plumper Rock (Saint John)   Lies offshore, northeast of POINT LEPREAU. On 5 December 1812, HMS

Plumper, with a cargo 'of much specie on board,' was wrecked on this navigational hazard. In the tragedy fifty people lost their lives. The contemporary *Bay of Fundy Pilot* still advises mariners to 'give this rock a berth of at least half a mile.'

Plumweseep (Kings)   East of SUSSEX. Like PENOBSQUIS, this is a coined name. Originally named Salmon River; however, since there were many other locations with this name in New Brunswick alone, it was decided during the course of railway construction 'to go with a translation, back to the Maliseet for Salmon River, *Plumwe-seep*' (Ganong).

Pocologan; Pocologan Harbour; Pocologan River (Charlotte) The river into Pocologan Harbour, an inlet of MACES BAY. The harbour may have been designated first, as the name is derived from the Passamaquoddy descriptive *Pekalugan*, 'enclosed harbour.' The settlement was named for the harbour.

Pocologan Harbour   *See* Pocologan.

Pocologan River   *See* Pocologan.

Point de Bute (Westmorland) On Fort Cumberland Ridge, overlooking the MISSAGUASH RIVER and the New Brunswick–Nova Scotia border. From the French Pointe à Buot, probably for a point in the nearby Missaguash River. May also be from Pont à Buot, 'Buots Bridge,' for an early Acadian settler, Pierre Buhot or Buot.

Pointe-du-Chêne (Westmorland) Northeast of SHEDIAC. It is a French descriptive for 'Oak Point' and dates from the early eighteenth century. In 1860 the community became the northern terminus for the European and North American Railway. For many years thereafter a line of steamers plied between Point-du-Chêne and Summerside. Parlee Beach, a noted resort and provincial park, honours T. Babbitt Parlee (1914–1956), provincial minister of Municipal Affairs and once MLA for MONCTON. He was killed in a plane crash while flying between FREDERICTON and Moncton. Parlee Beach is noted for its warm waters, caused by a combination of shallow water flowing over sand flats which become heated by the sun at low tide. The water temperature frequently reaches 20° Celsius at the height of the summer season.

Pointe-Sapin (Kent)   North of RICHIBUCTO. It was originally known as 'Point-aux-Sapins,' and as 'Point-Sapin' after 1873. It is a French descriptive for 'Fir Point.'

Point Escuminac   *See* Escuminac.

Pointe-Verte (Gloucester)   South of BELLEDUNE, near the RESTIGOUCHE COUNTY boundary. The name is also a French descriptive. The community possesses a unique facility in Atlas Park, located on the edge of an old quarry 30 metres deep. The cool, clear water attracts scuba divers in all seasons; in the winter months, under-ice scuba diving is practised.

Point Lepreau   *See* Lepreau Harbour.

Pokemouche River (Gloucester) Flows into the Gulf of St. Lawrence, south of CARAQUET. Traceable to the Mi'kmaq *Pocomooch*, translated by Silas T. Rand as 'salt water extending inward.' It was rendered as *Pakmouch* (Jumeau 1685), *Pocquemouche* (unknown surveyor 1754), and *Pokamouche* (Gesner 1847). By the late nineteenth century, the spelling had stabilized in its present form.

Pokiok; Pokiok Stream (York) The stream flows into MACTAQUAC LAKE, a section of the ST. JOHN RIVER, and is derived from

the Maliseet descriptive *Pokweok*, which was translated by William Francis Ganong as 'a narrow place or gorge.' He points out that the name occurs in several locations throughout the province (e.g., surburban SAINT JOHN) and 'that these are all alike in having a narrow gorge or narrows at the mouth of a stream.' The settlement was named for the stream.

Pokiok Stream   *See* Pokiok.

Pollett; Pollett River (Westmorland)   The river flows north into the PETITCODIAC RIVER; the community is located on Highway 905. Named for Peter Paulet, who was described as 'a Mi'kmaq medicine man who lived near the mouth of the river' (Ganong). An earlier spelling of the name was 'Pawlet.'

Pollett River   *See* Pollett.

Pont-Lafranc (Gloucester)   On the Big Tracadie River. Named after the Reverend François-Xavier-Stanislaus Lafrance (1814–1867), who served as parish priest at TRACADIE and was one of the founders of Collège Saint-Joseph. See also SAINT-JOSEPH.

Portage Island (Northumberland) In MIRAMICHI BAY. The origin is uncertain. It may be a variation of 'Passage' Island, or a reference to a local tradition that Acadian settlers stopped on the island to cook soup, or *potage*, while crossing the bay. During 1642–44, Jean-Jacques Enard, a Basque entrepreneur, established a seacow or walrus fishery on the island. See also SEA-COW POND, Prince Edward Island.

Port Elgin (Westmorland)   On BAIE VERTE. Named about 1850 in honour of Lord Elgin (1811–1867), governor general from 1846 to 1854. Replaced the earlier name Gaspereaux, from the GASPEREAU RIVER.

Pré-d'en-Haut (Westmorland) On the PETITCODIAC RIVER. A French Acadian descriptive for 'meadow on the heights.' In 1995 the village became part of the town of MEMRAMCOOK VALLEY.

Prince of Wales (Saint John) West of SAINT JOHN. The area was settled following the American Revolution by members of the Prince of Wales, Regiment, thus giving rise to the place name. The settlement predates the visit of Edward, Prince of Wales, to New Brunswick in 1860. The latter event is sometimes erroneously cited as the explanation for the name.

Prince William (York)   On the ST. JOHN RIVER, northeast of KINGS LANDING. Named for Prince William, later King William IV (1765–1837). He was patron of the regiment the Kings American Dragoons, some of whose members settled the area after 1783.

Pull and Be Damned Narrows (Charlotte)   The name arose from the difficulty experienced in rowing or paddling against the ebb tide in the Letang River, located east of ST. GEORGE. A similar name, Push and Be Damned Rapids, is found in GLOUCESTER and NORTHUMBERLAND counties for rapids on the NEPISIGUIT and Southwest MIRAMICHI rivers. These names depict the problems encountered in attempting to paddle a canoe against the onrushing water.

Push and Be Damned Rapids *See* Pull and Be Damned Narrows.

Quaco Bay; Quaco Head (Saint John)   An indentation of the BAY OF FUNDY, east of SAINT JOHN. Silas T. Rand traces the name to a contraction of the Mi'kmaq *Goolwagek*, meaning 'haunt of the hooded seal.' It appears on the Franquelin–DeMeulles map of 1686 as *Ariquaki*, from which, over time, the present spelling and pronunciation evolved. Quaco Head is located at the western entrance to the bay; there is a dangerous rip tide nearby.

Quaco Head   *See* Quaco Bay.

Quaker Brook (Victoria)   Flows into the TOBIQUE RIVER. Probably named for an early settler who was a member of the Society of Friends, or Quakers.

Queens County   Adjacent to KINGS COUNTY, and one of the eight counties established by legislation in 1786. The name was undoubtedly selected as an indication of loyalty to the monarchy. It may also have been inspired by the fact that some of its first settlers were Loyalists from Queens County on Long Island, New York.

Queensbury (York)   Northwest of FREDERICTON, on the ST. JOHN RIVER. The name was bestowed 2 February 1787 upon the parish settled by members of the Queens Rangers.

Queenstown (Queens)   South of GAGETOWN. The name evolved from the county in which it is located.

Quinton Heights (Saint John) On South Bay, in the western suburbs of SAINT JOHN. Named for James Quinton, son of Hugh and Elizabeth Quinton. He was born at Fort Frederick on 28 August 1762, the first child of English-speaking parents in the Saint John area.

Quisibis; Quisibis Mountain; Quisibis River (Madawaska)   A tributary of the ST. JOHN RIVER, at Sainte-Anne-de-Madawaska. It is derived from the Maliseet *Squee-seebisk*, of unknown meaning. The mountain is named for the river.

Quisibis Mountain   *See* Quisibis.

Quisibis River   *See* Quisibis.

Quispamsis (Kings)   Northeast of ROTHESAY. It is a coined descriptive formed by joining the Maliseet *Quispam*, for 'lake,' with *sis*, for 'little.' The lake in question is Ritchies Lake, which is 'little' in comparison with other nearby lakes. See also PENOBSQUIS.

Ranger Settlement (Victoria) Southwest of NEW DENMARK. Named for the Royal West India Rangers who settled here in 1819. The name was subsequently changed to Medford; however, the older name is also used.

Red Bank (Northumberland) On the Northwest MIRAMICHI RIVER. A descriptive for the red bank of the river. See also METE-PENAGIAG.

Red Head (Saint John)   Extends into SAINT JOHN harbour, southeast of the city. A descriptive, it was probably the *Cap Rouge* listed by Champlain on his map of 1612. There are a number of locations with the same name throughout the province, for example, in CHARLOTTE COUNTY, on CAMPO-BELLO, GRAND MANAN islands, and extending into the Bay of Fundy south of POCOLOGAN. All are descriptives.

Renforth (Kings)   On Kennebe-casis Bay. Named for James Ren-forth (1843–1871), stroke of a boat crew from Newcastle-upon-Tyne, England, who died follow-ing a race against a SAINT JOHN team on 23 August 1871. Renforth was internationally known as a champion rower, winning the singles event at the Thames Regatta in 1868. Before joining the four-oared English boat crew for a tour of Canada in 1871, Ren-forth was winner of the English single-scull championship. An ironworker, he was noted 'for his strength, enabling him to row at tremendous speed in almost any water': *New Brunswick Reporter*, 30 August 1871.

Renous; Renous River (Northumberland)   The river empties into the Southwest MIRAMICHI RIVER. The name is probably derived from that of a Mi'kmaq chief, 'Sock' Renou or Renard.

Renous River   *See* Renous.

Restigouche County   The county became a separate entity, detached from GLOUCESTER COUNTY, in 1837. Named for the RESTIGOUCHE RIVER.

Restigouche River   The river rises in MADAWASKA COUNTY, near QUISIBIS MOUNTAIN, flows in a northeasterly direction across RESTIGOUCHE COUNTY, and emp-ties into BAIE DES CHALEURS. The name may be traced to the Mi'kmaq *Lustagooch*; unfortu-nately, its precise meaning has become lost. The most accepted translation is 'good river.' It appears as *Restigoch* in the *Jesuit Relations* (1642); *Restigousche* (Des-Barres 1778); and *Restigouche* (Cooney 1832). A 55-kilometre section of the Restigouche, stretching from near the VICTORIA COUNTY line to the Québec bor-der, has been nominated by the provincial government to become a Canadian Heritage River. There were two basic rea-sons for the nomination: The Res-tigouche once formed part of the Mi'kmaq transportation route to the St. Lawrence River, and it pro-vides a habitat for a variety of rare plants, mosses, and lichens, and the Canada lynx and the osprey, which are both on New Brunswick's list of endangered species.

Reversing Falls (Saint John)
Created by the rise and fall of the
BAY OF FUNDY tide and the flow of
water from the ST. JOHN RIVER.
This descriptive name has been
attributed by Alan Rayburn to
'Sir Charles G.D. Roberts, who
wrote a description of its revers-
ible character in 1882.' The location is also celebrated in Mi'kmaq
lore and legend. Thus it was
Glooscap who created the falls
when he cleared away a dam
erected by his enemies. Non-
believers may still see a piece of
the dam, now PARTRIDGE ISLAND,
at the harbour's mouth.

Rexton (Kent)   South of RICHI-
BUCTO. First named for Kingston,
Yorkshire, England. The name
was changed in 1901 to Rexton,
thus avoiding confusion with
numerous other locations of the
same name. It was the birthplace
of Andrew Bonar Law (1858–
1923), who, at age twelve, emigrated to Scotland, later entered
politics, and became prime minister of Great Britain in 1922. Bonar
Law was victorious in the general
election of November 1922 but
was obliged to resign, due to ill
health, in May 1923. He died on
30 October 1923, having earned
the distinction of being the only
prime minister born outside of
the British Isles. The Bonar Law
homestead has been declared a
historic site and is open to the
public. As well, the local high
school is named Bonar Law
Memorial High School.

Richibucto; Richibucto River
(Kent)   The river flows in a
northeasterly direction into the
NORTHUMBERLAND STRAIT.
Although it is derived from the
Mi'kmaq, William Francis
Ganong points out that 'its
aboriginal form is unknown.' It
may be from *Lichibouktouck*, translated as 'the river which enters
the woods.' It is listed as *la Baye de
Regibouctou* in the *Jesuit Relations*
(1646) and as *Richibucto* on the
Mitchell map of 1755. Nicolas
Denys (1598–1688) was familiar
with this coast and has left a late-
seventeenth-century description:
'Continuing our route we went
into the river of *Rechibouctou*
which is about ten leagues from
[Cocagne]. The river has great
sand flats at its entrance, which
extend almost a league. In the
midst of them is a channel for the
passage of vessels of 200 tons.
Two other rivers [Charles and
Gaspereau Creek] fall into this
basin, one of which is little, the
other large.' An effort was made
in the early nineteenth century to
change the name of the village to
Liverpool; fortunately, the
attempt failed.

Richibucto River   *See* Richibucto.

Ripples (Sunbury)   Southwest of MINTO. Descriptive of the rapids in the nearby Little River. During the Second World War, there was an internment camp in this area.

River Charlo   *See* Charlo.

River Glade (Westmorland)   On Highway 2, southwest of SALISBURY. The name is descriptive and dates from 1904. See also THE GLADES.

Riverside–Albert (Albert)   On Highway 114, leading to FUNDY NATIONAL PARK. A locational name. The post office was called Albert, until 1875; River Side, from 1875 to 1932; and Riverside, from 1932. For derivation see ALBERT.

Riverview (Westmorland)   The descriptive name 'Riverview Heights' was adopted for this suburban MONCTON community in 1947. Amalgamated with the town of Coverdale in 1973. 'Heights' was dropped in 1974.

Rivières-des-Caches (Northumberland)   Flows south into MIRAMICHI BAY. The precise origin is in dispute. In all probability it is from the French *cache*, for boat. Thus, it may refer to an incident during the 1755 expulsion of the Acadians or to an earlier slaying of six English sailors who reputedly 'wandered away from their boat.' Early documents give the spelling as *Vieux Caichi* or *Old Caichi*. The contemporary spelling dates from William Francis Ganong 1896.

Rivière-des-Crocs   *See* Crocks Point.

Rivière-du-Portage (Northumberland)   South of the GLOUCESTER COUNTY boundary. Descriptive for a number of locations where it was necessary to 'portage' or 'carry' canoes and supplies around an obstruction, e.g., rapids, or from one waterway to another.

Rivière-Verte (Madawaska)   Flows into the ST. JOHN RIVER, southeast of SAINT-BASILE. A descriptive; it was first known as Green River. The name was changed in 1935 to Rivière-Verte.

Roachville (Kings)   West of SUSSEX. Named for Loyalist John Roach, a member of the Royal Fencible American Regiment, who was its first settler in the 1780s.

Robertville (Gloucester)   Northwest of BATHURST. The name honours Abbé François-Antoine Robert (1820–1888), who founded the local church in 1884.

Robichaud (Westmorland)   On the NORTHUMBERLAND STRAIT, at the mouth of the ABOUJAGANE and Kinnear rivers. The name was adopted in 1885 with the establishment of the post office. The first postmaster was Hippolite Robichaud, and the family name has remained common in the area.

Rockport (Westmorland)   Fronts on CUMBERLAND BASIN. The name is descriptive. It was described by Michael Collie as 'a natural rock cove with a caliper [measure] of broken stone that kept out all but the worst of weather.'

Rogersville (Northumberland)   North of Kent Junction, near the boundary with KENT COUNTY. The name honours the Reverend James Rogers (1826–1903), who was to become the first Roman Catholic bishop of CHATHAM. Site of a Trappist monastery founded in 1902.

Rollingdam (Charlotte)   Northeast of WAWEIG, on Highway 770. A descriptive that relates to lumbering. It was named for a special type of dam designed to protect lumber from the rocks.

Rothesay (Kings)   Northeast of SAINT JOHN, on KENNEBECASIS BAY. Named for the Prince of Wales, who was also Duke of Cornwall and Rothesay, later King Edward VII. He embarked from this location during the course of a royal visit to New Brunswick in 1860. See also MOUNT ACQUIN.

Royal Road (York)   Northwest of FREDERICTON, on Highway 620. The community's name may be traced to a scheme launched by Lieutenant-Governor Sir Archibald Campbell (1769–1843). He decided that, from a military standpoint, it was unwise to rely upon the ST. JOHN RIVER as the sole means of communication between Fredericton and GRAND FALLS. What was needed was a road 'where wheels would go, to be constructed in roughly a straight line, between the two points.' Begun in 1831–7, the 'Royal Road' was completed as far as STANLEY; however, the designation is still used for this stretch of highway. A local historian, Peter Thomas, writing in 1986, noted that, 'on 26 July 1977, I was driving back from a fishing trip, along the Royal Road, from Stanley to Fredericton.'

Sackville (Westmorland)   At the head of the BAY OF FUNDY, adjacent to the Tantramar Marshes. By the early 1740s the Acadians had established three settlements in the area: Pré des Bourcqs, or Bourgs; Pré des Richards; and

Tintamarre. Following the expulsion, New England Planters, settlers from Yorkshire, and Loyalists took their place. In typical New England style, the first town meeting was held 'on 20 July 1762 at the house of Charity Bishop.' Sackville township was proclaimed in 1772. It was named for George Sackville Germain, first Viscount Sackville (1716–1785), who served as colonial secretary from 1775 to 1782. The name itself is Norman in origin, and may be traced to Saqueneville, near Rouen in northern France. Sackville is the home of Mount Allison University, established in 1839 and the first university within the present Commonwealth to grant a degree to a woman. This honour fell to Annie Grace Lockhart (1855–1916), who graduated with a Bachelor of Science degree in 1875. The town was incorporated in 1903. The Sackville Waterfowl Park, located in the centre of the town, has become an important location for ornithological study and research. Within this preserve, 160 species of birds and 17 species of ducks have been sighted. It is the focal point for the Atlantic Waterfowl Celebration held each August. See also TANTRAMAR MARSHES, and SACKVILLE, Nova Scotia.

Saint-Amand (Madawaska) North of GRAND FALLS/GRAND- SAULT. Named for the first settlers, David and Joseph Saint-Amand, who came to the area in the 1890s.

St. Andrews (Charlotte)   At the mouth of the ST. CROIX RIVER, in the southwest corner of the county. The name predates the arrival of the Loyalists. According to tradition a French missionary landed here on St. Andrews Day, erected a cross, celebrated Mass, and named the location St. André. By 1770 the area was referred to by Captain William Owen as 'St. Andrew's Point.' It is one of the oldest towns in the province, its history beginning with the arrival, in October 1783, of the Penobscot Loyalists. These refugees, from all over New England, had first settled at Castine, farther down the coast. When it became clear that the St. Croix River rather than the Penobscot was to define the international boundary, they moved to St. Andrews. Several brought their own houses, which were taken down in sections and towed behind ships. A new town was surveyed and laid out in square blocks. The streets parallel to the waterfront were named Water, Queen, Prince of Wales, Montaque, Parr, and Carleton – the last three being names of colonial governors. The cross-streets were named for King George II and his twelve children. For the next century St. Andrews prospered as a principal shipping port with the West Indies, dealing particularly in timber, fish, sugar, and rum. Following the demise of the 'Golden Age of Sail,' in the late 1800s, the town was 'discovered' as a major tourist attraction and became known as St. Andrews-by-the-Sea. Aside from its superb physical setting, the town is noteworthy for its domestic architecture, which spans all periods from the colonial era to the present. Forty-eight per cent of the structures in the original town plot have been lived in for more than a century, and many are approaching their bicentennial of occupancy. Two outstanding architectural gems are Greenock Presbyterian Church (1824) and the Court House, with its beautifully gilded royal coat of arms over the portico (1840). The town was incorporated in 1903. See also MINISTERS ISLAND.

Saint-Antoine (Kent)   South of BUCTOUCHE. The name is traceable to an eighteenth-century French mission established near here *ca* 1700. It was named for the Recollet seminary at Saint-Antoine-de-Padoue, France. Saint-Antoine was the birthplace of the Honourable Louis J. Robichaud, who served as premier of New Brunswick from 1960 to 1970. There is

also a parish of Saint-Antoine-de-Padua in MADAWASKA COUNTY. It was founded in 1854. St. Anthony of Padua (1195–1231), a Franciscan friar, was canonized in 1226. He was noted for his charismatic presence and devotion to the poor.

Saint-Antoine-de-Padua   *See* Saint-Antoine.

Saint-Basile (Madawaska)   East of EDMUNDSTON. The community name dates back to a church named Saint-Basile, built in 1792. It is also noteworthy as the birthplace of international pop-music superstar Roch Voisine.

St. Croix River (Charlotte)   The river rises in the CHIPUTNETICOOK LAKES and flows 120 kilometres southeast to PASSAMAQUODDY BAY, forming a part of the boundary between New Brunswick and Maine. Discovered in 1604 by Pierre Du Gua de Monts and Samuel de Champlain, the first settlement in Acadia was built on an island in the river, now known as Dochet's Island (it is today part of Maine). They called both the island and the river Sainte-Croix because, upon exploration, they found that the river had three branches that formed an irregular cross. The first year on Île Sainte-Croix was a disaster. Of the seventy-nine settlers who attempted to 'overwinter,' thirty-nine had died from scurvy by spring. In the summer of 1605 the settlement was abandoned, the buildings dismantled and moved across the BAY OF FUNDY, to Port-Royal. For years following the American Revolution, the boundary between New Brunswick and Maine was in dispute. In 1797 the Americans put forward the claim that the St. Croix River, mapped by Champlain, was in reality the MAGAGUADAVIC, while the British insisted that the river then called the Scoodic (now the St. Croix) constituted the boundary. The matter was settled when Thomas Wright (*ca* 1740–1812), later surveyor general of Prince Edward Island, discovered and excavated (with the aid of Champlain's map) the foundation of the ill-fated outpost on Dochet's Island, thus verifying the British claim. See also WRIGHTS CREEK, Prince Edward Island.

St. David Ridge (Charlotte) North of ST. STEPHEN. It takes its name from the parish of St. Davids, established in 1786. The designation for the patron saint of Wales was undoubtedly suggested by its proximity to ST. ANDREWS.

Sainte-Anne (Kent); **Sainte-Anne-de-Madawaska** (Madawaska)   The various communities, such as these, that incorporate the name of Sainte Anne were doubtless inspired by the mother of the Blessed Virgin, and for the fact that Sainte Anne is the patron saint of the Acadians. Each July the faithful converge on Sainte-Anne-de-Madawaska for the annual Neuvaine de Sainte-Anne.

St. Francis River   *See* Saint-François-de-Madawaska.

Saint-François-de-Kent (Kent); **Saint-François-de-Madawaska** (Madawaska)   The name Saint-François-de-Kent, for the settlement at the mouth of the BUCTOUCHE RIVER, was officially adopted in 1893, replacing the earlier Dixons Landing, for an early settler. Saint-François-de-Madawaska is located west of Baker Brook, on Highway 205. For a time in the late nineteenth century, the community was known as 'Winding Ledges' or 'Ledges,' for the rapids in the ST. JOHN RIVER. The parish name was probably suggested by the St. Francis River, named *Petit Rivière St. François* by Bishop Jean-Baptiste de La Croix de Chevrières de Saint-Vallier (1653–1727), second bishop of Québec, who visited the area in 1686.

Saint-François-de-Madawaska *See* Saint-François-de-Kent.

St. George (Charlotte)   On the
MAGAGUADAVIC RIVER; named for
the patron saint of England. The
name stems from the parish,
which, in turn, was inspired by
the presence nearby of place
names dedicated to other saints.
Known for a time as 'Magaguadavic,' and later as 'Granite
Town,' for the presence of red-
granite quarries in the area.
The town was incorporated in
1904.

Saint-Hilaire (Madawaska)
Southwest of EDMUNDSTON. It is
named for the parish church built
in 1868 on land donated by
Hilaire Cyr. The name was suggested by Bishop James Rogers
(1826–1893) in recognition of this
fact and to honour Saint Hilaire, a
fourth-century saint who was
bishop of Poitiers, France.

Saint-Isidore (Gloucester)   On
Highway 160. The parish was
established in 1881 and was
named for the patron saint of
farmers.

Saint-Jacques (Madawaska)
When you are approaching New
Brunswick from Québec on the
Trans-Canada Highway, Saint-
Jacques is literally the 'Gateway
to the Province.' It takes its name
from the parish church, which
was consecrated in 1877 by
Bishop James Rogers. The village

is noted for Le Jardin Botanique
du Nouveau Brunswick, established in 1993; one may find here
thousands of annual and peren-
nial plants, arranged in nine gardens, one of which is an arbor-
etum.

Saint John (City and County)
During the French colonial
period the only serious attempt at
settlement at the mouth of the
strategic ST. JOHN RIVER occurred
in 1631, when Charles de Saint-
Étienne de La Tour erected a fortified trading post as a base for
his commercial interests. Permanent English settlement began
with the arrival of pre-Loyalist
settlers from New England in the
1760s. Later, in 1783–4, some
18,000 Loyalists arrived, establishing themselves on the east
side of the harbour, in Parr Town,
and on the west side, in Carleton. In 1785 the two took the
name of Saint John (from the
river); with the new city being
officially granted a royal charter
on 17 May 1786, making it the
first incorporated city in Canada.
Ever since then, it has been popularly known as the 'Loyalist City.'
The early economy was based on
the timber trade and shipbuilding. The *Marco Polo*, which
earned the title 'the fastest ship in
the world,' was perhaps the most
famous constructed there. A ship
of 1,625 tonnes, it was launched

in April 1851 at nearby COURTE-
NAY BAY. Operating on the
England-to-Australia run, the
ship was able to complete the
round trip in less than six
months. The *Marco Polo* was
unfortunately to be wrecked off
CAVENDISH, Prince Edward
Island, in 1883. Four years later,
the 'Great Fire' of 1887 destroyed
over half of the city. Many of the
replacement buildings still stand
and are being restored in the late
twentieth century. Thus, much of
the contemporary cityscape is an
architectural reflection of the late
nineteenth century. A campus of
the University of New Brunswick was established in the city
in 1964. In 1969 Saint John
expanded to incorporate Lancaster and part of the parish of
Simonds. More recently, the construction of a modern through-
way, a new harbour bridge, and
an inner-city renewal project cen-
tring on historic Market Square
have added greatly to the attrac-
tiveness of the city. Saint John
County, a narrow rectangle of
territory that surrounds the city
on the east, north, and west, was
established by legislation in
1786. See also PORT LA TOUR,
Nova Scotia.

St. John River   This river was
known originally to the Maliseet
as *Wolastoq*, 'the good river.' Its
French name, in translation St.

John River, was bestowed by the
Du Gua–Champlain expedition
after the date of discovery, the
feast of St. John the Baptist,
24 June 1604. It was Samuel de
Champlain, geographer, cartographer, and author of the narrative
of the expedition, who provided
the first description of the area by
Europeans: 'We came upon a fine
bay, running into the land, and
at its head lie three islands and a
rock. [One of the islands] was
at the mouth of the largest and
deepest river we had yet seen.'
Nearly a century later, in 1693,
Antoine Laumet, better known by
his assumed name, de Lamothe
Cadillac (1658–1730), made a
canoe voyage of '100 leagues up
the St. John River.' After describing its islands, intervales, and
species of trees, he concluded: 'It
... is the most navigible, the most
favoured, and the most beautiful
river in all Acadia.' The river, 673
kilometres long, rises in Maine
and flows northeast into MADA-
WASKA COUNTY, to EDMUNDSTON,
where it is joined by the Madawaska. For the next 110 kilometres, the St. John forms the
international boundary between
Maine and New Brunswick. Veer-
ing slightly eastward at GRAND
FALLS/GRAND-SAULT, the river
roughly parallels the boundary as
far as MEDUCTIC, where again it
flows more easterly, towards
FREDERICTON and on to GRAND

LAKE; from there it proceeds in a southerly direction to the city and harbour which also bear its name. The St. John, truly one of the world's great rivers, drains a basin of more than 55,000 square kilometres, an area larger than Switzerland, and draws water from fourteen of New Brunswick's fifteen counties. In 1992 the St. John River Society was established to 'foster an appreciation of the river and its tributaries as an important and distinctive watershed; and to emphasize environmental and historical stewardship.' On 24 June 1993, the bells of some sixty churches along the watershed pealed to celebrate the foundation of the society.

A note of explanation is necessary concerning the spelling 'St. John River' and 'St. John River Valley' used throughout this book. Although 'Saint John River' is the form sanctioned by the *New Brunswick Gazetteer*, the older form has been utilized here for several reasons. A search of the record from the early seventeenth century down to the present indicates that there is ample historical precedent for this decision. In 1609 Marc Lescarbot rendered the name as *R. St. Jean*, and succeeding French cartographers followed suit. By 1701 Jean-Baptiste-Louis Franquelin's interpretation, *Rivière St. Jean*, had become

fixed. The translation to the English 'St. John River' was made during the early eighteenth century. The shortened form was consistently used in documentation emanating from both sides of the Atlantic (see reference to the 1785 order-in-council establishing Fredericton as the capital of the colony on p. 76). The same spelling continued in the nineteenth century, both before and after Confederation, for example, in the reports of Edward Jack, crown-lands surveyor. In the twentieth century, historians James Hannay and William Francis Ganong used both forms, although a preference is shown the shortened version. On the other hand, Esther Clark Wright favoured 'St. John River' consistently, as did W.O. Raymond, W. Stewart McNutt, and George Frederic Clarke. In the 1980s and 1990s, historical geographer Graeme Wynn and historian T.W. Acheson, among others, have used 'St. John River.' In 1993, when the St. John River Society was formed, a search was made to ascertain the most consistent spelling. Before making a final decision, the society surveyed the contemporary press and found that, while both forms were followed, there was a greater frequency in the use of 'St. John River.' Thus, their comprehensive map of the St. John River

Watershed employs the shortened form. Two final points: on 10 August 1993, Canada Post issued a postage stamp in its River Heritage Series that included the spelling 'St. John River.' It is sometimes forgotten that this river is also shared with the state of Maine. Just under half of the watershed is actually outside New Brunswick, in Québec and Maine. In Maine the usual spelling is 'St. John River.' It is obvious that both 'Saint John' and 'St. John' will continue to be used for this important feature, and technically both are correct. In light of historical precedence, consistency, and current usage, 'St. John River' has been followed in *Place Names of Atlantic Canada*.

Saint-Joseph (Westmorland)
This was the site of the founding, on 10 October 1864, of Le Collège Saint-Joseph de Memramcook by Abbé Camille Lefebvre (1831–1895). A native of Québec, Lefebvre spent three decades in New Brunswick, which marked the beginning of an Acadian renaissance, to which the Collège Saint-Joseph was to contribute in no small measure. In 1963 the institution moved, to became the nucleus of the Université de Moncton. Its former buildings now house the Memramcook Institute. Following the death of Abbé Lefebvre in 1895, a project

was inaugurated to honour his memory. The result, a building known as the 'Monument Lefebvre,' now houses an auditorium and an exhibition centre, the Acadian Odyssey National Historic Site, developed by Parks Canada. It traces the evolution of Acadia from the first settlements through to the present. In addition, it is a reminder of the many accomplishments of the Acadian people. See also MEMRAMCOOK VALLEY.

Saint-Léonard (Madawaska)
On the ST. JOHN RIVER, opposite Van Buren, Maine. The first settlement, by Acadians in 1789, included both sides of the river and was known as 'Grande-Rivière' for the nearby stream of the same name. In 1842, a newly defined boundary between New Brunswick and Maine was proclaimed, and the now separated communities were renamed: Van Buren, Maine, for Martin Van Buren (1782–1862), eighth president of the United States, and Saint-Léonard, for local magistrate Leonard Reed Coombes. The two cross-border communities share a municipal flag, and each July a joint festival is held to celebate their common Acadian heritage.

St. Martins (Saint John)   On QUACO BAY, east of SAINT JOHN. The name derives from the parish established in 1786. The name may be after St. Martins, in Maryland. In 1942 this area earned a small footnote in the history of the Second World War. In the early hours of 14 May, the German U-boat *U-213* was successful in landing secret agent 'Lieutenant Langbein,' alias Alfred Haskins, near the mouth of the Salmon River to the east of St. Martins. As events transpired, the landing was the only successful aspect of the entire operation. At daybreak Haskins hiked to St. Martins, where he eluded suspicion, despite passing outdated Canadian currency. He then moved on to Saint John, MONCTON, Montreal, and eventually Ottawa, where he lived for two years, before turning himself in to the Naval Intelligence Directorate. Subsequent investigation revealed him to be 'the spy that never was,' for he did not engage in any espionage activities. Having lived in Canada before the war, he seems merely to have been motivated by a desire to get out of Germany. Haskins spent the remainder of the war in a Canadian internment camp and was repatriated at the end of hostilities. See also MARTIN BAY, Newfoundland.

St. Patricks Lake (Charlotte) North of KERR LAKE, in the parish of St. Patrick. The name originates with the parish and completes the quartet of patron saints, along with St. Andrews, St. George and St. Davids, within the bounds of one county. All four were established in 1786.

Saint-Pons (Gloucester)   Southwest of TRACADIE. A number of theories prevail as explanations for this place name. The most plausible attributes it to Antoinette de Pons, Marquise de Guercheville, the wife of Charles du Plessis, Duc de Liancourt, the governor of Paris in the early seventeenth century. A deeply religious woman, she was responsible for raising funds to send missionaries to Acadia.

Saint-Quentin (Restigouche) On Highway 17, near the VICTORIA COUNTY boundary; named for the battle of Saint-Quentin, March 1918, a notable Allied victory in the First World War. Originally known as 'Five Fingers,' for the nearby brook, it was renamed Andersons Siding in 1910, and changed to Saint-Quentin in 1919. The site of the battle lies in the old French province of Picardy, the original home of some of the first settlers in northern New Brunswick. See also EDMUNDSTON.

St. Stephen (Charlotte)   On the ST. CROIX RIVER opposite Calais, Maine. Settled by Loyalists in

1783, it was first known as 'Scoodic,' the Passamaquoddy name for this section of the St. Croix River. Later, Dover Hill was put forward as a new name, giving rise, in 1806, to the complementary name for Calais, Maine. However, the parish name, St. Stephen, adopted in 1786, proved to be more enduring and has remained as the accepted place name since 1825. This name may have been suggested by a survey party for one-time resident Stephen Pendleton, with the 'St.' being added as a facetious gesture. There is no historical evidence to connect the name, as is sometimes suggested, with Sir Charles St. Stephen, one of the Knights Baronet of Nova Scotia. During the early nineteenth century, this area of CHARLOTTE COUNTY became a major centre for the booming lumber industry. Historical geographer Graeme Wynn has pointed out that 'by 1830 the mills on the St. Croix were producing approximately 20 million feet of lumber per year ... perhaps 20 per cent of New Brunswick's lumber production came from the small area of Charlotte County west of St. Andrews.' The appropriately named adjacent community, Milltown, once boasted more than twenty sawmills. St. Stephen was incorporated as a town in 1871. A further incorporation occurred in 1973 as a result of an amalgamation with Milltown. For a time the town was known as 'St. Stephen–Milltown,' only to revert in 1975 to the older 'St. Stephen.'

Salem (Kings; Albert)   South of Highway 112 in KINGS COUNTY; southwest of HILLSBOROUGH, in ALBERT COUNTY. This place name is of biblical origin and was an ancient abbreviation for 'Jerusalem.' It is from the Hebrew *Salom*, for 'peace,' and its use in Nova Scotia and New Brunswick may have been inspired by Salem, Massachusetts. Salem, in Albert County, is also commemorated in the Salem and Hillsborough Railway; a steam train still operates on this route in the tourist season.

Salisbury (Westmorland)   West of MONCTON, on Highway 112. The community name was selected at the time of the establishment of the post office in 1840. Located within the bounds of Salisbury parish; the latter name may have been suggested by nearby Salisbury Cove, an indentation of the BAY OF FUNDY between CAPE ENRAGÉ and ALMA. The parish, established in 1787, was originally larger, and extended closer to the Bay of Fundy. The derivation of all three names goes back to the cathedral city of Salisbury, in Wiltshire, England.

Samp Hill (Kings)   West of HAVELOCK. The word *samp* is of Amerindian origin and refers to a porridge made from coarsely ground corn which was sweetened by maple sugar. Alan Rayburn quotes a reference from the William Francis Ganong papers to explain the place name: 'My grandfather got tired of the porridge and ... one morning said, *to Hell with the samp and hill!'* (Thorne to Ganong, 1903).

Saumarez (Gloucester)   West of TRACADIE. The name honours Major-General Sir Thomas Saumarez (1760–1845), who served as administrator of New Brunswick in 1813. He had seen service in the British army during the American Revolution, and at the time of his appointment was commander-in-chief of the British troops in New Brunswick.

Savoy Landing (Gloucester) Northeast of SHIPPEGAN. Named for Joseph and Noel Savoy, who were among the first grantees in the area.

Scotch Ridge (Charlotte)   At the junction of Highways 730 and 735, in the southwestern section of the county. In 1803 a group of emigrants from Sutherlandshire, Scotland, landed on the ST. CROIX RIVER. Discouraged by their inability to find satisfactory land, they immediately took passage to Nova Scotia. When this word was conveyed to St. Andrews, some Scottish merchants of the town fitted out a vessel, pursued the would-be settlers, and convinced them to return. They were eventually granted land at what is now Scotch Ridge.

Scoudouc (Westmorland)   East of MONCTON, on Highway 132. The name is of Mi'kmaq origin and was first applied to the Scoudouc River. It is traceable to the Mi'kmaq *Omskoodook*, of unknown meaning. The community is the site of a major industrial park that serves the Greater Moncton area.

Second Adder Lake (Northumberland)   Southeast of SERPENTINE LAKE. 'Probably named as a complement [to the latter]' (Rayburn).

Seeleys Cove (Charlotte)   An indentation of the BAY OF FUNDY, southeast of St. George. Named for Loyalist Justus Seeley, who served in the King's American Dragoons. The Seeley family moved to this area from Connecticut in 1783.

Serpentine Lake; Serpentine River (Northumberland); **Serpentine Mountain** (Victoria)   These features are situated near the

point where VICTORIA, NORTHUM-
BERLAND, and RESTIGOUCHE counties converge. Each is descriptive
of the feature's crooked appearance.

Serpentine Mountain   *See* Serpentine Lake.

Serpentine River   *See* Serpentine Lake.

Seven Days Work (Charlotte)
A cliff located at the northern end
of GRAND MANAN. It is descriptive
of seven contrasting layers of
basaltic rock. The name refers to
the creation story found in the
Book of Genesis.

Sevogle; Sevogle River
(Northumberland)   On Highway
425, near the mouth of the Big
Sevogle River. The name may be
traced to the Mi'kmaq *Sewokulook*,
'the river of many cliffs.' The
present spelling has appeared on
maps since 1826 and was officially
approved on 5 May 1949. An
unsuccessful campaign was
launched in 1964 to change the
name to Mount Kennedy, in
honour of U.S. president John F.
Kennedy (1917–1963): CPCGN Files.

Sevogle River   *See* Sevogle.

Shampers Bluff; Shampers Cove
(Kings)   The bluff projects into
BELLEISLE BAY. This area was first

settled by the Loyalist Andrew
and Ludweig (Lewis) Schomber
(later, Shampier) families. Over
time the name was further shortened to Shamper. It is the home of
the internationally renowned
photographer Freeman Patterson. Shampers Cove takes its
name from the same family.

Shampers Cover   *See* Shampers
Bluff.

Shannon (Queens)   East of
WASHADEMOAK LAKE. The name is
a corrupted form of Shanahan,
which can be traced to John Shanahan, who emigrated to this area
from Ulster in the late 1820s. The
contemporary spelling was in
use by 1877 when the post office
opened.

Shannonvale (Restigouche)   On
Highway 280, west of EEL RIVER
CROSSING. The name was inspired
by the River Shannon, the longest
in Eire. It marks the nineteenth-
century Irish emigration to New
Brunswick and dates from 1871.

**Shediac; Shediac Bay; Shediac
Cape; Shediac Island; Shediac
River** (Westmorland)   The town
fronts on NORTHUMBERLAND
STRAIT. The name, of Mi'kmaq
origin, is derived from *Esedeiik*,
translated by Silas T. Rand as
'running far in,' a reference to the
indented coastline. As early as

1685 Jumeau renders it as *Chédiac*, and this is repeated on the Couagne chart of 1749. By 1755 D'Anville's map had changed the 'c,' as in the contemporary 'Shediac.' The Shediac–Pointe-du-Chêne area is one of the province's most popular summer resorts. See also POINTE-DU-CHÊNE.

Shediac Bay   *See* Shediac.

Shediac Cape   *See* Shediac.

Shediac Island   *See* Shediac.

Shediac River   *See* Shediac.

Sheephouse Brook (Northumberland)   The brook flows in an easterly direction into South Branch LITTLE SEVOGLE RIVER. The descriptive name is derived from the foamy water which swirls around the base of a waterfall, giving the appearance of a sheepskin. A service road provides access to the area now being developed as a tourist site.

Sheffield (Sunbury)   Southeast of FREDERICTON, on Highway 2. Named for John Baker Holroyd, first Earl of Sheffield (1735–1821). His title originated with the home he purchased in 1769: 'Sheffield Place,' in Sussex.

Sheila   *See* Tracadie–Sheila.

Sheldrake Island (Northumberland)   At the entrance to the MIRAMICHI RIVER. It was named for the sheldrake, a species of duck common to the area. For much of the nineteenth century, this island housed a quarantine station. Each year, as ships arrived from overseas, the sick were dropped off and the healthy continued on upriver to CHATHAM and NEWCASTLE. There was great suffering among these people, especially those afflicted with leprosy. Eventually, to protest the lack of medical attention, the lepers burned down the buildings, and the lazaretto was transferred to Tracadie. See also TRACADIE.

Shemogue; Little Shemogue (Westmorland)   Adjacent to the NORTHUMBERLAND STRAIT. The name derives from the Mi'kmaq *Simooaquik*, which was subsequently spelled by the Acadians as 'Chimougoui.' Its meaning is uncertain, although 'a good place for geese' has been put forward as one translation. Since it lies on the migratory flight path for ducks and geese there may be some credence to this suggestion.

Shepody Bay; Shepody Mountain; Shepody River (Albert)   The bay is located at the mouth of the PETITCODIAC RIVER. The name is traceable to the Mi'kmaq *Esedabit*, 'the bay that turns back on itself.' Later versions were listed by New Brunswick poet Douglas Lochhead in his *Upper Cape Poems* (1989):

> The bay, Chiepody, Memoramcok, Chipodie, Shepody. In 1779 cast-
> iron
> DesBarres bobbing and squinting
> put it down for their Lordships
> as Shepody, in *The Atlantic
> Neptune.*

The spelling 'Shepody' has remained constant since 1779. The mountain and river take their name from the bay.

Shepody Mountain   *See* Shepody Bay.

Shepody River   *See* Shepody Bay.

Shikatehawk Stream Carleton) Enters the ST. JOHN RIVER at Bristol. The name stems from the Maliseet *Shigateehawg*, translated by most authorities as 'where he killed him.' The word is a legendary reference to a battle between the Mohawk and the Maliseet decided by a combat between their respective rival chiefs. In the end the Maliseet chief won the contest, and this fact is preserved in the place name. See also BRISTOL.

Shippegan; Shippegan Island (Gloucester)   The name may be traced to the island, located between MISCOU ISLAND and the mainland. It originates with the Mi'kmaq *Sepaguncheech*, which has been translated by Silas T. Rand as a 'duck road, or small passage through which ducks fly,' a reference to the migratory flight path of these birds. It was first applied to the harbour, and later extended by the English to the island. In 1755 D'Anville renders it as *Chipagan*, for the harbour, while DesBarres applies the word to the island. The spelling has evolved over the years to the officially recognized Shippegan. Shippegan Island is now officially known as ÎLE LAMÈQUE.

Shogomoc Lake; Shogomoc Stream (York)   The stream flows into MACTAQUAC LAKE, a section of the ST. JOHN RIVER. The name is traceable to the Maliseet *Seeogamook*, which may be a reference to a rock, once visible in the river prior to the flooding caused by the construction of the Mactaquac Dam. It marked the 'place of chiefs' and indicated a location where the Maliseet once held meetings.

Shogomoc Stream   *See* Shogomoc Lake.

Silverwood (York)   A suburban area first developed in 1961 and located west of FREDERICTON. The name is descriptive of the silver birch trees found in abundance on the hillside.

Skedaddle Ridge (Carleton) Southeast of KNOWLESVILLE. During the American Civil War (1861–5), this isolated area became a popular hideout for the first American 'draft dodgers.' Many individuals who were not in sympathy with the Northern cause 'skedaddled' to the community. A contemporary American reference (1864) defined the word as 'a disorderly retreat ... probably set afloat by some professor at Harvard' (*Dictionary of American Slang*).

Skoodoowabskook (York)   *See* Longs Creek.

Snowshoe Cove (York)   On the headpond of Mactaquac Dam. When the 1967 flooding for the dam covered the Snowshoe Islands, the name was transferred to the nearby cove. Maliseet legend has it that the islands were once the snowshoes of Glooscap.

Southern Wolf Island   *See* The Wolves.

Stanley (York)   On Highway 620, in the central section of the county. The name honours Lord Stanley (1799–1869), who was colonial secretary from 1833 to 1834. He became Earl of Derby in 1851 and served as British prime minister in 1852, 1858–9, and again in 1866–8. He was president of the New Brunswick and Nova Scotia Land Company, responsible for settlement in this area in 1833–4.

Sugarloaf Mountain (Restigouche)   At 282.2 metres in height, Sugarloaf Mountain dominates the city of CAMPBELLTON. It was known to the Mi'kmaq as *Squadichk*, for 'the highest point.' A 'Sugarloaf' Mountain is also to be found in KINGS and YORK counties, and is frequently repeated as a place name in Nova Scotia and Newfoundland. The name is descriptive and refers to a topographical resemblance to the pointed conical loaf that, during the early nineteenth century, refined sugar was sometimes shaped into. On 31 January 1972 Sugarloaf Provincial Park, a 1,200-hectare retreat for winter and summer recreation, was officially opened. However, many people are simply attracted by the panoramic view of Campbellton and surrounding countryside obtained by hiking to the summit.

Sunbury County   In 1765 the territory of the province of Nova Scotia north of the BAY OF FUNDY was divided into two counties. The ISTHMUS OF CHIGNECTO and lands adjoining the PETITCODIAC

RIVER and adjacent territory became part of CUMBERLAND COUNTY, which also embraced a section of peninsular Nova Scotia. Sunbury County included the ST. JOHN RIVER Valley and the PASSAMAQUODDY area. The name originated with George Montagu Dunk, second Earl of Halifax (1716–1710), who also numbered Viscount Sunbury as one of his titles. In 1786, following creation of the province of New Brunswick, Sunbury County was redefined to its present limits, bounded by the counties of YORK, NORTHUMBERLAND, QUEENS, and CHARLOTTE, and bisected by the St. John River.

Sussex (Kings)   On the KENNEBECASIS RIVER, northeast of HAMPTON. It was named in honour of Prince Augustus Frederick, Duke of Sussex (1773–1842), sixth son of King George III and Queen Charlotte. Its first settlers were from New England, augmented after 1783 by Loyalists. The parish was established in 1786, and the town incorporated in 1904. Sussex is the centre of one of the richest agricultural areas in New Brunswick and is known for the production of milk, butter, cheese, ice cream, and ginger ale. Within a few kilometres' radius of the town centre, there are seventeen covered bridges. See also COV-

ERED BRIDGE, HARTLAND, and NEWTOWN.

Swallow Tail (Charlotte)   This is a descriptive term for the shape of a point at the northeast tip of GRAND MANAN; it is also a favoured habitat for swallows. The landform was defined by the *Bay of Fundy Pilot* as 'a narrow and bold point,' and a lighthouse was erected at Swallow Tail as a warning to mariners of the rocky headland.

Tabusintac; Tabusintac River (Northumberland)   The river flows east into Tabusintac Bay and the NORTHUMBERLAND STRAIT. Originated with the Mi'kmaq *Taboosimkik*, 'a pair of them' or 'two of them,' a possible reference to the river and nearby FRENCH COVE. Appears as *Tabochemkek* (Jumeau 1685), *Taboquinquet* (Bellin 1774), and *Tabucintac* (*The Canadian Almanac* 1896). The modern spelling is consistent from 1931 onward.

Tabusintac River   *See* Tabusintac.

Tantramar Marshes; Tantramar River (Westmorland)   The Tantramar Marshes, on the ISTHMUS OF CHIGNECTO, near Sackville, comprise the largest of the North American tidal marshes. During the late 1600s, Acadians

drained some 500 square kilometres of fertile marshland in this
immediate area. In a real sense the
presence of these dykelands, three
centuries later, constitutes a tangi-
ble legacy of French occupation.
But more than this, they serve as a
symbol of a people who, though
exiled, were to return to become
an important segment in the population of Atlantic Canada. The
place name originates with the
French *Tintamarre,* for 'great
noise,' traced by William Francis
Ganong to the *Jesuit Relations*
(1647). It appears in the same form
on the Couagne chart of 1749, and
the English version Tantramar is
undoubtedly a corruption of the
French. The noise in question is a
reference to the rushing sound of
migratory birds on the marsh. See
also SACKVILLE.

Tantramar River   *See* Tantramar
Marshes.

Tay Creek (York)   Flows south-
east into the NASHWAAK. Named
in 1783 by Jacobina Drummond
Campbell, wife of Lieutenant
Dugald Campbell of the 42nd
Regiment (later known as the
Black Watch), for the River Tay,
Scotland's longest river.

Telegraph Hill (Kings)   There
are two features so named in
KINGS COUNTY, with five others
scattered throughout the province. The name was derived from
the semaphore–telegraph system
established between FREDERIC-
TON and HALIFAX by Prince
Edward, Duke of Kent, in the
1790s. He was then commander
of the armed forces in Nova
Scotia and New Brunswick. Of
limited military use, it was
reported that the system's main
purpose was to enable the eccentric prince, while travelling, to
send orders for the punishment of
the soldiers under his command.
Two of his best-known idiosyn-
crasies were an inflexible insis-
tence on punctuality and swift
punishment for the most minor
offences. See also PRINCES LODGE,
Nova Scotia.

Temperance Vale (York)   North
of NACKAWIC, on Highway 605.
The name is attributable to the
temperance movement, which
reached its peak in New Brunswick during the mid-nineteenth
century. The community was
founded about 1860 by the Nova
Scotia and New Brunswick Land
Company. Another community
near Harvey Station was once
called 'Teetotal Settlement'; however, this name disappeared, and
it is now known appropriately as
Cork, since most of the original
settlers came from Ireland.

Teneriffe Lake; Teneriffe Peak
(Northumberland)   Sometimes

known as 'Mount Teneriffe,' it is situated within the bounds of Mount Carleton Provincial Park. It was so named in 1849 by Sir Edmund Head (1805–1869), then lieutenant-governor of New Brunswick. The lake, 5 kilometres northwest, takes its name from the mountain.

Teneriffe Peak   *See* Teneriffe Lake.

Tetagouche River (Gloucester) Flows east, into BATHURST harbour. This place name is traceable to Mi'kmaq sources; however, the precise word and its meaning are uncertain. It may be from *Toodoogoosk*, suggested by William Francis Ganong, or *Odoodooguech*, quoted by Alan Rayburn. The evolution of the name is not helpful in deciphering possible origins. It appears first as *R. toutegouch*, or *tout-gouch* on the Franquelin–DeMeulles map of 1686. Delisle (1703) renders the name as *Tougouche*. Bayfield's survey of 1845 has *Tetagouch River*, with the Geographic Board of Canada confirming in 1901 'Tetagouche not Teteagouche or Tete à Gouche.'

The Barony. *See* Barony.

The Bishop (Charlotte)   A rock located at Northern Head, GRAND MANAN, that is said to resemble the figure of a seated bishop.

The Enclosure (Northumberland) Opposite BEAUBEARS ISLAND, 7 kilometres southwest of NEWCASTLE, on Highway 8; now a provincial park. In 1765 William Davidson (1740–1790) secured a grant of 40,000 hectares of land on the MIRAMICHI. Founder of the local salmon fishery, contractor of masts for the Royal Navy, lumber merchant, shipbuilder, and a member of the first New Brunswick Assembly, Davidson was buried in the cemetery that forms part of The Enclosure. The park was restored, named, and presented to the province by Lord Beaverbrook.

The Glades (Westmorland)   East of PETITCODIAC, on the POLLETT RIVER. When the first settlers arrived, they discovered tracts of low ground covered with grass, which gave rise to the descriptive place name. RIVER GLADE, 6 kilometres northwest of The Glades, is a place name with similar origins.

The Rocks (Albert)   Giant flower-pot shaped formations sculpted by the restless tides of the BAY OF FUNDY account for this descriptive name. It forms part of a provincial park at HOPEWELL CAPE. Caves and tunnels at the base of the sculptures, as well as the ocean floor, may be explored at low tide. At high tide the 'flower pots' become tiny islands surrounded by water 14 metres deep.

The Wolves (Charlotte)   The name refers to a series of three islands in PASSAMAQUODDY BAY: Eastern Wolf Island, Flat Wolf Island, and Southern Wolf Island. They have been associated with the designation 'Wolf' since at least 1707, when they so appear on the Captain Cyrian Southack map. However, there is a much earlier Glooscap legend accounting for their presence: Once, while watching three wolves chasing a deer and a moose, Glooscap noted that the pursued animals were tiring, whereupon he changed them all into islands. Deer Island, New Brunswick, and Moose Island, Maine, remain side by side in the bay; the three wolves are still in pursuit off-shore. See also DEER ISLAND.

Thomaston Corner (York)   East of MCADAM. Named in 1902 for Richard Thomas, the first post-master. The place name may also have been suggested by Thomaston, Maine.

Tide Head (Restigouche) Descriptive for a community at the confluence of Black Brook and the RESTIGOUCHE RIVER. First known as 'Head of Tide'; the name was changed to Tide Head in 1921.

Tide Head was incorporated as a village in 1967.

Tidnish Head   *See* Nova Scotia entry.

Tilley Ridge (Northumberland) South of the NEPISIGUIT RIVER. The name honours the career of Sir Samuel Leonard Tilley (1818–1896), premier of New Brunswick (1861–5 and 1866–7), a leading Father of Confederation, federal cabinet minister (1867–73), and lieutenant-governor of New Brunswick (1873–8). He re-entered federal politics as minister of Finance (1878–85) and was reap-pointed lieutenant-governor (1885–93). Tilley, north of PERTH–ANDOVER, and Tilley Road, west of TRACADIE, also mark his long public service.

Tobique River (Victoria)   Rises in the interior of VICTORIA and RESTIGOUCHE counties, and flows 137 kilometres eastward to enter the ST. JOHN RIVER at Tobique Narrows, above PERTH–ANDOVER. Esther Clark Wright has charac-terized it 'as more a river system in itself, with its own tributaries and magnificent hills. It has never become reconciled to being a trib-utary of the St. John, and retains an air of aloofness and of preoc-cupation with its own concerns ... its upper branches can only be reached by private roads and

canoes.' It was named for a Maliseet chief, Noel Toubic, or Tobec,
who once lived at the mouth of
the river.

Tormentine   *See* Cape Tormentine.

Tracadie; Tracadie–Sheila
(Gloucester)   On Highway 11,
paralleling the NORTHUMBER-
LAND coast. The name is from
the Mik'maq *Tulakadik*, for 'camping ground,' as the area was
used as a camp while fishing the
nearby Big and Little Tracadie
rivers. A number of variations of
the place name appear on early
maps: *Tregate* (Champlain 1603),
Tregatté (Champlain 1613), *Tracadi* (Jumeau 1685), and *Tracady*
(Franquelin–DeMeulles 1686).
'Tracadie' is consistent from the
1850s onwards. It was resettled in
1784 by Acadians who had
escaped the expulsion of 1755
and by others who returned
from exile. In 1849 the town
became the site of a lazaretto
(hospital for contagious diseases).
A collection of artefacts portray-
ing life in this institution is to be
found in the Tracadie Historical
Museum (see also SHELDRAKE
ISLAND). The neighbouring community of Sheila (pronounced
locally as SHY-La) has been amalgamated with Tracadie. Its name
may be traced to Sheila Foster,
an early resident of the area. See

also TRACADIE, Nova Scotia and
Prince Edward Island.

Tracadie–Sheila   *See* Tracadie.

Tracy (Sunbury)   South of FRED-
ERICTON, at the junction of Highways 101 and 645. Named for the
Tracy family, who moved here
from Maine in the late eighteenth
century. Founder of the dynasty
was Jeremiah Tracy (1744–1812);
his descendants became prominent in the lumbering industry.

Trousers Lake (Victoria)   North
of Highway 108. This descriptive
was bestowed by early lumbermen, for its trouser-like shape.
The two extensions are known as
the Right Hand Leg and the Left
Hand Leg.

Tweedside (York)   South of
HARVEY, on the shores of ORO-
MOCTO LAKE. Named by Scottish
settlers for the River Tweed in
Scotland.

Underhill (Northumberland)
On Highway 8, south of RENOUS.
It carries the name of the Under-
hill family. Among the first set-
tlers in this area, they were of
Loyalist stock from Westchester
County, New York.

Uniacke Hill (Westmorland)
Southeast of BAIE VERTE. This feature serves as a reminder of an

early chapter in the life of Richard John Uniacke (1753–1830). On the American side in the Eddy Rebellion, which broke out during the autumn of 1776, Uniacke was captured and sent to Halifax to be tried for treason. Later released, he returned to his native Ireland to complete his legal studies. He was admitted to the Nova Scotia bar on 3 April 1781. On 27 December of the same year, he was appointed solicitor general. In 1783 Uniacke was elected to the Nova Scotia House of Assembly for Sackville township. See also MOUNT UNIACKE, Nova Scotia.

Upham (Kings)   Southwest of HAMPTON. The name originates with Upham Parish, named for Loyalist Joshua Upham (1741–1808). A major in the King's American Dragoons, aide-de-camp to Sir Guy Carleton, and law graduate of Harvard College, Upham was named, in 1784, a judge of the Supreme Court and member of the legislative council.

Upper Kennedy Lakes   *See* Kennedy Lakes.

Upper Woodstock   *See* Woodstock.

Upsalquitch; Upsalquitch Lake; Upsalquitch River (Restigouche)

The river flows northward into the RESTIGOUCHE RIVER. Derived from the Mi'kmaq *Apsetkwechk*, translated as 'little or small river.' It appears for the first time on a 1786 survey map as *Upsatquitch*. Alan Rayburn theorizes that the Mi'kmaq reference to its size is a comparison with the larger Restigouche River.

Upsalquitch Lake   *See* Upsalquitch.

Upsalquitch River   *See* Upsalquitch.

Utopia   *See* Lake Utopia.

Val-Comeau (Gloucester)   Six kilometres south of TRACADIE–SHEILA, on the NORTHUMBERLAND STRAIT. Although the name originated in 1927 with the establishment of a post office and the appointment of the first postmaster, C. Comeau, it also serves to recognize one of the most common Acadian family names. The sand dunes of Val Comeau Provincial Park, north of the village, are noted for their abundance of migratory seabirds.

Val d'Amour (Restigouche) South of CAMPBELLTON, on Highway 270. Named for the Reverend L. d'Amour, who served this area as mission priest in the early twentieth century.

Verret (Madawaska)   Four kilometres west of EDMUNDSTON, on Highway 120. The name originated with that of the first postmaster, Joseph Verret.

Victoria County   Established in 1845 through a subdivision of CARLETON COUNTY, which was created in 1832. The name of the county honours Queen Victoria (1819–1901), the only child of Prince Edward, Duke of Kent, and Princess Victoria Maria Louise of Saxe-Coburg. The five other locations within the province that share this name also honour Queen Victoria.

Village-Saint-Laurent (Northumberland)   Northeast of CHATHAM. Named in 1949 for the Right Honourable Louis St. Laurent (1882–1973), prime minister of Canada from 1948 to 1958.

Wakem Corner (Carleton)   Northeast of CENTREVILLE. Both Wakem Corner and nearby Wakem Hill were named for Thomas Wakem, an early settler in this region.

Wakem Hill   *See* Wakem Corner.

Washademoak; Washademoak Lake (Queens)   The settlement is opposite CODYS, on the shore of WASHADEMOAK LAKE. The lake links the CANAAN with the ST. JOHN RIVER. From the Maliseet *Wasetemoik*, of uncertain meaning. The name was once applied to the entire river; however, the upper reaches have been called 'Canaan' for the past century.

Waterborough (Queens)   A coined name originally applied to the parish of Waterborough. Since the eastern shoreline of GRAND LAKE was within its bounds, the name may also be considered a descriptive. This area was first settled by Loyalists in 1784. One such grantee was Jacob Wiggins of New York, who named fourteen children as heirs in a will drawn up prior to his death in 1815.

Waterford (Kings)   Adjacent to Poley Mountain, southeast of SUSSEX. Formerly known as 'Seelys Mills,' it was renamed for Waterford, Ireland, in 1875.

Waterloo Corner (Queens)   East of CAMBRIDGE NARROWS, near the boundary with KINGS COUNTY. Named in commemoration of the Battle of Waterloo, 18 June 1815.

Waweig; Waweig River (Charlotte)   The river flows into OAK BAY, a section of the ST. CROIX RIVER. The name is traceable to the Passamaquoddy designation for Oak Bay, Wahquaheek, which has been translated as 'head of the bay.' It was subsequently transferred to the river and settlement.

Waweig River   *See* Waweig.

Welsford (Queens)   South of Canadian Forces Base GAGETOWN, on Highway 101. Marks the military career of Major Augustus Frederick Welsford (1811–1855), who lost his life on 8 September 1855 during the Battle of Sevastopol, one of the engagements of the Crimean War (1853–6). See also WELSFORD, Nova Scotia.

Welshpool (Charlotte)   On the western side of Campobello Island. It was named by David Owen in 1835, 'in remembrance of that place in Wales which was near his home.' See also CAMPOBELLO ISLAND.

Westcock (Westmorland)   On the Wood Point Road, west of SACKVILLE. First impressions to the contrary, the word is traceable to the Mi'kmaq *Oakshaak*, of unknown meaning. The Mi'kmaq was adopted by the French, who filtered it through their language and passed it on to the English, who familiarized it to its present form. The evolution may be seen in the spelling on various documents: *Ouskoc* (1746), *Ouskak* (1760), *West Coup* (1768), and finally *Westcock* (1792 onward). St.

Ann's Anglican Church, Westcock, is of both architectural and literary interest. Built in 1817, it is one of the oldest churches in southeastern New Brunswick. Sir Charles G.D. Roberts (1860–1943), son of a rector of St. Ann's, Canon Goodridge Roberts, spent his boyhood years at Westcock. This part of New Brunswick was to have a profound impact on both the poetry and prose of the younger Roberts.

Westfield (Kings)   At the south end of LONG REACH, a section of the ST. JOHN RIVER. The name may have been inspired by Westfield, Massachusetts, or simply by its location on the west side of the river.

Westmorland County   The county borders on Nova Scotia at the ISTHMUS OF CHIGNECTO. It was established in 1786 and, until the creation of ALBERT COUNTY in 1845, contained a larger area than at present. The name was selected because of its being contiguous to CUMBERLAND COUNTY (Nova Scotia), as was then the case with the two so-named counties in England.

White Head Island (Charlotte) Southeast of GRAND MANAN. The name is descriptive of White Head, a conspicuous cliff composed of white quartz close to the west of the island and joined to it by a flat.

Whooper Spring   *See* Dungarvon River.

Wickham (Queens)   On the ST. JOHN RIVER, north of the KINGS COUNTY boundary. Named for Wickham, Hampshire, England. One of the early grantees, Captain William Spry, was a native of Wickham, England.

Wicklow (Carleton)   On the ST. JOHN RIVER, opposite BATH. Named for the town of Wicklow on the east coast of Ireland.

Wilmot (York; Carleton)   Wilmot on the MAGAGUADAVIC RIVER and Wilmot northwest of HARTLAND have the same origin. They were named for Lemuel Allan Wilmot (1809–1878), long-time MLA for YORK COUNTY, who was a member and virtual head of the first administration under responsible government in the province. He left politics to become a judge, later serving as the first native-born lieutenant-governor of New Brunswick (1868–73).

Wilsons Point (Northumberland)   At the junction of the Northwest and Southwest MIRAMICHI rivers. Named for John Wilson, a New Jersey Loyalist who settled here in 1788.

Wirral; Wirral Lake (Queens)   The community is in the southwestern corner of the county, on Highway 101. Originally known as 'Gaspereau,' the name was changed to prevent postal confusion with other locations of the same name. In 1924, named for the Wirral Peninsula, Merseyside, England.

Wirral Lake   *See* Wirral.

Woodstock (Carleton)   On a point of land at the confluence of the MEDUXNEKEAG and ST. JOHN rivers. The name originates with Woodstock, a town northwest of Oxford, England. William Francis Ganong indicates that the name 'was probably suggested by its nearness to Northampton, as in England.' The examples of the same name in Maine, New Hampshire, and Vermont may have been a further factor. Others have suggested that it may have been inspired by the title of Sir Walter Scott's romantic novel of the English Civil War; however, since this book did not appear until 1826, the theory does not hold. Whatever the reason, the name was first assigned in 1786, when the parish was founded. It was then an appropriate designation, as the original place name may be translated from the medieval English as 'a place in the woods.' Today, it is one of the most progressive of the small towns of New Brunswick, and shares with a number of other centres, such as ST. ANDREWS, a well-preserved architectural heritage. This heritage is also evident in nearby Upper Woodstock, where the original 1833 county court-house still stands. The handsome building, carefully restored by the local historical society, was over the years the setting for New Brunswick's first county council; a stagecoach stop; and the scene of fairs, levees, and rallies. When CARLETON COUNTY was established in 1832, Upper Woodstock was, for a time, the shiretown; 1909 saw the transfer of shiretown honours to the larger community of Woodstock.

Woolastock Provincial Park (York)   At the mouth of LONGS CREEK, 25 kilometres north of FREDERICTON. Established in 1969, the park is named for the Maliseet for the ST. JOHN RIVER – *Wolastoq* or *Woolahs-ook*, 'good river.'

Yoho Lake (York)   Southwest of FREDERICTON, off Highway 640. The name, probably of Maliseet origin, is of unknown meaning. Appears on some early maps as *Yahoo Lake*.

York County   One of the original counties established by legislation in 1786. It was named for Prince Frederick Augustus (1763–1827), second son of King George III, who was created Duke of York in 1784.

Youghall (Gloucester)   North of BATHURST. Named for Youghal in County Cork, Ireland. The name originally meant 'yew wood.'

Zealand (York)   North of MACTAQUAC LAKE, on the KESWICK RIVER. Founded in 1867 by settlers from Britain under the sponsorship of the New Brunswick and Nova Scotia Land Company. The community was first known as 'New Zealand,' after the country. The latter name may be traced to *Nieuw Zeeland*, so-named by the Dutch after a province in the Netherlands. The New Brunswick name was inspired by contemporary British colonization efforts in the south Pacific. The post office became Zealand Station in 1885, and the name reverted to Zealand in 1961.

Zionville (York)   Northeast of TAYMOUTH. Settled about 1860 by Scottish and Irish immigrants and named for the biblical Mount Zion, a hill on the southwest side of Jerusalem. In poetic writings, the name Zion is often used to represent the city itself.

3

Newfoundland and Labrador

Abrahams Cove (Western)   On the south side of the PORT AU PORT PENINSULA. The baptismal name of an early Acadian settler is probably the derivation. The surname Abraham is also found in Newfoundland. See also ABRAMS VILLAGE, Prince Edward Island.

Adlavik; Adlavik Bay; Adlavik Islands (Labrador)   Northwest of CAPE HARRISON. Applied first to the bay and harbour, and later to the offshore islands. The name is of Inuit origin and has been translated by E.P. Wheeler as the 'place of killing Indians.'

Adlavik Bay   *See* Adlavik.

Adlavik Islands   *See* Adlavik.

Admirals Cove (Avalon)   North of FERRYLAND. This place name and several others that incorporate 'Admiral' are reminders of the title 'fishing admiral,' assigned to the captain of the first vessel to reach a particular Newfoundland harbour in a given season. Put in place by the First Western Charter of 1634, and more fully spelled out in the 1699 Act to Encourage the Trade to Newfoundland, the system lasted from the early seventeenth to the late eighteenth century. It gave the designated admiral supreme authority over all visiting fishermen.

Aguathuna (Western)   West of STEPHENVILLE. Noted for its limestone quarries. First known as 'Jack of Clubs Cove,' 'so named by sailors of the Royal Navy for the fancied likeness of the eroded limestone cliff to the gentleman in the pack of cards' (Seary). In a petition dated 24 October 1911 the electors of the district of St. George declared: 'The present name, Jack of Clubs Cove, though

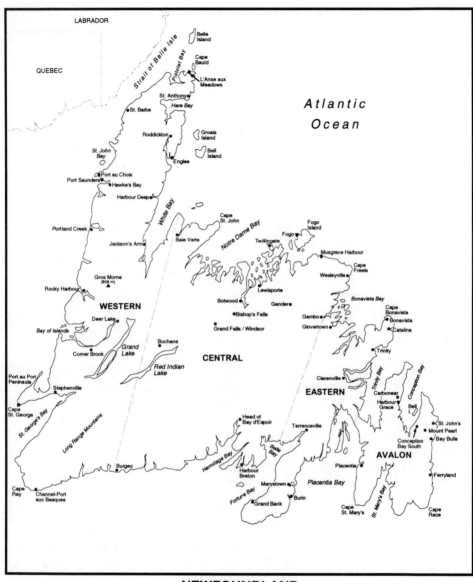

NEWFOUNDLAND

LABRADOR

perhaps picturesque, does not appear to be of any great antiquity, is not consecrated with any hallowed memories and is not suggestive of very elevated associations ... Your petitioners pray [that] it may be changed to *Aguathana*.' The new name was adopted 23 June 1914, replacing both Jack of Clubs Cove and Limeville. The former name is retained in nearby Jack of Clubs Brook. The latter informal designation was also in use locally. Aguathana may be traced to the Beothuk *aguathoonet* or *aguathoont*, meaning 'white rock' or 'grindstone.'

Aillik; Aillik Bay; Aillik Island (Labrador)   A settlement and cape north of MAKKOVIK. A Hudson's Bay Company post, known as 'Eyelich,' was established in 1840, with George MacKenzie as factor. The name is an Inuit descriptive and has been defined as 'a place having sleeves,' since the bay is shaped with two branches at its head. The island takes its name from the bay.

Aillik Bay   *See* Aillik.

Aillik Island   *See* Aillik.

Alcock Island (Central)   East of PILLEY'S ISLAND, NOTRE DAME BAY. Dates from the mid-nineteenth century, and the derivation is probably the surname of an early settler. There is no association with the famous aviator Sir John Alcock. See also LESTERS FIELD.

Alderburn   *See* Norris Arm.

Alexander Bay (Eastern)   An inlet of BONAVISTA BAY, northeast of GLOVERTOWN. It was named for William Alexander, a local merchant, replacing the earlier Bloody Reach or Bloody Bay. The latter names marked a conflict between the Beothuk and Europeans, still remembered in Bloody Point on the shores of the bay.

Alexander Point; Alexander River (Labrador)   The settlement is southwest of RIGOLET. Named for the Alexander plant or Scotch lovage (*Liguisticum scothicum*), an edible herb found on the Newfoundland and Labrador coastline. Captain George Cartwright (1739/40 –1819) named the Alexander River in Labrador for the same plant, which he found growing in abundance on its banks.

Alexander River   *See* Alexander Point.

Anchor Point (Western)   South of Deadmans Cove, on ST. BARBE BAY. The community, dating from *ca* 1750, is one of the oldest English settlements in the 'Straits

Area' of the NORTHERN PENIN-
SULA. The name may have
resulted from its importance
as an anchorage, since it has a
concealed harbour and is in a
strategic location in relation to
Labrador. The outport was visited by Anglican bishop Edward
Feild (1801–1876) in 1851. Of
Anchor Point he wrote: 'Alto-
gether the good things of both
earth and sea appear to abound in
this locality.'

Angels Cove (Avalon)   On the
eastern shore of PLACENTIA BAY.
The name may be a corruption of
'Angles or Angels Cove,' used in
1910 by historian and cleric the
Reverend M.F. Howley (1843–
1914) as a designation for the
community. The *Dictionary of
Newfoundland English* lists 'a
curved inlet' as one definition of
'angle.'

**Anguille Mountains; Cape
Anguille** (Western)   The range
parallels the west coast of Newfoundland in a northeasterly
direction from Cape Anguille.
The present name, of French origin for 'eel,' was first applied to
the cape. The latter is the most
westerly point on the island of
Newfoundland. It was sighted by
Jacques Cartier 'on the day of St
John,' 24 June 1534, and accordingly named Cap Sainct Jehan.
Selma Barkham points out that

the area was well known to the
Basques, and that Cape Anguille
was named Norteco burua, the
'north cape,' whereas modern
Cape Ray was the south cape. See
also CAPE RAY.

Annieospsquotch Mountains
(Western)   Southwest of RED
INDIAN LAKE. The name is derived
from a Mi'kmaq word for 'rocky
mountains,' or 'terrible rocks.'
The highest peak is 687 metres
above sea level.

Antelope Harbour (Labrador)
On the east side of CHATEAU BAY.
Named for an incident that
occurred during the American
Revolution. In 1780, HMS *Antelope*,
while patrolling the Labrador
coast, intercepted the American
ship *Mercury*. As the vessels came
to close quarters, a package was
thrown overboard from the latter.
One of the sailors on the *Antelope*
dived from the deck and rescued
the package, which contained
details of secret negotiations then
being conducted between America and Holland (Browne).

Appleton (Central)   Southeast of
GLENWOOD. First settled around
1910, and named for Appleton
Cleaves, manager of the local
sawmill.

Aquaforte (Avalon)   Southwest
of FERRYLAND. The name is of Por-

tuguese origin and may be traced to *R. de Aguea* for 'river of fresh water,' on the Reinel map of 1520. Aaron Thomas visited the area on 7 August 1794 and left a record of his impressions: 'Aquafort harbour is very properly named. Aquatic signifys abounding with water and Aquarius, the Waterman of old, was also one of the Twelve Signs [of the Zodiac]. The name of the place at once bespeaks its qualities. Here is good anchoring ground and plenty of room for a large fleet to moor and ride in safety. Several rivulets and small springs of fresh water discharge themselves into this harbour. There is also a very considerable cascade which emits about five tons of water every minute.'

Argentia (Avalon)   North of PLACENTIA. First known as 'Petit Plaisance,' and later 'Little Placentia.' The community was renamed about 1900 to mark the presence of a silver mine in the vicinity. The name is taken from the Latin for silver, *argentum*. A naval base was established here in January 1941, part of the lend–lease arrangement between Britain and the United States prior to the latter's entering into the Second World War. From 9 to 11 August of the same year, on the waters of nearby Placentia Bay, Prime Minister Winston Churchill and President Franklin Delano Roosevelt negotiated the historic Atlantic Charter. Eileen Hunt Houlihan has recounted the impact of the event on local residents: 'Maintaining strict secrecy during the three day stay was in itself a major feat. There was a total blackout in Argentia, no telephone communication was permitted, no person was allowed to either enter or leave the area, and even the train was held up at Marquise Neck' (Peter Neary, ed., 'Eileen Hunt Houlihan's Family Memoirs,' *Newfoundland Studies* 7/1 [Spring 1991], 48–64). During the summer months Marine Atlantic operates a ferry service between Argentia and NORTH SYDNEY, Nova Scotia.

Arnolds Cove (Avalon)   Southwest of COME BY CHANCE. Undoubtedly named for an early settler. Dr. E.R. Seary (1908–1984) has pointed out that Arnold is an English surname 'found elsewhere in Newfoundland but not locally, though the possibility that it is a baptismal name should not be overlooked.' Arnolds Cove was one of the so-called growth centres designated by the Newfoundland Resettlement Program (1967–75). Many of the inhabitants from the islands and smaller communities of PLACENTIA BAY were relocated here.

Aspen Cove (Central)   On HAMILTON SOUND, south of FOGO ISLAND. Prior to European settlement, this was the site of a Beothuk settlement. Named for the aspen trees once abundant in the community.

Assizes Harbour (Labrador)   On St. Lewis Sound. As the name implies, this was the setting for the first session in 1826 of the Labrador court established under authority of the governor of Newfoundland. It was presided over by William Patterson of the Royal Navy. In 1835, the harbour was visited by Captain Henry Bayfield (1795–1885), who, using local pronunciation, reported 'we encamped together at "Sizes" Harbour.'

Atikonak Lake; Atikonak River (Labrador)   The lake is in southwestern Labrador. Its name is taken from the Montagnais for 'whitefish lake.' The Atikonak River is a tributary of the CHURCHILL.

Atikonak River   *See* Atikonak Lake.

Avalon Peninsula   The name for the southeast corner of the island of Newfoundland. The peninsula's four major bays – TRINITY, CONCEPTION, ST. MARY'S, and PLACENTIA – were the earliest to be fished, and on their coastlines the first permanent settlements were founded. However, this place name does not appear until the Royal Charter of 7 April 1623, when the colony centred at Ferryland, and established by George Calvert, first Baron Baltimore (*ca* 1580–1632), was officially designated 'the province of Avalon.' Over time 'Avalon' was applied to the entire peninsula, and today it serves as a historical reminder of the long-standing links between Newfoundland and the West Country of England, site of Avalon, King Arthur's 'island of the blessed.'

Avalon Wilderness Reserve (Avalon)   This is the oldest wilderness reserve in the province. Located in the interior of the peninsula, it may be reached via an access road from LaManche Provincial Park. The reserve, of over 800 square kilometres, is home to a large herd of Newfoundland woodland caribou.

Avondale (Avalon)   Southeast of BAY ROBERTS. Originally known as 'Salmon Cove South.' It was renamed in 1906 by the Newfoundland Nomenclature Board for Avondale in County Wicklow, Eire.

Bacalhao Island; Baccalieu Island   One of the oldest place names of European origin on the Atlantic seaboard; it was an early-sixteenth-century designation for the island of Newfoundland. Over the years various cartographers and mapmakers simply applied the name to their own language. For example, the Portuguese adaptation was *bachalos*; the Basque, *bakailua*; the Spanish, *baccalao*; and the French, *baccalieu*. The word survives in four Newfoundland place names: Bacalhao Island, off the coast of Labrador and repeated again north of NEW WORLD ISLAND, NOTRE DAME BAY, and Baccalieu Island and Baccalieu Tickle, at the entrance to Conception Bay. See also BACCARO, Nova Scotia.

Baccalieu Island   *See* Bacalhao Island.

Baccalieu Tickle   *See* Bacalhao Island.

Badger (Central); **Badgers Quay** (Central)   Badger is located west of WINDSOR; while Badgers Quay is now part of Badgers Quay–Valleyfield–Pools Island, on the coast south of WESLEYVILLE. Badger is probably after the surname which stems from Badger, a hamlet in Shropshire, England. The animal is a member of the weasel family found in western Canada.

Badgers Quay   *See* Badger.

Baie Verte; Baie Verte Peninsula (Central)   The Baie Verte Peninsula lies between NOTRE DAME BAY and WHITE BAY. The name Baie Verte, or 'Green Bay,' is descriptive and dates from the period of French influence in Newfoundland. Highway 410, which traverses the peninsula, has been named 'The Dorset Trail' to underline the fact that the Dorset people once inhabited the area. There is also archaeological evidence that, even earlier, the region was home to the Maritime Archaic Indians (see PORT AU CHOIX). For many years the town of Baie Verte, at the head of the bay, was an important mining centre. Copper and asbestos, along with some silver and gold, were mined. See also BAIE VERTE, New Brunswick.

Baie Verte Peninsula   *See* Baie Verte.

Baine Harbour (Eastern)   On PLACENTIA BAY, northeast of MARYSTOWN. The name is descriptive and may be traced to the French *bain*, for 'bath.' The harbour is roughly shaped like a basin, thus giving rise to the name. It is rendered as *Havre Bane* or *Havre du Bane* on some early maps.

Bakeapple Bay (Labrador)   Within Kolotulik Bay. Named for the bakeapple or cloudberry (*Rubus chamaemorus*), which grows in abundance throughout Newfoundland and on the coast of Labrador as far north as HEBRON. 'The sweet flower of the bake-apple, and other pretty things grow quietly upon this ground, which is scarce habitable for man' (Lowell 1858). See also BAKEAPPLE BARREN, Nova Scotia.

Bannerman Lake; Bannerman River (Avalon)   The river flows southeast into HARBOUR GRACE. Named for Sir Alexander Bannerman (1788–1864), who was governor of Newfoundland from 1857 to 1864. Although he had considerable experience in the colonial service, having served as governor of Prince Edward Island (1851–4) and Barbados (1854–7), his record in Newfoundland was not impressive. Bannerman has been depicted by political scientist S.J.R. Noel as 'a grossly prejudiced near-octogenarian.' Accused by Prime Minister John Kent (1805–1872) 'of conniving with the opposition and bench' to defeat a government measure, the governor dismissed Kent (who refused to apologize) and called upon the opposition leader, Hugh William Hoyles (1814–1888), to form an administration. A dissolution was granted, and the Hoyles ministry was subse-

quently elected by a slim majority. Bannerman Lake takes its name from the river. Bannerman Park, on the north side of Military Road in ST. JOHN'S, was also named for the governor. In 1864 he agreed to allot this parcel of land for public use; however, the park was not officially opened until 1 September 1891.

Bannerman River   *See* Bannerman Lake.

Banting Lake (Central)   South of MUSGRAVE HARBOUR. Formerly known as 'Seven Mile Pond.' Commemorates the life of Sir Frederick Banting (1891–1941), a prominent Canadian scientist and co-discoverer of insulin, one of the important medical finds of the twentieth century. During the Second World War, Banting, a member of the Canadian Army Medical Corps, was *en route* to the United Kingdom on, as the press described it, 'a mission of high national and scientific importance' when his aircraft, a Lockheed Hudson Bomber, crashed in a remote area near Seven Mile Pond. Of the four men on board, only the pilot survived. He was rescued by a search party from Musgrave Harbour on 26 February 1941, four days after the crash.

Barachois; Barachoix; Barasway   This place name, sometimes rendered as *The Barachois*, occurs with frequency throughout Newfoundland, and is a testament to the Basque, and later French, impact on the nomenclature of the province. Joseph Jukes (1811–1869) decribed the feature in 1842 as 'a shallow lake at the back of a harbour that filled at the rise of the tide, and was called by the people a *barrasway*.' The name was originally coined by Basque fishermen to describe what was for them a new feature. Basque linguist Miren Egaña Goya traces it to the Basque '*barra + txo + a* or *barrachoa*' meaning 'a little bar' or 'sand bar.' Over time it was rendered in French as *barachois* and in English as *barasway*. The Barachois Provincial Park is located at the head of ST. GEORGE'S BAY in an area once called 'Cote des Basques.'

Barachoix   *See* Barachois.

Barasway   *See* Barachois.

Barbace Cove; Barbace Point (Western)   On the north side of the PORT AU PORT PENINSULA. The name may be traced to the Basque *barbaza*, which has been translated as 'a patch of vines.'

Barbace Point   *See* Barbace Cove.

Bareneed (Avalon)   Southeast of BAY ROBERTS. Two theories

exist as explanations for this place name. According to the Reverend Michael Howley, the community may once have been known as 'Barren Head.' This name occurs in several land deeds from the early nineteenth century, verifying this as a plausible explanation. However, E.R. Seary asserts that the original name of the community was Bearing Head, as it provided a navigational landmark for sailors in Bay de Grave. The first settlers were from Devon, and in their dialect the name would be pronounced 'Bareneed.' One fact is certain: over time the name became corrupted to Bareneed.

Barking Kettle Pond (Avalon) Southwest of WINDSOR LAKE. The name refers to the 'barking' procedure once used by fishermen. Writer Harold Horwood explains: 'It looks like something out of the witches' scene from *Macbeth*. In spring the [iron or copper kettle] is filled with a tarry mixture (it used to be bark from the forests), a fire is lighted underneath, and, while the aromatic smoke and steam drift down, crews cure their nets, steeping them in the hot liquid to ward off attacks by airborne fungi, bacteria, and marine organisms.' As early as 1795, Aaron Thomas described the same process: 'In every harbour, creek and cove there is what may be called a Parish Pott. It is filled with water and spruce bark, which is boiled together. They then dip the netts and sails into it, to which it is a great preservative.' See also OAKBARK COVE.

Barr'd Harbour (Western)   On ST. JOHN'S BAY. So called because of the reef that lies off the rocky exposed bay.

Barr'd Island (Central)   A village east of FOGO. This descriptive possibly refers to a narrow neck of land that partially blocks the BARR'D HARBOUR.

Bartletts Harbour (Western)   On the north shore of ST. JOHN'S BAY, on the ST. BARBE coast. This area was settled about 1800 by Robert Bartlett, from Yeovil, Somerset, England, which explains the name. He was later joined by his nephews Robert and Abraham Genge. Both surnames are still common on this coast.

Batteau (Labrador)   On the southeast shore of the Island of Ponds. One of the older names on the Labrador coast, it is traceable to the French *bateau* or *batteau*, and refers specifically to a type of fishing boat once common in this area. The place name was noted by Captain George Cartwright (1739/40–1819) in 1792.

Battle Harbour; Battle Island (Labrador)   In St. Lewis Sound. The name does not refer to a military engagement or to the surname Battle. On early maps it is spelled *batel*, from the Portuguese word for 'boat' or 'canoe'; this gradually became anglicized to 'battle.' In 1835 a visit was made by Captain Henry Bayfield, who reported: 'Battle Harbour, was full of small craft, brigs and schooners, 19 in all. The harbour is surrounded with fish stages & the huts of the fishermen. No one remains here during the winter, their [small] boats are hauled up and covered with spruce branches. The vessels return home, a few persons being left who winter up the bays of the main for the purpose of hunting for furs and to be in readiness for the seal fishery in the spring.' Although the winter population was to increase, the village remained much the same until 1930, when a major section was destroyed by fire. More recently it has reverted back to a summer fishery station. In 1990 the Battle Harbour Historic Trust was incorporated with the objective of developing this historic village, once called 'the capital of the Labrador, ' as a tourist attraction.

Battle Island   *See* Battle Harbour.

Bauline (Avalon)   Northwest of ST. JOHN'S, on the Marine Drive. The name is derived from the French *baleine*, for 'whale.' It appears as *Pt. aux Baleines* on the Bellin map of 1744 and, a century later, as *Balline* in census records. The contemporary spelling dates from the late nineteenth century. The Reverend Michael Howley suggests that that the name was first applied to a rock off the coast which 'appears and disappears in the swell of the waves [to] present the likeness of a whale breaching.'

Bay Bulls (Avalon)   A village south of ST. JOHN'S. According to E.R. Seary, this is the first Newfoundland place name of undisputable English origin and is therefore 'unique in an [early] nomenclature otherwise seemingly Portuguese.' Recorded first on the Hood manuscript map of 1592, it may be traced to the bull bird or ice bird (*Plautus alle alle*), sometimes called the 'dovekie' or 'little auk.' These birds follow the Labrador current down the Newfoundland coast and were obviously found at this location by early settlers. See also BULL ARM.

Bay d'Espoir; Head of Bay d'Espoir (Central)   An inlet north of HERMITAGE BAY. The name is derived from the French *Baie des Esprits*. During the nineteenth century, the area was resettled by the English, who anglicized the name to Bay Despair. Later the Newfoundland government, 'disliking the associations of this name and knowing that it was corrupted from a French original, decided to restore it. But instead of *Bay des Esprits*, and no doubt for the best of patriotic reasons, they made it Bay d'Espoir, "Bay of Hope" ' (Horwood). Ironically, it is still pronounced 'Bay Despair.'

Bay de Verde; Bay de Verde Peninsula (Avalon)   At the northern end of the Bay de Verde Peninsula. The location was noted as *Greene Bay* by John Guy in 1612, and later rendered as *Bay de Verde* by the Portuguese. When Joseph Jukes (1811–1869) visited in July 1839, he noted: 'We continued our voyage along the shore into *Bay de Verde*, or as the people call it, *Bay of Herbs*. This latter name is singularly inappropriate, as it is a wild desert place, composed entirely of bare red gritstone.' Fortunately, the earlier Portuguese translation prevailed.

Bay de Verde Peninsula   *See* Bay de Verde.

Bay l'Argent (Eastern)   On the northwest coast of the BURIN PENINSULA. The name dates from the period of French fishing rights on the south shore of Newfoundland and is mentioned in William Taverner's survey of the coast in 1714. It is a descriptive reference ('Bay of Silver'), for the high surrounding cliffs, which appear silver coloured when reflected in the sunlight. See also TOSLOW.

Bay of Exploits   *See* Exploits River.

Bay of Islands (Western)   A fiord on the west coast into which the HUMBER RIVER empties. There are numerous arms of the bay, the largest of which is the Humber, with the city of CORNER BROOK at its head. The area was explored by Jacques Cartier on 18 June 1534. He wrote: 'We came abreast of a bay full of round islands like dovecotes, and on this account we called them *Colombiers* and the Bay, St. Julians Bay [for the patron saint of travellers].' Bay of Islands is descriptive and dates from the Captain James Cook survey of 1767. Two years later, and half a world away, Cook was to repeat the place name in his survey of the coast of the North Island, New Zealand.

Bay Roberts (Avalon)   South of HARBOUR GRACE, on CONCEPTION BAY. For many years this area had strong commercial links with the Channel Islands. It was known as *Baye robert* or *Bay de Roberts* dur-

ing the seventeenth century, for a Jersey family of that name. Other modified Channel Island surnames may be found in settlements around Conception Bay and in other parts of the province: Guizot (Gushue); Poing destre (Puddister); LeGros (LeGrow); Fillier (Filleul); Nicolle (Nicol); Murrin (Mourant). Noel and LeDrew have remained unchanged. Bay Roberts was the model for Peterport in the novel *The New Priest in Conception Bay* (1858) by Robert Traill Spence Lowell (1816–1891). This name was taken from St. Peterport on the island of Guernsey. A native of Boston, Massachusetts, and brother of American poet and diplomat James Russell Lowell (1819–1891) he served as a missionary for the Anglican Society for the Propagation of the Gospel, in Bay Roberts (1843–7). The novel, a fascinating pen portrait of nineteenth-century Newfoundland, was reprinted in 1974 with an introduction by Dr. Patrick O'Flaherty. He comments: 'Although aspects [of it are] dated, the tale is not without pathos and is artfully told.' See also GUERNSEY COVE, Prince Edward Island.

Beachy Cove (Avalon)   South of PORTUGAL COVE, CONCEPTION BAY. A descriptive for a strip of sand and shingle edging the shore. Witch Hazel Ridge, Beachy Cove, was for many years the home of Newfoundland author Harold Horwood. The area figures prominently in his writings. Witch hazel (*Betula lutea*), sometimes called 'Newfoundland Oak,' was much sought after in shipbuilding.

Beau Bois (Eastern)   Southeast of MARYSTOWN. This area of the BURIN PENINSULA displays its heritage in a number of French descriptive place names: Beau Bois, Jean de Baie, and Bay l'Argent. The first two locations were rendered as *Boa Boa* and *havre John Dubois* in the William Taverner survey of 1714. Until 1713 most of the south coast of Newfoundland was under French control. See chapter 1, pages 17–18.

Bellburns (Western)   North of DANIEL'S HARBOUR, on the west coast of the NORTHERN PENINSULA. This area was first settled in the 1830s; the name is a variant of the surname Belben. According to E.R. Seary, this is a family name in Glenburnie, BONNE BAY. Thus the community was probably named after one of its early settlers.

Belle Bay (Eastern)   An arm of FORTUNE BAY. An early descriptive, 'beautiful bay,' dating from the period of French influence on the south coast of Newfoundland (see chapter 1, pages 17–18).

Bellevue (Eastern)   Near the head of TRINITY BAY. Originally known as 'Tickle Harbour.' Tickle is a descriptive name for a narrow stretch of salt water, usually with hazardous tides, currents, and rocks. It lived up to its reputation when visited by Joseph Jukes (1811–1869) on 15 July 1839: 'Weighed anchor and sailed along the shore toward Tickle Harbour. In the middle of the day a thick fog came on, and presently a deluge of rain. In the evening it began to blow ... [some fishermen] told us Tickle Harbour was a bad place to lie in and piloted us to a small cove called Chance Cove, a mile or two astern.' On 14 December 1896 the name was changed by order of governor-in-council to the coined name Bellevue, undoubtedly to avoid confusion with the many other locations incorporating the descriptive 'Tickle.' Bellevue Provincial Park is nearby. See also JIGGER TICKLE.

Bell Island (Avalon)   In CONCEPTION BAY. Although officially proclaimed by the Newfoundland Nomenclature Board on 26 April 1910, the name may be traced back over three centuries to John Guy's 1612 record of the *great Belile*. However, there is a possi-

bility of it being older and a
French transfer name from Belle
Isle off the coast of Brittany (see
STRAIT OF BELLE ISLE). Perhaps the
only certainty is the antiquity of
the name and its probable French
origin. The theory that it is
descriptive, from an immense
rock in the form of an inverted
bell, dates from the nineteenth
century. This may have served to
reinforce the older name; however, it was not its source. During
the Second World War, Bell
Island experienced two raids by
German U-boats – on 4 September and 5 November 1942. The
targets were ships loading iron
ore from the Bell Island mines. In
all, four ships were sunk, with a
loss of 33 lives. See also WABANA.

Belle Isle (Western)   *See* Strait of
Belle Isle.

Belleoram (Central)   In BELLE
BAY, on the west side of FORTUNE
BAY. This name, dating from the
the latter part of the seventeenth
or early eighteenth century, was
classified by the Reverend
Michael Howley as 'very euphonious but unintelligible.' In his
1714 survey, William Taverner
pointed out the origin of this
unusual place name: 'At Banda-
lore [Belleoram] there is a large
beech and severall houses wich
belong to a Monsr. Beloram, a
Malouin [from St. Malo] Gentle-

man who hath wintered in that
place 20 years successively one
after the other.' This 'small but
snug place' was also visited by
Captain James Cook (1728–1779)
during his survey of the south
coast in 1765. He noted that,
although the French had used
Bande l'Arier (now Belleoram), the
English had neglected it, even
though the harbour 'is allow'd to
be as good a place, as any in Fortune Bay, & it is certain a Fishery
might be carried on here to a
great advantage.' This place name
may be traced through a variety
of mispronunciations and misspellings, from: Bande l'Arier,
Bande de Laurier, and Bande
l'Arriéré, to eventually the euphonious Belleoram. There is also a
Belleoram Bank and Belleoram
Barasway.

Belleoram Banks   *See* Belleoram.

Belleoram Barasway   *See* Belleoram.

Biscayan Cove; Biscay Bay
(Avalon)   Biscay Bay is an arm of
TREPASSEY BAY; Biscayan Cove is
south of CAPE ST. FRANCIS. The
European Bay of Biscay lies adja-
cent to the Basque territory of
northern Spain and southwestern
France. The name is from the
Basque word *bizkar*, for 'moun-
tain country,' a reference to the

Pyrenees. The name was carried across the Atlantic by anonymous Basque fishermen of the sixteenth century.

Biscay Bay   *See* Biscayan Cove.

Bishop's Falls (Central)   On the EXPLOITS RIVER, northeast of GRAND FALLS–WINDSOR. Named for the Reverend John Inglis (1777–1850), Anglican bishop of the Diocese of Nova Scotia, which once included Newfoundland. In 1826, on an episcopal visit covering some 8,000 kilometres, Inglis visited this area, giving rise to the name. Newfoundland became a separate Anglican diocese in 1839. Bishop's Falls was incorporated as a town in 1961, and its motto, 'In the middle of the forest we remain,' is indicative of the importance of forestry to the local economy. The recent discovery nearby of commercial black granite, supplemented by pink granite from the Hermitage Peninsula and a yellow-green variety from THE TOPSAILS, has given rise to a new industry for the area.

Bishops Mitre   *See* Kaumajet Mountains.

Black Duck Brook (Western) On the PORT AU PORT PENINSULA, northeast of Lourdes. A descriptive for the black duck (*Anas rubripes*) common to the area. The community, largely French speaking, is known locally as 'L'Anse aux Canards.'

Blackhead (Avalon)   Northeast of CARBONEAR. The name, a common descriptive for a 'black'-appearing headland, was the site of the first Methodist church in Newfoundland and, since 1949, in Canada. It was erected in 1768–9, largely through the efforts of a charismatic and enigmatic missionary, Laurence Coughlan (?–1784?). He began life as a Roman Catholic, converted to Methodism, and was ordained on 27 April 1765 by the Church of England. During his years in the CONCEPTION BAY district, as a missionary of the Anglican Society for the Propagation of the Gospel (SPG), it is clear that he led a double life. On the surface he performed the rites of the Church of England; however, his theology and ecclesiastical approach were not always in conformity. In 1773 he returned to England and resigned from the SPG. Regarded as the 'Father of Methodism' in Newfoundland, Coughlan maintained close ties with the Methodist movement. Near the end of his tenure in Newfoundland, he wrote to John Wesley: 'I am and do confess myself to be a Methodist. The name I love and hope I ever shall. The plan which you first taught me, I have followed, both as to doctrine and discipline.'

Black Joke Cove (Western)   On the north shore of BELLE ISLE, in the STRAIT OF BELLE ISLE. Named for one of the most notorious of pirate ships. It is reputed that the ship used to lie at anchor in this cove, ready to pounce on unsuspecting merchant ships.

Blaketown (Avalon)   On DILDO POND, north of Highway 1. The name, officially changed from Dildo Pond in 1888, honours Sir Henry Arthur Blake (1840–1918), governor of Newfoundland from 1887 to 1889. Although Blake was of Irish ancestry, there does not seem to be any connection with Blakestown in County Kildare, Eire. Further, the suggestion that the name evolved from 'By the Lake Town [Dildo Pond]' is apocryphal.

Blow Me Down   A village northeast of CARBONEAR (Avalon), a range of hills northwest of CORNER BROOK (Central), a cove south of Mortier Bay (Eastern), a mountain southeast of RAMAH BAY (Labrador), and found in at least fourteen other locations throughout the province. This unusual place name has an undisputed nautical origin. William Francis Ganong, who made an exhaustive study of the name and

its variant, 'Blomidon,' concluded: 'The kind of places called Blow-me-Down are abrupt and more or less isolated mountains, headlands or bluffs, rising steeply from or near navigible waters and therefore are [locations] that render vessels under their lee liable to danger from squalls. This catchy phrase was applied, as is the sailor's wont, wherever appropriate.' See also CAPE BLOMIDON, Nova Scotia.

Blue Cove (Western)   Southwest of ANCHOR POINT. Originally a French settlement, the community was listed as Blue Guts Cove in the 1911 census. In the 1920s the name was 'reformed' by action of the Newfoundland Nomenclature Board to become Blue Cove.

Bonavista; Bonavista Bay; Bonavista Peninsula; Cape Bonavista (Eastern)   The cape is at the tip of the Bonavista Peninsula. It is recorded in the *Première Relation de Jacques Cartier*: 'On Sunday 10 May 1534, we reached Newfoundland, sighting land at *Cap de Bonne Vista* ... on account of the large blocks of ice along that coast, we deemed it advisable to go into *Havre Sainte-Katherine* [Catalina], lying about five leagues south-southwest of this cape [Bonavista], where we remained the space of ten days, biding favourable weather and rigging and fitting up our long boats.' Cartier's comments are important because they indicate a certain familiarity with the coastline and show that some place names were already known to him. Bonavista is of possible Spanish, Portuguese, or French origin. It may have been bestowed by Gaspar Corte-Real (*ca* 1450/55–1501?) about 1500, after one of the Cape Verde Islands – Boa Vista. The assertion that, in 1497 John Cabot exclaimed, *'buona vista* – O happy sight,' thus giving rise to the name, does not have any documentary support. The case for Newfoundland as Cabot's landfall is a strong one; however, it was probably more to the north. In the final analysis, and in the absence of specific evidence, E.R. Seary's verdict rings true: 'No decisive conclusion [about Cabot's landfall] has been, or perhaps can ever be, reached' (see also Cape Dégrat in chapter 1, pages 5–6). The town of Bonavista, strategically located south of Cape Bonavista, from the earliest days was a centre for the English fishery. The importance of Cape Bonavista as a navigational landmark was recognized on 11 September 1843, when the lighthouse became operational.

Bonavista Bay   *See* Bonavista.

Bonavista Peninsula   *See* Bonavista.

Bonne Bay (Western)   Between BAY OF ISLANDS and St. Pauls Bay. This name may be traced to Basque sources. It was listed as *Baya Ederra,* or 'beautiful bay,' on the Detchevery map of 1689, later to be rendered as *Belle Bay* by the French. In 1767, Captain James Cook (1728–1779) correctly translated the name as Bonne Bay – an apt descriptive for this location.

Botwood (Central)   On the BAY OF EXPLOITS, southwest of LEWISPORTE. Once a railway centre and now a major shipping port, the town was named Botwoodville (later simplified to Botwood) for Archdeacon Edward E. Botwood (1828–1901). Early in his career he served as Anglican minister at EXPLOITS RIVER. Aviation history was made in Botwood in the 1930s when it was selected by British and American air lines as the site for a seaplane base. In 1939 the Pan Am Yankee Clipper seaplane began passenger service across the Atlantic, using Botwood as a stopover. The base figures prominently in the novel *Night over Water* by Ken Follett, which depicts one of the last Pan Am flights prior to the outbreak of war in 1939. With the demise of the flying boat and the establishment of GANDER as an international air base, operations at Botwood were phased out.

Bowdoin Canyon; Bowdoin Harbour (Labrador)   The canyon is located south of CHURCHILL FALLS. In 1891 a party from Bowdoin College, in Brunswick, Maine, carried out surveys on the Hamilton (now Churchill) River. The harbour is located on the east side of KILLINIQ ISLAND. In 1938 a scientific survey party, also from Bowdoin College, charted the harbour and bestowed the name.

Bowdoin Harbour   *See* Bowdoin Canyon.

Branch (Avalon)   On ST. MARY'S BAY, northeast of Point Lance. The name is of French origin and may well refer to the French surname Branch or Branche.

Brandies (Central)   A group of hazardous rocks in TWILLINGATE harbour. It is a common term, found in many locations throughout Newfoundland, for a reef of rocks which may be partly under water. According to the *Dictionary of Newfoundland English*, it stems from *brandize*, an early name for a trivet or iron tripod that was subsequently applied to 'low-lying rocks.' The name is also found near the Saltee Islands, off the southeast tip of Ireland. Considering the Irish influence on Newfoundland, the name's appearance on this side of the Atlantic is not surprising.

Brent's Cove (Central)   On Confusion Bay, west of LA SCIE. An example of a transplanted English place name. In the West Country, 'brent' is used as a descriptive term for 'burnt hill,' as in Brent Knoll and South Brent in Somerset. Obviously the local topography reminded a West Country fisherman of home.

Brig Bay (Western)   On the GULF OF ST. LAWRENCE, south of Plum Point. A deep, sheltered harbour that is almost landlocked, it was listed by Captain James Cook (1728–1779) in 1767 as *Brigg Bay*. The name is a probable reference to a long-lost incident concerning a brig or brigantine.

Brig Harbour (Labrador)   On Brig Island, one of the White Bear Islands, south of Holton. Named by fishermen from HARBOUR MAIN who frequented this area in the nineteenth century. A derelict brig was moored close to the shore, and served for a time 'the purpose of residence, store and stage, whilst the nearby bawns [rocks on which salted cod was dried] served as flakes' (Browne).

Brighton (Central)   On NOTRE DAME BAY. Originally known as

'Dark Tickle,' the name was changed in the early twentieth century by the Newfoundland Nomenclature Board. There does not seem to be any local reason for the imposed name. Brighton Tickle Point and Brighton Tickle Islands are nearby.

Brig Island   *See* Brig Harbour.

Brigus (Avalon)   Southeast of BAY ROBERTS. The origin of this name is uncertain. It has been attributed to Brighouse, near Huddersfield, Yorkshire, England; however, it is more probably a derivative of the old French *brigas* or *brigues*, for 'intrigues.' The story behind the naming has, unfortunately, been lost. Two seventeenth-century references give the spelling as *Brega* (*ca* 1630) and *Brigues* (1677). The contemporary Brigus appears as early as 1693. There is a second Brigus located on the southern shore of the AVALON PENINSULA. Sometimes mentioned in early documents as 'Brigus by South,' its derivation seems to have been similar to that of the CONCEPTION BAY Brigus. The latter was the birthplace of Captain Robert Bartlett (1875–1946), famous Arctic explorer. Coming from a long line of seamen and explorers (both his father and grandfather had explored in the Arctic), Bartlett began sailing with Robert Peary in 1898 and was subsequently captain of the latter's ships. Bartlett accompanied Peary part of the way to the North Pole in 1909. Later he was in command of the *Karluk* with the Vilhjalmur Stefansson (1879–1962) Arctic expedition of 1913–14. Bartlett's former home in Brigus, 'Hawthorne Cottage,' has been designated a Historic Site.

Bristol's Hope (Avalon)   Northeast of HARBOUR GRACE. The origin of the name may be traced to the city of Bristol, whose Society of Merchant Venturers supported the early colonization efforts of native Bristolian John Guy. In 1615 Guy had a quarrel with the society, and members made application for a separate grant of land adjacent to Harbour Grace. It was named Bristol's Hope. Robert Hayman (1575–1629), who was appointed governor of the colony about 1618, is noteworthy as Newfoundland's first poet. While resident in Newfoundland, he wrote some verse and a series of epigrams. The word 'Hope,' common in English nomenclature, means 'a small enclosed valley.' As a place name, Bristol's Hope was revived in the mid-nineteenth century and officially sanctioned by proclamation on 16 August 1910.

Britannia (Eastern)   East of
CLARENVILLE, on RANDOM ISLAND.
The Roman name for Britain was
adopted as 'a mark of patriotism'
for this community during the
late nineteenth century. It was
known as 'Britannia Cove' until
1904. Birthplace of Dr. W.T. Ross
Flemington (1897–1971), long-
time president of Mount Allison
University (1945–62). Flemington
was later to serve as the first
ombudsman for the province of
New Brunswick.

Broom Point (Western)   Within
GROS MORNE NATIONAL PARK. The
origin of the name may stem from
the custom of attaching a birch
broom to the masthead of a vessel
to indicate that it was for sale. An
interpretation centre at Broom
Point, located in a restored cabin
and fish store, details the history
of the Mudge family summer
fishery from 1941 to 1975.

Buchans; Buchans Island
(Central)   On Highway 370,
north of RED INDIAN LAKE.
Buchans Island in Red Indian
Lake was named for David
Buchan (1780–1838?), naval
officer and colonial administrator.
In October 1810, Governor Thomas Duckworth (1748–1817)
selected Buchan to lead an expedition to the interior of Newfoundland with the objective of
winning the friendship of the
Beothuks. Contact was eventually
made on the shores of Red Indian
Lake. Later, due to a misunder-
standing, two of Buchan's men
were killed, and the Beothuks
fled. In 1819 Buchan was
involved in escorting a captured
Beothuk woman, Demasduit,
back to her home. She died on
the way, and her body and possessions were subsequently
placed in a tent on the shores of
the lake. The town of Buchans
(named for Buchans Island) was
established in 1927 to mine copper, lead, and zinc. The mines
have now closed, and the town is
largely a service centre for the
immediate area. A plant producing granite monuments and
other stone products has recently
opened in Buchans.

Buchans Island   *See* Buchans.

Bull Arm (Avalon)   An arm of
TRINITY BAY. The name is probably for the bull bird, common to
this part of Newfoundland (see
BAY BULLS). Great Mosquito Cove
on Bull Arm is a construction site
for the Hibernia offshore oil
project. It is here that the Gravity
Based Structure, a massive con-
crete platform, is being built. It
will eventually be located on the
Grand Bank, southeast of ST.
JOHN'S. The self-contained site
houses hundreds of employees
and provides everything from a

cafeteria, bank, tavern, barber-shop, medical centre, and fire hall, to an Olympic-sized swimming pool. It is one of the largest such construction sites in Canada.

Burgeo; Burgeo Bank; Burgeo Islands (Western)   The town, settled in 1798, is on the south-west coast, at the termination of Highway 480. For nearly two centuries Burgeo's only outside link was by sea. All this changed in 1979 when the 148-kilometre Caribou Trail was completed, connecting the town with the Trans-Canada Highway. The place name was applied first to the islands off the coast, once known as *Mill Virgines* (Chaves-Oviedo 1536), later as *Virgeo*, and eventually as *Burgeo*. The name may be traced to the medieval legend of the eleven thousand virgins. As explained by Harold Horwood, 'any sceptic who wonders where eleven thousand virgins might be found is reminded that they were recruited [by St. Ursula] to go on a crusade to the Holy Land in the belief that God would deliver Jerusalem into their sinless hands. They were, of course, kidnapped en route and sold into Moslem harems, where virgins commanded a good price.' Burgeo, Burgeo Islands, and Burgeo Bank are their unlikely memorial.

Burgeo Bank   *See* Burgeo.

Burgeo Islands   *See* Burgeo.

Burin; Burin Peninsula (Eastern) The town is on PLACENTIA BAY south of MARYSTOWN. Although the town was incorporated in 1950, it is one of the oldest communities on the Burin Peninsula. For some time this place name was thought to be traceable to the old French word *burine*, for an engraving or carving tool. However, Basque fishermen were using the coves and harbours of the peninsula by the mid-1600s, giving rise to a more probable origin. Recent research by Basque linguist Miren Egaña Goya suggests that *Burie* on the Detcheverry map of 1689 may be Burin. She concludes: 'In naming a cape, Detcheverry commonly employed *burua*, meaning "head" in Basque and used to name prominent geographical features such as the headland of a point or cape.' Further corroboration is found in a number of other local place names that are of Basque origin, such as Mortier (*Martiris*), Little St. Lawrence (*San Lorenz Chumea*), and Great St. Lawrence (*San Lorenz Andia*). The naming of Placentia Bay, on the east side of the peninsula, may also be traced to Basque sources.

Burin Peninsula   *See* Burin.

Burlington (Central)   On Highway 413, southeast of BAIE VERTE. The area was first permanently settled in the 1850s and was known as 'North West Arm.' Burlington was adopted as a place name in 1914. It is a variant of Bridlington, Yorkshire, England, and may have been suggested by Burlington, in Ontario.

Burnside (Eastern)   East of GLOVERTOWN. Settled in 1885, the district was composed of two communities: Squid Tickle and Hollets Cove. In 1921 the area was ravaged by a severe forest fire. This tragic event was to inspire the new name, adopted when the two communities amalgamated in 1921. The frequent use of 'Burn,' 'Burnt,' and the French, 'Brûlé' in place names is evidence of the prevalence of forest fires in many parts of Newfoundland.

Butter Pot Hill (Avalon)   This place name may be found in several locations on the AVALON PENINSULA and elsewhere in the province. Because of their distinctiveness, the features have always attracted considerable attention. Aaron Thomas, writing in 1794, gave the following description: 'Between Cape Broyle and Cape Race are singular, mountainous rocks call'd Butter Potts. They are situated on the edge of a mountain about five miles inland and extend in length, I suppose, three miles. There are a number of these huge rocks, and their sponsors [named] them Butter Potts from their resemblance to the domestic utensil.' The highest of these features, at 302 metres, lies south of Highway 13. Butter Pot Provincial Park is off the Trans-Canada Highway, near the junction with Highway 13.

Byron Bay (Labrador)   Northwest of Holton. Named for Vice-Admiral John Byron (1723–1786), who served as governor of Newfoundland from 1769 to 1772. He took an interest in the Labrador fishery and issued several proclamations relating to whaling in the STRAIT OF BELLE ISLE. His grandson was the poet Lord Byron (1788–1824).

Cabot Strait   *See* chapter 1, page 5.

Calvert; Calvert Bay (Avalon) The village is northwest of FERRYLAND. First known as 'Capelin Bay,' it was officially renamed in 1922 in honour of Sir George Calvert, first Baron Baltimore (1580?–1632), 'planter of the province of Avalon.' He visited his fledgling colony in 1627, returning the next year prepared to settle permanently. However, one year's residence proved sufficient. By 19

August 1629, he was ready to leave because, in his words, 'the winter lasts from October to May; half of the company of 100 are sick, and 10 of them dead.' In 1632 Calvert was granted territory 'in warmer climes' north of the Potomac River in what was to become the province, later state, of Maryland. He died before receiving the charter for the new colony. The family title is perpetuated in Baltimore, Maryland.

Calvert Bay   *See* Calvert.

Campbells Creek (Western)   On the south coast of the PORT AU PORT PENINSULA. The community was settled in 1853 by a Campbell family from Cape Breton, which expains the name.

Campbellton (Central)   Northeast of LEWISPORTE. Situated on Indian Arm, NOTRE DAME BAY, the village was established in the early twentieth century and named for John Campbell, manager of the local sawmill.

Canada Bay (Western)   An inlet northeast of HARBOUR DEEP. Appears first as *Canarie* (Cordier 1696) and, by 1775 as *Baie de Canadaou des Canaries* (1765). It is apparent that this name has evolved from the Latin *Canaria*, for 'dog.' This may have been mistakenly imposed when mem-

bers of the grey wolf family (*Canis lupus*) were first sighted.

Cannings Cove (Eastern)   On the south shore of NEWMAN SOUND, TERRA NOVA NATIONAL PARK. Settled in the 1870s; originally known as 'Cannons Cove,' after an early settler, over time this name evolved to Cannings Cove.

Cape Anguille   *See* Anguille Mountains.

Cape Bauld (Western)   Headland on the north side of QUIRPON ISLAND, off the tip of the NORTHERN PENINSULA. Sighted, but not named, by Jacques Cartier on his first voyage in 1534. On the Reinel and other early Portuguese maps, it appears as *C de Marco*, appropriately, 'cape of the landmark.' The present name, a descriptive, is a common designation in many parts of Atlantic Canada. See also CAPE DÉGRAT.

Cape Bonavista   *See* Bonavista.

Cape Broyle (Avalon)   Northeast of FERRYLAND. Listed as *Cape Broile* by John Guy in 1612, and on the French maps of the period as *Cabreuil* or *C. Brolle*. By the time of the 1836 census, the name had evolved to Cape Broyle. The name is a descriptive that may be traced to the old English *broile*, meaning a confused disturbance, tumult, or turmoil, referring to the waters around the cape. Another explanation is provided by the Reverend Michael Howley, who asserts that the name is a corruption of the Portuguese *Abrohlo*, meaning 'rock.' See also DEVILS STAIRWAY.

Cape Chapeau Rouge (Eastern) Southeast of ST. LAWRENCE. A descriptive dating from the period of the French migratory fishery. On 11 July 1792, seaman Aaron Thomas 'passed within a league of Cape Chapeau Rouge or the Mountains of the Red Hatt. It is the most remarkable cape and is an immense heap of ragged, craggy rocks placed one upon the other. When viewed from the sea every fathom of your move gives it a new shape. It [can] appear like a Dutchman without legs, afterwards like a Hatt, then a Lion Rampant, a Bust, a broken Turret, a rough Dome and lastly, a craggy inaccessible mountain.'

Cape Chidley (Labrador) First listed on early French charts as *Cap Predrix*, or 'Cape Partridge.' The present name was assigned in 1587 by the explorer John Davis (1550–1605), 'after the Worshipfull Mr. John Chidley of Broad Clyst, near Exeter, in the countie of Devon' (CPCGN files). Chidley, also an explorer, died while in command of an expedition to the South Seas, via the Strait of Magellan. The cape, sometimes erroneously placed on the mainland, is actually on KILLINIQ ISLAND, the most northerly location in Newfoundland and Labrador. The provincial boundary passes across Killiniq, so that the eastern section is within Labrador and the remainder is part of the Northwest Territories. In 1905 the area was explored by Sir Wilfred Grenfell (1865–1940). 'We not only visited the coast as far north as Cape Chidley,' he wrote, ' but explored the narrow channel which runs through the land into Ungava Bay, and placed Cape Chidley itself on a detached island.' See also GRENFELL SOUND.

Cape Cormorant (Western)   At the southeastern tip of the PORT AU PORT PENINSULA. Named first by Jacques Cartier in 1534 *Cap de Latte*, after Fort La Latte, west of St. Malo. *Latte* refers to the batten or thin strip of wood or metal placed around the hatch to hold down a tarpaulin. Cape Cormorant, for the presence of the seabirds, was an eighteenth-century designation.

Cape Dégrat (Western)   Southeast of CAPE BAULD, on QUIRPON ISLAND. Sometime in the late fifteenth or early sixteenth century, Basque fishermen, who had been whaling for centuries in the BAY OF BISCAY, reached the Labrador coast and the STRAIT OF BELLE ISLE (their *Gran Baya*) in search of whale and walrus. *En route* they spotted a high cliff rising from the sea, which they named Cap dé Grat. *Dé grat* refers to the stage where fish are landed and the platform on which they are dried. Jacques Cartier, on his first voyage in 1534, refers to the location as *cap Dégrat*, indicating that it was already known as such. See also PETIT-DE-GRAT, Nova Scotia.

Cape Fogo (Central)   The eastern tip of FOGO ISLAND. *See* Fogo.

Cape Freels (Avalon; Central) The first is located west of CAPE PINE, at the entrance to TREPASSEY BAY. It was originally named by the Portuguese *Ilha de frey Luis,* 'the island of Brother Lewis,' which, over time, became anglicized to 'Freels.' By 1713 the Michael Lane survey recorded the location as *Cape Freels South*, to distinguish it from the second Cape Freels, northeast of WESLEYVILLE. The latter is probably of Breton origin for Cape Fréhel on the coast of Brittany.

Cape Harrigan (Labrador)   On NUNAKSALUK ISLAND, north of HOPEDALE. The explanation that it 'owes its name to an Irishman named Harrigan' is incorrect.

'Harrigan' is a corruption of 'hurricane,' and the pronunciation may be traced to the Devonshire-accented 'harricane.' Thus the name is descriptive for the stormy conditions that prevail locally.

Cape Harrison (Labrador)   The origin of the name of this headland, situated northwest of Holton, is shrouded in mystery. It has been attributed to Benjamin Harrison, once director and later deputy-governor of the Hudson's Bay Company. Several locations in the Northwest Territories were named for this individual. However, there is no documentary evidence to link him with the Labrador location. It may possibly be named for a Captain Harrison, from Newcastle, England, known to have led whaling expeditions to DAVIS STRAIT and Labrador in the 1840s. The cape is a conspicuous bluff faced by a reddish cliff that rises to UIVALUK PEAK, 350 metres high. *Uivaluk* is of Inuit origin and has been defined by Wheeler as 'big cape facing the open sea.' It has also been interpreted to mean a promontory 'with sides too steep to cross,' thus forcing the traveller to 'go around it.' Cape Harrison was, for a time, known as Cape Webec, a corruption of the Inuit *Uivaluk*. See also WEBECK.

Cape Lahune (Central)   On the south coast southwest of François. The name is of French origin and means literally 'top mast.' In like fashion, English sailors applied terms such as 'topsail' to geographic features.

Cape Makkovik; Makkovik; Makkovik Bank (Labrador) The settlement is northeast of POSTVILLE. The name is of Inuit origin, and it is the opinion of Wheeler that it is derived from *maxok*, meaning 'two.' The suffix *vik* in Inuit means 'place of' or 'where.' Thus, Makkovik is, in all probability, an Inuit descriptive for a bay that is divided in two sections. It was formerly thought to be a variation of the name of Pierre Marcoux (1757–1809), a merchant once active on the Labrador coast; however, the Inuit explanation is more plausible. The settlement and offshore bank take their names from the cape.

Cape Mugford (Labrador)   On the mainland, opposite Cod Island. This 671-metre-high bluff was probably named for Captain Francis Mugford, who was in command of the *Jersey Packet*, a ship which carried a group of Moravian missionaries to the coast of Labrador in 1770.

Cape Norman (Western)   The northernmost point of the island of Newfoundland. The high cliffs of the cape have long provided an excellent landmark for the southeastern entrance to the STRAIT OF BELLE ISLE. Thus, it was named *cap Normand* early in the sixteenth century by unknown French mariners from the province of Normandy. The cape was scaled by Captain James Cook (1728–1779) in August 1764. He noted 'that the land [round about] is of barren soil, for many miles into the country.' While surveying near Cape Norman, Cook met with a serious accident 'when a large powder horn exploded in his hand ... which shattered it in a terrible manner.' The first lighthouse here was erected by the government of Canada in 1869. This federal intervention was made because of the importance of the Strait of Belle Isle to Canadian shipping and the reluctance of Newfoundland authorities to become involved with lighthouse construction until jurisdiction of the 'French Shore' was settled.

Cape Onion (Western)   At the entrance to SACRED BAY. The name appears on early maps as *C de Ognon* or *Cape Dognon*, a corruption of the French *oignon*, for the 'onion shape' of the headland.

Cape Pine (Avalon)   At the entrance to TREPASSEY BAY. The name is undoubtedly of Portuguese origin and is listed in 1592 as *C de pena* on the Petrus Plancius 'representation' of North America derived from earlier Portuguese charts. Translated as 'cape of punishment or sorrow,' it was to appear in English as *Cape Pine* on the Henry Southwood map of 1675. The original name was prophetic, as, over the centuries, this dangerous headland claimed its toll of ships and lives. To illustrate: in the autumn of 1816, HMS *Comus* and HMS *Harpooner* were lost off Cape Pine (see MARINES COVE). Agitation mounted for construction of a lighthouse and, in August 1847, Captain Henry Bayfield (1795–1885) selected a site at the tip of the cape. He recounts in his journal that 'there had been 22 wrecks in the space of 20 years and the number of lives lost was very great.' In addition to dense fog, the reason was a combination of 'the tide, irregular in strength,' and the 'heave of the long rolling sea from the southwest, that causes so many heavily laden homeward [England] bound ships to be wrecked.' The construction of the lighthouse alleviated but did not totally solve the problem. It was not until 1914 that the lighthouse on the 'cape of punishment or sorrow' was supplemented by a foghorn. See CAPE RACE.

Cape Porcupine (Labrador) Northwest of Huntington Island. Historian explorer Helge Ingstad has written of this area: 'We continued our voyage northward along the coast; to the west there was a wide, white beach, bordered on the other side by the forest. After some hours we approached a promontory [which] seemed to jut out like a spear into the ocean. It had a curious shape; in the middle it could have been as much as three hundred feet in height ... the terrain sloped down evenly on both sides.' This was Cape Porcupine, earlier named for its resemblance to the animal. But, more important, Ingstad became convinced that this 60-kilometre-long beach, not duplicated elsewhere on the North Atlantic seaboard, was the *Furdustrandir*, or 'Wonder Strands,' of the Norse sagas, and that Cape Porcupine was their *Kjalarnes* or *Keelness*. To the Norse, unfamiliar with the porcupine, its shape undoubtedly resembled an upturned boat. Samuel Eliot Morrison reached the same conclusion following an exhaustive sea, land, and air reconnaissance of the North Atlantic coast.

Cape Race (Avalon) East of TREPASSEY BAY; the southeast tip of the island of Newfoundland. The name could be of either Portuguese or French origin, or a combination of both. The headland makes its appearance as *Capo raso* (Vespucci 1505–6) and *cap de raze* (Cartier 1535–6). As *Capo raso*, it might have been inspired by the name of the last Portuguese territory seen by a ship leaving Lisbon to cross the Atlantic; or it might have been named by early French mariners for Pointe du Raz on the coast of Brittany. In any event, the meaning has a nautical 'twist' and refers to a headland which has to be literally 'shaved by.' Since it lies to the east of Trepassey Bay, which is named for Baie des Trépassés in Brittany, the case for the Breton origin is stronger, with *Capo raso* as a translation. As with CAPE PINE, the need for the construction of a lighthouse became tragically obvious, and Captain Henry Bayfield (1795–1885) was also instructed in 1847 to survey Trepassey Bay and the Cape Race area. In 1851 an unlit wooden structure was erected as a beacon at Cape Race; however, it was totally ineffective. Unfortunately, it took two major marine disasters to bring about the erection of a lighthouse. In the autumn of 1854, an American ship, the *City of Philadelphia* ran aground with 540 people on board. This time the seas were relatively calm, and all were eventually rescued. Not so lucky were those on board the 2,800-tonne steamer *Arctic*, which

struck a French ship, the *Vesta*, with a loss of more than 300 lives. Finally, on 15 December 1856, following an expenditure of more than £5,000 the Cape Race light shone for the first time. Ironically, ten days later, on Christmas day, in a dense fog, the *Welsford* from SAINT JOHN, New Brunswick, bound for Liverpool, struck a reef near the lighthouse. Only four from a crew of twenty-six were saved by the lightkeeper. It was not until the spectacular loss in April 1863 of the liner *Anglo Saxon*, which claimed more than 350 lives, that further action was taken. By 1872 the all-essential fog whistle had been installed at Cape Race.

Cape Ray (Western)   South of CAPE ANGUILLE; the southwest tip of Newfoundland. The name may possibly be traced to *c de Roi* on the Abraham Ortelius map of 1564. According to William Francis Ganong, 'this is the earliest use of the name on a map, and in a form suggesting an origin from Cartier's [1535–6] *C Royal* [at the southern entrance to the Bay of Islands].' Another, and more plausible, theory suggests that the name is of Basque/Portuguese origin, and may be traced to the Basque Cap de Ray, Cap d'Array, or Cadarrayco hegoaco burua, for 'South Cape Ray.' In turn the Basque place name may have been inspired by the Portuguese Cabo do Rei, 'Cape of the King.' On the Levasseur map of 1601 the feature is listed *c raye*, and is usually *c raye* or *Cape Ray* thereafter. The area was described by Joseph Jukes (1811–1869) on 24 September 1839: 'Cape Ray is a very conspicuous object at a distance, in consequence of the bold flat-topped ridge of hills that come down to it, ending in two or three detached conical elevations, from the foot of these about a mile of flat ground stretches out to sea, forming the point of the cape.' Over the years, Cape Ray has been the scene of numerous shipwrecks and marine disasters. One of the worst occurred in June 1831, when the *Lady Sherbrooke*, out of Londonderry and bound for Quebec, went aground with the loss of 350 lives. Because of the danger the location posed to Canadian shipping, the government of Canada erected a lighthouse on Cape Ray in 1871. Earlier, Cape Ray became the terminal of the first submarine telegraph cable to Newfoundland. Completed in 1856, the cable linked Newfoundland with the rest of North America. See also CODROY.

Cape Rouge (Western)   On the northeastern coast, south of HARE BAY. Discovered and named by Jacques Cartier on his first voyage in 1534. The name is derived from the headland of reddish sandstone. According to D.W. Prowse, the sheltered cove between Cape Rouge and the Conche Peninsula was called by the French 'Carouge,' a corruption of Cap Rouge. Eventually this became anglicized to Crous, and today is spelled 'Crouse.'

Cape St. Charles (Labrador) Southeast of PORT HOPE SIMPSON. First known in the early eighteenth century as 'Cap Charles'; the exact origin has been lost. In 1743 Louis Fornel (1698–1745), a Québec merchant and entrepreneur, anchored 'entre les Iles des terres des Cap Charles.' Possibly because of the prevalence nearby of capes and headlands named for saints, its beatification occurred at the hands of some later cartographer.

Cape St. Francis (Avalon)   At the entrance to CONCEPTION BAY. This name appears to be an English translation of the earlier Portuguese *c de s francisco*. It was listed by John Guy in 1612 as *Cape St Fraunces* and appears as *Cape St Francis* on the Robinson map 'Of the Province of Avalon 1669.'

Cape St. George; St. Georges; St. George's Bay; St. George River (Western)   The cape is at the northwestern point of St.

George's Bay; the town and river are at the head of the bay. On the surface, these names would seem to be undisputably English in origin; however, their evolution is more complex. A small island opposite CAPE CORMORANT and MAINLAND, on the PORT AU PORT PENINSULA, was known to the Basques as 'Isla de San Jorge'; the modern town St. George's was called (possibly in a fit of late-spring 'desperation') Uiycilho or Ulicillo, 'fly hole.' The name Cabo de San Jorge was applied to the cape and later translated into English as the name for the cape, bay, town, and river (Barkham). See also RED ISLAND.

Cape St. John (Central)   At the entrance to NOTRE DAME BAY. The name Sam Joham was first attached by the Portuguese to a feature much farther north (GROAIS ISLAND); it was later translated and transferred by cartographers to the mainland as Cape St. John. In 1884 the Newfoundland government erected a lighthouse on Gull Island, off the tip of Cape St. John.

Cape St. Lewis (Labrador)   At the north entrance to St. Lewis Sound. Described by *The Newfoundland and Labrador Pilot* as 'a promontory rising in precipitous and dark red granite hills to a height of 122 metres.' The precise

origin of the name is in doubt; however, since 'St. Lewis' is not listed in the canon of saints, the name may be a mistaken anglicization of 'Baie St Louis,' which was once the French name for HAMILTON INLET, farther north. The community name, St. Lewis, was applied on 19 June 1981 to the settlement formerly known as 'Fox Harbour.'

Cape St. Mary's (Avalon)   On the east side of PLACENTIA BAY. Known locally as 'the Cape Shore.' The name Cabo de Sancta Marie was first bestowed by the Portuguese, after their patron saint. By the sixteenth century, the French had translated the name to Cap de Saincte Marie, and eventually it was anglicized as Cape St. Mary's. The name has been immortalized in Otto Kelland's hauntingly beautiful song 'Let Me Fish Off Cape St. Mary's.' Because of the cape's strategic location close to the major shipping lanes, a lighthouse was erected in the mid-nineteenth century and became operational on 20 September 1860. Shortly thereafter it was noticed that a nearby sea stack known as 'Bird Rock' had became home to thousands of seabirds, principally gannets. It has been speculated that the gannets relocating here were from the famous colony on Funk Island, off the east coast of Newfoundland. Today, this is the centre-piece of the Cape St. Mary's Ecological Reserve, internationally known as a location to study, not only gannets, but murres, kittiwakes, the razor-billed auk, and other seabirds. See also FUNK ISLAND.

Cape Spear (Avalon)   The most easterly point in North America. The name is derived from the Portuguese *Cauo de la Spera* (Olivieriana 1505–8), which has been translated as 'cape of waiting.' The name Cape of Sper was in popular usage at the time of the visit of John Rut in 1527. In the French version this became *Cap d'espoir* (Alfonse 1541), and still later *c spare*, or *c spear* in English. During the first session of the Newfoundland House of Assembly in 1833, legislation was passed authorizing the erection of a lighthouse at Cape Spear. This may be cited as the major achievement of the session, as the Assembly and Council were deadlocked over the right of the former to pass revenue bills. So acrimonious was the debate that the session was dubbed the 'Bow Wow Parliament,' after a famous cartoon depicting 'the honourable members' as a pack of snarling Newfoundland dogs. The Cape Spear light shone for the first time on 1 September 1836; it is the oldest existing lighthouse in the province. The area is now a National Historic Park.

Cape White Handkerchief (Labrador)   At the entrance to NACHVAK FIORD. The name is descriptive of a large and very conspicuous square of light-coloured rock.

Caplin Cove (Avalon)   There are more than twenty-five Caplin Coves scattered throughout the province. Of the six to be found on the Avalon, Caplin Cove southwest of BAY DE VERDE is cited by way of example. As with the others, it was named for the small deep-water fish *Mallotus villosus*, resembling a smelt. Harold Horwood has described them as 'a seven inch fish, dark green and silver and iridescent, and shaped like slender torpedoes.' Caplin are netted for bait; used for fertilizer; or dried, salted, smoked, or frozen for eating. The migration of the fish from the deep sea to inshore, known as the 'caplin scull,' occurs each year as 'June begins to mellow toward July.'

Cappahayden (Avalon)   South of FERRYLAND. First known as 'Broad Cove'; the name was changed by proclamation 23 December 1913 to honour Cappahayden, in County Kilkenny, Eire. Now part of Renews–Cappahayden. See also RENEWS.

Capstan Island (Labrador) Southwest of RED BAY. Named for some long-lost incident concerning a capstan or windlass, a cylindrical device that stands on the forecastle of a ship and is used for hauling anchors or winding ropes or cables. Since a capstan may also be used on land for hauling up boats, it is logical to assume that this practice may be the origin of the name.

Captain Orlebars Cairn (Avalon) A hill northeast of BAY BULLS. Cairns and stone effigies were often erected by surveyors and others as landmarks. When utilized as place names, they were called cairns, such as 'Merican Man, American Man, and sometimes The Naked Man. The practice was common among American fishermen on the Labrador, which provided an explanation for some of the names. Captain John Orlebar (1810–?) began his career as an assistant to Captain Henry Bayfield (1795–1885), who paid him the following tribute: 'I find that he is well prepared for the duties of an Assistant Surveyor, by education, habits of study and application, and by previous voluntary practice in observations.' Orelebar was later to follow in Bayfield's footsteps as one of the major surveyors of the eastern Canadian coast. In 1877 he was placed in charge of the Newfoundland Survey. See also NAKED MAN HILL and PILLAR ISLAND.

Carbonear (Avalon)   On the western shore of CONCEPTION BAY. The name is of uncertain origin. It may be a variation of Cape Caroeiro on the coast of Portugal, Carboneras in southern Spain, a French family name, or the site of a charcoal industry. There is considerable circumstantial evidence to support the last-noted theory. Included among the early settlers were West Country fishermen and a number of Channel Islanders. Thus, the name may be a corruption of 'Charbonnier,' used on Jersey to denote the location of a charcoal pit. Documents exist indicating that there were such pits on the shore of Conception Bay. As early as 1612, John Guy reported that colonists were 'cutting wood for the collier [charcoal burner], and in coling [preparing charcoal].' Carbonear became a major fishing and shipbuilding centre in the nineteenth century, enjoying much of the same prosperity as nearby HARBOUR GRACE. Incorporated as a town in 1948, it is now a major service centre for the immediate area. See also SADDLE HILL.

Carmanville (Western)   Southwest of MUSGRAVE HARBOUR. The

former name of the community
was Rocky Bay. Renamed by
proclamation on 18 June 1906 for
the Reverend Albert Carman
(1833–1917), who was named
General Superintendent of the
Methodist Church in 1883, serving until 1915. This section of
Newfoundland has strong Methodist roots.

Cartwright (Labrador)   A village
at the entrance to Sandwich Bay.
Named by George Cartwright
(1739/40–1819), entrepreneur and
author. Born at Marnham, Not-
tinghamshire, England, Cartwright saw service in the British
army. He later entered into a partnership with a Bristol firm, Perkins, Coghlan, Cartwright and
Lucas, engaged in the Newfoundland–Labrador trade. In all he
made six voyages to Labrador,
establishing a trading post first at
Cape Charles. Here he carried on
'a cod seal and salmon fishery, a
furring business, and a friendly
and commercial intercourse with
the Eskimo and Indians.' In an
age not noted for its enlightened
attitude towards aboriginal people, Cartwright was an exception. Four years later he moved
farther north, to the location
which he named Cartwright. Fortunately for posterity he kept a
record of his experiences. This
lively, observant, and humane
journal, published in 1911, pro-

vides valuable insight, not only
on Labrador, but on his expeditions to the interior of the island
of Newfoundland. It was the estimate of George Story (1927–1994)
that 'among writings from the
New World a more singular eighteenth century document ... is
hard to find.' See also MOUNT
CAUBVICK.

Castle Hill (Avalon)   North of
Placentia. *See* Placentia.

Castors River (Western)   Flows
west, into ST. JOHN BAY. The place
name is derived from the French
'castor,' for beaver. It is another
reminder of the French presence
on this section of the west coast of
the NORTHERN PENINSULA.

Catalina; Little Catalina (Eastern)
On TRINITY BAY, southeast of
BONAVISTA. The area was visited
by Jacques Cartier and was
already known as 'Havre Sainte-
Katherine.' 'On Thursday the
twenty-first day of May [1534] we
set forth from this harbour with a
west wind, and sailed north, one
quarter northeast of Cape
Bonavista as far as the *Isle of Aves*
[Funk Island].' Obviously, the
harbour was frequented by other
west European fishermen, and
the Spanish form, Cataluña, was
to supersede the French and survive as the modern Catalina and,
to the northeast, Little Catalina.

Cavendish (Avalon)   West of CARBONEAR. First known as 'Shoal Bay,' the community was renamed by proclamation 1 June 1905 for Sir Cavendish Boyle (1849–1916), who served as governor from 1901 to 1904. Boyle is remembered as the author of the anthem 'Ode to Newfoundland':

> When sun rays crown thy pine clad hills,
> And summer spreads her hand,
> When silvern voices tune thy rills,
> We love thee smiling land.
> When blinding storm gusts fret thy shore,
> And wild waves lash thy strand,
> Though spindrift swirl and tempest roar,
> We love thee windswept land.

Centreville (Central)   Southwest of WESLEYVILLE. This community, a twentieth-century creation, is a rarity in Newfoundland, for it dates from 1959 and the resettlement program of the provincial government. Situated offshore are the Fair Islands, once populated by fishermen engaged in the Labrador fishery. With the decline of the latter in the 1950s, many people were resettled on the mainland. Centreville is a locational name.

Change Islands (Central)   West of FOGO ISLAND, NOTRE DAME BAY.

The name applies to a group of islands and to the chief settlement built along the tickle and the causeway that connects the two largest islands. It originates with the practice of local fishermen who lived on the outer islands during the summer, then moved, or 'changed,' to other locations to access wood and shelter during the winter (Handcock). This lifestyle, which lasted well into the twentieth century, is portrayed by Roland W. Abbott in *The Million Dollar Rock: A Brief History of Offer Wadham Island* (St. John's 1994). A native of Change Islands, Arthur Scammell (1903–1995) composed, at age fifteen, one of Newfoundland's most famous songs, 'The Squid Jiggin' Ground.'

Chamberlains (Avalon)   Southwest of ST. JOHN'S; now part of CONCEPTION BAY SOUTH. The name is traced to the Chamberlain family from Gloucestershire, England. It is always spelled as the possessive form.

Champney's Cove (Eastern) On TRINITY BAY. Named for Sir Ralph Champney Williams (1848–1927), who served as governor of Newfoundland from 1909 to 1913. See also WILLIAMSPORT.

Channel–Port aux Basques (Western)   At the tip of the

southwest coast. Formerly two separate communities, their incorporation took place in 1945. Channel is a descriptive for the stretch of water bounded by a string of islands lying close to the land. *Port aux Basques* is found on a 1612 map drawn by Samuel de Champlain. The name may be attributed to the fact that this was the last harbour visited by Basque fishermen before rounding Cap d'Array, or Cape Ray, *en route* to La Cote des Basques. In 1765, Captain James Cook (1728–1779) described Port aux Basques as 'a small snug commodious harbour for fishing vessels.' Today it is the main western port of entry for the province and the terminal for the Marine Atlantic ferry service from NORTH SYDNEY, Nova Scotia.

Chapel Arm; Chapel Cove
(Avalon)   Chapel Arm, situated southwest of BAY ROBERTS, has a nautical origin and refers to a seaman's term, current in the eighteenth century. Chapelling was the turning of a ship in a light breeze, and was caused by the act of a careless helmsman or by a sudden change of wind. The name of Chapel Cove, northeast of HARBOUR MAIN, is attributable to a West Country English family name, either Chappell (Somerset) or Chappelle (Devonshire).

Chapel Cove   *See* Chapel Arm.

Charlottetown (Eastern; Labrador)   South of GLOVERTOWN, and within TERRA NOVA NATIONAL PARK. Originally Brown's Cove, the name was changed to Charlottetown towards the end of the nineteenth century, for an early settler, Charlotte Spracklin. A second Charlottetown is located in Labrador, northeast of PORT HOPE SIMPSON. Formerly known as 'Olds Cove'; the new name was suggested in 1949 by a local resident, Benjamin Powell, after CHARLOTTETOWN, Prince Edward Island. Known locally as 'Uncle Ben,' Powell has written extensively about life in Labrador.

Chateau Bay; Chateau Island
(Labrador)   On the STRAIT OF BELLE ISLE. The location was already known as *baie des Châteaux* to Jacques Cartier, who stopped here during the course of his first voyage in 1534. Chateau Island, at the entrance, with its sheer cliff of vertical columns of basaltic rock, crowned by a flat top resembling the glacis of a castle, provided inspiration for the name. Once considered 'the key to the Labrador fishery,' it was fortified at various times by both France and England.

Chateau Island   *See* Chateau Bay.

Chimney Tickle (Labrador)
Southeast of PORT HOPE SIMPSON.

This narrow strait is sometimes referred to as the 'Hole in the Wall.' The name is descriptive, for the shape of the tickle.

Churchill Falls; Churchill River (Labrador)   The falls were first named 'Grand' by their discoverer in 1838, John MacLean (1797–1890), an employee of the Hudson's Bay Company. Later designated Hamilton Falls and River, for Sir Charles Hamilton (1767–1849), governor of Newfoundland from 1818 to 1824 (see HAMILTON INLET). The river and falls were renamed by Premier Joseph Smallwood (1900–1991) on 4 February 1965. As Smallwood explained: 'I had been to the funeral [of Sir Winston Churchill], Edmund de Rothschild taking me in his car to the lying in state at Westminster. He was deeply affected and so was I. I told him that I thought the least Newfoundland could do was to call our great falls and river after him.' Unfortunately for this spontaneous decision, three points were overlooked: Canada already possessed a Churchill River and confusion would result, as the previous name was one of long-standing usage, and the appropriate bodies (the CPCGN and Newfoundland Nomenclature Board) had not been consulted. After Smallwood made a public announcement, it was too late, and although the change was subse-quently approved by the Newfoundland legislature, an air of controversy surrounded the issue for many years.

Churchill River   *See* Churchill Falls.

Clarenville (Eastern)   On the Northwest Arm of TRINITY BAY. The name was adopted about 1900 for the amalgamated settlements of Lower Shoal Harbour, Dark Hole, Brook Cove, and Red Beach. After Clarence Whiteway, son of Sir William Whiteway (1828–1908), who served as prime minister of Newfoundland in 1878–85, 1889–94, and 1895–7. The community was first known as 'Clarenceville' and was later shortened to Clarenville. Incorporated as a town in 1951.

Cochrane Pond (Avalon)   South of WINDSOR LAKE. Named for Sir Thomas Cochrane (1789–1872), who was governor of Newfoundland from 1825 to 1824. He was described by historian and jurist Daniel Prowse (1834– 1914) as 'universally admitted to have been the best governor ever sent to Newfoundland.'

Codner (Avalon)   Southwest of ST. JOHN'S. The community was first listed as *Middle Bight* in census records. The new name was proclaimed 18 June 1906, in honour of Samuel Codner (1806–1858), founder, in 1823, of the Newfoundland School Society. He was a wealthy Devonshire merchant and summer resident of St. John's. In 1820, while *en route* home to England, he narrowly escaped shipwreck. In thanksgiving for his rescue, Codner vowed to devote his time and resources to assisting the poor through the establishment of schools. Codner is now part of CONCEPTION BAY SOUTH.

Codroy; Codroy Valley (Western) The name Codroy is applied to an island, pond, river, provincial park, valley, and settlement in the area south–southeast of the ANGUILLE MOUNTAINS. The name is a contraction of Cap de Ray, pronounced and spelled as one word, 'Cadarri' (see CAPE RAY). Over time several variations of the word emerged, until the Captain Cook survey of 1765. On his maps and charts he used *Cod Roy*, and Codroy it has remained. The valley was settled first by Mi'kmaq from Nova Scotia, followed by Acadians fleeing the expulsion of 1755, and finally by an influx of second- and third-generation Scots Canadians drawn largely from the MARGAREE VALLEY in INVERNESS COUNTY, Cape Breton. They were attracted to this region because its potential for farming, and the salmon fishery, reminded them of their former homes on the Margaree. This demographic mix has contributed, along with its natural resources and superb scenery, to make the Codroy Valley a distinctive region of Newfoundland.

Codroy Valley   *See* Codroy.

Coleys Point (Avalon)   South of BAY ROBERTS. It would appear that this place name evolved linguistically from an early descriptive, Coldeast Point, or as it was sometimes rendered *Cole Lees Point*. The area is noteworthy as the birthplace of author Edward Russell (1904–1977) and playwright David French. Russell is best known for his *Chronicles of Uncle Mose*, first heard on CBC Radio. They provide a vivid and humorous account of life in outport Newfoundland. French's trilogy of plays – *Leaving Home, Of the Fields, Lately*, and *Salt-Water Moon* – focuses on the generational conflict within the fictional Mercer family. Along the way, this family became 'uprooted and transplanted Newfoundlanders,' as have so many others, including the playwright. Although French's plays contribute greatly to an understanding of the Newfoundland psyche, they go far beyond. As drama critic Urjo Kareda explained: 'Because he does not lie, David French has found a way to speak to all Canadians.'

Colinet; Colinet Passage; Colinet River; Great Colinet Island; Little Colinet Island (Avalon)   The village on Highway 91, east of PLACENTIA. The name may be a variation of the French family name Colenet. An André Colenet was master of the French vessel *Le Montoran*, active in Newfoundland waters in the 1760s. It may also be a corruption of 'La Collinette,' on the island of Sark in the Channel Islands, a theory given credence by the Channel Island presence in the region. The names Great Colinet Island, Little Colinet Island, Colinet Passage, and Colinet River are all from the same source.

Colinet Passage   *See* Colinet.

Colinet River   *See* Colinet.

Colliers; Colliers Bay; Colliers Point; Colliers River (Avalon) The village is southeast of BAY ROBERTS. There is a possibility that the name might be traced to a 'collier' or charcoal burner (see CARBONEAR). In this instance, it is more likely after the common English surname, and, as with CHAMBERLAINS, the possessive form is always used. The name is repeated in a bay, point, and river.

Colliers Bay   *See* Colliers.

Colliers Point   *See* Colliers.

Colliers River   *See* Colliers.

Come By Chance (Avalon)   At the head of PLACENTIA BAY. First designated as *Passage Harbour* by John Guy in 1612. It also rated an important mention in William Taverner's survey of 1714–15. His entry for 9 July 1714 reads: 'Fair wind and good weather, we sail'd for the bay of Carinole, which the English call Come By Chance. At the bottom of this Bay, the French in the late Warr did frequently haul boats overland to Bay Bulls [Sunnyside] in Trinity Bay, with which boats they plundred [*sic*] the English at Hearts Content, New Perlican, Scily Cove, Hans harbour, Old Perlican, Trinity, Bonavista and several other places. Its about two miles over. What plunder they gott of the English they often carried it overland, from Bay of Bulls, to come by Chance and from thence to Placentia.' W. Gordon Handcock is of the opinion that 'there is an implicit explanation here which derives from the use of the harbour by the French. It includes the factor of surprise [come by chance].' Further, '*Carinole* may be derived from the French *carriole*, meaning, carry all, a reference to the use of boats being dragged overland loaded with plunder.' The English spelling was firmly rooted by the eighteenth century and is used by both Captain James Cook (1728–1779) and Michael Lane (?–d. 1794 or '95). Archdeacon Edward Wix (1802–1866) refers to Come by Chance River in 1835. The town made the headlines in the 1970s when it was selected as the site for a deep-water oil terminal and oil refinery. The refinery went into receivership in 1976 and reopened again in 1987. See also CHANCE HARBOUR, New Brunswick.

Conception Bay; Conception Bay South; Conception Harbour (Avalon)   The name is probably from the Portuguese *B de Comceica* or *B de Concicao* (Bay of Conception) and was bestowed for the Feast of the Conception, 8 December. It appears as *Consumption Bay* on some seventeenth-century maps, giving rise to the suggestion that it was named on 15 August, Assumption Day. Evidence favours the first theory, and the name Consumption Bay possibly resulted from cartographic guesswork or poor penmanship, or both. The town of Conception Bay South is an amalgamation of nine communities on the southeast shore of Conception Bay. In 1980 TOPSAIL, CHAMBERLAINS, CODNER, Long Pond, MANUELS, KELLI-

GREWS, Upper Gullies, Indian Pond, and Seal Cove became a single municipal unit.

Conception Bay South   *See* Conception Bay.

Conception Harbour   *See* Conception Bay.

Conche (Western)   Northeast of ENGLEE. Probably named for the Abbey of Conches in Normandy; the local tradition that it is named for the conch shell, commonly found in the Caribbean, is highly unlikely. William Francis Ganong has suggested that Conche may be 'an early French descriptive which seems to have escaped the dictionaries, but may be an equivalence with the English "bight" or "road" in its navigational sense.'

Conne River (Central)   South of HEAD OF BAY D'ESPOIR. In the late eighteenth century, the name *rivière le con* was assigned to this feature by Captain James Cook (1728–1779). Over time the designation was anglicized as 'Conne River.' It is today the site of the only Mi'kmaq community in Newfoundland, although there has been a Mi'kmaq presence at Conne River since at least the visit of Archdeacon Edward Wix (1802–1866) in 1835. He noted in his journal finding 'the wigwams of two Indian families.'

Cooks Cove (Western)   In Humber Arm; **Cooks Cove** (Avalon) North of old PERLICAN, in TRINITY BAY; **Cooks Harbour** (Western)   a settlement on the STRAIT OF BELLE ISLE. These place names commemorate the career of Captain James Cook (1728–1779), whose charts and observations of the coast of Newfoundland add greatly to an understanding of its topography and toponymy during the late eighteenth century. Cooks Cove in Humber Arm lies in the BAY OF ISLANDS, where, in 1767, he completed a detailed coastal survey supplemented by a five-day exploratory mission to DEER LAKE. At Skerwink Head, Cooks Cove, on Trinity Bay, he took observations during a 1762 survey of Trinity Harbour. Not to be overlooked is Cook's personal contribution to the nomenclature of the province. Wherever possible he used designations already in existence; otherwise he bestowed names in the traditional manner: for similar features in England, royalty, politicians, admirals, naval commanders, and ships in the Royal Navy. A number of Newfoundland place names were to be repeated during later surveys in the South Pacific. Some New Zealand examples are Bay of Islands, Port Saunders, Cape Palliser, and Hawke Bay.

Cook's sense of humour was also evident in his place-naming, as witnessed by NAMELESS COVE, Newfoundland, and Doubtless Bay, New Zealand. Captain James Cook is further recognized by a National Historic Site monument on Crow Hill, overlooking Humber Arm, an area which he visited in 1767. However, the best testimonial to his work came from the pen of Captain Henry Bayfield (1795–1885), who was to resurvey many of the same areas. Repeatedly throughout the Bayfield journals, the accuracy of Cook's soundings, observations, and survey work is noted. *A General Chart of the Island of Newfoundland with rocks and soundings*, drawn by Cook and his assistant Michael Lane, was published in London in 1775. This remarkable feat of cartography was the first to depict an accurate outline of the island.

Cooks Harbour   *See* Cooks Cove.

Cooks Lookout (Eastern)   Adjacent to BURIN. During the course of Captain James Cook's survey of the south coast of Newfoundland in 1765–66, he established a 'lookout' on this hill which bears his name. See also NAKED MAN HILL.

Cormack; Cormack Trail (Western)   Born in ST. JOHN'S, and educated in Scotland, William Eppes Cormack (1796–1868) was the first 'European' (his wording) to cross Newfoundland on foot, travelling from TRINITY BAY to ST. GEORGE'S BAY, and noting the natural and geological resources along the way. The overland trek began on 5 September 1822 and concluded with his arrival at St. George's Bay on 6 November 1822. Later, in 1856, Cormack published a narrative of his travels. A classic in travel literature, over a century later it is still a 'good read.' In describing the previously unexplored interior, he wrote: 'The eye strides over a succession of northerly and southerly ranges of green plains, marbled with woods and lakes of every form and extent, a picture of all the luxurious scenes of national cultivation, receding into invisibleness ... There was no will but ours.' Once characterized as a 'rover by nature' Cormack had an extraordinary career, which included, in addition to exploration in Newfoundland, settlement schemes in Prince Edward Island (see NEW GLASGOW) and in British Columbia, where he died in 1868. In the 1830s and 1840s he was involved in a variety of ventures in Australia, New Zealand, and California. Cormack's other major contribution, which placed him generations ahead of his contemporaries, was an appreciation of

and affinity with the Mi'kmaq and Beothuk people. He was accompanied on his trans-Newfoundland trek by a Mi'kmaq, Joseph Sylvester, and on 2 October 1827 he founded the Beothic Institution in the hope of opening communication with the few remaining Beothuks. In 1827, Cormack undertook a second trip into the interior, accompanied by a Canadian Abenaki, a Labrador Montagnais, and a Newfoundland Mi'kmaq. Although this trip and two later forays were unsuccessful in locating Beothuk survivors, Cormack's actions were without precedent in an age noted for antipathy and indifference towards indigenous people. The basic humanity of the man shone through in a love of field sports, fishing, and skating. Late in life Cormack wrote a treatise on skating and could still, at age seventy, 'astonish his friends by graceful evolutions on the ice.' Cormack, located north of DEER LAKE, is a post-1945 community named for the explorer. Its first settlers were veterans of the Second World War. His memory has been further perpetuated by the appropriate designation of the Cormack Trail, a 182-kilometre coastal hike linking Petites, on the south coast, with ST. GEORGE'S, on the west. In 1992 an expedition funded by the Royal Canadian Geographical Society retraced the route taken by Cormack and Sylvester in their 1827 trek (Note: Don Cayo and Ray Fennelly, 'Crossing The Rock,' *Canadian Geographic* 112/3 [May–June], 38–49). See also JAMIESON HILLS, MOUNT CORMACK, MOUNT MISERY, and MOUNT SYLVESTER.

Cormack Trail   *See* Cormack.

Corner Brook (Western)   At the southern head of the Humber Arm. The brook which flows through the city was so named in 1767 by Captain James Cook (1728–1779). For many years it remained a relatively unnoticed settlement, until a sawmill began operations in 1864. A more dramatic change occurred in 1923, when Corner Brook was selected as the site for one of the world's largest pulp-and-paper mills. Today it is Newfoundland's second-largest city, capitalizing on the paper industry and a superb location on a fiord framed by the surrounding hills. The city is noted for its excellent recreational facilities. A major event is the annual winter carnival, which has been described as the largest of its kind in Atlantic Canada (see also MARBLE MOUNTAIN). Corner Brook has become the major commercial and distributing centre for western Newfoundland. Sir Wilfred Grenfell College, an affiliate of Memorial University, was established here in 1975. Included within the city, incorporated in 1956, are the former communities of Curling, Corner Brook West, and East and West Townsite. Curling, once known as Birchy Cove, changed its name to honour the Reverend Joseph J. Curling (1844–1906), an Anglican clergyman who once served in the area.

Cottles Island   *See* Cottrells Cove.

Cottlesville   *See* Cottrells Cove.

Cottrells Cove (Central)   On South Arm, NOTRE DAME BAY. This community has been variously known as 'Cottle Cove,' 'Cuttrell Cove,' and 'Cottrell Cove.' The name may be derived from *cotterall*, or *cottle*, a notched metal bar hung in a fireplace. The names Cottlesville and Cottles Island, NEW WORLD ISLAND, appear to have the same origin.

Cow Head (Western)   A peninsula north of St. Pauls Inlet. On Tuesday, 16 June 1534, Jacques Cartier, sailing 'through fog and thick weather' on the west coast of Newfoundland, spotted 'a break in the coast line, like the mouth of a river between the mountains and a cape. This cape is all eaten away at the top, and at the bottom towards the sea is pointed, on which account we named it *Cap Pointe* or Pointed Cape.' This feature is now known as Cow Head, for a boulder, not unlike a cow's head in appearance, which once stood on the southern part of the peninsula.

Coxs Cove (Labrador)   On the eastern shore of Stony Island. Named for the first settlers, George, John, and William Cox, herring and lobster fishermen who arrived on the Labrador coast in the early 1840s. The Cox family was originally from Dorset, England.

Cranky Point (Western)   On the western shore of St. Anthony Bight. Sometimes known as 'Craniky' Point; the name is traceable to an old English nautical term meaning 'liable to turn over or capsize,' the fate of many sailors who experienced difficulty in rounding the point.

Creston (Eastern)   On the BURIN PENINSULA, southwest of MARYS-TOWN. A proclamation dated 22 September 1914 stated: 'That the western section of Mortier Bay, extending from Wests Point to Glendon (including Butlers Cove), be renamed Creston.' This name was deliberately coined and is without a local association. There is no foundation for the suggestion that the mainly

Protestant settlement was once known as 'Christ's Town,' as opposed to nearby Marys-town, which was largely Roman Catholic.

Croque (Western)   South of ST. ANTHONY, on the east coast of the NORTHERN PENINSULA. Once one of the principal stations of the French Petit Nord; the name is descriptive and derived from *Croc*, an old French word for 'boat-hook.' The bay is long, narrow, and curving towards its head – in shape, somewhat like the traditional boat-hook. The first permanent English residents were Patrick Kearney and James Hope, who settled on the bay in the 1850s. This location was later known as 'Kearney Cove.' The present community of Croque was established in 1959, when the people of Kearney Cove moved farther into the bay.

Culls Harbour (Eastern)   Northeast of GLOVERTOWN. Cull is a Newfoundland family name; however, in this instance, the place name is a diminutive of the surname of the first settler, John Culleton, a native of Prince Edward Island. Culleton operated a sawmill in the area around 1900.

Cupids (Avalon)   Southeast of BAY ROBERTS. John Guy (?–*ca* 1629) was appointed governor, and commissioned by the London and Bristol Society to establish a colony in Newfoundland. Guy had earlier visited the island and, in August 1610, selected Cupers's Cove for the new settlement. Over the years it was variously known, in addition, as 'Cupitts Cove,' 'Cuperts Cove,' 'Coopers,' and 'Cubbits Cove'; however, by the early eighteenth century 'Cupids Cove' became the accepted spelling. Although the colony's formal existence lasted only eighteen years, it was not without significance. On 27 March 1613, a son born to Nicholas Guy and his wife was possibly the first English child born in Newfoundland. After six years, John Guy was succeeded as governor by John Mason (1586–1635). In 1616, Mason produced the first English map of Newfoundland. As part of Cupids's tricentennial celebrations in 1910, the Newfoundland Historical Society erected a monument in honour of 'John Guy, first governor of Newfoundland, and master of the Bristol Society of Merchants.'

Curlew Harbour (Labrador) East of Sandwich Bay. Named for the curlew (*Numenius borealis*), a shore bird having a long slender bill that curves downward. The curlew, once common to the Labrador coast, is now rarely seen, if not totally extinct. A fisherman at Independent (north of Huntington Island) reported on their great numbers in the nineteenth century: 'We once saw a flock of curlew which may have been a mile long and nearly as broad; there must have been in this flock four or five thousand. The sum total of their notes sounded at times like the wind whistling through the ropes of a thousand ton vessel; at others, the sound seemed like the jingling of sleigh bells' (Browne). 'Curlew' appears in six other place names on the coast of Labrador.

Curling   *See* Corner Brook.

Cut Throat Harbour; Cut Throat Island (Labrador)   The settlement is on the south shore of Cut Throat Island. This unusual name originates with the 'cut-throater,' the individual in the assembly line which prepared codfish for salting. It has been in use since at least 1794, when seaman Aaron Thomas described 'the process of curing fish,' and noted the various roles of 'Header, Cutt [*sic*] Throat, Carver, Splitter and Salter.' The knife used in the process has been described as 'double bladed, not unlike a stiletto; while the splitter uses a curved knife.'

Cut Throat Island   *See* Cut Throat Harbour.

Daniel's Harbour (Western)
On Highway 430, north of PORT-
LAND CREEK. It may be after Captain Charles Daniel (?–1661), sea
captain and member of the
Compagnie des Cent-Associés,
who were trading in the GULF OF
ST. LAWRENCE during the mid-
seventeenth century. Since Captain Daniel may not have pene-
trated this far north, the local
tradition that it was named for
Daniel Regan, who reputedly
sought refuge in the harbour
during the 1820s, has plausi-
bility.

Davidsville (Central)   On GAN-
DER BAY; previously known as
Mann Point. See also MAIN POINT–
DAVIDSVILLE.

Davis Inlet (Labrador)
Northwest of HOPEDALE; named
for John Davis (1550?–1605). During the course of three voyages
(1585–7), Davis explored the
shores of present-day Davis
Strait, Cumberland Gulf, and Baffin Bay. In addition he reconnoitred the coast of Labrador as far
south as HAMILTON INLET.
Although unsuccesssful in his
quest for a northwest passage,
Davis remains one of the most
important of the early Arctic
explorers. Prior to its establishment in 1926, the community was
known by its Inuit name Utshi-
massit, which translates as 'store-

keeper's place.' See Also CAPE
CHIDLEY.

Deep Bight (Eastern)   On Northwest Arm, south of CLARENVILLE.
The name, which literally means
'deep water,' is a descriptive for
an indentation in the shoreline of
the arm. This lumbering community was settled in the mid-
nineteenth century.

Deer Lake (Western)   The town,
situated at the northern head of
Deer Lake, is named for the lake,
which great herds of caribou once
swam across during the course of
their annual migration. Although
the southern end was visited by
Captain James Cook (1728–1779)
in September 1767, settlement of
the townsite did not take place
until the 1860s. By 1867 it was
known as 'Nicholsville,' for the
first settler, George Nichols. In
1923 Deer Lake was selected as
the site for a power plant to supply electricity for the pulp-and-
paper mill at CORNER BROOK. The
completion of the Trans-Canada
Highway and the Viking Trail to
the NORTHERN PENINSULA, along
with the opening of an airport in
1957, have made the town a major
distribution centre for western
and northern Newfoundland. The
town was incorporated in 1950.

Devils Dancing Table (Central);
Devils Dining Table (Labrador);

Devils Dressing Table (Avalon);
Devils Stairway (Avalon)   The
'devil' or 'le diable' occurs in
numerous place names in Newfoundland and Labrador. Devils
Dancing Table is a hill on the
western shore of North Bay, BAY
D'ESPOIR; Devils Dining Table is
a precipitous basaltic cliff on
Henley Island, in CHATEAU BAY;
and Devils Dressing Table is a
marsh on the AVALON PENINSULA.
The first two have a physical
resemblance to a gigantic table;
the third is waiting to lure the
unwary into its boggy depths.
The Devils Stairway is a rock formation at CAPE BROYLE, where
Satan reputedly left his footprints
in the face of the cliff. In 1909 the
Reverend Patrick W. Browne
(1864–1937) climbed the Devils
Dining Table and reported: 'As
the afternoon waned, the atmosphere became hazy ... whether
his Satanic Majesty was concerned in the transformation we
do not say; but as the sun went
down in a blaze of glory, the
mountains and rocks seemed to
dwarf; an indescribable tint
o'erspread the landscape, and a
brownish mist came in from the
sea and settled over the hills giving them a sinister appearance.'
See also JOBS COVE.

Devils Dining Table   *See* Devils
Dancing Table.

Devils Dressing Table   *See* Devils Dancing Table.

Devils Stairway   *See* Devils
Dancing Table.

**Dildo; Dildo Arm; Dildo Cove;
Dildo Island; Dildo Pond**   The
village is west of BAY ROBERTS.
This place name was first
applied to Dildoe (Dildo Island)
and dates from at least 1711. It
was also recorded in the survey
of Michael Lane in 1775. The
name is of obscure origin, and a
number of theories have been
advanced to explain its meaning.
The *Oxford English Dictionary* provides several definitions. It may
be 'a word of obscure origin,
used in the refrain of ballads; a
cylindrical glass; a tree or shrub
of the genus *Cereus,* as the Dildo-
tree; or the name of a penis or
phallus substitute.' Both Captain
James Cook (1728–1779) and his
assistant Michael Lane, who succeeded him, had a keen sense of
humour and were not above
enshrining descriptive names
that might offend the overly sen-
sitive. While the precise origin of
this place name is lost, some comfort can be found in the fact that a
number of twentieth-century
campaigns 'to expurgate' the
name have failed. The colourful
nomenclature of the eighteenth
century stands on its own
merits.

Dildo Arm   *See* Dildo.

Dildo Cove   *See* Dildo.

Dildo Island   *See* Dildo.

Dildo Pond   *See* Dildo.

Doting Cove (Labrador)   At the mouth of HAMILTON SOUND. The name is derived from 'doater,' an obsolete spelling of a word which meant 'an old seal.' In Captain George Cartwright's 1792 journal he noted: 'After breakfast, I went up the river again; looked at the traps ... and killed a doater with my rifle.' The word is now spelled 'dotter' or 'doting.'

Dover (Central)   On Freshwater Bay. The former name of this community was Shoal Bay. Since more than 100 other locations in the province incorporate the word 'shoal,' confusion abounded, and the name was changed to Wellington, for Arthur Wellesley, first Duke of Wellington (1769–1852). After 1949 it was noted that the latter was a common place name within Canada, and the post office was named Dover. The new name was undoubtedly suggested by Dover, England, and was not in use elsewhere in the province. However, the dual names led to additional problems. After considering a new name, Port Charles, the matter was set-

tled in 1973 with the approval by the Newfoundland Nomenclature Board of 'Dover' as the community name.

Dunfield (Eastern)   South of TRINITY, on TRINITY BAY. Formerly known as 'Cuckolds Cove.' The name was changed to Dunfield, after the Reverend Henry Dunfield, an Anglican clergyman.

Dunville (Avalon)   Northeast of PLACENTIA. Possibly traceable to the River Dun, in Eire, or after the surname of one of the first settlers, Dun or Dunn.

Durrell (Central)   On the north shore of TWILLINGATE ISLAND. The present community is an amalgamation of Durrells Arm, Harts Cove, Jenkins Cove, Gillesport, and BLOW ME DOWN. For a time, Durrells Arm and Gilliesport were known as 'Grand River.' The name Durrell is probably that of an early settler.

Eastern Meelpaeg Lake   *See* Meelpaeg Lake.

Eastport; Eastport Peninsula (Eastern)   On SALVAGE BAY, and formerly known as such. The descriptive name for this village stems from its location on the east side of Salvage Bay. It was renamed by an amendment to the Newfoundland Post Office Act of

1915. Along with GLOVERTOWN, Eastport has evolved as a service centre for nearby TERRA NOVA NATIONAL PARK.

Eastport Peninsula   *See* Eastport.

East St. Modeste   *See* West St. Modeste.

Eclipse Harbour (Labrador) South of CAPE CHIDLEY; **Eclipse Island** (Central)   South of BURGEO. Eclipse Island was named by Captain James Cook (1728–1779) as the location where he witnessed an eclipse of the sun on 5 August 1776. Subsequently he presented a paper on his observations to the Royal Society of the Arts. This helped establish his reputation as an astronomer and mathematician. Eclipse Harbour, Labrador, was named by a United States Coast Survey team which went north to observe another eclipse of the sun, on 18 July 1880.

Eclipse Island   *See* Eclipse Harbour.

Elliston (Eastern)   Southeast of BONAVISTA. Formerly Bird Island Cove. The name was changed in 1892 to honour the Reverend William Ellis (1780–1837), who is credited with conducting the first Methodist service in the community, in 1812.

Emily Harbour (Labrador) Southeast of HOLTON. Named for Emily Warren, wife of an early settler, whose remains were interred in nearby Reynolds Cove.

Englee (Western)   On CANADA BAY, at the end of Highway 433. The name is a corruption of the French *anglais*, and as such serves to underscore the conflict between the French and English for control of the fishery in the Petit Nord (see chapter 1, pages 17–18). By the Treaty of Utrecht in 1713, the French had gained the right to use the coast from CAPE BONAVISTA to POINTE RICHE for fishing, but not for settlement. Between Bonavista and TWILLINGATE, the coast was effectively occupied and controlled by the English. However, north of Twillingate, the French summer fishery held sway, and the English were considered intruders. The matter was not to be finally settled until the Anglo-French Convention of 1904.

Epaves Bay (Western)   Off L'ANSE AUX MEADOWS, and forming the eastern end of SACRED BAY. The name, dating from the French migratory fishery in the STRAIT OF BELLE ISLE, translates as 'Shipwreck Bay.'

Epworth (Eastern)   Southwest of BURIN. The community was first known by the descriptive Spoon Cove, as it resembled the handle and ladle of a spoon. It was renamed for Epworth, Lincolnshire, England. The rectory at Epworth was once the home of John Wesley (1703–1791).

Esker (Labrador)   Northeast of LABRADOR CITY, on the Québec North Shore and Labrador Railroad line. Named for the geological feature, a winding ridge of sand and gravel thought to have been deposited by the retreating glaciers of the Ice Age. See also WABUSH.

Exploits River (Central)   Begins at the northeast outlet of RED INDIAN LAKE and flows into the Bay of Exploits, on NOTRE DAME BAY. At 264 kilometres, it is the longest river on the island of Newfoundland. The name is of unknown origin and was in use at the time of the Cook survey of 1774. For a detailed account of the toponymy of this area see W. Gordon Handcock, 'The View from Mount Janus: John Cartwright's 1768 Exploits River Toponymy,' *Canoma* 14/1 (July 1988), 6–11.

Fair Haven (Avalon)   On the Eastern Channel of PLACENTIA BAY. Originally known as 'Famish Gut,' it was probably a companion name for PINCHGUT POINT, which lies to the north. In all probability

both names were applied by Michael Lane in the 1770s as a joke, during a period when his survey crew were experiencing a shortage of rations. Famish Gut was later bowdlerized or expurgated to Famish Cove, and eventually, by proclamation of 29 June 1940, it became the harmless and banal Fair Haven. In addition to this location, the name Pinchgut was to be repeated at least a dozen times, in all parts of the province, from Pinchgut Bank, on the Labrador, to Pinchgut Tickle, on ST. MARY'S BAY.

Falaise Point (Western)   On the north coast of HARE BAY and again on the east shore of PISTOLET BAY. From the French *falaise*, for 'cliff.' It may have been inspired by the town of Falaise, south of Caen in Normandy. Both Newfoundland locations were frequented by Norman sailors and fishermen.

Father Duffys Well Provincial Park (Avalon)   On Highway 90, between Salmonier and HOLYROOD. The park is named for the Reverend James Duffy (*ca* 1797–1860), once parish priest at ST. MARY'S. During construction of a new church, he became embroiled in an argument over its location with a local merchant, John Hill Martin. However, the church was built where Father Duffy wanted it. In retaliation, Martin erected a fish flake or platform blocking the church entrance. Thereupon, Duffy ordered his parishioners to tear down the flake. The matter went to court, and Duffy reputedly discovered a well of clear spring water on one of his many treks to ST. JOHN'S for court appearances. Eventually, Father Duffy was acquitted of 'inciting to riot,' and this provincial park remains as his memorial.

Fermeuse (Avalon)   Southwest of FERRYLAND. Of probable Portuguese origin, the name appears as *R formoso*, 'beautiful river,' on the Reinal map of 1519. A century later, Champlain renders it as *C Frinouse*. By the end of the seventeenth century, the English spelling had stabilized as 'Fermeuse.' During the early 1600s, Fermeuse was part of the Sir William Vaughan settlement scheme. See also RENEWS.

Ferolle Point (Western)   Northwest of BARTLETTS HARBOUR. The original name, Amuix or Aumixco Punta, was imposed by the Basques and may be traced to Amuix, an island near the border of Spain and France. Selma Barkham explains the transition to Ferolle Point, after Ferrol, a town and naval station in northwestern Spain. 'Since Amuix was hard to pronounce for non-Basques, the harbour of Old Ferolle, or *Ferrol Çaraharra*, gradually became the dominant place name for the area, effacing the term *Amuix*, and replacing it with New Ferolle and Ferolle Point.' She concludes that the location 'must have reminded Basque sailors of the port in Galacia [Ferrol] where they went each year for the winter whaling season.'

Ferryland (Avalon)   South of CAPE BROYLE. The name appears as *Farilham* or *Port Farilhao* (1529 Portuguese), *Forillon* (1547 French), and *Ferriland* (1627 English). In the Michael Lane survey of 1773, the spelling is 'Ferryland.' Thus the contemporary name is undoubtedly a distillation of all these early sources. In the beginning, it was probably a descriptive, traceable to the Portuguese *Farelho*, for 'steep rock' or 'reef.' Aaron Thomas visited Ferryland in 1794 and left this description: 'It is a considerable settlement. Near two hundred Houses and Hutts constitute the place. Here are some good stores and much trade is carry'd on in fish. There is a harbour of difficult access; before it lyes Ferryland Head and the Isle of Boise.' See also ISLE AUX BOIS.

Fischot Island (Western)   Southeast of HARE BAY. Of uncertain origin; however, it may be for the

French surname Fichot. The settlement is known as Fischot Island.

Flat Rock (Avalon)   Northeast of TORBAY, on Highway 20. The settlement dates from at least 1689. The name is descriptive as Joseph Jukes (1811–1869) explains: 'Along the south side of this little cove, the thick red sandstone dips at a slight angle towards the sea, forming a long, smooth, sloping pavement, whence the name of the place.' It is also the location of Flat Rocks Grotto, a shrine dedicated to Our Lady of Lourdes.

Fleur de Lys (Central)   The most northerly village on the BAIE VERTE PENINSULA. The name is descriptive for a striking rock formation 249 metres high. Three hummocks on the cliff are said to resemble a fleur-de-lis. The name is a very old one, appearing as *Flower de Luce* on the Fitzhugh chart of 1693. As late as the 1871 it was still being described in *Lowell's Directory* as '*Flower de Luce* a fishing station on the French Shore with a fine harbour.'

Flowers Cove (Western)   North of ST. BARBE BAY. It has been suggested that, in view of the local topography, 'the name is a misfit,' or at best 'an attractive name bestowed to lure settlers.' However, in this instance, the reference is not to flowers. The area was first known as 'French Island Harbour.' In 1764 this coast was charted by Captain James Cook (1728–1779), who bestowed the names 'Flour Cove,' for the breakers flowing shoreward, and 'Flour Ledge,' for a rock formation offshore. Both names may be traced to an old English meaning for the word *flour*: 'a scum caused by the action of breakers on the shore.' Before the completion of the west-coast highway, Flowers Cove was accessible only by sea. The extreme isolation of the community led to the establishment in 1920 of a nursing station and clinic by the Grenfell Mission. Thereafter, those in need of medical attention no longer had to cross the STRAIT OF BELLE ISLE to FORTEAU.

Fogo; Fogo Island (Central) Fogo Island, the largest of Newfoundland's offshore islands, is located to the east of NEW WORLD and Change islands. The name, of Portuguese origin, is first listed as *y do fogo*, 'of the fire,' in the so-called Miller I Atlas by Jorge Reinel (1516–22). This may well be an early reference to a forest fire. The island is surrounded by the shallow Fogo Shelf, attractive to cod, salmon, and other species of fish. Thus the area was well known to European fishermen from the early 1500s onward. By the eighteenth century, West Country mercantile interests were established at Fogo Harbour (now Fogo). For Fogo Brandies, see BRANDIES.

Fogo Island   *See* Fogo.

Forbes Sound   *See* Grenfell Sound.

Fore Topsail   *See* the Topsails.

Forteau; Forteau Bay (Labrador) The village is southwest of RED BAY. The name originated with the early French navigators and is descriptive of the 'strong ' tides characteristic of the area. These have been noted as 'very irregular, occasionally running in one direction at the rate of five knots close to the shore, and in the opposite direction a short distance off. Sometimes three distinct streams are met within a distance of two miles; and the tide rips are of considerable strength' (Browne). The eighteenth- and nineteenth-century fishery at Forteau Bay was carried on largely by a group of merchants from Jersey, Boutillier, DeQuetteville Bros., and Dehaume being the principal firms represented.

Forteau Bay   *See* Forteau.

Fortune; Fortune Bay (Eastern) West of the BURIN PENINSULA. The name stems from the Portuguese *Fortuna,* or 'luck,' and may refer to a now-unknown incident in the seafaring history of Newfoundland. Because of its proximity to the Grand Banks, fishermen from Portugal, France, and England frequented the area from the 1500s onward. In 1765 Captain James Cook (1728–1779) reported that 'Fortune Village was sited behind a barrasway like that of Grand Bank with very near as many inhabitants.' Today a regular ferry sevice operates between Fortune and Saint Pierre, 50 kilometres away. See BAY FORTUNE, Prince Edward Island.

Fortune Bay   *See* Fortune.

Fourche Harbour (Western) Northeast of HARBOUR DEEP. This descriptive name was imposed by French migratory fishermen and may be traced to *fourchu,* for 'forked.' It appears as *Fourchée* on the Bellin map of 1744. See also FOURCHU and CAPE FORCHU, Nova Scotia.

Foxtrap (Avalon)   Now part of the town of CONCEPTION BAY SOUTH. A local tradition suggests that Foxtrap was so called because 'the settlement grew up in a previously unnamed district where only foxes were caught in rabbit snares' (Seary). During the construction of the Newfoundland Railway, in 1880, the community achieved notoriety for the so-called Battle of Foxtrap. According to the press, rumours were spread by those opposed to the railway that 'farmers would be dispossessed of their lands,' '... the Queen planned to give up the country to Canada,' and further that 'a toll gate was to be erected on the road from Conception Bay to St John's to force people to travel by rail.' When the survey crews reached Foxtrap, towards the end of July 1880, they were met by 'a noisy mob, armed with sticks and sealing guns, and women whose aprons were filled with stones.' After five days the constabulary managed to restore order; the rumours were quelled, and construction of the railway went forward (*Morning Chronicle*, 29 July 1880).

French Shore   *See* chapter 1, pages 17–18.

Freshwater (Avalon)   A common descriptive place name in Newfoundland. Examples on the AVALON PENINSULA include two villages, one northeast of CARBONEAR and the other northwest of PLACENTIA. The latter is a relatively new town, established because of relocation caused by the construction of the Argentia

military base during the Second World War. The name undoubtedly refers to the search by fishermen and settlers for fresh water.

Funk Island (Central)   Northeast of CAPE FOGO. This isolated island has long attracted attention. On 21 May 1534, Jacques Cartier spotted 'the isle of aves': 'Our two longboats were sent off to the island to procure some of the birds, whose numbers are so great as to be incredible, unless one has seen them; for although the island is about a league in circumference, it is so exceeding full of birds that one would think they had been stowed there. ' Similar experiences were later reported by Captain George Cartwright (1739/40–1819) and seaman Aaron Thomas, both of whom visited the island in the 1790s. The bird called 'l'apponat' by Cartier was the Great Auk (*Platus impennis*), extinct since 1844. According to Thomas: 'The islands are called the Funks or Stinking Islands from the quantity of Dung which the Birds occasion which in warm weather sends forth a terrible stench.' Despite Thomas's firsthand account, present scholarship suggests that the name may be traced to a Norse or Icelandic word for 'small haycock,' which the island is said to resemble.

Gaff Topsail *See* The Topsails.

Gambo (Central) Northeast of
GLOVERTOWN. On 3 October 1980,
the communities of Dark Cove,
Middle Cove, and Gambo were
amalgamated to form the town of
Gambo. The precise origin of the
name remains uncertain. The
most plausible theory would suggest that it is a corruption of the
Portuguese Baie de las Gamas, or
'bay of the does,' although some
sources attribute it to 'gambo,'
a type of sled. One of the first
settlers was David Smallwood
(1839–1928), who moved to
Newfoundland from SOUTHPORT,
Prince Edward Island, in 1860
and established a sawmill at
Gambo in 1863. His grandson, J.R.
'Joey' Smallwood (1900–1991),
was to become chief architect
of Newfoundland's entry into
Confederation and long-time
(1947–72) premier of the province.
Although both revered and
reviled during his lifetime, few
politicians have had a greater
impact on their province than 'the
little fellow from Gambo.' Plans
are under way to honour the community's most famous son by the
erection of a monument to J.R.
Smallwood's memory on a hill
overlooking the town.

**Gander; Gander Bay; Gander
Lake; Gander River** (Central)
The town and major international airport are on the Trans-
Canada Highway, adjacent to
Gander Lake. The name, which
appears on a map of Gander Bay
by John Cartwright (1767), is for
the male of the goose family. In
1935, Gander was selected by the
British and Canadian governments as a site for an airport to
handle the growing transatlantic
air traffic. By the outbreak of the
Second World War, the base was
operational and played a pivotal
role in anti-submarine warfare
and the defence of the North
Atlantic. In an age of jet travel,
the airport is not as important as
formerly; however, because of its
relatively 'fog free' status and
strategic location, it remains an
important link in international air
travel and communication. East
of Gander, on Highway 1, are two
reminders of tragedies associated
with the air base. In the Commonwealth War Graves Commission
cemetery, the service personnel
lost in the line of duty in the Second World War lie buried. Three
kilometres farther along is Peace-
keeper Park, with its Silent Witness Memorial in remembrance of
the 259 members of the U.S. 101st
Airborne Regiment who lost
their lives in a 1985 plane crash.
En route home following peacekeeping duties in the Middle East,
their aircraft mysteriously
crashed shortly after take-off
from Gander. The main Gander

River, 44 kilometres long, begins at the north side of the lake, and enters the Atlantic at Gander Bay. The Northwest Gander flows 97 kilometres into the west end of the lake, where it is joined by the 77-kilometre-long Southwest Gander River. Both branches are popular with sports enthusiasts for canoeing, hunting, salmon and trout fishing, and the observation of wildlife.

Gander Bay   *See* Gander.

Gander Lake   *See* Gander.

Gander River   *See* Gander.

Garden Cove (Eastern)   On PLACENTIA BAY, southeast of Swift Current. In Newfoundland, where arable land is at a premium, the word 'garden' takes on special significance. In place names it indicates, as in this instance, a long-time site of cultivation and seasonal habitation. Still today in many parts of the province, and most notably on the NORTHERN PENINSULA, well-tended garden plots, principally for root crops, are found along newer highways. They are so sited to capitalize on the soil upturned by road construction. See also SWIFT CURRENT.

Gargamelle (Western)   Northwest of PORT SAUNDERS. Garga-

melle (French for 'throat') was the mother of Gargantua, the giant who is the central character of Rabelais's great sixteenth-century satire *Gargantua and Pantagruel*. How the name came to be applied to this cove is uncertain; however, it may be a French or Basque designation.

Garnish; Garnish River; Garnish Tolt; Great Garnish Barrasway (Eastern)   The fishing settlement is northwest of MARYSTOWN. The name is found on the Cook survey, and thus probably predates 1765. It also appears in Great Garnish Barrasway (see BARACHOIS) and Garnish Tolt. The word 'tolt,' still in common usage, refers to an isolated rounded hill. The Garnish River is an important salmon stream.

Garnish River   *See* Garnish.

Garnish Tolt   *See* Garnish.

Gaskiers (Avalon)   Southwest of Point La Haye. Over the years two names, Gascoigne and Gaskiers, have been applied to this community. The latter, in use consistently in recent years, is the most favoured. Early spellings were 'Castries Bay,' 'Gastries Bay,' 'Gasters,' and 'Gastries.' There are two possible theories as to origin. Gaskiers may originate with Gasquié, a variant of

Gasquet, the French surname. Alternatively, it may stem from the Marquis de Castries (1727–1801), who, as French minister of marine, was involved with the reoccupation of nearby St. Pierre and Miquelon. The interchange of an initial letter is not unusual in place names. See BURGEO, which was once Virgeo.

Gaultois Central)   Northwest of HARBOUR BRETON. The name is descriptive and is taken from the Norman French *galtas*, meaning 'pinnacle,' or 'dormer.' The present spelling dates from the Cook survey of 1764. The Newman Company, employing fishermen from Jersey, once operated a factory for the processing of whale oil at Gaultois. See NEWMAN SOUND for other ventures of this firm.

Glenwood (Central)   Northwest of GANDER. Dates from the 1890s, and is named for the Glenwood Lumber Company, which moved here from Glenwood, YARMOUTH COUNTY, Nova Scotia. The town was incorporated in 1962. The coat of arms depicts a salmon fly crossed with a pulp hook – thus recognizing its two major industries.

Glover Island   *See* Glovertown.

Glovertown (Eastern)   Southeast of GAMBO. The first name,

Flat Island, was changed in honour of Sir John Hawley Glover (1829–1885), governor of Newfoundland in 1875–81 and 1883–5. Glover Island in GRAND LAKE has the same origin.

Goobies (Eastern)   Northeast of SWIFT CURRENT; probably named for the Gooby or Goobie family; part of the West Country Dorset migration to this part of the province. There is also a Gobeys on the island of Guernsey, which may have given rise to the name; however, the West Country origin is the most plausible.

Goose Bay   *See* Happy Valley–Goose Bay.

Goulds (Avalon)   South of ST. JOHN'S, on Highway 10. So called from a 'gold or yellow flower which grows abundantly on some brooks' (Jukes). This is a probable reference to the marsh marigold.

Grand Bank (Eastern)   The town of Grand Bank (as distinct from *the* Grand Bank, see chapter 1, pages 11–12) is located on the BURIN PENINSULA, facing FORTUNE BAY. The name is descriptive and dates from the late seventeenth century. It refers to the hill or bank on the west side of the harbour. By the time of the Cook survey in 1765, the settlement was well established and had 'the

greatest Fishery in Fortune Bay.'
Incorporated as a town in 1943.

Grand Bruit (Western)   A village west of BURGEO. The name was imposed by the French and is descriptive of the noise (*bruit*) made by the large cascade which leaps down over cliffs 300 metres high. The location was described by William Eppes Cormack (1796–1868) as 'a good little harbour with two entrances, the west being the better.'

Grand Codroy River   *See* Codroy.

Grand Falls–Windsor (Central) An amalgamated town on the EXPLOITS RIVER. Grand Falls is descriptive of its 'spectacular falls' and was developed as a company town by the Anglo-Newfoundland Development Company. Here Newfoundland's first pulp-and-paper mill was officially opened with due ceremony on 11 October 1909. Three months later, the London *Daily Mail* announced: 'For the first time yesterday [28 January 1910] an English newspaper was printed on paper produced in England's oldest colony.' The mill, now owned by Abitibi-Price, continues to provide an economic base for the town. Grand Falls was the birthplace of noted Canadian actor and playwright Gordon Pinsent (1930–). Windsor, first known as 'Grand Falls Station' for its position on the Newfoundland Railway, was probably renamed for the royal house of Windsor. Historically, this area was a centre of Beothuk culture, a fact commemorated in the Mary March Regional Museum, named in honour of one of the last of this race. Adjacent to the museum is a re-created Beothuk village, with summer and winter *mamateeks* (wigwams), a sweat lodge, and related exhibits. See also MARY MARCH'S BROOK.

Grand Lake (Western)   At 539 square kilometres, this is the largest lake in Newfoundland, and thus was 'named by nature.' In combination with Birchy and Sandy lakes, which lie to the northeast, Grand Lake provides a magnificent 145-kilometre waterway much appreciated by canoe enthusiasts. There is also a 'smaller' Grand Lake in Labrador, adjacent to the community of NORTHWEST RIVER.

Great Brehat; Great Brehat Bay (Western)   The town is northeast of ST. ANTHONY, on Great Brehat Bay, in an area of the Petit Nord once occupied by Channel Islanders. During the eighteenth century, there were no safe 'wintering anchorages' on the islands of Jersey and Guernsey; accordingly, the port of Brehat, south-west of Guernsey on the Nor-mandy coast, was used. This summer fishery station in north-eastern Newfoundland obvi-ously reminded the Channel Islanders of their winter haven. Brehaut, as a surname, is found in both Newfoundland and Prince Edward Island. See also GUERNSEY COVE, Prince Edward Island.

Great Brehat Bay   *See* Great Bre-hat.

Great Colinet Island   *See* Coli-net.

Great Garnish Barrasway   *See* Garnish and Barachois.

Great Paradise   *See* Paradise.

Great St. Lawrence   *See* Burin.

Green Bay (Central)   At the western end of NOTRE DAME BAY. It is thought that Gaspar Corte-Real (1450?–1501) was the origi-nal explorer of this area, and that this is the *baia verde* of the *terra verde* which he reported discover-ing around 1500. It survives in English translation as an arm of Notre Dame Bay.

Greenspond; Greenspond Island (Central)   The town is south of WESLEYVILLE, on Greenspond Island. Derived from the names of the first two families to settle in the district – Green and Pond. The name is listed on a 1709 map by Herman Moll, indicating that the settlement dates from the early 1700s.

Greenspond Island   *See* Greens-pond.

Grenfell Sound (Labrador)   This body of water, located between the mainland and KILLINIQ ISLAND, was explored in 1905 by Sir Wilfred Grenfell (1865–1940) and, for a time, was known as 'Grenfell Tickle.' Following settle-ment of the Labrador–Québec boundary in 1927, Killiniq Island was divided between Newfound-land and the Northwest Territory; thus most of the channel or tickle was technically within Canadian jurisdiction. In 1938 the Geo-graphic Board of Canada desig-nated the eastern entrance Grenfell Sound; while the west-ern entrance was named Forbes Sound, for Alexander Forbes (1882–1965), who headed a 1931–5 National Geographic aerial survey of northern Labrador. However, the tickle was sur-prisingly designated McLelan Strait, after the Honourable A.W. McLelan (1824–1890), a Nova Scotian politician who held a number of minor portfolios in the federal cabinet during the 1880s.

He died in 1890 while serving as lieutenant-governor of Nova Scotia (CPCGN Files). See also SEA-PLANE COVE.

Groais Island (Western)   Opposite CAPE ROUGE. Named for Île de Groix, off the coast of Brittany. It, in turn, may be traced to the Breton word *groac'h*, for 'witch.' BELL ISLAND, to the south, and Groais Island are sometimes referred to by the descriptive Grey Islands. These two 'belle isles that are near Cap Rouge' were sighted by Jacques Cartier in 1534. The principal settlement on Bell Island is Grey Islands Harbour.

Gros Morne   *See* Gros Morne National Park.

Gros Morne National Park (Western)   Established in 1970, Gros Morne National Park has earned an international reputation as a showcase of Canada's natural and geological heritage. The name, part of the French legacy in Newfoundland nomenclature, is taken from Gros Morne – at 806 metres, the highest point in the LONG RANGE MOUNTAINS. The phrase, literally 'large bluff or hill,' may be traced to the Creole for 'a large rounded mountain that stands alone.' Other examples are found on the Caribbean islands of Haiti and Martinique. There is also a second Gros Morne in Newfoundland, on the BAIE VERTE PENINSULA. In its over 1,800 square kilometres, the national park offers a mingling of contrasts, from glacier-scarred barrens to fiord valleys, from woodland caribou to the rare Arctic hare, from boreal forest to coastal dunes, from the tucka-more (wind-stunted fir and spruce trees that grow in exposed areas along the coastline) to delicate alpine flowers, from mossy bogs to deep mystery-shrouded lakes. Western Brook Pond is typical of the latter as it demonstrates how glacial action carved a lake 16 kilometres long, 165 metres deep, and enclosed by cliffs that rise 656 metres above the surface. Gros Morne was selected in 1987 by UNESCO as a World Heritage Site, largely on the strength of its geological significance. Fascinating geological features go back billions of years, giving evidence of continental drift. In addition fossils from the Precambrian to the Paleozoic era may be found. One of the best known of the park hiking trails is the Callaghan which begins at sea level and rises to the top of Gros Morne. Although not an approved name, it was assigned on 16 September 1976, in honour of the Right Honourable James Callaghan, British prime minister from 1976 to 1979. See also BROOM POINT and LOBSTER COVE HEAD.

Groswater Bay (Labrador)   At the entrance to HAMILTON INLET. This French/English descriptive is a reminder of the French migratory fishery on the Labrador.

Gulf of St. Lawrence   *See* chapter 1, page 9.

Gulnare Hill (Central); **Gulnare Island** (Labrador)   Gulnare Hill is southwest of BAIE VERTE; the island lies north of Comfort Head. *Gulnar* is the Persian word for 'pomegranate' and was the name of Captain Henry Bayfield's survey vessel used in charting sections of the Labrador and Newfoundland coastline. It had become popular through the name of a character in Lord Byron's poem 'The Corsair.'

Gulnare Island   *See* Gulnare Hill.

Guernsey Island (Western) At the entrance to the BAY OF ISLANDS. Named by Captain James Cook (1728–1779) for HMS *Guernsey*, the flagship of Sir Hugh Palliser (1722/3–1796), who served as governor of Newfoundland from 1764 to 1768. Cook's service in Newfoundland coincided with Palliser's term in office. Nearby Pearl and Tweed islands were also named by Cook for ships of the Royal Navy.

Ha Ha Bay (Western)   East of PISTOLET BAY. This place name occurs five times within the province; four in the immediate vicinity of Ha Ha Bay, and the other, an inlet, northeast of BURGEO. Apocryphal stories abound as to its origin; however, it may be traced to an old French expression for an unexpected obstruction or dead end. In this example, a sand bar acts as the obstruction, preventing direct passage to Pistolet Bay. In England and Australia, 'ha ha' has a slightly different meaning. It is used to designate a dry moat that prevents livestock from coming onto a lawn, while at the same time not obstructing the view. As a place name it is also found in several Québec locations, the best known being St. Louis-du-Ha! Ha!

Hamilton Falls; Hamilton Inlet; Hamilton River (Labrador) Together with LAKE MELVILLE, the inlet is the largest on the Labrador coast. First known as 'Baie des Esquimaux,' it was renamed, in 1743, Baie-Saint Louis by Québec entrepreneur and explorer Jean-Louis Fornel (1698–1745). The name was again changed in July 1821 by Captain William Martin, for Sir Charles Hamilton (1767–1849), who served as governor from 1818 to 1824. At this time the governor of Newfoundland had jurisdiction over the coast of Labrador. The river and falls were later named for the inlet. The offshore Hamilton Bank takes its name from the inlet. See also CHURCHILL FALLS and CHURCHILL RIVER.

Hamilton Inlet　*See* Hamilton Falls.

Hamilton River　*See* Hamilton Falls.

Hamilton Sound (Central) South of FOGO ISLAND; it also commemorates the career of Governor Sir Charles Hamilton (see HAMILTON FALLS).

Hampden (Western)　Southwest of BAIE VERTE. Formerly known by the descriptive 'Riverhead,' it was renamed by proclamation on 16 August 1910. The name was probably inspired by Hampden, Buckinghamshire, England.

Hant's Harbour (Avalon)　Northeast of WINTERTON. Appears as *L'Ance Arbe* or *Ance Arbre* on early French records, and as *Hans Harbour* in the Taverner survey of 1714–15. The present spelling results from the English pronunciation of the original French. There is no connection with Hants, the abbreviated form of 'Hampshire.'

Happy Adventure (Eastern) East of GLOVERTOWN. It is thought that this euphonious name was suggested by Captain George Holbrooke during a survey of this coast. He was forced by a fierce northeast gale to seek shelter in the cove and reputedly described his good fortune as a 'Happy Adventure.' Holbrook Head at the entrance of NEWMAN SOUND adds credence to this theory. Holbrooke was later named surveyor general of Newfoundland. See also MOUNT PEARL.

Happy Valley–Goose Bay (Labrador)　In the summer of 1941 aerial surveys of Labrador were undertaken in the search for an airport site that might provide a shortened route to Britain and as an alternative to GANDER. Eventually a sandy plateau at the western end of LAKE MELVILLE was selected. In what has been classified as 'one of Canada's remarkable wartime engineering feats,' the base was operational by that December, although the runways were not yet paved. During the remainder of the Second World War, Goose Bay played a key role in North Atlantic defence and was, by the end of 1943, the world's largest airport. More recently it has been used as a training base by the American, British, German, and Dutch air forces. In 1942 the euphemistic name 'Happy Valley' was selected for the townsite housing workers at the air base. Happy Valley and Goose Bay were amalgamated in 1975.

Harbour Breton (Central)   At the end of Highway 360. Named by fishermen from Brittany, who arrived here in the early 1600s. In 1848, Anglican Bishop Edward Feild (1801–1886) visited the south coast and described the community as 'a picturesque harbour, so completely land-locked that a stranger could hardly guess the passage to the sea, and surrounded by hills of bold and fantastic outline.' Incorporated as a town in 1952.

Harbour Deep (Western)   On the eastern side of the NORTHERN PENINSULA, this isolated community is not linked with the provincial highway system. From June to January, access is by ferry, from JACKSONS ARM; for the remainder of the year, the community is served by bush plane. The name is descriptive and may be traced to 1693, when it appeared as *Harver Deep* on the *Chart of Newfoundland and the Fishing Banks* by Augustine Fitzhugh.

Harbour Grace (Avalon)   South of CARBONEAR, on CONCEPTION BAY. The name is an anglicization of Havre de Grace, now Le Havre, in France. John Guy lists the name as *Harbor de Grace*, which gradu-

ally evolved to Harbour Grace. For a time (1610–13), the port served as headquarters for the pirate Peter Easton. Following his departure, settlement was begun by former members of the nearby Cupers (CUPIDS) colony. Thereafter, for many years, the economic foundation of Harbour Grace was to be found in fishing, sealing, and associated mercantile interests. Prominent among the latter were three Jersey family firms: Guizot (Gushue), DeQuetteville, and LeSeur. While in Harbour Grace, Peter LeSeur was converted to Methodism by Lawrence Coughlin, and later introduced the denomination in Jersey. Although the demise of the seal fishery, vanishing fish stocks, and automation have taken their toll, the town still retains architectural and historical reminders of its storied past. Today it functions largely as a service centre for the immediate area. Harbour Grace also occupies a firm place in aviation history. Numerous pioneering transatlantic flights began at the local airstrip, the first facility of its kind in Newfoundland. Among the famous aviators associated with Harbour Grace were Charles Kingsford Smith (1897–1935) and Amelia Earhart (1897–?1937). In 1930 the Australian aviator (later Sir Charles) Kingsford Smith touched down at Harbour Grace *en route* from Ireland to New York on a flight around the world. On 20 May 1932 Amelia Earhart took off from here to became the first woman to fly solo across the Atlantic. The town was incorporated in 1945.

Harbour Le Cou (Western)   East of CHANNEL–PORT AUX BASQUES. The name, of French origin, is descriptive of the harbour. It has been described as 'an hour glass shaped body of water' – hence, 'le cou,' for 'neck.' Captain James Cook (1728–1779) reported the presence of fishing stages at Harbour Le Cou in 1765. The village is celebrated in a famous folksong of the same name. See also ROSE BLANCHE.

Harbour Main (Avalon)   Southeast of BAY ROBERTS, at the head of CONCEPTION BAY. Two theories exist as to the origin of this place name. It has been attributed by the Reverend Michael Howley to 'the harbour of St. Méen, a small town near St. Malo'; while E.R. Seary suggests that it may well be 'a French family name.' St. Méen was a sixth-century Breton priest whose feast day is 21 June. Now part of the district of Harbour Main–Chapel Cove–Lakeview, established in 1977.

Harbour Mille (Central)   South of TERRENCEVILLE, on FORTUNE BAY. Fishermen from the Channel Islands were active on this section of the coast in the early eighteenth century. Harbour Mille (pronounced 'millay') was named for Millais, a common surname on Jersey. See also JERSEYMANS HARBOUR.

Harbour Round (Central)   On NOTRE DAME BAY, at the end of Highway 416. Described in Lovell's 1871 *Directory* as 'a small fishing station on the French Shore.' The name is descriptive of the configuration of the harbour.

Hare Bay (Western; Eastern) The name of the bay on the northeastern coast of the NORTHERN PENINSULA dates from the seventeenth century and appears on French charts of the period as *B aux Livres*, a reference to the Arctic hare (*Lepus americanus*). In late April 1908, a drama of daunting proportions unfolded on the ice floes of Hare Bay. Word was conveyed to Dr. Wilfred Grenfell at the St. Anthony medical mission that a patient in the isolated community of ENGLEE required immediate attention. Grenfell set out with a dog team to make the long journey. The route was overland to Lockes Cove, on Hare Bay; across the bay; and overland again to Englee. On reaching the shore of Hare Bay, Grenfell attempted a short-cut across the ice floes to Hare Island. Unfortunately, the wind shifted direction and he was carried out to sea. Grenfell's survival and subsequent rescue in the face of almost insurmountable odds were detailed in his book *Adrift on an Ice Pan*. It became a best-seller and greatly enhanced Grenfell's international reputation. Almost a century later, the book is still in print. The origin of the name of the town northeast of GAMBO, on Freshwater Bay, may also be traced to the Arctic hare, although the animal is now extinct in this part of the province. The numerous other Hare Bays have the same origin.

Hatchet Cove (Eastern)   On Southwest Arm, TRINITY BAY. The name probably stems from 'hatchet' or 'hatchet face,' a Newfoundland term for the common puffin (*Fratercula arctica*) (Handcock).

Hawke's Bay (Western)   Southeast of PORT SAUNDERS, on the NORTHERN PENINSULA. So named by Captain James Cook (1728–1779) in 1767 in honour of the first lord of the Admiralty, Edward Hawke, first Baron Hawke (1705–1781). The name was repeated by Cook in 1769 for a bay off the east coast of the North Island, New Zealand. See also TORRENT RIVER and HOGAN TRAIL.

Head of Bay d'Espoir   *See* Bay d'Espoir.

Hearts Content; Hearts Delight; Hearts Desire (Avalon)   These three similarily named communities are located west–northwest of CARBONEAR, on TRINITY BAY. Hearts Content was recorded by John Guy in 1612 as *Hartes Content* and may possibly have been the name of a ship. The remaining two, probably inspired by the existing Hearts Content, were in place by the time of the Michael Lane survey of 1775. Hearts Content occupies an important niche in the history of communications. In 1866 the transatlantic cable was successfully landed there. Shortly thereafter a cable station was established and operated for nearly a century, until outmoded by modern technology. The station was phased out in 1965 and the building is now a museum. Hearts Delight and nearby Islington (named for the London borough) were amalgamated and incorporated as a town in 1972.

Hearts Delight   *See* Hearts Content.

Hearts Desire   *See* Hearts Content.

Hebron (Labrador)   On the north side of the entrance to Hebron Fiord. Site of a Moravian mission established in 1829. It was named for the biblical Hebron, located southwest of Jerusalem. The name is derived from the Hebrew *havor*, 'to join' or 'unite.' The mission has been closed and relocated to NAIN.

Hermitage; Hermitage Bay (Central)   The bay is on the south coast, north of Connoire Bay. The bay was named by Channel Islanders who saw in an island in the bay a resemblance to the Hermitage, off the port of St. Helier, in Jersey. The settlement (now the amalgamated community Hermitage–Sandville) is on Highway 364, facing Hermitage Bay.

Hermitage Bay   *See* Hermitage.

Hibbs Cove (Avalon)   Northeast of BARENEED, formerly known as 'Hibbs Hole.' Dating from the eighteenth century, it is for an English surname. E.R. Seary noted that the generic 'hole' was steadily being ousted in favour of 'cove,' 'a word, in Roget's phrase, less offensive to ears polite.'

Highlands of St. John   *See* St. John Highlands.

Hodges Hill (Central)   Northeast of BADGER. This feature was named Mount Labour-In-Vain by Captain John Cartwright (1740–1824) on an expedition into the EXPLOITS RIVER territory in 1768. The prosaic name Hodges Hill, of uncertain origin, may predate the Cartwright expedition.

Hogan Trail (Western)   This hiking trail, which begins at HAWKE'S BAY, runs through marshy bogs and heavily forested areas, at times paralleling the Torrent River. The trail is an appropriate memorial to the heroic saga of John Hogan, a member of the Newfoundland Rangers. On 8 May 1943, Ranger Hogan, who was stationed at GOOSE BAY, was on an RCAF flight to GANDER. Somewhere over the foothills of the LONG RANGE MOUNTAINS, east of Hawke's Bay, the aircraft filled with smoke, and all on board were forced to bail out by parachute. Hogan landed safely in dense forest with only minor injuries. The following day he encountered another survivor, Corporal Butt, who had landed in water, and whose feet were frozen. Without food or equipment, Ranger John Hogan managed to keep himself and his injured companion (who was unable to travel) alive by trapping rabbits and brewing spruce tea. Fifty-two days later, on 25 June, they were accidentally spotted and were rescued by a survey team. See also TORRENT RIVER.

Holyrood (Avalon)   At the head of CONCEPTION BAY. Formerly thought to be a transfer name from Holyrood House, Edinburgh. It is now believed to be after Holyrood, in the parish of Crewkerne, southwest of Yeovil, in Somerset, England (Handcock).

Hooping Harbour (Western) Northeast of HARBOUR DEEP. During the period of French control, the harbour was known as *Sans Fond*, 'without bottom.' The later English name is a reference to 'hooping,' the placing of hoops on casks and barrels. It dates from the Cook and Lane survey of 1775.

Hopedale (Labrador)   On the north side of the entrance to Deep Inlet. In 1752 the ship *Hope* carried the first Moravian missionaries to Labrador. The settlement was founded in 1782.

Horse Islands (Central)   Off FLEUR DE LYS, at the entrance to WHITE BAY. Since there were never horses on these islands, we have to look elsewhere for an explanation of the name. According to folklorist P.K. Devine, the name 'is a poetic illusion to the white rolling waves that dash on the land in a storm.' Such waves were once called 'white horses' by seamen.

Howe Harbour (Western)   On the north shore of HARE BAY. Honours the career of British Admiral Richard Howe (1726–1799). Named a rear-admiral in 1775, Howe served in North America during the American Revolution. He was first lord of the Admiralty (1783–8) and became an earl in 1788.

Howley (Western)   At the end of Highway 401; the access point for canoeists wishing to try the waters of GRAND LAKE. Named for James P. Howley (1847–1914), a geologist and surveyor who explored the Grand Lake area in the 1890s. His brother was archbishop and historian Right Reverend Michael Howley (1843–1914). A specialist on Newfoundland nomenclature, the latter has been frequently quoted in this book.

Humber River (Western)   The river, 153 kilometres in length, rises in the LONG RANGE MOUNTAINS, west of WHITE BAY; drains the GRAND LAKE and DEER LAKE areas; and then flows into Humber Arm and BAY OF ISLANDS. Named for the English Humber River by Captain James Cook (1728–1779) in 1767.

Igluksoatulligarsuk Island (Labrador)   Within Deep Inlet, south of HOPEDALE. Of Inuit origin, the name may be translated as 'a collection of sod houses.'

Ingornachoix Bay (Western) Southwest of ST. JOHN BAY. *The Newfoundland and Labrador Pilot* describes the bay thus: 'From the eastern point of Gargamelle Cove to Two Hills Point, the bay is bordered by a rocky bank ... which extends as much as 3/4 of a mile offshore and must be approached with caution.' This contemporary description would have been seconded by the early Basque fishermen and navigators who named the location *Aingura Charreco portua* – literally, 'bad anchorage.' Over time the original Basque became anglicized to Ingornachoix.

Ireland's Eye (Eastern) An island and abandoned settlement in TRINITY BAY. The precise origin of the name has been lost. 'Eye' is sometimes used in a nautical sense, as 'keeping an open eye' for danger; thus, the name may relate to the island as a navigational hazard. One area legend attests that the name can be traced to the 'claim' by homesick residents that 'Ireland could be seen by looking eastward through the narrow channel at the entrance to the harbour.' Ireland's Eye is also the name of a small island in the Irish Sea, east of County Dublin.

Isle Aux Bois (Avalon) At the entrance to FERRYLAND harbour. The name is descriptive. Because of its strategic location, the island was fortified by the English early in the eighteenth century, only to be captured twice by the French. Later the island was granted to Robert Carter, an ancestor of Sir Frederick Carter (1819–1900), who served as prime minister of Newfoundland in 1865–70 and 1874–8. In 1762, under Robert Carter's leadership, a French attack was repulsed by local fishermen; tradition has it that his wife managed to fire a direct hit on the mainmast of the French lead ship. By 1792 Aaron Thomas reported: 'the fort is now in Ruins, and the Guns cover'd with rubbish and weeds.'

Isle aux Morts (Western) East of CHANNEL–PORT AUX BASQUES. Although this aptly named 'isle of the dead' has witnessed numerous tragedies, in 1828 it did not live up to its reputation. The passenger ship *Despatch*, out of Liverpool and bound for Québec City, ran aground on a nearby reef. Its distress signals were spotted by a local fisherman, George Harvey, who, with his son and daughter plus a heroic Newfoundland dog, was responsible for rescuing the 152 people on board. The dog is reported to have, on command of his master, struggled through the water to the ship, captured a line, and swum back to shore. A breeches buoy was subsequently rigged, and the passengers and crew reached safety on land. The Harveys were awarded the gold medal of the Royal Humane Society, a reward of 100 gold sovereigns, and a letter of commendation from Governor Sir Thomas Cochrane (1789–1872). Joseph Jukes (1811–1869) visited Harvey on 26 September 1839, when 'the medal and letter were exhibited with pride.'

Jack of Clubs Brook   *See* Aguathuna.

Jacksons Arm (Western)   An inlet on WHITE BAY. Until the completion of Highway 420, Jacksons Arm, named for an early settler, was dependent on contact by sea. Today it is the terminal for the ferry to DEEP HARBOUR.

Jacques Fontaine (Eastern)   On the BURIN PENINSULA, south of BAY L'ARGENT. The origin of this place name is uncertain; in all probability it was named for a French fisherman once located here. On some charts the name was anglicized to Jack's Fountain.

Jamieson Hills (Central)   East of MEELPAEG LAKE. Named by William Eppes Cormack (1796–1868) Jamieson's Mountains on 10 October 1822, for his teacher and mentor Robert Jamieson (1744–1854), noted professor of mineralogy at Edinburgh University. Jamieson inspired Cormack's lifelong interest in natural history.

Jean de Baie; Jean de Baie Head; Jean de Baie Island (Eastern)   The settlement is northeast of MARYSTOWN. As with JACQUES FONTAINE, it traces its name to an anonymous French fisherman. Known locally as 'John the Bay.' The name is also perpetuated in Jean de Baie Head and Jean de Baie Island offshore.

Jean de Baie Head   *See* Jean de Baie.

Jean de Baie Island   *See* Jean de Baie.

Jeffreys (Western)   On ST. GEORGE'S BAY. First known as 'Bear Cove' and changed in 1891 to Crabbes East. It was renamed in 1911 after the Reverend Charles Jefferys (1847–1926), an Anglican clergyman who once served in the area. The shoreline roundabout was described as 'The Barrisways' by the Reverend Edward Wix (1802–1866) during the course of a visit in 1836. See also BARACHOIS.

Jens Haven Island (Labrador)   In SAGLEK BAY. Commemorates the career of Jens Haven (1724–1796), a founder of the Moravian Mission in Labrador. In 1764, Haven, who had earlier served in Greenland, made his first trip to Labrador; however, it was not until 1770 that the first mission was established, at Nain. For the next thirteen years, Haven played a pivotal role in the successful development of the mission. One measure of his success is found in the active role still being played by the Moravian Brethren on the coast of Labrador. See also NAIN.

Jersey Island   *See* Paradise.

Jerseymans Harbour (Central); **Jerseyside** (Avalon)   Jerseymans Harbour, now shortened to 'Jersey Harbour,' lies east of HARBOUR BRETON; Jerseyside is across the harbour from PLACENTIA. Both names give indication of the impact of Channel Islanders on the eighteenth- and nineteenth-century development of the Newfoundland fishery. The Reverend Michael Howley asserts: 'The Jerseymen were close followers of the Bretons and the Westcountrymen. They left their mark on almost every harbour on the south coast.' In addition to the south shore of the province, Channel Islanders were also active around CONCEPTION BAY and on the northwest and northeast coasts. See also HARBOUR GRACE, HERMITAGE BAY, and PAR-

ADISE. For the Channel Island impact on Nova Scotia place names, see JANVRIN ISLAND.

Jerseyside   *See* Jerseymans Harbour.

Jigger Tickle (Labrador)   Between Jigger Island and the mainland. The combination of these two words has produced what is arguably one of the most distinctive of Newfoundland–Labrador place names. Although the terms are also found in Nova Scotia, they are of Newfoundland origin. Further, 'tickle' and 'jig' or 'jigging,' and their variants, appear countless times in place names around the coastline of the province. The perceptive Joseph Jukes (1811–1869) provides a clear description of 'jigging': 'A jigger is a plummet of lead, with two or three hooks stuck at the bottom, projecting on every side, and quite bare. This is let down by a line to the proper depth, and then a [fisherman], taking a hitch of the line in his hand, jerks it smartly in.' Arthur Scammell's famous song 'The Squid Jiggin' Ground' has served to familiarize the procedure. A 'tickle' is simply a narrow, hazardous strait between two islands, or between an island and the mainland. See BELLEVUE for Jukes's experience at what was then known as 'Tickle Harbour'.

Jobs Cove (Avalon)   Northeast of CARBONEAR. Originally known as 'Devil's Cove'; the name was changed by a petition of the inhabitants, dated 29 May 1812. According to their sworn statement, it was 'the unanimous resolve' of the inhabitants to 'alter the barbarous, execrable, and impious name of Devil's Cove [to] the ancient, venerable, and celebrated name of Job's Cove.' The first name, embedded in nautical lore, was a reference to the sailors 'devil of a problem' with the prevailing easterly wind on entering the cove. It is not known whether 'Job' was for a local family name or bestowed as a mark of piety, in reference to the Book of Job in the Old Testament. The change is noteworthy as the official beginning of 'place-name reform' in Newfoundland. Although in this instance an interesting name was expunged for the sake of posterity, many other such efforts failed. For the Devil's survival see DEVILS DINING TABLE and L'ANSE-AU-DIABLE.

Joe Batts Arm (Central)   On the north shore of FOGO ISLAND. The settlement dates from the mid-eighteenth century. It was named for Joseph Batt, a native of Ringwood, in Hampshire, England, who was sentenced in 1754, at BONAVISTA, to receive fifteen lashes for stealing a pair of shoes and buckles, valued at 7s/6p. In 1901 a successful campaign was launched to rename the community 'Queenstown to honour Queen Victoria.' Since there were a few other place names both within and without Newfoundland honouring the queen, 'the new name did not catch on,' and the name Joe Batts Arm was later restored.

Journois; Journois Brook (Western)   The brook flows west into ST. GEORGE'S BAY. This place name is a reminder of an unplanned transatlantic crossing with a happy ending. On the evening of 18 April 1886, Louisa Journeaux (1878?–1939), a native of St. Helier, Jersey, along with a friend, Jules Farné, went rowing on the placid waters of the harbour. Subsequently one oar was lost overboard and, in the effort to retrieve it, the second became lost. Thereupon, Jules swam for help, leaving Louisa in the boat. Unfortunately, the boat drifted out to sea, and Louisa was stranded for two days until rescued by the *Tombola* from St. Malo, *en route* to St. George's, Newfoundland. It was not until 10 May that word was conveyed to the Journeaux family in St. Helier that Louisa was safe in St. George's. The name commemorates this event.

Journois Brook   *See* Journois.

Jubilee Lake (Central)   Southwest of LAKE MEELPAEG. Named by geologist J.P. Howley (1847–1918), whose visit on 10 August 1887 coincided with the observation of Queen Victoria's Golden Jubilee.

Kaegudeck Lake (Central)   West of EASTERN MEELPAEG LAKE. The name is from the Mi'kmaq and has been translated as 'on the top.' See MEDONNEGONIX LAKE.

Kaumajet Mountains (Labrador) A coastal mountain range ending at CAPE MUGFORD. The name is of Inuit origin and means 'shining top' or 'shining mountains.' Väinö Tanner, who explored the area in the late 1930s, recalled: 'This name suits them exactly, because the brilliancy of the crests is grand especially when covered with a fresh fall of snow.' He also considered one of the major peaks in the range, the descriptive Bishops Mitre, as 'a scene in its way unrivalled in Labrador.'

Keels (Eastern)   A village northwest of CATALINA; originally spelled 'Keeles.' The definitive origin of this name has been lost. It may be a descriptive for the shape of the rocks at the harbour entrance, a corruption of the surname Keough, or for the family name Keel, a surname found in the early parish records of BONAVISTA and TRINITY (Handcock).

Kelligrews (Avalon)   Now part of the town of CONCEPTION BAY SOUTH. The name was first applied to Kelligrews Head and is undoubtedly for a Conception Bay family. The name itself may be traced to the Cornish Killigrews, a hamlet in St. Erme Parish, Cornwall. According to E.R. Seary, there is evidence that a family named Kelligrews from Port de Grave had a summer plantation for the shore fishery at this location. Handcock has confirmed this, with affirmation of a William Kelligrews, who resided there in the 1760s. During the twentieth century, the community became celebrated in the well-known song 'The Kelligrew's Soiree' by Johnny Burke (1851–1930).

Kellys Island (Avalon)   In CONCEPTION BAY. Once the rendezvous of Captain Kelly, a notorious Cornish pirate, for whom it was named. In the nineteenth century the island was known for its sandstone quarries. In 1839, Joseph Jukes reported: 'When I landed I found several workmen were getting stone for the projected Cathedral [Basilica of St. John the Baptist] in St. John's.'

The court-houses in ST. JOHN'S and HARBOUR GRACE were also constructed from the same stone.

Keppel Island (Western)   In INGORNACHOIX BAY. This name was bestowed by Captain James Cook (1728–1779) in honour of Augustus, first Viscount Keppel (1725–1786), an admiral of the British navy. Keppel Bay in Queensland, Australia, was also so named by Cook.

Kiglaplait Mountains (Labrador) North of South Aulastivik Island. The coastal mountains 'begin to rise with steep sides and jagged crests directly out of the sea' (Tanner). Thus the name is descriptive of the very rugged and serrated skyline; its meaning in Inuit is 'Dog-Tooth Mountains.'

Kikkertasoak Island (Labrador) North or Cape Kiglaplait. The island was once known as 'Spracklings Island,' after a CONCEPTION BAY sealer of that name. The Inuit name is descriptive and means 'the very big island off to sea.'

Killick Island (Labrador)   In St. Lewis Sound. The name comes from the 'killick,' an anchor made with a stone secured by pliable pieces of wood tied at the top.

Even more descriptive is Killick Stone Island, located west of NEW WORLD ISLAND in central Newfoundland. It was a likely place to find the required stone for killicks.

Killiniq Island (Labrador)   At the tip of the Labrador peninsula. This descriptive name is of Inuit origin and has been translated by E.P. Wheeler as 'the big seaward one.' See also CAPE CHIDLEY.

King George IV Lake (Western)   West of Highway 480; named by William Eppes Cormack (1796–1868) on 31 October 1822 for King George IV (1762–1830).

Kings Cove (Eastern)   Southwest of BONAVISTA. According to folklorist P.K. Devine (1859–1950), this place name may be a corruption of the surname Canning. Thus, it may have originated with 'the pronunciation becoming "Kings Cove" in the West Country tongue.'

Kippens (Western)   West of STEPHENVILLE. This name is of uncertain origin. It may possibly be derived from an old English word for 'a bundle of hides' or an English surname not traced in Newfoundland (Seary). One additional theory that exists locally suggests that it may be

traced to a 'Captain Kippen supposedly shipwrecked here in
the 1840s.' However, it would
appear that the name is much
older.

Knob Lake (Labrador)   South of
Schefferville, Québec. A descriptive named for 'a great knob of
rock' located at the end of the lake
and visible for a great distance.

Labrador City (Labrador)
Northwest of Wabush, near the
Labrador–Québec border. For
derivation of Labrador see chapter 1, pages 6–7. The presence of
deposits of iron ore in this area
was discovered as early as 1892.
In 1958 mining began, and the following year a settlement was
established on the shore of Carol
Lake. With incorporation in 1961,
the name Carol Lake was
changed to Labrador City for the
territory in which it was situated.
The motto of the city is the
Naskapi *Kamistaitusset*, meaning
'Land of hard-working people.'
See also WABUSH.

Lake Cormack; Mount Cormack
(Central)   The lake is north of
KING GEORGE IV LAKE. The 318-
metre-high mountain is west of
Middle Ridge. Lake Cormack and
Mount Cormack were named by
John Guille Millais (1865–1931)
for William Eppes Cormack
(1796–1868), explorer, entrepre-

neur, and author. Of Cormack's
work, Dr. George Story has written: 'He described the interior
with an accuracy no subsequent
traveller has matched; his *Narrative* is the undisputed classic of
Newfoundland travel.' Millais, as
well, was a travel writer of note.
His *Newfoundland and Its Untrod-
den Ways*, published in 1907, is
still worth reading. See also COR-
MACK, MOUNT MISERY, and MOUNT
SYLVESTER.

Lake Melville (Labrador)   A
large saltwater lake connected
with the sea by HAMILTON INLET.
Honours Henry Dundas, first Viscount Melville (1742–1811), who
served as lord of the Admiralty
from 1804 to 1805.

Lake Michikamau (Labrador)
North of CHURCHILL FALLS. The
name is traceable to an Inuit
descriptive, *meshikamau*, which
has been translated as 'big lake.'
The name is appropriate, considering that the lake covers 150,000
hectares. It is now part of SMALL-
WOOD RESERVOIR.

Lamaline (Eastern)   At the
southern tip of the BURIN PENIN-
SULA. The name may be of Portuguese origin, after *le belim*, or
possibly a corruption of *La
Maligne*, the French for 'malignant.' On 18 November 1929, the
area was struck by an earthquake

which registered 7.2 on the Richter scale. Although its centre was 250 kilometres south of Lamaline, the resulting tidal wave, measuring 5 to 15 metres in height, did considerable damage along the coast. The effects were felt as far away as HALIFAX, where it was reported in the *Halifax Herald* that 'buildings started shaking like topsails in a storm.' Lamaline is the birthplace of Canadian playwright Edwin R. Procunier. Although now a resident of London, Ontario, he set many of his plays in 'Peace Harbour,' a fictional Newfoundland outport.

Lamanche (Avalon)   South of ARNOLD'S COVE, on PLACENTIA BAY. The name, derived from the French word for 'sleeve,' is also the term used in France for the English Channel. During exploratory work seeking a transatlantic cable terminal site, lead was discovered at this location. Subsequently a mine was opened and operated for a time during the late nineteenth century. The name is repeated north of FERRYLAND.

Lance Cove (Avalon)   East of CAPE ST. MARY'S. The name may be derived from 'lance,' a small fish or sand eel; it may be a corruption of the common 'l'anse' (see L'ANSE-AU-CLAIR), or for an implement used in killing fish or harpooned whales. The word is incorporated in many place names throughout the province.

L'Anse-au-Clair; L'Anse-au-Diable; L'Anse-au-Loup; L'Anse-Amour (Labrador)   A collection of four villages situated southwest of RED BAY. L'Anse-Amour has changed both in spelling and meaning and is a corruption of the original Pointe aux Mortes, or 'Deadmans Point.' L'Anse-Amour has the distinction of being the earliest verified site of human habitation in Labrador. Maritime Archaic artefacts dating back 7,500 years have been discovered here. Among other items discovered in a child's burial mound was a 'toggling' harpoon – a sophisticated seal-hunting device that twists, or toggles, in the wounded animal and prevents it from escaping. The name L'Anse-au-Clair has also evolved over the centuries. The original name was L'Anse Eau Claire, or 'Clearwater Cove.' L'Anse-au-Diable was, according to the Reverend Patrick Browne, an early twentieth-century visitor, 'well named ... for the frightful reputation of the headland,' then and now, a navigational hazard. He reported that, in the local dialect, the name was pronounced 'Nancy Jawble.' L'Anse-au-Loup simply means 'Wolf Cove.' All four place names help document the French presence on the Labrador coast. The term *Anse* for cove or bay is common to all four Atlantic provinces, with more than fifty examples in Newfoundland and Labrador.

L'Anse-au-Diable   *See* L'Anse-au-Clair.

L'Anse-au-Loup   *See* L'Anse-au-Clair.

L'Anse-Amour   *See* L'Anse-au-Clair.

L'Anse aux Meadows (Western) Southwest of CAPE BAULD. Site of a pre-Columbian Norse settlement discovered and excavated in 1961–8 by the Norwegian team of historian-explorer Helge Ingstad and his archaeologist wife, Anne Stine. The name is a French–English descriptive which can be translated as 'the bay with the grasslands.' It may also be a misspelling of an earlier French designation, L'Anse aux Meduses, 'the bay of jellyfish.' Managed by Parks Canada, L'Anse aux Meadows was declared a World Heritage Site by UNESCO in 1978, as it offers verification of the Norse discovery of America about A.D. 1000. In addition, the excavation established that the site was occupied year round. One of the eight building sites excavated was a smithy where local bog iron was smelted. Following radio-carbon tests, it was found to date between A.D. 860 and 1070. Additional proof of a settled existence came with the discovery of a sauna and, from among the more than 2,000 authenticated artefacts, items such as a bronze pin, a stone lamp, and a spindle whorl. Adjacent to the site, Parks Canada has reconstructed three sod houses of the period. These structures, with their warm smoky atmosphere, along with an interpretation centre, provide a realistic glimpse into one of the earliest chapters of Canadian history.

Lark Harbour; Lark Island (Western)   In the BAY OF ISLANDS. Named by Captain James Cook (1728–1779) for HMS *Lark*, one of his ships used in the Newfoundland coastal surveys of the 1760s.

Lark Island   *See* Lark Harbour.

La Scie (Central)   A village east of BAIE VERTE. This area was first settled by the French; thus, the descriptive name, which means 'saw,' is a reference to the nearby jagged or saw-like hills.

Latine Point (Avalon); **Latin Point** (Western)   Latine Point is located north of Point Verde, on PLACENTIA BAY. This name probably has a nautical origin and is for the Latin sail, defined as a type of triangular sail suspended by a long yard at an angle of about 45° to the mast. Although common to the Mediterranean, it was used in Newfoundland. There is another Latin Point on the eastern shore of Conche Harbour, on the NORTHERN PENINSULA. Another explanation prevails for Latine Point (sometimes Point Latine). This suggests that it was named 'because a ship named Latine was wrecked off the point' (Houlihan).

Latin Point   *See* Latine Point.

Lawn (Eastern)   West of St. Lawrence. The name has been traced to a case of mistaken identity. An early French fishermen mistook a doe caribou for a donkey and named the community L'Âne, 'the ass.' In 1714 William Taverner (*ca* 1680–1768) referred to the location as 'Great Laun.' Over time the name evolved to Lawn. By the early nineteenth century, the contemporary spelling was in use. On 18 February 1942, the people of Lawn and nearby St. Lawrence participated in a sea-rescue and life-saving operation of epic proportions. Two American destroyers, USS *Wilkes* and USS *Truxton*, and the supply ship *Pollux* ran aground in a severe storm. In the struggle to reach land, 203 American

sailors died. The 185 survivors owed their lives to the local people, who defied all odds in rescuing and caring for them. Their dramatic story is well told in *Standing into Danger*, written in 1985 by Newfoundland author Cassie Brown. See also ST. LAWRENCE.

Lesters Field (Avalon)   Now part of the city of ST. JOHN'S, it was originally named for its owner. The field included an area between Cornwall Avenue and Blackmarsh Road. Used as an airstrip on 14 June 1919 by Captain John William Alcock and Lieutenant Arthur Whitten Brown for the beginning of the first non-stop transatlantic flight from St. John's to Clifden, Ireland.

Lethbridge (Eastern)   Northeast of CLARENVILLE. The village was first known as 'Southeast Arm,' and later 'Hopedale.' The change to Lethbridge was approved by the Newfoundland Nomenclature Board in 1911. The name honours the then oldest resident, James Lethbridge.

Lewins Cove (Eastern)   Southwest of MARYSTOWN. Originally the village was known as 'Loons Cove'; the change occurred as a result of local pronunciation. See COLEYS POINT for another example of an oral name change.

Lewis Hills (Western)   A section of the LONG RANGE MOUNTAINS, situated southwest of CORNER BROOK. Lewis Hill, at 825 metres, is the highest mountain on the island of Newfoundland. The name is possibly derived from a common first name among the Mi'kmaq.

Lewisporte (Central)   On Burnt Bay, an inlet of the BAY OF EXPLOITS. The community was once known as 'Burnt Bay'; later the name changed to Marshall-ville, for the Reverend William T. Marshall (1811–1846), a pioneer Methodist missionary. About 1900, Lewis Miller (1819–1909), a native of Belloch, Scotland, estab-lished a logging company nearby and began using the port for the export of lumber. The name was changed again in his honour. From Lewisporte, ferries and coastal boats travel to Labrador. See also MILLERTOWN.

Little Catalina   See Catalina.

Little Colinet Island   See Colinet.

Little Hearts Ease (Eastern)   On Southwest Arm, TRINITY BAY. This small fishing community was first known as 'Hearts Ease.' It is thought that the derivation may be a ship's name.

Little Paradise   See Paradise.

Little St. Lawrence   See Burin.

Lobster Cove Head (Western) At the entrance to BONNE BAY, part of Gros Morne National Park. Named for the presence of the lobster fishery. In 1990 the lightkeeper's cottage, adjacent to the now automated lighthouse, was opened. The purpose, in the words of the park brochure, is 'to interpret how people have lived along this coast and harvested the sea for more than 4,000 years.' The lighthouse was erected in 1897 to mark the approach to Rocky Harbour. The centre also pays tribute to Lobster Cove Head lighthouse keepers. See also GROS MORNE NATIONAL PARK.

Lobstick Lake (Labrador)   Part of the SMALLWOOD RESERVOIR, in western Labrador. Named for the lobstick, used by the Montagnais–Naskapi (among others) as a marker. It was usually a conspic-uous tree from which all but the topmost branches were removed. The name was possibly assigned by John McLean (1797–1890), an employee of the Hudson's Bay Company.

Logy Bay (Avalon)   North of ST. JOHN'S. Since it appears as *Lugy Bay* on early maps, E.R. Seary suggests that the name was prob-ably derived from the Cornish *lugh-ogo*, for 'cave calf or seal.'

The *Dictionary of Newfoundland English* lists 'a fish of inferior quality; a large codfish' as another meaning for 'logy.' The community is the site of Memorial University's Ocean Science Centre, established in 1967. The centre's circular architecture, designed to resemble the sea anemone, and its dramatic setting on the Atlantic coastline symbolize its mission, the study of oceanography.

Long Range Mountains (Western)   This 'long range' extends for 500 kilometres along the west coast, from CAPE RAY to the WHITE BAY area. On 16 June 1534, Jacques Cartier recorded: 'We came to a region of very high and rugged mountains, among which was one in appearance like a barn and on this account we named this region [les montes de Granches] the Barn Mountains.' Cartier was probably referring to the ST. JOHN HIGHLANDS opposite ST. JOHN BAY. Some authorities suggest that the name *Granches* was a reference to Cartier's wife, Catherine des Granches; however, the record does not support this suggestion. By the time of the Jukes expedition in 1842, the English descriptive Long Range Mountains was in popular usage.

Lumsden (Central)   North of WESLEYVILLE. This area was first known as 'Cat Harbour,' for the 'cat' or newly born seal. The name was changed in 1915 to honour the Reverend James Lumsden (1854–1915), who was the local Methodist minister from 1885 to 1888. Lumsden, a native of Glasgow, Scotland, served Methodist congregations on Newfoundland's east coast for a decade before moving to Nova Scotia in 1892. His experiences, including a shipwreck and the loss of all personal possessions, were chronicled in *The Skipper Parson*, published in 1906. In 1966–7 the people of Lumsden North (the original Cat Harbour) resettled in Lumsden South, which is today known as 'Lumsden.' See also LUMSDEN DAM, Nova Scotia.

McLelan Strait   *See* Grenfell Sound.

Maiden Hair Cove (Eastern) In Sweet Bay, at the head of BONAVISTA BAY. Named for the Maiden Hair (*Gaultheria procumbens*), commonly known as the wintergreen or teaberry.

Mainland (Western)   West of STEPHENVILLE, on the PORT AU PORT PENINSULA. It is possibly derived from La Grand'Terre, the name given to the community by the first French settlers. However, Selma Barkham points out that it may well go back to a translation of the Basque *certan*, their generic name for 'mainland.'

Main Point–Davidsville (Central)   On the east side of GANDER BAY. Main Point, to the south of Mann Point, is a descriptive name; the latter was named for a local family. Davidsville is after St. David's Anglican Church. In 1956, Mann Point was renamed Davidsville by the Canadian Board on Geographical Names on the advice of the Department of the Postmaster General; the justification was probably the similiarity of the two place names. Of the change, E.R. Seary wryly commented that the reason was one which 'only the bureaucratic mind could fathom.' The official name of the amalgamated community is now Main Point–Davidsville.

Main Topsail   *See* The Topsails.

Makkovik   *See* Cape Makkovik.

Makkovik Bank   *See* Cape Makkovik.

Manuels (Avalon)   Now part of the town of CONCEPTION BAY SOUTH; named for 'Emmanuels,' which appeared 'on an early land deed' (Handcock). The suggestion that it was named for King Manuel I of Portugal, who reigned from 1495 to 1521, is unfounded.

Marble Mountain (Western)   At the head of the BAY OF ISLANDS, 11 kilometres from CORNER BROOK. The name is a descriptive for a location that has become one of Atlantic Canada's major ski resorts. The mountain has a top elevation of 472 metres and a vertical drop of 520 metres. Unlike many other Eastern Canadian ski resorts, Marble Mountain has a dependable snowfall each winter.

Marines Cove (Avalon)   On the southeast shore of ST. MARY'S BAY. In the autumn of 1816, HMS *Harpooner*, a Royal Navy troop carrier, went aground in a dense fog near CAPE PINE. The ship was *en route* home with British marines and their families, following service in the War of 1812. More than 350 people were lost in the disaster which gave rise to the place name.

Markland (Avalon)   On Highway 81 south of WHITBOURNE. Established in May 1934 and named 'Markland ... the wooded land,' after the Norse designation for Labrador. The new community, a Utopian land-settlement scheme for the unemployed, began as a private trust but soon received government funding as an experiment in social reconstruction. As such it was to be the

Commission of Government's 'beacon of hope' in combating the Depression. Two of its members, Thomas Lodge (1882–1958), Commissioner for Public Utilities, and Sir John Hope Simpson (1868–1961), Commissioner for Natural Resources, were enthusiastic supporters of the project. On 8 September 1934, Sir John wrote: 'We are hoping great things from Markland. If successful we hope to multiply it by ten or twenty. After all, the salvation of this country lies in the land, though I suppose the major industry will always be the fisheries.' Further ventures were launched during 1934–41, at Browns Arm, Haricot, Lourdes, Point au Mal, SANDRING-HAM, and Winterland. Although these projects experienced a measure of success, the economic problems of the 1930s were beyond any resettlement scheme, however idealistic in conception.

Marquise (Avalon)   The *Newfoundland Pilot* lists Marquise as 'the name for the narrow isthmus joining Little Placentia [Argentia] to the mainland.' Altnough it appears as *Marquess Harbour* on early charts, E.R. Seary is of the opinion that it was named for a village northeast of Boulogne, France, or for Marquès, a variant of a French surname. The isthmus is sometimes referred to as 'The Marquise' or 'Marquise Neck.' See also ARGENTIA.

Martin Bay (Labrador)   An indentation in Hutton Peninsula, east of Ikkudliayuk Fiord. Possibly named by Captain William Martin of HMS *Clinker* during exploration of the coast of Labrador in 1821. The bay became a significant footnote in the history of the Second World War when it was revealed in the 1980s that U-boat 537 of the German navy had secretly entered Martin Bay on 22 October 1943 and established an automatic weather station. See ST. MARTINS, New Brunswick, for another U-boat assignment.

Martin Point (Western)   North of Woody Point, on BONNE BAY. Visited by Captain James Cook (1728–1779) in 1767. The name is for an early settler. On 10 December 1919, the SS *Ethie* ran aground 'off Martin's Point about one o'clock.' Although the passengers and crew were eventually rescued, the incident provoked controversy on two counts. The seamanship of the captain was called in question, and the press were 'fed' graphic, but totally erroneous, reports of the role of a Newfoundland dog in the rescue. These accounts, later discredited, were suspiciously similar to those of an 1828 rescue on the south coast. See also ISLE AUX MORTS.

Mary March's Brook (Central) Flows south into Red Indian

Lake. The name commemorates Demasduit (*ca* 1796–1820), one of the last of the Beothuk. She was the wife of the chief Nonosbawsut; her anglicized name was given following her capture in March 1819. Demasduit died in captivity, on 8 January 1820. The extermination of the Beothuk is retold in the novel by Peter Such, *Riverrun* (Toronto 1973) and in F.W. Rowe's, *Extinction: The Beothuks of Newfoundland* (Toronto 1977). See also RED INDIAN LAKE and SHANADITHIT BROOK.

Marystown (Eastern)   On Mortier Bay, off PLACENTIA BAY. First known as 'Mortier Bay,' the name was changed to Marystown, as there is another Mortier Bay nearby. In addition to being a service centre for the BURIN PENINSULA, Marystown is also the location of a major shipbuilding and ship-repair facility.

Marysvale (Avalon)   South of BRIGUS. Formerly known as 'Turks Gut' or 'Turkish Gut,' for the Turkish or Barbary pirates who were a menace in Newfoundland during the seventeenth century. *Gut* is a straightforward term for a narrow passage or channel of water. The name was changed to Marysvale by proclamation on 7 November 1919. This act of 'place-name reform' was

not totally effective, as Turks Gut Long Pond still survives as a reminder of the older name. See also PINCHGUT POINT and FAIRHAVEN.

Mealy Mountains (Labrador) Southeast of HAMILTON INLET. The name, of uncertain origin, may be a descriptive. In the late eighteenth and early nineteenth centuries, one meaning of the word *mealy* was 'covered with flour,' an apt description of snow-covered mountains. This area has been designated for future development as a national park. See also NORTHWEST RIVER.

Medonnegonix Lake (Central) Southwest of EASTERN MEELPAEG LAKE. The name is derived from a Mi'kmaq descriptive indicating that its location is roughly halfway on the canoe route between the Head of Belle Bay and KAEGUDECK LAKE.

Meelpaeg Lake (Central)   South of RED INDIAN LAKE. Sometimes referred to as 'Meelpaeg Reservoir.' The name is of Mi'kmaq origin and may be translated as 'lake of many bays or coves.' It was visited by William Eppes Cormack (1796–1868) on 18 October 1822 during the course of his trek across Newfoundland. Eastern Meelpaeg Lake is located east of Mount Sylvester.

Merasheen Island (Eastern)
This, the largest island in PLACEN-
TIA BAY, was once home to hundreds of people. During the
Resettlement Program of the
1950s and 1960s, the inhabitants
were moved to mainland centres
such as PLACENTIA, JERSEYSIDE,
and FRESHWATER. The name may
be traced to the period of French
influence and Mer aux chiens, a
reference to sea dogs or seals. See
also NAKED MAN HILL.

Michikamau Lake (Labrador)
A large lake in western Labrador,
now part of the SMALLWOOD RES-
ERVOIR. The name is of Inuit origin, and is an anglicization of the
original *Meshikamau*, which has
been translated as 'Big Lake.
Labradorite is found along the
northeast shore.

Millertown (Central)   Southeast
of BUCHANS, on RED INDIAN LAKE.
Established and named after the
lumber firm of Lewis Miller and
Company. The site of Millertown
is referred to by John Cartwright
in his 1768 narrative of an expedition to the region. One of Cartwright's guides was a capable
Beothuk whose English name was
Tom June. June knew the local
topography well and told Cartwright that this location was
'where his father once dwelt.'
Cartwright assigned the name
June's Cove; however, the desig-

nation was destined to disappear.
See also EXPLOITS RIVER and
LEWISPORTE.

Milton (Eastern)   North of CLAR-
ENVILLE, on Smith Sound. Formerly known as 'King's Cove,' for
the family who first established a
logging operation here. Renamed
Milton (for the sawmill) in 1910.
William Eppes Cormack (1796–
1868) began his epic journey
across Newfoundland from a
point south of the village. A cut-
stone monument marks this historic event.

Ming's Bight (Central)   Northeast of BAIE VERTE. Three explanations for the name have been put
forward. It may be for the Breton
Saint Méen, or a corrruption of
the French La Baie des Pins, or a
geographical use of the old
English verb 'to ming,' or to mix.
This could be a reference to lands
owned by a 'mixture' of different
proprietors. ' Bight' is an old
English word for cove or bay.
Since St. Anthonys Bight, near ST.
ANTHONY, was once known as St.
Méins Bight, the Breton origin
would appear as the most plausible. See also HARBOUR MAIN.

Mizzen Topsail   *See* The Topsails.

Moreton's Harbour (Central)
On NEW WORLD ISLAND. It was

probably named for Moreton, a village in Dorset, England. The suggestion that it was named for the Reverend Julian Moreton (1825–1900), an Anglican missionary, is incorrect. The cleric published his memoirs, *Life and Work in Newfoundland*, in 1863; the place name predates his career by at least a century.

Mortier   *See* Burin.

Mount Caubvick (Labrador) Spans the Labrador–Québec boundary, south of NACHVAK FIORD. At 1,650 metres, this is the highest peak in the province, and until recently was unnamed. In 1971 the Québec government designated the feature Mont d'Iberville, for soldier and adventurer Pierre Le Moyne d'Iberville et d'Ardillières (*ca* 1661–1706). Ten years later, Dr. Peter Neary, a native Newfoundlander and now Dean of Social Science, University of Western Ontario, recommended that the mountain be named for one of the five Inuit who accompanied George Cartwright (1739/40–1819) to England in 1772. This suggestion was accepted, and Mount Caubvick was appropriately added to the nomenclature of Newfoundland and Labrador (CPCGN Files). See also CARTWRIGHT.

Mount Cormack   *See* Lake Cormack.

Mount Misery; Mount Sylvester (Central)   Mount Misery, in the vicinity of LAKE MEELPAEG, was so named by William Eppes Cormack (1796–1868) 'in remembrance of an unpleasant night [16–17 October 1822] snowbound at this location.' Mount Sylvester, northeast of KAEGUDECK LAKE, was also named by Cormack on 14 September 1822, in honour of his Mi'kmaq guide, Joseph Sylvester.

Mount Moriah (Western)   On HUMBER ARM, west of CORNER BROOK. Formerly known as 'Giles Point.' Named for the biblical Mount Moriah, where Abraham made preparations to sacrifice his son. Later it was the site of Solomon's temple.

Mount Musgrave (Western) West of GRAND LAKE; **Musgrave Harbour** (Central)   First knowrr as 'Muddy Hole'; northwest of LUMSDEN; **Musgravetown** (Eastern)   Originally named Goose Bay, an arm of BONAVISTA BAY, on which the town is situated.   All three locations were renamed for Sir Anthony Musgrave (1828–1888), who served as governor of Newfoundland from 1864 to 1869. Alexander Murray (1810–1884), in the 1866 report of the Geological Survey, noted that Mount Musgrave was so called 'in honour of your Excellency's recent visit to that part of the country.'

Mount Pearl (Avalon)   Southwest of ST. JOHN'S. In 1834 the area now known as 'Mount Pearl' was granted by the British government to Commander James Pearl (1790–1840) of the Royal Navy. Pearl had a local connection as the father-in-law of George Holbrooke, provincial surveyor general. Immediately he named his estate 'Mount Cochrane,' for then governor Thomas Cochrane. Later, in 1837, following a quarrel with the governor, he changed the name to 'Mount Pearl.' A native of KELLEYS COVE, near YARMOUTH, Nova Scotia, Pearl entered the navy at the age of eleven and rose quickly through the ranks. He was knighted in 1836 for his lengthy naval career, which included service aboard HMS *Neptune* at the Battle of Trafalgar, on 21 October 1805. Pearl's seafaring ancestors were New England Planters who migrated to Yarmouth from Saybrook, Connecticut, in 1764. Mount Pearl was incorporated as a city 21 July 1988.

Mount Peyton (Central)   This 482-metre-high mountain lies southeast of NORRIS ARM. It was named by Governor Sir Charles Hamilton for John Peyton, Jr. (1793–1879), who was responsible for returning the body of Demasduit (Mary March) to RED INDIAN LAKE.

Mount Pownal   *See* Paul Island.

Mount Sylvester   *See* Mount Misery.

Musgrave Harbour   *See* Mount Musgrave.

Musgravetown   *See* Mount Musgrave.

Nachvak Fiord (Labrador)   A 20-kilometre-long fiord which divides into two arms at its head. The name is probably an Inuit descriptive, of uncertain meaning.

Nain (Labrador)   On Tikkoatokak Bay. The most northerly settlement in Labrador. Site of the first Moravian Mission, founded in 1771 and named for the biblical Nain, a small village southeast of Nazareth. A school was established in 1791 and, from this point onward, the Moravians strove to make the Inuit literate in their own language. This was not an easy assignment, owing to the complexity of the language and the need to translate abstract ideas in a meaningful way. Over time the Moravians were successful, and today there is almost no illiteracy among the Labrador Inuit. In recent years the population of Nain has been augmented by the resettlement of the former missions at NUTAK and HEBRON.

The Reverend Patrick Browne, a frequent visitor to Labrador between 1890 and 1909, has left these impressions: 'The entrance to the Nain fiord is so contorted that you hardly realize that you are sailing on an arm of the sea; it rather resembles a huge mountain lake, from which retreat seems impossible. Astern are immense cliffs which shut out the view of the sea; whilst right ahead are tumbled mountains bathed in sunshine ... Whilst at Nain we heard a great deal of music, chin and instrumental, from the Inuit. At all the Moravian missions there are brass bands and violins are a feature of the church service.' One of the reasons for the success of the Moravian Mission was their interest in the preservation of Inuit culture, a culture that might otherwise have disappeared.

Naked Man Hill (Eastern)   On MERASHEEN ISLAND, in PLACENTIA BAY. From 13 to 19 June 1840, Joseph Jukes (1811–1869) and his survey party explored this island and its neighbourhood. He reported: 'It is very long, narrow and lofty, and about [9 kilometres] from Merasheen Harbour there is a peak where Captain Cook had a station when he surveyed this coast.' On 17 June, they 'arrived at Captain Cook's station, at a spot called, from a tall pile of stones, "Naked Man Hill." The view was bold and extensive, but the land all along the west side of Placentia Bay was bare and rugged in the extreme. We walked down to Merasheen Harbour by a precipitous track, and found the sun very hot.' The erection of stone effigies, or 'Naked Men,' was followed by other surveyors such as John Orlebar and Michael Lane and also by fishermen on the Labrador. See CAPTAIN ORLEBARS CAIRN and PILLAR ISLAND.

Nameless Cove (Western) North of FLOWERS COVE, on the NORTHERN PENINSULA. This name was bestowed by Captain James Cook (1728–1779) in 1764 and provides further evidence of his sense of humour. See also NAKED MAN HILL.

Napartokh Bay (Labrador) South of HEBRON. This is the northern limit of the tree line; thus, the name is traceable to the Inuit word for 'tree.' This feature is sometimes referred to as 'Black Duck Bay.'

Naskaupi River (Labrador) Flows southeast into GRAND LAKE, an arm of LAKE MELVILLE. It was known originally as the 'North West River,' for the trading post North West River House, established at its mouth. The more recent name, Naskaupi, originates with the Naskapi who inhabit this part of Labrador. They 'migrate seasonally from the interior of Labrador to the coast' (*Dictionary of Newfoundland English*).

Newfoundland Dog Pond (Central)   East of LAKE MEELPAEG. As early as 1839 it was noted by Joseph Jukes (1811–1869) that 'the term pond is [here] applied indiscriminately to all pieces of freshwater, whatever may be their size.' This area was visited by William Eppes Cormack (1796–1868) in October 1822. He noted the presence of a large Newfoundland dog at a Mi'kmaq encampment and subsequently applied the name to the pond. The Newfoundland dog was developed over the centuries by crossing dogs from Europe with a local breed. The result was a distinctive animal which in time became a national symbol, appearing on Newfoundland postage stamps prior to its joining Confederation.

Newman Sound (Eastern)   On BONAVISTA BAY and within the bounds of Terra Nova National Park. Named for the Newman family of Dartmouth, England, who for many generations were involved in trading in Bonavista Bay and the south coast of New-foundland. Other members of the Newman family were associated with the shipping of wine from Oporto, Portugal, to Newfoundland. It was discovered that the rolling of the vessels blended and married the older vintage years with the younger wines. Upon arrival, the fortified wines were placed in bond for four years, as the local climate was deemed to have a beneficial effect on the product. Subsequently, the wine (which became known as 'port,' from its origin in Oporto) was shipped back to England and 'Newman's Port matured in Newfoundland' remains one of the firm's most celebrated products. See also GAULTOIS and TERRA NOVA NATIONAL PARK.

New Perlican (Avalon)   North of HEARTS CONTENT. *See* Old Perlican.

Newtown (Central)   On BONAVISTA BAY. Formerly known as 'Inner Islands,' the current name was adopted in 1892 upon the suggestion of John Haddon, operator of the local lobster cannery. The Barbour family of Newtown produced several generations of prosperous sea captains. The Alphaeus Barbour Queen Anne–style home, open to the public as a museum, illustrates what has been described as 'an outport aristocracy of the sea.'

In November 1929, Captain Job Barbour, while *en route* from ST. JOHN'S to Newtown on his schooner *Neptune II*, went adrift in a storm. Barbour's account of his adventures and eventual arrival in Tobermory, Scotland, is retold in *Forty-Eight Days Adrift*.

New World Island (Central)   In NOTRE DAME BAY. Prior to the early sixteenth century, there was considerable cartographic confusion as to whether the 'new found lands to the west' were actually part of Asia. Samuel Eliot Morison credits Giovanni da Verrazzano, an Italian explorer under commission by King Francis I of France, as the first to put forward the 'New World' theory. During 1523–4, Verrazzano explored the coast, from Cape Fear, North Carolina, to Newfoundland, and concluded 'that the coast between Florida and Newfoundland belonged to a completely New World.' This lends credence to the suggestion by the Reverend Michael Howley that the place name 'New World Island' may be traced to Verrazzano's *Novus Mundus* map of 1528.

Nippers Harbour (Central)   On NOTRE DAME BAY. On a visit to the area in 1854, Bishop Edward Feild (1802–1876) declared: '[This] name is rather an alarming one, particularly to thin skinned Southerners, as the Nipper is the largest and most formidable of the mosquitoes.'

Noddy Bay; Noddy Point (Western)   The point is southwest of CAPE BAULD, on the STRAIT OF BELLE ISLE. Named for the Northern fulmar (*Fulmarus glacialis*). This common seabird is referred to locally as the 'noddy.'

Noddy Point   *See* Noddy Bay.

Norris Arm (Central); **Norris Point** (Western)   At first glance both place names might appear to be derived from the surname; however, this is true only of Norris Arm, a village southwest of LEWISPORTE. It was founded in 1892 and named for James Norris. Norris Point, BONNE BAY, is a corruption of 'North Point,' which dates from the Cook survey of 1767. Cook described the location as 'a snug harbour for small vessels.'

Norris Point   *See* Norris Arm.

North Aulatsivik Island (Labrador) Southeast of CAPE CHIDLEY. The name is derived from the Inuit for 'place of dominance,' a reference to the height of land that rises above the adjacent channel. South Aulatsivik Island, northeast of NAIN has a similar origin.

Northern Peninsula (Western) A descriptive for the peninsula extending from BONNE BAY in a northerly direction to CAPE BAULD, and southward to the head of WHITE BAY. It is often referred to as the 'Great Northern Peninsula.'

Northwest River (Labrador)   A settlement at the head of LAKE MELVILLE, on the north shore of GRAND LAKE. The first fur-trading post at this location was probably established by Louis Fornel (*ca* 1698–1745) around 1745. In 1836 it came under the jurisdiction of the Hudson's Bay Company and was briefly known as 'Fort Smith,' for Donald Smith (1820–1914), later Lord Strathcona. The post was renamed North West River House in 1840. In the twentieth century, the Grenfell Mission erected a small hospital at Northwest River. The community has been well described by Dr. Anthony Paddon, son of Dr. Harry L. Paddon (1881–1939), both of whom served the mission at Northwest River: 'The land is well wooded, and a wonderful contrast to the barren islands of the coast. It is a gentler country with the magnificience of the Mealy Mountains (generally snowcapped) on its south side, and to the north, endless forests of evergreen and birch, stretching westward all the way to Hud-

son's Bay. It was a paradise for my brothers and me ...'

Notre Dame Bay (Central) Extends from CAPE ST. JOHN to CAPE FREELS; some authorities limit its eastern boundaries to CAPE FOGO. Although the name, translated as 'Our Lady Bay,' would appear to be French, it may be even older than the arrival in Newfoundland of Breton and Norman fishermen. Notre Dame Bay is thus possibly a French translation of an earlier Portuguese place name. It appears in this form from about 1550.

Nunaksaluk Island (Labrador)   A high conical island located east of DAVIS INLET. The name has been translated by E.P. Wheeler as 'inhabited land' or 'the big habitable place.'

Nutak (Labrador)   An abandoned settlement on Martin Island, in OKAK BAY. A Hudson's Bay Company post was established here in 1928 and adopted the Inuit name for 'the new one.' In recent years the inhabitants were relocated to NAIN. Nutak is used today for the summer fishery.

Oakbark Cove (Western)   On ST. JOHN BAY. Traditionally the bark of the oak was used in tanning and as an astringent. Although the oak is not native to Newfoundland, the process of using bark in the treatment of nets was followed and explains the name. See also BARKING KETTLE POND.

Ochre Pit Cove (Avalon); **Ochre Pit Island** (Central)   The cove is situated on CONCEPTION BAY, northeast of CARBONEAR, and is named for the red ochre that was once extracted there. The substance was mixed with salt water to produce red building paint. Ochre Pit Island, in EXPLOITS BAY, along with other place names incorporating 'ochre' or 'red' in the interior of the province, have an association with the Beothuk. They used red ochre to colour their bodies, bows, arrows, and canoes, and in their burial practices. See RED INDIAN LAKE.

Ochre Pit Island   *See* Ochre Pit Cove.

O'Donnells (Eastern)   Southeast of PLACENTIA. The name may originate with the fact that, during the nineteenth century, four O'Donnell brothers were serving as parish priests in Newfoundland. More probable is the suggestion that the name honours Bishop J.L. O'Donel (1737–1811).

Offer Wadham Island (Central) To the east of FOGO ISLAND. Of the seven islands in the chain known as 'The Wadhams,' Offer Wadham is the largest and the most important. Although today all are uninhabited, in the summers of the early twentieth century as many as 450 people were engaged in the summer fishery on the Wadhams. 'Offer' is an old English word meaning 'outer,' 'offshore,' or 'away from the land,' and is frequently found in sea-coast place names throughout the province. Wadham originates with the English surname; members of the family were ship captains and owners in NOTRE DAME BAY in the 1720s. The famous 'Wadham's Song' chronicles the navigational hazards from CAPE BONAVISTA to the Stinking Isles (FUNK ISLAND) and thence, by way of JOE BATTS ARM and Fogo, to PILLEY'S ISLAND. The song, dating from the late eighteenth century, was placed on the Admiralty records in London 'as the best guide to that portion of the coastline.' Peckfords Island, also in the Wadhams group, achieved fame on 26 June 1977 as the landfall for Tim Severin's *Brendan Voyage* across the Atlantic. See also ST. BRENDAN'S.

Oil Jacket Cove (Western)   On French Bay, northeast of ST. ANTHONY. The name refers to the jackets once made from flour sacking soaked in raw linseed oil to make them waterproof. The garment gave rise to a nineteenth-century proverb: 'When the weather is fair, your oil jacket bear.'

Okak Bay (Labrador)   Northeast of NUTAK. The name, from the Inuit *okhakh*, is a descriptive meaning 'tongue.' Once the site of a large Moravian mission founded in 1775, its population was almost wiped out in the influenza epidemic of 1918–19. The mission was subsequently abandoned.

Old Ferolle Harbour (Western) Northeast of ST. JOHN BAY. *See* Ferolle Point.

Old Perlican (Avalon)   West of BAY DE VERDE, on TRINITY BAY. Known as 'Parlican' in 1597, it is one of the oldest place names on Trinity Bay. The name probably originates with 'Pelican,' a popular name for a ship. Since the pelican is not native to Newfoundland, any association with the bird is ruled out. 'Old' was later added to distinguish the community from New Perlican, north of HEARTS CONTENT.

Packs Harbour (Labrador) Northeast of Sandwich Bay. Named for Robert Pack (1786–1860), one of the first West Country English merchants to establish

permanent residence in Newfoundland. By the 1850s the firm Pack, Gosse and Fryer was the largest in CARBONEAR, and an active participant in the Labrador fishery.

Palliser Point (Labrador)   North of RIGOLET. Commemorates the career of Sir Hugh Palliser (1723–1796), governor of Newfoundland from 1764 to 1768. The coast of Labrador was placed under the jurisdiction of the governor of Newfoundland in 1763. Palliser subsequently paid two visits to Labrador during his term in office. See also PITTS HARBOUR.

Paradise (Avalon); **Paradise**; **Paradise River**; **Paradise Sound** (Eastern)   The name Paradise is repeated many times in both Newfoundland and Labrador. In most instances the reason is simply euphemistic, or to create a good impression. This explains the origin of the first example, a village west of ST. JOHN'S. Paradise, Paradise Sound, Paradise River, Little Paradise, and Great Paradise are found on the west side of PLACENTIA BAY. Their source may be traced to Paradis, a community north of St. Sampson's, on Guernsey in the Channel Islands. Other nearby locations with a Channel Island connection are Petit Forte, west of Paradise Sound, a variation of

Petit Port, also on Guernsey; while offshore from Rushoon is Jersey Island. This collection of names is indicative of the strong Channel Island influence on the fishery in Placentia Bay.

Paradise River   *See* Paradise.

Paradise Sound   *See* Paradise.

Parsons Pond (Western)   North of GROS MORNE NATIONAL PARK. It echoes a Newfoundland surname common in this area and elsewhere on the NORTHERN PENINSULA.

Pasadena (Western)   Southwest of the town of DEER LAKE. The community was first settled in the 1930s and named after Pasadena Farm, owned by Lawrence Earle. It, in turn, was inspired by the city of Pasadena in California. The latter name is a coined or manufactured name incorporating the endings of four Amerindian words: *pa, sa, de, na*.

Paul Island (Labrador)   East of NAIN. First known as 'Pownal Island,' after John Pownal, who served as secretary to the Board of Trade and Plantations in 1758–61. Later the island was renamed for the Reverend Paul Hettasch, a Moravian missionary in the area for over fifty years. The original name was retained in Mount Pownal, the highest point on the island. In 1774 the Society for the Propagation of the Gospel wrote to the Moravian Mission concerning a mysterious item forwarded in a shipment from Nain. This was 'a stone when turned to the light in a certain position showed a blue lustre ... the stone attracted the attention of many, not for its intrinsic value, but because it had never been seen before.' The reference was to a sample of a precious gemstone, later to be officially named labradorite, which was first found on Pownal (Paul) Island by Brethren of the Moravian Mission. This region is renowned for its deposits of anorthosite, a granite-like rock composed almost entirely of labradorite crystals. See also POWNAL, Prince Edward Island.

Pearl Island   *See* Guernsey Island.

Penetanguishene (Avalon) Adjacent to St. John's Airport and sometimes referred to locally as 'Tanguishene.' The village was founded in the 1950s and named for Penetanguishene, a town on an arm of Georgian Bay, Ontario. The name may be traced to an Ojibwa word translated as 'white falling sand.'

Petit Forte   *See* Paradise.

Petit Nord   See reference to French Shore in chapter 1, pages 17–18.

Petitsikapau Lake (Labrador) East of KNOB LAKE. Originates with a Montagnais–Naskapi word meaning 'willow-fringed.' The name of the lake was mentioned by Hudson's Bay Company factor John MacLean, who visited here in 1839.

Petty Harbour (Avalon)   South of ST. JOHN'S. This picturesque harbour is reputedly one of the most photographed places in Newfoundland. The name is very old and may be of Basque origin. Once known as 'Pettits Harbour,' later contracted to 'Petty Harbour,' the name is descriptive of its size in relation to the much larger St. John's harbour.

Piccadilly (Western)   West of STEPHENVILLE. This is a classic example of a place-name origin that transcends the obvious, for it has no connection with Piccadilly Circus in London. The location was first known as 'Pic à Denis,' a name bequeathed by the first Acadian settlers and later 'anglicized' to Piccadilly. The area between the community and ABRAHAMS COVE is known as Piccadilly Slant; the latter word is an old English term for incline.

Pillar Island (Labrador)   Northeast of HOPEDALE. Named for the 'stone pillars' once found there. The island is known as 'Inuksuktut,' sometimes shortened to 'Inuksuk.' This Inuit word means 'a pile of rocks built to resemble a man' and refers to the practice followed by Labrador fishermen of erecting stone cairns and effigies. These served as landmarks for fishing schooners. Captains Cook and Orlebar, among others, also followed the same custom. See also CAPTAIN ORLEBARS CAIRN and NAKED MAN HILL.

Pilley's Island (Central)   In NOTRE DAME BAY and connected to the mainland by causeway. The derivation is the surname Pilley. The island figures prominently in the essays of native son Dr. Cyril F. Poole, former principal of Sir Wilfred Grenfell College in CORNER BROOK.

Pinchgut Point (Avalon)   On the eastern shore of PLACENTIA BAY; a notable survivor of 'place-name reform.' See the fate of nearby Famish Gut, now FAIR HAVEN. Pinchgut Point endures as a reminder of an eighteenth-century nautical expression for 'a scarcity of food' or a 'miserly purser.'

Pinware; Pinware Bay; Pinware River (Labrador)   The river flows into the STRAIT OF BELLE ISLE, near WEST ST. MODESTE. The name is a corruption of *Pied Noir*, 'black foot,' for a rock resembling a foot at the entrance to the bay. It is a reminder of the once-thriving French migratory fishery.

Pinware Bay   *See* Pinware.

Pinware River   *See* Pinware.

Pipers Hole River (Eastern) Northwest of SWIFT CURRENT. According to local legend, the name Pipers Hole dates back to the eighteenth century. Ever since a battle between the French and English at nearby GARDEN COVE, a lone French piper is reputed to still haunt the area, mournfully playing a pipe. See also SWIFT CURRENT.

Pipestone Pond (Central)   East of MEELPAEG LAKE. According to William Eppes Cormack (1796–1868) this location 'was known to the Mi'kmaqs by the name, Stone Pipe Lake, for their procuring here serpentine rock and other magnesium rocks out of which they carved or chiseled their tobacco pipes.'

Pistolet Bay (Western)   Southeast of CAPE NORMAN. This name also dates from the period of the French migratory fishery. It is probably after a French surname.

In the 1760s, Captain James Cook (1728–1779) reported that 'the shore is almost everywhere cloath'd with wood, [the fishermen] frequently come here from Quirpon to get timber.'

Pitts Harbour (Labrador)   In CHATEAU BAY. The name may be traced to British statesman William Pitt 'The Elder' (1708–1778). In 1756 he became nominally secretary of state, but was virtually prime minister, with three short breaks, until 1768. It was first bestowed on Fort Pitt, located on the shores of the Arm. The fort was the temporary residence of Governor Sir Hugh Palliser while on duty on the Labrador. From here he issued several proclamations relating to the Labrador fishery.

Placentia; Placentia Bay (Avalon) The town occupies a picturesque setting on the east side of Placentia Bay. By the later part of the sixteenth century, it had become a centre for the Basque fishery, which, at its peak, employed 6,000 men. The name may originate with Plascenzia, a town in Salamanca, Spain, but more probably is for Plentzia, in the Basque province of Bizkia. From 1624 to 1713 it was Plaisance, the capital of the French colony in Newfoundland. Following the Treaty of Utrecht in 1713, the English assumed control, and France transferred its attention to the construction of Fortress Louisbourg, in Cape Breton. On 14 July 1792, Aaron Thomas visited Placentia, as it became known to the English. He wrote: 'The Town is, in importance, next to St. John's. There are about 200 Houses or Hutts huddled together, built on a kind of sand beach, which is nearly surrounded by water. The inhabitants nearly all come from Waterford in Ireland. The face of the country is unusually Mountainous and Rocky. The Town at the back of it, has a narrow arm of water which is overhung by a Precipice. Here is a small fort with about twenty Artillery men. There are two old forts in ruins, one on Castle Hill, the other on the Larboard hand, going into the Northeast Arm.' Today Castle Hill Park, situated between JERSEYSIDE and FRESHWATER, affords a superb view of the setting described by Thomas. The park is host to an annual Canada Day Folk Festival.

Placentia Bay   *See* Placentia.

Pleasantville (Avalon)   Now part of the city of ST. JOHN'S. Named for the meadowland north of QUIDI VIDI LAKE. During the First World War, Pleasantville became the site of a training camp for the Royal Newfoundland Reg-iment, and, as Fort Pepperell, from 1941 to 1965 it was a U.S. Air Force base. The latter was named for Sir William Pepperell (1696–1759), commander of the colonial forces at the capture of Louisbourg in 1745.

Pointe à l'Aurore (Western) Northwest of ST. JULIEN'S. Known for a time as 'Little St. Julien's.' The name provides an indication of the dramatic impact of the *aurora borealis* throughout Newfoundland and Labrador. To Väinö Tanner, Finnish scholar and explorer, the northern lights were 'the searchlights of God ... most brilliantly displayed after dark, and at all seasons, provided the moonlight does not neutralize them. We found that radio signals and compass disturbances were greatest when the Northern Lights were especially intensified.'

Point Leamington (Central) North of BOTWOOD, at the head of South West Arm. Named after Leamington, in Warwickshire, England.

Pointe Riche (Western)   A headland on the southeastern tip of the PORT AU CHOIX PENINSULA. The point was sighted and named by Jacques Cartier on 15 June 1534. He wrote: 'We saw ... a large cape doubled one part above the other [a reference to the St. John Highlands in the rear], and on this account we named it *Cap Double.'* The present name is traceable to early settlers with the surname Rich or Riche.

Port au Choix; Port au Choix Peninsula (Western)   A village northwest of PORT SAUNDERS. Derived from the Basque descriptive *Portuchoa,* 'little harbour' and the nearby *Portucho caharra,* 'old little harbour.' Aside from its role as an important Basque fishing station, this area is also of considerable historical and archaeological significance. In the late 1950s, at nearby Phillips Garden, relics were uncovered of a Dorset culture dating from between A.D. 200 and 600. The Dorset people were neither Amerindian nor Inuit, but take their name from artefacts first collected at Cape Dorset on Baffin Island in 1925. (See also BAIE VERTE.) The Dorset culture has been described as one of the most beautiful and skilful in the ancient world. Their carvings of stone and bone may be classified as masterpieces and are among the earliest examples of true art yet found in Atlantic Canada. The second archaeological find, a large cemetery, was discovered at Port au Choix in 1967 and has added greatly to our understanding of the Maritime Archaic culture, which flourished in this area some 3,000 years ago. Thanks to the local climate, geography, and soil conditions, many bones, tools, weapons, ornaments, and other artefacts have survived the centuries. Other discoveries indicate that the intellectual development of the Maritime Archaic people matched their technology and was particularly noticeable in their burial practices. The graves were always lined with red ochre and marked or protected by slabs of rock. They usually contained collections of artefacts for use by the dead in the afterlife. Memorial University archaeologist James Tuck, who was largely responsible for the excavation of the site, has concluded: 'Their history is only beginning to be understood.' See also L'ANSE AMOUR.

Port au Choix Peninsula   *See* Port au Choix.

Port au Port; Port au Port Bay; Port au Port Peninsula (Western) A village, bay, and peninsula north of ST. GEORGE'S BAY. The name, of Basque origin, is a corruption of 'Oporportu,' which has been freely translated as 'port of relaxation' or 'port of rest in time of storm.' A Basque linguist, Miren Egaña Goya, has concluded that 'Oporportu' means a 'harbour for ships.'

Port au Port Bay   *See* Port au Port.

Port au Port Peninsula   *See* Port au Port.

Port aux Basques   *See* Channel–Port aux Basques.

Port Blandford (Eastern)   Northwest of CLARENVILLE. The village was named for Captain Darius Blandford (1840–1909), prominent sealing captain and at one time a resident of GREENSPOND.

Port de Grave (Avalon)   East of BAY ROBERTS. Traceable to the French *grève* or *grave*, for 'pebbly beach.' Early French fishermen frequently dried their cod on the shingle, or beach.

Port Hope Simpson (Labrador) On the south side of Alexis River. Marks the career of Sir John Hope Simpson (1868–1961), who served as Commissioner for Natural Resources in the Commission of Government in 1934–6. In August 1934, Sir John visited a logging operation started by the Labrador Development Company at the mouth of the Alexis River. At the request of the company 'he named its headquarters Port Hope Simpson.'

Portland Creek; Portland Creek Pond (Western)   Between DANIEL'S HARBOUR and THE ARCHES. Name assigned in 1767 by Captain James Cook (1728–

1779) after Portland, in Dorset, England.

Portland Creek Pond   *See* Portland Creek.

Port Saunders (Western)   Northwest of HAWKES BAY. Honours Admiral Sir Charles Saunders (1713?–1775), who served as commodore and commander-in-chief of the Newfoundland station in 1752. Today, Port Saunders is a regional service centre and location of a major marine-repair depot.

Portugal Cove; Portugal Cove South (Avalon)   The first location is a town on the northeast side of CONCEPTION BAY. The name dates from the early seventeenth century and is evidence of Portugal's long association with the Newfoundland fishery. In the 1890s, with the advent of iron-ore mining on nearby Bell Island, a regular ferry service was established with the mainland. The town was incorporated in 1977. The second Portugal Cove, east of TREPASSEY, also dates from the early seventeenth century. The name Portugal Cove South was officially adopted on 30 August 1913 to distinguish this location from the other Portugal Cove.

Portugal Cove South   *See* Portugal Cove.

Port Union (Eastern) South of CATALINA, on TRINITY BAY. In 1908 a group of fishermen joined with their leader, William Coaker (1871–1938), to form the Fishermen's Protective Union. Coaker realized that the outport fishermen faced even greater hardships on land than on the stormy north Atlantic. Their lives were held in economic bondage by a credit system controlled by ST. JOHN'S merchants. Coaker was eventually successful in enrolling some 20,000 fishermen in a union and in founding the town. In addition, he was responsible for the organization of light and power, publishing, shipping, and cold-storage companies. Less successful were his efforts to found a political party; his political dreams were never realized. The town he named Port Union remains as his most enduring monument.

Postville (Labrador) Southwest of MAKKOVIK. The name is derived from the use of this location for many years as a fur-trading post. Originally known as 'The Post,' it was for a time (1830–7) operated by the Hudson's Bay Company. The contemporary name dates from about 1941.

Pouch Cove (Avalon) Northwest of ST. JOHN'S. The precise origin of the village name is unknown; however, E.R. Seary suggests that it may be for the French surname Pouche. Fortunately, it survived an attempt by eighteenth-century English cartographers to rename the location 'Port Choice.' One of the earliest records of the name as *Pouche Cove* was by Joseph Jukes (1811–1869) in 1840.

Princeton (Eastern) On Southern Bay, an inlet of BONAVISTA BAY. The community was first known as 'Seal Cove,' but was renamed about 1910 to prevent confusion with the numerous other locations of the same name. Commemorates the Samuel Prince family, who were residents and landowners at Seal Cove in the 1840s.

Prowestown *See* Sibleys Cove.

Queen's Cove (Eastern) On the south side of North West Arm, TRINITY BAY. Settled in the 1860s and named in honour of Queen Victoria's Silver Jubilee in 1862.

Queen's Lake (Labrador) The archipelago, or 'sea of many islands,' west of Dog or High Island, was known on the Labrador as 'Queen's Lake,' for Queen Victoria.

Quidi Vidi (Avalon) A village northeast of ST. JOHN'S. Once classified by the Right Reverend

Michael Howley as an 'uncommon name of uncertain origin,' Quidi Vidi has endured more than twenty-five variations in spelling, ranging all the way from 'Quilli widdi' to 'Quidy Vidy.' The phonetic rendering, 'Kitty Vitty,' is common in early documents – for example, 'Colonel Amherst marched to Kitty Vitty and made himself master of that important post' (dispatch of Rear-Admiral Lord Colville, 20 September 1762). E.R. Seary theorized that Quidi Vidi is 'a conjectural derivation from the French family name which occurs variously as Quédville in Normandy and Picardy and Quetteville in Jersey.' The prominence of Channel Island firms in the development of the Newfoundland fishery, and in particular the role of the DeQuetteville family of Jersey, might be cited as circumstantial evidence to verify this conclusion. However, another and stronger theory is that it is from the Latin phrase *Que divide*, for 'here divides.' Thus, the name resulted from a division, at this point, of the original grant of the London and Bristol Company in the seventeenth century (Cell and Le Messurier). See also KITIWITI SHOAL, Nova Scotia.

Quirpon; Quirpon Island (Western)   The settlement is on the mainland, while the island lies off the tip of the NORTHERN PENINSULA. This area was visited by Jacques Cartier on 27 May 1534, when he reported 'on account of unfavourable weather and the large number of icebergs we met with, we deemed it advisable to enter ... a harbour called Karpont, where we remained, without being able to leave until 9 June.' It is significant that the harbour was *already* known to Cartier as 'Karpont,' so named because of its resemblance to the port of Le Kerpont, near St. Malo, France. Over the centuries the name has been anglicized to 'Quirpon' and pronounced locally as 'Carpoon.'

Quirpon Island   *See* Quirpon.

Raleigh (Western)   On HA HA BAY, northwest of ST. ANTHONY. The name was proclaimed on 23 June 1914 in honour of Sir Walter Raleigh (or Ralegh; 1522–1618), the famous Elizabethan courtier, navigator, and author. The assignment of this name is not as far-fetched as it might appear. Sir Walter Raleigh was a half-brother of Sir Humphrey Gilbert's (1537?–1583) and provided financial backing for the latter's 1583 exploratory voyage, which culminated in Gilbert's taking possession of Newfoundland, in the name of Queen Elizabeth I, on

3 August 1583 at ST. JOHN'S. Later, in 1600, Sir Walter Raleigh was appointed governor of Jersey, about the time Channel Islanders began to play an active role in the Newfoundland fishery.

Ramah Bay (Labrador)   South of NACHVAK FIORD. A settlement on Ramah Bay was founded in 1871 as a Moravian mission and named for the biblical Ramah, located on the border between the ancient kingdoms of Judea and Israel. Because of its extreme isolation, the mission was abandoned about 1901.

Ramea; Ramea Islands (Central) Southeast of BURGEO. Over the years this name has been spelled in various ways: 'Ramie,' 'Ramee,' and 'Ramea.' Because of the involvement of Channel Islanders in the south-shore fishery, the name is probably for Le Ramée, northwest of St. Peterport, on the island of Guernsey. There the word means 'vetch plant' (*Vicia cracca*). In 1766, Captain James Cook (1728–1779) noted: 'In [Ramea] & about these islands are many convenient places for erecting Stages & Drying of Fish & are well situated for the Cod Fishery.' See also REN-CONTRE.

Ramea Islands   *See* Ramea.

Random Island; Random Sound (Eastern)   On the west side of TRINITY BAY. The name may be traced to the old English word *randan*, which meant 'riotous or disorderly behaviour,' a possible reference to some long-forgotten revelry or 'spree.' See also RANTEM.

Random Sound   *See* Random Island.

Rantem (Avalon)   A small cove at the head of TRINITY BAY. It is also used to designate the narrow isthmus that links the AVALON PENINSULA with the main island of Newfoundland. E.R. Seary held the opinion that its origin is similar to that of RANDOM ISLAND. Both place names probably have an association with *rantum-scantum*, defined by the *Oxford English Dictionary* as 'a boisterous spree.' Such an event has long been known in Newfoundland as 'a time.'

Rattling Brook (Central)   This example of the numerous 'Rattling' Brooks found in the province flows eastward into Southeast Arm, GREEN BAY. In 1792, George Cartwright (1739/ 40–1819) provided a definition of the phenomenon: 'where there is a succession of falls in a river ... the falling water makes a great noise; such a place is called a rattle.' This place name, with the same meaning, is repeated several times in Nova Scotia.

Red Bay (Labrador)   Northeast of PINWARE BAY, on the STRAIT OF BELLE ISLE. The name is a descriptive for the red granite bluffs that surround the bay. It was first known to the French as 'Havre des Buttes,' later changed in Basque documents to *Buytres*. From 1550 to 1600, the location was literally 'the whaling capital of the world,' as each year ships sailed from the Basque provinces in search of whales in the Strait of Belle Isle. Much credit for our knowledge of the 'Basque chapter' in Canadian history must go to Selma de Lothbinière Barkham. Through extensive research in the departmental archives of France and Spain, she was able not only to pinpoint the major Basque whaling sites on the coast of Labrador, but also to ascertain details surrounding the operation of the industry. Subsequent archaeological studies on location were to add further insight. Thus, their distinctive red roof tiles (named 'Basque calling cards' by Barkham) led investigators to sites ranging from PLEASURE HARBOUR (Puerto Nuevo) to EAST ST. MODESTE (Los Hornos). Within Red Bay, underwater archaeologists discovered the wreck of the *San Juan*, also men-

tioned in archival documents. For her ground-breaking research, Selma Barkham was awarded, in 1980, the Gold Medal of the Royal Canadian Geographical Society. For another example of her research see RED ISLAND.

Red Indian Lake (Central) South of Highway 370. First known as 'Lieutenant's Lake.' This name was bestowed by Lieutenant John Cartwright (1740–1824) for his rank. Not so well known as his brother George (see CARTWRIGHT); he led an important expedition to the EXPLOITS RIVER area in 1768 in search of the Beothuk. The current name of this lake stems from the Beothuk attachment to the use of red ochre. This led the first Europeans to use the epithet 'red' to describe all Amerindians. The shore of the lake was also the site of a major Beothuk winter encampment. See also OCHRE PIT COVE and OCHRE PIT ISLAND.

Red Island (Western)   Opposite MAINLAND, on the PORT AU PORT PENINSULA. In 1767 this island, long known by its Basque name, Sen Georgeco Irla or Isla de San George, was renamed Red Island by Captain James Cook (1728–1779). In his words it was so called because 'the steep cliffs around it are of reddish colour.' More than a century earlier, on

7 June 1632, a Basque ship, the *San Pedro*, lay at anchor off Red Island. On board was a dying man who dictated his last will and testament to the captain. This document, one of the hundreds uncovered in the research of Selma Barkham, is important as 'the first known document written on the West Coast of Newfoundland.' Further, as she points out, because of the other legal papers related to proving the will, 'we have a fairly clear picture of ... the lives of these early visitors.'

Rencontre Bay (Central)   Northeast of CAPE LAHUNE. The name is traceable to *rencontre*, for 'meeting or meeting bay.' It was probably first assigned as a place name by Channel Islanders. H.W. LeMessurier points to the presence of two hills at the mouth of Rencontre Bay which are called St. Aubin and St. Helier, after the two towns in Jersey.

Renews (Avalon)   South of FERRYLAND; now part of Cappahayden. On 16 June 1536, Jacques Cartier, *en route* to France, rounded CAPE RACE and 'entered a harbour called *Rougnouse,*' where wood and water were taken on for the Atlantic crossing. On Monday, 19 June, the expedition 'set forth from this harbour and were favoured with such good weather that [they] reached

St. Malo 16 July 1536, thanks be to God.' The place name may be traced to the French *rougneux*, for 'scruffy, as a rock covered with weeds, slime or shells.' Over time the pronunciation and spelling evolved to 'Renoose,' and eventually to 'Renews.' E.R. Seary points out that 'there is a rock off the coast of Brittany having the same name and in the harbour of Renews there is a large rock with the same description.' See also CAPPAHAYDEN.

Rigolet (Labrador)   At the head of HAMILTON INLET. Prior to the settlement of the Labrador–Québec boundary dispute in 1927, the Geographic Board of Canada maintained files on some Labradorian names. On 5 December 1901, it reported this 'settlement name appears to be descriptive and relates to the narrow channel beside which the place is situated. The term *rigolet* is used in the sense of *un petit ruisseau*, an extension of the usual meaning of the French noun *rigole.*'

River of Ponds (Western) Southwest of HAWKE'S BAY. This feature was named by nature. The nearby River of Ponds Provincial Park was set aside because of its environmental interest. In particular, this section of the west coast of the NORTHERN PENINSULA is noted for the presence of tucka-more, or 'tuck.' Similar in appear-ance to the *krummholz* of the Alps, the stunted spruce and fir trees have been shaped by the fury of wind and sea to provide a closely matted ground cover.

Robert's Arm (Central)   On NOTRE DAME BAY. The community was first known as 'Rabbits Arm' since it was a popular location for trapping. By the late nineteenth century, it had been changed to Roberts Arm, after a common Newfoundland surname.

Robinsons (Western)   A village southwest of ST. GEORGE'S. Two theories exist to explain the name's origin: it may be for an early settler, or, more probably, it was bestowed in 1767 by Captain James Cook (1728–1779) for one of his fellow naval officers.

Rocky Harbour (Western)
Northwest of NORRIS POINT, on BONNE BAY. The name is descrip-tive of the shoreline, which is bor-dered by rocky ledges. It appears on the Admiralty chart of 1897 as *Roche* or *Rocky Harbour*.

Roddickton (Western)   North of ENGLEE. Once known as 'Easter Bay.' Named in the early twenti-eth century in honour of Sir Thomas George Roddick (1846–1923), a native of HARBOUR GRACE,

who emigrated to Canada while still in his teens. Following a med-ical education, he went on to achieve fame as a surgeon in Montreal. In addition to his medi-cal career, Roddick served eight years as the member of Parliament for Montreal–St. Antoine. He was also responsible for the establish-ment of the Medical Council of Canada. A strong supporter of Sir Wilfred Grenfell, Roddick pre-sented the mission, in 1894, with 'a splendid twenty foot jolly boat.' Grenfell recorded his enthusiasm for the gift: 'I have sailed the seas in ocean greyhounds, and in float-ing palaces, and in steam yachts, but better than any other voyage [was] the memory of that first summer cruising the Labrador.' Later, when a Grenfell nursing station was established at the head of CANADA BAY, Roddick's name was enshrined in the new place name.

Romaine River (Labrador)   The headwaters of this river (which flows south into the GULF OF ST. LAWRENCE) are in Labrador, and for the first portion of its length, it forms the boundary with Québec. The name is a corruption of the Amerindian *alimun*, which trans-lates as 'difficult,' a reference to the problems in navigating the river.

Rose Blanche (Western)   East of CHANNEL–PORT AUX BASQUES. The harbour, and Rose Blanche Bank off shore, were once frequented by French migratory fishermen. The name originates with the out-croppings of white granite char-acteristic of the shoreline and is a corruption of *Roche Blanche,* 'white rock.' In recent years the two communities Rose Blanche and nearby Harbour Le Cou have been amalgamated. See also HAR-BOUR LE COU.

Rushoon (Eastern)   Northeast of MARYSTOWN. The precise origin of the name, possibly traceable to French or Channel Island sources, has been lost. The Right Reverend Michael Howley suggests that it may have evolved from *ruisseau,* for 'brook'.

Sacred Bay (Western)   South-west of CAPE BAULD. The name appears on eighteenth-century charts as *B de Sacre*; subsequently rendered as *Sacred Bay* by Captain James Cook in 1764. It probably originates with the French sur-name Sacré. Sacrey is a family name still found on the NORTH-ERN PENINSULA.

Saddle Hill (Avalon)   Between HARBOUR GRACE and CARBONEAR. A common descriptive, in New-foundland and elsewhere, for a hill or island having a depression in the middle, and thus resem-bling a saddle. In 1835 Saddle Hill was the setting for an incident involving Henry Winton (1815–1866), the ultra-Protestant editor of the ST. JOHN'S *Public Ledger.* Known as 'the war horse of New-foundland journalism,' he had been, for a number of years, embroiled in a battle of words against Roman Catholic mem-bers of the legislature. As Winton later described it: 'On 15 May 1835 ... I was set upon by a gang of ruffians, hideously disguised with painted faces at the Saddle or Saddle Hill.' In the ensuing struggle he was struck to the ground; his left ear was cut off and his right ear badly mutilated. Not easily silenced, Winton lived for another twenty years to, in his words, 'unflinchingly advocate the principles of civil and reli-gious liberty' (*Public Ledger,* 1852–4; 1855–60).

Saglek Bay; Saglek Fiord (Labrador)   The bay is a major indentation in the coastline south of NACHVAK FIORD. Saglek Fiord is at the head of the bay. From the Inuit for 'low land,' so named in comparison to the adjacent high mountains. Saglek Bank offshore takes its name from the bay.

Saglek Fiord   *See* Saglek Bay.

St. Alban's (Eastern)   On BAY D'ESPOIR. First known as 'Ship Cove,' the name was changed in

1915. The Reverend Stanislaus St. Croix (1882–1968), the local priest, selected St. Alban's as an approprite name for the parish, composed largely of English Roman Catholics. St. Alban was a third-century martyr who reputedly was murdered on the site of St. Alban's Cathedral, in the city of the same name in Hertsfordshire, England.

St. Anthony (Western)   North of Hare Bay. The name was bestowed by Jacques Cartier on St. Anthony's Day, 13 June 1534, for a location on the present Canadian mainland, west of Blanc Sablon, now known as 'Rocky Harbour.' The name St. Antoine was later transferred to the northeast coast of Newfoundland, and over time became St. Anthony's. In 1900, Dr. Wilfred Grenfell (1865–1940) selected this village as the site for a hospital and, later, in 1912, the headquarters for the International Grenfell Mission. For decades, until the medical and social-service work of the mission was assumed by government, the Grenfell Mission was literally the 'beacon of hope' for thousands of isolated residents of northern Newfoundland and Labrador. Even today, in St. Anthony one can still catch something of the mystique of the paradoxical Dr. (later Sir) Wilfred Grenfell. Here may be found his home, now the Grenfell House Museum, full of artefacts that chronicle a long and storied life. Letters from prime ministers, presidents, and kings vie for space with medical memorabilia and reminders of adventures on land and sea. Then, farther up the hill, one encounters a rock face to which a brass tablet is fixed, marking where his ashes were interred. It simply bears his name, the date, and an inscription 'Life Is a Field of Honour.' Grenfell, a man of grim determination and not a little controversy, remains to many an enigma. A balanced assessment comes from his most recent biographer, Ronald Romkey, of Memorial University. It is Romkey's contention that Grenfell can best be understood 'not as a doctor or even as a missionary or as a hero, but as a social reformer whose instruments were political and cultural.' The transitional years of the International Grenfell Association, renamed the Grenfell Regional Health Services in 1978, are well described in *From Sled to Satellite* (Toronto 1987), by one of Grenfell's successors, Dr. Gordon W. Thomas. See also GRENFELL SOUND and HARE BAY.

St. Barbe; St. Barbe Bay (Western)   A settlement and bay southeast of ANCHOR POINT. Prior to the eighteenth century, this area was known as 'Ste. Marie,' and more generally as 'Point aux Anchres.' By the 1730s the name St. Barbe, for the second-century saint and martyr, had become fixed. A pilgrimage is held in her honour at Roscoff, in Brittany, on the third Monday in July. There is a seasonal ferry from St. Barbe to Blanc Sablon on the Quebéc–Labrador boundary.

St. Barbe Bay   *See* St. Barbe.

St. Brendan's (Central)   On COT-TLES ISLAND, BONAVISTA BAY. Named for the sixth-century Irish St. Brendan, known as 'the voyager.' In 1976–7 Tim Severin, an Irish historian and explorer, set out with a crew of four to re-enact the legendary Brendan voyage in a curragh or coracle made of oxhides. Their route took them from Brandon Creek, Ireland (on the day following St. Brendan's Day, 17 May 1976), to the Hebrides, to the Faeroe Islands, and on to Iceland, across to Greenland, and from there to the east coast of Newfoundland. Of their successful feat Severin commented: '*Brendan* touched the New World at 8:00 PM on 26 June 1977 on the shore of Peckford Island [in the Offer Wadham Islands]. The exact spot of her landfall has no particular significance [other than] it was the place where the wind and current had

brought a 20th century replica of the original Irish skin vessels.' That it is difficult to sift fact from fiction in the Brendan sagas does not in any way detract from the singular achievement of Severin and his crew. In the spirit of Thor Heyerdahl, they proved that such a voyage *could* take place.

St. Bride's (Avalon)   North of CAPE ST. MARY'S. The earlier name for St. Bride's was the descriptive Distress. The sea coast was treacherous, and inland travelling not much better. Geologist J.P. Howley recalled: 'We left Distress early in the morning to cross overland to Branch, and a hard tramp over barrens and marshes. The country is nearly level with scarcely any wood except occasional patches of tucking bushes [Tucking or Tuckamore: see RIVER OF PONDS].' The contemporary name was taken from the titular saint of the Church of St. Bridget. The fifth-century St. Brigit or St. Bride was one of the patron saints of Ireland.

St. Chads (Eastern)   Northwest of EASTPORT, on BONAVISTA BAY. Named for a seventh-century Northumbrian bishop; however, the community did not always possess a 'saintly' name. It was originally called Damnable Harbour and was known as such to

Joseph Jukes (1811–1869) in 1839. According to local legend, which may well have apocryphal overtones, the name is traceable to an incident in the earliest days of settlement. On one occasion the harbour afforded shelter to a pirate ship under pursuit by the Royal Navy. The pirate ship was safely hidden behind a small island until a crew member accidentally bumped into the ship's bell. The noise caused by 'the damnable bell' alerted the searching sailors and resulted in the eventual capture of the pirates. In 1879 the name listed was Dangerous Cove, which was changed to St. Chads by the time of the 1911 census report.

St. David's (Western)   Southwest of ROBINSONS, on ST. GEORGE'S BAY. Named for the patron saint of Wales and the only native Welshman to be canonized.

Ste. Genevieve Bay (Western) South of ST. BARBE. Probably goes back as far as the French migratory fishery. Commemorates the life of the fifth-century French saint who was noted as the patroness of Paris. The settlement receives first mention in the census report of 1874.

St. George's   *See* Cape St. George.

St. George's Bay   *See* Cape St. George.

St. George's River   *See* Cape St. George.

St. John's (Avalon)   The name of the capital city of Newfoundland and Labrador, is one of the oldest in the province, and is derived from its supposed date of discovery by John Cabot on the Feast of St. John the Baptist, 24 June 1497. It made its first official appearance on the Portuguese Reinel map of 1516–20 as *R de Sam Johem*. A few years later, on 3 August 1527, John Rut, commander of an English expedition, entered 'into a good haven called Saint John,' giving indication that the name was already in popular usage. Over time it survived a series of translations, from the Portuguese to English, to French, and back to the English. Today, St. John's, replete with apostrophe, is the official designation of the city, thus distinguishing it from SAINT JOHN, New Brunswick. On a continent where many of the larger cities are not easily distinguishable one from the other, St. John's is an exception. Shaped by its long history and a landlocked harbour with an amphitheatre-like setting, the city must be visited to be fully appreciated. Memorial University of Newfoundland was founded at St.

John's in 1925 as Memorial University College, in commemoration of Newfoundlanders who died in the First World War. Located first in downtown St. John's, Memorial achieved university status following Newfoundland's entry into Confederation. In 1961 the university moved to a spacious new campus in the northern section of the city. See also SIGNAL HILL.

St. John Island; St. John Bay; St. John Highlands (Western)   St. John Island is located in St. John Bay, on the west coast of the NORTHERN PENINSULA. The mountains on the nearby mainland are known as St. John Highlands. According to Selma Barkham: 'The name [of Basque origin] seems to have made its first cartographic appearance in 1602 as *San Ian.*'

St. John Bay   *See* St. John Island.

St. John Highlands   *See* St. John Island.

St. Jones Within; St. Jones Without (Eastern)   The first community is located inside (within) RANDOM SOUND, TRINITY BAY; the second is outside (without) the Sound. Originally, 'St. Jones' was 'St. John's'; thus, it is an interesting example of evolutionary linguistic change. The change had the particular advantage of producing toponyms that were distinctive from St. John's. E.R. Seary points out that the names 'echo those of the twin parishes of St. John's Within and St. John's Without in Waterford, Ireland.

St. Jones Without   *See* St. Jones Within.

St. Julien's (Western)   Northeast of CROQUE. Sometimes known as 'Great St. Juliens Harbour.' Named for a Breton saint; the place name is also common in Brittany and elsewhere in France. The inhabitants of Great St. Julien's were resettled at Grandois in the 1960s; however, the post office retains the older name, St. Julien's.

St. Lawrence (Eastern)   Southwest of BURIN. The name, undoubtedly a reminder of the saint and martyr who died at Rome in A.D. 258, may be traced to the Portuguese *a baia de sa lourenço.* The name passed, in translation, to its present rendering in English. For many years in the late eighteenth and early nineteenth centuries, the Jersey firm of DeGrouchy, Nicolle and Company had a thriving business at nearby Little St. Lawrence. The coincidence of the parish name St. Lawrence on Jersey helped reinforce the earlier name. The people of St. Lawrence, along with others from neighbouring Lawn, achieved international fame on Ash Wednesday, 18 February 1942. In the midst of a savage snow and sleet storm, they managed to help rescue 185 shipwrecked American sailors (see LAWN). On 6 June 1954, in grateful appreciation, the government of the United States presented the two communities with a $400,000 fully equipped hospital. A plaque commemorating the event reads in part: 'It is hoped that the hospital will serve as a living memorial to the 203 officers and men of the United States Navy who lost their lives in the disaster and as a vital reminder of the inherent courage of mankind.'

St. Lewis   *See* Cape St. Lewis.

St. Lunaire (Western)   Northeast of ST. ANTHONY. It was settled and named by Breton fishermen in the early sixteenth century. The designation was undoubtedly inspired by the town near St. Malo in northwestern France. In turn it was named for St. Leonorius, a Breton bishop of the sixth century. Near St. Lunaire, a stone with an undecipherable inscription has been found. There has been some speculation that the letters may be of ancient Irish or Celtic origin. Archaeologist James Tuck has concluded that 'all that

we can really say is that we do not know how to explain the St. Lunaire inscription.' It is now part of the amalgamated community of St. Lunaire–Griquet.

St. Mary's; St. Mary's Bay (Avalon)   The indentation between CAPE ST. MARY'S and CAPE FREELS known as St. Mary's Bay undoubtedly takes its name from the earlier named cape. See Cape St. Mary's.

St. Mary's Bay   *See* St. Mary's.

St. Patricks (Central)   On Highway 392, northeast of SPRINGDALE. Settled in the late nineteenth century, it first appears in the 1911 census report. The name comes from the fifth-century bishop who became patron saint of Ireland.

St. Phillips (Avalon)   On CONCEPTION BAY, southwest of PORTUGAL COVE. Originally known as 'Broad Cove'; the name was changed by proclamation on 1 June 1905 to St. Philips or St. Phillips, after the apostle. The local Anglican church is dedicated to this saint.

St. Shores; St. Shotts (Avalon)   These two coves northwest of CAPE FREELS have long constituted a place-name puzzle. However, E.R. Seary has traced St. Shotts back to the old French *cince,* or *cinche,* a reference to the 'ragged or shoal ridden coast.' The name appears on some early maps as *Chinchette* or *Cap de Chinette;* however, it was not until the Cook and Lane surveys of the 1770s that canonization to *St. Shots* took place. By the time of the Jukes expedition in 1839–40 it was in common use. On 26 October 1839, he wrote: 'We passed near St. Shotts. This place, a small rocky cove or bay, is the terror of mariners on this coast.' The evolution of the name St. Shores is more straightforward. It began as South Shores, sometimes shortened to S. Shores, and eventually to St. Shores. Thus both names underwent changes that created saints unknown in the ecclesiastical calendar.

St. Shotts   *See* St. Shores.

St. Vincent's (Avalon)   Southwest of ST. MARY'S. Listed as early as 1519 on Portuguese maps as *Porta da Cruz.* During the late nineteenth century, the settlement was known as 'Holyrode South.' The name was changed in 1910 because of postal confusion with Holyrood, CONCEPTION BAY. St. Vincent was a fourth-century Spanish martyr.

Sally's Cove (Western)   North of BONNE BAY, on the western coast of the NORTHERN PENINSULA. The old English word *sally* has a number of meanings. It may refer to a projection of land or to species of trees resembling the willow. Either of these may account for the place name; or it may be after the first name of an early settler, reputedly one Sally Short. In the provincial election of 28 October 1971, the village earned a place in Canadian electoral history. The Liberals, under J.R. Smallwood, won twenty seats; the Conservatives, led by Frank Moores, captured twenty-one and the New Labrador Party held the remaining seat. A recount was called in St. Barbe South, where the winning Conservative, Ed Maynard, was elected by four votes. During a recount it was discovered that the returning officer at Sally's Cove had burned all 107 ballots cast at this poll. Eventually matters were sorted out: the Conservatives retained the seat, and the Smallwood government resigned in January 1972.

Salmonier Arm; Salmonier River (Avalon)   The arm is an extension of ST. MARY'S BAY; the river flows into the arm. Salmonier, for 'one who fishes salmon,' is derived from the French *saumonier* and frequently occurs in place names throughout the province. The Salmonier Line refers to the highway from the Head of St. Mary's Bay to CONCEPTION BAY.

Salmonier River *See* Salmonier Arm.

Salvage; Salvage Bay (Eastern) On BONAVISTA BAY at the tip of the EASTPORT PENINSULA. The name is one of the oldest in this immediate area. In all probability it is traceable to the Spanish *salvaje*, for 'savage,' a probable reference to an early sighting or contact with the Beothuk. The local pronunciation is 'Salvadge,' which is also an early spelling of the place name.

Salvage Bay *See* Salvage.

Sandringham (Eastern) East of GLOVERTOWN. Named for the royal residence, Sandringham House, in Norfolk; the name was imposed to mark the Queen Victoria's Diamond Jubilee. The settlement dates from 1939–40 and was one of the projects launched by the Commission of Government. See also MARKLAND.

Seaplane Cove (Labrador) In Seven Islands Bay. The name was suggested by Alexander Forbes (1882–1965) of the National Geographical Society Aerial Survey of northern Labrador 'because of its fitness for seaplane operations.' He was recruited by Sir Wilfred Grenfell to carry out this mission during the years 1931 to 1935. Forbes was accompanied on his aerial surveys by Charles Hubbard, and occasionally by Sir Wilfred himself.

Searston (Western) Northwest of CHANNEL–PORT AUX BASQUES. This community was first known as 'Grand River Gut.' In an act of place-name 'reform' following establishment of the Newfoundland Nomenclature Board in 1904, it was changed to honour Monsignor Thomas Sears (1824–1885). Sears, a native of Ireland, grew up near ANTIGONISH, Nova Scotia. He served among the Cape Breton emigrants to the CODROY valley. See also TOMPKINS.

Seary Peak (Avalon) A hill, 240 metres high, west of Bellevue Provincial Park on the isthmus that joins the AVALON PENINSULA to the mainland of Newfoundland. It was named in October 1984 by the Newfoundland and Labrador Names Board to mark the contribution of Dr. E.R. Seary (1908–1984) to the toponymy of his adopted province. A native of Sheffield, England, Seary was appointed head of the Department of English at Memorial University in 1953. From this point onward he was to be in the forefront of linguistic and place-name research relating to Newfoundland. The selection of this feature to honour his work was singularly appropriate for it stands at the gateway to the Avalon. Of the many distinguished publications that bear Seary's name, none ranks higher than his monumental *Place Names of the Avalon Peninsula of the Island of Newfoundland* (1971). Not only will this volume remain for many years the definitive study on Avalonian place names, it will continue to be a model in toponymic methodology and research. A more complete note of appreciation for Seary's contribution to toponymy is found in the Bibliographical Essay.

Seldom Come By (Central)   On the south coast of FOGO ISLAND. The precise origin of this interesting place name, dating from at least the eighteenth century, has been lost. Since it was the first sheltered harbour north of GREEN-SPOND, local residents have suggested that the name arose because 'the port was seldom passed by.' The name may also have been invoked because of the isolation of the community. In 1840 Joseph Jukes (1811–1869) noted that forest fires were raging 'in the woods near Seldom Come By Harbour.'

Sepoy Hill (Avalon)   On the northwest shore of ST. MARY'S BAY. This place name has nothing to do with the traditional meaning of *sepoy*, an Indian soldier in the

British colonial service. Rather, it is a corruption of *sea-pie*, a fish-eating bird, sometimes called the American oystercatcher (*Haematopus palliatus*). This distinctive black and white shore bird with a red bill is today native to the southern United States. However, no less an authority than J.J. Audubon (1785–1851) points out that it once ranged as far north as Labrador.

Shamblers Cove (Central)   On the northwest coast of BONAVISTA BAY. The name is that of a New-foundland family once common in this area. In the 1720s Samuel Shambler pioneered the salmon fishery in Bonavista and NOTRE DAME bays. By the 1740s salted salmon was being exported to Italy and Spain.

Shanadithit Brook (Central) Flows into RED INDIAN LAKE. Named after Shanadithit, a Beothuk woman who was captured in 1823. She died in 1829 and was reputedly the last survivor of her race. See also MARY MARCH'S BROOK.

Shearstown (Avalon)   West of BAY ROBERTS. First known as 'Spaniard's Bay Pond,' the town was renamed for the Reverend W.C. Shears (1839–1905), who served as Anglican rector in the area from 1868 to 1903.

Sibleys Cove (Avalon)   Southwest of OLD PERLICAN. The settlement was first named after an early settler. By proclamation, on 22 September 1914, it was renamed Prowsetown, after Daniel Woodley Prowse (1834–1914), a prominent jurist and historian. When recording his death, the *Newfoundland Quarterly* stated that Prowse 'was a man of sterling qualities and of unflagging industry.' Although Prowsetown is still sometimes used locally as a place name for this community, it was never universally popular. For a time it was called Davidsons, after Sir Walter Davidson (1859–1923), who served as governor from 1913 to 1917. It was later to revert to Sibleys Cove, which is today the officially recognized name.

Signal Hill (Avalon)   At the entrance to St. John's harbour. This prominent landmark is so named because it was the location from which the approach of ships to St. John's was signalled. One responsibility of the lightkeeper at CAPE SPEAR was to be on the lookout for inbound shipping. When a ship was sighted, a visual signal was relayed to a watchman on present-day Signal Hill. From there the information was quickly relayed to the appropriate St. John's merchant. Today Signal Hill is dominated by Cabot Tower, built in 1897 to mark the 400th anniversary of John Cabot's discovery of Newfoundland and to celebrate the 60th year of Queen Victoria's reign. It was here on 12 December 1901 that Guglielmo Marconi (1874–1937), the inventor of wireless telegraphy, received the first transatlantic wireless signal, a simple 'S' in Morse Code. Signal Hill is now a National Historic Park and provides a spectacular view of city, harbour, and coastline. The opposite scene, looking towards Signal Hill, can also be spectacular. From a vantage point on the fifth floor of the first Newfoundland Hotel, Lady Hope Simpson, wife of the Commissioner for Natural Resources, described the setting on 16 October 1935: 'The sun is on [Signal Hill] and it is golden and purple and silver. Above it are higher slopes with Cabot Tower and the Marconi aerial and the guns and the old arsenal; below are cultivated fields sloping steeply to quaint wooden houses, climbing winding roads. I find these wooden houses most picturesque; the colours are delicately lovely; faded reds and blues & greens & greys & the roads all up and down & no two houses ever alike or quite in line.' Although the details have changed after a half-century and more, the ambience of Signal Hill, in whatever season or hour, remains as compelling as ever. See also ST. JOHN'S.

Slambang Bay (Labrador)   On the eastern shore of OKAK ISLAND. The origin of this name is best described in the words of Dr. Anthony Paddon, who served as director of Northern Medical Services for the Grenfell Mission from 1960 to 1978. 'The curious name Slambang was coined by disillusioned schooner captains who had been driven ashore by "williwaws," furious gusts from the high hills of the area, or had found their vessels on their beam ends, their cargoes of salt fish tumbled in a useless heap. It was also notorious for the destruction of traps and fishing gear by rough water and other hazards.' Paddon's medical career began in the Royal Canadian Navy during the Second World War. He then returned to the Labrador, to follow in the footsteps of his father, Dr. Harry L. Paddon (1881–1939), who had been recruited by Sir Wilfred Grenfell to serve with the medical mission. The son was to cap his career by serving as lieutenant-governor of Newfoundland and Labrador from 1981 to 1986; the first Labradorian to fill this post. Paddon's years with the Grenfell Mission are vividly chronicled in his *Labrador Doctor* (1989). See also NORTH-WEST RIVER.

Smallwood Reservoir (Labrador)   In western Labrador. Named for the Honourable J.R. Smallwood, premier of Newfoundland from 1949 to 1972. In his own words: 'It is the principal water storehouse for the Churchill Falls hydro-electric power development and is the third-largest man-made lake in the world.' See also CHURCHILL FALLS and GAMBO.

Somerset (Eastern)   On the north shore of Smith Sound, Trinity Bay, and originally known as 'Broad Cove.' In 1917, by action of the Newfoundland Nomenclature Board, a change was made to avoid postal confusion with other communities of this name. The name Somerset was selected to mark the strong West Country influence on Newfoundland.

Sops Arm; Sops Island (Western)   The arm is an indentation of WHITE BAY; the island lies offshore. Named during the course of the Cook and Lane survey of 1765, after an old English word which meant 'a lump or mass of black lead in the ground.'

Sops Island   *See* Sops Arm.

South Aulatsivik Island   *See* North Aulatsivik Island.

Spaniard's Bay (Avalon)   Northwest of BAY ROBERTS, on CONCEPTION BAY. The name is much older than 1836, when it was noted by Archdeacon Edward Wix as *Spaniards Bay Beech*. Like numerous other names that dot the Newfoundland coastline, it is locational, providing linguistic evidence of Spanish involvement in the fishery. It was known to be frequented by Basque and Portuguese fishermen in the late seventeenth century. Upon occasion the latter were sometimes mistakenly identified as 'Spanish.' The town of Spaniard's Bay was incorporated in 1965. See also SPANISH ROOM.

Spanish Room (Eastern)   Northeast of MARYSTOWN. The word *room*, widely used throughout the province, is defined by the *Dictionary of Newfoundland English* as 'a parcel of land on the waterfront of a cove or harbour from which a fishery is conducted.' Historically it has its origin in the division of the foreshore among fishing crews, each nationality (e.g., Spanish) having their designated 'room' or area. The transfer to a place name was inevitable, Spanish Room being a typical example. The word was also used to describe a practice once followed by leading Newfoundland mercantile houses. According to historian D.W. Prowse, 'a great institution on the merchant's premises, always called in the vernacular, "The Room," was the periodical serving of grog, in the morning at eleven o'clock, and in the afternoon, [all employees] had a glass of rum.'

Springdale (Central)   On Halls Bay, an arm of NOTRE DAME BAY. This lumbering and fishing town has become a service centre for the immediate area. The name is a coined descriptive and was adopted in 1896.

Stearing Island (Western) North of St. Pauls Bay, on the west coast of the NORTHERN PENINSULA. The name refers to the northern common tern (*Sterna hirundo*). Many islands and coves in Newfoundland/Labrador provide breeding grounds for these birds; thus, the variants, 'stearing,' 'steering,' and 'stearin' are employed in place names throughout the province.

Stephenville (Western)   On the north shore of ST. GEORGE'S BAY. Settlement in the area dates from about 1845; the name was assigned by the Reverend Thomas Sears (1824–1885), Roman Catholic missionary, after Stephen LeBlanc, the first child to be baptised in the new community. During the Second World War, it was selected as the site for Harmon Air Force

Base, opened in 1941 by the United States. The base was named for Captain Ernest H. Harmon, an aviation pioneer who had served in the American Air Corps during the First World War. The base officially closed on 31 December 1966.

Storehouse Island (Central) West of NEW WORLD ISLAND. One specialized meaning for 'storehouse' in Newfoundland is a place for storing fishing gear in winter. Storehouse Islets in NOTRE DAME BAY have the same origin.

Storehouse Islets   *See* Storehouse Island.

Strait of Belle Isle (Western) The strait that separates Newfoundland from the coast of Labrador was known to the Basques as 'Gran Baya,' although sometimes this designation included a portion of the present GULF OF ST. LAWRENCE. Early in the sixteenth century, *Belle Isle,* for the island off the northern tip of Newfoundland, began to appear on maps and charts. In Jean Fonteneau dit Alfonse's *La Cosmographie* of 1544, he notes *Belle Isle de la Grand Baye.* Clearly this was not a descriptive, for the island cannot be described as beautiful. In all probability it was a transfer name from Belle-Île, off the coast of Brittany. Gradually the island was to lend its

name to the strait. The strait is sometimes referred to locally as 'Iceberg Alley' for the frequency with which icebergs are sighted offshore.

Sugarloaf (Eastern)   A promontory on the eastern side of TRINITY BAY. The name is found in many other locations throughout the province. It is common as well in New Brunswick and Nova Scotia. For origin see SUGARLOAF, New Brunswick.

Summerside (Western)   On the north shore of the Humber Arm. Its picturesque setting provides a panoramic view of CORNER BROOK. The name appears in the 1870s and may have been inspired by SUMMERSIDE in Prince Edward Island. Incorporated in 1970 and amalgamated with nearby Irishtown in 1991.

Swift Current (Eastern)   On PLACENTIA BAY. The community was formerly known as 'Pipers Hole.' It was changed to the descriptive Swift Current early in 1920. The older name has been preserved in Pipers Hole Provincial Park and PIPERS HOLE RIVER.

Swoilers Cove (Western)   In St. Anthony Bight. Among the words used to designate 'seal' are 'swale,' 'swile,' and 'swole.' Thus Swoilers Cove is, in translation, simply 'Sealers Cove.' The frequent appearance of these words in place names is a testament to the importance sealing once held in the economy of Newfoundland and Labrador.

Tasisuak Lake (Labrador) Northwest of VOISEY BAY. Sometimes spelled 'Tessisoak,' the name is of Inuit origin and means 'the large lake.'

Tasse L'Argent (Eastern)   On PLACENTIA BAY. *See* Toslow.

Terrenceville (Central)   Northeast of HARBOUR MILLE. First known as 'Head of Fortune Bay' and 'Fortune Bay Bottom.' The settlement dates back to the eighteenth century. It was renamed for Sir Terence O'Brien (1830–1903), who served as governor of Newfoundland from 1889 to 1896. Once a relay point for the southshore telegraph line, it is now a port of call for coastal ships that serve isolated communities from Terrenceville to PORT AUX BASQUES.

Terra Nova; Terra Nova National Park (Central)   *Terra Nova* or *Terre Neuve* is one of the oldest designations for the island of Newfoundland. Among the first references is that found in Hakluyt's *Voyages* of 1576. The community of Terra Nova, on Terra Nova Lake, is at the end of Highway 301. The national park, the most easterly in Canada, was established in 1957. It consists of 400 square kilometres of striking scenery and boreal-forested landscapes that inevitably lead to the sea. The hiking and nature trails are noted vantage points for bird and animal watching or examining wild flowers and plants. There are also opportunities for scuba diving and golf at Twin Rivers. As late as July, gigantic icebergs brought southward by the Labrador Current, may still be seen. A year-round facility, Terra Nova also offers a wide range of winter activities. See also NEWMAN SOUND.

Terra Nova National Park   *See* Terra Nova.

The Arches (Western)   Between PARSONS POND and PORTLAND CREEK on Highway 430. A descriptive name for a natural geological formation carved out of limestone rock. The Arches were formed thousands of years ago by a combination of glacial action, erosion by wind, the pounding of the sea, and other geological changes. Site of a day-use provincial park.

The Droke (Avalon)   South of MARYSTOWN. Listed in the 1869 census report. This unusual name goes back to a West Country (Cornish) descriptive meaning 'a valley with steep sides.' E.R. Seary notes that it may sometimes refer to 'a clump of trees.'

The Keys (Avalon)   South of BAY BULLS. The name of the settlement is traceable to an anglicization of the Spanish *cayo*, referring to a sharp point of land or a low island. Key West in Florida has the same origin.

The Motion (Avalon)   This phenomenon has been well described by Howley: 'The sea off the south point of Petty Harbour is known ... as "The Motion" or Petty Harbour Motion. The name is quite expressive as there is almost always a sort of "under tow" which causes the sea to be somewhat rough.'

The Rooms (Western)   Northeast of HAMPDEN, on WHITE BAY. For derivation see SPANISH ROOM.

The Spout (Avalon)   Midway between BAY BULLS and Little Bay. The name is descriptive of a phenomenon caused by the rush of the sea into an underwater cave, whence it then escapes into the air. It is a very old designation, being clearly marked on the Fitzhugh *Chart of Newfoundland and the Fishing Banks* in 1693.

On 18 July 1794, The Spout impressed seaman Aaron Thomas: 'The waters rise into a Column and is to all intents a grand and magnificent Fountain, view'd from the sea. In the distance there is a rise of land, and when ting'd with azure blue, which it generally is ... shows off this Column of water to the greatest of advantage.'

The Topsails (Western)   In the interior east of DEER LAKE. This is a collective term for four hills known individually as 'Fore Topsail,' 'Main Topsail,' 'Mizzen Topsail,' and 'Gaff Topsail.' The names were assigned at the time of the construction of the railway by an unknown surveyor with a keen sailing background. According to the Reverend Michael Howley: 'At a distance ... [the hills] present a rude resemblance to the topmasts of a ship under sail and seen hull down on the horizon.' On 11 March 1934, Sir John Hope Simpson was travelling on the Newfoundland Railway when he recorded: '[At] a place called Topsails ... we passed through a drift where the snow was level with the carriages.' See also TOPSAIL and CAPE LAHUNE.

The Tickles (Eastern)   Off Long Island, PLACENTIA BAY. For the origin of *Tickle* see JIGGER TICKLE.

Thrum Cap Island (Eastern)   In BELLE BAY. For derivation see THRUMCAP ISLAND, Nova Scotia.

Tilt Cove; Tilting (Central); **Tilton** (Avalon)   Tilt Cove is on NEW WORLD ISLAND; Tilting is northwest of CAPE FOGO, on FOGO ISLAND; Tilton is a village northwest of BAY ROBERTS. All three names are derived from 'tilt,' a shelter or lean-to which may be covered with a sail, skins, bark, or boughs. Often of a temporary nature, they were and still are used by fishermen and woodsmen. Tilting is the process of erecting a tilt. Aaron Thomas's 1794 journal contains an interesting description of a 'tilting or skating party' on Twenty Mile Pond, near ST. JOHN'S. 'To this lake the inhabitants of St. John's repair ... lapped up in furs and warm clothing, they bid defiance to the piercing winds.' Obviously 'tilts' would be required for shelter, thus giving rise to this synonym for a skating party. See also WINDSOR LAKE. Tilton is also traceable to 'tilt.' E.R. Seary quotes Canon William Pilot (1841–1913) 'that at a meeting of the Newfoundland Nomenclature Board in the early 1900s [he gave] the name "Tilton" to the settlement, which had been formerly called "The Tilts."'

Tilting   *See* Tilt Cove.

Tilton   *See* Tilt Cove.

Tompkins (Western)   North of CHANNEL–PORT AUX BASQUES. The CODROY valley was settled towards the end of the nineteenth century by Scots-Canadians from the Margaree Valley in INVERNESS COUNTY, Cape Breton. The predominant surnames in this migration were Scottish: MacIsaac, Campbell, MacDonald, and MacNeil. The exception was Irish Canadians William Tompkins and his family, who gave their name to this village. It had been formerly known as Little River. See MARGAREE VALLEY, Nova Scotia.

Topsail (Avalon)   Now part of the town of CONCEPTION BAY SOUTH. The name was first applied to Topsail Head, described by Joseph Jukes (1811–1869) as 'a bold height, chiefly a mass of pure white quartz rock.' It was this feature, resembling a topsail, which gave rise to the name.

Torbay (Avalon)   Site of St. John's Airport and located north of the city. The name serves to highlight the contribution of England's West Country to Newfoundland–Labrador nomenclature. Dating from the early seventeenth century, it is a descriptive, after Tor Bay in Devon, and means 'the bay at the hill or tor.' The English Tor Bay is derived from a hill called 'Torre,' that also gave its name to nearby Torquay. On 1 May 1942, an important link between New-foundland and Canada was forged with the arrival of the first Trans-Canada Air Lines (prede-cessor to Air Canada) flight at Torbay airport. The authorized spelling of the bay, as distinct from the settlement, is 'Tor Bay.'

Torngat Mountains (Labrador) The range parallels the coast, from Hebron Fiord to CAPE CHID-LEY. Sometimes referred to as the 'Devils Mountains'; the name is derived from the Inuit word for 'spirits.' In Inuit legend they are considered to be the home of *Tor-nassoag*, the ruler of all sea animals. Within Canada, the Torngats con-stitute the highest range east of the Rocky Mountains.

Torrent River (Western)   Flows westward into HAWKE'S BAY. The name of this river, a well-known salmon stream, is descriptive. The Torrent River Nature Park fol-lows the river from its junction with the salt water inland to a salmon ladder. A 3-kilometre boardwalk (part of the Hogan Trail) terminates at the salmon ladder. The ladder allows the Atlantic salmon to traverse the Torrent River Falls. See also HOGAN TRAIL.

Tors Cove (Avalon)   North of FERRYLAND. This is a very old place name, dating from the late seventeenth century, when it was known as 'Toth Cove.' Two cen-turies later, according to census returns, the name had evolved to Toads Cove. By proclamation, dated 18 January 1910, it was renamed Tors Cove. The Rever-end Michael Howley states that this was done in the mistaken belief that 'Tors was the original specific and for its more pleasing connotations.'

Toslow (Eastern)   On PLACENTIA BAY, northeast of LITTLE PARADISE. This community, now abandoned as a result of the Smallwood resettlement program, lives on in the folk-song of H.W. LeMes-surier (1848–1931):

> We'll rant and we'll roar like true
>   Newfoundlanders:
> We'll rant and we'll roar on deck
>   and below,
> Until we see bottom inside the two
>   sunkers [submerged rocks],
> When straight through the channel
>   to Toslow we'll go.

It also lives on in the beautiful place name selected by the first French settlers: La Tasse de l'Argent – 'the Cup of Silver.' Unfortunately, the name became corrupted to the point where any resemblance to the original was lost, evolving from Tasse l'Argent to Toslow John, to Toslow. However, the immortality of this, and the dozens of other names of resettled communities, is conveyed in the burnished prose of Harold Horwood: 'No dusty road with cars or trucks will ever bring 20th century Canada into Toslow. It will be Newfoundland for all time to come. It is safe in the years that were. It will remain forever inviolate, the village that gave us birth, that shaped us, that made us what we are, this happy breed of men that came, somehow, out of the fire and the ice of the past, and stood upon this iron-black land, and looked fearlessly upon the sea and the surrounding hills, and called a little cove a cup of silver.'

Tourlinguet Head   *See* Twillingate.

Traytown, BONAVISTA BAY (Eastern); TRINITY BAY (Eastern)   *See* Triton.

Trepassey; Trepassey Bay (Avalon)   The village is north of Trepassey Bay. This name is derived from Baie des Trépassés, near Point du Raz in Brittany. According to the Reverend Michael Howley, the name is singularly appropriate (from the French *trépassé* – 'the dead or departed'), considering the large

number of shipwrecks on this stretch of coastline. He suggested that the Baie des Trépassés was 'the Bay of Souls, the launching place where the departed spirits sail off across the sea.' See also CAPE RACE.

Trepassey Bay   *See* Trepassey.

Trinity; Trinity Bay; Trinity East (Eastern)   The name is frequently credited to Gaspar Corte-Real (*ca* 1450/5–*ca* 1510), who is reputed to have entered the bay on Trinity Sunday, 1500; however, there is no documentary evidence to this effect. In 1615 Richard Whitbourne held the first Court of Admiralty in the New World at Trinity, providing evidence that the harbour was being utilized by overseas fishing fleets. It may possibly be Whitbourne who bestowed the name. Much later, by the late eighteenth and early nineteenth centuries, the town of Trinity had emerged as a major fishing and mercantile centre. Prominent among those who made this possible were a group of merchant/entrepreneurs from Poole in Dorset. Another milestone was achieved in 1800, when the Reverend John Clinch (1748/9–1819), both a medical doctor and clergyman, carried out a successful innoculation against smallpox. Edward Jenner (1749–1823), a friend of Clinch's, supplied the vaccine for this first vaccination in North America. The ubiquitous Joseph Jukes (1811–1869) visited Trinity in July 1839 and pronounced its harbour as 'one of the finest in the world, having three spacious basins entirely landlocked.' Today much of the old town has been designated a national historic site and attracts tourists interested in its narrow lanes, period architecture, and sense of history. Trinity was incorporated as a town in 1969.

Trinity Bay   *See* Trinity.

Trinity East   *See* Trinity.

Triton (Central)   On NOTRE DAME BAY. Local sources suggest that the community was named for HMS *Triton*; however, since the name appears in early records as *Troytown* or *Traytown*, it is undoubtedly yet another example of linguistic change in place names. According to the *Oxford English Dictionary*, 'Troy Town' was 'a Devonshire room with its furniture disarrayed.' The latter arose because the village of Troytown near Dorchester was noted for a maze cut into turf. Eventually 'Troy Town' came to mean a maze or labyrinth of streets. Since Notre Dame Bay appeared as a 'maze' of headlands and islands, the transition effected by West Country fishermen becomes clear.

Traytown, BONAVISTA BAY, and Traytown, TRINITY BAY, have the same West Country origin.

Turkish Gut Pond   *See* Maryside.

Tweed Island   *See* Guernsey Island.

Twillingate Island (Central) North of NEW WORLD ISLAND. Until 1713, a French fishing station named Toulinguett. The immediate locale reminded the first Breton fishermen of Pointe de Toulinguet, at the entrance to the harbour at Brest. Following British control, the name was anglicized, and the station developed by fishing and mercantile interests from Poole in Dorset (see TRINITY). Over time, Twillingate became important as a centre for the Labrador cod fishery and sealing operations. A stone cross in the Anglican cemetery marks the grave of Twillingate native Georgina Stirling (1867–1935) who became known as 'the nightingale of the north.' Trained as an opera singer in France and Italy, she enjoyed international fame, under her stage name, Marie Toulinguet. Unfortunately her operatic career was cut short by illness, and she gave her last performance in ST. JOHN'S in 1904. Twillingate is now linked by causeway to the mainland, and has developed as a regional service centre. The town was incorporated in 1962.

Uivaluk Peak (Labrador)   The summit of Cape Harrison. See CAPE HARRISON.

Valleyfield (Eastern)   Southwest of WESLEYVILLE. This is a coined or manufactured name and is now part of Badgers Quay–Valleyfield–Pools Island.

Victoria (Avalon)   North of CARBONEAR. Originally known as 'Beaver Pond.' The name was changed to Victoria Village, at the time of the Queen's Silver Jubilee in 1862. By the early twentieth century, the name had been simplified to Victoria. There are also two Victoria Coves, a Victoria Lake, and a Victoria River in Newfoundland. See also SANDRINGHAM and JOE BATTS ARM.

Virgin Arm (Central); **Virgin Rocks** (Avalon)   There are at least fifteen features scattered throughout the province that bear this specific. In some instances the names may date from the period of the French migratory fishery and have a religious significance, relating to the Blessed Virgin. In other cases they may simply indicate that a new or 'virgin' feature had been discovered. The two examples cited fall in this latter category. Virgin Arm is on the northwest coast of NEW WORLD ISLAND; Virgin Rocks are off POINT VERDE, in PLACENTIA BAY. See also BURGEO, and chapter 1, page 12, for a discussion of Virgin Rocks on the Grand Bank.

Virginia Lake (Avalon)   To the east of WINDSOR LAKE. Once known as 'Downings Pond,' later as 'Virginia Waters,' and now as 'Virginia Lake.' It takes its name from the former summer residence of the governors of the province. The name is after 'Virginia Waters,' the estate of the Duke of Cumberland (1721–1765), located near Staines, in Surrey, England.

Voisey Bay (Labrador)   South of NAIN. The bay is named for Amos Voisey, a native of Plymouth, England, who emigrated to Labrador in 1850. This area achieved prominence in the 1990s with the discovery of major deposits of nickel, copper, and cobalt. The copper reserves alone may be sufficient to supply one-sixth of the world's demand for this mineral. The *Globe and Mail Report on Business Magazine* (November 1995, 122–34) noted that this 'base metal discovery is shaping up to be a spectacular mining rush of near-Klondike proportions.' Meanwhile, local residents are anxious to ensure that the discovery 'delivers lasting prosperity without destroying the traditional [Inuit] way of life.' The report concludes: 'Voisey Bay is a chance for the mining industry to get everything right: to respect the traditional lifestyle of aboriginal peoples, protect the environment and improve the lot of the local population.' For this reason, the Voisey Bay operation will be closely monitored, not only by Labradorians but by the wider world.

Wabana (Avalon)   On BELL ISLAND, in CONCEPTION BAY. In the 1890s an iron-ore mine was opened on the island. Thomas Cantley (1857–1945), an official of the Nova Scotia Steel and Coal Company, selected Wabana, an old Mi'kmaq designation, as a name for the community that grew up round the mine. It is a contraction of *Wabunaki*, 'east land,' or *Wabana*, 'the dawn.'

Wabush (Labrador)   Southeast of LABRADOR CITY. The origin of the name may be traced to the Naskapi *Waban*, meaning 'rabbit ground.' The completion of the Québec North Shore and Labrador Railway in 1954 helped make possible the development of the natural resources of this region. In the 1960s the establishment of Wabush and adjacent Labrador City resulted from the exploitation of local iron-ore deposits. See also LABRADOR CITY.

Wadham Islands (Central) East of FOGO ISLAND. *See* Offer Wadham Islands.

Waterford River (Avalon) Flows northeast into ST. JOHN'S harbour. Originally known as 'Little Castors [Beaver] River,' it was renamed for the city of Waterford in southeast Eire, since the area was settled largely by Irish immigrants. Waterford was a popular port of call for West Country ships *en route* to Newfoundland, thus allowing for the recruitment of Irish fishery workers.

Watts Point (Western)   Off Highway 430, northeast of Eddies Cove. Probably named for an early settler. The area is now the site of an important ecological reserve, a protected habitat for many unique Arctic-alpine plants, sub-Arctic orchids, and lichens. Some of these are very rare and not found elsewhere in the province.

W Cove (Western)   In Prince Edward Bay, an inlet of HARE BAY. A descriptive so named for its resemblance to the letter 'W.'

Webeck Harbour; Webeck Island (Labrador)   The name is a variation of the Inuit *Uvialuk*, 'a cape,' and was for many years an important rendezvous for fishermen on the Labrador. It was visited by the Reverend Patrick Browne in the 1890s. He reported: 'The view from the top of Cape Webec (now Cape Harrison) is one of the most charming sights I have ever visited. Away to the north lay the archipelago of *Tikaloaik,* and westward an undulating plateau whose surface, dotted with numberless tarns, seemed to fade away and dissolve into the azure of the sky. The [view] differs from any other section of the Labrador coast which I have visited.' See also CAPE HARRISON.

Webeck Island   *See* Webeck Harbour.

Wellington (Central)   On Freshwater Bay. *See* Dover.

Wesleyville (Central)   Northeast of BADGERS QUAY. The settlement was first known as 'Coal Harbour' but was renamed in 1884 in honour of John Wesley (1703–1791), the founder of Methodism. Wesleyville is the birthplace of noted Canadian artist David Blackwood. Although he is now a resident of Port Hope, Ontario, many of his most acclaimed prints and etchings have his native Wesleyville and other Newfoundland scenes as their subject-matter.

Western Bay; Western Bay Head (Avalon)   The head appears first as 'Point Prime,' so named since it was the first important headland seen on rounding CAPE ST. FRANCIS. The bay was, for a time, known as 'Green Bay'; the transition to Western Bay began with the Lane survey of 1774. Eventually, the names Point Prime and Green Bay were replaced by Western Bay Head and Western Bay. One of Newfoundland's and Canada's most important poets, E.J. Pratt (1883–1964), was born at Western Bay on 4 February 1883, the son of a Methodist clergyman Reverend John Pratt and his wife, Fanny Pitts Knight. Pratt spent his first twenty-four years in Newfoundland before emigrating, in 1907, to study and pursue an academic career in Toronto. Although the remainder of his life was spent inland, the early outport years in communities such as Western Bay and MORETON'S HARBOUR left an indelible imprint, later reflected in his poetry. A major preoccupation, the struggle of life against the sea, is a theme that echoes throughout much of Pratt's work. His grand-nephew, artist Christopher Pratt, continues the family's creative tradition in his portrayal on canvas of the stark reality of Newfoundland.

Western Bay Head   *See* Western Bay.

Western Brook Pond   *See* Gros
Morne National Park.

West St. Modeste (Labrador)
Southwest of RED BAY. The names
of both West St. Modeste and East
St. Modeste (now abandoned) may
be traced to the Basque *Semadet*.
Selma Barkham points to the 'odd
historical puzzle [that] has been
bequeathed to us by the contraction of Ste. Modeste to Semadet.
The name Semadet is applied by
modern fishermen to East St. Modeste; but that name seems to have
slipped over to the east side of Pinware Bay. Old maps and rutters
[sailing directions] show *Semadet*
or *Saumadet* to the *west* of Pinware
River.' This is one instance where
early maps are not helpful in
unravelling the puzzle. All that we
can say is that Ste. Modeste, an
obscure eighth-century abbess,
has been immortalized on the
Labrador. References relating to
the Basque contribution to Canadian toponymy may be found in
the work of Selma and Michael
Barkham, cited on pages 36–7.

Weybridge (Eastern)   On North-
west Arm, TRINITY BAY. Formerly
known as 'Foster's Point.'
Renamed in 1952 for Weybridge,
Surrey, southeast of London,
England.

White Bay (Western)   A large
indentation that forms part of the
eastern shoreline of the NORTH-
ERN PENINSULA. The area was visited by Samuel de Champlain in
1612 and named by him *Baye
Blanch*. The name is undoubtedly
descriptive for white limestone
outcroppings on the coastline of
the bay. The translation to White
Bay occurred with the Cook and
Lane survey of 1775.

Whitbourne (Avalon)   On
Highway 81, south of the Trans-
Canada Highway. The assignment of this name was suggested
by Sir Richard Bond (1857–1927).
Bond was described by political
scientist S.J.R. Noel as 'an aristo-
cratic politican who combined
intellect with moral passion.' He
served as the Liberal prime minister from 1900 to 1909. The election
of 1908 resulted in a tie with the
People's Party, led by Sir Edward
Morris (1859–1935). The latter
was able to form a new government, and Bond led the opposition until his retirement in 1914.
He died at his country estate in
Whitbourne on 16 March 1927.
The place name originates with
Sir Richard Whitbourne (fl. 1579–
1628), merchant, colonizer, and
governor of Sir William
Vaughan's colony at AQUAFORTE,
Newfoundland, from 1618 to 1620
(Cell).

Whiteway (Avalon)   A village
on TRINITY BAY, southwest of

HEARTS DELIGHT. It was previously known as 'Witless Bay,' and the name was changed by proclamation on 13 August 1912 in honour of Sir William Vallance Whiteway (1828–1908), who served as prime minister in 1878–85, 1889–94, and 1895–7. Soon after his defeat in the election of 1895, Whiteway was replaced as Liberal leader by Sir Robert Bond. See also WHITBOURNE.

Williamsport (Western)   Southwest of ENGLEE, on WHITE BAY. The name of this community, formerly known as 'Greenspond,' was changed by proclamation on 8 August 1911 to avoid confusion with another GREENSPOND, south of WESLEYVILLE. It marks the career of Sir Ralph Campney Williams (1848–1927), who served as governor from 1909 to 1913.

Wiltondale (Western)   Northwest of DEER LAKE. Named for Norman Wilton, who settled here in 1927. The surname may be traced to Wilton, once the principal town of Wiltshire, England.

Windsor   *See* Grand Falls–Windsor.

Windsor Lake (Avalon)   East of ST. PHILLIPS. Formerly known as 'Twenty Mile Pond.' This designation still persists locally despite the fact that the first reference to

the approved name, Windsor, dates from 1812. On 28 January of that year, 'a large party of gentlemen from St. John's assembled at the home of Thomas Kearney, Twenty Mile Pond.' After partaking of a 'plentiful refreshment ... they took some excellent Old Maderia [*sic*] Wine, and pouring generous libations, called the village *Windsor*, with many good wishes for its prosperity and increase.' For good measure, and before donning their skates, 'they also named Windsor Lake.' E.R. Seary, who quotes the account cited above from the *Royal Gazette*, 6 February 1812, laments that 'no information is given as to the source of the name.' He conjectures that the answer might 'lie in the fact that the father of the then governor [Admiral Sir John Duckworth (1748–1817)] was sometime canon of Windsor.' More likely, in line with the convivial nature of the occasion, it was after a member of the party named Windsor. This surname is still found on the AVALON PENINSULA and in other parts of the province. For another party on the same lake see TILTING.

Winterton (Avalon)   Southwest of HANTS HARBOUR. The original name of the community, Sillee Cove, later changed to Scilly Cove, dates from 1675, and is one of the oldest names on the

AVALON. By proclamation, on 16 August 1912, in keeping with 'place-name reform,' and 'in deference to the sensibilities of its inhabitants,' the name was changed to Winterton. The new designation honoured Sir James Spearman Winter (1845–1911), who served as prime minister from 1897 to 1900. Winter died on 6 October 1911, and the desire to honour his memory may have been a factor in the renaming.

Witless Bay (Avalon)   South of ST. JOHN'S. There are three possible explanations for this unusual place name. According to the Reverend Michael Howley, it may be 'a corruption of Whittle's Bay, either from [a Dorsetshire surname], or from the prevalence of the shrub which grows abundantly in our woods, the *virburnum nudum*, called by the Westcountrymen, the wit-rod or wittle.' Seary adds a third possibility – that it may be 'used metaphorically to describe the [crazy, lunatic] sea.' This latter explanation bears the ring of logic. Witless Bay is the site of an Ecological Reserve, where seabirds and humpback and minke whales may be seen. As early as 1794, seaman Aaron Thomas reported a sighting: 'Looking towards the sea, I saw a thick vapor or mist rise in a narrow compass out of the ocean near the shore. I thought it was the smoke which issued from a gun when fired, only it rose in a larger column. I pointed it out to the person who was with me, who immediately said, "It is a whale blowing." Presently, we saw the fluke of his tail and the enormous fins on his back. He kept blowing and rolling about in chase of a fish called capelin.' A second Witless Bay (on TRINITY BAY) was changed to Whiteway. See also WHITEWAY .

Zoar (Labrador)   Northwest of DAVIS INLET. Established as a Moravian Mission in 1865 but later abandoned. In keeping with the Moravian custom, it was named for the biblical Zoar, located on the Dead Sea and mentioned in the Book of Genesis.

4

Nova Scotia

Aalder Island *See* Aldersville.

Aalders Lang Meadow *See* Aldersville.

Abercrombie (Pictou) On a point jutting into PICTOU harbour. This district was settled in the late eighteenth century by emigrants from Scotland. The name, of Scottish origin, commemorates the career of Captain James Abercrombie of the 42nd Regiment of the Royal Highlanders. This regiment was later to be popularly known as the Black Watch, so called because of the dark colour of its tartan. Abercrombie served as aide-de-camp to General Jeffrey Amherst during the American Revolution and was killed in action at the battle of Bunker Hill, 17 June 1775.

Aconi Island *See* Point Aconi.

Addington Forks (Antigonish) Southeast of ANTIGONISH. Named for Henry Addington, first Viscount Sidmouth (1757–1844), an obscure figure who served briefly (1801–4) as prime minister of Great Britain and was described by British historian Arthur Cross as 'a dull though well meaning man.' His administration's major achievement was the negotiation, with France, of the Treaty of Amiens (1802), which held for barely a year. This area was part of a large land grant in 1804 to a prominent Loyalist and Halifax merchant, Lawrence Hartshorne (1775–1822), one of the MLAs for HALIFAX COUNTY. The constituency then included this part of Nova Scotia.

Admiral Rock (Hants) On the SHUBENACADIE RIVER. Once noted for shipbuilding and the export of gypsum. The name marks the career of Admiral Sir Alexander

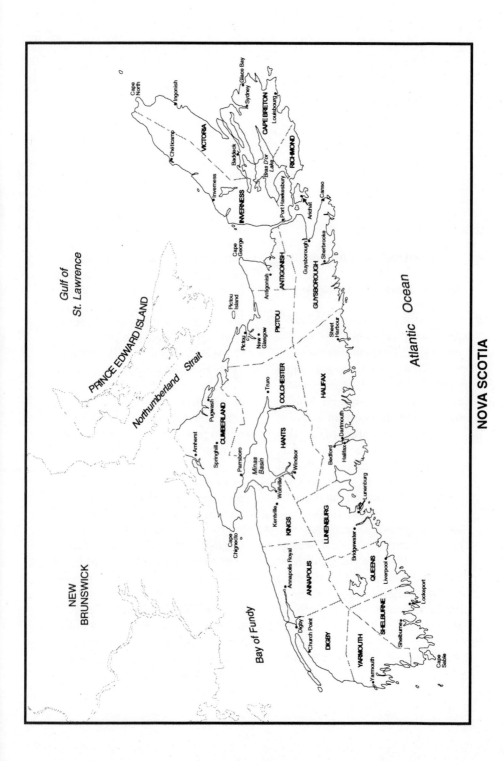

NOVA SCOTIA

Forrester Inglis Cochrane (1758–1832). Cochrane held a command in the British navy in the West Indies and American station from 1805 to 1815. During this period he encouraged Scottish emigration to Nova Scotia. The settlement dates from 1806.

Advocate Harbour (Cumberland)   Between CAPE CHIGNECTO and CAPE D'OR. One of the oldest place names on MINAS BASIN. It was called by the French *Havre à l'Avocat*, on the Franquelin–DeMeulles map of 1685. In 1604, the area was visited by Samuel de Champlain, who noted 'in a harbour on the north side of the Minas Basin [possibly Advocate] we found a very old cross, all covered with moss, and almost wholly rotted away, an unmistakable sign that formerly Christians had been here.' In 1607, as an illustration in his *Voyages*, Champlain drew a sketch of 'Port des Mines,' the first name of Advocate Harbour. However, the discovery of the cross later led William Francis Ganong to speculate that the area had been visited by João Alvares Fagundes in 1522 and that the name suggested a 'corrupted survival' of Alvares. In the absence of definitive proof of a Fagundes visit, all that can be noted is that Advocate Harbour is an English adaptation of a much earlier French name. The first

English-speaking settlers were New England Planters and Loyalists who arrived in the late eighteenth century. By this time the anglicized spelling was in common usage.

Africville (Halifax)   Once located on BEDFORD BASIN, within the HALIFAX city limits. This settlement of blacks, which went back nearly two centuries, was first known as 'Campbell Road,' for the street leading to the area. Over time the name Africville evolved, possibly first evoked as a place name by the whites. By the dawn of the twentieth century, the name was firmly established, although housing and living conditions had deteriorated. In the 1960s a decision was made by the city to acquire the land, demolish the homes, and relocate the inhabitants. As with other resettlement schemes, this one was not without controversy. One uprooted resident spoke for many, if not most, residents: 'When the city rushed us out and tore [Africville] down, they tore our hearts away. But we are surviving right to this day, and we still survive and we will go on forever.' This indomitable sense of endurance, a characteristic of so many dispossessed and dislocated peoples, is well captured in a publication of the Africville Genealogy Society, *The Spirit of*

Africville. While the community may have been physically 'erased,' not so the place name, and efforts to supplant 'Africville' by 'Seaview' have been resisted. In 1995, when a map appeared bearing the name Seaview Point instead of the earlier Negro Point, it was pointed out by the local black community that there had been no consultation with them and, further, that Negro Point was the historically correct name for this extension of land into Bedford Basin.

Albany Cross (Annapolis) South of MIDDLETON, on Highway 10. The area was surveyed and laid out in lots during the years 1801–4 by Phineas Millidge, a son of Loyalist Thomas Millidge (*ca* 1735–1816). Before the Revolution, the latter was a member of the New Jersey Assembly, and also the surveyor general. The family settled in Granville, near Annapolis, where he became a long-serving (1785–1806) member of the Nova Scotia Assembly. The first settlers in New Albany were also Loyalists from New Jersey and upstate New York; thus, in all likelihood, Phineas Millidge named the community for Albany, New York. The word 'cross' simply indicates a crossroad. See also MILLIDGEVILLE, New Brunswick.

Aldershot (Kings)   North of KENTVILLE. In the late 1860s a militia-training centre was established on the AYLESFORD plain, near present-day Canadian Forces Base GREENWOOD. It was named for the Aldershot military base in Hampshire, England, established during the Crimean War (1853–6). In 1904 both the camp and its name were transferred to a new site near Kentville. The new Camp Aldershot was to play an important role in the training of the Canadian army in the two world wars.

Aldersville (Lunenburg)   On the military road that once linked HAMMONDS PLAINS and ANNAPOLIS ROYAL. Originally spelled 'Aaldersville.' The name, later shortened to Aldersville, may be traced to Peter Aalders (1785–1834), a native of Gorinchem, Holland, who served in the 7th Battalion, 60th Regiment, posted to Nova Scotia during the War of 1812. Later, in 1822, Aalders returned to take up a land grant in the area destined to bear his name. His descendants became scattered throughout KINGS, LUNENBURG, and HANTS counties. The surname may also be found in nearby Aalders Lang Meadow, northeast of NEW ROSS, and Aalder Island, in GOLD RIVER.

Allains Creek   *See* Lequille.

Alma (Pictou)   West of NEW
GLASGOW. Although settled by
Scots as early as 1773, this district
was not named until the end of
the Crimean War (1853–6). In
September 1855, the Allied armies
(Britain, France, and Turkey)
landed in the Crimea. Subsequently, on 20 September 1855,
the Russians were defeated in the
Battle of Alma River, one of the
first major engagements of the
Allied march towards the fortress of Sevastopol. The place
name marks this battle.

Alton (Colchester)   South of
TRURO. The land in the community of Alton was conveyed in a
grant in 1821 to William Polley.
For a time the district was known
as 'Polley's Bog' which is still
used to designate a local land feature. In 1880 the name, on petition
of local residents, was changed to
Alton, for a village in Hampshire,
England. Alton is traceable to an
old English word which means
'the source of a stream.'

Amet Island; Amet Sound
(Pictou)   The island is in Amet
Sound, between CAPE JOHN and
MALAGASH POINT. This small
island appears on the earliest
French maps of the region and
rates a mention in Nicolas
Denys's (1598–1688) description
of the coast of Acadia published
in 1672. Its name goes back to the

old French *l'armet,* 'helmet,' a
reference to the island's shape. It
is given as *Île l'Armet* on the
D'Anville map of 1755; thereafter,
the 'r' is usually dropped. From
the mid-nineteenth century to the
First World War, there was a
manned lighthouse on the island.
On 26 December 1868, the brig
Isabella, out of TATAMAGOUCHE,
bound for Buenos Aires with a
cargo of lumber, was spotted by
the lightkeeper on Amet Island.
Thereafter no trace of the ship,
crew, or cargo was ever found.
There are those who maintain
that the 'phantom ship' of the
NORTHUMBERLAND STRAIT, said to
frequent these waters, is the ill-
fated *Isabella.*

Amet Sound   *See* Amet Island.

Amherst (shiretown of Cumberland County)   Travelling from
New Brunswick on the Trans-
Canada Highway, one catches
the first glimpse of Amherst
midway across the ISTHMUS OF
CHIGNECTO. The LaPlanche Street
exit approximates the name of the
original French settlement, Les
Planches, and leads directly to the
town. After the expulsion of the
Acadians, the area was resettled
in 1761 by a group of New
England Planters, followed by
emigrants from Yorkshire who
arrived between 1772 and 1775.
The new name, Amherst, was

bestowed to mark the career of Jeffery, Baron Amherst (1717–1797). Following the capture of Fortress Louisbourg on 26 July 1758, Amherst was appointed commander-in-chief of the British forces in North America; on the surrender of Montreal in 1760, he became the governor general of British North America. Later, following brief terms as governor of Virginia and Guernsey, he rose to be commander-in-chief of the army in England and achieved the rank of field-marshal. Amherst Point, Amherst Head, Amherst Marsh, and Amherst Shore are all named for the town. In addition, Amherstburg and Amherst Island, in Ontario, and Amherst County, in Virginia, are further reminders of the career of the baron. The town was incorporated in 1889.

Amherst Head   *See* Amherst.

Amherst Marsh   *See* Amherst.

Amherst Point   *See* Amherst.

Amherst Shore   *See* Amherst.

Amiraults Hill (Yarmouth)   East of YARMOUTH, in the municipality of ARGYLE. This community recalls the resilience of the Acadian people, who returned in numbers to Nova Scotia following the expulsion of 1755. Nearby PUBNICO was an important Acadian settlement both before and following the expulsion, for this was one area where their lands had not been confiscated by others. As the population of settlements such as Pubnico expanded, the settlers moved farther along the shore. Thus, about 1800, Jacques Amirault of Pubnico settled in the district which bears his name.

Annapolis County   When first created, on 17 August 1759, it extended from the source of the Annapolis River to the northeastern boundary of the township of YARMOUTH. Eventually, in 1836–7, with the creation of Yarmouth and DIGBY counties, it assumed its present size. The name was inspired by that of ANNAPOLIS ROYAL.

Annapolis Basin; Annapolis River; Annapolis Royal (shiretown of Annapolis County)   The area surrounding Annapolis Royal and nearby Port Royal comprise the oldest continuous European settlement north of St. Augustine, Florida. Settled first by Samuel de Champlain and Pierre Du Gua de Monts in 1605, Port Royal remained in French hands for most of the seventeenth century. However, it was subject to frequent capture by the British, only to be restored time after time by subsequent recapture or treaty negotiations. By the Treaty of Utrecht (1713), Port Royal was granted to the British for the last time. The present name was bestowed in 1710 in honour of Queen Anne (1665–1714). It was formed by dropping 'Port' and combining the queen's name with that of *polis*, the Greek word for 'city.' Annapolis Royal served as the capital of Nova Scotia from 1710 until the founding of HALI-FAX in 1749. Incorporation took place in 1893. See also LEQUILLE and PORT ROYAL. Annapolis Basin and Annapolis River take their name from the town.

Annapolis River   *See* Annapolis Basin.

Annapolis Royal   *See* Annapolis Basin.

Antigonish (shiretown of Antigonish County)   Nicolas Denys (1598–1688), in his *Description géographique et historique des costes de l'Amérique septentrionale* (Paris 1672), may be credited with the first reference to this place name, rendering it as *Articougnesche*. The word is of Mi'kmaq origin and may be traced through French and English sources to N'*alegihooneech*, translated by Silas T. Rand as 'where branches are torn off,' a possible reference to a location where bears came to eat beechnuts

or hazelnuts. An anonymous map of Acadia dating from about 1738 mentions a portage from *la Rivière Chebenacady à Artigoniche*. By the end of the eighteenth century, the name was being given as *Antigonich*. In 1784, Colonel Timothy Hierlihy, who had served on the Loyalist side in the American Revolution, was granted land at what was to become known as 'Antigonish Harbour.' He named the new settlement Dorchester, for Sir Guy Carleton, first Baron Dorchester (1724–1808), who had served as commander-in-chief of the British forces in North America. This settlement was not successful, and the name disappeared. A more favourable location, farther inland, at the junction of two rivers, began to attract settlers, and eventually became the town of Antigonish. It was incorporated in 1889. Antigonish is the home of St. Francis Xavier University. Originally located in ARICHAT, the institution moved to its present site in 1855 and was accorded full university status in 1866. Since 1863 the Antigonish Highland Society has been hosting the annual Highland games, the oldest such event in Canada.

Antigonish County   In 1759 five counties were created on peninsular Nova Scotia. At first, the entire eastern section of the colony was included within the bounds of HALIFAX COUNTY. In 1785, 'all that part which lies to the east of St Mary's River became the county of Sydney.' The new county was named for Thomas Townshend, Viscount Sydney (1733–1800). Later, in 1823, Sydney County was was divided into upper (northern) and lower (southern) districts. A further rearrangement took place in 1836 (see GUYSBOROUGH COUNTY). In 1863 Sydney County disappeared when the upper district became Antigonish County by act of the provincial legislature. For origin of the name see ANTIGONISH.

Arcadia (Yarmouth)   North of YARMOUTH. Originally known as 'Upper Chebogue.' The change to Arcadia was made in 1863. While the word itself may be traced to the classical name for a land of peace and contentment, the place name was suggested by the brig *Arcadia*, built and launched here in 1817.

Argyle (Yarmouth)   A municipality in the southeast of the county. One of the first landholders, Captain Ranald McKinnon (1737–1805), saw service in the British army during the Seven Years War (1757–63). Later he was engaged in surveying lands in southwestern Nova Scotia for New England Planters. On 1 April 1766, McKinnon received a grant of 800 hectares, 'including the islands commonly called LaTour's islands.' He named his new holdings Argyle, for his native county in Scotland. In 1771 the area was granted township status. The literal translation of Argyll or Argyle is 'land of the Gaels'; however, this was never an accurate reflection of the population, as the majority were and are Acadian French.

Arichat (shiretown of Richmond County)   On Isle Madame. In a letter dated 12 August 1800 to Bishop Joseph-Octave Plessis (1763–1825), Father François Lejamtel, missionary at Arichat, wrote: 'You ask me why I write *Arischat* while the people say *Narischaque*. When I arrived in this country in 1792 I saw all sorts of spellings applied to the place: *Neireichak, Narichat, Narachaque, Anarachaque* etc. What made me decide to write Arischat was the government spelling, and I thought the other spellings should yield to it.' Over the years Father Lejamtel's version, with the exception of one 's,' has prevailed. Unfortunately, the meaning of the original Mi'kmaq name has been lost. An early French name for the harbour was Port Sainte Marie. In the late 1700s and early 1800s, many Channel Islanders were attracted to

Arichat and vicinity because of its strategic location for pursuit of the fishery. Among these emigrants was Isaac LeVesconte (1822–1879), who emigrated from Jersey in 1834. Employed by the firm of DeCarteret and LeVesconte, he was to settle permanently at Arichat; be elected to the Nova Scotia legislature as MLA for RICHMOND; serve as financial secretary in the Tupper administration; and, from 1869 to 1874, to represent RICHMOND COUNTY in the House of Commons. See ISLE MADAME and JANVRIN ISLAND for the early commercial development of the area.

Arisaig (Antigonish)   Southwest of CAPE GEORGE. In 1783, Angus MacDonald Gillis, of South Morar, Inverness-shire, Scotland, received a land grant on the north shore of ANTIGONISH COUNTY, and 'landing at a point which had a resemblance to his native place, he named it Arisaig.' The Scottish name is of Norse origin and means 'bay at the mouth of a river.' Arisaig was the site of the first Roman Catholic parish in the diocese of Antigonish. See also FRENCHMANS BARN.

Armdale (Halifax)   A district within the city of HALIFAX, at the head of the northwest arm of the harbour. 'Armdale,' the house that gave the area its name, still stands at the intersection of Tupper Grove and Armview Avenue. It was once the home of Charles Tupper (1821–1915), pre-Confederation premier of Nova Scotia; long-time federal cabinet minister; and briefly, in 1896, prime minister of Canada. Although the original structure and its once spacious grounds have been altered and changed, the community name is still widely used.

Aspotogan; Aspotogan Mountain; Aspotogan Peninsula (Lunenburg)   The peninsula extends into ST. MARGARETS BAY. The name is derived from the Mi'kmaq *Ukpudeskakum*, meaning 'where they block the passageway' for the purpose of killing and trapping seals. Aspotogan Mountain, behind the village, is the highest point on the south shore of Nova Scotia. A nineteenth-century geologist named Poole described the setting : 'I climbed the deep path that leads to the summit of Aspotogan. There, spread out beneath, lies beautiful Mahone Bay, dotted in all directions with its hundreds of islands; whilst far away on the western shore, the steam from the mill at Gold River rises into the morning air like a pillar of cloud. Looking down upon [Deep Cove] beneath, one sees every tree mirrored in the silent depths.'

Aspotogan Mountain   *See* Aspotogan.

Aspotogan Peninsula   *See* Aspotogan.

Aspy Bay (Victoria)   At the northeastern tip of CAPE BRETON ISLAND. Two place names once shown on early charts of this coast, *Baxes* ('shoals') *aux Basques* and *Basque Cove*, have disappeared from today's maps; however, nearby is Aspy Bay, a name with a strong Basque connection. Although the name has been credited to both Mi'kmaq and various western European sources, recent research points to a Basque origin. Aspy may be for Pic d'Aspé in the Pyrenees, or the monastery of Santa Maria de Axpe, in the Basque province of Bizkaia. The name also appears as *Aispe* on a Basque map of the early seventeenth century.

Atwoods Brook (Shelburne) Flows into BARRINGTON PASSAGE. The name may be traced to a New England Planter, Joseph Atwood, of Cape Cod, who settled here in 1767. On 19 October 1776, Atwood, along with several others, petitioned the Council of Massachussetts Bay, noting that 'in the course of these Unhappy Times we have done everything in our power to ... assist the free and generous sons of America.'

Through the petition they hoped for safe passage of a schooner laden with 'fish and liver oyl' and eventual sale of the produce. The petition illustrates the dilemma of the New England Planters in Nova Scotia during the American Revolution.

Auburn (Kings)   West of BERWICK. The name stems from a line in 'The Deserted Village,' a poem by the anglo-Irish poet Oliver Goldsmith (1728–1774): 'Sweet Auburn! loveliest village of the plain.' The community is noteworthy for St. Mary's Anglican Church, erected in 1790. The building is an adaptation in wood of a design created by the master architect Sir Christopher Wren (1632–1723). It was the second Anglican church in British North America to be consecrated. See also GOLDSMITHS STREAM, New Brunswick.

Aulds Cove (Antigonish)   This community straddles the ANTIGONISH–GUYSBOROUGH boundary, although the cove itself lies in the latter county. Named for Alexander Auld, an early settler, the area was once known as 'Porcupine Cove.' This is the mainland terminal of the Canso Causeway, completed on 13 August 1955.

Avondale (Hants); **Avonport** (Kings); **Avon River**   The Avon

River forms part of the boundary between KINGS and HANTS counties. It was known during the French period as 'Rivière Pisiquid,' from the Mi'kmaq *Pesegitk*, which has been translated by Silas T. Rand as 'flowing into the sea' or 'where the tidal flow forks.' Avon is the most common river name in the British Isles, with examples in England, Scotland, Wales, and Ireland. The Nova Scotia Avon dates from the creation of the township of Windsor on 24 December 1764, and was probably conferred for the river of the same name in England. The communities of Avonport and Avondale were named because of their location in relation to the river. See also WINDSOR and FALMOUTH.

Avonport   *See* Avondale.

Avon River   *See* Avondale.

Aylesford (Kings)   Off Highway 101, between BERWICK and KINGSTON. On 6 October 1786, a proclamation was issued by the executive council of Nova Scotia indicating that 'the part of the township of Wilmot which lies in Kings County is to be called Aylesford.' The name marks the career of an undistinguished English nobleman, the Earl of Aylesford, Lord of the Bedchamber to King George III, who, in

turn, took his title from the village of Aylesford in Kent.

Baccaro (Shelburne)   East of CAPE SABLE ISLAND. *Pointe de Bacareau* is a prominent feature on Lalanne's *Carte d'une partie de la côte méridionale de l'Acadie* of 1684. However, the name is older and probably of Basque origin. It stems from one of the many designations for codfish, such as *baccalaos*. In 1896 the local postmaster reported to the Geographic Board of Canada: 'We are of the opinion that this name is derived from the obsolete word *baccalieu* [for 'codfish'] which was in olden times given to this region. The point of land now called Baccaro is in close proximity to the old [French] Fort St. Louis and was corrupted to Baccaro by the English.' See also BACCALIEU ISLAND, Newfoundland.

Baddeck (shiretown of Victoria County)   Fronts on BRAS D'OR LAKE. The only certainty concerning the source of this name is its Mi'kmaq roots, and several definitions have been cited to explain its meaning. William Francis Ganong asserts that it may be traced to the Mi'kmaq root *petek*, which means 'a turn' or 'bend backwards.' He further suggests that the name has 'a broad descriptive sense and alludes to the fact that a reverse turn must be made in order to enter the the harbour.' The French interpretation of the name on the anonymous *Plan de l'ile Royale* of 1751 was *La Badecque*. See also BEINN BREAGH, and BEDEQUE, Prince Edward Island.

Baileys Brook (Pictou)   Flows into the NORTHUMBERLAND STRAIT at LISMORE. In 1788, John Baillie, a native of Sutherlandshire, Scotland, and a member of the 82nd Regiment during the American Revolution, received a grant of 60 hectares in the northeastern section of PICTOU COUNTY. The community which grew up around his farm was known as 'Baillie Brook'; however, over time, the Scottish spelling, 'Baillie,' changed to 'Baileys.'

Bakeapple Barren (Inverness) East of Cap Rouge, in CAPE BRETON HIGHLANDS NATIONAL PARK. Named for a low, bog-dwelling plant (*Rubus chamaemorus*). Sometimes called the 'cloudberry,' it has a white flower, followed by a light amber-coloured berry. The plant also grows on barrens and bogs in Newfoundland and Labrador (see BAKEAPPLE BAY, Labrador). Nearby is Cranberry Barren, named for the wild cranberry also native to this area of Cape Breton.

Bakers Settlement (Lunenburg) On Highway 325, northwest of BRIDGEWATER. The Becker family was numbered among the Foreign Protestants of French, Swiss, and German origin, who, in the mid-eighteenth century, settled in LUNENBURG COUNTY. The name was gradually anglicized to Baker – hence, the name of the community. Members of the family moved here in 1835.

Baleine (Cape Breton)   Northeast of LOUISBOURG. Because of its strategic location near the easternmost tip of CAPE BRETON, 'Port de la Baleine,' as it was known in the French period, figured prominently in the early history of the region. It was originally a French fishing station, but an attempt was made in the seventeenth century to establish a Scottish colony on the site. In 1629, Sir James Stewart, one of the Knights Baronet of Nova Scotia, erected Fort Rosemar, only to have it destroyed by an expedition under the command of Captain Charles Daniel of Dieppe, a member of the Compagnie des Cent-Associés. The name was inspired by a baleine (whale)-shaped rock once located at the harbour entrance.

Ballantynes Cove (Antigonish) Near the tip of CAPE GEORGE. It was named for an early settler, Captain David Ballantyne, a native of Strathaven, Scotland, who served with the 82nd Regiment in the American Revolution. His wife, Mary Morrison, daughter of George Morrison, was one of the Highland emigrants who came to Pictou on the *Hector* in 1773. Descendants still live in the area.

Balmoral (Richmond); **Balmoral Brook** (Pictou); **Balmoral Mills** (Colchester)   Balmoral Mills, in north COLCHESTER COUNTY, was settled by emigrants from Sutherlandshire, Scotland, in the 1820s and 1830s. It became noted for the several grist mills built on Mathesons Brook, which flows through the community. One of these, erected about 1874, is still in existence. This mill was operated by the MacDonald family until 1954; in 1966 it became part of the Nova Scotia Museum complex. The name stems from Balmoral Castle, near Braemar, Scotland. Balmoral in RICHMOND COUNTY and Balmoral Brook in PICTOU COUNTY have the same origin.

Balmoral Brook   *See* Balmoral.

Balmoral Mills   *See* Balmoral.

Barachois (sometimes spelled 'Barrachois'; Colchester)   East of TATAMAGOUCHE. This is a common place name found in all four Atlantic provinces. There are more than thirty toponyms in Nova Scotia that incorporate the word. Of Basque origin, it may be traced to their word *barratxo* or *barrachoa*, for 'little bar' or 'sand bar.' Later it was adapted and spelled 'barachoix' or 'barachois' by the French and extended to mean a shallow body of fresh or salt water, sheltered from the sea by a sand spit or strip of land. Writing in 1760, Thomas Pichon (1700–1781) noted: 'They give the name *barachois* in this country to small ponds near the sea, from which they are separated by only a kind of causeway.' The name is sometimes rendered as 'The Barachois.' See SOI POINT, and BARACHOIS, Newfoundland.

Barneys River (Pictou)   Flows into the NORTHUMBERLAND STRAIT, near the PICTOU–ANTIGONISH county line. First known as 'East River Merigomish,' it was renamed in 1779 for an early settler, Barnabas 'Barney' MacGee, a member of the Philadelphia Company. A native of Ulster, MacGee first emigrated to Pennsylvania, thence to Lyons Brook, near Pictou; from there he moved to the community that now bears his name. See also LYONS BROOK.

Barrachois   *See* Barachois.

Barra Glen (Victoria); **Barra Head** (Richmond); **Barra Mens Cove**

(Inverness); **Barra Strait** (Cape Breton)   The original Barra is a hilly island in the Outer Hebrides, and the translation of the Celtic word is exactly that, 'hilly island.' Since many nineteenth-century emigrants came from the Hebrides, it is not surprising that the place name is found in all four counties on Cape Breton. The ancestral home of Clan MacNeil, a clan well represented on Cape Breton, it has become nationally known through the Barra MacNeils, a contemporary folk-music group. In 1758 the region bordering on ST. ANDREWS CHANNEL was visited by Donald Og MacNeil and Donald MacNeil, soldiers in the British army at the capture of Fortress Louisbourg. They took back to Barra 'an enthusiastic and precise description' of the land, and thereby encouraged fellow islanders to emigrate to Coalas nam Barrach, the Barra Mens Cove, a name it still bears. See also WASHABUCK CENTRE.

Barra Head   *See* Barra Glen.

Barra Mens Cove   *See* Barra Glen.

Barra Strait   *See* Barra Glen.

Barrington; Barrington Bay; Barrington Passage (Shelburne) Prior to the completion of a causeway in 1949, CAPE SABLE ISLAND was separated from the mainland by 'The Passage' which echoed its Acadian name, Le Passage. The descriptor was later to be incorporated in the community name Barrington Passage. Following the expulsion in 1755, this area, so important to the fishery, was resettled by fifty New England families from Marblehead, Plymouth, Cape Cod, and Nantucket. One of their first actions was to erect, in 1765, a meeting-house, which still stands in Barrington. Both communities were named in 1767 for William Wildman Barrington (1717–1793), Viscount Barrington, who served briefly as chancellor of the exchequer (1761–2). Barrington Bay takes its name from the settlement.

Barrington Bay   *See* Barrington.

Barrington Passage   *See* Barrington.

Barss Corner (Lunenburg) Northeast of NEW GERMANY. The community was established in the late eighteenth century by the second generation of Foreign Protestant settlers from the LUNENBURG area. It was named for one of the first landholders.

Barton (Digby)   Near the head of ST. MARYS BAY. Named for an early Loyalist settler, Joseph Barton. He received his land grant in 1787. The first post office was called Spechts Cove; however, this name was short-lived and the original was restored by 1887.

Bass River (Colchester)   West of GREAT VILLAGE, on Highway 2. The first settler was James Fulton, who earlier had emigrated from Londonderry, Ulster, to New England. A land surveyor, he worked in Pennsylvania before coming to Nova Scotia, where he surveyed and subdivided the township of LONDONDERRY, an area to be later settled largely by Ulster Scots. For this work he was allowed a free land grant of his choice and selected the area that later became Bass River. The name was assigned because of the quantities of bass found there.

Bayfield; Bayfield Beach; Bayfield Road (Antigonish)   On the Northumberland coast, between MONKS HEAD and TRACADIE. Named for Captain Henry Wolsey Bayfield (1795–1885), who was responsible for coastal surveys of Prince Edward Island, the Magdalen Islands, Cape Breton, Sable Island, and Nova Scotia, from Halifax to the Strait of Canso. See also BAYFIELD, New Brunswick, and BAYFIELD, Prince Edward Island.

Bayfield Beach   *See* Bayfield.

Bayfield Road   *See* Bayfield.

Bay of Fundy   See chapter 1, pages 9–10.

Bay St. Lawrence (Victoria) Fronts on the GULF OF ST. LAWRENCE. The name was originally applied by Jacques Cartier to Baie-Saint-Laurent on the north shore of the present Gulf of St. Lawrence. Over time the name was gradually applied to the gulf and river. During his second voyage in 1534–5, Cartier explored the northern tip of CAPE BRETON, naming Cap de Lorraine and Cap de Sainct Paul (later renamed Cape St. Lawrence and CAPE NORTH, respectively). Both Bay St. Lawrence and Cape St. Lawrence take their name from the gulf.

Bear River (Annapolis)   Flows into the ANNAPOLIS BASIN. Although named Rivière Saint-Antoine in 1605 by Champlain, four years later it was being referred to by Lescarbot as Rivière Hébert. The name commemorates the career of Louis Hébert (1575?–1627), apothecary and a member of the Gua de Monts expedition to Acadia. The modern name is an English corruption of the original French. See also RIVER HÉBERT.

Bedford; Bedford Basin (Halifax)   From 1749 until 1856, the land at the head of CHEBUCTO BAY was known as 'Fort Sackville,' after the defences established in 1749 to protect the overland trail from HALIFAX to the ANNAPOLIS VALLEY. Following English settlement, the basin was known briefly as 'Torrington Bay,' for John Byng, Viscount Torrington (1704–1757). The name Bedford was applied first to the basin in honour of John, fourth Duke of Bedford (1710–1771), secretary of state (southern department) at the time of the founding of Halifax in 1749. In 1856 the name Fort Sackville was replaced by Bedford. The town was incorporated in 1980 (see LOWER SACKVILLE). In 1996 it became part of the Regional Municipality of Halifax.

Bedford Basin   *See* Bedford.

Beinn Breagh (Victoria)   This name was selected by Alexander Graham Bell (1847–1922) for his estate on the outskirts of BADDECK. The translation from Gaelic is 'beautiful mountain,' an apt description of the setting. As Bell's fame and importance grew, the descriptive achieved the status of a place name. A many-sided genius, Bell is best known for the invention of the telephone. However, while in residence at Beinn Breagh, he turned his attention to a variety of research projects, ranging from genetics to the science of sound, and from the hydrofoil to manned flight. Bell founded the Aerial Experiment Association and was the driving force behind the first flight in the Commonwealth of 'a heavier than air machine under power.' This occurred at Baddeck on 23 February 1909. His exploits are commemorated in the Alexander Graham Bell Museum at Baddeck. Included in the display is Bell's original HD-4 hydrofoil boat. See also MOUNT McCURDY.

Belle Côte (Inverness); **Belleisle** (Annapolis); **Belle Marche** (Inverness)   Belle Côte, on the northeast side of the MARGAREE RIVER, marks the entrance to the Acadian section of INVERNESS COUNTY. The name, in translation 'beautiful hill,' is a descriptive applied by the Acadians who returned to this part of CAPE BRETON following their expulsion in 1755. Some 25 kilometres farther north, on the Cabot Trail, another descriptive, Belle Marche, for 'beautiful walk,' may be found. On the other hand, Belleisle, in ANNAPOLIS COUNTY, is not a descriptive. It was named for Alexandre Le Borgne de Belle-Isle (*ca* 1643–1693), onetime acting governor and seigneur of Port-Royal. In 1669 'a piece of land and meadow' was conveyed to the first settlers, Pierre and Matthieu Martin, by Sieur de Belle-Isle. See also BELLEISLE, New Brunswick.

Belleisle   *See* Belle Côte.

Belle Marche   *See* Belle Côte.

Belliveaus Cove (Digby)   In the municipality of CLARE, within DIGBY COUNTY. The community was named in the late eighteenth century for Jean Belliveau and his three sons, Charles-Martin, Joseph-Jacques, and Frédéric. The Belliveau family was among the first to settle in the area.

Ben Eoin (Cape Breton)   On the eastern shore of East Bay, an arm of BRAS D'OR LAKE. The name, after an early settler, is Gaelic in origin and may be translated as 'Jonathan's Mountain.'

Berwick (Kings)   In the Annapolis Valley, west of KENTVILLE. Although often attributed to Berwick, Scotland, this town name is for Berwick, Maine. During the first half of the nineteenth century, the community passed through a series of name changes: Congdon Settlement, Curries Corner, and Davisons Corner – all for early settlers. In 1851 the people decided to opt for a permanent name. A letter in the CPCGN files states: 'One of our residents once travelling in the United States passed through [Berwick, Maine] and ... pleased with its neat and tidy appearance, [he] suggested the

name.' The town was incorporated in 1923.

Bible Hill (Colchester)   A suburb of TRURO. Its name has given rise to a number of apocryphal stories concerning its origin. It actually stems from the ministry of the Reverend Dr. William McCulloch (1811–1895), who served Truro's First Presbyterian (now First United) Church from 1839 to 1885. He lived across the Salmon River in the district later to become known as 'Bible Hill.' His father, Dr. Thomas McCulloch (1776–1843), was one of the founders of the Nova Scotia Bible Society and passed on an interest in the distribution of the Scripture to his son. Thus, it became the custom of McCulloch to give out, to any who might want them, copies of Holy Scripture, free of charge. Following McCulloch's ministry of nearly a half-century, the name Bible Hill became fixed.

Big Intervale (Inverness)   North of SUGARLOAF MOUNTAIN. Once known as 'Scotch Intervale' and 'Big Intervale Margaree.' The name, a descriptive, is frequently found as part of place names throughout northeastern Nova Scotia and CAPE BRETON. Intervale, derived from 'interval,' refers to a low-lying area adjacent to a stream. As early as 1774, two Yorkshire visitors to Nova Scotia,

John Robinson and Thomas Rispin, commented on the feature: 'Good intervale land [is] not much inferior to the marsh, when properly cultivated. What [Nova Scotians] call intervale land, lays by the brooks, which, in the spring of the year, at the melting of the snow, is frequently overflowed, which greatly enriches the ground.'

Big Pond (Cape Breton) On East Bay. The community was first known as 'Anse de Charbon' (Coal Cove) during the French colonial period. The contemporary name is a descriptive. The community was the home of Rita MacNeil, well-known Canadian pop-singer.

Birchtown (Shelburne) On the western outskirts of SHELBURNE. This community, settled in 1783 by black Loyalists, was named in honour of Brigadier-General Samuel Birch, British commandant of New York City during the latter stages of the American Revolution. He earned the goodwill of the black refugees by providing them with rations and shelter prior to their departure for Nova Scotia. In 1993–4 the Birchtown area was the site of an extensive archaeological dig undertaken by a team from St. Mary's University. When the project is completed, a better understanding of

this important settlement will be obtained.

Blanche (Shelburne) One of the older names on the south shore of Nova Scotia, this fishing harbour was noted on the Lalanne map of 1684. *Pointe Blanche* was also listed by Jean-Baptiste-Louis Franquelin (1697–1768), hydrographer royal, for the stretch of 'white' sand in the vicinity.

Blockhouse (Lunenburg) West of MAHONE BAY. This community was the site of a blockhouse built by Captain Ephraim Cook in 1754. Described by historian Winthrop Pickard Bell (1884–1964) as a 'cantankerous character,' Cook spent most of his life embroiled in litigation. At various times he was charged with crimes ranging from embezzlement to fraud, to acting as a justice of the peace after the revoking of his commission. In an application to Governor Charles Lawrence for the grant of a 'vacant spot of land [near] Mahone Bay,' Cook detailed grandiose settlement plans and noted 'having had the timbers of a blockhouse prepared, ready for erection' on location. This achievement, and through it, the bequeathing of a place name, were to be the most important legacies of Captain Ephraim Cook, 'of notorious memory.'

Blomidon   *See* Cape Blomidon.

Blue Mountain (Pictou)   Southeast of NEW GLASGOW. Blue Mountain was first settled in 1815 by William Urquhart, a native of Glen Urquhart, Scotland. He was soon followed by other Scottish immigrants, one of whom, William Ross, was to suggest the descriptive name for the community. It should be noted that the mountain is more normally green than blue, and its name resulted from a mistranslation into English from the original Gaelic.

Blue Rocks (Lunenburg)   On Lunenburg Bay. In 1937 Clara Dennis wrote: 'A few miles out of Lunenburg, I am in the most unique of fishing hamlets. It is mostly rocks, blue rocks, the dwellings and fish houses are all perched on rocks.' The settlement dates from 1760, and the name is descriptive. Nearby Stonehurst was originally known as 'Black Rocks.' Dennis also noted: 'The rocks there are just as black as they are blue here.' For the record, the rock colour is not always obvious; thus local residents tire of answering the question: 'Can you tell us where the Blue Rocks are, please?'

Boisdale (Cape Breton)   On the south side of ST. ANDREWS CHANNEL; an arm of BRAS D'OR LAKE. It was named in 1823 for Boisdale, in South Uist, Scotland, original home of the first settlers.

Bon Portage (Outer) Island (Shelburne)   A small island off SHAG HARBOUR, near the southern tip of Nova Scotia. The location was known to early French navigators, who gave the island and the anchorage of which it forms the outer breakwater the name Bon Portage. It was listed as *Île Mouillées* on the Lalanne map of 1684. Also known locally as 'Outer Island,' it became the focal point for the novels and non-fiction of Evelyn Richardson (1902–1977), award-winning author, and wife of the lightkeeper during the 1940s and 1950s. Described as a birder's paradise, the island was deeded by Mrs. Richardson to Acadia University as an 'on site' laboratory for botanical and ornithological studies. The lighthouse dates from 1874.

Boularderie (Victoria); **Boularderie Island** (Cape Breton and Victoria)   Although seigneuries were not established on Île Royale (Cape Breton) during the French period, substantial land grants were made to specific individuals. One of these conveyed the island and the adjacent eastern shore of the La Petit Brador (ST. ANDREWS CHANNEL) to Louis-Simon Le Poupet de La Boularderie (1674–1738). Boularderie served as commandant at Port d'Orléans (North Bay Ingonish) from 1719 to 1738. His colonization efforts and those of his son, Antoine, were not particularly successful, and their main legacy is the place name. Boularderie takes its name from the island.

Boularderie Island   *See* Boularderie.

Boylston (Guysborough)   On the east side of GUYSBOROUGH harbour. On 31 October 1765, this district became part of an 8,000-hectare land grant to Benjamin Hallowell, a wealthy customs official in Boston. Before settlement could begin, the American Revolution intervened, and Hallowell returned to England. One of his sons, Ward Hallowell (1749–1828), 'by the particular desire of his maternal uncle, Nicholas Boylston, dropped the name Hallowell and assumed that of Boylston.' It was this association that led his father to 'give to the town which he planned the name that it now bears' (Hart). In 1800, Nicholas Ward Boylston returned to the United States to live in Boston. Boylston Street and Boylston Market in that city are both named for him.

Bras d'Or Lake (Cape Breton)   Writing in 1829, T.C. Haliburton

(1796–1865) points to 'a connection' between the name Bras d'Or Lake and Labrador. As early as 1671, Nicolas Denys (1598–1688) gave the following description of the lake: 'That which is called *labrador* is a stretch of the sea cutting in half the island of Cape Breton.' The explanation of the 'connection' lies in an error made by several sixteenth-century cartographers. Ignorance of local geography placed 'Labrador' much farther south on certain maps, and over time it survived in the shortened form 'Bras d'Or. See also chapter 1, pages 6–7.

Bridgetown (Annapolis)   In 1803 a bridge was built across the Annapolis River, 25 kilometres above Annapolis. Originally the community was known as 'Hicks Ferry,' after an early settler. The new descriptive name was adopted at a public meeting held on 15 January 1824. According to the *Acadian Recorder*: 'it was held at the local place of entertainment [the tavern] ... The evening was convivially spent and many loyal toasts given. The name was chosen by reason of the appreciation of the residents [for] the bridge.' Incorporation as a town occurred in 1897.

Bridgewater (Lunenburg) Strategically located at the main bridging point on the LAHAVE

RIVER, this area attracted settlers from the LUNENBURG area shortly after the founding of the latter. It was included in a grant to Joseph Pernette (*ca* 1728–1807), a native of Alsace, who served as MLA for LUNENBURG COUNTY from 1761 to 1770. The name is descriptive of its location near a bridge over the LaHave River. It became an incorporated town in 1899.

Brier Island (Digby)   Adjacent to Long Island, in the BAY OF FUNDY. This name is of uncertain origin and appears first as *Bryer Island* on the DesBarres chart of 1775. By 1809, when the Nova Scotia legislature passed an act 'to provide for the support of a lighthouse on the island,' the spelling was 'Brier.' It was settled as early as 1769, when David Welch and Robert Morrell emigrated from Maine in search of fish. Later they were joined by a group of Loyalists in the 1780s. The name is probably derived from the wild brier rose, which grows in profusion on the island. A lighthouse was erected at West Point in 1809. See also LONG ISLAND.

Broad Cove (Lunenburg)   Midway between East Port Medway and PETITE RIVIÈRE . Broad Cove dates from 1791,when it was settled by Martin Tiel, Nicholas Reinhardt, and John Michael Schmitt and their families.

They were part of the second-generation expansion of the original LUNENBURG settlement. The name is a descriptive, as the cove is broad or triangular in shape.

Brookfield (Colchester; Queens) The Colchester Brookfield, south of TRURO, was first settled by William Hamilton (1758–1838), a native of Vicar's Cairn, Armagh, in Ulster. He emigrated to Nova Scotia in 1771, moving to this area in 1784. Hamilton named the community for a brook which flowed through his property. In 1798 a road was opened between the township of LIVERPOOL on the south shore of Nova Scotia and NICTAUX in the Annapolis Valley. One of those interested in this project was William Burke, who 'brought to the notice of the people of Liverpool the benefit of opening up the northern portion of the county' (More). Later he settled near the bridge on the MEDWAY RIVER and assigned the descriptive Brookfield to the community. It is now known as South Brookfield. See also MOLEGA.

Brooklyn (Queens)   This is a common descriptive that occurs at least six times in Nova Scotia. Its popularity may have been inspired by a borough of the same name in New York City. The name of this Brooklyn was derived, over time and many misspellings, from Breukelyn in the Netherlands. In QUEENS COUNTY, Brooklyn is located 5 kilometres east of LIVERPOOL and was formerly known as 'Herring Cove.' The community dates from the late eighteenth century.

Brora Lake (Pictou)   North of GARDEN OF EDEN. This lake, named for Brora in Sutherlandshire, Scotland, serves as a reminder that much of PICTOU and north COLCHESTER counties was settled by Scots who were forced to emigrate in the early nineteenth century. The root causes of this emigration and the associated Highland Clearances were many and varied. Overpopulation, land hunger, near starvation following a series of bad harvests, and 'grinding' poverty contributed to the exodus. Unfortunately, in the words of Scottish historian J.D. Mackie, 'some of these emigrants were forcibly evicted from homes in which they wished to stay in spite of everything.' Many emigrants came from the Sutherlandshire parishes of Clyne, Rogart, Golspie, Lairg, and Dornoch, all in the vicinity of Brora.

Broughton (Cape Breton)   In the Cochran Lake area, southwest of PORT MORIEN. In the early 1900s a small seam of coal was discovered here. This event led to one of the most spectacular fiascos in the history of Nova Scotia. Before adequate exploration had taken place, and prior to the acquisition of adequate capital, officials of the Cape Breton Coal, Iron and Railway Company put forward a scheme to build a town designed for 10,000 to 12,000 people. Noted Prince Edward Island architect William Critchlow Harris (1854–1913) was hired to develop plans for the model town, and about fifty buildings were actually built. The new town was named after 'Broughton Hall' in Cheshire, England, the country seat of Horace Mayhew, an English mining entrepreneur recruited to head the company. By 1907 the entire enterprise had collapsed, leaving a solitary place name as a reminder.

Brule Point (Colchester); **Brûlé Point** (Richmond)   Fronting on AMET SOUND. This district in north COLCHESTER COUNTY was named by the French Pointe Brûlé, because they found that the forest had been burned over in the early eighteenth century. The anglicized version (*Point Brouley* on some early maps) prevailed following the expulsion of the Acadians in 1755. The origin of the RICHMOND COUNTY name is the same; however, in this instance the French spelling and pronunciation have been maintained.

Brûlé Point   *See* Brule Point.

Burntcoat Head (Hants)   A promontory between Tennycape and Noel Head on the MINAS BASIN shore of HANTS COUNTY. It was reputedly so named in 1795 when two early settlers, Thomas and Robert Faulkner, were burning marshland and lost a coat in the ensuing fire. The world's highest tide (16.1 metres) has been recorded at Burntcoat Head, where the average tide reaches 10 metres. This phenomenon once inspired Joseph Howe (1804–1873) to advise Nova Scotians: 'Brag of your country. When I'm abroad I brag of everything that Nova Scotia is, has, or can produce; and when they beat me at everything else, I say, how high does your tide rise?'

Caledonia (Guysborough)   On the west branch of the ST. MARYS RIVER. It was settled in 1810 by a group of Scots who moved there from PICTOU COUNTY. It was the Roman name for north Britain and is used in poetic and literary contexts for Scotland. Appropriately, the place name occurs eight times in various parts of Nova Scotia.

Cambridge (Kings)   West of KENTVILLE. The community was first known as 'Cambridge Station,' for its location on the former Dominion Atlantic Railway. Named for Cambridge, Massachusetts, and now part of CORNWALLIS SQUARE.

Canard; Canard River (Kings)   The river flows into the MINAS BASIN. Prior to 1755 Canard was the thriving Acadian parish of La Rivière-aux-Canards, with some 150 families. The name has been traced by Silas T. Rand to a Mi'kmaq phrase meaning 'a place abounding in ducks.' This was later rendered in French as *Canard*, for 'duck,' and was subsequently retained by the New England Planters who arrived in the 1760s.

Canard River   *See* Canard.

Canning (Kings)   On the HABITANT RIVER. The community was first known as 'Apple Tree Landing,' because of a landmark apple tree surviving from the earlier Acadian settlement. A later name, Habitant Corner, was replaced in 1830 by public vote in favour of Canning. The new name honoured George Canning (1770–1827), who served briefly as British prime minister in 1827.

Canso; Cape Canso (Guysborough); **Strait of Canso**   Although Canso, the easternmost point on mainland Nova Scotia, appears in Marc Lescarbot's *Histoire de la Nouvelle France* (1609), the name is clearly of much earlier origin. It may be traced to Mi'kmaq sources and is a French interpretation of *kamsok*, which means 'opposite a high bluff' or 'the place beyond the cliffs.' This is an apt description of its position along the south side of CHEDABUCTO BAY. On some French maps it is variously known as *Campseau*, *Camseau*, and *Canceau*. The present spelling has been in use since the 1700s. The designation Strait of Canso, for the waters between CAPE BRETON and the mainland, became common in the early nineteenth century. The name was also adopted in 1955 for the Canso Causeway. See also GRASSY ISLAND.

Cape Blomidon (Kings)   At the end of the NORTH MOUNTAIN range; the dominant feature of the MINAS BASIN landscape. The Mi'kmaq people believed that this was the home of their deity Glooscap. It was Glooscap, as the legend goes, who created man from an ash tree and who was responsible for the mighty tides of FUNDY. According to William Francis Ganong, 'the place name may be traced to 'blow me down,' a nautical phrase.' This expression meant a headland rising steeply from the sea and subject to sudden down draughts of wind. See also FIVE ISLANDS, and BLOW ME DOWN, Newfoundland.

Cape Breton (Cape Breton) Originally named Cap Breton, the specific feature that is today known as 'Cape Breton' is situated at the easternmost point of the island of the same name. There are several theories as to its origin. The most common suggests that it commemorates the Bretons of Brittany, who were known to be among the earliest fishermen in the area. William Francis Ganong, as part of his argument for Cape Breton as Cabot's landfall, was emphatic that the use of 'Breton' referred to a sixteenth-century designation for the English people. Citing the *Concise Oxford Dictionary*, he pointed out that, during this period, 'the English were called, among themselves at least, Bretons, Brytons, or Bretones.' The final theory points to a possible Basque origin for the name. In the old Basque province of Les Landes, located between Bordeaux and Bayonne, there was an important town and fortress known as 'Cap Breton.' As time went on, the mouth of the adjacent Adour River silted up and the town became an insignificant village; however, the headland remained. Thus, it is reasoned that Cape Breton was so named because Basque sailor-fishermen recalled the last land that they had seen as they sailed from the southeast coast of France, site of the original Cap Breton. All that can be confirmed is that Basque fishermen frequented the coastline of both Cape Breton and Newfoundland during the pre-1600 period. In the absence of documentary evidence, the Basque theory, while entirely plausible, remains unproven. As a result, the Breton origin remains the most convincing.

Cape Breton County; Cape Breton Island   By proclamation dated 7 October 1763, Cape Breton Island was formally annexed to Nova Scotia and became part of HALIFAX COUNTY. On 10 December 1765, Cape Breton Island was set apart as a separate county, a division that lasted for nineteen years. From 1784 to 1820, Cape Breton Island existed as a colony in its own right, with a lieutenant-governor and appointed council, but without an elected Assembly. Following reannexation to Nova Scotia in 1820, the entire island was again considered to be Cape Breton County; however, by legislation proclaimed on 2 April 1824, it was subdivided into three separate and distinct sections, to be known

as the Northeastern, Southern, and Northwestern districts. Later, in 1835, the three districts were accorded county status: Cape Breton County (Northeastern); RICHMOND COUNTY (Southern); and Juste-au-Corps, later INVERNESS COUNTY (Northwestern). A final subdivision took place in 1852, with the separation of VICTORIA COUNTY from Cape Breton County. In 1995 all municipal units within Cape Breton County were amalgamated to form one 'super city,' the Regional Municipality of Cape Breton.

Cape Breton Highlands National Park   The origin of this national park goes back to 1934, when Donald MacIntosh deeded 40 hectars of land east of PLEASANT BAY with the stipulation 'that the government maintain a park in the intervale and construct a crofter's cottage such as was used on the Isle of Skye.' By 1936, the 'Lone Shieling' was constructed, and the land became the nucleus for the park which stretches across the northern tip of CAPE BRETON ISLAND. On a map of Cape Breton dated 1835, this section of the island was designated 'high bold land,' a description that has not changed significantly, even with man's intrusion over the years. The park consists of 950 square kilometres of forested mountains and craggy red cliffs, barrens, and bogs; stream-lined valleys; and sea vistas. It is encircled by the Cabot Trail, a modern highway 300 kilometres in length. See also chapter 1, page 5.

Cape Breton Island   *See* Cape Breton County.

Cape Canso   *See* Canso.

Chignecto (Cumberland)   At the eastern entrance to Chignecto Bay. Originally called Cap des Deux Bayes by Samuel de Champlain, a literal description of its situation at the entrance to Chignecto Bay and the MINAS BASIN. The later name, Cape Chignecto, is of Mi'kmaq origin. See also CHIGNECTO BAY, New Brunswick.

Cape d'Or (Cumberland)   At the entrance to Minas Basin. In 1603 Jean Sarcel de Prévert and François Gravé Du Pont explored the coastline of Acadia. They brought back to Champlain mineral specimens found on the shores of present-day Minas Basin. This find and the subsequent search for minerals in the area gave rise to the name Cap des Mines, later Cape d'Or, in the mistaken belief that the copper they found was gold. See also MINAS BASIN.

Cape Forchu (Yarmouth)   At the entrance to Yarmouth harbour.

Named Cap Fourchu in 1604 by Champlain 'because it was formed like a fork.' *Cap Fourchu* appears consistently thereafter on all major French maps; for example, Lalanne 1684 and Franquelin-DeMeulles 1687. The intrepid Nicolas Denys (1598–1688) provided the following description in 1672: 'Vessels can there be placed under shelter. The fishery for cod is abundant, and not far off shore; [the cod] comes here earlier than any other place in Acadia.' The anglicized spelling dates from the late nineteenth century. The first lighthouse was built in 1839. See also FOURCHU HARBOUR and YARMOUTH.

Cape George (Antigonish) Extends into NORTHUMBERLAND STRAIT. Originally known as 'Cape St. Louis,' it appears first, in Latin, on the Creuxius map of 1660. Nicolas Denys (1598–1688) described the setting in 1672: 'The cape is extremely high, and it is visible for twenty leagues. I ascended to its top, where there are fine trees very tall and stout, although from below they only seem like bushes.' The change to Cape St. George was made by J.F.W. DesBarres (1722–1824) on his charts for *The Atlantic Neptune*. Later it was shortened to Cape George. The name of the bay separating Cape George and CAPE BRETON remains St. Georges Bay.

Cape Jeddore   *See* Jeddore Harbour.

Cape John; River John (Pictou)
A promontory on the east side of
AMET SOUND. The name is of unknown French origin and appears
as *Cap Jean* on early-eighteenth-
century maps. The river and village take their name from the
nearby cape. The anglicized spelling dates from the 1777 DesBarres
survey of the northern coast of
Nova Scotia. River John was first
settled by four families from
Montbéliard who were part of the
1753 Foreign Protestant migration
to LUNENBURG. Later, they
moved to TATAMAGOUCHE, and
from there to River John. Descendants of these families, two
named Petrequin (Patriquin), one
Langill (Langille), and one Gretaux (Gratto), are still to be found
locally.

**Cape LaHave; LaHave; LaHave
Islands; LaHave River** (Lunenburg)   The river flows into the
Atlantic, at LaHave. The name
Cap de la Have, applied by Pierre
Du Gua de Monts (1588?–1628),
was the first location on mainland
North America sighted by Champlain and de Monts on their 1604
voyage. It was suggested by Cap
de la Hève, 3 kilometres north–
northwest of the entrance to
Havre-de-Grâce (now Le Havre,
France), the port of embarkation

for the expedition. In 1632 a fort
was constructed at Cap de la
Have by Isaac de Razilly (1597–
1635) which became known as
'Fort Sainte-Marie-de-Grâce.' The
name was selected to mark the
date of their landing, 8 September, the feast of the Nativity of the
Virgin. This location is now
known as Fort Point. Later seventeenth- and eighteenth-century
maps indicate the evolution of the
place name: *Port de la heve*
(Lalanne 1684), *Port de la Haive*
(Bellin 1744), and *La Have Road*
and *Harbour* (Southack undated
[mid-1700s]). Southack, a New
England cartographer, displayed
great enthusiasm in his description of 'La Have Road [a partly
sheltered inlet] and Harbour with
a Fine River Navigable for Ships
and small vessels, a place to
bould [*sic*] a fine Town ... Trade,
Cod fishing, Herring, Mackerel,
Bass, Salmon, and masts for His
Majesty's Navy.' Over time the
anglicized LaHave was applied
not only to the cape but also to a
number of settlements, a group of
islands, and the river.

**Cape Morien; Morien Bay; Port
Morien** (Cape Breton)   Southeast
of GLACE BAY. The name was first
applied to the cape. In origin it
may be a corruption of the Portuguese for St. Martin. On the Goldfrap map (1767), part of the
Holland survey of Cape Breton

Island, *Le Cap Mordienne* and *Bay de Mordienne* are listed as the French names. However, Holland's suggested replacements, Granby Bay and Gage Point, did not survive, and the anglicized spelling 'Morienne' began to appear. For a time in the nineteenth century, the prosaic Cow Bay was in popular usage. Matters were regulated in 1895 by provincial statute to coincide with the establishment of a post office, and the names Cape Morien, Morien Bay, and Port Morien were officially adopted.

Cape Negro (Shelburne) Between SHELBURNE harbour and BARRINGTON BAY on the Atlantic coast. Named by Champlain in 1604 for the black rocks opposite the cape; appears as *Port de Cap Naigre* in Nicolas Denys 1672. Although considered a pejorative word today, 'negro' was in general use in the seventeenth century. See also AFRICVILLE.

Cape North (Victoria)   At the northern tip of CAPE BRETON. Although named Cap St. Paul by Cartier, this designation did not last. The earliest reference to Cap de Nort is in Nicolas Denys's 1672 description of this coastline. The English translation later replaced the French and has remained.

Cape Porcupine (Guysborough) Near AULDS COVE, on the STRAIT OF CANSO. This precipitous headland takes its name from a fancied resemblance to the shape of its namesake animal, the fir trees with which it is covered representing the spines.

Cape Roseway; Roseway; Roseway Beach; Roseway River (Shelburne)   Roseway and Roseway Beach are located near the western entrance to Shelburne harbour; Cape Roseway is on the southeastern tip of McNUTTS ISLAND; and the Roseway River enters the Atlantic Ocean at Shelburne. During the French colonial period, Jean-Baptiste-Louis Franquelin, hydrographer royal, was the first to use Port Rasoir as the name for the area. It may have been suggested by the razor clam, a narrow, elongated mollusk with a sharp-edged shell, and common to this coast. Another theory is that the shape of the harbour reminded the French of a partly folded razor. Whatever the origin of the name (variously spelled as 'Rasior' and 'Razair'), it was to be interpreted by the English as Rasway, then Rosaway, and eventually the euphonious Roseway. A lighthouse was erected at Cape Roseway in 1788. See also SHELBURNE.

Cape Sable; Cape Sable Island (Shelburne)   Cape Sable is the southern extremity of Nova Scotia; it is also the name of the southernmost point of the continental United States, at the tip of Florida. According to William Francis Ganong, the earliest known use of this descriptive for the island off BARRINGTON PASSAGE, may be found on the Lopo Homen map of 1550. It reappears on Champlain's charts as *Bay du Cap de Sable* and *Cap de Sable*, surviving as possibly the oldest place name on mainland Nova Scotia. It is derived from the French word *sable*, for 'sand.' The first lighthouse was built at Cape Sable in 1861. On August 1949, the Cape Sable Island causeway, linking the island to the mainland, was officially opened by Premier Angus L. Macdonald. See also SABLE ISLAND.

Cape Sable Island   *See* Cape Sable.

Cape St. Lawrence   *See* Bay St. Lawrence.

Cape Sambro   *See* Sambro.

Cape Smokey (Victoria)
Extends into the Atlantic at Ingonish harbour. William Francis Ganong suggests that this place name is 'one of the oldest' on CAPE BRETON ISLAND. He notes that on various sixteenth-century maps the words *fumdos*, *fumides*, and *fumos* appear. 'The word conforms so closely to that of the place called *Enfumé* [on later

French maps] as to leave scant doubt of their identity. *Enfumé* takes its name from the high greyish banks in the elevated land south of Ingonish ... that present from a distance a striking resemblance to clouds of smoke.' The name survives in translation as 'Cape Smokey.' In recent years the area has become renowned as a year-round tourist resort (see INGONISH). During the winter, skiing is an attraction at Cape Smokey, with its 1,234-metre double chair lift.

Cape Spencer; Spencers Island
(Cumberland)   In GREVILLE BAY, off the north shore of MINAS BASIN. Named for George Spencer (1758–1834), who served as first lord of the Admiralty (1794–1801). The present village of Spencers Island is on the mainland, northeast of the island. During the nineteenth century the community was noted for shipbuilding. Perhaps the most famous vessel ever launched here was the ill-fated brigantine *Amazon* (1861), later renamed the *Mary Celeste*. The *Mary Celeste* was discovered in 1871 off the Azores sailing erratically, but with no one on board. There was no evidence of foul play, nor had there been storms in the area. The only items missing were the ship's papers and chronometer. A definitive explanation of the fate

of those on board has never been found.

Cap Le Moine   *See* St. Joseph du Moine.

Caribou Island (Pictou)   On the NORTHUMBERLAND STRAIT, west of PICTOU. Originally *Cariboo Island* and *Cariboo Harbour*, on the Arrowsmith map of 1838, the earlier spelling persisted locally until the 1950s. 'Caribou' is now the official designation. The area was described by Nicolas Denys (1598–1688): 'The cove is furnished with a number of islands of unequal sizes; some are covered with trees, the others with meadows and an infinity of birds of all kinds.' The name is said to have arisen from the presence of herds of deer, mistaken by early settlers for caribou. It is the Nova Scotia terminal for the ferry from Prince Edward Island. See also WOOD ISLANDS, Prince Edward Island.

Carleton; Carleton Lake (Yarmouth); **Carleton Village** (Shelburne)   Carleton is located 22 kilometres northeast of YARMOUTH, on Highway 340. The popularity of the total abstinence movement in the early nineteenth century led to its designation as Temperance. The new community name, adopted in 1834, was after nearby Carleton Lake. The latter name honoured Sir Guy Carleton, Baron Dorchester (1724–1805; see DORCHESTER, New Brunswick). Carleton Village, south of the town of SHELBURNE, was named for Sir Guy's brother Thomas Carleton (1735–1817; CPCGN Files). See also GUYSBOROUGH, and CARLETON COUNTY, New Brunswick.

Carleton Lake   *See* Carleton.

Carleton Village   *See* Carleton.

Catalone; Catalone Gut; Catalone Lake (Cape Breton)   North of LOUISBOURG and adjacent to MIRA BAY. First known as 'Barachois de Catalogne'; the names may be traced to Captain Gédéon de Catalogne (1662–1729), once an important landholder in the area. A soldier and engineer, he was associated with the Comte de Saint-Pierre, proprietor of Île Saint-Jean in 1720–3. In 1723 he was posted to Louisbourg, where he became involved in the construction of its defences. On the fertile soil of his Miré (Mira) River estate, he grew vegetables, oats, barley, melons, and tobacco. De Catalogne died at Louisbourg on 5 July 1729.

Catalone Gut   *See* Catalone.

Catalone Lake   *See* Catalone.

Centre   *See* First Peninsula.

CFB **Cornwallis**   *See* Cornwallis River.

Charles Lake   *See* Lake Banook.

Chaswood (Halifax)   West of MIDDLE MUSQUODOBOIT. By act of the Nova Scotia legislature in 1901, Gays River Road and Taylorville were declared to be 'hereafter known as Chaswood.' This was done to perpetuate the memory of Charles Wood, a native of HALIFAX and the first Canadian soldier to be killed in action in the South African War (1899–1901). Wood was a grandson of General Zachary Taylor, briefly president of the United States (1849–50).

Chebucto Bay; Chebucto Head (Halifax)   The original Mi'kmaq name for HALIFAX is perpetuated by the headland at the entrance to the harbour. It is taken from *Chebookt*, meaning 'chief bay or harbour.' Samuel de Champlain noted its importance in 1604 and declared it to be 'une baie fort saine,' "a good safe bay.' Writing in 1687, M. de Gargas (the principal recorder in Acadia during this period) called it 'Chibouctou the finest harbour in Acadie.' A 1711 description was given by De-

Labat, an engineer who served at Port Royal: 'This bay is practically in the middle of the coast between Cape Breton and Cape Sable [and is] very recognizable because of *Cap St. Sembre* [modern Sambro] which is a whitish rock bare of all verdure [vegetation]. The entrance is quite safe provided one passes nearer *Cap Sembre* than the beaches or isles on the starboard.' This advice is as valid for contemporary sailors as it was for DeLabat in 1711. See also GEORGES and McNABS islands.

Chebucto Head   *See* Chebucto Bay.

Chedabucto Bay (Guysborough) At the eastern extremity of mainland Nova Scotia. The name of this large bay is of Mi'kmaq origin. It is traced by Silas T. Rand to the word *Sedabooktook*, meaning 'a bay running far back.' In July 1687, M. de Gargas disembarked at 'Chedabouctou,' which he recommended 'only for its bay ... [and] the upper part of the river, which is pleasant.' See also GUYS-BOROUGH.

Chester; Chester Basin (Lunenburg)   Northeast of MAHONE BAY. On 18 October 1759, the township of Shoreham, for Shoreham, Sussex, England, was

created. It stretched from HUB-
BARDS to Martins River on the
south shore of Nova Scotia. Less
than a year later, the name was
changed to Chester, probably for
the town of the same name in
Pennsylvania. It, in turn, was
named for the city in England.
The first settlers were a group of
New England Planters who
arrived in 1760–1. Chester Basin
was named for the township.

Chester Basin *See* Chester.

Cheticamp; Cheticamp Island
(Inverness)   The village is on the
Cabot Trail. The first reference to
this place name as *Le Chadye*
occurs in Nicolas Denys's
description of the coastline of
Acadia (1672). By 1752 there was
a fishing station here, and the
spelling had changed to 'Chéti-
can.' During the 1760s there was
an influx of Acadian settlers, and
by the late eighteenth century the
contemporary spelling was in
use. The name is of uncertain origin; however, it may stem from
the French *chétif*, for 'poor' – a reference to the lack of productive
soil. It was first applied to Cheticamp Island, lying parallel to the
coast. In this predominantly Acadian village the tradition of *La Mi-
Carême* is carried out at mid-Lent.
On this night, people in disguise
travel from house to house, bringing treats to children. Sometimes
the visiting *Mi-Carêmes* try to
keep their identity secret.

Cheticamp Island   *See* Cheticamp.

Chetigne Island   *See* Shut-In
Island.

Cheverie (Hants)   On the MINAS
BASIN shore of HANTS COUNTY. An
adaptation of the Basque family
name d'Etcheverry or d'Chevery.
It is evident that a member of this
family settled here in the early
1700s. By the middle of the century, *Vil Cheverie* was noted in
French records, and the name
passed on unchanged, from the
final French form to the English,
following 1755.

**Chezzetcook Harbour; Chezzet-
cook Inlet; Chezzetcook Lake;
Chezzetcook River; Head of
Chezzetcook** (Halifax)   The
inlet is on the eastern shore of
HALIFAX COUNTY. The name is
derived from the Mik'maq *Cheset-
kook* or *Sesetkook*, which has been
translated by Silas T. Rand as
'flowing rapidly in many channels.' Appears as *Shezetcook Harbour* on the Morris survey of 1755.
The harbour, lake, and river take
their name from the inlet.

Chezzetcook Inlet   *See* Chezzetcook Harbour.

Chezzetcook Lake   *See* Chezzet-cook Harbour.

Chezzetcook River   *See* Chezzet-cook Harbour.

Chignecto   *See* Chignecto, New Brunswick.

Christmas Island (Cape Breton)
Off the ST. ANDREWS CHANNEL coastline of Lake Bras D'or. The island was named for a Mi'kmaq chief who adopted the name Noel. He was buried on Christmas Island, opposite the mainland community of the same name.

Church Point (Digby–Clare)
The settlement, originally named Pointe de l'Église,was founded in 1771 and named for Saint Mary's Church, which occupied a prominent location in the community. Home of Université Sainte-Anne (for the patron saint of Acadians). It was founded as Collège Sainte-Anne by the Eudist Fathers in 1890. Earlier, in 1860, an attempt was made through an act of the legislature to rename the community Port Acadia. The suggested new name lacked public acceptance, and Church Point remains in the *Nova Scotia Gazetteer*. In recent years use of the French version, Pointe-de-l'Église, has become common.

Clare (municipality within Digby County)   Following their expulsion in 1755, the Acadians were permitted by order-in-council, dated 28 September 1764, to return to Nova Scotia and obtain land. In 1768, Governor Michael Francklin designated the District of Clare as their future home. Clare takes its name from County Clare, a division of the old kingdom of Munster in Ireland.

Clark's Harbour (Shelburne)
On the southwestern side of CAPE SABLE ISLAND. Named after Captain Jonathan Clark, originally from New England, an early settler who is credited locally 'as the first to discover the harbour.' In the early 1900s, the community survived several attempts to change its name. The first suggesion was Port Minto in 1901, followed by Clarkton, Clarksboro, Southport, Atlantic, and Seaton. None of the suggestions caught the public's fancy, and Clark's Harbour remains on the map. It has the distinction of being one of a very few Nova Scotian place names to have official approval to use the apostrophe.

Clements (former township in Annapolis County); **Clementsport; Clementsvale; Upper Clements**   The township of Clements, fronting on Annapolis Basin, was created in 1784 and settled immediately thereafter by German mercenaries, mainly from the states of Hesse and Waldeck. Their services had been sold by their princes to Britain during the American Revolution. The township may have been named for an early Loyalist family, although there is some evidence that it might be of earlier origin. In 1642 Charles de Saint-Étienne de La Tour's supply ship the *Saint Clement* was anchored at the mouth of the river, near Clementsport. However, it seems unlikely that such an incident could survive both the expulsion and the passage of more than a century to give rise to the name. Clementsport, Clementsvale, and Upper Clements take their name from the township. See also WALDECK.

Clementsport   *See* Clements.

Clementsvale   *See* Clements.

Clyde River; Port Clyde (Shelburne)   The river rises in the interior of SHELBURNE COUNTY and flows into the Atlantic at Negro Harbour. Named in 1785 for the River Clyde in Scotland. The area was settled by Loyalists in 1783.

Cobequid Bay; Cobequid Mountains (Northern Nova Scotia) The bay is an extension of the BAY OF FUNDY. The range of mountains bisects CUMBERLAND, COLCHESTER, and PICTOU counties. The name was spelled *Cocobequy* in a land grant to Mathieu Martin in 1689, and as *Gobetik* by Abbé Jean-Louis Le Loutre (1709–1772). It is of Mi'kmaq origin, and is traced by Silas T. Rand to *Wakobetgitk*, 'end of flowing or rushing water,' a reference to the tidal bore common to the streams and rivers that flow into Cobequid Bay. The bay takes its name from the mountains.

Cobequid Mountains   *See* Cobequid Bay.

Cockerwit Channel (Passage) *See* Woods Harbour.

Coffin Island (Queens)   At the entrance to LIVERPOOL harbour. First known as 'Île du Rossignol' for Captain Jean Rossignol. The present name dates from the 1760s, when Peleg Coffin, a New England Planter grantee from Liverpool, established a fishing station on the island. The first lighthouse was erected in 1812.

Colchester County   First known as Cobequid District (see COBEQUID BAY); the name was changed to Colchester in 1780, after the city in England. It was raised to the status of a county in 1835. The name Colchester dates back to Roman times, when the

English garrison town was named for its location on the River Colne.

College Grant (Pictou; Antigonish); **College Lake** (Antigonish) All three communities take their name from large land grants made 'to the Governors, President and Fellows of Kings College, Windsor' in 1813. See also DENMARK.

College Lake   *See* College Grant.

Collingwood Corner (Cumberland)   On RIVER PHILIP, southeast of SPRINGHILL. The village was named for Vice-Admiral Cuthbert Collingwood, later Baron Collingwood (1750–1810). He took command on Admiral Horatio Nelson's death at the Battle of Trafalgar, 21 October 1805, the most famous naval engagement of the Napoleonic Wars. Following this battle, Napoleon's hopes for invading England were dashed.

Concession (Digby)   Northeast of SAULNIERVILLE. In 1799 *une concession* of land was made in the centre of Clare to Major François Comeau and associates. The community was first referred to as 'Les Concessions'; over time this was gradually shortened to 'Concession.'

Conquerall Bank; Conquerall Mills (Lunenburg)   Conquerall Bank is on the west side of the LAHAVE RIVER; Conquerall Mills is located near Fancy Lake and the headwaters of PETITE RIVIÈRE. This area was part of a late-eighteenth-century grant to Joseph Pernette (1728–1807), MLA for LUNENBURG COUNTY from 1761 to 1770. He later granted a portion of his holdings to George Fancy. Two local stories, possibly apocryphal, purport to account for this unusual name. One relates that Fancy, for whom Fancy Lake was named, traced Petite Rivière to its source in 1805. When he reached his destination, he reputedly exclaimed: 'This conquers all.' Another, more probable version, attributes 'Conquerall' to a trade name adopted by Fancy to indicate the superiority of the lumber produced in his mill. The Conquerall Bank post office dates from 1855; Conquerall Mills was opened in 1883.

Conquerall Mills   *See* Conquerall Bank.

Corberrie (Digby)   In central CLARE. This community traces its name to the birthplace of Abbé Jean-Mandé Sigogne (1763–1844). A much-beloved figure, Abbé Sigogne was known as 'the apostle of the Acadians' for his forty-five years of service (1799–1844) among them. Thus, Corberi, a suburb of Beaulieu-Indre-et-Loire, France, gave its name to the Nova Scotia Corberrie.

Cornwallis River; Cornwallis Valley (Kings); CFB **Cornwallis** (Annapolis)   The river flows into MINAS BASIN; it was known to the Acadians as 'Rivière des Habitants.' The new name was assigned in honour of Colonel Edward Cornwallis, who became governor of Nova Scotia on 9 May 1749. He returned to England in 1752 and was succeeded by Colonel Peregrine Hopson. The valley takes its name from the river. The former Canadian Forces Base Cornwallis, located on the shore of Annapolis Basin, at Deep Brook, was established in 1942 as a training base for the Royal Canadian Navy. In 1994 the base was recommissioned for the training of international peacekeeping forces. On 24 April 1995, the appropriately named Pearson International Peacekeeping Centre was opened to conduct research, education, and training in this field. The new facility honours Canada's fourteenth prime minister, Lester B. Pearson (1897–1972), who held office from 1963 to 1968. However, his greatest diplomatic achievement occurred earlier, in 1956, while serving as minister of External Affairs. Pearson proposed a

United Nations Peacekeeping Force as a means of easing the British and French out of Egypt during the Suez crisis. For this endeavour he was awarded the Nobel Peace Prize in 1957.

Cornwallis Square (Kings)   On 8 July 1993 the communities of Waterville, Cambridge, and Grafton were amalgamated to form the village of Cornwallis Square. The name comes from that of the CORNWALLIS RIVER and CORNWALLIS VALLEY.

Cornwallis Valley   *See* Cornwallis River.

Country Harbour (Guysborough) East of SHERBROOKE. This harbour is considered to be one of the finest on the eastern shore of Nova Scotia. Its importance was reflected in the Mi'kmaq descriptive *Moolaboogwek*, translated by Silas T. Rand as 'deep and gullied.' The area was first settled in 1783 by disbanded soldiers of the Royal North and South Carolina regiments and the Carolina Rangers. Until 1914 it was known as 'Green Harbour.' The name was then changed to Country Harbour, or *the* harbour of the country, to avoid confusion with other locations of the same name. In 1995, Country Harbour was selected as the site for landing an underwater pipeline conveying natural gas from wells near SABLE ISLAND, located 225 kilometres southeast.

Craigmore; Creignish; Creignish Rear (Inverness)   North of PORT HASTINGS, on ST. GEORGES BAY. Craigmore, sometimes spelled 'Creigmore,' for 'great rock,' was named for a location in Perthshire, Scotland. 'Creignish,' the Gaelic for 'rocky place,' is also named for its counterpart in Argyllshire, Scotland. It is the home of Ashley MacIsaac, an acclaimed Cape Breton fiddler.

Cranberry Barren   *See* Bakeapple Barren.

Creignish   *See* Craigmore.

Creignish Rear   *See* Craigmore.

Cross Island (Lunenburg)   At the entrance to Lunenburg Bay. When the first lighthouse was erected in 1834, the *Novascotian* carried the following notice: '... the tower is white and it is intended to paint on it a black cross 5 feet wide, to designate it from Sambro or Liverpool in day time,' thus giving rise to the name. Earlier designations were Prince of Wales Island and Cunninghams Island.

Crousetown (Lunenburg)   North of Green Bay, on the PETITE RIVIÈRE. Named after the first settlers, John and Philip Crouse. The Kraus, or Crouse, family, originally from southwestern Germany, were part of the migration of Foreign Protestants to LUNENBURG.

Crystal Cliffs (Antigonish)   On Highway 337, northeast of ANTIGONISH. The name is descriptive for the fine-grained white and flesh-coloured gypsum bluffs that rise to form a beautiful cliff fronting the sea. For a number of years, the Massachusetts Institute of Technology maintained a geological summer school here. The property is now owned by St. Francis Xavier University.

Cumberland (County and Basin) This name originated with Fort Cumberland, as Fort Beauséjour was renamed, following its capture by the British in 1755. The fort commemorates the career of the 'infamous' Prince William Augustus, Duke of Cumberland (1721–1765), nicknamed 'Butcher Cumberland,' who crushed Jacobite forces under Prince Charles Edward Stuart at the Battle of Culloden in 1746. An indication of the antipathy towards the Duke may be found in another nickname, 'Stinking Willie,' still applied to a noxious weed found in both Scotland and Nova Scotia. Cumberland was later applied to the bay, township, and county. The county was formed in 1759. See also KNOYDART; WESTMORLAND COUNTY, New Brunswick; and CULLODEN, Prince Edward Island.

Dalhousie (Kings, Annapolis, and Pictou)   From 1816 to 1819, George Ramsay, Earl of Dalhousie (1770–1838), served as lieutenant-governor of Nova Scotia, moving to become governor-in-chief of Canada (1819–28). Most colonial governors left behind evidence of their tenure in the form of place names. In this instance, names in three Nova Scotian counties provide examples: East Dalhousie and Lake Dalhousie (Kings); Dalhousie Hill, Dalhousie Lake, Dalhousie West (Annapolis); Dalhousie Mountain (elevation 340 metres) and Dalhousie Settlement (Pictou). The KINGS and ANNAPOLIS locations are situated on a road ordered surveyed by Dalhousie for the settlement of soldiers following the Napoleonic Wars. In 1818, before leaving Nova Scotia, he was instrumental in the founding of Dalhousie University in HALIFAX. See also EARLTOWN and LAKE RAMSAY.

Darling Lake (Yarmouth)   Six kilometres north of YARMOUTH. This community was named in the 1790s by a member of the gar-rison at ANNAPOLIS, Colonel Michael Ashley Darling. On an inspection trip to Yarmouth, he camped at this location, liked the scenery, and called it Darling Lake.

Dartmouth (Halifax)   On the east side of HALIFAX harbour. The city was named for William Legge, Earl of Dartmouth (1672–1750), whose death occurred during the year of the city's founding. He served in a number of cabinet posts, including president of the Board of Trade and Plantations and as secretary of state. The name has been attributed to his son, the second Earl (1731–1801); however, this has no foundation, since the latter, then still a student at Oxford, succeeded to the title in 1750. Settlement began in August 1750, when the *Alderney*, out of Gravesend, England, dropped anchor with a complement of 353 new settlers. It became a town in 1873 and was, following annexation of several suburban areas, incorporated as a city in 1966. It became part of the Halifax Regional Municipality on 1 April 1996.

Debert (Colchester)   West of TRURO. During the Second World War, a bulldozer clearing land for Camp Debert uncovered Palaeo-Indian artefacts dating back over 10,000 years, to roughly 8600 B.C.

These people, however, were not related to the Mi'kmaq, who were here millennia later. In the colonial period, the French were also attracted to this district 20 kilometres west of Truro. The French place name Ville de Bourg, or Deburk, was gradually changed, after 1755, to Deburt (in Haliburton 1829), and eventually to the contemporary Debert. From 1941 to 1945, Camp Debert was a marshalling and embarkation centre for the Canadian army. In total, some 15,000 Canadian soldiers were stationed here.

Dedication Lake (Halifax)   In the Musquodoboit Valley, near Fraser Settlement. During 1972, students from Musquodoboit Rural High School visited the area, an expansion of Sherlock Brook, as part of a class project. Following their trip they expressed a wish to the CPCGN to name the lake visited 'Dedication Lake – as we are dedicated to our Valley and to protecting its future by finding solutions to its problems.' The name was approved by the CPCGN on 11 June 1973.

Deep Cove (Lunenburg)   An arm of the sea on the west side of the Aspotogan Peninsula. The name is descriptive. On 6 July 1799, 'the close covered with water called Deep Cove' was granted by the crown to Thomas James and William Cochran. Included in the deed were the lands surrounding the cove, 'together with the fishery and liberty of fishing commonly called the Deep Cove Fishery.' Later, when an attempt was made to convey these rights to others, the Supreme Court of Nova Scotia ruled in 1842 that 'the crown cannot grant the waters of a navigible arm of the sea, so as to give the right of fishing therein.' In rendering this judgment, Mr. Justice William Hill declared: 'The crown might as well grant the air around the cove.' See also ASPOTOGAN.

Delhaven (Kings)   North of KINGSPORT. Delhaven was originally known by the Mi'kmaq as 'Woogeech,' for 'white waters.' It was sometimes referred to by the French as 'Rivière des Vielles Habitants,' and later as 'Rivière Pereaux.' On 10 March 1880, by an act of the Nova Scotia legislature, Middle Pereaux was replaced by the coined name Delhaven. See also PEREAUX RIVER.

Denmark (Colchester)   Two kilometres north of AMET SOUND. There is no evidence to link the name of this community to the country Denmark. In the early eighteenth century, the land adjoining was granted to the Right Reverend Charles Inglis,

Anglican bishop of Nova Scotia, 'and his successors in office for a Dean and Chapter.' Lands immediately to the east were assigned to the 'Governors, President and Fellows of Kings College Windsor.' To distinguish between the two, the territory of the former was blazed with the 'Dean's Mark,' which over time evolved to the place name Denmark. See also COLLEGE GRANT.

D'Escousse (Richmond)   On ISLE MADAME. Established in the early 1700s by fishermen from St. Malo, France. Eighteenth-century census records list the name as *Decoust*, and Thomas Pichon (1700–1781), writing in 1760, referred to it as 'Decoux.' It has been incorrectly suggested that the name refers to a French officer named de Coux who served at LOUISBOURG. Since there are no records of such a surname, it seems more likely to have simply evolved into the French for 'stopping-place,' *d'escousse.*

Diamond Island   *See* Five Islands.

Digby (shiretown of Digby County); **Digby Gut; Digby Neck** The town and township were named for Admiral Robert Digby (1732–1815), commander of HMS *Atlanta*, flagship of the convoy which brought the Loyalist set-

tlers to found the town in 1783. Digby Gut, known locally as 'The Gut,' is a narrow channel at the entrance to Annapolis Basin. Digby Neck, extending from Point Prim to East Ferry, is a continuation of the NORTH MOUNTAIN range.

Digby County   Takes its name from the township of DIGBY. The county dates from 21 April 1837, when an act 'to divide the County of Annapolis and to regulate the representation thereof' was passed by the Nova Scotia legislature. In 1861, by provincial statute, Digby County was divided into two districts, Digby and Clare.

Digby Gut   *See* Digby.

Digby Neck   *See* Digby.

Diligent River (Cumberland) Flows into MINAS BASIN. During the French colonial period, this area was known as 'Rivière Gascogne,' for Gascony, an old province in southwest France. The first settlers following 1755 were Loyalists soldiers who had seen service with the New Jersey Volunteers in the American Revolution. Two of these, Captain Samuel Wilson and Lieutenant Elizear Taylor, were visited by Governor John Parr in 1785. 'So pleased was [the governor] with the progress and diligence of the settlers that he decided to name the community Diligent River' (Brown).

Dingwall (Victoria)   On ASPY BAY. Originally called Youngs Cove, for one of the first grantees, Walter Young. By act of the Nova Scotia legislature in 1883, the name was changed to Dingwall, the surname of Robert Dingwall, the first postmaster. Dingwall is also a place name in Ross and Cromarty, Scotland.

Dominion (Cape Breton) Northwest of GLACE BAY. The town grew up around a coal mine, Dominion Number 1 Shaft, opened by the Dominion Coal Company in 1894. By provincial statute, the name Dominion Number 1 was changed to the simpler Dominion in 1906.

Donkin (Cape Breton)   Southeast of GLACE BAY. This mining community evolved around the coal mine known as 'Dominion Number 6,' operated by the Dominion Coal Company. To avoid confusion with DOMINION, the name Donkin was assigned, for Hiram Donkin, a civil engineer who served as manager of the company.

Dublin Bay   *See* New Dublin.

Dublin Shore   *See* New Dublin.

Dunmaglass (Antigonish)   In the northwest corner of the county. First known as 'Back Settlement of Knoydart,' and later as 'Summerville.' The replacement name, Dunmaglass, originated with the ancestral home of Clan McGillivray in Lochaber, Scotland. The name was suggested in 1879 by native son Father Andrew McGillivray (1828–1900). It was approved by the legislature in the same year.

Dunvegan (Inverness)   Northeast of INVERNESS. First known as 'Broad Marsh Cove' until the establishment of the post office in 1885, when the community was renamed Dunvegan. Dunvegan Castle, the inspiration for the name, is on the Isle of Skye and is the traditional home of the chiefs of Clan Macleod. Dunvegan was the birthplace of Angus L. Macdonald (1890–1954), premier of Nova Scotia from 1933 to 1940. He then entered the federal cabinet as minister of National Defence for Naval Services. After filling this portfolio with great distinction, he returned to Nova Scotia politics in 1945, serving again as premier until his death on 13 April 1954. Macdonald's great-grandfather, Alisdair, was part of the Highland migration to CAPE BRETON; on his maternal side his ancestors were Acadian. Thus, in him were fused the two ethnic strains that are so much a part of the history of Nova Scotia. The mesmeric hold of 'Angus L.,' ever the consummate politician, over two decades of Nova Scotia's political life can be explained in part by this heritage, which was combined with a deep understanding of the province, along with well-honed oratorical skills in both the Gaelic and the English language.

Earltown (Colchester)   Northeast of TRURO. In 1820 a request was made to the Earl of Dalhousie, the lieutenant-governor, that a Scottish settlement in north COLCHESTER COUNTY be named in his honour. In reply he stated: 'I have already given [my name] to the Dalhousie military establishment near Annapolis, and it would cause confusion or inconvenience to have two places of the same name. If I may suggest a name allusive to my own, I would say Earlstown ...' The suggestion was accepted; however, by 1836, the 's' had been dropped. East and West Earltown take their name from Earltown. This area was settled by emigrants drawn largely from the Sutherlandshire parishes of Rogart, Clyne, and Lairg, all in the vicinity of Brora. See also BRORA LAKE and DALHOUSIE.

East Earltown   *See* Earltown.

East Ironbound Island (Lunenburg)   To the east of TANCOOK ISLAND. The name is a descriptive for the iron-grey stone characteristic of the landscape. It is important as the setting for Frank Parker Day's (1881–1950) novel *Rockbound*, first published in 1928.

East Side of Ragged Island   *See* Lockeport.

Economy; Economy Mountain (Colchester)   At first glance it might appear that this place name in west COLCHESTER is related to the word 'economy.' However, it is derived from the Mi'kmaq *kenomee*, which translates as 'a long point jutting out into the sea.' Settled later by the Acadians, it was known as 'Vil Conomie' in 1755. Following resettlement in the 1770s by emigrants from New England and Ulster, the English spelling became accepted.

Economy Mountain   *See* Economy.

Ecum Secum (Guysborough)   Near the GUYSBOROUGH–HALIFAX county boundary. This unusual place name is of uncertain origin. In all probability it is a corruption of a lost Mi'kmaq designation. Early spellings were 'Ekamsagen' and 'Ekemsikam.' When the post office was established in 1873, the spelling had evolved to 'Ecum Secum.' See also NECUM TEUCH.

Egg Island   *See* Five Islands.

Egypt Falls   *See* Pipers Cove.

Elderbank (Halifax)   Southeast of MIDDLE MUSQUODOBOIT. Once known as 'Little River'; the present name was taken from a coined name adopted by a local farm. It was later applied to the Anglican church, which was known as 'St. Andrew's of Elderbank.' The new name was sanctioned by an act of the Nova Scotia legislature passed in 1912.

Ellershouse (Hants)   Off Highway 101, southeast of WINDSOR. This community takes its name from a mansion built in 1865 by Baron Franz von Ellershausen. A mining engineer, he was attracted to Nova Scotia by the discovery of gold. The house, a two-storey building with hip roof, in the colonial style, still stands. The post office, dating from 1866, was first known as 'Ellershausen,' which gradually became anglicized to Ellershouse.

Elmfield (Pictou); **Elmsdale** (Hants)   Both names are coined descriptives for the abundance of elm trees to be found in each location. Elmfield, in west PICTOU COUNTY, was first settled in 1796 by James McCara, a Loyalist soldier. Elmsdale, on the SHUBENACADIE RIVER, was settled by John Archibald in the early 1800s. The name was probably suggested by his property, which was called Elmsdale Farm.

Elmsdale   *See* Elmfield.

Enfield (Hants)   North of the Halifax International Airport. The name Enfield, for the borough in London, England, crossed the Atlantic in 1683 and was assigned to a town in Connecticut. Almost two centuries later, in 1863, it was put forward by Thomas Donaldson, a native of Enfield, Connecticut, as the name for this community near the headwaters of the SHUBENACADIE RIVER.

Eskasoni (Cape Breton)   On East Bay, an inlet of BRAS D'OR LAKE. Site of a Mi'kmaq settlement before the arrival of the Europeans, Eskasoni has been, since the 1830s a designated Mi'kmaq community. The name is derived from the word *Eskasoognig*, which has been translated by Silas T. Rand as 'green boughs.' Eskasoni is the home of the award-winning Mi'kmaq poet Rita Joe.

Eureka (Pictou)   North of
HOPEWELL. The word is from classical Greek and may be traced to
Archimedes. He is said to have
used it as an exclamation of triumph following the discovery of
the principle of buoyancy. This
place name has a more ordinary
derivation. In 1883 the Eureka
Milling Company was established here and gave its name to
the community.

Falmouth (Hants)   West of WIND-
SOR. As the population of the first
Acadian settlements increased,
new generations migrated to areas
where they might continue to
reclaim land from the sea. By 1685
settlers from Rivière aux Canards
and Grand Pré moved to the river
valleys that flowed into the MINAS
BASIN at Pisiquid (Windsor).
On the west bank of the Rivière
Pisiquid (Avon), the parish of
Sainte-Famille was founded.
By 1714 the population of the
Pisiquid district was listed as 53
families, totalling 344 people.
Following the expulsion of 1755,
the area was resettled by New
England Planters from Rhode
Island and Connecticut. Their first
'town meeting' was held on 8 July
1760. The new name, Falmouth,
honoured Admiral Edward Bos-
cawen, Viscount Falmouth (1711–
1761), who was commander-in-
chief at LOUISBOURG in 1758. In
1763 surveyor, colonizer, and

colonial administrator J.F.W.
DesBarres (1721?–1824) received a
grant of land in Falmouth township. A house was erected overlooking the Avon River, which he
grandly named 'Castle Frederick.'
Nearby, DesBarres erected what is
believed to be the first optically
equipped astronomical observa-
tory in the Western hemisphere.
Recently, the original name for
Falmouth has been revived by
Sainte-Famille Wines Limited,
whose vineyards are located on
lands once tilled by the Acadians.
See also AVON RIVER and WIND-
SOR; and DESBARRES POINT, Prince
Edward Island.

Fancy Lake   *See* Conquerall
Bank.

Fenwick (Cumberland)   South
of AMHERST. Named for Sir William Fenwick Williams (1800–
1883), lieutenant-governor
of Nova Scotia from 1865 to
1867. See also KARSDALE, PORT
WILLIAMS, and WILLIAMSDALE.

First Peninsula; First South
(Lunenburg)   On 15 September
1753, a plan depicting a number
of lots adjacent to the town of
LUNENBURG was presented to the
Executive Council in HALIFAX.
Winthrop Pickard Bell notes that
'a memento of these subdivisions
of 1753–4 is to be found in some
place names near Lunenburg.'

For example: First Peninsula is the first peninsula north of the town. Further, several of the ranges of lots were 'named according to their direction with reference to the town or their situation with reference to the range system as a whole.' Thus the origin of several 'unusual' LUNENBURG COUNTY place names is revealed. They are descriptors of the location of the community in relation to the 1753 subdivision plan. Thus 'First South' perpetuates its situation as the first lot in the south subdivision; while 'Centre' and 'Back Centre' are reminders of the centre range of lots.

First South   *See* First Peninsula.

Five Islands (Colchester)   The name is a direct translation of a Mi'kmaq descriptive. According to legend, Glooscap, in a fit of anger, once threw five rocks across the MINAS BASIN from his residence on CAPE BLOMIDON. The sceptical may still count the result. They are also known individually (east to west) by the prosaic names of Moose (said to resemble the hump of a moose), Diamond, Long, Egg, and Pinnacle islands (all descriptors of their shape). Writing in 1866, historian Israel Longworth described the view of Five Islands as seen from ECONOMY MOUNTAIN as 'of the most grand and striking character.' Five Islands Provincial Park fronts on Minas Basin and capitalizes on this panorama.

Florence (Cape Breton)   Northeast of SYDNEY MINES. This name is sometimes erroneously attributed to Florence Nightingale. It was assigned in 1905, upon the opening of the local coal mine, for Florence, wife of the Honourable D.D. MacKenzie (1859–1927), then the member of Parliament for Cape Breton North–Victoria. He was later to serve as federal Liberal House leader, following the death of Sir Wilfrid Laurier in 1917.

Florida Road (Colchester and Cumberland)   Dates from the mid-nineteenth century as the original name for Highway 246, which links TATAMAGOUCHE and WENTWORTH. The older name, still used locally, appears on the A.F. Church map of COLCHESTER COUNTY (1874). It may be traced to the Florida Inn, a stagecoach stop located in NEW ANNAN, approximately halfway between the two communities. It was so called because Katherine Ramsay, wife of the innkeeper, Alexander Munro, was a native of Florida.

Folly Lake; Folly Mountain; Folly River (Colchester)   Folly Lake is adjacent to Highway 104.

This name originates with the 'folly' of an early farmer, James Flemming, a native of Peebles, Scotland, who, against all advice, settled on a tract of stony land in west COLCHESTER. 'Flemming's Folly,' as the location became known, has survived a number of changes in spelling – from 'Folly' to 'Fawleigh' to 'Folleigh' and back to the original. The community name was later changed to Glenholme; however, the first spelling survives in the name of a lake, mountain, and river.

Folly Mountain   *See* Folly Lake.

Folly River   *See* Folly Lake.

Fort Lawrence (Cumberland) On the Nova Scotia–New Brunswick border. The community name is traceable to the fort erected in 1750. A memorial cairn summarizes its history: 'Erected by Major Charles Lawrence, afterward lieutenant governor of Nova Scotia, for the defense of the Isthmus of Chignecto; garrisoned by British troops until after the capture of [nearby] Fort Beausejour in 1755, when it was abandoned. Immediately south was the village of Beaubassin, one of the oldest French settlements in Nova Scotia, founded by Jacques Bourgeois and others from Port Royal in 1672, evacuated and burned by the French in 1750.'

See also FORT BEAUSÉJOUR, New Brunswick.

Forties Settlement (Lunenburg) West of NEW ROSS, on the military road surveyed under direction of the Earl of Dalhousie (1770–1838) while serving as lieutenant-governor of Nova Scotia (1816–19). 'Forty' lots were reserved for veterans of the Napoleonic Wars, giving rise to the name. See also DALHOUSIE.

Fort Point   *See* Cape LaHave.

Fourchu Harbour (Richmond) On the eastern coast of CAPE BRETON ISLAND. This harbour was a haven for French fishermen from the early eighteenth century onward. On early maps it is listed as *Le Hâvre de Fourché*. The name is a descriptive for 'forked' or 'crooked,' and is not to be confused with CAPE FORCHU in YARMOUTH COUNTY. Nearby Fourchu Head has the same origin. See also FRAMBOISE.

Fourchu Head   *See* Fourchu Harbour.

Framboise (Richmond)   About 15 kilometres southeast of FOURCHU HARBOUR. In 1752 this area was visited by the census-taker Joseph Sieur de la Roque. He noted that the year-round resident population was smaller

than the summer seasonal population. A total of 450 persons were
engaged in the offshore fishery in
the Fourchu–Framboise district.
Framboise is French for 'raspberry,' and is probably an early
descriptive name.

Freeport (Digby)   At the southern end of LONG ISLAND, on the
eastern side of GRAND PASSAGE.
First known as 'Lower Cove'
because of its location at the
lower end of the island; the name
was changed to Freeport in 1865.
Because of the many links
between Long and BRIER islands
and New England, the new name
was undoubtedly suggested by
Freeport, Maine.

French Cross Point (Kings)   On
the BAY OF FUNDY coast, midway
between MARGARETSVILLE and
Harbourville. A cross made of
beach stones marks the site of a
tragedy that occurred in 1755–6,
following the expulsion of the
Acadians. A number of refugees
from BELLEISLE sheltered here for
five months during the winter of
1756. They existed on shellfish
and food provided by Mi'kmaq.
On 18 March 1756, the survivors
escaped in canoes and travelled
across the MINAS CHANNEL to
what is still known as 'Refugee
Cove.' It is located east of CAPE
CHIGNECTO. See MORDEN.

Frenchmans Barn (Antigonish)
An early designation for ARISAIG;
the name is used as a descriptive
for a large, barn-like rock off the
coast. Many tall tales surround
this landmark. One Scottish legend suggests that a prosperous
Acadian farmer, once resident
here, fell into disfavour with the
sithichean, or 'fairies.' Consequently, his barn was turned into
stone, and so it remains to this
day.

French River (Pictou, Colchester,
Victoria); **French Village** (Halifax)   French River, found in
three Nova Scotia counties, is
simply an indelible reminder of
settlements that existed during
the French colonial period.
French Village, at the HEAD OF ST.
MARGARETS BAY, marks the resettlement of part of the 'Foreign
Protestant' population of LUNEN-
BURG COUNTY. Numbered among
them were families with such
names as Bouteiller (Boutilier),
Harnisch (Harnish), Darés
(Dorey), and Dauphinee, among
others. Many were natives of
Montbéliard, an area in southwestern France bordering on
Switzerland. According to Winthrop Pickard Bell, by the 1790s
the district had become known as
'French Village.'

French Village   *See* French
River.

Gabarus; Gabarus Bay (Cape Breton)   The settlement is southwest of LOUISBOURG, on Gabarus Bay. A number of conflicting theories have been advanced to explain the meaning of Gabarus. William Francis Ganong speculates that it may be 'a gallicized version of Cabot's Cross,' indicating yet another landing site for Cabot! Others have suggested that it may be for François Cabbarus, one-time French Finance minister; however, the place name predates his birth in 1752 by a century. The most logical explanation is that it is a corruption by the English of the French Chapeau Rouge or *Cap Rouge*. The northern side of Gabarus Bay was the landing site for the armies that captured Louisbourg in 1745 and 1758.

Gabarus Bay   *See* Gabarus.

Gairloch; Gairloch Lake (Pictou); **Gairloch Mountain** (Pictou, Victoria)   The settlement is southeast of SALTSPRINGS. In 1805 a group of Scots emigrated from Gairloch, in Ross and Cromarty (Wester Ross), to PICTOU COUNTY. In keeping with their Celtic roots, they perpetuated the name of their home community in the New World. In translation the Gaelic *Gair Loch* means 'short lake.' The lake and mountain were named for the community.

There is another Gairloch Mountain in VICTORIA COUNTY.

Gairloch Lake   *See* Gairloch.

Gairloch Mountain   *See* Gairloch.

Garden of Eden (Pictou)   To the north of Eden Lake. First settled in 1830 by William MacDonald, a native of Caithness, Scotland. The location, one of great natural beauty, gave rise to his nickname 'Adam in the Garden.' Thereafter, the evolution of the community name was almost inevitable. It is the one place name that all Nova Scotians are happy to claim.

Gaspereau; Gaspereau Lake; Gaspereau River (Kings)   The river flows from Gaspereau Lake, on Highway 12, into MINAS BASIN, near GRAND PRÉ. The word occurs in several Nova Scotia and New Brunswick place names and was first used as a descriptive for this river. In the early eighteenth century, there was a sizeable settlement on the banks of the Gaspereau River named by the Acadians for the *gasperot* or *gaspareau*, a species of herring. Less than a kilometre from the mouth of the Gaspereau River is the historic embarkation point for many of the exiled Acadians in 1755.

Gaspereau Lake   *See* Gaspereau.

Gaspereau River   *See* Gaspereau.

Georges Island (Halifax)   A prominent landmark in HALIFAX harbour. In the DeLabat survey of 1711, the island is called *Île Ronde ou Racquette*, for 'Round or Snowshoe Island.' It appears as *Georges Island* on Thomas Jefferys's *Composite map of Chebucto Harbour* (1750). Named in honour of King George II (1683–1760). See also McNABS ISLAND.

Glace Bay (Cape Breton)   The *Plan de l'ile Royalle* by Franquet (1751) gives this place name as *B. de Glace*. On some early maps it is called *Glass Bay*; however, the French descriptive has survived. It was taken from *glace*, for 'ice,' a possible reference to the fact, that when discovered, it was frozen over. In 1902, from nearby Table Head, Marconi first established official transatlantic wireless communication. Incorporated as a town in 1901; now a part of Cape Breton Regional Municipality.

Glen Bard (Antigonish)   Off Highway 104, near the PICTOU–ANTIGONISH boundary. The only community in Nova Scotia to be named for a resident poet. John 'the Bard' MacLean (1787–1848) was a native of the Island of Tiree, Argyllshire, and was appointed by the laird of Coll as family bard. Lured by the promise of land, he emigrated to Nova Scotia in 1819 and settled at BARNEYS RIVER, moving to the community that was later to incorporate his name, in 1830. Of his poetry Charles W. Dunn has written: 'he might have come to be considered a classic exponent of the pioneer life had he written in English rather than Gaelic.'

Glencoe (Inverness)   Northeast of JUDIQUE. This place name is also found in PICTOU and GUYSBOROUGH counties, in New Brunswick and Prince Edward Island, and around the world, from the United States to Australia, or wherever Scots have migrated. All locations commemorate the 13 February 1692 massacre of thirty-eight members of Clan Donald, including some women and children, in the pass above Loch Leven, Argyllshire, by soldiers (Campbells) of the Duke of Argyll's regiment. The latter had accepted MacDonald hospitality during the previous ten days.

Glencoe (Pictou)   The second Glencoe is on the Upper East River. For the origin of the name, see the INVERNESS COUNTY entry. In 1947 a cairn was erected at Glencoe, PICTOU COUNTY, honouring the MacDonald family, who were among its first settlers. By 1994 the cairn had fallen into disrepair and had to be refurbished by members of the Clan Donald Society of Nova Scotia. A plaque on the cairn bears the inscription 'Dedicated to the memory of John A. MacDonald and his four sons, Duncan, James, Alexander and Ewen – all of the 84th Royal Highland Regiment, who served with the Loyalists in the Revolutionary war of 1776. Descendants of John MacDonald of Glen Urquhart, Scotland – a survivor of Glencoe 1692.' Another Glencoe lies south of ROMAN VALLEY in GUYSBOROUGH COUNTY. For origin of the name, see the Inverness County entry.

Glendyer (Inverness)   Northeast of MABOU. This district was once the site of an important pioneer industry. In 1848, Donald MacLean MacDonald moved here from NEW GLASGOW and erected a mill for dyeing and fulling (cleaning and thickening) handmade cloth. MacDonald became known as the 'Dyer,' to distinguish him from others with the same name. The name of his home, 'Dyers Glen,' was later transposed to the attractive place name Glendyer.

Glenelg (Guysborough); **Glengarry** (Pictou); **Glenholme** (Colchester); **Glenora** (Inverness) It is not surprising to find many place names in Nova Scotia that begin with the prefix 'Glen.' Originally, in Scotland, *glen* meant 'valley' and was usually followed by the name of a river. The vast majority of such names (including the first three cited in this entry) are transfer names from Scotland, often the home community of the first settlers. A few are coined names, such as Glendyer, while others may be traced to other Scottish sources; for example, Glenora, is a contraction of Glenmore. Nova Scotia's Glenora carries on a fine Scottish tradition as the home of North America's only single-malt whisky distillery.

Glengarry   *See* Glenelg.

Glenholme   *See* Glenelg.

Glenora   *See* Glenelg.

Goldboro; Goldenville (Guysborough); **Gold River** (Lunenburg)   Goldboro is located on ISAACS HARBOUR; Goldenville is on the west side of ST. MARYS RIVER, near SHERBROOKE. The search for minerals, most notably gold, led to the exploration and settlement of several sections of Nova Scotia. In 1861, the discovery of the mineral in eastern GUYSBOROUGH COUNTY led to an influx of settlers. Unfortunately, the diggings were soon exhausted but the place names remain. Gold River, which flows into CHESTER BASIN, was originally known as 'Goulds River,' after an early settler. The name was shortened to Gold River before the discovery of gold in 1861.

Goldenville   *See* Goldboro.

Gold River   *See* Goldboro.

Gore; West Gore (Hants)   Northeast of RAWDON. Named for Sir Charles Stephen Gore (1793–1869) and not, as sometimes attributed, for Francis Gore (1769–1852), who served as lieutenant-governor of Upper Canada. Sir Charles Gore's first contact with Nova Scotia came with his appointment as aide-de-camp to Lieutenant-Governor Sir James Kempt in 1820. While in this post he married Sarah Fraser, daughter of the Honourable James Fraser, a member of the Nova Scotia legislative council. Later he was deputy quartermaster general in Lower Canada during the Rebellion of 1837. From 1852 to 1855, Gore was again posted to HALIFAX, serving with the Nova Scotia command.

Goshen (Guysborough)   Near the ANTIGONISH–GUYSBOROUGH boundary. The settlement dates from the mid-nineteenth century and was so named for the Goshen

Society (for the proverbial 'land of plenty,' as described in the Book of Genesis). It was the duty of a delegation of its members to travel twice annually, to Halifax, to bring back supplies to the community.

Goulet Beach; The Goulet (Richmond)   On ISLE MADAME, east of D'ESCOUSSE. A descriptive defined by the CPCGN as 'a body of water, often a salt water harbour, with a narrow entrance.'

Grande Anse (Richmond); **Grand Étang** (Inverness)   The word *anse* appears frequently on the map of Atlantic Canada. It means 'cove,' or small indentation along a coastline, and is another indication, not only of the French presence in the region, but of the durability of place names. *Etang*, another descriptive, denotes a small landlocked body of water or a pond.

Grand Étang   *See* Grande-Anse.

Grand Passage   *See* Long Island.

Grand Pré (Kings)   East of WOLFVILLE. Grand Pré, an Acadian descriptive for 'great meadow,' is known internationally as the setting for the poem 'Evangeline' by Henry Wadsworth Longfellow (1807–1882). According to William Francis Ganong, the name is a French translation of an earlier Mi'kmaq descriptive *mskeg-a-kadik*, literally 'grass at its occurrence place.' Paul Mascarène (1684–1760), writing in 1720, described Grand Pré as a prosperous location with a 'platt of meadow, part of which is damn'd in from the tide, and produces very good wheat and pease.' The history of the area is depicted in the replica of St. Charles Church, a museum located within Grand Pré National Historic Park. The community was the birthplace of Sir Robert Laird Borden (1854–1937), who served as the eighth prime minister of Canada from 1911 to 1920.

Granville Centre   *See* Granville Ferry.

Granville Ferry (Annapolis) Named for John Carteret, Earl of Granville (1690–1763), and located on the site of an earlier Acadian village. It was resettled by New England Planters in 1760, supplemented in the 1780s by Loyalists, largely from Massachusetts and New Hampshire. The name was first applied to the township; however, today it is remembered in Granville Centre and Ferry, along with Upper and Lower Granville, all situated north of the Annapolis Basin and River.

Grassy Island (Guysborough) One of a chain of islands protecting CANSO harbour and now a National Historic Site. In the eighteenth century, it was known as 'Fort Island,' after the fortifications first erected in 1732. Today it marks the important role of the Canso fishery in the Anglo–French rivalry for North America. Visits to the island are made by boat from the Interpretation Centre in Canso. On Grassy Island a trail links a number of historic sites. The present name is a descriptive dating from the mid-nineteenth century.

Great Village; Great Village River (Colchester)   The town is on a river of the same name which flows into COBEQUID BAY, and occupies the site of a pre-1755 Acadian settlement. The name is descriptive, marking a comparison with other villages in Londonderry Township. Although there are occasional references to 'Port of Londonderry' as the place name, the latter did not prevail. The post office dates from 1855. In recent years, Great Village has received recognition as the childhood home of the American poet Elizabeth Bishop (1911–1979). Tragic circumstances, the death of Bishop's father when she was eight months old and the permanent confinement of her mother to hospital, dictated that Bishop would spend the first six years of her life and many summer vacations with her maternal grandparents and other relatives in Great Village. Later, Great Village and its people were to figure prominently in Bishop's writing. During her lifetime she was the recipient of numerous literary awards, including the coveted Pulitzer Prize for poetry in 1956.

Great Village River   *See* Great Village.

Greenfield (Queens); **Green Harbour** (Shelburne); **Green Hill** (Pictou)   The vast number of names with the prefix 'Green' are descriptives, such as the first and third cited, and date from the nineteenth-century settlement period. Green Harbour, located between JORDAN BAY and LOCKEPORT harbour, although also a descriptive, is of much earlier origin. It appears on the anonymous 1703 *carte de l'Acadie* as *Havre Vert.*

Green Harbour   *See* Greenfield.

Green Hill   *See* Greenfield.

Greenwich (Kings)   West of WOLFVILLE. First known as 'Noggin's Corner.' The name originated with a store once located in the community which became renowned for the sale of 'noggins'

(wooden mugs) of rum. During the 1830s, one patron who imbibed too freely fell from his horse and was killed. This incident, plus the advent of the temperance movement, spelled the end for both the shop and the name. A new name was selected to mark the fact that many of the original New England Planter settlers came from Greenwich, Connecticut. However, the original name lives on in the Noggin's Corner Farm and adjacent fruit and vegetable market. It is owned and operated by the Avard Bishop family, whose ancestors were part of the Connecticut New England Planter migration.

Greenwood (Kings)   South of KINGSTON. First known as 'Greenwood Square' because the early settlers found their lands heavily forested. Over time the name was shortened to Greenwood. The Canadian Forces Base dates from 1942, when it opened as an operational training base for the Royal Air Force.

Greville Bay; Port Greville (Cumberland)   East of CAPE D'OR. The village takes its name from Greville Bay, which in turn, was named for Charles Cavendish Fulke Greville (1794–1865), clerk of the council (1821–59), famous political diarist, and confidant of two prime ministers,

Wellington and Palmerston. In common with many other harbours that ring the BAY OF FUNDY, Port Greville was once an important shipbuilding centre. The Age of Sail Heritage Museum is located at Port Greville.

Grosses Coques (Digby)   Fronts on ST. MARYS BAY, in the District of Clare. It was settled by Acadian refugees who returned to Nova Scotia following their expulsion in 1755. The area became renowned for the large clams or quahogs found on the tidal flats offshore. 'Coque' is French for 'shell' and this gave rise to the name.

Gulf Shore (Cumberland)   East of PUGWASH, on the NORTHUMBER-LAND STRAIT. The name is descriptive for a community settled by Scottish emigrants in the early nineteenth century.

Guysborough (shiretown of Guysborough County)   On the west side of CHEDABUCTO BAY. Originally known as 'Chedabucto'; the name may be traced to the Mi'kmaq descriptive *Chebuktook* or *Sedaboktook*. The translation rendered by Silas T. Rand is 'a bay running far back.' During the French period, this was the location chosen by Nicolas Denys (1598–1688) 'for constructing storehouses in order to establish a sedentary fishery' in the late seventeenth century. After Loyalist resettlement, the name was changed to Guy's Borough (later Guysborough) in honour of Sir Guy Carleton (1724–1808), commander-in-chief of the British forces in New York towards the end of the American Revolution. Carleton supervised the evacuation of the Loyalists from New York in 1783.

Guysborough County   The county was established by act of the provincial legislature in 1836. By this legislation, 'the lower division [of the then Sydney County] was to be called Guysborough County.' For origin of the name, see GUYSBOROUGH. See also ANTIGONISH COUNTY.

Habitant; Habitant River (Kings) The settlement is on the north side of the Habitant River, which flows into MINAS BASIN. As the name implies, this was once an Acadian settlement. It was resettled by New England Planters, mainly from eastern Connecticut, in the 1760s.

Habitant River   *See* Habitant.

Halifax   Halifax, possessing one of the finest natural harbours in the world, is strategically located almost midway between CAPE SABLE and CAPE CANSO, on mainland Nova Scotia's Atlantic coast. Founded on 21 June 1749 by Governor Edward Cornwallis (1713–1766) and named for George Montagu Dunk, Earl of Halifax (1716–1771), then president of the Board of Trade. Designated the capital of Nova Scotia on 14 July 1749 in place of Annapolis Royal; it was officially incorporated as a city in 1841. From its earliest days, Halifax has been both a garrison city and naval base, and played a pivotal role in the two world wars. On 6 December 1917, an unfortunate disaster gave the city international recognition. Two ships, one loaded with munitions, collided in the harbour. The explosion that followed killed 1,600 people, injured thousands more, and levelled the north end of Halifax and part of DARTMOUTH. In Rudyard Kipling's 'The Song of the Cities,' Halifax is called the 'The Warden of the Honour of the North'; during the Second World War, it was known internationally by the code name 'An East Coast Canadian Port.' As the twentieth century comes to a close, Halifax continues to maintain its place in history, having played host to the G7 Economic Summit in 1995. The mystique of the city was caught by author/ historian Thomas Raddall: 'The old clock tower stands on the slope, still ticking off the hours and reminding the city of the punctilious Duke of Kent ... And the green cone of Citadel Hill stands over all like a volcano, extinct now but still the finest watch-post in the city, a witness to the changing life and the unchanging duty of the Warden of the North.' Halifax is also noteworthy as the home of a large number of post-secondary institutions, including University of King's College (1789), Dalhousie University (1818), St. Mary's University (1841), Mount St. Vincent University (1873; degree-granting in 1925), and the Technical University of Nova Scotia (1907). On 1 April 1996 the city became part of the Halifax Regional Municipality – an amalgamation of Halifax, Dartmouth, Bedford, Lower and Middle Sackville, and Halifax County. The new 'super-city' has a population of 330,000, making it the largest metropolitan area in Atlantic Canada. In the amalgamation legislation there is provision for changing the name to Halifax Regional Municipality, if deemed necessary by the new city council. For some time, letters to the editor in the local press have been preoccupied with suggestions, ranging from Harbour City to the ancient Mi'kmaq Chebucto (see CHEBUCTO).

Halifax County   The county was established in 1759 and originally contained what is now COLCHESTER, PICTOU, ANTIGONISH, and GUYSBOROUGH counties. The subdivision into individual counties took place in 1837. The county was named for the city (see HALIFAX).

Halls Harbour (Kings)   On the MINAS CHANNEL. In the period between 1799 and 1813, this harbour was a favoured rendezvous for Captain Samuel Hall, a native of KINGS COUNTY, who emigrated to New England 'and took up privateering.' According to local legend, some of his treasure lies buried near the shoreline.

Hammonds Plains (Halifax) West of BEDFORD. The name marks the career of Sir Andrew Snape Hamond (1738–1828), lieutenant-governor of Nova Scotia from 1780 to 1782. The military road to ANNAPOLIS, constructed in the early nineteenth century, began at this location. Settlement dates from 1786; since the earliest days the contemporary spelling has been in use.

Hants County   Originally a part of KINGS COUNTY, it became separate in 1781, when the townships of Windsor, Newport, Falmouth, and adjacent territory along COBEQUID BAY were constituted to form a new county by act of the legislature. The name is an abbreviation for 'Hampshire' and was probably inspired by the state of New Hampshire, which had been named for Hampshire, England. The abbreviated form, Hants, goes back to the Domesday Book of 1086.

Hantsport (Hants)   First known as 'Halfway River' for its location midway between GRAND PRÉ and WINDSOR. This is a coined name to underline the importance of the port in the nineteenth-century Age of Sail. The name change occurred in 1849 upon the suggestion of Captain (later Senator) Ezra Churchill (1806–1874), 'because the place had become the chief port of Hants County.' The Churchill shipyard was reputed, at one point, to be the fifth-largest in the world.

Harmony (Colchester)   Southeast of TRURO. Settled in the 1820s. According to local information, the name describes the fact that 'the first residents lived in harmony,' and was selected as a place name for that reason.

Havre Boucher (Antigonish) Northeast of TRACADIE. Bishop Joseph-Octave Plessis (1763–1825) visited the area in 1812 and reported that the place took its name from Captain François

Boucher of Québec, 'who was overtaken on this coast by the winter of 1759, and had to stay there until spring.'

Hazel Hill (Guysborough)   On the outskirts of CANSO. In the pre-satellite era, this community was an important link in transatlantic communications. From 1883 to 1962, it was the North American terminal for the Commercial and Western Union cable companies. The name is a descriptive for the abundance of hazelnut shrubs once found in the vicinity.

Head of ...   For names beginning with 'Head of' see the reference for specific features; for example, for 'Head of Chezzetcook,' see CHEZZETCOOK.

Heatherton (Antigonish)   East of the town of ANTIGONISH. The community was first known as 'Pomquet Forks' 'by reason of the number of roads converging at this point,' and was settled largely by Scots. The change to Heatherton occurred by act of the Nova Scotia legislature in 1879. The new name was suggested by local merchant 'Big' Christopher MacDonald for his ship, the *Heather*, which 'carried the fame of the village to the far corners of the Maritimes.'

Hebron (Yarmouth)   Immediately to the north of YARMOUTH. This community takes its name from 'Hebron House' built near the junction of Highway 1 and Route 340 by shipbuilder and owner Captain Anthony Landers. A number of the first settlers were New England Planters from Hebron, Connecticut.

Henry Island   *See* Port Hood.

Herring Cove (Halifax)   South of SPRYFIELD, on the Purcells Cove Road. This area was settled shortly after the founding of HALIFAX. On of the early grantees was Thomas Herring; hence, the name. Nearby Tribune Head was the scene of a marine disaster on the night of 22 November 1797, when HMS *Tribune* was wrecked. Of the 250 persons on board, a mere 10 survived the ordeal.

Hopewell (Pictou)   South of NEW GLASGOW. Several sources credit the late-eighteenth-century emigrant ship *Hopewell* as the origin of the name of this community in south PICTOU COUNTY. However, this ship is more closely associated with the Ulster–Scot migration to neighbouring COLCHESTER COUNTY. More plausible is the theory that the name was suggested by that of a Halifax firm, Hopewell & Co.

Hopewell replaced the prosaic name Milltown about 1800.

Hubbards (Halifax)   Overlooking ST. MARGARETS BAY, on the HALIFAX–LUNENBURG county boundary. First known as 'Hubbards Cove.' It takes its name from one of the first families to settle in the area.

Hunts Point (Queens)   Southwest of LIVERPOOL. This area was conveyed in 1788 to Deacon Samuel Hunt (?–1800), one of the original proprietors of Liverpool. In 1873 it was reported that 'this place is favourably situated for the prosecution of the fisheries and ... agriculture.' Today it is well known as a seaside resort.

Ingonish; Ingonish Bay; Ingonish Beach; Ingonish Island (Victoria)   The settlement is on the northeast coast of CAPE BRETON. This place name may be traced to *Niganis*, a Mi'kmaq word, of unknown origin, first recorded by Samuel de Champlain. By 1672, Nicolas Denys (1598–1688) gives *Niganiche* as the spelling, applying the name to what is now Ingonish Island. For a brief period in the early eighteenth century, it was also known as 'Port d'Orléans,' although the earlier name continued to be used and has survived as the contemporary Ingonish. Middle Head, a for-

ested headland extending into Ingonish Bay, is the site of the Keltic Lodge resort. Nearby is one of the continent's finest golf courses. This facility, combined with the excellence of Ingonish Beach, make the area one of the province's premier tourist attractions. See also CAPE SMOKEY.

Ingonish Bay   *See* Ingonish.

Ingonish Beach   *See* Ingonish.

Ingonish Island   *See* Ingonish.

Inner Sambro Island   *See* Sambro.

Inverness   *See* Inverness County.

Inverness County   The county was established by act of the legislature in 1835 under the name Juste au Corps; a subsequent act in 1837 changed the name to Inverness, for the Scottish county. For the derivation of the former name, see PORT HOOD. The suggestion for renaming originated with Father Alexander MacDonnell of JUDIQUE, a native of Inverness-shire, and marks the fact that the area was settled largely by emigrants from that part of Scotland. The name change was formally proposed by Sir William Young (1799–1887), its first MLA in the House of

Assembly. The town of Inverness (formerly Broad Cove) was incorporated in 1904 and took its name from the county.

Iona (Victoria)   Overlooks BARRA STRAIT, BRAS D'OR LAKE. This area was first settled by Scottish Hebridean immigrants. In 1891, when a name change from Grand Narrows was sought, it was appropriate that the choice fell on Iona, the Hebridean island that was the ancient centre of Celtic Christianity. Both Little and Grand Narrows were settled at the same time, the former by Presbyterian emigrants from the Island of Lewis and the latter by Catholic 'Barramen' from the Island of Barra. Iona is the site of the re-created Nova Scotia Highland Village.

Isaacs Harbour (Lunenburg) East of COUNTRY HARBOUR. Among the newcomers to the Country Harbour area in 1783 were several 'black Loyalists.' One of these settlers was Isaac Webb, who gave his name to the community of Isaacs Harbour.

Isle Haute (Cumberland)   At the entrance to MINAS BASIN. Discovered in 1607 by Samuel de Champlain, this island remains a major landmark. He named it Île Haute, 'in consequence of its elevation.' Later,

Nicolas Denys (1598–1688) described the island thus: 'Leaving the Baye des Mines, and continuing toward Port Royal, there occurs an island of great height [97 metres today], and of one and one quarter leagues of circumference or thereabouts. It is flat on top and despite its height a spring of water occurs there.'

Isle Madame (Richmond)   Off the southeast coast of CAPE BRETON. An early French name for the principal harbour on the island was Porte Sainte Marie (see Arichat). On the Crexius map of 1660, the island is called *I(nsula) S(ancte) Mariae*, the Franquelin–DeMeulles map of 1701 gives *Isle Notre Dame*, while the English rendering by Captain Cyprian Southack in 1720 was *I. Madam*. Consistently from 1720 onward it has been Isle Madame. After 1763 Isle Madame became a major centre for Channel Island fishing and mercantile interests. As early as 1764, Guernsey fishermen were active in the area and, by 1800, Francis and Philip Janvrin from Jersey had established a fishing station at Arichat. See also ARICHAT and JANVRIN ISLAND.

James River (Antigonish)   West of ANTIGONISH, near the boundary with PICTOU COUNTY. Two theories have been given as explanations for this name. One attributes it to the fact that three early settlers – James Miller, James Nichols, and James Macdonald – all owned land in the area. The second associates the name with that of the Reverend James Munro (1758–1819), an itinerant Presbyterian missionary who reputedly became lost in the woods and followed the river to safety. Munro served from 1808 until 1821 as Presbyterian minister in Antigonish and donated the land where St. James United Church (later named in his honour) now stands.

Janvrin Island (Richmond) West of Isle Madame. During the late 1700s and early 1800s the regional centre for the commercial and fishing interests of the Channel Islanders was the port of Arichat and Isle Madame. Adjacent Janvrin Island was named for a Jersey entrepreneur, John Janvrin (1762–1835), once its owner. His brothers, Francis and Philip Janvrin, along with the firm of DeCarteret and LeVesconte, were among the Jersey merchants on Isle Madame. Recent research by Rosemary Ommer (Newfoundland) and John Sarre (Guernsey) has drawn attention to the importance of the Channel Island mercantile interest in southeast CAPE BRETON. These firms were part of a consortium of merchants known as 'the Arichat and Gaspé Society.' Responsible for all activities connected with the fishery, they carried basic supplies, salt, clothing, and manufactured goods for the use of local fishermen; exported fish to the West Indies and Brazil (usually in their own vessels); brought return cargoes of wines from Brazil to England; and carried molasses, sugar, and rum from the West Indies to Nova Scotia. See also ARICHAT and ISLE MADAME.

Jeddore Harbour (Halifax) On the eastern shore of HALIFAX COUNTY. The name is of unknown origin. Originally referred to by Nicolas Denys in 1672 as 'Rivière Théodore ... which has a good entrance for ships'; the name has been filtered through more than one language to become the contemporary Jeddore. Associated local place names include Head of Jeddore, Cape Jeddore, and Jeddore Oyster Ponds.

Jeddore Oyster Ponds See Jeddore Harbour.

Jersey Cove (Victoria); **Jerseymans Island** (Richmond); **Jersey Point** (Richmond) Jersey Cove is on ST. ANNS BAY; Jerseymans Island is southwest of ARICHAT; Jersey Point (later to be known by its contemporary name, Joshuas Point) is southwest of PETIT-DE-GRAT. All three place names provide additional evidence of the Channel Island influence on the toponymy of Nova Scotia. Joshuas Point may well be named for an early settler from the island of Jersey.

Jerseymans Island   *See* Jersey Cove.

Jersey Point   *See* Jersey Cove.

Joggins (Cumberland; Digby) Joggins, CUMBERLAND COUNTY, is located on CHIGNECTO BAY. The name is derived from the Mi'kmaq *Chegoggin*, which has been translated as 'a place of fish weirs.' This refers to a method of fishing developed by the Mi'kmaq, which utilizes a fence of stakes or branches to catch fish. Such weirs may still be found on both sides of the BAY OF FUNDY to this day. On 28 May 1992, a memorial plaque was unveiled at Joggins to mark the 150th anniversary of the Geological Survey of Canada. It also serves as a reminder that this shoreline is internationally known as a prime location to study prehistoric fossils. The second Joggins, in DIGBY COUNTY, is a late-eighteenth-century descriptive referring to an inlet which 'jogs in' from the sea.

Jordan Bay; Jordan River (Shelburne)   The bay is west of GREEN HARBOUR. Despite its 'biblical' appearance, this place name has other origins and is one of the oldest on the south shore of SHELBURNE COUNTY. On the Lopo Homen map of 1554 the area was listed as *Ribera des Jardines*, while on the Franquelin–DeMeulles map of 1686 it is *R. des Jardines*. Over the centuries the name became anglicized as Jordan River and Bay.

Jordan River   *See* Jordan Bay.

Joshuas Point   *See* Jersey Point.

Judique (Inverness)   On ST. GEORGES BAY. The name is of French origin. During the early colonial period, the harbour was frequently closed in by sand. '... Heavy northerly storms would close up the channel and after a little time it would break through ... this gave rise to the name *playing channel* or *jou-jou-dique*, which eventually became shortened to Judique' (CPCGN Files). There are ten locations in the immediate vicinity, ranging from Judique Bank to Little Judique Rear, that incorporate the name.

Karsdale (Annapolis)   On the north side of Annapolis Basin. Named for ANNAPOLIS ROYAL native Sir William Fenwick Williams (1800–1883). In the Crimean War (1853–6), he distinguished himself by his defence of Kars and later served (1865–7) as lieutenant-governor of Nova Scotia. According to Peter Waite, in the *Dictionary of Canadian Biography*, 'it was widely believed at the time of his birth and throughout his career that [his] father was Edward Angustus, Duke of Kent and Strathearn [father of Queen Victoria and commander of the British forces in Nova Scotia, 1796–1800] ... Williams himself made no effort to discredit this possibility ...' See also FENWICK, PORT WILLIAMS, and WILLIAMS-DALE.

Kejimkujik Lake; Kejimkujik National Park   Near the junction of ANNAPOLIS, DIGBY, and QUEENS counties. The name is of Mi'kmaq origin. It was first applied to the lake and approved by the Geographic Board of Canada on 18 March 1909. The national park, established in 1968, covers 375 square kilometres of rolling forested hills, glacier-scarred rocks, and lakes without number. Because of its great natural beauty and diverse wildlife, this area was an important rendezvous for the Mi'kmaq, and their petroglyphs or rock pictures are still to be found within the park. Highway 8, linking ANNAPOLIS ROYAL and LIVERPOOL, was named in 1992 Kejimkujik Drive,

a fitting designation as it roughly parallels the historic water and portage route followed for hundreds of years by the Mi'kmaq as they travelled from the BAY OF FUNDY to the Atlantic coast. Thomas J. Brown suggests that the name may be traced to the Mi'kmaq *koojumkoojik*, meaning 'attempting to escape.' According to the CPCGN files, the word may also mean 'swelled private parts,' caused by exertion in the 8-kilometre paddle across the lake.

Kejimkujik National Park   *See* Kejimkujik Lake.

Kelleys Cove (Yarmouth)   On the east side of Yarmouth Sound. Named for Captain James Kelly or Kelley, a native of Manchester, Massachusetts, who received a local land grant in 1765. A year earlier, in 1764, another early settler, David Pearl, arrived from Saybrook in Connecticut. A descendant, James Pearl (1790–1840), rose to be a commander in the Royal Navy. See also MOUNT PEARL, Newfoundland.

Kempt (Queens); **Kempt Head** (Victoria); **Kempt Lake** (Queens); **Kempt Shore** (Hants); **Kemptown** (Colchester); **Kemptville** (Yarmouth)   All locations mark the career of Sir James Kempt (1764–1854), lieutenant-governor of Nova Scotia from 1820 to 1828.

In 1822 Sir James paid an official visit to north QUEENS, 'and visiting the settlements near Brookfield [he] named one for himself.' Two years later he ordered the construction of Kempt Road, the HALIFAX exit which also bears his name. It provided an alternative route from the city in place of the Windsor Road (Windsor Street).

Kempt Head   *See* Kempt.

Kempt Lake   *See* Kempt.

Kempt Shore   *See* Kempt.

Kemptown   *See* Kempt.

Kemptville   *See* Kempt.

Kennetcook; Kennetcook River (Hants)   Settled in 1784 by disbanded soldiers who served with the 84th Regiment of Foot (Royal Highland Emigrant Regiment) in the American Revolution. One of the grantees was Captain Allan MacDonald (?–1792), whose wife was the famous Scottish heroine Flora MacDonald (1722–1792). After the Jacobite Rebellion, she conducted Prince Charles Edward Stuart, 'Bonnie Prince Charlie,' to safety on the Isle of Skye. (See SELMA for details on the raising of the regiment by MacDonald's cousin, Captain Alexander MacDonald.) The community takes its name from the Mi'kmaq *kunetcook*, first applied to the river. This word has been translated as 'a place near or close at hand.' See also KNOYDART.

Kennetcook River   *See* Kennetcook.

Kennington Cove (Cape Breton) On the coast south of Fortress Louisbourg. First known during the French colonial period as 'L'Anse de la Cormorandière' (Cormorants Cove). It was renamed for HMS *Kennington*, part of the British naval force against Fortress Louisbourg. Here, on the morning of 8 June 1758, some 27,000 British soldiers, sailors, and marines, under the command of General Jeffrey Amherst, were landed. Once a bridgehead was established, the force went on to successfully capture Fortress Louisbourg. See also LOUISBOURG.

Kentville (shiretown of Kings County)   Originally the site of an Acadian settlement, the town owes its location to the fordable condition, at this point, of the Rivière des Habitants (now CORNWALLIS RIVER). In June 1794, Prince Edward, Duke of Kent (1767–1820), the father of Queen Victoria, visited the area *en route* to ANNAPOLIS ROYAL. In 1826, by a vote of the inhabitants, the name was changed from Horton Corner in commemoration of this visit. Two years later, Joseph Howe

(1804–1873) reported in his *Western Rambles:* 'We are now approaching the village of Kentville ... it is seated in a valley, and contains about 30 houses; near its centre, the Horton and Cornwallis streets cross each other, and hence arose the old name of Horton Corner.' Kentville was incorporated as a town in 1886. The area surrounding the town contains some of the richest farming land in Nova Scotia; therefore, a federal agricultural research station was established here in 1911. Because of the importance of the local apple orchards, the annual Apple Blossom Festival was launched in Kentville in June 1933. Held to mark the tricentennial of the apple industry, started by Acadian farmers near PORT ROYAL in 1633, the festival has grown to include events throughout the entire Annapolis Valley.

Keppoch Mountain (Antigonish and Pictou; Inverness)   Often referred to locally as 'The Keppoch.' All traces of the nineteenth-century Scottish settlement on the ANTIGONISH–PICTOU county boundary have disappeared. It is now the site of a well-known ski resort. The name is traceable to Keppoch on the west coast of Scotland, near Arisaig. A second community, in Inverness County, northeast of LAKE AIN-

SLIE, takes its name from the same source.

Kings Bay   *See* Kingsburg.

Kingsburg (Lunenburg)   On Kings Bay. Both the bay and settlement were named as an expression of loyalty to King George III. The first settlers were members of the Mossman, Keizer, and Knock families.

Kings County   When established on 17 August 1759, Kings County included all of contemporary HANTS, part of LUNENBURG, and sections of CUMBERLAND and COLCHESTER counties. The name was assigned in the reign of George II as an expression of loyalty to the monarchy. The first reduction in size occurred on 17 June 1781, when the new county of Hants was proclaimed. Portions of the original county adjacent to Lunenburg and across MINAS BASIN, next to Cumberland and Colchester counties, were subsequently reassigned to each. The present boundaries were defined by an act of the legislature in 1840.

Kingsport (Kings)   East of CANNING. The place name evolved as the 'Kings [County] port' for nineteenth-century ships which carried mail and passengers across the MINAS BASIN to PARRS-

BORO. The port was also an important shipbuilding centre. Perhaps its most notable example was the four-masted barque *Kings County*, built in 1890, one of only two such vessels ever to be built in Canada.

Kingston (Kings)   East of MIDDLETON. The name is derived from KINGS COUNTY and was adopted in the hope that the community might become a town. It was first known as 'Kingston Station' because of its location on the then Dominion Atlantic Railway line. By act of the legislature in 1916, the word 'station' was dropped.

Kitiwiti Shoal (Halifax)   Off Prospect Bay. This shoal is listed by the *Nova Scotia and Bay of Fundy Pilot* as one of the dangers in approaching anchorage, as it 'has a depth of 5 fathoms, on which the sea breaks in bad weather.' The name is probably a phonetic rendering of 'Quidi Vidi' and may have been bestowed by some anonymous Newfoundland fisherman (Brown). See QUIDI VIDI, Newfoundland.

Knoydart (Pictou)   On NORTHUMBERLAND STRAIT near the PICTOU–ANTIGONISH county boundary. Among the first set-tlers in 1791 were Angus Mac-Donald, Hugh MacDonald, and John MacPherson, natives of Knoydart, Inverness-shire, Scotland, thus explaining the origin of the name. All three were veterans of the Battle of Culloden, 16 April 1746. This encounter, the last major battle on British soil, marked the end of the Jacobite Rebellion, led by Prince Charles Edward Stuart, 'Bonnie Prince Charlie.' It also put an end to the Highlanders' hope that a Scot might ascend the British throne. Each year, on the anniversary of the battle, a cermony is held at a fieldstone memorial in Knoydart, 'to commemorate Culloden' and the three Scottish soldiers who were founders of the community. See also KENNETCOOK and MOIDART.

LaHave   *See* Cape LaHave.

LaHave Islands   *See* Cape LaHave.

LaHave River   *See* Cape LaHave.

Lake Ainslie (Inverness)   South–southeast of INVERNESS. During the years 1784 to 1820, CAPE BRETON existed as a colony separate from Nova Scotia. Its last lieutenant-governor was General George Robert Ainslie (1776–1839). Beyond an undistinguished career in the British army and colonial service, Ainslie is remembered for bestowing his surname on this lake, previously known to the French as 'Marguérite.' Certainly he did not hold the Cape Bretoners of his day in high regard, describing the recent Loyalist settlers as 'a set of deceitful, unprincipled aliens imbued with Yankee qualities,' while the remainder were nothing more than 'the refuse of the three kingdoms.' The factional quarrelling that characterized his administration of the colony was one reason for its reunification with the mainland in 1820. Ainslie then returned to England, where he happily pursued his hobby of coin collecting, becoming an expert in the field of Anglo-Norman coinage. Lake Ainslie is the largest freshwater lake in the province.

Lake Banook (Halifax)   On 31 July 1922, the Halifax *Morning Chronicle* reported that a contest for the renaming of First, Second, and Third lakes had been completed. These lakes formed part of the Shubenacadie canal system, begun almost a century earlier, in 1826. This enterprise was designed to provide inland navigation between MINAS BASIN and HALIFAX harbour; however, financial and engineering problems intervened and it was never completed. The three names

selected – Banook, Micmac, and Charles – were approved by the Canadian Geographic Board on 5 September 1922. Since the canal project was 'part of the chain of lakes that was the Micmac [*sic*] highway or route of travel,' two of the names, Micmac and Banook (for the Mi'kmaq *Bahnook* or *Ponhook*, meaning 'the first lake in a chain'), highlighted this heritage. The name Charles was selected to mark the career of Charles Fairbanks (1790–1841), the entrepreneur responsible for the canal project. In the 1990s the Shubenacadie Canal is being restored for recreational and historical purposes. See also PONHOOK LAKE.

Lake Charlotte (Halifax)   East of SHIP HARBOUR. The name, bestowed in the early nineteenth century, honours Princess Charlotte Augusta, the only daughter of King George IV and Queen Caroline, who died in childbirth 6 November 1817. In 1937 the name of the community Ship Harbour Lake was changed to Lake Charlotte by act of the Nova Scotia legislature.

Lake George (Kings; Yarmouth) The first is southeast of AYLESFORD; the second, north of YARMOUTH. Both commemorate the long and controversial reign of King George III, from 1760 to 1830.

Lake Mulgrave (Annapolis; Halifax)   The first lies parallel to the ANNAPOLIS–DIGBY county line; the second is to be found north of SHEET HARBOUR. The two are named for George Phipps, third Earl of Mulgrave (1819–1890), lieutenant-governor of Nova Scotia (1858–63). See also MULGRAVE.

Lake Ramsay (Lunenburg)   To the north of the military road ordered surveyed by George Ramsay, ninth Earl of Dalhousie (1770–1838), lieutenant-governor of Nova Scotia from 1816 to 1819. The name probably commemorates the earl's family name. There is a local tradition that the lake was named for 'an Anglican rector named Ramsay'; however, in view of its location and the earl's fondness for place-naming, the Dalhousie explanation is more likely correct. See also DALHOUSIE and EARLTOWN.

Lake Rossignol (Queens) Northwest of Liverpool. Marc Lescarbot, in his *Histoire de la Nouvelle France*, published in 1609, writes of an incident that occurred on 6 May 1604: 'They [the Champlain–Du Gua de Monts expedition] made land at a certain harbour in 44° of latitude, where they found one Captain Rossignol of Havre-de-Grâce, who was bartering for furs ... contrary to the King's intention. The result was that they confiscated his ship, and called the harbour Port Rossignol; whereby in this disaster he had the consolation that a good and safe harbour on those coasts bears his name.' Unfortunately for Captain Jean Rossignol's 'consolation,' the place name was subsequently changed (see LIVERPOOL); however, his name, if not his deed, has been perpetuated in Lake Rossignol (the largest lake on mainland Nova Scotia) and in the Rossignol River. See also COFFIN ISLAND.

Lake Uist (Richmond)   On the RICHMOND–CAPE BRETON county boundary. Named for either of two islands, North Uist or South Uist, in the Outer Hebrides. The first settlers were from this part of Scotland.

Lansdowne (Pictou; Digby)   The PICTOU COUNTY community, located southwest of WESTVILLE and settled in 1803 by immigrants from the parish of Lairg in Sutherlandshire, Scotland, was first known as 'New Lairg.' The name was changed in 1884 by act of the Nova Scotia legislature to honour Henry Charles Petty-Fitzmaurice, fifth Marquis of

Lansdowne (1845–1927), who served as governor general of Canada from 1883 to 1888. Lansdowne was the first governor general to travel widely throughout Canada, visiting the Maritimes on several occasions and making a westward trip on the new Canadian Pacific Railway. The DIGBY COUNTY Lansdowne (near BEAR RIVER) was also named during his tenure in Canada.

Lantz (Hants)   Off Highway 101, near ELMSDALE. This area has been noted for brick and tile manufacturing since 1898, when the first such plant was built by Harvey and Croft Lantz. The community which grew up around the industry was named for them. The Lantz enterprise was bought out by James B. Miller in 1905 to become the Elmsdale Brick and Tile Company, and was later absorbed as part of the Nova Scotia Clay Works. The operation was purchased in 1913 by L.E. Shaw.

L'Ardoise (Richmond)   South of ST. PETER'S. This district was named during the French colonial period for the slate (*ardoise*) cliffs found along the coast. It achieved importance during the early 1700s as a supply depot for the construction of Fortress Louisbourg. The slate quarry supplied roofing material, firewood was cut for the fortress, and some agricultural items were produced. The census of 1752 indicated 252 residents.

Larrys River (Guysborough)   On Highway 316. It was settled in 1767 by an Irish immigrant, Lawrence (Larry) Keating; hence, the name.

Lawrencetown (Annapolis; Halifax)   These communities, one west of MIDDLETON, the other east of DARTMOUTH, were named for Governor Charles Lawrence (1709–1760). His term, from 1754 to 1760, coincided with the expulsion of the Acadians (1755), the establishment of representative government (1758), and the coming of the New England Planters (1760s), all major milestones in Nova Scotian history. Lawrencetown Beach (within a provincial park) is noted for its breakers and is used by surfers the year round.

Lennox Passage (Richmond)   Separates ISLE MADAME from CAPE BRETON ISLAND. The name commemorates the career of Charles Lennox, third Duke of Richmond and Lennox (1735–1806). He served in a variety of posts in the British cabinet, including that of secretary of state. His nephew, the fourth Duke, was to serve briefly as governor-general of Canada (1818–19). See also RICHMOND COUNTY.

Lequille; Lequille River (Annapolis)   There has been some confusion surrounding the location of these two place names. The name Rivière de l'Equille was first bestowed by Champlain on what is today the Annapolis River. It was so called because of an abundance of small smelt-like fish (*l'esquille*) found there. Marc Lescarbot has several references to the river in his *Histoire de la Nouvelle France*. Describing the particularly mild winter of 1608–9, he wrote: 'Up to January we always went about in our doublets, and I remember on a Sunday afternoon, the 14th of that month, we amused ourselves by singing music along the banks of the Rivière Lequille ... we [also] paid a visit to the cornfields and dined joyously in the sunshine.' The French were later to change the name to Rivière Dauphin, honouring the eldest son of a king of France; however, the old name lives on in the community Lequille, located south of ANNAPOLIS ROYAL, on Allains Creek, or as the latter is sometimes called 'the Lequille River.'

Lequille River   *See* Lequille.

Liscomb Mills; Liscomb River (Guysborough)   All references suggest that this area was named for 'Liscomb House, a Tudor mansion, [supposedly] located somewhere in Buckinghamshire, England.' The problem is that nobody knows why it was so named or by whom. If there is a Buckinghamshire connection, it may stem from a misspelling of 'Lipscombe,' a surname common to that part of England. Liscomb Lodge is a well-known riverside retreat noted for salmon and trout fishing.

Liscomb River   *See* Liscomb Mills.

Little Harbour (Pictou)   On the NORTHUMBERLAND STRAIT, northeast of NEW GLASGOW. The area was the site of early Mi'kmaq and Acadian communities and was resettled by Highland Scots in 1773. The name is descriptive of its size in relation to MERIGOMISH and PICTOU harbours.

Little Hope Island (Queens)   A small island located off PORT JOLI POINT. It was the site of numerous shipwrecks until 1866, when the government of Nova Scotia erected a lighthouse. The name is a satirical reference to the possibility of survival prior to the erection of the lighthouse.

Little River (Cumberland)
Joins RIVER PHILIP at OXFORD.
Descriptive of its size with reference to the Black River and River
Philip in central CUMBERLAND
COUNTY.

Little Tancook Island   *See* Tancook Island.

Liverpool; Liverpool Bay
(Queens)   The present town site
at the mouth of the MERSEY RIVER
was known to the Mi'kmaq as
Ogukegeok, which translates as
'the place of departure,' an allusion to the harbour (Rand). Later
designated Port Rossignol in 1604
by Champlain, for Captain Jean
Rossignol (see LAKE ROSSIGNOL).
It was settled in 1760–3 by New
England fishermen, largely from
Nantucket and Cape Cod. A town
meeting was held on 1 July 1760,
and one of the first acts was to
adopt a coat of arms. It 'had as its
device a codfish, salmon & pine
tree with a sheaf of wheat for a
crest.' The new township and settlement were named for Liverpool, England, being at the
mouth, as was its namesake, of
the MERSEY RIVER. Liverpool's
most famous early resident was
merchant, politician, and diarist
Simeon Perkins (1735–1812). For
thirty years a member of the
Nova Scotia Assembly, he
recorded, in 'Pepysian style,' a
detailed and intimate account of
life in colonial Nova Scotia. Published in five volumes by the
Champlain Society, it is an indispensable reference for historians,
and became the source for much
of the writing of local historical
novelist Thomas Raddall (1904–
1994). Once known as the 'privateering capital' of Nova Scotia,
Liverpool played a pivotal role in
the American Revolution and the
Napoleonic Wars. The town was
incorporated in 1897.

Liverpool Bay   *See* Liverpool.

Lochaber (Antigonish); **Loch Ban**
(Inverness); **Loch Katrine** (Antigonish); **Loch Lomond** (Richmond)
The Gaelic prefix *loch*, for 'lake,' is
found in abundance in overseas
areas settled by Scots. All of the
examples cited, with the exception
of Loch Ban – a descriptive, translating as 'white lake' – are transfer
names from Scotland.

Loch Ban   *See* Lochaber.

Loch Broom (Pictou)   On a point
of land between the West and
Middle rivers. Named by Alexander Cameron, a native of Loch
Broom, Ross-shire, Scotland, and
one of the passengers on the ship
Hector (see PICTOU). At Loch
Broom, Nova Scotia, there stands
a replica of the first log church
erected in 1787 by Presbyterian
Scottish settlers under the direc-

tion of their minister, Dr. James MacGregor (1759–1830). The building, dedicated in 1973, follows original specifications, with exterior, pulpit, and pews all made from hand-hewn logs. Loch Broom Islet, located offshore, was first known as 'Frasers Island,' after Alexander Fraser, another *Hector* passenger and early settler. This island, in common with many others in Nova Scotia, is reputedly a hiding-place for buried treasure. For a time in the nineteenth century, it bore the name Devils Island.

Loch Broom Islet   *See* Loch Broom.

Loch Katrine   *See* Lochaber.

Loch Lomond   *See* Lochaber.

Lockeport (Shelburne)   Southeast of SHELBURNE. Originally known by the descriptive 'Ragged' Island, for a coast encumbered with rocks, submerged rocks, and shoals. The name was changed to Locke's Island in the 1790s in honour of Jonathan Locke, a native of Rhode Island who moved here from Liverpool about 1767. During the 1770s, local residents were, according to historian J.B. Brebner, 'so American in sympathy as to serve as advance bases for American privateers and for the

disposal of their captures.' Eventually, as the revolution wore on, Ragged Island, along with many other South Shore ports, suffered at the hands of the same American privateers. So much so, that on 25 September 1779 a group of prominent residents, including Locke, petitioned the Massachusetts Council for relief from 'such incursions.' Eventually these raids did much to influence 'His Majesty's Yankees' here, and elsewhere in Nova Scotia, to turn against the revolutionary cause. On 16 February 1870, by public vote, the name Locke's Island was changed to Lockeport. However, the original name lives on, across Lockeport harbour, in East Side of Ragged Island.

Londonderry (Colchester) North of GREAT VILLAGE. The Ulster Scots were an important element in the settlement of the township of Londonderry, and the individual most responsible was the colonizer–entrepreneur Alexander McNutt (1725–*ca* 1811). Of Ulster origin, he emigrated first to Virginia, and later served at the final capture of LOUISBOURG in 1758. McNutt recruited settlers for Nova Scotia from Ulster and New Hampshire, the latter settled in part by his countrymen. The majority of immigrants to this part of Nova Scotia came from New England; thus the new community was named for Londonderry, New Hampshire. A deposit of iron ore was discovered here in 1844. From 1849 until mining ceased fifty-six years later, the area prospered, reaching a peak population of 2,600 by 1891. The community was designated Acadian Mines in 1849, later Acadia Mines, for the Acadian Charcoal Mining company. A further change occurred in 1877, when, by act of the provincial legislature, Acadia Mines became 'Siemens,' honouring the inventor/engineer Wilhelm (William) Siemens (1823–1883), a director of the local mining company and co-discoverer of a process for developing steel. Siemens, a native of Germany, was a member of the family that founded the multinational firm now known as Siemens AG. Today one of the world's largest companies, it specializes in electric technology and electronics. Siemens, who became a British citizen and changed his name to William, came to Canada to promote the manufacture of steel and the laying of a transatlantic cable to Halifax in 1875. Despite its international prominence, the name Siemens was never popular locally and, in 1902, when the iron ore deposits began to dwindle, the name was officially changed back to Londonderry. See also McNUTTS ISLAND, ONSLOW, and TRURO.

Long Island (Colchester)   *See* Five Islands.

Long Island (Digby)   DIGBY NECK, Long Island, and BRIER ISLAND are a continuation of the NORTH MOUNTAIN range of mainland Nova Scotia. According to Mi'kmaq legend, the deity Glooscap was responsible for the creation of Long Island. In a dispute with his arch-rival, the Beaver, Glooscap hurled two gigantic stones in the direction of the latter. Both missed; however, in landing, they created PETIT PASSAGE, separating Long Island from the mainland, and GRAND PASSAGE, between Long and Brier islands. The three names Île Longue, Petit Passage, and Grand Passage were first assigned by Champlain in 1604. Ever since, mariners have told tales of the treacherous tides in this area. In attempting to navigate Grand Passage, Nicolas Denys (1598–1688) reported: 'I wished to have the anchor cast, even though there were only two and a half fathoms of water in the entrance. The current was so strong that we lost it along with our cable which ran out to the end.' Long Island was granted in 1783 to Captain Neil MacNeill, a New York Loyalist who served as commandant of a company of pro-British troops. Many of his descendants may be found throughout DIGBY and ANNAPOLIS counties.

Longspell Point (Kings)   North of KINGSPORT. The name dates from the French colonial period and is an English adaptation of the French *longue pelle*, for 'long shovel,' descriptive of the local topography. The suggestion that it was so named when some early settlers started to walk to CAPE BLOMIDON and found to their dismay that it was 'a long spell' is purely apocryphal.

Lorne (Pictou); **Lornevale** (Colchester); **Lorneville** (Cumberland); **Port Lorne** (Annapolis) These place names commemorate the career of the Marquis of Lorne (1845–1914), governor general of Canada from 1878 to 1883. Port Lorne was first known as 'Port Williams'; the name change occurred to avoid confusion with the better-known PORT WILLIAMS in KINGS COUNTY.

Lornevale   *See* Lorne.

Lorneville   *See* Lorne.

Louisbourg (Cape Breton)   On the eastern coast of CAPE BRETON. This seaport was first called, ironically, Havre à l'Anglais, because of its role as an occasional haven for English fishermen. In 1713 it was selected by the French as the site for a major military base. In 1745 the fortress, named after Louis XIV, was captured by a force of New Englanders, supported by a squadron of the Royal Navy. The fortress was ceded back to France by the treaty of Aix-la-Chappelle, and again captured by the British, under Major-General Jeffrey Amherst, in 1758 (see KENNINGTON COVE). The fortifications were destroyed in 1760. Two centuries later, in 1961, Parks Canada began an authentic reconstruction based on detailed historical and archaeological studies. Aside from the obvious attention to detail and authenticity, the interpretation program at the restored Fortress Louisbourg involves people – soldiers and government officials, artisans and clergy, women and children – simulating life as it was in 1745. Even the food served is from period recipes. Thus, Louisbourg has become one of Canada's premier examples of historic restoration, attracting thousands of visitors each year. The town of Louisburg was incorporated in 1901, and this spelling was in use until 6 April 1966, when, following approval of the CPCGN and royal assent by the lieutenant-governor of Nova Scotia, the original spelling was reintroduced.

Louisdale (Richmond)   North of LENNOX PASSAGE. This area appears in early records as *The Barachois* or *Barrasois St. Louis*. To avoid confusion with other similarly named communities, the name was changed by act of the provincial legislature in 1905 to Louisdale, a coined or manufactured name.

Lower Granville   *See* Granville Ferry.

Lower River Inhabitants (Richmond)   Traceable to the French Rivière des Habitants, the contemporary name is a direct translation of the original. It was also sometimes listed as River Inhabitants. In an 1861 census report, the area is described: 'The River Inhabitants on the East side of [Richmond] County is a Pretty large River with extensive Entervale [*sic*] and where large stocks of cattle are kept it is decidedly a farming country, there are no fish in the river. But in the Bay below large quantities of lean Mackerel are taken.'

Lower Sackville; Middle Sackville (Halifax)   North of HALIFAX, off Highway 101. Sometimes referred to as 'The Sackvilles,' these communities comprise the fastest-growing area in the province, ideally situated for the majority of people who live here who commute daily to Metro Halifax or DARTMOUTH. The place name may be traced to Fort Sackville, which once guarded the Windsor road leading from Halifax to the Annapolis Valley (see BEDFORD). In turn, it was named for George Sackville Germain, first Viscount Sackville (1716–1785), who served as secretary of state for the colonies in the British cabinet (1755–82). In common with HALIFAX COUNTY, this area became part of the Halifax Regional Municipality in 1996. See also SACKVILLE, New Brunswick.

Lower Shinimicas; Shinimicas Bridge; Shinimicas River (Cumberland)   The river drains into the NORTHUMBERLAND STRAIT, at Northport. The name is derived from a Mi'kmaq word meaning 'shining waters.' Shinimicas Bridge and Lower Shinimicas take their name from the river.

Lucasville (Halifax)   Approximately 18 kilometres northwest of HALIFAX. Named Lucas Settlement for one of its first settlers, James Lucas. As the population grew, 'settlement' was dropped to be replaced by 'ville.'

Lumsden Dam (Kings)   Southeast of KENTVILLE. Named in 1941 for James Freeman Lumsden (1890–1929), who was manager of the Nova Scotia Power Company at the time of his death on 15 May 1929. Born in Trinity, Newfoundland, the son of the Reverend James Lumsden (1854–1915), he graduated from Mount Allison University and Nova Scotia Technical College. Of his early death, the *Halifax Herald* commented in an editorial: 'Lumsden had considerable and varied experience as an electrical engineer, including duty overseas in the [first world] war; his service with the Nova Scotia Power Company was particularly meritorious.' See also LUMSDEN, Newfoundland.

Lunenburg (shiretown of Lunenburg County)   In early 1753 Governor Peregrine Hopson (?–1759) ordered a survey of lands once occupied by Acadians 'at the Bay of Merligash' on the south shore of Nova Scotia. This name, of Mi'kmaq origin, was recorded by Nicolas Denys (1598–1688) as *Mirligaiche* and is said to mean 'white or milky surf,' referring to its appearance in a storm. Following the survey, the area was resettled by some 1,400 'Foreign Protestants' who were recruited from southwestern Germany and the Montbéliard region of France and Switzerland. Prior to their arrival, the governor and council decreed that the new settlement would be called Lunenburg, for the royal house of Braunschweig–Lüneburg (in English: Brunswick–Lunenburg). In 1714 the elector of Hanover, Duke of

Brunswick–Lunenburg, became King George I of England. Unfortunately, historians, from Haliburton (1829) to McNutt (1965), have perpetuated the myth that the town was named for the city of Lüneburg, in Hanover, 'home of the original settlers.' There were few Hanoverians among the Foreign Protestants; the name was assigned before their arrival, and its selection was the prerogative of the governor and council. Lunenburg's leading historian, Winthrop Pickard Bell (1884–1964), points to a 'political' reason for the choice of name. Only eight years earlier, in 1745, Prince Charles Edward Stuart had landed in Scotland and proclaimed his father, 'the Old Pretender,' as King James III. Although the 'Forty-Five Rebellion' failed, the choice of a name derived from the reigning house was 'a demonstration of devotion to the Settlement of 1701 ... and of loyalty to the existing monarchy.' For long one of Atlantic Canada's major fishing ports, Lunenburg has had its seafaring past documented in the Fisheries Museum of the Atlantic, with displays that cover two centuries of ocean-going history. An engraving of the championship Lunenburg racing schooner *Bluenose* is to be found on the Canadian ten-cent coin. For a number of years, a view of the town was depicted on the Canadian one-hundred-dollar bill. The annual Folk Harbour Festival and Nova Scotia Fisheries Exhibition and Fishermen's Reunion are further reminders of the town's heritage. Another of Lunenburg's assets is a wealth of nineteenth-century architecture, which has resulted in its listing as a National Heritage Historic District. A further honour came in 1995 when the town was designated a World Heritage Site by UNESCO. The incorporation of the town took place in 1888.

Lunenburg County   The county, named for the town, was formed on 17 August 1759. Three years later it was reduced in size when QUEENS COUNTY was established.

Lyons Brook (Pictou)   On the outskirts of PICTOU. Named for the Reverend James Lyons. A graduate of Princeton, and a member of the Philadelphia Land Company, he was responsible for bringing a group of emigrants from Pennsylvania to the Pictou area in the spring of 1767. Lyons later returned to New England. See BARNEYS RIVER.

Mabou (Inverness)   Northeast of Port Hood. The name is from an obscure Mi'kmaq word *Malabo* or *Malabokak*. This area was settled by Scottish immigrants in the 1820s. On the 1794 Miller map of Cape Breton, the place name *Hunting River* was given for Mabou harbour; however, this name did not achieve permanent status. The post office dates from 1835 and was first known as 'Mabou Bridge'; however, soon thereafter, it was shortened to Mabou. This area has been called with justification the fountainhead of Cape Breton culture and music. The Gaelic language is spoken here, and scores of singers and musicians, from John Allan Cameron to the internationally recognized Rankin Family, call the Mabou area home.

Maccan (Cumberland)   On Highway 302, south of AMHERST. Site of an earlier Acadian settlement; the name is traceable to Mi'kmaq sources. They called the location *Makaan*, for 'fishing place,' applying it to the river. Eventually the spelling took the present anglicized form.

McNabs Island (Halifax)   In the entrance to HALIFAX harbour. In 1711 Jean DeLabat, a military engineer stationed at PORT ROYAL, completed a survey of Chebucto (Halifax) harbour. The large island at the entrance he lists as *Île de Chibouqueto*. In 1749 the island was named Cornwallis, not for the then governor Edward Cornwallis, but for his brother Frederick (1713–1783), who became Archbishop of Canterbury in 1768 and to whom the island had been granted. In 1783 the island was purchased by John McNab for £1,000 and has borne the name McNabs since then. See also GEORGES ISLAND.

McNutts Island (Shelburne)   In the entrance to SHELBURNE harbour. During the 1760s and 1770s, Alexander McNutt, the famous Ulster Scot colonizer–entrepreneur, lived on this island, which was named for him. Self-promoted from captain to 'colonel,' and once described as 'an erratic individual lacking in mental ballast,' McNutt flirted with the the American cause in the revolutionary war. In 1778 his property suffered a raid by 'a party of armed ruffians' from an American privateer, the *Congress*, out of Boston. In travelling to Massachusetts to seek restitution, he was further humiliated by his arrest as a 'doubtful' character. After several attempts to play both sides in the conflict, he came back to McNutts Island in 1787, later returning to Virginia, where he died in 1811. See also LONDONDERRY, ONSLOW, and TRURO.

Mahone Bay (Lunenburg) Southwest of CHESTER. On some early French maps this location appears as *La Baye de Toutes Iles*, or 'Bay of Many Islands.' The present place name was derived from the French word *mahonne*, which refers to 'a particular type of low-slung pirate ship.' With reputedly 365 islands in the bay, it became a favourite haven for pirates. On 27 June 1813, a British warship chased the notorious pirate ship the *Young Teazer* into Mahone Bay, where it was subsequently scuttled. There are those who maintain that a phantom ship returns, each year, on the anniversary of this event. An unsuccessful attempt was made in the nineteenth century to impose the banal name Kinburn on the community. Since the establishment of a post office in 1848, the euphonious Mahone Bay has been fixed. During the last week of July, a Wooden Boat Festival is held to celebrate the local shipbuilding heritage.

Main-à-Dieu; Main-à-Dieu Passage (Cape Breton)   Main-à-Dieu Passage separates SCATERIE ISLAND from mainland CAPE BRETON, and the community takes its name from this sea feature. It is of Mi'kmaq origin and, ironically, is a French corruption of *menadou*, for 'evil spirit or the devil.' It was first rendered as *Main-a-Dieu*, 'hand of God,' by DesBarres during his survey of Cape Breton in 1786 (Davy).

Main-à-Dieu Passage *See* Main-à-Dieu.

Maitland (Hants; Lunenburg); **Maitland Bridge** (Annapolis); **Maitland Forks** (Lunenburg); **Port Maitland** (Yarmouth); **South Maitland** (Hants)   All of these locations commemorate the career of Sir Peregrine Maitland (1777–1854), who served as lieu-tenant-governor of two colonies, Upper Canada (1818–28); and Nova Scotia (1828–34). Historian Arthur Lower categorized him as 'an impecunious soldier who eloped with the daughter of the Duke of Richmond. When the couple were duly forgiven, the Duke [who was to become gover-nor general] packed [Maitland] up with his baggage and brought him along as lieutenant gover-nor.' Closely identified with the right-wing Family Compact, Maitland's tenure in Upper Can-ada was noted for political unrest. By contrast, during his six-year term in Nova Scotia, he left little mark beyond place names on the province's history. Maitland in HANTS COUNTY was originally the site of the Acadian settlement Ville Robert. The Mi'kmaq desig-nations for the area were *Mene-satung*, 'healing waters,' and *T'witnook*, 'the place where the river runs fast.' Both names refer to the tidal waters of the nearby SHUBENACADIE RIVER. Maitland

was once a noted shipbuilding centre: the *W.D. Lawrence*, Can-ada's largest wooden ship, was launched there in 1874. The nineteenth-century heritage of the area is reflected in its architecture. On 15 July 1995, Maitland was proclaimed Nova Scotia's first provincial Heritage District. See also RICHMOND COUNTY.

Maitland Bridge   *See* Maitland.

Maitland Forks   *See* Maitland.

Malagash; Malagash Point (Cumberland)   The name of this peninsula in the northeast corner of the county is derived from a Mi'kmaq word, *Malegaawach*, meaning 'place of games.' It was the custom of the Mi'kmaq to leave their winter encampments in the COBEQUID MOUNTAINS and spend the summer at locations such as Malagash, with its excel-lent beaches, warm salt water, and abundance of shellfish – a perfect 'place for games.' At Mal-agash Point, on 2 September 1918, the first rock-salt mine in Canada began operation. It was closed in 1959 to coincide with the opening of another salt mine in nearby PUGWASH.

Malagash Point   *See* Malagash.

Malagawatch (Inverness)   On a peninsula fronting West Bay, an arm of BRAS D'OR LAKE. Although the original Mi'kmaq name has been lost, it is probably descriptive for a triangular point of land. The present spelling dates from the establishment of the post office in 1852.

Malignant Cove (Antigonish) In the autumn of 1774 a British warship, HMS *Malignant*, was shipwrecked on the NORTHUMBERLAND coast, midway between CAPE GEORGE and the present PICTOU COUNTY boundary. Despite two efforts to change the name, the community has remained Malignant Cove. In 1892 local historian the Reverend Ronald MacGillivary suggested 'the people of the place ought to ... substitute for the malignant old name a new appellation.' He suggested Barradale (for the Scottish island of Barra) as an alternative, but nothing came of the proposal. In 1915 an attempt was made to change the name (by act of the legislature) to the prosaic Milburn. Fortunately, history prevailed, and the original name was retained by popular usage.

Mapleton (Cumberland)   A striking feature of the interior of CUMBERLAND and COLCHESTER counties is the heavily wooded COBEQUID MOUNTAINS. One of the predominant hardwood trees is the sugar maple, and there are thirty or more maple-sugar camps scattered throughout the region. Mapleton, in central Cumberland County, derives its name from this industry. First known as 'Maccan Mountain,' Mapleton was adopted by an act of the legislature in 1789.

Marble Mountain (Inverness) Overlooks West Bay, an arm of BRAS D'OR LAKE. In 1942 Clara Dennis wrote: 'I see a marble quarry. Its walls rise sheer above the village – a majestic ruin ... No sound of busy work is heard. Rusted and broken machinery lie all around. Here then is the explanation of the deserted houses in the village [and the place name].' The marble seam was accidentally discovered in 1868 by Nicholas Brown, a geologist from Prince Edward Island. For a time around the end of the nineteenth century, the quarry employed 750 people; it ceased operations in 1921.

Margaree Harbour; Margaree Island; Margaree River; Margaree Valley (Inverness)   The river, which enters the Gulf of St. Lawrence at Margaree Harbour, is internationally known for its scenery and salmon fishery. The name goes back to the 1780 French settlement known as 'Mâgré,' thought to be a variation of Marguérite. It appears variously on early maps as *Madré*

(1751) and *Magarie* (1813); and from this evidence it would appear that the modern spelling is a corruption of the original French place name. Another interpretation in the CPCGN files cites a local tradition that the name stems from a shipwrecked crew who were forced against their will (*malgré eux*) to remain for a time in the area. The valley was later resettled by emigrants from Scotland. Two generations later, in the 1880s, some of their descendants were to migrate to western Newfoundland and establish a Scottish presence in the CODROY valley. Natives of the Margaree area, the Reverend J. J. Tompkins (1870–1953) and Dr. Moses Coady (1882–1959), achieved fame through their pioneering work with co-operatives and credit unions during the Depression of the 1930s. Coady was also responsible for developing the 'Antigonish Movement,' a successful blend of economic co-operation and adult education. The work continues through the Coady Institute at St. Francis Xavier University, ANTIGONISH. See also CODROY and TOMPKINS, Newfoundland.

Margaree Island   *See* Margaree Harbour.

Margaree River   *See* Margaree Harbour.

Margaree Valley   *See* Margaree Harbour.

Margaretsville (Annapolis)   On the BAY OF FUNDY coast, near the ANNAPOLIS–KINGS boundary. Site of the summer residence of Sir Brenton Halliburton (1775–1860), who served as chief justice of Nova Scotia from 1833 to 1860. The name originates with his wife, Margaret Inglis, eldest daughter of the Anglican bishop Charles Inglis. The lighthouse dates from 1859. There is divided opinion within the community as to the proper spelling of the name. Some suggest that the 's' should be deleted; however, 'Margaretsville' is the official spelling as found in the most recent issue of the *Nova Scotia Gazetteer*.

Marshy Hope (Pictou)   Close to the PICTOU–ANTIGONISH boundary. This community was first settled by Robert Mappel or Maple. His farm consisted mainly of marshland and, when frequently advised 'to leave that marshy place,' his stock reply was always: 'I hope t'will improve.' This optimism is cited locally as the origin of an unusual place name. In the 1830s and 1840s, a number of immigrants from Sutherlandshire settled in this area.

Martinique Beach (Halifax) South of MUSQUODOBOIT HARBOUR, at the end of the Petpeswick Road. This 5-kilometre beach of white sand, the longest in the province, is within a provincial park. The name is a probable reference to the British capture of Martinique in 1794. The Duke of Kent served in this campaign just prior to his appointment as commander of the British forces in Nova Scotia and New Brunswick.

Martock; Martock Mountain (Hants)   Southeast of WINDSOR, on Highway 14, a handsome Greek revival mansion is to be found. Situated on a slight rise, it overlooks the site of the pre-expulsion Acadian village of LeBreau. Following 1765 this area became part of a land grant to John Butler, a wealthy Halifax merchant. He named his estate 'Martock,' after his birthplace in Somerset, England. His nephew and grand-nephew, who inherited 'Martock,' remodelled the original mansion in the 1840s, adding the Greek Revival details. Part of the house still stands, and the estate name has been transferred to the community, now a well-known ski resort.

Martock Mountain   *See* Martock.

Massacre Island (Queens)   A small island off PORT MOUTON. According to local legend, a French ship was once wrecked on the island and the survivors were killed by the Mi'kmaq. From time to time, human bones have been discovered on the island, giving credence to the 'massacre' legend.

Masstown (Colchester)   In 1689 a seigneury at the head of COBEQUID BAY was granted to Mathieu Martin of PORT ROYAL. Strategically located at the mouth of the Chiganois River was the seigneury church of St. Peter and St. Paul, giving rise to the local place name, Cove d'Eglise. The population in 1707 was 81; by 1714, 175; and, by mid-century, nearly 300. On 2 September 1755, 'the ancient as well as yong [*sic*] men and lads were ordered to repair to the church tomorrow at 3 pm and hear what is to be said to them.' Thus the tragic drama of the expulsion began to unfold in this area. Following 1755, the memory of the 'mass house' or church remained in the anglicized name Masstown.

Mavilette (Digby)   Near Cape St. Mary, on ST. MARYS BAY. Once known as 'Cape Cove Corner'; by the time of the establishment of the post office in 1864, the name Mavilette was in general use. It may derive from the combination of *ma* and *villette*, the latter a diminutive of *ville*. Thus, 'the name "my little town" would be descriptive of this charming, compact, rural community' (Deveau).

Meaghers Grant (Halifax) Northeast of DARTMOUTH, on the MUSQUODOBOIT RIVER. According to Bruce Fergusson, on 7 June 1783, Martin Meagher, a Loyalist from North Carolina, received this land grant. However, the CPCGN files suggest that the grant was not made until after the War of 1812 and was given because Meagher had lost a ship in the conflict. There is, however, agreement that the community was named for Martin Meagher.

Medway; Medway Head; Medway River; Port Medway (Queens)   The Medway River parallels the QUEENS–LUNENBURG boundary; Port Medway is a village on Medway harbour, into which the river drains. It was also the site of Port Maltais during the French colonial period, part of a 1705 grant to François de Beauharnois de La Chaussaye, Baron de Beauville (*ca* 1665–1746). Following 1755, the area was resettled by New England Planters. During the American Revolution, remaining true to their heritage, local residents were almost unanimously in support of the Ameri-

can cause. The place name is probably for the River Medway in England. It has been suggested that its location, 'midway' between Liverpool and Bridgewater, was the inspiration; however, the English association is the more likely. A lighthouse was erected at Medway Head in 1851.

Medway Head   *See* Medway.

Medway River   *See* Medway.

Melmerby Beach (Pictou)   On a sandbar that links Roy Island with the mainland. Scene of a marine disaster on 1 October 1890, when the barque *Melmervy*, out of Quebec and bound for Greenock, Scotland, was shipwrecked here. Fifteen men, including the captain, were drowned. Over time the spelling has become 'Melmerby.'

Melvern Square (Annapolis) Northeast of MIDDLETON. Originally known as 'Milltown'; the name of this community was changed in 1853. In 1906 the local postmaster reported to the Geographic Board of Canada: 'At a public meeting called for the purpose of selecting a new name, Melvern, a favourite with those present, was adopted.' The designation may well be an adaptation of the English 'Malvern.'

Merigomish; Merigomish Island (Pictou)   Northeast of NEW GLASGOW. The name is traceable to the Mik'maq *mallegomichk,* which has been translated as 'a place of merrymaking,' indicative of the fact that there was once a major Amerindian encampment here. The first European settlers were Loyalists, augmented later by emigrants from Scotland. The post office dates from 1838.

Merigomish Island   *See* Merigomish.

Merland (Antigonish)   Southwest of Monastery, near the GUYSBOROUGH COUNTY border. Named in 1868 by act of the legislature for the Reverend Vincent de Paul Merle (1768–1853), founder and superior of the nearby Trappist monastery. See also MONASTERY.

Mersey Point; Mersey River (Queens)   Flows into Liverpool Bay, at Liverpool. Named for the River Mersey in England, which also enters the sea at Liverpool. Historically, it was sometimes referred to as the 'Liverpool River' and appears as such on the Arrowsmith map of 1839. Mersey was officially sanctioned by the Geographic Board of Canada on 7 December 1937. A settlement on Liverpool Bay is known as Mersey Point. See also LIVERPOOL.

Mersey River   *See* Mersey Point.

Meteghan (Digby)   On ST. MARYS BAY. Founded by Prudent Robichaud in 1785 as part of the resettlement of the returned Acadians. The name is derived from a Mi'kmaq word, *Mitihikan,* meaning 'blue rocks or stones.' A letter in the CPCGN files indicates that 'the smooth stones along the shores ... of St. Marys Bay are of a remarkably blue tinge.'

Micmac Lake   *See* Lake Banook.

Middle Musquodoboit   *See* Musquodoboit.

Middle Sackville   *See* Lower Sackville.

Middleton (Annapolis)   The name was chosen by public vote on 18 September 1854, replacing Wilmot Corner. It denoted the fact that the town is midway between ANNAPOLIS ROYAL and KENTVILLE, and nearly in the centre of what was once Wilmot township. Incorporated as a town in 1909.

Milford (Hants; Annapolis); **Milford Lake** (Annapolis)   The HANTS COUNTY village was probably named for Milford in Hampshire (Hants), England. It was first known as 'Milford Station,' for its position on the Intercolonial Railway built in 1858. Milford in ANNAPOLIS COUNTY was first designated Thomas Mills, until the new name (a descriptive) was selected on 2 April 1860. The local inn, 'Halfway House,' was renamed 'Milford House' shortly thereafter; well over a century later, it is still in operation.

Milford Lake   *See* Milford.

Mill Village (Queens)   On the MEDWAY RIVER. First known as 'Port Mills,' and then as 'Mills Village.' The names arose because the first settlers erected a saw- and grist mill in the community. When the post office was established in 1847, it was renamed Mill Village.

Milton (Queens)   On the MERSEY RIVER. Until 1830 the village was known as 'The Falls.' As early as 1762 there were three sawmills in operation, indicative of the importance of lumbering in the local economy. Over time the name Milltown, and later Milton, evolved. The first post office in 1855 was called Milton as a means of distinguishing the community from the numerous other 'Milltowns.'

Minas Basin; Minas Channel; Minasville (Hants); **New Minas** (Kings)   A preoccupation of the French during the early 1600s was the search for minerals and precious stones. Champlain visited the area now known as Minas Basin on three occasions and, although no great mineral wealth was found, this fixation led to some enduring place names, principally Cap des Mines (later Cap de Or), Le Bassin des Mines, and Les Mines or Minas. When used as a regional land name, the French first applied Les Mines to the entire shoreline of the Basin; later it became the area between CAPE BLOMIDON and the AVON RIVER; and eventually it was narrowed to the two parishes St. Joseph's (CANARD) and St. Charles (GRAND PRÉ). This area was first settled in 1682; by the end of the century, the population had gown to approximately 300. In 1755, 2,743 people were listed for expulsion. Minasville is near BURNTCOAT HEAD; Minas Channel is found at the entrance to Minas Basin. New Minas (between KENTVILLE and WOLFVILLE) dates from the mid-nineteenth century. All take their names from the basin. See also CAPE D'OR.

Minas Channel   *See* Minas Basin.

Minasville   *See* Minas Basin.

Minudie (Cumberland)   The large marsh located on a peninsula in CUMBERLAND BASIN, an inlet of Chignecto Bay, was called by the French *le champs élysées* and is still known locally as the 'Elysian Fields.' Minudie began as the Acadian settlement of Menoudie, traceable to the Mi'kmaq *Munoode*, 'a sack or bag.' Silas T. Rand speculates that this may be a reference to the shape of the local marsh. Following the expulsion, the area became part of the vast landholdings of J.F.W. DesBarres (1721?–1824) and later, in 1834, it was purchased by Amos 'King' Seaman (1788–1864), who developed a model village for his employees. An entrepreneur of the first rank, he amassed a fortune operating a quarry producing stone, grindstones, and flywheels for the American market. His wealth, accumulated in a mercantile and shipping network that spanned the world, enabled him to divide his time between a townhouse in Boston and his Minudie estate. Part of this estate and the surviving buildings from the village are being developed as a Heritage Site and conservation park.

Mira Bay; Mira Lake; Mira River (Cape Breton)   South of MORIEN BAY. The lake and river take their name from *La baie de Miray* (Juneau 1685). Later versions include *Baie de Mirai* (Franquelin 1701); *Miré* (Bellin 1744); *La Bay de Miray* (Bishop Plessis 1815).

Miré, to denote the settlement, is common in early ecclesiastical records. The name, like many others of early origin, is a puzzle. The files of the Geographic Board of Canada suggests it may be traced to a surname. 'The person commemorated may be *Jean de Miré, sieur de l'Argenterie* or his brother *Etienne de Miré, lieutenant d'un détachment de la Marine.'* Other explanations range from an Amerindian origin (Ganong) to a transfer name from Spain (Fergusson). The only firm conclusion is that the precise origin has been lost.

Mira Lake   *See* Mira Bay.

Mira River   *See* Mira Bay.

Missiguash River   *See* New Brunswick entry.

Mistake Lake; Mistake River (Digby)   In 1828 John Heavyside, a merchant from SAINT JOHN, moved across the BAY OF FUNDY and began lumbering on the SISSIBOO RIVER. One of his foremen, William Hassett, reached a stream which he thought was the Sissiboo. Finding that he was incorrect, he bestowed the name Mistake River; later applied to the lake.

Mistake River   *See* Mistake Lake.

Mochelle (Annapolis)   Between
LEQUILLE and ROUND HILL. The
place name is a survivor from the
French colonial period. Mochelle
was the name of a family that
lived in this area in the pre-1755
period.

Molega; Molega Lake (Queens)
Off Highway 8, near SOUTH
BROOKFIELD. The name is traceable to the Mi'kmaq *Maligeak*,
meaning 'fretful water.' On some
early maps it appears as *Malega*;
however, over time the present
spelling was accepted. Site of a
late-nineteenth-century gold
mine, the community had a population of 500 in 1888. During this
period a small steamer plied the
waters of Molega Lake, linking
BROOKFIELD, GREENFIELD, and
Molega. Between 1888 and 1900,
the local mines produced 18,562
ounces of gold, worth more than
$350,000. By the turn of the cen-
tury, the 'gold boom' was over,
and Molega reverted to a small
rural community.

Molega Lake   *See* Molega.

Monastery (Antigonish)   Just off
Highway 104, near TRACADIE. As
the name implies, this community
is the location of a monastery.
Founded as Point Clairvaux
by French Trappists in 1825, it
was abandoned in 1919, to be
reopened in 1938 by the Augus-
tinian Fathers, under whose religious rule it is now known as
St. Augustine's Monastery. The
Augustinians came to Nova
Scotia to escape Nazi persecution
prior to the outbreak of the Second World War. See also MER-
LAND.

Monks Head (Antigonish)   A
point of land north of POMQUET,
on the NORTHUMBERLAND coast.
Although only a few kilometres
distant from MONASTERY, there is
no connection between the two
names. Another explanation, its
purported resemblance to a
'monk's head,' is also incorrect.
On 29 March 1784, Major George
Henry Monk (*ca* 1748–1823) was
granted '1,000 acres of land on the
east side of Antigonish harbour
entrance.' A lawyer by profession
and a prominent Loyalist, he
served in the British army during
the American Revolution. It is not
known whether he occupied this
grant, as the remainder of his life
was spent elsewhere; however,
his name has been perpetuated in
the headland. Elected in 1792 as
the MLA for HANTS, he subsequently served as a justice of the
Supreme Court (1801–16).

Montrose (Colchester)   North of
PORTAPIQUE. First known as 'Portapique Rear'; the name was
changed in 1890 with the establishment of the post office.

Named for Montrose in Angus-
shire Scotland.

Moose Island   *See* Five Islands.

Moose River Gold Mines (Halifax)   In eastern HALIFAX COUNTY,
on the highway linking TANGIER
and Elmsvale. One of many
former gold-mining communities,
Moose River (a descriptive)
achieved a special niche in Canadian history on 12 April 1936.
On that date a sudden cave-in
trapped three prospectors
inspecting an abandoned mine
shaft. Rescue teams of draegermen were summoned and, after
six days, it was discovered that,
miraculously, the men were still
alive. Eventually two were rescued, while the third died in the
rescue attempt. Regular news bul-
letins were conveyed to the outside world by a Canadian
Broadcasting Corporation mobile
radio crew. The impact of these
broadcasts by J. Frank Willis
established both 'on the spot'
radio reporting and the reputation of the fledgling CBC.

Morar (Antigonish)   On the
north side of CAPE GEORGE. Formerly known by the descriptive
North Side Cape George. The
community was renamed in 1888
by an act of the legislature for the
district of Morar located on the
Sound of Sleath, opposite the Isle

of Skye. Many of the first settlers
came from this part of Scotland.

Morden (Kings)   This area, on
the BAY OF FUNDY coast, was once
known as 'French Cross' (see
FRENCH CROSS POINT); it is now
part of Morden. On 10 September
1783, James Morden, keeper of
HM Ordinance stores in Halifax,
received a grant of 2,000 hectares
in the vicinity, giving rise to the
new name.

Morien Bay   *See* Cape Morien.

Morristown (Kings; Antigonish)
The first, on SOUTH MOUNTAIN,
south of AYLESFORD, was probably named for Charles Morris I
(1731–1802), surveyor general of
Nova Scotia and MLA for KINGS
COUNTY at the time of its settlement by New England Planters in
the early 1760s. The second community, northeast of ANTIGONISH,
was designated Morriston, for
James Morris, who was responsible for the first land survey of the
area. It was settled by disbanded
Loyalist soldiers, later supplemented by immigrants from
Scotland. By 1855 the name had
changed to Morristown.

Moser River (Halifax)   On Highway 7, near the GUYSBOROUGH
COUNTY boundary. Traceable to
Henry Moser, son of Jacob Moser,
a native of Switzerland who set-

tled in KINGSBURG, LUNENBURG COUNTY. The Moser family came to Nova Scotia in 1751, along with other Foreign Protestant immigrants on the vessel *Speedwell*. Henry Moser moved to what was to become Moser River in 1796.

Moshers Island (Lunenburg) Nicolas Denys, writing in 1672, described the easterly approach to LAHAVE: 'There was only a point [Gaff Point] to round in order to enter the harbour of *La Haive*. At the entrance, on the left, there is an island which is called *Isle aux Framboises* [Raspberry Island], its top being nothing but raspberry bushes.' In the 1770s the island was conveyed to the Mosier or Mosher family; hence, the name.

Mount Denson (Hants)   In the lower section of FALMOUTH. The name Henry Denson (1715–1780), one of the original grantees, gave his estate. His mansion, 'Mount Denson,' was built about 1772, and the name was applied to the community shortly thereafter. Denson served as MLA for Falmouth Township (1761–5); NEWPORT Township (1769–70); and KINGS COUNTY (1770–80).

Mount Hanley (Annapolis)   Part of the NORTH MOUNTAIN range. Named for an early settler, John Handley or Hanley. The current spelling has prevailed since 1870 with the opening of the post office.

Mount McCurdy (Victoria)   Off the Cabot Trail, to the north of NORTH RIVER Bridge. Named in 1974 for aviation pioneer and associate of Alexander Graham Bell's, J.A.D. McCurdy (1886–1961). He served as lieutenant-governor of Nova Scotia from 1947 to 1952. See also BEINN BREAGH.

Mount Thom (Pictou)   On Highway 104. Sometimes credited to Thomas Troop, who made a trek through the forest between TRURO and PICTOU in 1767 to bring supplies to settlers recently arrived from Philadelphia (see LYONS BROOK). However, the evidence indicates that the name was bestowed in 1829 to honour William Thom, who, with three associates, received a grant of 400 hectares in the area.

Mount Uniacke (Hants)   Northwest of Upper Sackville. Several reminders exist throughout the province of the long career of Richard John Uniacke (1753–1830). Uniacke's magnificent country home still stands in the community which bears his name. Completed in 1815 and filled with original furniture and memorabilia of the family, it is now part of the Nova Scotia

Museum complex. In addition, Mount Uniacke Gold Mines, and Uniacke Lake and River (all in HANTS COUNTY), along with Uniacke Point, in CAPE BRETON COUNTY, were named for him. Uniacke's long political career began with his election to the Nova Scotia Assembly in 1783. In 1793 he was named attorney general, an appointment he kept for the rest of his life. In 1806 Uniacke retired from the Assembly to be appointed a member of the executive council. Details of his career may be gleaned from Brian Cuthbertson's *The Old Attorney General: A Biography of Richard John Uniacke*. See also UNIACKE HILL, New Brunswick.

Moydart Point (Antigonish) Between KNOYDART and ARISAIG, on Highway 245. Named for Moidart, a district on the western coast of Scotland, southeast of the Isle of Skye. The name is traceable to two Gaelic words: *Mouid*, for 'sea spray,' and *ard*, for 'high.' This part of Scotland was Jacobite country and figured prominently in the Rebellion of 1745, when Prince Charles Edward Stuart attempted to regain the throne of the United Kingdom for the house of Stuart, only to be defeated at Culloden. Two veterans of this battle, Donald Macpherson and Angus Macdonald, were among the first settlers in the

Nova Scotia Moydart. Unfortunately, the contemporary spelling has deviated from the original. See also KNOYDART.

Mulgrave (Guysborough) On the mainland side of the STRAIT OF CANSO. First known as 'Port Mulgrave' in honour of George Phipps, third Earl of Mulgrave (1819–1890), who was lieutenant-governor of Nova Scotia from 1858 to 1863. In 1863 he returned to England on succeeding to his father's title as Marquis of Normanby. He remained in the colonial service, subsequently holding governorships in New Zealand and Australia. While he was governor of Queensland, the Normanby River was named for him.

Murder Island (Yarmouth) Off PINKNEYS POINT. On early eighteenth-century maps, this island was identified as *Isle Massacre*. Throughout succeeding years, human remains have been frequently found here, giving credence to the name and its retension. Local legend has it that there is a connection between this site and the more famous OAK ISLAND, in LUNENBURG COUNTY (see entry). Following construction of the mysterious subterranean passages on the latter, the construction workers were reputedly taken to this secluded area and systematically killed, thus protecting the 'secret' of Oak Island.

Musquodoboit Harbour; Musquodoboit River; Musquodoboit Valley (Halifax)   The river flows through the valley to enter the Atlantic at Musquodoboit Harbour. Of Mi'kmaq origin, the name may be traced to *Mooskudoboogwek*, translated by Silas T. Rand as 'rolling out in foam' or 'suddenly widening out after a narrow entrance at its mouth.' Lands in the vicinity of Musquodoboit Harbour, known to the French as 'Mouscoudabouet,' were conveyed to Mathieu des Goutins in 1691. English settlement dates from the 1750s, and the contemporary spelling has been consistent since then. The river, valley, and settlement, Middle Musquodoboit, take their name from the harbour.

Musquodoboit River   *See* Musquodoboit Harbour.

Musquodoboit Valley   *See* Musquodoboit Harbour.

Nappan (Cumberland)   South of AMHERST. Traceable to the Mi'kmaq *Nepan*, and filtered through the French and English languages to become Nappan. There was a small Acadian settlement here known as 'Napane.' The original Mi'kmaq has been interpreted by Silas T. Rand as meaning 'a good place to obtain camp or wigwam poles.' Site of an Agriculture Canada Experimental Farm since 1888.

Necum Teuch (Halifax)   On Highway 7, east of MOSER RIVER. The original Mi'kmaq spelling of this place name was *Noogoomkeak*, referring to 'a beach of fine or soft sand.' The contemporary spelling evolved from 'Nicamteau,' to 'NecumTach,' and eventually 'NekumTough.' When the post office was established in 1885, the present spelling was adopted.

Neils Harbour (Victoria)   On the Cabot Trail, north of INGONISH. The location of an earlier French settlement. This area is mentioned by Thomas Pichon in his *Lettres et Mémoires ... du Cap Breton* (1760) as '*Quarachoque* [situated] between *Niganiche* (Ingonish) and *Aspre* (Aspy Bay).' Resettled by Scottish immigrants, it was named Neils Harbour for an early grantee, Neil McLennan. The post office dates from 1867.

New Albany   *See* Albany Cross.

New Annan (Colchester)   On Highway 246, midway between TATAMAGOUCHE and WENTWORTH. Named in 1815 by John Bell, an early settler, and native of Annandale, Dumfries, Scotland.

Soon other Scottish immigrants arrived, principally from Annandale, but also from Elgin, Aberdeen, Paisley, and Kilmarnock. These settlers were, according to historian Israel Longworth, 'possessed of little or no wealth, but were hardy and industrious, and of sterling integrity. They emigrated to Nova Scotia to enjoy the privilege of cultivating more acres, than in their wildest dreams they could ever possess in Scotland.' See also FLORIDA ROAD.

New Dublin (Lunenburg)   The township of New Dublin, on the west bank of the LAHAVE RIVER, and from which West Dublin, Dublin Shore and Dublin Bay take their name, was created on 21 May 1760. Altough some of the first settlers were Ulster Scots lured to Nova Scotia by Alexander McNutt (see McNUTTS ISLAND), the name, for the city of Dublin, Ireland, was applied to the township before their arrival. According to Winthrop Pickard Bell, 'the name appeared both as Dublin and as New Dublin, eventually the latter designation became the one generally used.' Although the original intent behind the establishment of the township was to attract '260 Connecticut Proprietors,' only a few New England fishermen came for the summer season of 1761. Eventually 'when it was discov-ered that the settlers had flown, [the lands were granted] to the German overflow from Lunenburg.'

Newellton (Shelburne)   On the west side of CAPE SABLE ISLAND. Named for the Newell family, who settled here early in the nineteenth century. In 1893, Arnold Newell designed an improved lobster 'car,' used for keeping lobsters alive until the time for shipment to market. The Newellton post office was opened in 1889.

New France (Digby)   Approximately 25 kilometres southeast of WEYMOUTH. Although it flourished for a mere two decades following its establishment in 1895, this community lives on in the place name and the legends that surround it. Emile Stehelin (1837–1918), a French entrepreneur from St. Charles, near Gisors, in Normandy, conceived the idea of establishing a model community based on the lumbering industry, in the interior of DIBGY COUNTY. Attracted to the area by members of the Eudist order, who had earlier founded Collège Sainte-Anne in nearby CHURCH POINT, Stehelin, his wife, eight sons, and three daughters succeeded in fulfilling his dream. No expense was spared in building a mansion for the family, accommodation for workmen, a sawmill, a forge, and all related facilities. New France was linked to Weymouth, the nearest seaport, by a company railway. Known locally as 'the Electric City,' the site had its own plant for the generation of electricity in 1895, a convenience that did not reach Weymouth until 1926. Today little remains of this once important enterprise. Overextension of resources, a collapse of the lumber market, and the impact of the First World War (six of the sons were called for active duty in France) were contributing factors to its downfall. Paul Stehelin, grandson of the founder, has commented in his history of the community: 'As much as the family assimilated into their new environment and enjoyed it, they did not adopt the lifestyle of Canada ... None would have wanted to give up their French cuisine, the wine with meals, long evening dinners, the quiet time in the salon over black coffee, cigars and good reading.' The forest, the reason for the creation of New France, was destined to reclaim it.

New Germany (Lunenburg) Fifteen kilometres from the ANNAPOLIS COUNTY boundary, on Highway 10. This community was established about 1805. The first families, second- and third-generation settlers from the LAHAVE area, bestowed the name in honour of their ancestral homeland. The New Germany post office dates from 1854.

New Glasgow (Pictou)   On the East River. Named after Glasgow, Scotland, by William Fraser, who first surveyed the townsite. From his farm at Frasers Mountain, overlooking the location of the future town, 'in forecasting the future [he] saw in a vision another Clyde [the East River] and another Glasgow' (CPCGN Files). Settlement by Scottish immigrants began in the 1780s and continued for the next several decades. For a time in the mid-nineteenth century, the area prospered as a major shipbuilding centre. Prominent among the local shipbuilders was Captain George McKenzie (1798–1876), who became known as 'the father of shipbuilding' in PICTOU COUNTY. His business flourished during the period when wooden vessels were needed for the timber trade with Great Britain and for the export of coal to the United States. This prosperity led to the incorporation of the town in 1875. McKenzie served as MLA for Pictou County (1855–9) and for Pictou County Eastern Division (1859–63). New Glasgow continues to be the major distribution centre for Pictou, ANTIGONISH, and GUYSBOROUGH counties. The town was incorporated in 1875.

New Minas   *See* Minas Basin.

Newport; Newport Corner; Newport Landing (Hants)   The township of Newport was established in 1761 'from the part of Falmouth east of the Pisiquid [Avon] which was known as East Falmouth.' It was named by Charles Morris, chief surveyor, on 31 March 1761. He wrote: 'I have proposed to have it named Newport from my Lord Newport, a friend of Mr. Belcher's [Jonathan Belcher, Chief Justice] and I believe that it will be agreeable to the people.' Since many of the first settlers were New England Planters from Newport, Rhode Island, the name found popular acceptance. Two years later, Morris reported: ' The inhabitants have imported large quantities of cattle and have this year cut hay sufficient for supporting them. The river Pisiquid running through [this township] is navigable for sloops to all the settlements. The town [Avondale] is situated in the centre.' Although the township disappeared, Newport community names have survived.

Newport Corner   *See* Newport.

Newport Landing   *See* Newport.

New Ross (Lunenburg)   On Highway 12, northwest of CHESTER BASIN. First named Sherbrooke, in honour of Sir John Coape Sherbrooke (1764–1830), who served as lieutenant-governor of Nova Scotia from 1811 to 1816. In 1859, during the Mulgrave administration, the name was changed to avoid confusion with Sherbrooke in GUYSBOROUGH COUNTY. The new name had a double significance: it marked the governor's second title, held by his son, and derived from New Ross, Wexford, Ireland, and also the career of Captain William Ross of the Nova Scotia Fencibles, who arrived in Sherbrooke in 1816 with 172 disbanded soldiers to found a new settlement. In 1817, Ross built 'Rosebank,' a one-and-one-half storey Cape Cod–style cottage, which still stands. After five generations of ownership by the Ross family, the farm was taken over in 1967 by the Nova Scotia Museum. The farm depicts the evolution of agriculture within the province.

New Waterford (Cape Breton)   Northwest of GLACE BAY, near Low Point, the eastern headland of SYDNEY harbour. In 1908 the Dominion Coal Company opened a mine at what was then known as 'Barrachois.' In 1913 the town was incorporated and the new name, 'Waterford,' was put forward by the mayor, J.J. Hinchey, a native of Waterford, Ireland. To avoid confusion, the post office suggested that the prefix 'New' be added to the name.

Nictaux: Nictaux Falls; Nictaux River (Annapolis)   South of MID-DLETON. The village was settled in the early 1800s. The name is traceable to the Mi'kmaq word *niktak*, meaning 'the forks of a river.' It appears on the Arrowsmith map of 1838 as *Nictou*, and on the Church map of 1860 as *Nictoux*, and is listed as *Nictaux* in the *MacAlpine Gazetteer* of 1883. The last was confirmed by the spelling of the post office in 1889.

Nictaux Falls   *See* Nictaux.

Nictaux River   *See* Nictaux.

Noel (Hants)   On Highway 215, east of BURNTCOAT. By the mid-eighteenth century, Acadian settlement had spread from Pisiquid (WINDSOR) along the south shoreline of MINAS BASIN to COBEQUID, and from there in a westerly direction to present-day ECONOMY. In 1748 the estimated population of Vil Noel was fifty. Following the expulsion, the area was resettled by the O'Brien family from Londonderry, Ireland. They moved here from the Nova Scotia LONDONDERRY, directly across the Minas Basin, in 1771. The old Acadian name was retained, a silent reminder of the earlier settlement.

North Gut St. Anns   *See* St. Anns.

North Mountain; South Mountain (Kings, Annapolis, and Digby)   The North Mountain extends for 190 kilometres along the BAY OF FUNDY, from CAPE BLO-MIDON to BRIER ISLAND, the westernmost extension of DIGBY NECK. A narrow ridge of volcanic trap rock, the name reflects its position in relation to the South Mountain. The latter, in reality the northern side of the southern uplands, runs southwestward from the MINAS BASIN to the ANNAPOLIS–DIGBY county boundary. In between lies the fertile CORNWALLIS–ANNAPO-LIS valley. Both mountain names have been in common usage since the late eighteenth century. They were officially approved by the Canadian Board on Geographic Names in 1926.

North Range (Digby)   A descriptive arising from its location at the northern end of a range of hills that runs parallel to ST. MARYS BAY.

North River (Colchester; Lunenburg)   North River, in central COLCHESTER COUNTY, north of TRURO, is so named because its flow was almost directly north to south. The LUNENBURG COUNTY name is derived from its location

near the north branch of the
LAHAVE RIVER.

**North Sydney; Sydney; Sydney
Mines; Sydney River** (Cape Breton)   In 1784, in anticipation of
an influx of Loyalist settlers, CAPE
BRETON became a separate colony
from mainland Nova Scotia. The
first lieutenant-governor, J.F.W.
DesBarres (1721?–1824), selected
La Baye des Espagnols, or Spanish Harbour, as it was then
known, to be the capital. It was
subsequently renamed for Thomas Townshend, first Viscount
Sydney (1733–1800), home secretary in the British cabinet at the
time of its founding. Sydney,
Australia, was also named for the
same individual, inspiring the
conclusion that immortality was
thus given (doubly) to an obscure
minister. Sydney remained the
capital of Cape Breton until 1820,
when the colony was again reannexed to Nova Scotia. Later it was
named the shiretown of Cape
Breton County, being incorporated as a town in 1886 and as a
city in 1904. The nearby towns of
Sydney Mines (1889) and North
Sydney (1885) take their names
from Sydney. The latter is the terminus of the ferry service to PORT
AUX BASQUES, Newfoundland. In
1974 the University College of
Cape Breton was founded by the
amalgamation of the local campus of St. Francis Xavier University with the Nova Scotia Eastern
Institute of Technology. Degree-granting status was awarded in
1982. In 1995 the three Sydneys
became part of the Regional
Municipality of Cape Breton.

Northumberland Strait   *See*
chapter 1, page 21.

Nyanza; Nyanza Bay (Victoria)
The bay is an indentation of St.
Patricks Channel, BRAS D'OR LAKE.
The name, first applied to the settlement, was adopted in 1883 at
the time the post office was established. It was undoubtedly
selected for its euphonious sound
and because it was not repeated
elsewhere in Canada. The inspiration was Lake Nyanza or Nyasa,
now in Malawi, but then part of
what later became the Nyasaland
Protectorate. The name is derived
from the Bantu word for any
water area of great size; it is now
known as 'Lake Malawi.'

Nyanza Bay   *See* Nyanza.

Oakfield (Halifax)   On SHUBEN-ACADIE GRAND LAKE. The community takes its name from
'Oakfield,' a model estate established in 1865 by Colonel John
Winburn Laurie (1835–1912).
Born in England, he served in the
British Army during the Crimean
War (1853–6) and the Fenian
raids. He came to Canada in 1861,

retiring from the army in 1887 with the rank of lieutenant-general. Laurie represented SHELBURNE in the House of Commons from 1887 to 1891.

Oak Island (Lunenburg)   There are five Oak Islands in Nova Scotia, but only one, located off the western shore of MAHONE BAY, enjoys an international reputation. First known as 'Smiths Island,' after an early settler, it was renamed Gloucester by J.F.W. DesBarres, in his 1778 survey of the Nova Scotian coastline. In common with a number of names assigned by DesBarres this suggestion was not accepted locally and was soon replaced by Oak Island. The mystery of Oak Island stems not from its name, a common descriptive, but from the discovery in 1795 of a saucer-shaped depression in the ground. In the course of an exploratory dig, a platform of oak logs was found, and still others were encountered at regular intervals to a depth of 29.5 metres. Then, suddenly and without warning, water rushed into the pit. From that day onward, numerous efforts to solve the mystery have failed. Whatever the motive behind this intriguing project, considerable engineering skill was required to design and build the subterranean passages that continue to guard its secret. See also MURDER ISLAND.

Oban (Richmond)   North of ST. PETER'S. Named for the resort town in Argyllshire, Scotland. It, in turn, is derived from the Gaelic for 'little bay.' The town was settled in the 1830s; the post office dates from 1884.

Ohio (Shelburne, Yarmouth, and Antigonish).   All three place names were inspired by the Ohio River in the United States. The word is Iroquois in origin and means 'beautiful or fine river.' It was occasionally rendered on early French maps as *belle rivière*. It is believed that the SHELBURNE COUNTY Ohio was a transfer name bestowed by Loyalist settlers, while the YARMOUTH COUNTY example was associated with the 'Ohio Fever,' which gripped the northern United States and the British North American colonies in the 1820s, luring thousands of settlers west of the Alleghenies. According to local legend, Nehemiah and Benjamin Churchill moved from the settled area of the county to establish a new homestead, which they called Ohio. According to local information, the name was applied to the river in ANTIGONISH COUNTY because it was literally 'beautiful.'

Old Barns (Colchester)   Between
TRURO and the SHUBENACADIE
RIVER. The area was the site of an
Acadian village prior to 1775.
When the first British settlers
arrived in 1761, they found two
Acadian barns still standing,
which led to the name of the com-
munity.

Old Cobequid Road (Colchester
and Halifax)   This was the name
of the first trail, and later, from
about 1800, the post road linking
Cobequid (TRURO) and HALIFAX.
The route joined the road to
WINDSOR at LOWER SACKVILLE
and ran in an easterly direction
towards WAVERLEY. It continued
northward, roughly parallel with
the present Highway 102, to
ENFIELD, thence easterly to Gays
River, STEWIACKE East, and
ALTON, to Truro. Sections of this
route are still in use, and the part
from Lower Sackville to Waverley
continues to be known as the 'Old
Cobequid Road.'

Onslow; Onslow Mountain
(Colchester)   The name was first
applied to the township north–
northwest of TRURO and created
26 July 1759. It honoured Arthur
Onslow (1691–1768), who served
as speaker of the British House of
Commons (1728–61). According
to T.C. Haliburton: 'The first British settlers, who came from the

province of Massachusetts, and
were of various origin, landed at
Onslow in the summer of 1761, to
the number of thirty families, and
brought with them twenty head
of horned cattle, eight horses and
seventy sheep.' Onslow County
in North Carolina was named for
Arthur Onslow at the same time.

Onslow Mountain   *See* Onslow.

Orangedale (Inverness)   On
BRAS D'OR LAKE, south of WHYCO-
COMAGH. First known as 'Mull
Cove,' for the Isle of Mull in the
Inner Hebrides. The new name,
Orangedale, was put forward by
members of the local Orange
Lodge. The post office dates from
1879.

Osborne Harbour (Shelburne)
Near LOCKEPORT. First settled by
Loyalists in 1785. It has been sug-
gested that it was named for
Osborne House, Queen Victoria's
residence on the Isle of Wight;
however, the name predates
Victoria's reign by many years.
Osborne was a common New
England Planter–Loyalist sur-
name; thus this is a more proba-
ble origin.

Ostrea Lake (Halifax)   On the
eastern shore of MUSQUODOBOIT
HARBOUR. This area was once
noted for its oyster beds; thus, the

name is traceable to *Ostreidae*, the root word for 'oyster.' An earlier name for the community was Williams Settlement; the new name dates from 1887.

Outer Bald Tusket Island (Yarmouth)   Beyond Big Tusket Island, a few kilometres off PINKNEYS POINT, lie four small islands descriptively named Half Bald, Mossy Bald, Inner Bald, and Outer Bald Tusket islands. The last has given rise to one of the best fishing stories on record. Outer Bald was once owned by an American sportsman and fishing enthusiast, R.M. Arundel of Washington, DC. One day when the tuna were noticeably absent, he concocted, with the help of a few friends, an international hoax. The principality of Outer Baldonia was proclaimed and a declaration of independence drawn up. Arundel arranged for stationery to be printed bearing a gold-embossed letterhead replete with the great seal of Outer Baldonia. Its 'embassy' was listed in the Washington telephone directory, and 'ambassador' Arundel was soon on the diplomatic invitation list. Keeping up the spirit of the hoax, passports, stamps, and coinage (tunars) were designed. Eventually the press learned of the story; the charade was over, and Arundel deeded the 'principality' to conservation

interests. Today the Nova Scotia Bird Society has jurisdiction over the island.

Outer False Harbour (Yarmouth) At the end of CAPE FOURCHU. This suitable descriptive is exactly what it says. In foggy weather, mariners frequently mistake the harbour for YARMOUTH.

Overton (Yarmouth)   The name is descriptive of the fact that the community is located across, or 'over,' the harbour from the town of YARMOUTH. The post office was established in 1882.

Owls Head Harbour (Halifax) Southwest of SHIP HARBOUR. Known briefly as 'Kepple [*sic*] Harbour,' for Admiral Augustus Keppel (1725–1786), who became first lord of the Admiralty in 1782. The more enduring original name is said to have originated from the figure of an owl implanted on a rock at the entrance to the harbour.

Oxford (Cumberland)   Settled in 1791 by Richard Thompson, a Yorkshire immigrant, who reached the area by canoe coming up the RIVER PHILIP to the head of the tide. The community was first known by the descriptive 'Head of the Tide.' The new name, although probably inspired by Oxford, England, is a reference to this location as a convenient one for oxen to ford the river.

Paradise (Annapolis)   On the Lalanne map of 1684, *Paradis Terrestre* appears as an Acadian village on the south side of the *Rivière Dauphin*, later the ANNAPOLIS RIVER. Gargas, in his census of 1688, refers to the same location as *Au Bout du Monde*, or 'the end of settlement on the river.' The Acadian descriptive name survived the expulsion to become the anglicized Paradise, resettled by New England Planters in the 1760s.

Parrsboro (Cumberland)   The northern shore of MINAS BASIN witnessed a few scattered Acadians settlements from the 1670s onward. By 1730, Jean Bourg and François Arsenault operated a primitive ferry service across the basin from Partridge Island. The latter name was a direct translation of the Mi'kmaq *pulowech*, for 'partridge' (Rand). This location was, for the next twenty-five years, a strategic link between the French settlements at the head of CHIGNECTO BAY and those at Minas. Following the expulsion in 1755, and the ensuing influx of New England Planters and Loyalists, the major focus of settlement gradually shifted 3 kilometres eastward, to MILL VILLAGE. In 1784, Governor John Parr (1725–

1791), a Loyalist, visited the area. Two years later when a new township was established, the name Parrsborough was selected in his honour. This spelling is still used locally when referring to 'the Parrsborough Shore.' In 1889, upon incorporation of a new town, the name Mill Village was replaced by the abbreviated spelling 'Parrsboro.'

Partridge Island   *See* Parrsboro.

Peggys Cove (Halifax)   On Highway 333, at the entrance to ST. MARGARETS BAY. The permanent settlement of this well-known tourist mecca dates from the early nineteenth century. The name appears to have been derived from the nickname of an early settler, Margaret (Peggy) Rodgers, wife of William Rodgers or Rogers. There has been a lighthouse at Peggys Cove since 1868. See also SOI POINT.

Pentz (Lunenburg)   On the south side of the LAHAVE RIVER. The name originates with the Pintz or Pentz family, who settled here following the founding of LUNENBURG in 1753.

Pereaux River (Kings)   Flows into the MINAS BASIN, to the south of CAPE BLOMIDON. In all probability named for François-Marie Perrot (1644–1691), who served as governor of Acadia from 1684 to 1687. See also DELHAVEN.

Perotte (Annapolis)   Southeast of ANNAPOLIS ROYAL. Lands in this area were granted in 1821 to Captain James Perrot, a Loyalist 'of some consideration' and member of the Annapolis garrison. The community was first known as 'Perrot Settlement'; however, the second word was dropped early in the twentieth century.

Pesaquid Lake (Hants)   This name was adopted for the artificial lake created by the erection of a causeway across the AVON RIVER in 1970–1. It is a Mi'kmaq descriptive, traced by Silas T. Rand to *Pisiquid*, the 'place where the tidal flow forks.' Approved by the CPCGN on 14 July 1971.

Petit Anse   *See* Grande Anse.

Petit Etang   *See* Grand Etang.

Petit-de-Grat (Richmond)   On the southeast coast of CAPE BRETON ISLAND. This place name is a reminder of the early Basque presence in the area. According to E.R. Seary, *degrat* is a Basque word that refers to the stage where the fish were landed and the platform on which they were dried. Nearby may be found Petit-de-Grat Island, Petit-de-Grat Shoal, Basque Island, and Basque

Shoal. On an ecclesiastical visit in 1814, Bishop Joseph-Octave Plessis (1763–1825) noted in this area Le Barachois des Basques, a place name that has disappeared. In common with ARICHAT, Petit-de-Grat was a base for Channel Island fishing and mercantile interests. See also JANVRIN ISLAND, and CAPE DÉGRAT, Newfoundland.

Petite Rivière (Lunenburg) Flows into Green Bay. Named by Samuel de Champlain in 1604. Later in the century the area was visited by Nicolas Denys (1598–1688), who described 'the little river' as located in 'a beautiful and very excellent region.' Today, only the spelling remains as a legacy from France, for local usage has corrupted the pronunciation to 'Pateet Reveer.'

Petit Passage   *See* Long Island.

Petpeswick Harbour; Petpeswick Inlet (Halifax)   The community is south of MUSQUODOBOIT HARBOUR, on Petpeswick Inlet. Derived from a Mi'kmaq word *Koolpijwik*. Over time, the first syllable was left off and the name Port Piswick evolved into Petpeswick. The contemporary spelling dates from the establishment of the post office in 1879.

Petpeswick Inlet   *See* Petpeswick Harbour.

Pictou (shiretown of Pictou County)   Fronts onto Pictou Harbour, an arm of the NORTHUMBERLAND STRAIT. The name is of Mi'kmaq origin and is traceable to *Piktook* or *Piktuk*, for an 'explosion' or 'fire.' One of the oldest place names on the north shore of Nova Scotia, it is listed by Nicolas Denys (1598–1688) in 1660 as *La rivière de Pictou*. There is a distinct possibility that the place name may predate European settlement. This area ia a prime location for sightings of the 'phantom ship of the NORTHUMBERLAND STRAIT.' Thus the Mi'kmaq reference to 'fire' may allude to the appearance of a fireball on the water, a documented precursor of the 'phantom ship.' In 1763 a land grant was made to the Philadelphia Company, whose first settlers arrived from Pennsylvania on the brigantine *Betsey* four years later. Then followed the first wave of Highland Scots, on the *Hector*. This ship arrived from Loch Broom, Scotland, on 15 September 1773. For the next half-century, Pictou became the entry point for thousands of Scottish immigrants who went on to populate north COLCHESTER, Pictou, and ANTIGONISH counties. Because of its historical significance, a replica of the *Hector* is now under construction as the focal point for the Hector Heritage Quay on Pictou's waterfront. Shortly after the first settlement, a determined effort was made to replace the original name. The following were put forward as substitutes: Coleraine, New Paisley, Alexandria, Donegal, Teignmouth, Southampton, and Walmsley. None of the suggested replacements had local associations, and the Mi'kmaq 'Pictou' was to outlive them all. Pictou's Scottish heritage is enshrined in the Hector National Exhibit Centre and nearby Sherbrooke Cottage (1806), once the home of Dr. Thomas McCulloch (1776–1843), founder of Pictou Academy (1816) and first president of Dalhousie University (1838–1843). McCulloch's campaign for nonsectarian higher education, along with his scientific and literary achievements, earned him an important place in the history of Nova Scotia. The town was incorporated in 1887.

Pictou County   The area which eventually became Pictou County was a part of HALIFAX COUNTY from 1759 to 1835. Named for the town, it was elevated to the status of a county by provincial statute in 1835.

Pictou Island (Pictou)   In the NORTHUMBERLAND STRAIT, northeast of CARIBOU. The name, for the town of Pictou, was assigned by the DesBarres survey in the 1760s. The island was first settled in 1814 by four Irish families, followed in 1819 by a series of migrations from the Scottish Highlands. Unfortunately, ancient Celtic rivalries led to local feuds, and the Irish families moved away. More Scottish settlers, principally from the islands of Mull and Tiree, arrived in the 1820s and 1830s, thus preserving the Scottish character of the island community. For several generations these settlers and their descendants carried on the largely self-sufficient life of the Highlands. However, almost total dependence on the fishery and subsistence agriculture, combined with the isolation of a largely ice-bound island during the winter, led to considerable out-migration. Since 1921, when there was a peak of 227 people, there has been a steady decline in population. Today only a handful of year-round residents live on Pictou Island.

Piedmont (Pictou)   Southeast of MERIGOMISH. Named by the Reverend Dugald McKeichan, the first clergyman in the area. It describes the location of the community, at the foot of a range of hills. It is based on the French *pied-mont*, literally 'foot mountain,' or 'at the foot of the mountain.' For a time it was known as 'Piedmont Valley'; however, the shorter name prevailed.

Pinkneys Point (Yarmouth) Forms the eastern side of Chebogue Harbour. Named for John Pinkney, a second-generation New England Planter, who settled there in 1777.

Pinnacle Island   *See* Five Islands.

Pipers Cove (Cape Breton); **Pipers Glen** (Inverness)   Pipers Cove is located east of BARRA STRAIT, on the north side of BRAS D'OR LAKE. Norman MacNeil, official piper to the chief of Clan MacNeil, emigrated from Barra to Pictou in 1802, moving to CAPE BRETON the following year. The place name proclaims his prowess as a piper. Pipers Glen, northeast of LAKE AINSLIE, was also named for a piper of fame, Neil Jamieson. Near Pipers Glen is Egypt Falls, reached at the end of a hiking trail. According to local lore it was so named when a farmer, Ira Hart, divided his property among his five sons. All received adjacent lands, except one, who had to travel some distance and was said 'to have gone down to Egypt' for his inheritance.

Pipers Glen   *See* Pipers Cove.

Pleasant Bay (Inverness)   Northeast of CHETICAMP. Before the adoption of the present descriptive in 1871, this community was known as 'Grand Anse,' and later as 'Limbo Cove.' There was a certain appropriateness in the latter name as the area was approachable only by sea until the 1930s. On 15 October 1932, the Cabot Trail through to CAPE NORTH was opened, ending over a century of isolation. During the early twentieth century, Pleasant Bay was often snowbound during the winter months, and the only access by land was on foot or by snowshoe.

Plymouth (Pictou)   Adjacent to Stellarton. This community was named for Plymouth, England. It achieved tragic recognition at 5:18 A.M. Saturday, 9 May 1992, when a massive explosion 350 metres underground wrecked the Westray coal mine. Despite heroic efforts on the part of draegermen, the death toll stood at twenty-six miners. When rescue efforts were terminated, eleven bodies remained underground. See also STELLARTON.

Plympton (Digby)   On ST. MARYS BAY. This area was formerly known as 'Everette Settlement.' The name was changed about

1864 on the suggestion of native son Judge Alfred Savary (1831–1920). The Savary family was Loyalist and had lived in Plympton, Massachusetts, prior to the American Revolution. The name can be traced to a town in Devon, England.

Pockwock; Pockwock Lake (Halifax)   At the south end of lake of the same name. The name is derived from the Mi'kmaq *Pogwek*, translated as 'smoky' or 'dry lake.' In 1974, 38,400 hectares of watershed were expropriated, and the lake became a reservoir, the major source of water for Metropolitan HALIFAX.

Pockwock Lake   *See* Pockwock.

Point Aconi (Cape Breton)   A descriptive suggested by the sharp, needle-like promontory that juts into the Atlantic, north of SYDNEY MINES. The name is taken from the Greek *aconi*, for 'dart.' On the *Plan de L'isle Royale* of 1751, the location is called *Pt. aux Canets*.

Pointe-de-l'Église   *See* Church Point.

Point Edward (Cape Breton)   On the Northwest Arm of SYDNEY harbour. Named in the 1790s for Prince Edward, Duke of Kent (1767–1820), father of Queen

Victoria. He served as commander of the British forces in Nova Scotia from 1794 to 1800.

Point Tupper (Richmond) Adjacent to PORT HAWKESBURY, on the STRAIT OF CANSO. This place name has been erroneously attributed to Sir Charles Tupper (1821–1915), pre-1867 premier of Nova Scotia, a leading Father of Confederation, and briefly prime minister of Canada in 1896. Recent research by John Sarre, a Guernsey historian, proves that it was named for Ferdinand Brock Tupper, who received a land grant in the area on 5 February 1824. Tupper, a nephew of Sir Isaac Brock (1769–1820), the hero of the battle of Queenston Heights in 1812, wanted the location named Brock Point; however, the lieutenant-governor, Sir James Kempt, issued a proclamation on 2 April 1824 assigning the name Point Tupper. Tupper was a native of Guernsey and served as the agent for the Channel Island–owned Arichat and Gaspé Society at ARICHAT before moving to Point Tupper (see JANVRIN ISLAND). Prior to the completion of the Canso Causeway in 1955, this was the terminus of the railway ferry across the Strait of Canso.

Pomquet (Antigonish) East of ANTIGONISH. Originally a Mi'kmaq word variously rendered as *Popumkek* and *Pogomkooigitk*. The French spelling, 'Pomquette,' was gradually shortened to 'Pomquet.' The name is a descriptive and refers to 'a sand beach' or a 'good place for landing.' The first Acadian settlers came in 1762 by way of St. Malo, France. Following the expulsion, they had been exiled to France; however, having once experienced the freedom of the New World, they were not content to remain overseas. Since their former lands were now occupied, they were forced to relocate. The first settlers were members of five families: Bourque, Broussard, Daigle, Lamarre, and Vincent – names still to be found among the Acadian population.

Ponhook Lake (Queens) Northeast of LAKE ROSSIGNOL, near Highway 8. The name is of Mi'kmaq origin and is derived from *Bahnook* or *Ponhook*. It refers to 'the first lake in a chain.' There is also a lake in HALIFAX COUNTY with a similar origin. See also LAKE BANOOK.

Portapique (Colchester) On COBEQUID BAY, east of BASS RIVER. Site of an Acadian village prior to 1755. The name is derived from the French *porcépic*, for 'porcupine.' On the Morris survey map, it is rendered as *Ville Porcapic*, later to be anglicized as 'Portapique.' Following the expulsion, the area was resettled by Ulster Scottish immigrants from both Ireland and New Hampshire.

Port Bickerton (Guysborough) On the eastern shore of GUYSBOROUGH COUNTY, near COUNTRY HARBOUR. Honours Sir Richard Hussey Bickerton (1759–1832), who served as British naval commander on the West Indies and Newfoundland station in 1794. The post office dates from 1876.

Port Clyde   *See* Clyde River.

Port Dufferin (Halifax)   East of SHEET HARBOUR. First known as 'Salmon River.' The name of this community east of Sheet Harbour was changed in 1899 by act of the legislature to honour Frederick Blackwood, first Marquis of Dufferin and Ava (1826–1902). He served as governor general of Canada from 1872 to 1878.

Port Felix (Guysborough) Southwest of CANSO. The area was first named Molasses Harbour. According to local legend the name referred to a keg of molasses which once washed ashore. In 1869 it was changed by an act of the legislature to honour the Reverend Felix Van Blerk, the popular parish priest. He was a native of Belgium and a member of the Trappist Order.

Port George (Annapolis)   Settled by members of the Oldham Gates family, who were part of the New England Planter migration to the ANNAPOLIS area in the 1760s. The first name for the locality was Gates Breakwater; however, this was changed, in keeping with the pro-British sympathies of the family, to honour King George III (1738–1820). A prime location on the BAY OF FUNDY was to lead to the opening of a shipyard. Ironically, the first vessel to be built at Port George ended its days as a privateer and was captured by the Americans in the War of 1812.

Port Greville   *See* Greville Bay.

Port Hastings (Inverness)   The CAPE BRETON terminus for the Canso Causeway, opened in 1955. At one time known as 'Plaster Cove,' for deposits of gypsum found in the area; the name was changed by act of the legislature in 1869. It was renamed in honour of Sir Charles Hastings Doyle (1804–1883), who served as lieutenant-governor of Nova Scotia from 1867 to 1873.

Port Hawkesbury (Inverness) On the STRAIT OF CANSO. Formerly called Ship Harbour. This area was first developed as a shipbuilding and trading centre by Guernsey native Nicholas Paint, Jr. (1790–1832). In 1817 he requested and received, on behalf of the Guernsey merchant firm of Thoume, Moullin & Company, a grant of land and adjacent water lots at Ship Harbour (Sarre). The extent of trade undertaken by Channel Island firms can be seen in their ports of call. These covered a great circle route: from Cape Breton, the West Indies, South America, the Mediterranean, the Channel Islands, North Sea ports, and back to Cape Breton. The community name was changed by an act of the legislature in 1860 to avoid confusion with another Ship Harbour in HALIFAX COUNTY. However, Ship Harbour remains on the map as the name for the harbour. The new name honoured Charles Jenkinson, first Baron Hawkesbury (1727–1808), who served as president of the Board of Trade in the British cabinet. The town was incorporated in 1889. Until 1955 Port Hawkesbury was the Cape Breton terminus of the highway ferry that linked Cape Breton with the mainland.

Port Hood; Port Hood Island (shiretown of Inverness)   Southwest of MABOU. Known to the French as 'Juste au Corps,' loosely translated: 'up to the waist.' This unusual place name was a satiri-cal reference to the lack of a wharf. This meant that those coming ashore had to wade waist deep in the water. For a time Juste au Corps was the name of the electoral district, until it was renamed Inverness in 1837. The community name was changed by DesBarres, during the course of his survey of Cape Breton, to honour Admiral Samuel Hood (1724–1816), who became Viscount Hood in 1796. Port Hood Island, located offshore, was first named in 1786 Smiths Island, for Loyalist Captain David Smith, from Cape Cod, Massachusetts. The island is still occupied, generations later, by a direct descendant. Perhaps the most famous member of the family was Dr. Sydney Smith (1897–1959), president of the University of Toronto from 1945 to 1957 when he entered the federal cabinet as minister of External Affairs. Adjacent Henry Island was also named by DesBarres for Henry Hood, son of Admiral Hood. During the French colonial period, stone from quarries on Port Hood Island was used in the construction of Fortress Louisbourg. See also INVERNESS.

Port Hood Island   *See* Port Hood.

Port Howe (Cumberland)   On the west side of the RIVER PHILIP.

This place name has been attributed to Admiral Lord Howe (1726–1799), once British naval commander-in-chief on the North American station. Since the name was assigned by an act of the legislature in 1883, it seems more likely that it marks the career of Joseph Howe (1804–1873), advocate of responsible government, premier and later lieutenant-governor of Nova Scotia. Howe served as MLA for CUMBERLAND COUNTY (1851–5).

Port Joli; Port Joli Point (Queens) Off Highway 103, near the SHELBURNE COUNTY boundary. Listed as *St Catherines River* (a name still found in the area) on the Lalanne map of 1684. However, the name Port Joli is much older, and was assigned by the Du Gua de Monts expedition in 1604. Although early maps are unreliable, it would appear that the same location was called *Baya Formose* by the Portuguese, and *Le Beau Baia* by the Spanish, both close in meaning to the French version. It was settled by New England Planters in the 1760s.

Port Joli Point   *See* Port Joli.

Port Latour (Shelburne)   Southeast of BARRINGTON. This place name, the site of Fort St. Louis (later Fort La Tour), is a lasting reminder of the amazing career of Charles de Saint-Etienne de La Tour (1593–1666), adventurer, trader, and colonizer. La Tour came to Acadia while in his teens, and for a time lived a nomadic life, marrying a Mi'kmaq and pursuing the fur trade. The vendetta between La Tour and his arch-rival, Charles de Menou d'Aulnay (*ca* 1604–1650), for control of the fur trade in Acadia not only dominated events in the colony between 1632 and 1654, but incorporated all the elements of *opéra bouffe*. Bungling Paris bureaucrats, ignorant of local geography, added vague territorial and political definitions to the controversy. In 1635, La Tour moved his headquarters from Fort La Tour to SAINT JOHN, in 'd'Aulnay territory,' while the latter retained control of posts at LAHAVE and PORT ROYAL, in 'La Tour territory.' There then followed a series of skirmishes, ambushes, fort-stormings, and intrigues without number. The climax came with the death of La Tour's second wife, Françoise-Marie Jacquelin (1602–1645), following her gallant defence of the Saint John fort in his absence; the death of d'Aulnay, following a near-drowning incident at Port Royal; and the *mariage de convenance* between La Tour and d'Aulnay's widow, subsequently to be blessed by five children. La Tour has been characterized by historian George MacBeath as 'a controversial figure, ambitious and the possessor of great natural ability and determination, a born leader with the happy faculty of making friends. His associations with the French court, Boston merchants, and d'Aulnay's widow, if not d'Aulnay, testify to his diplomatic persuasiveness. The pages of Acadia's history are much richer for his presence.'

Port Lorne   *See* Lorne.

Port Maitland   *See* Maitland.

Port Medway   *See* Medway.

Port Morien   *See* Cape Morien.

Port Mouton; Port Mouton Head; Port Mouton Island (Queens) The community is on Highway 103; the island is directly offshore. This name was bestowed by Du Gua de Monts in 1604 'because here a sheep [mouton] was drowned, recovered, and eaten by the company.' The name Port Mouton has prevailed over the years despite efforts to impose others. It was designated St. Lukes Bay in 1623 for the name of a ship which brought Scottish colonists recruited by Sir William Alexander (*ca* 1602–1638) to Nova Scotia. Later, in the 1770s, surveyor J.F.W. DesBarres attempted to rename it Gambier Bay, for

Admiral James Gambier (1756–1833), then naval commander-in-chief of the North American station. However, neither suggestion gained acceptance, and the earlier French name lives on, although pronounced locally as 'Port Matoon.'

Port Mouton Head   *See* Port Mouton.

Port Mouton Island   *See* Port Mouton.

Port Philip; River Philip (Cumberland)   The river rises in the COBEQUID MOUNTAINS and flows into the NORTHUMBERLAND STRAIT, at PORT HOWE and Port Philip. The name is mentioned in Haliburton's *History of Nova Scotia* and may be traced to an early settler 'named Philip to whom with others, a grant of land was made in 1785.' The community was first known as 'Mouth of River Philip'; the shortened form, Port Philip, was enacted by the legislature in 1867.

Portree (Inverness)   On the northeast MARGAREE RIVER. Named for Portree, on the Isle of Skye. The name can be traced to the Gaelic *port righe*, for 'royal harbour,' a reference to a sixteenth-century visit to the Scottish port by King James V. An unsuccessful attempt was made in the late nineteenth century to rename the community Kingsburgh.

Port Royal (Annapolis; Richmond)   The ANNAPOLIS COUNTY community is part of the district so named by Samuel de Champlain in 1604 (see ANNAPOLIS ROYAL). In 1949 the name was officially adopted for the immediate area surrounding the replica of Champlain's Habitation. Thus an original French designation was restored, replacing the name Lower Granville, which dated from the 1760s. The RICHMOND COUNTY Port Royal is located northwest of ARICHAT, on ISLE MADAME. It was adopted by provincial statute in 1867 in place of the name Grand Ruisseau.

Port Shoreham (Guysborough) On the shore of CHEDABUCTO BAY. Early names for this community were Ragged Head and Clam Harbour. The original Mi'kmaq name was *Assugadich*, which meant 'clam ground.' In 1901 a petition was passed by the Nova Scotia legislature 'that the name of Clam Harbour ... be changed to Port Shoreham.' The reason was 'the obvious confusion caused by the existence of a better known Clam Harbour in Halifax county.' Port Shoreham (after Shoreham in Sussex, England) is the ancestral home of Charles Bruce (1906–

1971), noted Canadian poet and novelist. His novels, *Channel Shore* and *The Township of Time*, along with an award-winning collection of poems, *The Mulgrave Road*, were largely inspired by his early life in Port Shoreham. Harry Bruce, his son, has also written eloquently about the same area in the semi-biographical *Down Home*.

Port Wade (Annapolis)   On the north side of ANNAPOLIS BASIN. The site of the Acadian community of Pré des Bourgeois. It was known as 'West Ferry' until 1905. The name was then changed to honour the local member of Parliament, Fletcher Bath Wade (1852–1905).

Port Williams (Kings)   Northwest of WOLFVILLE. The earlier name was Terrys Creek, for a New England Planter family that settled here in the 1760s. In August 1856, at a public meeting, the new name was selected to commemorate the career of General Sir William Fenwick Williams (1800–1883). A native of ANNAPOLIS ROYAL, Williams achieved fame during the Crimean War (1853–6) and later served as lieutenant-governor of Nova Scotia (1865–7). See also FENWICK, KARSDALE, and WILLIAMSDALE.

Preston (Halifax)   Northeast of DARTMOUTH. Probably named for Preston in Lancashire, England, this community was settled by a group of black Loyalists following the American Revolution. In 1796 a group of Maroons (slaves and descendants of escaped slaves) were expelled from Jamaica and settled in Preston. Their tenure was short-lived, and many moved on to Sierra Leone in 1800. Following the War of 1812, a third group of black immigrants came to the province from the United States, many of whom settled in this area. In 1993 the provincial constituency of Preston was created. In the ensuing election, Wayne Adams, the first black MLA in Nova Scotia history, was elected. He was later named to cabinet as minister of Supply and Services and now serves as minister of the Environment.

Princeport (Colchester); **Princes Lodge** (Halifax)   Princes Lodge, on the shore of BEDFORD BASIN, takes its name from Prince Edward, Duke of Kent (1767–1872), who lived on the estate while commander of the British forces in Nova Scotia, 1794 to 1800. The Lodge was a favoured retreat of the prince and his consort, Thérèse-Bernadine Montgenet (1760–1830), who was also known as Madame Julie St. Laurent. Later, the prince, 'for reasons of state,' was forced to set her aside and marry a German noblewoman, Victoria Maria Louisa, Princess of Saxe-Coburg. Their daughter was to ascend the throne as Queen Victoria. In addition to the place name, there are two other reminders of this famous royal romance. The round, domed music room of the estate still stands, and the heart-shaped pond created by the prince for Julie can also be seen. One section, including the pond, has been set aside as the Hemlock Ravine Conservation Area. It is a unique example of a relatively undisturbed forest ecosystem within a metropolitan area. See also ROCKINGHAM, and TELEGRAPH HILL, New Brunswick. Princeport is located on the east bank of the SHUBENACADIE RIVER. It marks the visit of another Prince Edward, later King Edward VII (1841–1910), the eldest son of Queen Victoria, who visited Nova Scotia in 1860.

Princes Lodge   *See* Princeport.

Prospect (Halifax; Kings)   The first is southwest of HALIFAX, between PEGGYS COVE and TERENCE BAY. In referring to this location, first named by the Mi'kmaq, Nicolas Denys (1598–1688) noted: 'This place is called *Passepec*. Along the sea coast there is nothing but rocks, which are all bald for the space of four or five leagues.' Although the topography has changed but little in the intervening centuries, this place name, of unknown meaning, has evolved into the very English-sounding Prospect. The KINGS COUNTY Prospect, located southeast of WATERVILLE, is descriptive of its location on the SOUTH MOUNTAIN.

Pubnico (Yarmouth)   Southeast of YARMOUTH. There are at least fifteen distinct communities that incorporate the name Pubnico. One of the oldest European settlements in the province, this area was included in the barony of Pobomcoup granted to Philippe Mius d'Entremont (*ca* 1601–1700) in 1653 by Charles de Saint-Étienne de La Tour (1593–1666). The Pubnicos escaped the first wave of expulsion in 1755; their turn came in 1758–9. A few people escaped deportation and, because these particular Acadian lands were never occupied by others, the majority of the exiled returned in the 1760s. The name is derived from the Mi'kmaq *Pogomkook*, of uncertain meaning. The earliest French form was Pobomcoup, from which the modern spelling has evolved. The barony remained in the d'Entremont family until the expulsion; after more than three centuries, some one hundred families of this

name may be counted in the Pubnicos. Simon d'Entremont (1788–1886), from West Pubnico, was elected MLA for ARGYLE in 1836, one of the first two Acadians to achieve this honour. A second Acadian, Frédéric Robicheau (*ca* 1786–1863), was also elected in ANNAPOLIS; however, he was ill and missed the swearing-in ceremony of the fifteenth Assembly on 31 January 1837. Robicheau was unable to take his seat until the next session, thus making d'Entremont the first Acadian legislator.

Pugwash (Cumberland)   On the NORTHUMBERLAND STRAIT. This name is traceable to the Mi'kmaq *Pagweak*, meaning 'shallow water or shoal.' This later evolved as Pugwash. In 1826 the press noted that there was a move 'to change [this] uncouth name to Waterford'; however, the attempt failed, and the original designation survived. It the mid-twentieth century, the name Pugwash achieved worldwide significance when the village became the site for native son Cyrus Eaton's (1883–1979) 'Thinker's Conferences,' designed to foster peace and understanding between the then USSR and the West and to seek an end to nuclear proliferation. The Pugwash Movement, funded by multi-millionaire industrialist and humanitarian Eaton, remains active, promoting the ideals of global cooperation in a world that still finds it lacking. In 1995 formal international recognition came when the Nobel Peace Prize was awarded to nuclear physicist Joseph Rotblat and the Pugwash Movement for its long campaign against nuclear weapons. Rotblat, along with Albert Einstein (1879–1955) and Bertrand Russell (1872–1970), was one of the signatories of the original anti-nuclear manifesto that led to the first Pugwash Conference sponsored by Eaton in 1957. Thus, an ancient Mi'kmaq word lives on as an international synonym for peace.

Quaker Island (Lunenburg)   In MAHONE BAY. Among the New England emigrants to Nova Scotia in the 1760s were several groups of Quakers from the whaling towns of Massachusetts, principally Nantucket and New Bedford. Areas where they settled included BARRINGTON, CAPE SABLE ISLAND, and DARTMOUTH. It was also their intent to establish a fishery on this island; however, having been unable to secure title to it, they abandoned the scheme and returned home. The place name remains as a legacy.

Queens County   On 21 July 1762, by a minute of the Nova Scotia executive council, 'the townships of Liverpool, Barrington and Yarmouth [were] erected into a county to be called Queens.' When SHELBURNE COUNTY was established in 1784 (and included Yarmouth and Barrington townships, along with the new township of Shelburne), the present boundaries of Queens County came into effect. The name was selected as an expression of loyalty to the monarchy.

Queensland (Halifax)   East of HUBBARDS, on ST. MARGARETS BAY. It was named for Queen Victoria (1819–1901) shortly after her accession to the throne on 20 June 1837.

Queensport (Guysborough)   On CHEDABUCTO BAY. First known as 'Crow Harbour.' The name was changed by a 1898 provincial statute to mark the Diamond Jubilee of Queen Victoria, celebrated the previous year.

Queensville (Inverness)   North of PORT HAWKESBURY. It was named for Queen Victoria's Silver Jubilee in 1862. The post office dates from 1865.

Quinan (Yarmouth)   Once called Tusket Forks for its location on the TUSKET RIVER. The name was changed 15 May 1885 to commemorate the career of the Reverend John L. Quinan, who served the local parish from 1860 to 1868.

Quoddy Harbour; West Quoddy Harbour (Halifax)   This name, found in several forms between PORT DUFFERIN and MOSER RIVER on the eastern shore of HALIFAX COUNTY, is a corruption of the Mi'kmaq *Noodaakwade*, for 'the seal hunting place.' Variations over the centuries have included Noody Quaday, Noody Quodoy and, Quoddy. Settlement in the area dates from the 1820s.

Rainbow Haven (Halifax) On the western shore of Cole Harbour, southeast of DART-MOUTH. The name originated with a summer camp for under-privileged children incorporated in 1921 by the *Halifax Herald*. The driving force behind the endeav-our was a *Herald* reporter, Laura P. Carten. Her popular children's column, written under the pseud-onym Farmer Smith, was called 'The Rainbow Club.' Rainbow Haven Provincial Park is located nearby.

Rawdon (Hants) Originally a township and later a community name in central HANTS COUNTY. It was first settled by Loyalist sol-diers and their dependents, who served under Lord Francis Raw-don-Hastings, second Earl of Moira (1754–1826), during the American Revolution. Lord Raw-don was the commander of the British army in the American South during the siege of Fort Ninety Six in South Carolina. He was responsible for the rescue of those inside the fort, a fact never to be forgotten by them. The sol-diers, who had been drawn largely from this immediate area, were evacuated to Charlestown and quartered in a temporary camp named Rawdon. Later they were conveyed to their lands in Nova Scotia, and the crown grant for the township of Rawdon was registered on 3 August 1784. For a period in the nineteenth century, gold was mined in the area; how-ever, the deposits were soon exploited. See also SELMA.

Rear ...   Use of 'rear' as part of a place name is common in CAPE BRETON and the eastern Nova Scotia mainland, and to a lesser extent on Prince Edward Island. It indicates the 'back section of the settlement, or those lands gener-ally less advantageously located.' These names have not been included in the text; see the main entry for origin of each.

Reserve Mines (Cape Breton) Between GLACE BAY and SYDNEY. The name evolved from the fact that the General Mining Associa-tion which once owned all coal in Cape Breton, held certain coal fields in reserve for future operations. Mining in this area began in 1872; the Reserve Mines post office opened in 1873.

Richmond County   Named for Charles Lennox, fourth Duke of Richmond, who served briefly (1818–19), as governor general of Canada. Described as a 'broken down nobleman,' he is best remembered for the numerous locations named for him in Ontario, Quebec, and the Maritimes. The Duke died of hydrophobia, contracted from the bite of a pet fox, on 28 August 1819, near Richmond, in eastern Ontario. In 1835, by provincial statute, the former southern district of Cape Breton was set apart as Richmond County. See also MAITLAND.

Rissers Beach (Lunenburg) Fronts on Green Bay. Originally settled by members of the Rieser (Risser) family who were part of the Foreign Protestant emigration from southwestern Germany to the LUNENBURG area in 1753. Site of Rissers Beach Provincial Park, with an interesting interpretative centre and marsh boardwalk.

River Bourgeois (Richmond) Near ST. PETERS. Known first as 'Rivière à Bourgeois.' Members of the Bourgeois family, a common Acadian surname, were among the first settlers. During the French regime, lumber and firewood were shipped from here to Fortress Louisbourg. The Guernsey firm of Thoume, Moullin & Company was active at River Bourgeois during the early nineteenth century. The post office dates from 1838.

River Denys; River Denys Basin (Inverness)   The river flows into the basin, an inlet at the southeastern end of BRAS D'OR LAKE. The attribution of this place name to Nicolas Denys (1595–1688) has been questioned; however, the evidence, along with his importance in the history of Cape Breton, indicates that the river was probably named *after* him, but not *by* him. The confusion arises because Denys did rename Rivière des Espagnols (later SYDNEY) as La R. Denys, after himself. The latter name was never in common usage. On the River Denys Mountain Road (which linked the communities on the Bras d'Or with JUDIQUE), is St. Margaret of Scotland Church, once the centre a thriving community. It stands today as a memorial to the dozens of lost Scottish Highland communities which dotted the interior of INVERNESS COUNTY. On the Sunday before Labour Day each summer, a Mass is said to honour the indomitable pioneers who lived here during the nineteenth and early twentieth centuries.

River Hébert (Cumberland) The village is on the river, which flows into Cumberland basin. The river was named for Louis Hébert, a member of the Du Gua de Monts expedition to Acadia in 1604. An apothecary by profession, he was interested in herb culture and farming and deserves the title of first Canadian farmer. While at PORT ROYAL, he treated both Mi'kmaq and French patients, ministering to Chief Membertou in his last illness. Later he was to settle at Québec, where he continued his interest in agriculture. He died there 25 January 1727.

River John   *See* Cape John.

River Philip   *See* Port Philip.

Riverport (Lunenburg)   On the east side of the LAHAVE RIVER. First known as 'Henrici's Cove.' Among the early settlers was Captain Johan Philip Henrici, a member of the Foreign Protestant migration to LUNENBURG. Over time, the Henrici family name became known as 'Ritcey,' and the village 'Ritcey's Cove.' The place name was changed by provincial statute in 1904 to Riverport, a descriptive.

Rockingham (Halifax)   A district of HALIFAX, located on the west side of BEDFORD BASIN. In 1795, Prince Edward, Duke of Kent, erected a barracks on the edge of the Prince's Lodge estate, which he had leased from Governor Wentworth. It housed two companies of his regiment, the 7th Foot, or Royal Fusiliers. Following his return to England in 1800, the property reverted to Wentworth, who converted one of the barracks to an inn. This hostelry was home to the Rockingham Club, a men's dining-club that attracted the Halifax élite. Later the building became known as the 'Rockingham Inn,' serving the community until its destruction by fire in 1833. This name, eventually to be that of the community, was selected by Wentworth as a tribute to Charles Watson-Wentworth, second Marquis of Rockingham (1730–1782). See also PRINCES LODGE.

Rodney (Cumberland)   Southeast of SPRINGHILL. It was named for George Brydes Rodney, first Baron Rodney (1719–1792), an eighteenth-century naval hero who served as governor of Newfoundland from 1748 to 1752. The post office dates from 1891.

Roman Valley (Guysborough) Between Guysborough Intervale and the boundary with ANTIGON-

ISH COUNTY. This area was settled in the 1820s by Irish immigrants from Newfoundland. Since they were Roman Catholics, the community received the name Roman Valley.

Rose Bay (Lunenburg)   Southwest of LUNENBURG harbour. The name may be a corruption of Ross Bay; however, it is more likely a descriptive for the prevalence of wild roses in the summer. On 3 June 1794, the brig *Falmouth*, bound for Belfast, Ireland, anchored in the bay. The master, William Corran, who was accused of murdering a passenger, was landed and later conveyed to Halifax. He was tried by the Admiralty Court, found guilty, and, on 22 July 1794, was executed by hanging in Point Pleasant Park.

Roseway   *See* Cape Roseway.

Roseway Beach   *See* Cape Roseway.

Roseway River   *See* Cape Roseway.

Rossignol River   *See* Lake Rossignol.

Round Hill (Annapolis)   On the Annapolis River, east of MOCHELLE. The area was once known as 'La Rosette,' after the nickname of Jacques Léger, a French drummer from the Port Royal garrison. Later it was replaced by a French descriptive Pré Ronde, or 'Round Meadow,' because the meadow at the base of a nearby hill formed a horseshoe-shaped bend in the Dauphin (later Annapolis) River. Following the expulsion in 1755, the New England Planters renamed the community Round Hill.

Sable Island (Halifax)   Lies 300 kilometres south–southeast of HALIFAX. Known to mariners for centuries as 'the graveyard of the Atlantic.' A crescent-shaped series of sand-dune ridges stretching from east to west, it is the only visible portion of the Continental Shelf. (Note comments on Sable Bank, encircling the island, in chapter 1, pages 13–15.) The first recorded shipwreck on Sable Island occurred in 1583, when one of Sir Humphrey Gilbert's ships was claimed by the shoals that surround the island. In 1800, and shipwrecks without number later, Nova Scotia lieutenant-governor, Sir John Wentworth (1737–1820), called for 'an establishment on the Isle of Sable for the relief of the distressed and the preservation of property.' He pointed out that 'the facts furnish a melancholy account and a lamentable list of lives and property that have perished for want of assistance and relief; and that list [will] increase as navigation increases between the countries in Europe and America and from British America to the West Indies ... in the track of which the Isle of Sable lies.' On the basis of this appeal, a rescue station was established, to be supplemented by two manned lighthouses erected in 1873. Following automation of the lighthouses in the 1960s, federal meterological and navigation personnel, supplemented by members of scientific expeditions in the summer, account for the present population of Sable Island. See also CAPE SABLE ISLAND and WALLACE.

St. Alphonse (Digby)   Part of this community, south of METEGHAN, on ST. MARYS BAY, was once known as 'Cheticamp'; the other section, 'Bear Cove.' In order to avoid postal confusion with CHETICAMP, CAPE BRETON, a merger took place between the community and parish names early in the twentieth century, and for a time it was known as 'St. Alphonse de Clare.' The church had been named St. Alphonse in honour of the Reverend Alphonse Benoit Côté, of Meteghan, who was responsible for the erection of the building. In recent years, St. Alphonse has become the official community name.

St. Andrews Channel (Cape Breton)   This division of BRAS D'OR LAKE was named, along with St. Georges Channel (Richmond) and St. Patricks Channel (Victoria), in honour of the patron saints of Scotland, England, and Ireland.

St. Anns; St. Anns Bay (Victoria) The village is at the head of St. Anns Bay. This name first appears as a result of Samuel de Champlain's exploration in 1604 and has persisted to this day. It is currently listed in the *Nova Scotia Gazetteer* as St. Anns, not Ste. Anne. Nicolas Denys (1598–1688) described the location in the 1660s: 'The Harbour of Sainte-Anne is good and very spacious. Vessels of three or four hundred tons can enter at all tides. ' Following the end of the French colonial empire, the area was settled by Sutherlandshire Scots. Famous among these was the charismatic and indefatigable Reverend Norman McLeod (1780–1866), who led a group of his followers (known as Normanites) from Scotland to Loch Broom, near Pictou, and from there to St. Anns in 1820. In 1851, McLeod uprooted his flock again to relocate at Waipu, about 80 kilometres north of Auckland, New Zealand. Here he lies buried among his followers, whose tombstones proudly list the various parishes once known as

'home': Assynt, Lochalsh, Apple-
cross, Skye, and Harris, in Scotland; St. Anns, BADDECK, and
BOULARDERIE, in Nova Scotia.

St. Anns Bay   *See* St. Anns.

St. Bernard (Digby)   Adjacent to
WEYMOUTH. The community name
is taken from that of the local
parish. The present cathedral-like
St. Bernard's Church was begun
in 1910 by Reverend Edouard
LeBlanc (1870–1935). On 10
December 1912, he was named
Bishop of Saint John, the first
Acadian elevated to episcopal
rank. Built of SHELBURNE granite,
which was transported to the site
by rail and ox-cart. After thirty-
two years of construction, the
debt-free church was consecrated
on 24 September 1942.

St. Catherines River (Queens)
Near the entrance to the seaside
section of KEJIMKUJIK NATIONAL
PARK. The name of this small
stream dates from the seventeenth century and appears as
Rivière Ste. Catherine on the
Lalanne map of 1684. St. Catherines River Beach is a major nest-
ing area for the endangered
piping plover.

Ste. Anne du Ruisseau
(Yarmouth)   East of TUSKET.
Originally known as 'Eel Brook';
the name was an English transla-

tion of the original Mi'kmaq
descriptive. It was changed in the
1950s to conform to the name of
the local parish. *Ruisseau* is translated as 'a small brook.'

St. Georges Bay   *See* Cape
George.

St. Joseph du Moine (Inverness)
North of MARGAREE HARBOUR.
Part of the name may be traced to
nearby Cap Le Moine, a toponym
that is descriptive of the headland
and may be literally translated as
'Cape Friar.' The parish was separated from CHETICAMP in 1879
and was named in honour of St.
Joseph. The first settlers were
Acadians who relocated in the
area following the expulsion.
They were drawn largely from
the Chiasson, LeBlanc, Doucet,
and Aucoin families.

**St. Margarets Bay; Head of St.
Margarets Bay** (Halifax)   Lies 20
kilometres to the west of HALIFAX.
The name is traceable to Champlain's *Le Porte Saincte Marguerite*,
which survives in English translation as the name for this bay. The
community Head of St. Margarets
Bay was first settled by second-
generation Foreign Protestants
from LUNENBURG COUNTY. The
post office dates from 1860. See
also FRENCH VILLAGE.

St. Marys Bay (Digby)   Between DIGBY NECK, LONG ISLAND, BRIER ISLAND, and the mainland. Explored and named *La Baie Saincte Marie* by Samuel de Champlain in 1604.

St. Mary's Municipality (Guysborough)   By provincial statute passed in 1840, the western section of GUYSBOROUGH COUNTY was set aside as the township, later the municipality, of St. Mary's. The name originates with that of ST. MARYS RIVER. It has the distinction of retaining the apostrophe as part of its approved name.

St. Marys River (Guysborough) Enters the Atlantic 15 kilometres below Sherbrooke. The name originated with *Fort Saincte Marie*, established by the French adventurer Charles Baye de la Giraudière. The fort was captured by the English in 1669, and the name eventually became attached to the river. See also SHERBROOKE.

St. Paul Island (Victoria)   Some 18 kilometres off the northern tip of CAPE BRETON ISLAND. The name was first applied by Jacques Cartier in 1536 to the nearby headland now known as 'Cape North.' Over time the name became attached to the island offshore. From earliest days this island has attracted the attention of cartog-raphers, mariners, and writers because of its danger to navigation. In 1829, T.C. Haliburton called the island 'the fatal St. Paul, a barren and rocky isle, the precipitous shores of which have been the unseen grave of thousands.' Unfortunately, no action was taken until 1837 when two lighthouses and a life-saving station were erected.

St. Peter's (Richmond)   On Highway 104. Founded as a Portuguese fishing station (San Pedro) in 1521. The name has survived both time and translation. From 1650 onward, to 1713, it was known as 'St. Pierre.' Following the Treaty of Utrecht, the English form was imposed. During the mid-seventeenth century, the adventurer Nicolas Denys (1598–1688) established his headquarters at St. Peter's, until its destruction by fire in the winter of 1668–9. Although Denys was a merchant, explorer, and, for a time, 'governor of the coasts and islands of the Gulf of St. Lawrence from Canso to Gaspé as well as Newfoundland,' his niche in history was to be confirmed by a two-volume work, *Description géographique et historique des costes de l'Amérique septentrionale*, published in Paris in 1672. Nicolas Denys's vivid description of the topography of seventeenth-century Acadia has added greatly to our understanding of both the history and the toponymy of the region. See also BATHURST, New Brunswick.

Saltsprings (Pictou) On the Upper West River, near the foot of MOUNT THOM. It is a descriptive for the presence in the area of saline springs. The name occurs for the same reason in CUMBERLAND and ANTIGONISH counties.

Sambro; Sambro Head; Inner Sambro Island; Sambro Island (Halifax) Sambro is on Highway 349, southwest of HERRING COVE. Sambro Head (Cape Sambro) is 7 kilometres to the south. Inner Sambro and Sambro islands lie offshore. The name was first applied to the island and appears on Nicolas Denys's map as *Isle de Saint Cembro*. The feature was noted earlier by Samuel de Champlain, who explained that 'the name was given by people from Saint Malo.' Thus, it can be concluded that it is traceable to the island of Cèzembre, off St. Malo, France. Jean DeLabat renders Sambro Head as *'Cape St. Sembre*, a whitish rock bare of all verdue.' By 1698 the headland was being called Cap Sambre, and the transition to the anglicized Sambro was completed following the Treaty of Utrecht in 1713, when mainland Nova Scotia was ceded to England. The first lighthouse

was erected on Sambro Island in 1758.

Sambro Head *See* Sambro.

Sambro Island *See* Sambro.

Saulnierville (Digby) A coastal community north of METEGHAN. Among the first landholders were six Acadian families bearing the name Saulnier; hence, the place name. This surname is traceable to fifteenth- and sixteenth-century workers on the salterns, or saltworks, of Saintonge in southwest France. Over time they became known as 'sauniers,' later 'saulniers.' This expertise was carried overseas, and saulniers among others, were responsible for dyking the famous salt marshes of Acadia.

Scaterie Island (Cape Breton) Off MAIN-À-DIEU. Sometimes called 'Little Cape Breton,' this island has always posed a threat to navigation. Writing in 1829, T.C. Haliburton described it as 'a triangular island projecting two of its points to the Atlantic and the third toward Main-à-Dieu ... it is the most easterly dependency of Cape Breton and consequently of Nova Scotia.' Recent research by Miren Egaña Goya has confirmed the Basque origin of its name. She writes: '*Escatarai* is a common Basque noun to indicate a steep coast or a line of cliffs.' It can therefore be classified as descriptive of the local topography. The first lighthouse was erected on the island in 1839.

Scots Bay (Kings); **Scotsburn** (Pictou)   Scots Bay on the west side of CAPE BLOMIDON marks the fact that a group of Scottish immigrants were shipwrecked here in 1764. The name of Scotsburn, southwest of PICTOU, was adopted in 1867 to replace Rogers Hill. It was suggested by Hugh Ross, an early settler, in honour of his birthplace in Ross-shire, Scotland. The post office dates from 1874.

Scotsburn   *See* Scots Bay.

Seabright; (Halifax) **Seafoam**; (Pictou) **Seaforth**; (Halifax)   All three names were suggested by their location on the seacoast. Seabright, for a community on the west side of ST. MARGARETS BAY, was proclaimed by an act of the provincial legislature in 1902. Seafoam is exposed to the winds off the NORTHUMBERLAND STRAIT and is descriptive of their effect, especially during autumn storms. Seaforth faces the Atlantic Ocean near the mouth of CHEZ-ZETCOOK INLET. The post office was established in 1882.

Seafoam   *See* Seabright.

Seaforth   *See* Seabright.

Seal Island (Yarmouth)   A cluster of five small islands due west of CAPE SABLE ISLAND. Named *Îles aux Loups Martins* by Samuel de Champlain in 1604. The name has survived in its English translation for the largest island. As one recent lightkeeper, Chris Mills, expressed it: 'Seal Island ranks with the other graveyards of the Atlantic – St. Pauls, Scaterie, and Sable Island – as a seducer of ships and a claimant of lives.' In 1823, Mary Crowell Hitchen, wife of a sailor who experienced such a shipwreck, along with other members of the Crowell–Hitchen families, moved to the island and established a primitive life-saving station. Numerous lives were saved as a result, and eventually a lighthouse was built. On 28 November 1831, Seal Island Light shone for the first time.

Second Peninsula   *See* First Peninsula.

Selma (Hants)   At the mouth of the SHUBENACADIE RIVER, below MAITLAND. Originally the site of an Acadian settlement. Following the 1755 expulsion, the area remained unsettled until 1784. In 1774, Colonel John Small (1726–1796), who previously served with the 42nd Highlanders

(Black Watch), joined with Captain Alexander MacDonald to form a colonial regiment composed of Highlanders resident in the Thirteen Colonies. Recruiting took place principally among Scottish settlements in the Carolinas and resulted in the formation of the 2nd Battalion of the 84th Regiment of Foot (Royal Highland Emigrant Regiment). Following the Revolution, Colonel (later Major-General) Small purchased lands on COBEQUID BAY and erected a manor house on his estate, which he named 'Selma.' Since he was a native Scot, the name was undoubtedly inspired by 'Selma,' the residence of the ancient Celtic King Fingal at Morven, Scotland. Upon Small's death, his landholdings in HANTS COUNTY were sold. See also KENNETCOOK and RAWDON.

Shag Harbour (Shelburne) Northwest of CAPE SABLE ISLAND. The name of this community dates back to the French colonial period and is derived from the old French word for 'cormorant.' The first permanent settlers were New England fishermen who emigrated here during the mid-eighteenth century. 'Shag' as part of a place name appears frequently in both Newfoundland and Nova Scotia.

Shearwater (Halifax) On Eastern Passage, adjacent to DARTMOUTH. This is an appropriate designation for the Canadian Forces Base. Named in 1952 for the medium-sized seabird noteworthy for its distinctive flight pattern as it skims the water in search of food. Only the Manx shearwater (*Puffinus puffinus*) breeds in Canada; there is one known colony in Newfoundland. However, the shearwater is fairly common along the north Atlantic seaboard from June to October.

Sheet Harbour (Halifax) On Highway 7. Two theories have evolved to explain the origin of the name for one of the major harbours on the Atlantic coast of Nova Scotia. One suggests that it is a descriptive assigned because of a large white cliff at the harbour entrance which appeared like a sheet spread out to dry. Another theory traces the name to the DesBarres survey of the coast of the province, published in 1777. DesBarres recorded that, at the entrance, 'there is a spacious *sheet* of water broader than the harbour.'

Sheffield Mills (Kings) West of CANNING. Named for the Sheffield family, who were part of the New England Planter migration to Nova Scotia in the 1760s. The founder of the KINGS COUNTY branch of the family was Amos Sheffield (1733–1815), a native of Newport, Rhode Island.

Shelburne (shiretown of Shelburne County)   The harbour was once known as 'Port Razoir,' later anglicized to 'Port Roseway' and settled by Loyalists in the years following the American Revolution. The first group arrived on 4 May 1783. On 20 July the lieutenant-governor, John Parr (1725–1791), arrived to inspect the site and announced his intention to name the new town Shelburne, in honour of William Petty, second Earl of Shelburne (1737–1805), named prime minister of Great Britain the previous year. On this occasion, 'toasts were drunk to the King's health, the prosperity of the town, the district of Shelburne and to the Loyalists; each toast being greeted with cheers and the rumble of cannon.' Despite this auspicious beginning, Parr's choice of name was not greeted with approval. Many Loyalists felt that Shelburne was not sympathetic to their cause, and a few refused to use the name, referring to the location as 'Port Roseway *alias* Shelburne.' Although shortly afterward Shelburne was voted out of office and became a minor footnote in history, the place name has prevailed. The town was incorporated in 1907.

Shelburne County   The county as first created on 16 December 1785 was larger than the present boundaries and included the townships of Yarmouth, Argyle, and Barrington. The first two were set apart as YARMOUTH COUNTY in 1836. The name evolved from the town.

Sherbrooke (Guysborough); **Sherbrooke Lake** (Guysborough; Lunenburg)   Sherbrooke in GUYSBOROUGH COUNTY is located near the site of Fort Sainte-Marie, established 'three leagues above the entrance of St. Marys River at the head of the tide' by Charles Baye de La Giraudière during the French colonial period. The fort was abandoned after its capture by the English in 1669. The first English settlers arrived in the early 1800s, and the new community was named for Sir John Coape Sherbrooke (1764–1830), who served as lieutenant-governor of Nova Scotia (1811–16) and later (1816–18) as governor general (see also ST. MARYS RIVER). In 1969 the Nova Scotia government, impressed by the number of nineteenth-century buildings to be found in Sherbrooke, began a restoration of the village to conform to the 1860–80 period. Today, Sherbrooke Village is an important link in the network of Nova Scotian heritage sites. Nearby Sherbrooke Lake takes its name from the village. The second Sherbrooke Lake (also named for Sir John) is near the LUNENBURG–KINGS county boundary.

Sherbrooke Lake   *See* Sherbrooke.

Shinimicas Bridge   *See* Lower Shinimicas.

Shinimicas River   *See* Lower Shinimicas.

Ship Harbour (Halifax)   East of MUSQUODOBOIT HARBOUR. Settled in 1783 by a group of North Carolina Loyalists. The name was inspired by a cliff known as 'Ship Rock' at the entrance to the harbour. From a distance and under the right weather conditions, it gave the illusion of a full rigged vessel.

Shubenacadie; Shubenacadie Grand Lake; Shubenacadie River (Hants and Halifax)   The river flows into COBEQUID BAY, at MAITLAND; the village (off Highway 102) is on the river; the lake is west of the Halifax International Airport. The name, of Mi'kmaq origin, may be traced to *Segubunakadik*, translated by Silas T. Rand as 'the place where ground nuts occur.' An early spelling, 'Chicabenacadie,' gradually evolved to the modern spelling. It appears as *Shubenaccadie* as early as 1748 on the Charles Morris *Draught of the Upper Part of the Bay of Fundy*. See also LAKE BANNOOK.

Shubenacadie Grand Lake   *See* Shubenacadie.

Shubenacadie River   *See* Shubenacadie.

Shulie (Cumberland)   Southwest of RIVER HÉBERT, on CHIGNECTO BAY. The precise origin of the place name is unknown; however, it may be an English corruption of the French *joli*. In early records it is sometimes spelled 'Sholee' or 'Shoulie.'

Shut-in Island (Halifax)   Off THREE FATHOM HARBOUR, on the eastern shore of HALIFAX COUNTY. Occasionally referred to as 'Chetigne Island.' The name is undoubtedly an example of an English corruption of the spoken French; thus, to some ears 'Chetigne' sounded like 'Shut-In.' In 1916 the area was the subject of a novel by Margaret McLaren entitled *Chetigne Island*. Although the latter name has disappeared from official gazetteers, both Chetigne and Shut-In Island continue to be used locally.

Sissiboo River (Digby)   Enters ST. MARYS BAY at Weymouth North. The name is traceable to the Mi'kmaq *Cibou*, for 'big,' and is descriptive of the river. The legend that it was derived from 'six owls' (six *hiboux*) is apocryphal. See also WEYMOUTH.

Skir Dhu (Victoria)   On the Cabot Trail, north of Breton Cove. The name is a Gaelic descriptive for 'black rock.'

Skye Glen; Skye Mountain (Inverness)   Adjacent features on Highway 252, northwest of WHYCOCOMAGH. Both were named for the Isle of Skye, the largest of the Hebrides Islands. A number of Hebrideans were among the first settlers of INVERNESS COUNTY.

Skye Mountain   *See* Skye Glen.

Smiths Cove (Digby)   On the Annapolis Basin west, of Bear River. The cove takes its name from Joseph Smith, a Loyalist from New York, who settled here in 1784.

Smugglers Cove (Digby)   South of METEGHAN. For a time in the nineteenth century, this small cove, surrounded by high cliffs, was known as 'Anse-aux-Hirondelles,' as the cliffs were a nesting-place for swallows. However, it is referred to locally as 'Smugglers Cove,' since the topography has lent itself to illegal activities. A seaward-facing cave in the cliffs was used to advantage by rum runners during the Prohibition era of the 1920s and 1930s. Southwestern Nova Scotia, by virtue of its close proximity to the United States, figured prominently as a transshipment point for liquor destined for 'thirsty' Americans during this period. Smugglers Cove Provincial Park is adjacent.

Soi Point (Halifax)   Three place names incorporating the term 'soi' are to be found southwest of HALIFAX: Soi Point, Dover Soi, and Peggys Cove Soi. Recent research indicates that there is a connection between 'Soi' and 'Barachois' (see entry for latter). Although 'Barachois' is commonly found in areas settled by the French, the word is traceable to Basque sources. It was also spelled 'Barrasoi' by T.C. Haliburton in 1829 for locations in the ASPY BAY area of CAPE BRETON. Thus, Alan Rayburn points out: 'the spelling used by Haliburton suggests the origin of the term soi.' Further, Aspy is also of Basque origin, and there are additional Basque names in the vicinity. Yet another link may be found in the similar meaning of the two words. 'Soi' denotes a basin-like water feature connected to the open sea; 'barachois' is a body of water with a very narrow entrance partially enclosed by a sandbar.

South Brookfield   *See* Brookfield.

Southampton (Cumberland) Southwest of SPRINGHILL. Originally part of MACCAN, this community was named by provincial statute, in 1872, for Southampton, England. The post office was established the following year.

South Mountain   *See* North Mountain.

Spanish Ship Bay (Guysborough)   On the north side of Liscomb harbour. This place name may have been inspired by the nearby headland which reputedly once resembled a Spanish galleon. If true, there are three such topographical connections along the Eastern Shore (see also SHEET HARBOUR and SHIP HARBOUR). More plausible is the explanation that a Spanish ship was once wrecked here.

Spa Springs (Annapolis)   North of Highway 101, between KINGSTON and Middleton. First known as 'Salem,' this community changed its name when mineral springs were developed in the early nineteenth century. The springs were originally discovered by the Mi'kmaq, who used the bubbling water and mud for medicinal purposes. In 1832 an inn was built for visitors, bath houses erected, and mineral water piped in for hot and cold treatments. For a time the resort catering to those who wished 'to take the waters' flourished, only to collapse following a disastrous fire in 1889.

Spencers Island   *See* Cape Spencer.

Springhill (Cumberland)   A former coal-mining town in central CUMBERLAND COUNTY. The name is a descriptive; the hill on which the town developed once contained numerous springs. Incorporated as a town in 1889. Over the years 'Springhill' has become a symbol for bravery in the face of misfortune. A coal-mine explosion in 1891 killed 125 miners; another in 1956 killed 39; a devastating fire swept the town in 1957; a 'bump' in 1958 claimed 76 lives. In this last disaster, 12 miners were rescued after six days of entombment; 7 more were rescued two days later. Throughout all of these adversities and numerous other accidents and incidents underground, the people of Springhill have maintained their spirit and sense of resolution. On a happier note, in 1989, the Anne Murray Centre, honouring the Springhill native and international pop-music star, was opened. The centre was dedicated by her 'to the people of Springhill for their strength, their courage and their resilience.'

Spryfield (Halifax)   A district of HALIFAX situated on the west side of the North West Arm. Named for Captain William Spry, who served at the siege of Fortress Louisbourg in 1758 and was the commander of the Royal Engineers at Halifax (1775–83). Spry's farm came to be known as 'Spry's Field,' and eventually the name became applied to the community.

Stanley (Hants)   In central HANTS COUNTY. Named for Lord Frederick Arthur Stanley (1841–1908), governor general of Canada (1888–93). Lord Stanley is remembered for his donation of the Stanley Cup, the oldest trophy competed for by professional athletes in Canada. It was first awarded in 1893. The award-winning Canadian poet and novelist Alden Nowlan (1933–1983) spent his boyhood years in this community.

Starrs Point (Kings)   East of PORT WILLIAMS. Known as 'Boudreau's Bank' during the period of Acadian occupancy. Resettled in 1760 by Major Samuel Starr (1749–1799), a New England Planter and native of Norwich, Connecticut.

Stellarton (Pictou)   South of NEW GLASGOW. The original name, Albion Mines, was changed as a result of a public meeting held on 1 February 1870. The new name denotes the fact that 'stellar' coal was mined locally. The coal is known as 'stellar' or 'oil' coal because, when burning, it gives off sparks like stars. The town was incorporated in 1889. As in SPRINGHILL, tragedy has constantly stalked the Stellarton coal mines. The Foord seam, one of the richest sources of coal, is also one of the most dangerous. From 1880 to 1957 a total of 650 miners lost their lives in Stellarton mines. In 1992 the Westray mine (in nearby Plymouth), which also tapped the Foord seam, ended in tragedy (see PLYMOUTH). 'Albion Mines' is the setting for a collection of locally evocative short stories by Leo McKay, Jr. The book was nominated for the 1995 Giller Prize.

Stewiacke; Stewiacke River (Colchester)   The town is south of TRURO. The name, applied first to the river, is a corruption of the Mi'kmaq *Esiktaweak*, translated by Silas T. Rand as 'whimpering or whining as it goes along.' The town was incorporated in 1906.

Stewiacke River   *See* Stewiacke.

Stonehurst   *See* Blue Rocks.

Strait of Canso   *See* Canso.

Strathlorne (Inverness)   Near LOCH BAN, an inlet of LAKE AINSLIE. It was once known as 'Broad Cove Intervale.' The new name, adopted in 1880, honours John Douglas Sutherland Campbell, Marquess of Lorne and ninth Duke of Argyll (1845–1914), who served as governor general from 1878 to 1883. 'Strath' is from the Gaelic *scrath*, which means 'valley.' Strathlorne was the birthplace of writer and raconteur James D. Gillis (1870–1965). Known to generations as the bard Jimmy Dubh, Gillis taught school and played both the violin and bagpipes. Noted for his 'unconscious humour,' Gillis wrote a series of books that have become collector's items. Representative titles include *The Cape Breton Giant*, *The Great Election*, and *A Sketch of My Life*. In the last named he confided: 'I was twice to the United States; I do not say so for the sake of boast.'

Sugarloaf Mountain (Inverness) North of PORTREE. This descriptive is repeated some twenty times throughout the province. For derivation, see New Brunswick entry.

Sunny Brae (Pictou)   On the East Branch of the East River, south of NEW GLASGOW. First known as 'Pleasant Valley'; the more original descriptive name, Sunny Brae, was coined and adopted in 1878 with the establishment of the post office. The East River Valley is sometimes referred to as 'A Gleann Boidheach,' the Gaelic for 'beautiful valley.'

Surettes Island (Yarmouth) South of TUSKET, in Lobster Bay. In 1801 a land grant was made to a group of Acadians from Eel Brook (now STE. ANNE DU RUISSEAU). Included among the grantees were Frédéric and Charles-Baronne Surette, who settled on the island which now bears their name.

Sydney   *See* North Sydney.

Sydney Mines   *See* North Sydney.

Sydney River   *See* North Sydney.

Table Head   *See* Glace Bay.

Tancook Island (Lunenburg) Approximately 11 kilometres from CHESTER by ferry. The name originates with the Mi'kmaq *k'tanook*, which means 'out to sea.' Over time, this became Tancook. Little Tancook Island, first known as Queen Charlotte Island, later reverted to its Mi'kmaq descriptive *Ukantook*; which evolved to Little Tancook. The islands were settled in the 1790s by New England fishermen and second-generation Lunenburgers. Tancook Island is noted for its production of sauerkraut.

Tangier; Tangier Harbour; Tangier Island; Tangier River (Halifax)   East of SHIP HARBOUR. The name of the settlement, harbour, island, and river may be traced to the 1830 shipwreck of the schooner *Tangier*. In September 1858, gold was discovered at Mooseland, on the Tangier River, by Lieutenant Charles L'Estrange and his Mi'kmaq guide, Joe Paul. For the next thirty years, gold mining was carried on in this area.

Tangier Harbour   *See* Tangier.

Tangier Island   *See* Tangier.

Tangier River   *See* Tangier.

Tatamagouche (Colchester)   On Highway 6, west of RIVER JOHN. This name stems from a Mi'kmaq descriptive, *Takumegooch* or *Takamegootk*, which has been freely translated as 'the meeting of the waters,' since two rivers, the French and the Waughs, flow into the harbour at this point. Its literal meaning has been deciphered by William Francis Ganong and Frank Patterson as 'the lying across place' or 'at the place which lies across,' a reference to the fact that 'the rivers lie across from each other and eventually meet in the harbour.' Ganong points out that this 'unusual geographical feature would have been noticed by the Mi'kmaq and used in their nomenclature.' Silas T. Rand's interpretation differs; he suggests that the word means 'barred across the entrance with sand.' The present spelling has evolved over the years. Some variations have been *Tahamigouche* (LeLoutre 1738), *Tatmagouch* (Morris 1755), and *Tatamagouche* (Plan of DesBarres Estate 1837). During the French colonial period, the port was a transshipment point for supplies from the Bay of Minas settlements to Fortress Louisbourg. Its strategic importance was confirmed when Tatamagouche became the first Acadian settlement singled out for destruction and the expulsion of its inhabitants in 1755. On 25 August 1765, J.F.W. DesBarres received a grant of 8,000 hectares in the immediate area. The DesBarres family was 'an old and honored Montbéliardian one'; thus, he was able to persuade a number of Foreign Protestant families from the vicinity of

408 Terra Nova, NS

LUNENBURG to relocate on his estate. In 1772 families such as the Grattos, Langilles, Jollymores, Millards, and Mattatalls settled in the area, where their descendants may still be found. In the late eighteenth century, the population was augmented by an influx of Scottish immigrants. One of these settlers, Wellwood Waugh (1741–1824), who also acted as DesBarres's local agent, attempted unsuccessfully to have 'Southampton' substituted for the original name. Shipbuilding was a major industry here in the late nineteenth century.

Terra Nova (Cape Breton) Northeast of LAKE UIST. Settled in the mid-nineteenth century by the 'overflow' of second-generation Scottish settlers. The name is indicative of the fact that it was then new land.

Terence Bay (Halifax) Southwest of HALIFAX. The name of this community has evolved through various spellings. It was probably named for an early settler as it was sometimes recorded as Turner Bay, later as Tenants Bay, and eventually as Terence Bay. The present spelling can be documented with the establishment of the post office in 1865.

Terre Noire (Inverness) An Acadian settlement on the Cabot Trail, between BELLE CÔTE and GRAND ETANG. The name is a descriptive for 'black earth.'

The Churn (Yarmouth) Off Highway 304, leading to CAPE FOURCHU. This descriptive refers to the 'churning' or agitation of the water.

The Falls (Colchester) Southeast of TATAMAGOUCHE. Settled by emigrants from Sutherlandshire in the 1820s. It takes its name from 'the falls,' a prominent topographical feature in the area. Site of a twentieth-century hydroelectric development.

The Goulet *See* Goulet Beach.

The Gut *See* Digby.

The Hawk (Shelburne) On the southern tip of CAPE SABLE ISLAND. It was named for a schooner that was shipwrecked on this headland. The post office was opened in 1888.

The Look Off (Kings) Strategically situated on the southeast side of CAPE BLOMIDON. The aptly named location provides a panoramic view of six rivers and five counties, and of the MINAS BASIN.

The Ovens (Lunenburg) This descriptive name was explained in Lovell's *Gazetteer* (1871): 'At the entrance of Lunenburg harbour, rises a promontory fifty feet in height which contains a dozen or more cavities facing the sea. These cavities or caves, from some fancied resemblances, are called ovens. The regularity at which these openings occur almost confutes the idea of their being created merely by the action of the waves; they appear rather to have been made by human efforts, though for what purpose, unless for mining, it is difficult to conjecture.'

The Shoughbac (Lunenburg) Near the entrance to the LAHAVE RIVER, there is a noticeable land feature known locally as 'The Shoughbac.' The area is described in *The Nova Scotia Pilot*: 'At the right in entering from Gaff Point, the eastern side of the entrance trends northward to a conspicuous bank 38 metres high and thence westward and northward to The Shoughbac, another conspicuous bank 25 metres high.' Nicolas Denys (1598–1688) described the same scene three centuries earlier: 'At the right in entering [the LaHave River] there is a great rocky cape which is called Cape Doré, because when the sun strikes it on the top it seems all gilded.' Writing in 1908, William Francis Ganong noted: 'Shou Bay Hill is about 100 feet high, and is composed of yellow clay which gives it a gilded appearance when the sun strikes it.'

The Tickle (Richmond); **The Tittle** (Yarmouth)   By definition 'the tickle,' or as it is sometimes called 'the tittle,' is a narrow, hazardous strait or channel between two islands or between an island and the mainland. The Tickle in RICHMOND COUNTY, in LENNOX PASSAGE, divides Birch Island from the mainland. The Tittle in YARMOUTH COUNTY lies between SURETTES ISLAND and adjacent islands. See also JIGGER TICKLE, Newfoundland.

The Tittle   *See* The Tickle.

Thorburn (Pictou)   East of NEW GLASGOW. Formerly known as 'Vale Colliery,' for the company which once owned and operated the local coal mines. The present coined name was approved by provincial statute in 1886. It is derived from 'Thor,' god of thunder, and 'burn,' for brook.

Three Fathom Harbour (Halifax); **Three Mile Plains** (Hants) Both are descriptive names. Three fathoms (5.4 metres) was literally the depth of this harbour east–southeast of DARTMOUTH; Three Mile Plains is located 5 kilometres from WINDSOR.

Three Mile Plains   *See* Three
Fathom Harbour.

Thrumcap Island (Guysborough)
Thrumcap, a small, rounded rock
or island, is utilized as a place
name in many locations throughout Nova Scotia, and Newfoundland. One of several Thrumcap
islands is found off Little Dover
Island, south of CANSO. There are
two further examples at the
entrance to HALIFAX harbour,
where Big and Little Thrumcap
islands are hazards to navigation.
In the nineteenth century Maine
and Maritime sailors frequently
wore 'thrumcaps,' cloth caps
embroidered with thrums, the
waste ends of the warp. This may
account for the frequency of the
place name.

Tidnish (Cumberland)   Of
Mi'kmaq origin, it is probably
derived from *Mtagunich*, for 'paddle.' Tidnish was to be the eastern
terminus of the Chignecto Marine
Railway, designed to cross the
Isthmus of Chignecto. Construction began in the 1890s; however,
the project was never completed.
See also TIGNISH, Prince Edward
Island.

Tiverton (Digby)   On LONG
ISLAND, directly across PETIT PAS-
SAGE from East Ferry. The village
was once known as 'Petit Passage'; the new name was adopted

in 1867 after Tiverton, in Devon,
England.

Tobeatic Lake (Queens)   In the
northwestern corner of QUEENS
COUNTY. The name stems from
the Mi'kmaq *Toobeadoogook*, of
uncertain meaning. Nineteenth-
century references use Tobigadic,
from which the contemporary
spelling has evolved. The name
has also been incorporated in the
Tobeatic Wildlife Management
Area at the junction of five counties (Queens, SHELBURNE,
YARMOUTH, DIGBY, and ANNAPO-
LIS). It covers the headwaters of
the CLYDE, JORDAN, MERSEY, ROSE-
WAY, and TUSKET rivers.

Toney River (Pictou)   On the
NORTHUMBERLAND STRAIT,
between RIVER JOHN and PICTOU.
Named for a French adventurer,
Captain Toney, who lived among
the Mi'kmaq and reputedly
helped to negotiate a peace treaty
in 1761.

Tor Bay (Guysborough)   Southeast of CANSO. Named for Tor
Bay, in Devon, England. This area
was explored by Champlain and
quite probably was the location of
his *Porte de Savilette*. He bestowed
this name for, 'a Basque captain,
who since 1564 fished every year
at a port four leagues to the south
of Canso.' The latter name died

out in the eighteenth century. See also TORBAY, Newfoundland.

Tracadie (Antigonish)   Northwest of MONASTERY. This place name appears in all three Maritime provinces and is from a Mi'kmaq place name (see New Brunswick entry for derivation). There is a local tradition that Tracadie, Nova Scotia, was named for Joseph Tracady, the captain of a crew that 'in early times called in the harbour for the purpose of buying cordwood.' It has also been suggested that it may be a modification of 'acadie,' with the prefix 'tr' added. The evidence favours its Mi'kmaq origin.

Trenton (Pictou)   North of NEW GLASGOW. The name was selected in 1882 by Henry Graham when the new townsite was laid out. It was inspired by Trenton, the capital of the state of New Jersey. The town was incorporated in 1911.

Tribune Head   *See* Herring Cove.

Truemanville (Cumberland) On Highway 6, east of AMHERST. The Trueman family was prominent among the Yorkshire emigrants to CUMBERLAND and WESTMORLAND counties in the 1770s. The settlement takes its name from this family, who were among the first settlers.

Truro (shiretown of Colchester County)   On the site of the pre-1755 Acadian settlement of COBEQUID. Its situation was described by John M'Gregor during his British North American travels as 'the most beautiful village in Nova Scotia, and as far as my impressions go, the prettiest that I have seen in America.' The new name was suggested in 1759 upon the resettlement of the area by New Englanders and Ulster Scots. Named for Truro in Cornwall, England, it is often referred to as 'the Hubtown' for its strategic location in relation to the rest of the province. Incorporated as a town in 1875. One of Nova Scotia's leading political dynasties, the Stanfields, have become synonymous with the town of Truro. Spanning seven decades, the succession began with John Stanfield (1868–1934), MP for COLCHESTER (1907–17) and senator (1921–34); his brother, Frank Stanfield I (1872–1931), was MLA for Colchester (1911–20, 1925–30) and lieutenant-governor of Nova Scotia (1930–1). They were followed by the latter's sons: Frank II (1903–1967), MP for Colchester–Hants (1945–53), and Robert L. Stanfield, who served as premier of Nova Scotia (1956–67) and federal Progressive Conservative leader (1967–76).

Tupperville (Annapolis)   The
Tupper family was part of the
New England Planter migration
to Nova Scotia in the 1760s. Three
brothers, Elisha, Miner, and Asa,
settled at Clarks Ferry, east of
ROUND HILL. The name was subsequently changed in their
honour.

**Tusket; Tusket Falls; Tusket
Islands; Tusket River** (Yarmouth)   The town is situated on
the Tusket River, which flows
into the Atlantic at this point. The
name was first applied to the
river, and then to adjacent features such as Tusket Falls and the
Tusket Islands. It is derived from
the Mi'kmaq *Tukseit* or *Neketaouk-
sit*, meaning 'a great forked tidal
river.' It is rendered as *Touquechet*
on the Sanson map of 1656, and as
Tousquet by Denys (1672) and
Lalanne (1684). See also OUTER
BALD Tusket Island and WEDGE-
PORT. Site of a pre-1755 Acadian
settlement, the area was resettled
by Dutch Loyalists from New Jersey and New York in 1785. The
Tusket court-house, erected in
1805, is the oldest standing structure of its kind in Canada.

Tusket Falls   *See* Tusket.

Tusket Islands   *See* Tusket.

Tusket River   *See* Tusket.

Ulva (Inverness)   In the MARGA-
REE VALLEY. Named for the island
of Ulva, off the coast of Argyllshire, Scotland. Many of the early
settlers came from this part of
Scotland.

Uniacke Lake   *See* Mount Uniacke.

Uniacke Point   *See* Mount Uniacke.

Uniacke River   *See* Mount Uniacke.

Upper Clements   *See* Clements.

Upper Granville   *See* Granville
Ferry.

Urbania (Hants)   Between South
Maitland and ADMIRAL ROCK.
This community was once known
as 'Carleton.' To avoid confusion,
the name was optimistically
changed in the 1860s to the coined
'Urbania,' traceable to the Latin
urbis, for 'city.'

Usige Ban Falls (Victoria)
North of Forks Baddeck. The
name is Gaelic for 'white water'
and refers to the cascade of water
that tumbles down a sheer rock
cliff.

Valley (Colchester)   East of
TRURO, in the Salmon River
valley. Originally Teviotdale
Station, for Teviotdale, Scotland;

the name was changed to Valley Station with the building of the Intercolonial Railway. The new name defined its location. In the twentieth century the place name was shortened to 'Valley.'

Victoria Beach; Victoria Vale (Annapolis)   Victoria Beach is on DIGBY GUT; Victoria Vale is north of MIDDLETON. Nova Scotia is particularly well endowed with place names honouring Queen Victoria; in addition to the two listed, there are at least twelve others that incorporate her name. Both of the examples cited were assigned following the Queen's Silver Jubilee in 1862.

Victoria County   One of the two counties that comprise the northern section of CAPE BRETON ISLAND. It was set apart from CAPE BRETON COUNTY in 1851 and named for Queen Victoria (1819–1901). Much of the northern section of the county lies within the boundaries of the CAPE BRETON HIGHLANDS NATIONAL PARK.

Victoria Vale   *See* Victoria Beach.

Voglers Cove (Lunenburg)   On the eastern side of MEDWAY harbour. This cove was named for Frederick Vogler, one of its first settlers. He was probably a descendant of John George Fogeler or Vogeler, one of the Foreign Protestant immigrants to the LUNENBURG area.

Waldeck (Annapolis)   Originally there were two settlements in the western section of the township of Clements referred to as the 'Waldeck' and 'Hessian' lines. Both were settled following the American Revolution by disbanded soldiers, from the states of Waldeck and Hesse, in Germany, who had fought on the British side. Today, only the place name Waldeck serves to remind us of this late-eighteenth-century settlement. The Hessian Line is now called Clementsvale. See also CLEMENTS.

Wallace (Cumberland); **Wallace Lake** (Halifax)   Wallace is on Highway 6, east of PUGWASH. This name, for Michael Wallace (1747–1831), long-time provincial treasurer of Nova Scotia, was assigned in 1810. It replaced the earlier Mi'kmaq designation, Remsheg, which had been retained as a place name for the Acadian village in the same general location. Following the American Revolution, the area was resettled largely by Loyalists. Wallace, also a Loyalist, moved from Norfolk, Virginia, to HALIFAX, and soon became a central figure in the oligarchy of early-nineteenth-century Nova Scotia.

Throughout his career, Wallace was able to maintain a position of power through an adroit use of patronage and an aggressive personality. One indication of his success may be found in the twenty-five place names attributed to him and scattered throughout ten of Nova Scotia's sixteen counties. Wallace Lake, on SABLE ISLAND, is a reflection of his position as a member of the commission responsible for the island's life-saving station.

Wallace Lake   *See* Wallace.

Walton (Hants)   On the shore of the MINAS BASIN. Settled in the 1790s by second-generation New England Planters from the Newport district. It was named for James Walton Nutting (1787–1870), a native of nearby KEMPT and a major landholder in this part of the county.

Washabuck Centre (Victoria) On a promontory in BRAS D'OR LAKE; bounded on the east by St. Patrick Channel and on the west by ST. ANDREWS CHANNEL. Also known as 'Washabuckt'; the name is of Mi'kmaq origin, and is a descriptive which means 'an angle of land formed between a river and a lake.' Settled by members of the MacNeil and MacLean clans from Barra, in the Hebrides, in 1818. Neil MacNeil's *The High-*

land Heart of Nova Scotia is a personal memoir of late-nineteenth- and early-twentieth-century life in Washabuck. He is at his best when describing the local folk culture: 'Gaelic was a grand language in which to curse, for it provided a range of denunciation and damnation that was at once alarming and magnificent. It was also a grand language in which to pray, for it had an intimacy and a depth of devotion that no other language can approach. The good people of Washabuck were great cursers and prayers, moving from one to the other with great dexterity.' See also BARRA GLEN.

Waterville (Kings)   Off Highway 101, between KENTVILLE and BERWICK. The name is a local descriptive, adopted at a public meeting on 21 November 1871. It replaced an earlier name, Pineo Village, for an early settler. Now part of Cambridge Square.

Waughs River (Colchester) Flows into Tatamagouche Bay, an arm of the NORTHUMBERLAND STRAIT. Named for Wellwood Waugh (1741–1824), a native of Lockerbie, Scotland, who settled here in 1781 as agent for the J.F.W. DesBarres estate. It was partly settled by tenants from Montbéliard who migrated from the LUNENBURG area in the 1770s. See also TATAMAGOUCHE.

Waverley (Halifax)   Northeast of
BEDFORD BASIN. The name originated with 'Waverley,' a cottage
built by Charles P. Allen. It was
assigned for the Waverley novels
of Sir Walter Scott (1771–1832).
Scott, in turn, derived the name
from the ruined Waverley Abbey,
near Farnham, in Surrey,
England.

Wedgeport (Yarmouth)   Southeast of YARMOUTH. This community was first known as 'The
Wedge,' or 'Tusket Wedge,' a
descriptive for a strip of land that
narrows to a point. Over time the
form Wedgeport gradually
evolved and has been in common
usage since the mid-nineteenth
century. From 1936 until the
1960s, Wedgeport was the home
of the International Tuna Cup
Matches. For reasons unknown,
the tuna disappeared from this
area and the matches were dis-
continued. See also OUTER BALD
TUSKET ISLAND.

Wellington (Queens)   East of
PONHOOK LAKE. It is one of three
Nova Scotian communities
named for Arthur Wellesley, first
Duke of Wellington (1769–1852).
The others are in HALIFAX and
YARMOUTH counties. Wellington,
a noted general and politician,
served as British prime minister
(1828–30) and as foreign secretary
(1834–5). However, it was his

famous military exploits, most
notably a victory over Napoleon
at the Battle of Waterloo in 1815,
that gave rise to these, and a number of other associated place
names. See chapter 1, pages 26–7.

Welsford (Kings; Pictou)   The
KINGS COUNTY community is
north of BERWICK and was originally known as 'Back Street.' The
name was changed in honour of
WINDSOR native and Crimean War
hero Major Augustus Frederick
Welsford (1811–1855), who was
killed in action during the Battle
of Sevastopol, 8 September 1855.
Welsford near RIVER JOHN, in
PICTOU COUNTY, was named for
the same reason. On 17 July 1860,
the Welsford–Parker Monument
was unveiled in St. Paul's Cemetery, HALIFAX. It commemorates
the heroism of Welsford and
another Nova Scotian officer,
William Buck Carthew Augustus
Parker, who lost his life in the
same encounter.

Welshtown (Shelburne)   Northwest of SHELBURNE. As the name
implies, this area was originally
settled by Welsh emigrants from
Carmarthenshire and Cardiganshire in 1818. The settlement was
first known as 'New Cambria';
however, the earlier name has
been gradually replaced by
Welshtown. Canadian poet and
novelist Margaret Atwood is a

descendant of David Davis, a Carmarthenshire native and one of the early settlers in Welshtown. Ms Atwood has acknowledged her roots with the comment, 'Every time I write a poem, I wonder which of my ancestors had the poetic gene and passed it along to me. I suspect it was one of the Welshtown settlers.' The story of the Welshtown–New Cambria settlement has been well told by historian Peter Thomas in *Strangers from a Secret Land*. See also CARDIGAN, New Brunswick.

Wentworth (Cumberland); **Wentworth Creek** (Hants); **Wentworth Lake** (Digby); **Wentworth Valley** (Cumberland)   The settlement and valley in central CUMBERLAND COUNTY were named for Sir John Wentworth (1737–1820), lieutenant-governor of Nova Scotia from 1792 to 1808. Wentworth Lake, in DIGBY COUNTY, south of CORBERRIE, also commemorates his career. Most colonial governors sought to enshrine their careers through place names; however, in the case of Loyalist Sir John, who had earlier served as governor of New Hampshire and surveyor general of the King's woods in North America, there was considerable justification. Wentworth Creek, east of WINDSOR, in HANTS COUNTY, has a different origin. It evolved from 'Winckworth,' the estate of Winckworth Tonge (1728–1792), father of William Cottnam Tonge (1764–1832). Both father and son served as members of the Nova Scotia Assembly. Ironically, the latter was to be an important leader in the first round of the constitutional struggle for responsible government, and thus directly challenged the power and position of then governor Wentworth, who was backed by his appointed legislative council.

Wentworth Creek   *See* Wentworth.

Wentworth Lake   *See* Wentworth.

Wentworth Valley   *See* Wentworth.

West Branch (Pictou)   This section of western PICTOU COUNTY was first settled by Sutherlandshire Scots in 1813–17. The name is descriptive of its location on the west branch of the RIVER JOHN. See also EARLTOWN and BRORA LAKE.

Westchester (Cumberland)   The name of this central CUMBERLAND COUNTY village was chosen in 1784 by the first Loyalist settlers from Westchester County, New York. The post office dates from 1838.

West Dublin   *See* New Dublin.

West Earltown   *See* Earltown.

West Gore   *See* Gore.

Westmount (Cape Breton)   A descriptive derived from its location on the west side of SYDNEY RIVER.

West Newdy Quoddy   *See* Quoddy Harbour.

West Quoddy Harbour   *See* Quoddy Harbour.

Westport (Digby)   On the west side of GRAND PASSAGE. Originally known as 'Brier Island Settlement.' The new name, a descriptive for its location, was adopted in 1839, the date of the establishment of the post office. Captain Joshua Slocum (1844–1909), sea captain and author of the marine classic *Sailing Alone around the World,* lived his boyhood years at Westport. Later, after his memorable voyage, a first in the annals of sailing, he returned to Westport to visit, and to complete the writing and editing of his manuscript. It was published in 1900 and is still in print.

Westville (Pictou)   The early name, Acadia Mines, was replaced on 25 February 1868 by a coined descriptive for this the westernmost of the mining towns of PICTOU COUNTY. The town's act of incorporation was passed by the provincial legislature in 1888; however, no action was taken until 1894, when the first civic elections were held.

Weymouth (Digby)   On the SISSIBOO RIVER. The village, once known by the name of the river was renamed Weymouth. According to 'the Squire,' a character in T.C. Haliburton's *The Clockmaker,* 'Sissiboo sounded too uncouth to the ears of the inhabitants and they changed it to Weymouth, but they must excuse me for adopting the old [spelling] ... I am no democrat; I like old names and the traditions belonging to them.' Despite this literary foible, the 'new' name was to prevail. The area was first settled by New England fishermen in the summer of 1765. One of their number, Christopher Strickland, was a native of Weymouth, Massachusetts; hence, the name. Following the American Revolution, the population was augmented by Loyalist settlers. Prominent among their numbers was Lieutenant-Colonel James Moody (1744–1809), a native of Delaware, and later, from 1793 to 1806, a member of the Nova Scotia Assembly. He wrote a narrative account of his service on the British side. It is a gripping story of stealthy marches by night, of ambuscades, of rearguard actions, and, on one occasion, a narrow escape in intercepting Washington's dispatches to Congress. The post office dates from 1833.

Weymouth Falls (Digby)   On the SISSIBOO RIVER, east of WEYMOUTH. A local resident, Sam Langford (1882–1956), achieved fame as a championship lightweight boxer. Langford fought at a time (1902–24) when black fighters battled not only their ring opponents, but prejudice as well. Thus, Langford, the 'trail blazer,' made an important contribution in the competitive-sports world.

White Hill (Victoria)   Northeast of INGONISH, in CAPE BRETON HIGHLANDS NATIONAL PARK. At 532 metres, the highest point in Nova Scotia. The name is descriptive.

White Point Beach (Queens)   On the eastern side of PORT MOUTON harbour. It was named for the extensive white-sand beaches characteristic of the area.

White Rock (Kings)   On the GASPEREAU RIVER, southeast of NEW MINAS. The name is descriptive and refers to the rushing cataracts of water over rocks which give the appearance of a 'white' rock.

Whitney Pier (Cape Breton) Adjacent to SYDNEY. First known as 'International Pier,' for the shipping docks of the Dominion Steel and Coal Company, but was changed with the establishment of the post office in 1895. The new name was for Henry M. Whitney, first president of the coal company.

Whycocomagh (Inverness) On Highway 105. A Mi'kmaq descriptive which stems from *Wakogumaak*, translated by Silas T. Rand as 'end of the bay' or 'beside the sea.' Settled in the 1820s by Scottish immigrants, principally from the Isle of Skye and Tiree. A direct descendant of one of the first settlers, Jonathan MacKinnon, founded and edited *Mac-Talla* (Echo), a newspaper published in Sydney from 1892 to 1924. *Mac-Talla* was unique because the complete publication was in Gaelic and no other similar newspaper had survived for such a long period of time.

Whynotts Settlement (Lunenburg)   On Highway 3A. Originally 'Weihnachts Settlement'; the anglicized version is cited by Winthrop Pickard Bell 'as an example of a name that was transmuted in the course of two centuries in Nova Scotia.' Members of the Weihnacht (Whynot) family, from southwestern Germany, were among the first settlers of this community.

Williamsdale (Cumberland) East of COLLINGWOOD CORNER. The first name, East Branch River, was replaced by act of the Nova Scotia legislature in 1867 in honour of Sir William Fenwick Williams (1800–1883), lieutenant-governor at the time. See also FENWICK, KARSDALE, and PORT WILLIAMS.

Williamswood (Halifax)   West of HALIFAX. This name, officially adopted in 1993, honours the first settler, William Thompson, a Loyalist.

Wilmot (Annapolis)   Between MIDDLETON and KINGSTON. It takes its name from Wilmot Township, one of four townships into which the county was originally divided. It was named for Montagu Wilmot (?–1766), who served as lieutenant-governor from 1763 to 1766. Wilmot died in office; however, the Assembly refused to pay the cost of his state funeral, which amounted to more than £245.

Windham Hill (Cumberland) Southeast of SPRINGHILL, in central CUMBERLAND COUNTY.

Named by John Bragg, local justice of the peace and lumberman, for General Sir Charles Ash Windham (1810–1870), who commanded the British forces in Canada from 1867 until his death in 1870.

Windsor (shiretown of Hants County)   On the AVON RIVER, off Highway 101. The name was adopted on 24 December 1764, for Windsor, England. It was also the name of one of the original townships of the later HANTS COUNTY. The designation replaced the Mi'kmaq *Pisiguit* or *Pisiquid*, from *Pesegitk*, which had been retained by the Acadians as their name for the area. Windsor was the birthplace of Thomas Chandler Haliburton (1796–1865), historian, jurist, and author, whose observations on Nova Scotia have been frequently quoted in this work. His estate, 'Clifton,' now part of the Nova Scotia Museum complex, is open to the public. In the late eighteenth century, Nova Scotia's first institution of higher learning, King's College, was established at Windsor. Sanctioned by an act of the legislature in 1788, King's College opened in 1790 and was granted a royal charter in 1802. Following a disastrous fire in 1920, the institution moved to HALIFAX. As the University of King's College, it continues as an autonomous affiliate of Dalhousie University. The original Windsor campus is now occupied by King's–Edgehill, a private secondary school. On nearby Long Pond, it is claimed that the first game resembling modern ice hockey was played. The Windsor Hockey Heritage Centre marks this event, along with an impressive collection of related memorabilia. The town of Windsor was incorporated in 1878. See also AVON RIVER and PESAQUID LAKE.

Winging Point (Cape Breton) South of Cape Gabarus. Named 'for the many wild duck shot there on the wing' (CPCGN Files). The place name is repeated several times in both Nova Scotia and Newfoundland.

Wolfe Island (Lunenburg); **Wolfes Island** (Halifax)   Wolfe Island, one of the LaHave Islands, was named for an early grantee, Wendel Wolff (later Wolfe), a member of the Foreign Protestant migration to the LUNENBURG area. Wolfes Island is situated some 6 kilometres off the entrance to SHIP HARBOUR. It was named for an early settler, John Wolfe, who served in the Nova Scotia Volunteers during the American Revolution. Other members of this regiment settled at nearby Ship Harbour. A lighthouse was established on Wolfes Island in 1895.

Wolfes Island   *See* Wolfe Island.

Wolfville (Kings)   Off Highway 101. On 21 May 1759, the township of Horton was created. It was named for 'Horton Hall,' the residence of George Montagu Dunk, second Earl of Halifax (1716–1771) and president of the Board of Trade in the British cabinet. Joseph Howe (1804–1873), then editor of the *Acadian Recorder*, penned the following description of the township, famous for its natural setting, in 1828: 'We ride on through Horton, and a prettier scene no man need desire – now you catch a glimpse of the [Minas] Basin, and Blomidon and the Cornwallis River, and then in a moment more, a stretch of marsh ... and you almost forswear mingling in the city again.' In 1829, Upper Horton, on Mud Creek, was officially renamed Wolfville, in honour of the DeWolf family, one of whom, Elisha DeWolf, was the local postmaster. Although the contemporary spelling of the family name is 'DeWolfe,' the place name 'bears silent testimony to the original spelling' (Kirkconnell). In 1838, Wolfville was selected as the location for Queen's College, later to become Acadia University. The town was incorporated in 1893. A major attraction is the Nature Centre, named for a local naturalist Robie

Tufts (1884–1982), containing an intrepretive display relating to chimney swifts. At dusk during the summer, these birds perform complicated aerobatic manoeuvres before resting in the chimney that forms part of the centre. The Atlantic Theatre Festival, occupying well-designed facilities in what was once the university rink, began a run of classical drama in the summer of 1995. The 'brainchild' of artistic director Michael Bawtree, the festival has attracted the support of theatrical personalities such as Christopher Plummer, Michael Langham, and Peter Donat.

Woods Harbour (Shelburne) North of SHAG HARBOUR. Originally the community was known as 'Cockouquit,' from a Mi'kmaq word for a species of duck. The new name was adopted in honour of the Reverend Samuel Wood, an early settler. The first name survives in nearby Cockerwit Channel or Passage.

Yarmouth (shiretown of Yarmouth County)   Off Highway 103. First designated as Port Fourchu or Forked Harbour (a translation of the Mi'kmaq *Maligeak* by Samuel de Champlain, the new name was transferred from Yarmouth, Massachusetts, by New England Planters and fishermen. It

appears first in the document 'A Grant for a Township at Cape Forchue call'd Yarmouth [1 September 1759].' For many years, Yarmouth was the major shipbuilding centre of Nova Scotia. By the 1870s Yarmouth reached its pinnacle of fame and possessed more tonnage per capita than any other seaport in the world. All of this was swept aside by the advent of steam and the consequent decline of Golden Age of Sail. Evidence of the prosperity of this bygone era may be found in the surviving domestic architecture of Yarmouth town and county. In addition, the Yarmouth County Museum depicts much of this history through displays of ship portraits, models, an archives, and other artefacts. Yarmouth is also home to the Firefighters Museum of Nova Scotia, which houses a rare collection of early equipment and memorabilia. Incorporation of the town took place in 1890. It is the terminus for ferry service across the Gulf of Maine to Bar Harbour and Portland.

Yarmouth County   The county, taking its name from the original township of 1759, was established by statute in 1836. According to this legislation, it was 'to contain, comprise, and comprehend the two townships of Yarmouth and Argyle ...'

Zwicker Island (Lunenburg) In MAHONE BAY. Named after an early settler, Peter Zwicker. The Zwicker family, from south-western Germany, were numbered among the 1751–3 Foreign Protestant migration to Nova Scotia.

5

Prince Edward Island

Abegweit Passage   *See* chapter 1, page 33.

Abells Cape (Kings)   Extends into ROLLO BAY, between Howe Point and Rollo Point. First named in the Samuel Holland survey of 1765 *Eglington* [*sic*] *Point*, for Alexander Montgomerie (1723–1769), tenth Earl of Eglinton. It was renamed Abells Cape in the early nineteenth century, as a historical reminder of an incident involving a land agent, Edward Abell, and a tenant farmer, Patrick Pearce. According to a contemporary newspaper account, Pearce owned a fine carriage horse, coveted by Mrs. Abell. When Pearce refused to sell the horse, Abell demanded immediate payment of the annual rent. Pearce, with the help of neighbours, raised the amount; however, the agent now was unwilling to accept payment, suggesting that some of the coins

were counterfeit. By this time Pearce's patience 'had worn thin, he went into his house and brought out a musket with a bayonet attached. He stabbed Abell first in the arm and then in the groin.' Following the agent's death, Pearce fled the province. Despite the offer of a reward of £20, he was not apprehended (*Prince Edward Island Register*, 8 September 1819; *Prince Edward Island Gazette*, 2 February 1820).

Abrams Village (Prince) Southwest of WELLINGTON, on Highway 124. Called Abrahams Village, for an Acadian, Abraham Arsenault, who settled here in 1824. Sometimes referred to as 'Abram Village'; it has remained a predominantly Acadian settlement.

Afton Lake; Afton Road (Queens)   Northwest of MOUNT STEWART. Named for Afton

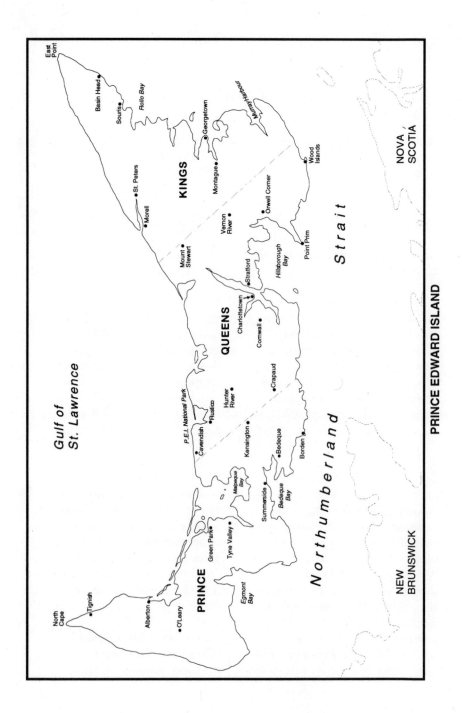

PRINCE EDWARD ISLAND

Water, a river in southern Scotland. In 1789 this river was immortalized in a poem, 'Flow Gently Sweet Afton,' by Robert Burns (1759–1796); ever afterward it became a popular place name for Scottish settlements overseas.

Afton Road   *See* Afton Lake.

Albany (Prince)   On Highway 112, northeast of BORDEN. Named for Prince Leopold (1853–1884), fourth and youngest son of Queen Victoria and Prince Albert. He was created Duke of Albany in 1881.

Alberry Plains (Queens)   East of VERNON RIVER. The name was adopted with the formation of a new school section in 1862. It is descriptive and, according to Robert Douglas, means 'all berry plains, from the large variety of wild fruit to be found in the area.'

Alberton; Alberton Harbour (Prince)   Alberton Harbour, on the northeast coast of the county, was designated Holland Cove by surveyor Samuel Holland, not for himself but for for Henry Fox, first Baron Holland (1705–1774). Holland, a minor figure in British politics, was once described as 'the most unpopular of contemporary statesmen' (see also FOXLEY RIVER). Possibly because of his lack of fame and importance, the name was discarded in favour of nearby Alberton. The latter was first known as 'Cross Roads' or 'The Cross', since two blazed trails met each other at this point. On 27 June 1862, 'the inhabitants of The Cross met in the Temperance Hall to choose a more suitable name for their community' (*Charlottetown Islander*, 13 July 1862). The name selected was in honour of Prince Álbert Edward, later King Edward VII (1841–1910), who visited Prince Edward Island on 10–12 August 1860. Alberton was once a centre for the silver-fox breeding industry. A National Historic Site monument marks the importance of this industry in Prince County. See also OULTONS ISLAND and SUMMERSIDE.

Alberton Harbour   *See* Alberton.

Albion Cross (Kings)   At the crossroads of Highways 4 and 327. The name was undoubtedly suggested by the ancient poetic designation for Britain. It, in turn, may be traced to the white or light-coloured cliffs (from the Latin *albus*), characteristic of the south coast of England and visible from France. Mount Albion in QUEENS COUNTY has the same origin.

Alexandra; Alexandra Bay; Alexandra Point (Queens)   The section of HILLSBOROUGH BAY between Alexandra Point and Crown Point. During the French colonial period, the bay was known as 'Anse de Matelot,' 'Sailors Cove.' The names for the community, bay, and point all honour Queen Alexandra (1844–1925), a Danish princess, who married Edward, Prince of Wales (later Edward VII), in 1863. The name Alexandra Point was adopted in 1991, replacing the earlier pejorative designation of Squaw Point. See also ALBERTON.

Alexandra Bay   *See* Alexandra.

Alexandra Point   *See* Alexandra.

Alma (Prince)   Northwest of ALBERTON, on Highway 2. A suggestion has been made that this community was named for the Crimean battle of Alma River, 20 September 1855. It is more likely that the name was in honour of the exploits of the 365-ton brigantine *Alma*, built by the famous PRINCE COUNTY shipbuilder James Yeo (1789–1868). Although the ship's name was probably inspired by the battle, it was the former that had local significance. In 1857 the ship, under command of William Richards, made a passage from PORT HILL, Prince Edward Island, to Mumbles, near Swansea, on the Bristol Channel in fourteen days. Unfortunately, the vessel was later shipwrecked and lost in the GULF OF ST. LAWRENCE.

Amherst Cove; Amherst Point (Prince) East of Borden and adjacent to Northumberland Strait. Commemorates the career of Jeffrey, first Baron Amherst (1717/18–1797). See also FORT AMHERST and AMHERST, Nova Scotia.

Amherst Point   *See* Amherst Cove.

Anglo Rustico (Queens) and **Anglo Tignish** (Prince)   The prefix 'anglo' is used to indicate an anglophone area in a predominantly francophone district. See also RUSTICO and TIGNISH.

Anglo Tignish   *See* Anglo Rustico.

Annandale (Kings)   On BOUGHTON BAY. Named about 1868 for Annandale, Dumfries, Scotland, the home of James Johnston, an early settler. See also NEW ANNAN, Prince Edward Island and Nova Scotia.

Ardgowan National Historic Park (Queens)   In the Parkdale district of CHARLOTTETOWN. 'Ardgowan,' built in 1850, was the home of William Henry Pope (1825–1879), one of Prince Edward Island's Fathers of Confederation, and a prominent lawyer, politician, and newspaper editor. Pope named his estate for the Gaelic for 'hill of the daisy.' During the 1864 Charlottetown Conference, the local press reported that he hosted at Ardgowan 'a grand *déjeuner à la fourchette*, featuring lobster, oysters, champagne and other Island luxuries.' The house and its extensive gardens have been designated a national historic site. Ardgowan is now the district headquarters for Parks Canada (*Parks Canada Report*, PAPEI)

Argyle Shore (Queens) Fronts on NORTHUMBERLAND STRAIT, between CANOE COVE and DE-SABLE. This area was settled in the early 1800s by immigrants from Argyllshire, Scotland. The new name was selected at a public meeting held on 30 August 1847. One of the prime locations for sighting the 'Phantom Ship of the Northumberland Strait,' Argyle Shore Provincial Park is also located here. See also AMET ISLAND, Nova Scotia.

Augustine Cove (Prince) On the NORTHUMBERLAND STRAIT between CUMBERLAND COVE and PREVOST COVE. The two place names, Augustine and Prevost, honour the career of Major General Augustin Prévost (1723–1786), father of Sir George Prévost (1767–1816), governor-in- chief of Canada from 1811 to 1815. The

elder Prévost, a French-speaking Protestant, saw service in the British army and was wounded at the siege of Québec in 1759.

Bacon Cove (Queens) At the mouth of Nine Mile Creek. Designated in 1765 by Samuel Holland for Edward Bacon, who served as Lord Commissioner of Trade and Plantations from 1759 to 1765.

Baglole Point (Prince) Extends into the GRAND RIVER. Named for Charles Baglole, an early settler, one of a family of four sons and several daughters who accompanied their father, William Baglole, to Prince Edward Island about 1840. They came from north Devonshire, near Bideford. William is ancestor to all Bagloles in North America.

Baltic; Baltic River (Prince) The river flows north into DARNLEY BASIN. The name is of uncertain origin. Robert Douglas suggests that 'the name appears to date from the Napoleonic wars when there was a heavy timber export trade from the Maritime Provinces owing to the Baltic ports being closed to British commerce.' Alan Rayburn counters with: 'Possibly it, and other places called Baltic, are derived from the Gaelic *bailteacch*, "belonging to a village."' There is also a Baltic in KINGS COUNTY, an inland community on Highway 302. In both cases the name may have been selected because it was short and easy to pronounce!

Baltic River   *See* Baltic.

Barachois Run; The Barachois (Prince)   In Lot 15, a predominantly Acadian section of the county. The name, traceable to Basque sources, is found in all four Atlantic provinces. It means a small salt-water pond or bay, usually protected from the sea by a barrier of sand or gravel. For more detail concerning its origin, see entries for the other three provinces.

Barbara Weit River (Prince) Flows west into MALPEQUE BAY. There are several explanations for this interesting and unusual place name. Over the years it has been spelled as: 'Barbara Weed,' 'Barbary Weed,' 'Barbara Wiot,' 'Barbary Weit,' and 'Barbara Weit.' It seems certain that these renderings are merely varied spellings of the original 'Barbara Waite.' Thus, the name commemorates the wife of an early settler, George Waite, who came to this area in 1804. She was buried in a cemetery in nearby NEW ANNAN.

Basin Head (Kings)   Ten kilometres east of SOURIS, near KINGSBORO. The name is descriptive and evolved from the shape of Basin Head Harbour. It is the site of Basin Head Fisheries Museum, which chronicles the changing nature of the province's inshore fishery. Included are artefacts, dioramas, a saltfish box factory, and a 1930s-style cannery. The museum is part of the PEI Museum and Heritage Foundation. Along this section of coastline the phenomenon of the 'singing sands' may be experienced. Because the sand has a high silica content, when one walks or hikes on them, the 'sands appear to sing.'

Bayfield; Bayfield Point (Kings) On Highway 16, between Priest Pond and ROCK BARRA. Honours the career of Admiral Henry Wolsey Bayfield (1795–1885), who surveyed the entire coastline of Prince Edward Island during the period 1841 to 1848. Following retirement he continued to live in CHARLOTTETOWN and the Bayfield home still stands at 269 Queen Street. In addition to his work on Prince Edward Island, Bayfield was responsible for surveys of Lakes Erie, Huron, and Superior; the GULF OF ST LAWRENCE; NORTHUMBERLAND STRAIT; STRAITS OF BELLE ISLE; and the coast of LABRADOR, CAPE BRETON, SABLE ISLAND, and Nova Scotia from the STRAIT OF CANSO to HALIFAX. Bayfield is also remembered in fourteen place names in Ontario, four in Québec, and three in Nova Scotia. A monument on the grounds of Province House, Charlottetown, bears this tribute: 'Few men have made greater contributions to hydrography and navigation.' His journals, also noteworthy for a wealth of observations on place names, have been published in two volumes by the Champlain Society of Canada (1984, 1986). See also BAYFIELD, New Brunswick and Nova Scotia.

Bayfield Point   *See* Bayfield.

Bay Fortune (Kings); **Fortune Cove** (Prince); **Fortune River** (Kings)   The river flows in an easterly direction to empty in Bay Fortune and the NORTHUMBERLAND STRAIT. The first Acadian settlement dates from the 1740s and was known as 'Havre de Fortune.' The name appears as *Rivière à la Fortune* (de la Roque 1752) and was later applied to Bay Fortune at the mouth of the river. It is possible that the name may have originated with that of a schooner named *La Fortune*. Fortune Cove is in PRINCE COUNTY, on the south side of MILL RIVER. It also originated during the French colonial period, when it appeared as *Anse à la Fortune*. See also FORTUNE BAY, Newfoundland.

Bedeque; Bedeque Bay (Prince) Adjacent to NORTHUMBERLAND STRAIT, southwest of SUMMERSIDE. The name may be traced to Mi'kmaq sources, and is traceable to *Petekook,* an earlier version of a word later influenced by French spelling. It is thus descriptive of the position of the harbour in relation to travel along the shore from the eastward. De la Roque has *Bedecque* in 1752; as late as 1841, Bayfield uses the shortened form *Bedec*. From the mid-nineteenth century onward, 'Bedeque' has been the accepted spelling. See also BADDECK, Nova Scotia.

Bedeque Bay   *See* Bedeque.

Belfast (Queens)   Two kilometres from the Trans-Canada Highway, on the PINETTE RIVER. Resettled in 1803 on the abandoned site of an earlier Acadian village by Scots from Skye, Uist, Ross-shire, and Inverness. The colony was the project of Scottish philanthropist Thomas Douglas, fifth Earl of Selkirk (1771–1820). It is generally thought that the name was earlier assigned by Captain James Smith, for Belfast, Ireland. However, there is also a contending claim that it may be traced to French sources and is a corruption of 'La Belle Face.' Local historian Jean M. MacLennan asserts: 'Whatever its origin, the name has acquired a well loved significance of its own.' The community is dominated by St. John's Presbyterian Church, erected in 1824. The crowning feature of this structure is the tower, said to be based on a design by Sir Christopher Wren (1632–1723).

Belle River   (Queens) Flows into NORTHUMBERLAND STRAIT northwest of WOOD ISLANDS. The name is a descriptive, and may be traced to the French 'Belle Rivière.' It is on the southern fringe of the Selkirk Settlement (see BELFAST) and was settled in 1803 by Highland Scots.

Bells Point   *See* Cape Traverse.

Belmont Lot 16 (Prince)   Northwest of SUMMERSIDE and within Lot 16. The community was first known as 'the Lower Lot' and as 'the Shore Road.' In 1888, 'the inhabitants thought that the time had come to have a more distinctive and outstanding name. Mr. Murray Auld proposed "Belmont" and the name was subsequently accepted.' It may have been suggested by BELMONT, Nova Scotia, named at about the same time. Writer L.M. Montgomery was once a teacher in the Belmont school. She later recounted her experience: 'I boarded in a very cold farmhouse. In the evening I would be too tired to write. So I religiously

arose at an hour early for that purpose ... I would put on a heavy coat, sit on my feet to keep them from freezing, and with fingers so cramped I could scarcely hold the pen, I would write my "stint" for the day.'

Bideford; Bideford River (Prince)   The river flows eastward into LENNOX CHANNEL. The river and community were named in 1818 for the port of Bideford, in Devon. This section of the province was settled largely by West Country emigrants from Devon, Cornwall, and Somerset.

Bideford River   *See* Bideford.

Bloomfield (Prince)   Southwest of ALBERTON on Highways 2 and 145. The community was first known as 'O'Halloran Road' for James O'Halloran, an early settler. With the establishment of the post office in 1873, the new name was selected. Site of Bloomfield Provincial Park. It may be for Bloomfield in Prince Edward County, Ontario.

Blooming Point (Queens) Projects into TRACADIE BAY. The settlement name dates from at least 1876, when it was noted in the *Island Argus*. The new name replaced the earlier Tracadie Sand Hills and was taken from the descriptive for the 5-kilometre sand spit at the eastern end of the PRINCE EDWARD ISLAND NATIONAL PARK. In summer the dunes are covered with lichens and wild roses, thus giving rise to the name.

Bonshaw (Queens)   North of ARGYLE SHORE, on Highway 1. On 10 November 1837 William Walter Irving, a recent emigrant from near Kirtlebridge, Scotland, purchased 80 hectares on the WEST RIVER, in Lot 30. He called his new home after 'Bonshaw Tower' (southeast of Kirtlebridge), the ancestral home of the Irvings in Dumfries-shire, Scotland. See Ian MacQuarrie, *The Bonshaw Hills* (Charlottetown 1989), for an in-depth look at this section of the province.

Borden (Prince)   Fronts on the NORTHUMBERLAND STRAIT, opposite CAPE TORMENTINE, New Brunswick. The Prince Edward Island terminal for the Marine Atlantic ferry service and the Fixed Link with New Brunswick. The ferry terminal was first established in 1917 and named for Sir Robert Borden (1854–1937), then prime minister of Canada. It replaced the earlier name, Carleton Point. See also CARLETON COVE.

Boughton Bay; Boughton Island; Boughton River (Kings) The bay

is adjacent to NORTHUMBERLAND STRAIT, between LAUNCHING POINT and SPRY POINT. For John, Lord Brudenell (1735–1770), who was created Lord Montagu of Boughton in 1762. 'Boughton House' is located near Geddington, in Northamptonshire, England. The island and river take their name from the bay. See also CARDIGAN and MONTAGUE.

Boughton Island   *See* Boughton Bay.

Boughton River   *See* Boughton Bay.

Bouquet Point (Prince)   Extends into SEVENMILE BAY. The name was assigned by Samuel Holland, for General Henry Bouquet (1719–1765), a commander in the British army who served in North America from 1759 to 1762, during the course of the Seven Years War. His papers are an important source of information concerning this campaign.

Brackley Bay; Brackley Beach (Queens)   Adjacent to PRINCE EDWARD ISLAND NATIONAL PARK. Named for Arthur Brackley (?–1776), who arrived in the province on 30 August 1770, and served as first clerk of the legislative council from 1772 until his death by drowning (possibly in this bay) in 1774.

Brackley Beach   *See* Brackley Bay.

Brae; Brae Island; Brae River (Prince)   On the Brae River, which flows into NORTHUMBERLAND STRAIT. This area was settled in the 1820s by immigrants from Scotland. The name is descriptive and is taken from the Gaelic for 'sloping land ... as the area slopes in gradual ascent from its shorefront on the Northumberland Strait' (Douglas). Brae Island is a sand bar located at the mouth of the river.

Brae Island   *See* Brae.

Brae River   *See* Brae.

Breadalbane (Queens)   On Highway 231. First known as 'Holm's Mills,' after an early settler. Renamed in 1887, for Breadalbane, Perthshire, Scotland.

Bridgetown (Kings)   On the BOUGHTON RIVER. The name stems from the fact that a bridge across the river was built about 1860 (Rayburn).

Brookfield (Queens)   Southeast of HUNTER RIVER, on Highway 2. The name was bestowed by the Reverend Alexander Sutherland, minister of the local Presbyterian church. It was descriptive of the church's location in relation to the WHEATLEY RIVER, which becomes a 'brook' at this point.

Brookvale (Queens)   On Highway 13, northeast of CRAPAUD. The name is descriptive. The community is the site of Brookvale Provincial Ski Park, the only such facility on Prince Edward Island. In 1991 Brookvale hosted the Canada Winter Games cross-country-ski competition.

Brudenell Point; Brudenell River (Kings)   The river flows into CARDIGAN BAY and was named by Samuel Holland in honour of George Brudenell, Earl of Cardigan (1712–1790). In 1731, Jean-Pierre de Roma (fl. 1715–1757), together with three associates, was granted all the land drained by the rivers now known as Brudenell, MONTAGUE, and CARDIGAN. His settlement, known as 'Trois-Rivières,' and sometimes as 'La Romanie,' was located on present-day Brudenell Point. Roma founded a substantial settlement, consisting of two piers, houses, storehouses, bakery, and forge. Roads were blazed in all directions to Saint-Pierre (ST. PETERS); Rivière des Sturgeons (STURGEON RIVER), Souris, and Port-la-Joie (FORT AMHERST). The settlement was destroyed on 20 June 1745 by an invading force of New Englanders.

Brudenell River   *See* Brudenell Point.

Bunbury (Queens)   On the HILLSBOROUGH RIVER, opposite CHARLOTTETOWN. Bestowed by John Bovyer, a grandson of the Reverend Stephen Bovyer, a Loyalist from Providence, Rhode Island, who came to Prince Edward Island following the American Revolution. Named for the Bovyer ancestral home in Cheshire, England. In 1995 Bunbury became part of the new town of STRATFORD, an amalgamation of several communities southeast of Charlottetown.

Burlington (Prince)   On Highway 101, near the QUEENS COUNTY boundary. First known as 'Eel River,' and later as 'Morrisons Cross'; the name was changed to Burlington on 26 April 1867. The name is a corruption of Bridlington, Yorkshire, England, and may have been inspired by Burlington Bay, in Ontario, or by Burlington House, Piccadilly, London.

Cable Head (Kings)   Northwest of ST. PETERS, on the GULF OF ST. LAWRENCE. Takes its name from an incident in the early colonial period when a group of Scottish settlers 'found a piece of hemp cable on the shore, evidently from some vessel' (Douglas).

Cabot Provincial Park (Prince)   At the tip of MALPEQUE PENINSULA. As the name implies, this is reputedly the site of John Cabot's landfall in 1497. Unfortunately, there is no documentary evidence to substantiate the claim. It is, however, the site of an interesting provincial park which fronts on MALPEQUE harbour and the GULF OF ST. LAWRENCE. See chapter 1, page 5, for details concerning the Cabot-landfall controversy.

Caledonia (Queens)   On the boundary between QUEENS and KINGS counties, at the junction of Highways 24, 315, and 325. Originally known as 'County Line'; the name was changed in 1873 to Caledonia, the historic name for Scotland – an appropriate designation in the most 'Scottish' province in Canada. From 1798, when Scots comprised one-half of the population, through to the present, they have formed the largest ethnic group in the province.

Campbells Cove; Campbells Point (Kings)   The cove is west of EAST POINT, on the GULF OF ST. LAWRENCE. It was named for members of the clan Campbell who settled the area in the early 1800s. When approaching the coast of what is now Prince Edward Island in 1534, Jacques Cartier reported: 'We caught sight of land in appearance like two islands, which lay some nine or ten leagues to the west–south-west of us.' Various commentators have suggested that these two points were Campbells Point, adjacent to the cove, and nearby Sylvester Point. Present scholarship disagrees and places the sightings farther westward; possibly Capes Turner and Tryon, prominent headlands east and west, respectively, of NEW LONDON BAY. See also CAPE KILDARE.

Campbells Point   *See* Campbells Cove.

Canavoy; Canavoy Island (Kings)   The settlement is northeast of MOUNT STEWART, on Highway 350. The name is possibly a corruption of Canonbie, Dumfries-shire, Scotland, ancestral home of early settlers. The island is in adjacent SAVAGE HARBOUR.

Canavoy Island   *See* Canavoy.

Canceaux Cove; Canceaux Point (Queens)   The point adjoins Fort Amherst–Port La Joie National Historic Park, on ROCKY POINT. Both names may be traced to that of the survey ship which brought Captain Samuel Holland from England to HILLSBOROUGH BAY in October 1764. According to Holland, 'the vessel was unrigged

and laid up in a cove a mile distant from the fort, where she is out of danger from the ice.' See also HOLLAND COVE.

Canceaux Point   *See* Canceaux Cove.

Canoe Cove (Queens)   Fronts on NORTHUMBERLAND STRAIT, west of RICE POINT. During the French colonial period, the area was known as 'Anse Canot' (Canoe Cove), and this name has persisted despite efforts to supplant it. In 1765 an attempt was made by Captain Holland to rename the location Allen Cove, for Admiral John Carter Allen, who was present at the capture of Fortress Louisbourg in 1758. Although Robert Douglas insists that the prosaic 'Allen Cove' is the correct designation, it has never found popular acceptance, and Canoe Cove remains on the map.

Cape Egmont; Egmont Bay (Prince)   The bay fronts on the NORTHUMBERLAND STRAIT, between Cape Egmont and WEST POINT. Both bay and cape were named for John Perceval, second Earl of Egmont and Baron Lovel and Holland (1711–1770). Described as a shrewd and conniving man, he was responsible for initiating a plan that ultimately led to the infamous land question. In 1763 Egmont presented a memorial to King George III in which he modestly requested 'a grant of the whole island of St. John, estimated at two million acres, with all rights, royalties, privileges, franchises and appurtenances, with all criminal and civil jurisdiction.' He then went on to outline a feudal system of landholding, with himself installed as the 'Lord Paramount ... residing in a strong castle, mounted with ten pieces of cannon, each carrying a ball of four pounds.' Although this scheme was denied, the British government did adopt, following a survey completed by Captain Samuel Holland in 1765, a system only slightly less preposterous than that proposed by the earl. On 23 July 1767, all but one of the townships or lots into which the Island had been divided were 'assigned by lottery to some one hundred individuals, the vast majority of whom were land speculators completely disinterested in the real estate they had so effortsly acquired' (Bolger). The result, the installation of a system of absentee landlords, the majority of whom had little or no interest in the Island beyond collecting rent, was not finally settled until the Land Purchase Act of 1875. By 1878 the last of the descendants of the winners of the 'grand lottery' of 1767 were paid off. Ironically, the names Cape Egmont, Egmont Bay, ENMORE, and PERCIVAL BAY are the Island's only reminders of the 'clever but quixotic earl.' In a fit of pique, when the lottery to assign lands was held, he refused to participate.

Cape Gage (Prince)   Juts into NORTHUMBERLAND STRAIT, north of MIMINEGASH. It was named for General Thomas Gage (1721–1787), commander-in-chief of British forces in North America from 1763 to 1772. Approximately 20 kilometres to the south is Cape Wolfe, named for General James Wolfe (1727–1759), who lost his life at the siege of Québec. Both names were assigned by Holland in 1765.

Cape Kildare; Kildare Capes; Kildare Point; Kildare River. (Prince) The river flows into ALBERTON harbour, at Kildare Point; Cape Kildare and Kildare Capes are north of JACQUES CARTIER PROVINCIAL PARK. All were named by Samuel Holland for James, Earl of Kildare (1722–1773), a son-in-law of Charles Lennox, Duke of Richmond. The cape is the 'very fine headland, the cap d'Orléans,' named by Jacques Cartier on 1 July 1534.

Cape Traverse (Prince)   East of BORDEN, on NORTHUMBERLAND STRAIT. The name dates from the French colonial period and is noted as *Rivière de la Traverse* by de la Roque in 1752, and *Cape Traverse* by Holland in 1765. Its application to the cape indicated that this was the nearest point on the Island to the mainland. The name is now applied to the settlement, the site of a National Historic Monument commemorating the iceboat service that linked the Island with the mainland from 1827 until 1917. The cape has been known since 1965 as 'Bells Point,' for the Bell family, early grantees in the area.

Cape Tryon (Queens)   On the GULF OF ST. LAWRENCE. For origin see TRYON HEAD.

Cape Wolfe   *See* Cape Gage.

Cardigan Bay; Cardigan River (Kings)   The bay is located at the mouths of Cardigan, Brudenell, and MONTAGUE rivers. The name was bestowed in 1765 by Captain Samuel Holland, for George Brudenell (1712–1790), Earl of Cardigan. See also BRUDENELL RIVER.

Cardigan River   *See* Cardigan Bay.

Carleton; Carleton Cove; Carlton Point (Prince)   The cove is north of BORDEN, adjacent to SEVENMILE BAY. Named after General Sir Guy Carleton (1724–1808),

who served as governor of Canada (1768–78, 1786–96). The community of Carleton, east of Borden, traces its name to Carleton Point (now the site of Borden). The point was originally named for the adjoining cove.

Carleton Cove   *See* Carleton.

Carleton Point   *See* Carleton.

Cascumpec; Cascumpec Bay (Prince)   The bay fronts on the GULF OF ST. LAWRENCE, from which it is protected by the Cascumpec Sand Hills. Of Mi'kmaq origin, the name is traceable to *Kaskamkek*, for 'bold sandy shore.' Appears in the early seventeenth century as *Caisiqupet*, and in 1760 as *havre de Cachecampec* (Thomas Pichon). Samuel Holland renders it as *Holland Bay*, after the French Kascumpeck (1765). An attempt was made in 1966 to standarize the spelling as Cascumpeque; however, the shortened form is cited in the 1990 *Prince Edward Island Gazetteer*.

Cascumpec Bay   *See* Cascupec.

Cavendish (Queens)   'Cavendish is a narrow farming settlement fronting on the Gulf of St. Lawrence. It is about three miles long and one wide ... The shore is very beautiful; part of it is rock, where the rugged red cliffs rise steeply from boulder-strewn coves. Part is a long, gleaming sandshore, divided from the fields and ponds behind by a row of rounded sand-dunes, covered by course grass.' L.M. Montgomery (1874–1942), author, poet, creator of *Anne of Green Gables*, and Prince Edward Island's most famous author, penned this description of Cavendish in 1917. Despite the intrusion of the tourist industry, the description, in large measure still stands. The name may be traced to William Winter, an army officer who, in 1771, was granted Lot 23, including the site of Cavendish, by Governor Walter Patterson (*ca* 1735–1798). Winter subsequently named his residence in honour of his patron, Field-Marshal Lord Cavendish (1729–1803).

Cedar Dunes Provincial Park
See West Point.

Central Bedeque   *See* Bedeque.

Central Lot 16 (Prince)   Northwest of SUMMERSIDE. In 1767 Prince Edward Island was subdivided into sixty-seven townships. These were raffled by a lottery and were most often referred to by lot and number, as in Lot 16. See also CAPE EGMONT.

Charlottetown (Queens)   In 1720 Robert-David Gotteville de Belile

(fl. 1696–1724), commandant of the Compagnie de Île Saint-Jean, established a settlement on ROCKY POINT, between the present WEST RIVER and HILLSBOROUGH BAY. It was named Port la Joie, as an expression of joy upon the safe arrival of the expedition in the New World. In 1763, Île Saint-Jean was officially ceded to the British and its name anglicized to St. John's Island. During the course of a survey of the island, Captain Samuel Holland made the following recommendation: 'The capital, to be called Charlotte Town, is proposed to be built on a point of the harbour of Port la Joie, betwixt York [North] and Hillsborough Rivers ... The ground designed for the Town and Fortifications is well situated upon a regular ascent from the water side; a battery some distance advanced, will entirely command the harbour.' The new town was named in honour of Queen Charlotte, consort of King George III. Charlottetown was incorporated as a town in 1855, and as a city in 1875. During early September 1864, the provincial legislative building was the site of a conference that considered the union of the British North American colonies, thus earning Charlottetown the title 'Birthplace of Confederation.' To mark the centennial of this event, in 1964, the Confederation Centre was built, funded by the federal and provincial governments. It houses a memorial hall, theatre, and library, and an art gallery that includes an important collection of the work of Island artist Robert Harris (1849–1919), along with drawings, sketches, and plans done by his brother, architect William Critchlow Harris (1854–1913). The first season of the Charlottetown Festival was held in 1965, with a musical version of L.M. Montgomery's *Anne of Green Gables* as the main attraction. This musical continues to play to capacity audiences each summer. The national importance of the complex has been eloquently stated by Dr. T.H.B. Symons: 'The Centre provides visitors with a rare opportunity to experience the sense of place and heritage that give expression to the spirit of a nation. [It] is a pan-Canadian endeavour that portrays and interprets our experience as a nation, reminding us of our substantially shared identities and opportunities.' In 1969 the University of Prince Edward Island was established in Charlottetown through the merger of Prince of Wales College (1834) and St. Dunstan's University (1855). The campus of the latter institution became the nucleus of the new university, while the facilities of the former were transferred to the newly established Holland College, a community college named for Samuel Holland (see HOLLAND COVE). As a result of legislation which took effect on 1 April 1995, the boundaries of the city were enlarged to include West Royalty, East Royalty, Winsloe, Hillsborough Park, Parkdale, and Sherwood.

Cherry Hill (Kings)   Near the head of the HILLSBOROUGH RIVER. It was named for the abundance of wild cherry trees in the vicinity.

Cherry Valley (Queens)   At the junction of Highways 1 and 3. This area was known during the French colonial period as 'Marguerite.' In 1785 it was granted to Henry Beers, a Loyalist from New York, and renamed by him Cherry Valley. According to family tradition the Beers family originally came from Cherry Valley, in Devonshire, England.

Chichester Cove (Prince)   At the mouth of INDIAN RIVER, which flows into MALPEQUE BAY. Name assigned by Samuel Holland in 1765 for Chichester, England. 'Goodwood,' seat of Charles Lennox, third Duke of Richmond (1735–1806), was in Chichester.

China Point (Queens)   Extends into ORWELL BAY. The precise origin of this place name has been lost; however, either of two theories may possibly provide an explanation. During the French colonial period, there were settlers on Île Saint-Jean with the surname Chesnay or Chainey, and some early documents spell the name of the location 'Chiney Point.' Another theory, put forward by Robert Douglas, notes that china tableware was once called 'chaney' and this may have inspired the name. Given the permanence of some French place names, the surname theory would appear the most plausible. For another example of place-name endurance see CANOE COVE. Considering the age of this place name, the further suggestion that it stems from the use of local clay for pottery does not ring true; nor does this suggestion appear to have any documentation.

Christopher Cross (Prince) North of TIGNISH, at the junction of Highways 2 and 14. Named for Patrick Christopher, who once owned a blacksmith shop at the crossroads.

Churchill (Queens)   Next to Strathgartney Provincial Park. At a public meeting held on 11 August 1900, Churchill was selected as the name for the new post office, replacing West River. Winston Spencer Churchill (1874–1965) was already well known as a Boer War correspondent. The same year also saw his election to Parliament, and the beginning of more than a half-century of public service. While prime minister, Churchill was informed of this early recognition and responded in writing: 'I am gratified to hear of the honour which the community of Churchill did me in 1900.' Some disbelief has been expressed as to the accuracy of the details sketched above. However, they were first verified by the research of Robert Douglas in 1925, long before Winston Churchill achieved his greatest fame (CPCGN Files).

Clyde River (Queens)   Flows south into the WEST RIVER. It was first known as 'Edward River,' a name bestowed by Samuel Holland for Edward, first Baron Eliot (1727–1804), who served as a commissioner of the Board of Trade and Plantations at the time of the infamous 1767 land lottery (see CAPE EGMONT). The name was little used, and for a time the prosaic Dock River, later corrupted to Dog River, sufficed. The replacement name, dating from the 1860s, is for the River Clyde in Scotland.

Colville Bay (Kings)   At the mouth of the SOURIS RIVER. Known during the French colonial period as 'Havre a la Souris,' it was renamed by Samuel Holland for Alexander, seventh Baron Colvill of Culross (1717/18–1770). Colvill, or Colville, joined the Royal Navy as a cadet at age fifteen and rose rapidly through the ranks to become a rear-admiral. He participated in the siege of Québec in 1759 and, from then until 1762, was senior naval commander in North America.

Conway; Conway Narrows (Prince)   The community is located northwest of TYNE VALLEY; Conway Narrows parallels the coast and lies directly behind Conway Sand Hills. All were named for Henry Seymour Conway (1721–1795), who served briefly as secretary of state for the Southern Department in 1765. Samuel Holland attempted to bestow the name Cavendish Channel for the Narrows; however, this name was never in popular usage. The Sand Hills were named because of their proximity to Conway Narrows.

Conway Narrows   *See* Conway.

Cornwall (Queens)   West of CHARLOTTETOWN in a fast-growing surburban area. Named after the Duchy of Cornwall in the late eighteenth century, and later reconfirmed with the establishment of the school section in 1849 and the post office in 1855.

The community became an incorporated village in 1966. Effective 1 April 1995, the three communities of Cornwall, ELIOT RIVER, and NORTH RIVER were amalgamated to form the new town of Cornwall. Initially a number of other names were suggested, including three that were eliminated: Homestead, North Riverview, and Harmony. On 6–8 February 1995, a plebiscite was held to select one of the three most popular names: Cornwall, Fairfield, and Westwood. Cornwall emerged as the clear winner, supported by 86 per cent of the electorate.

Corran Ban (Queens)   Southeast of GRAND TRACADIE. This community exemplifies the Scottish impact on Prince Edward Island nomenclature. Dating from 1773, when the area was settled by Scottish Highlanders, the name is Gaelic for 'white sickle' and refers to the appearance of the froth-covered shoreline in the autumn. When the post office was established in 1865, the community was known as 'Corran Ban Bridge'; the word 'bridge' was dropped shortly thereafter.

Courtin Island (Prince)   In MALPEQUE BAY. Abbé Courtin (?–1732) , a member of the Missions Etrangères of Paris, came to Québec in 1723 and later served as missionary to the Native peoples on Île Saint-Jean. He spent the winter of 1731 at Malpeque Bay and was responsible for translating part of the catechism, along with some prayers into Mi'kmaq. According to Joseph de la Roque he was granted an island in the bay 'from which fact it bears the name of Île à Monsieur Courtin.' For a time it was known as 'Bunbury Island,' for Sir Charles Thomas Bunbury (1740–1821); however, this name fell into disuse. Little Courtin Island is southeast of the main island.

Crapaud (Queens)   On the boundary between PRINCE and QUEENS counties. The name Rivière aux Crapauds, literally 'river of toads,' was applied to the nearby WESTMORLAND RIVER by the French. However, the name was probably inspired by the Acadian phrase *le crapaud de mer*, meaning 'eel'; thus, it is more logical to assume that the river was named for an abundance of eels rather than toads. Spelled 'Crappaux' in a memorial dated 20 February 1818. Crapaud has existed as a community name since the establishment of the post office in 1857.

Crowbush Cove (Kings)   On the GULF OF ST. LAWRENCE, east of SAVAGE HARBOUR. It is the site of Crowbush Cove Provincial Park and the Crowbush Golf Club. The name stems from a nickname once applied to John MacDonald, who was among the early Scottish settlers in the area. To distinguish him from numerous others with the same name, he became known as 'Johnnie Crowbush MacDonald.' Reputedly the nickname was applied because of the derelict appearance of the farm and the abundance of crows inevitably observed overhead. The Crowbush Golf Club, designed by Tom McBroom, has been described as 'a visual and competitive masterpiece.'

Culloden (Queens)   Northwest of WOOD ISLANDS. Named for the Battle of Culloden, 16 April 1746. This battle saw the Scottish Highlanders crushed by a superior force of English and Lowland Scots under command of the infamous Prince William Augustus, Duke of Cumberland (1721–1765). In a province populated by a high percentage of Highland Scots, this is a predictable place name. See also CUMBERLAND, Nova Scotia.

Cumberland Cove (Prince) West of TRYON HEAD. Not named for 'the infamous Duke' (see CULLODEN), but rather for Richard Cumberland (1732–1811), dramatist and civil servant. He was a friend of surveyor Samuel Holland, who bestowed the name. In the 1767 ballot for townships, Lot 61 was won by Cumberland. Nearby RICHARD POINT, also assigned by Holland, marks the career of the same individual.

Cymbria (Queens)   On the west side of RUSTICO BAY. In 1822 a Welsh settler, William Hodges, named his new home 'Cymbria Lodge,' after the poetic name for Wales. It was subsequently applied to the community.

Dalvay Beach; Dalvay Lake; Dalvay Pond (Queens)   On the GULF OF ST. LAWRENCE, at the eastern end of PRINCE EDWARD ISLAND NATIONAL PARK. In 1895, Alexander MacDonald, of Cincinnati, Ohio, vice-president of the Standard Oil Company and an associate of John D. Rockefeller's, built a summer residence here. He named it 'Dalvay-By-The-Sea,' for his ancestral home in Scotland. In 1937 it became part of the park and operates as a hotel during the tourist season. Dalvay Pond and Lake are adjacent.

Dalvay Lake   *See* Dalvay Beach.

Dalvay Pond   *See* Dalvay Beach.

Darnley; Darnley Basin (Prince) The basin faces the Malpeque Sand Hills and the GULF OF ST. LAWRENCE. The Mi'kmaq description-

tive name for the area was *Kijeboogwek*, for 'enclosed,' as the basin is practically enclosed from the gulf by a sand bar. The feature was named by Samuel Holland after Charles Lennox (1735–1806), Duke of Richmond; one of the Duke's titles was Earl of Darnley.

Darnley Basin   *See* Darnley.

Derby (Prince)   Near the mouth of the BRAE RIVER. Named for Edward George Geoffrey Smith Stanley, fourteenth Earl of Derby (1799–1869), who served briefly as prime minister of Great Britain on three separate occasions: 1852, 1858–9, 1866–8. The name was selected at a public meeting on 20 March 1869 as a replacement for Brae East. See also DERBY, New Brunswick.

DeSable; DeSable River (Queens)   Between BONSHAW and HAMPTON, on Highway 1. The DeSable River enters the Northumberland Strait at this point. The name dates from the French colonial period, when it was Rivière de Sable, or 'river of sand.'

DeSable River   *See* DeSable.

DesBarres Point (Kings) Extends into NORTHUMBERLAND STRAIT, north of MURRAY HAR-

BOUR. The name commemorates the lengthy career of Joseph Frederic Wallet DesBarres (1721?–1824). During his lifetime DesBarres was an army officer, military engineer, surveyor, artist, landholder, and colonial administrator. Although he served as lieutenant-governor of Cape Breton (1784–7) and as governor of Prince Edward Island (1804–12), his greatest contribution, both generally and in the field of toponymy, was *The Atlantic Neptune*. Published between 1774 and 1784, this *magnum opus* consists of four series of charts covering Nova Scotia, New England, the GULF OF ST. LAWRENCE, and Prince Edward Island. The *Dictionary of Canadian Biography* makes the claim of the work: 'it is in their artistic quality that the charts and views especially shine, since their accuracy is combined with an aesthetic character that places DesBarres among the more notable of the century's minor artists.' During his long career he amassed vast land holdings totalling some 32,000 hectares. These were located at Falmouth, Tatamagouche, MINUDIE, and MACCAN in Nova Scotia; yet another tract was at PETITCODIAC, in present-day New Brunswick. These lands were administered by his mistress, Mary Cannon (*ca* 1751–1827), whom he installed at his home, 'Castle Frederick,' in Falmouth. Five daughters and a son were born of this relationship. He had an additional eleven children with his wife, Martha Williams. DesBarres died in Halifax on 24 October 1824, reputedly aged 103. He is also said to have 'danced a jig on a table top' at a birthday celebration three years earlier. However, recent research indicates that his purported birthdate was 'inflated' by about eight years (*Nova Scotia Historical Review* 14/2 (1994), 108–22). More detail on DesBarres's colourful career may be found in the sources mentioned in the Bibliographical Essay. See also FALMOUTH, SYDNEY, and TATAMAGOUCHE, Nova Scotia; MOUNT DESBARRES, New Brunswick.

Devils Punchbowl Provincial Park (Queens) Northwest of FREDERICTON. Named by John Hawkins for an incident in the pioneer period when reputedly 'the devil ordered him to cut loose a cargo of rum.' Unfortunately, the story was 'met with considerable doubt,' although the 'encounter' did survive as a colourful name for the physical feature, a hollow or depression in the hills (CPCGN Files). There is also a combe, or hollow, with the same name near Haslemere, in Surrey, England; however, there is no apparent connection between the two names.

Dundas (Kings)   On Highway 2, between BRIDGETOWN and ALBION CROSS. Honours the career of George Dundas (1819–1880), who served as lieutenant-governor from 1859 to 1868. He held office during a dramatic period in Island history, characterized by controversy over the land question and the continuing debate over Confederation. In 1869 he was transferred to the governorship of the Island of St. Vincent.

Dundee (Kings)   Southwest of MORELL. Named by early Scottish settlers for the city on the River Tay in Scotland.

Dunedin (Queens)   On the WEST RIVER. Commemorates the old Gaelic name for Edinburgh. The name dates from the establishment of the post office in 1892.

Dunk River (Prince)   Flows into BEDEQUE BAY, at Ross Corner. Named by Samuel Holland for George Montagu Dunk, Earl of Halifax (1716–1771). Such diverse locations as HALIFAX, Nova Scotia, and Dunk Island, off the coast of Queensland, Australia, were also named for the same individual. *Watershed Red: The Life of the Dunk River* by biologist Kathy Martin is an engaging study of the natural history of this area. See also SUNBURY.

Dunstaffnage (Queens)   Northeast of CHARLOTTETOWN, on Highway 2. The first settlers from Argyllshire named the community for Dunstaffnage Castle, northeast of Oban, Scotland. This castle once housed the 'Stone of Destiny' before the artefact was moved to Scone, and eventually to Westminster Abbey.

Durrell Point   *See* Spry Point.

Duvar (Prince)   South of BLOOM-FIELD, on Highway 146. The name honours John Hunter-Duvar (1821–1899), a Scotsman who emigrated to Prince Edward Island in 1857 and settled at 'Hernewood,' on MILL RIVER, now part of the Mill River Resort. During his Island years he commanded the Prince County Militia, edited the *Summerside Progress* (1875–9), and served as federal Supervisor of Fisheries (1879–89). Hunter-Duvar also established a reputation as a poet and dramatist. His 'The Emigration of the Fairies' has been classified by poet and critic Fred Cogswell as 'the most aesthetically satisfying poem to be published in the Maritimes before 1890.' Of equal significance was the mystery that surrounded his wife, Annie Carter (1826–1901). Well educated in music, art, and literature, she received a quarterly allowance from a firm of English solicitors and steadfastly refused to provide any clue as to her parentage. Although she was happily married to Hunter-Duvar for over fifty years, a veil of secrecy surrounded her early life. The only clue was a scribbled note on the back of her husband's will 'that she was a first cousin of Queen Victoria' and, by deduction, one of the numerous illegitimate grandchildren of King George III and Queen Charlotte. While editing the Hunter-Duvar diaries in the 1970s, Dr. George Dewar undertook extensive genealogical and historical research in an effort to find the answer to her parentage. Nothing was found, and he concluded: 'so rests the saga of "Annie Carter" until some day the full epic story may be revealed and the chatelaine of Hernewood will be portrayed in all her royal prerequisites.'

Earnscliffe (Queens)   At the junction of Highways 267 and 268. The settlement was originally known as 'Gallas' or 'Gallows Point.' Robert Douglas is of the opinion that this name is a corruption of the family name Gillis, common in the area. He notes the first reference to Gallas Point in 1861. The name change occurred in 1897, when the new designation was selected in homage to Sir John A. Macdonald. His residence in Ottawa, known as 'Earnscliffe,' is today the official residence of the British high commissioner in Canada.

East Lake; East Point (Kings)   A descriptive for the most easterly point on the Island. The name of nearby East Lake is also a descriptive. The point was known to the Mi'kmaq as *Kespemenagek* for 'the end of the Island.' During the French colonial period, Pointe de l'Est was further westward, near present-day NORTH LAKE. The East Point Lighthouse, built in 1857, is a 19.5-metre-high octagonal tower with a range of 32 kilometres.

East Lake   *See* East Point.

Eglington Cove (Kings) Between Howe Point and ABELLS CAPE. Named for Alexander Montgomery, tenth Earl of Eglinton (1723–1769), who was Lord of the Bedchamber to King George III. As late as 1925, Robert Douglas cites the correct spelling as 'Eglinton'; however, in recent years, the phonetic rendition 'Eglington' has prevailed.

Egmont Bay   *See* Cape Egmont.

Eldon (Queens)   On Highway 1, between ORWELL CORNER and PINETTE. Eldon is a district name for the Belfast area and is of uncertain origin. It may be for John Scott (1751–1828), created

Baron Eldon in 1799, and receiving the title Earl of Eldon in 1821. The new name dates from 1862 and replaced Belfast Cross and Belfast Crossroads.

Eliot River *See* West River.

Ellerslie (Prince) North of TYNE VALLEY. There is agreement that this place name can be traced to a manor house once owned by Sir William Wallace (*ca* 1270–1305), the popular national hero of Scotland. The monument to his exploits is at Abbey Craig, near Stirling, Scotland, scene of his dramatic defeat of the English on 11 September 1297. The manor house once stood at Elderslie, or Ellerslie, in Roxburghshire. Wallace was later captured by the English; tried and convicted at Westminster Hall, London, on 23 August 1305, and executed the next day. His body was subsequently gibbeted at Berwick, Stirling, and Perth. Thus, through place names, Scots continue to honour their heroes.

Elmira (Kings) Northeast of SOURIS. First known as 'Portage,' for the route between NORTH and SOUTH lakes. The new name was suggested in 1872 by George B. MacEachern, the local teacher. The name had no local significance 'but was selected for its euphony from a gazetteer'

(Douglas). The local railway station was once the end of the line for the PEI Railway. Today it houses memorabilia and displays depicting the history of railroading in the province. The Elmira Railway Museum is part of the PEI Museum and Heritage Foundtion.

Emerald Junction (Queens) Southeast of KENSINGTON. The name honours Ireland and was applied because of that country's bright green vegetation. It also serves as a reminder that the Irish comprise the Island's third-largest ethnic group. When the Prince Edward Island railway was built, this location was the junction point for a branch line to BORDEN.

Emyvale (Queens) Northeast of CRAPAUD. Settled by the Irish, and named for Emyvale, County Monaghan, Ireland.

Enmore; Enmore River (Prince) The river flows south into EGMONT BAY; the settlement is on Highway 11, at Robbs Creek. Named for John Perceval (1711–1770), second Earl of Egmont. His other titles included Baron Lovel and Holland of Enmore. See also CAPE EGMONT.

Enmore River *See* Enmore.

Fairview (Queens) Southwest of CHARLOTTETOWN, overlooking the WEST RIVER. This descriptive was selected in 1889 to replace the earlier Webster Creek because the location provided a 'fair view' of the city of Charlottetown.

Fanning Bank (Queens); **Fanning Brook** (Kings)   Fanning Brook is located southeast of MOUNT STEWART. Named for Edmund Fanning (1739–1818), lieutenant-governor of Prince Edward Island from 1786 to 1804 and a landowner in the area. Fanning is also remembered for setting aside a point of land jutting into CHARLOTTETOWN harbour as a site for a future residence for the lieutenant-governor. The residence, eventually to be called 'Fanning Bank' in his honour, was not built until 1834, following plans drawn up by architect Isaac Smith (1795–1871). In 1873 the remainder of this land was set aside as Victoria Park, 'for the use and benefit of all Her Majesty's subjects, as a park, a promenade and a pleasure ground.'

Fanning Brook   *See* Fanning Bank.

Farmington (Kings)   On Highway 2, between ST. PETERS and BAY FORTUNE. This place name was coined in the late nineteenth century for the local school section. Highway 2 was, and still is, known as the 'Fortune Road.' Farmington is noteworthy as the

home of Lawrence Doyle (1847–1907), Prince Edward Island's farmer–poet 'who lived all his sixty years along the Fortune Road.' Included among his folk-songs are: 'The Picnic at Groshaut,' 'The Merchants of the Bay,' and 'When Johnny Went Plowing for Kearon.' Edward D. Ives, his biographer, has summarized Doyle's significance: 'His story is especially valuable because part of his response to life was to interpret it for others by making songs, and through his songs he has given us many remarkably sharp pictures of his world ... The songs show us the paradox of the uncommon common man.' See also GROSHAUT.

Five Houses (Queens)   East of ST. PETERS, on Highway 2, in an area originally settled by the French. The descriptive name may be traced to the Holland Survey of 1765, when a 'ruined village of five houses' was noted at this location. For a similar name see OLD BARNS, Nova Scotia.

Flat River (Queens)   Flows into the NORTHUMBERLAND STRAIT, at GASCOIGNE COVE. The name is indicative of the local landscape. It is a direct translation of the French place name Rivière Platte.

Fort Amherst (Queens)   At ROCKY POINT, on the site of the

French settlement Port La Joie, captured by the British in 1758. On 10 October 1758, Lieutenant-Colonel Andrew Rollo, fifth Baron Rollo (1703–1765), reported the completion of Fort Amherst, named for his superior Major-General Jeffrey Amherst (see ROLLO BAY). It is now part of the Fort Amherst–Port La Joie National Historic Park.

Fort Augustus (Queens)   Southwest of MOUNT STEWART. Named for Fort Augustus, in Inverness-shire Scotland. Ironically, it was named after Prince William Augustus, Duke of Cumberland (1721–1765), 'Butcher Cumberland,' to the Scots. Considering the Scottish antipathy towards the Duke, the survival of this place name on Prince Edward Island is surprising. See also CULLODEN.

Fortune Cove   *See* Bay Fortune.

Fortune River   *See* Bay Fortune.

48 Road (Kings)   Northwest of CARDIGAN. This unusual place name describes its location, on the road leading to Lot 48. Before the closure of the railway, the community was known as '48 Road Station.'

Foxley River (Prince)   Flows northwest into CASCUMPEC BAY.

The name was assigned by Samuel Holland in 1765, for Henry Fox, first Baron Holland of Foxley (1705–1744). Fox held a number of minor posts in the British civil service before being elevated to the cabinet as secretary of state in 1755. He resigned in 1756 to accept the post of paymaster general, a position that reputedly led to his making a large fortune. Fox Island, at the mouth of the MILL RIVER, was probably named for the same individual. See also ALBERTON.

Fredericton (Queens)   West of HUNTER RIVER. Alan Rayburn suggests that it was 'possibly named for Fredericton, New Brunswick.' Technically, since it appears as 'Frederick Town' on early documents, it may well have the same origin as the New Brunswick city, being named for Prince Frederick Augustus, Duke of York (1763–1827), second son of King George III.

French Creek (Kings); **Frenchfort** (Queens); **French Marsh Point** (Kings)   The eight or more place names that incorporate the prefix 'French' are all reminders that the Island was once Île Saint-Jean, part of the colonial empire of France. For example: French Creek flows north into the MONTAQUE RIVER. Holland renamed this feature 'Elibank Creek,' possibly for Patrick Murray, fifth Baron Elibank; however, this name did not survive. Frenchfort, northeast of CHARLOTTETOWN, on Highway 260, is exactly what it says: the site of an early French fort. French Marsh Point borders on Murray Harbour and, although not a major French settlement site, it is indicative of the French presence in the immediate area.

Frenchfort   *See* French Creek.

French Marsh Point   *See* French Creek.

Gallas Point   *See* Earnscliffe.

Garfield (Queens)   On Highway 207, between BELFAST and MELVILLE. This area, settled by Scots, was earlier known as 'Gairloch,' after a parish in Ross-shire, Scotland. For a brief period in the 1870s, the post office was called 'Selkirk Road.' The new name, 'Garfield,' was adopted in 1881, the year that James A. Garfield, twentieth president of the United States, was assassinated after only six months in office. However, Robert Douglas, writing in 1925, noted: 'it is still called Gairloch by the old people.'

Gascoigne Cove (Queens)   At the mouth of the FLAT RIVER. The name was bestowed by Samuel Holland in 1765 for Bamber Gas-

coyne (1725–1791), Lord Commissioner of Trade and Plantations (1763–79). Over time, the spelling changed to 'Gascoigne,' in the mistaken view that the name was for a 'Gascoigne,' that is, someone from Gascony in France. See also DILIGENT RIVER, Nova Scotia.

Gaspereau (Kings)   On ST. MARYS BAY, south of PANMURE ISLAND. The name occurs in all three Maritime provinces and is for the gasperot or gaspereau, a species of herring. See also GASPEREAU RIVER, in Nova Scotia and New Brunswick.

Georgetown (Kings)   On CARDIGAN BAY. The name George Town was assigned by Samuel Holland in 1765, for King George III (1738–1820) in anticipation of its becoming the capital of KINGS COUNTY. At this time a domain or 'royalty' was also attached to the projected town. Despite many natural advantages, Georgetown was destined not to flourish. As early as 1820 Walter Johnstone, in his *Letters from Prince Edward Island*, wrote: 'This is the best harbour on the Island. It has the greatest depth of water, easiest of entrance, the best shelter, earliest open in the spring, and latest shutting down in the fall ... But [as yet] no man of property or enterprise has pitched his tent here so as to give the town and port a beginning, although it is certainly the most eligible situation on the Island.' See also MALPEQUE and WEST ROYALTY.

Glencoe (Kings)   Northwest of MONTAGUE. Named for Glencoe, Argyllshire, Scotland. This place name is enshrined in Scottish lore and legend as the site of the 1692 massacre of thirty-six MacDonalds by members of Clan Campbell (see GLENCOE, Nova Scotia). The name was selected in 1869, proving the enduring quality of folk memory.

Glencorradale (Kings)   On Highway 302, between BALTIC and Priest Pond. Settled by Scottish immigrants from the Isle of Skye. The name was suggested by an incident in the conflict over the land question. In the 1840s the government sent a detachment of soldiers to quell a 'disturbance' among the tenants in northern KINGS COUNTY, forcing the latter into hiding. To the Scottish settlers, this was reminiscent of Prince Charles Edward Stuart's concealment from the English at Glen Caradel on the Isle of Skye following his defeat at Culloden on 16 April 1746. As further proof of the longevity of Scottish historical memory, a century later, in 1846, Glencorradale was selected as the name for this community.

Glenfinnan; Glenfinnan Island; Glenfinnan Lake; Glenfinnan River (Queens)   All are on the east side of the HILLSBOROUGH RIVER, in Lot 35. Named by Captain John MacDonald (1742–1810), who was once laird of Glenfinnan and Glenaladale in Scotland. His father, Alexander, his predecessor as chieftain of the Clan MacDonald of Clanranald, was a supporter of Prince Charles Edward Stuart. Glenfinnan at the head of Loch Shiel, Scotland, was where the Prince raised his standard on 19 August 1745. See also SCOTCHFORT.

Glenfinnan Island   *See* Glenfinnan.

Glenfinnan Lake   *See* Glenfinnan.

Glenfinnan River   *See* Glenfinnan.

Glengarry (Prince)   Southeast of CAMPBELLTON. Named by Alexander McDonald for Glengarry, in Inverness, Scotland.

Glenmartin; Glenwilliam (Kings)   Northwest of Murray River. Glenmartin was named for John Martin, from the Isle of Skye, one of the first settlers in the area. His brother-in-law William Matheson, also from Skye, is immortalized in nearby Glenwilliam.

Glenroy (Queens)   West of MOUNT STEWART. Named after Glen Roy, in Inverness, Scotland.

Glenwilliam   *See* Glenmartin.

Governors Island (Queens)   In the centre of HILLSBOROUGH BAY. A translation of the original French name Île Gouverneur, for Robert-David Gotteville de Belile (fl. 1696–1724), who was commandant of the Compagnie de l'Île Saint-Jean. He arrived in the colony in the autumn of 1720 and established headquarters for the company at Port La Joie. Additional settlements were started at Saint-Pierre (ST. PETERS) and Tranche-Montagne (now SOUTH LAKE).

Gowanbrae (Kings)   Northwest of SOURIS, on Highway 306. In 1830 John and William McGowan purchased 40 hectares of land and a millsite at the head of the Souris River. They were sons of Peter McGowan (*ca* 1763–1810), who served for many years as attorney general of the province. They called their farm 'Gowan Brae,' for 'mountain daisy.' Both 'gowan' and 'brae' are commonly combined in Scottish place names. See also ARDGOWAN and BRAE.

Grande Digue Point; Grande Digue Shore (Prince)   The point juts into PERCIVAL BAY. The name comes from the French colonial period and is a probable reference to the sand bar, which resembles 'a great dike.'

Grande Digue Shore   *See* Grande Digue Point.

Grand Pere Point (Queens) Extends into RUSTICO BAY. Named for an early Acadian settler, Simeon Gallant Grand-Père. Appears as *Grand-Père* or *Simeons Point* in the *Meacham Atlas* (1880).

Grand River (Prince)   Northwest of SUMMERSIDE, flowing into MALPEQUE BAY. Sometimes referred to as 'Ellis River,' the name bestowed by Samuel Holland for Welbore Ellis, first Baron Mendip (1713–1802), who served in a number of minor civil-service posts in the 1760s and 1770s. Known briefly as 'Quagmire River.' By the time of the Bayfield survey in 1850, the earlier descriptive, Grand River, was fixed.

Grand Tracadie   *See* Tracadie.

Green Gables (Queens)   Within the village of Cavendish. A simple diary entry – 'Elderly couple apply to orphan asylum for boy; a girl is sent them' – marked the origin of Lucy Maude Montgomery's immortal *Anne of Green*

Gables, first published in 1908. The establishment in 1953 of the Green Gables post office at Cavendish was simply bureaucratic recognition of the fame and popularity of the fictional Anne and her home. On an average day during the tourist season upwards of 600 or 700 people, from all corners of the globe, visit Green Gables. Their attitude speaks volumes, as one of the guides reported: 'As a rule tourists are noisy; they laugh and shout. At Green Gables they speak in hushed voices, as though at a shrine.' See also CAVENDISH and CHARLOTTETOWN.

Green Park Provincial Park (Prince)   On a peninsula extending into the estuary of the BIDEFORD RIVER and LENNOX CHANNEL. Established as a provincial park in 1960 to commemorate the nineteenth-century shipbuilding empire founded by James Yeo, Sr. (1788–1868). A native of Kilkhampton, Cornwall, he emigrated to Prince Edward Island in 1819. During his lifetime he was responsible for the construction of at least 155 ships, and was regarded as the 'greatest of Island shipbuilders.' Following his death in 1868, the dynasty was carried on by his younger sons, John and James Jr. The centre-piece of Green Park is a magnificent Gothic Revival–style home built by James Yeo, Jr. (1832–1916). It has been carefully restored to reflect its heyday in the Golden Age of Sail. James Yeo, Jr., was also active in politics. Following service in the provincial Assembly, he represented Prince in the House of Commons (1873–91). The name Green Park is a descriptive coined by Yeo for his property. It is part of the PEI Museum and Heritage Foundation. See also ALMA.

Groshaut (Kings)   East of Farmington. The community is now part of St. Charles. During the summer of 1898, a picnic to raise money for a new church was held at Groshaut. The parish priest, the Reverend Edward Walker, a strong temperance advocate, wanted to make certain that decorum would be observed and placed an order for fifteen kegs of sweet cider. However, the inevitable happened: hard cider was shipped 'by mistake.' The resulting mêlée became the subject of a celebrated song by Lawrence Doyle, the local farmer–poet. Although the place name Groshaut, which hearkens back to the French colonial period, has disappeared, the name and the incident live on in the folk-song. See also FARMINGTON.

Guernsey Cove (Kings)   On NORTHUMBERLAND STRAIT, southeast of Murray Harbour. Settled on 3 June 1806 by emigrants from Guernsey, and named by them for their home island. A number of distinctive Prince Edward Island surnames – for example, LeLacheur, Phillips, Machon, and Brehaut – may be traced to this migration. Robert C. Tuck has described the Guernsey Cove of today as 'a place of almost tree-less fields running in gentle undu-lation from a low horizon to a high bank along the shore. All the houses are old and several are empty ... It is quiet in Guernsey Cove.'

Haldimand River (Prince) Flows north into EGMONT BAY. Named by Samuel Holland in 1765 for Sir Frederick Haldimand (1719–1791), governor general of Canada from 1778 to 1786. Haldimand's nephew Peter Fred-erick Haldimand (1741–1765) served as Holland's assistant but was unfortunately drowned 'while sounding, at Louisbourg, 16 December 1765.' This accident may also have been a factor in the naming of the river.

Hampshire (Queens); **Hampton** (Queens)   Hampshire, on High-way 225, was named for the county in England. The choice of name was, no doubt, influenced by the presence of Wiltshire, 5 kilometres west. Hampton, on Highway 1, overlooking the NORTHUMBERLAND STRAIT, takes its name from HAMPTON, New Brunswick. The latter was named for Hampton in New York State.

Hampton   *See* Hampshire.

Hardys Channel (Prince) Between CONWAY and Malpeque Sand Hills. Named Conway Inlet by Samuel Holland, for Henry Seymour Conway (1721–1795), who served briefly as secretary of state (1765–6). In defiance of offi-cialdom, the name that has endured is that of a local 'squat-ter,' George Hardy.

Harmony (Prince); **Harmony Junction** (Kings)   On Highway 128. Reputedly selected in 1875 for the school district because 'the settlers got along peacefully, though of many nationalities: French, Irish, Highland Scottish, Lowland Scottish, English and Dutch' (Douglas). Harmony Junc-tion recalls the one-time site of a railway junction north of SOURIS. The name originates with nearby New Harmony Road, where the various nationalities 'also dwelt in harmony.' This name was also among those suggested for the new town created west of CHARLOTTE-TOWN in 1994. See also CORNWALL.

Harmony Junction   *See* Har-mony.

Haszard Point (Queens)
Extends into HILLSBOROUGH BAY,
east of KEPPOCH. Named for the
original Loyalist grantee, William
Haszard, who, with other
members of his family, emigrated
to Prince Edward Island
from Rhode Island in 1785.

Hay River (Kings)   Flows into the
GULF OF ST. LAWRENCE, between
ST. MARGARETS and Clearspring.
The descriptive name was
assigned for the hay prevalent
along its banks. During the 1830s
and 1840s, KINGS COUNTY was a
centre of agitation for a settlement
of the land question. On
20 December 1836, the issue was
the focus of a meeting at Hay
River attended by more than 700
tenants and presided over by the
3 local MLAS, William Cooper,
John LeLacheur, and John Mac-
Intosh. A petition was passed
demanding an immediate resolution
of the matter and encouraging
tenants to withhold rent
(details of the meeting may be
found in the *Royal Gazette*, 10 January
1837). When the members
subsequently refused to apologize
to the Assembly for what Governor
Sir John Harvey (1778–1852)
termed 'the dangerous, illegal and
unconstitutional' tone of the resolutions,
they were temporarily
barred from the House. Historian
Harry Baglole has commented:
'This [action] made them martyrs,
both in their own eyes and those of
the people.' Unfortunately
another fifty years were to pass
before a final resolution of the
land question was reached. See
also ABELLS CAPE and SAILORS
HOPE.

Hazelbrook (Queens); **Hazelgrove**
(Queens)   On Highway 2,
between HUNTER RIVER and FREDERICTON.
Both are coined names
for the prevalence of hazelnut
trees in their respective areas.
Hazelgrove became the name of
an inn on what is now Highway
1, east of CHARLOTTETOWN, first
operated by Richard Bagnall, son
of Samuel Bagnall, Loyalist. The
building was torn down around
1900.

Hazelgrove   *See* Hazelbrook.

Head of ...   For all features
beginning with 'Head,' see main
entry.

Heatherdale (Kings)   Southwest
of MONTAGUE, on Highway 316.
The first settlers were Scottish;
they selected this coined name
upon the opening of the post
office in 1891.

Hebron (Prince)   Facing Indian
Point Sand Hills and EGMONT
BAY. The name is biblical in origin
and was selected as the name for
the school section in the late nineteenth
century. It refers to the city

on the west bank of the Jordan River frequently mentioned in the Old Testament.

Herring Island (Kings)   One of a chain of islands located within Murray Harbour. Named for William Herring, who emigrated from Cornwall, England, and settled here in 1828. Herring, and adjacent Thomas Island, linked by a sand bar, were owned in recent years by Lieutenant-Colonel Patrick Wootton, of STRATFORD, Prince Edward Island. He had formerly operated successful youth camps on the island of Lihou, off the coast of Guernsey, in the Channel Islands. These camps were designed to promote sustainable development and the encouragement of positive values and attitudes among young people. It is Wooton's view that 'on small islands one gets a clearer view of what the world is about.' Thomas Island has been deeded by him to the Prince Edward Island Nature Trust.

High Bank (Kings)   Fronts on NORTHUMBERLAND STRAIT, between WHITE SANDS and LITTLE SANDS. A descriptive name for 5 kilometres of shoreline featuring red sandstone cliffs 25 metres high.

Hillsborough Bay; Hillsborough River (Queens)   The river emp-ties into CHARLOTTETOWN harbour. The bay is adjacent to NORTHUMBERLAND STRAIT and is partially sheltered by POINT PRIM. Both were named by Samuel Holland in 1765 for Wills Hill (1718–1793), Earl of Hillsborough, who was commissioner of Trade and Plantations (1763) and secretary of state for the colonies (1768–72). It was called *ance à la pointe Prime* during the French colonial period (de la Roque 1752). The river was the *Rivière du Nord-Est* in the French regime.

Hillsborough River   *See* Hillsborough Bay.

Holland Cove (Queens)   On HILLSBOROUGH BAY, south of ROCKY POINT. To the French this feature was L'Anse à Sanglier. Later it was known briefly as 'Observation Cove,' for the location of the home of Samuel Johannes Hollandt (1728–1801) while surveying the Island. On 14 November 1764, he wrote: 'I was in hopes of finding a lodging in the fort [Amherst] but it is is only a poor stockaded redoubt, with barracks scarcely fit to lodge the garrison ... I have [chosen] a spot in the woods near the sea-shore for a house properly situated for making astronomical observations.' Hollandt (later Holland) was born at Nijmegen, in The Netherlands, and first served in the Dutch army, transferring in 1754 to the British forces. Following service in the Seven Years War (1756–63), he was appointed surveyor general of the northern district of North America, with specific instructions to survey St. John's (Prince Edward) Island, Îles-de-la-Madeleine, and CAPE BRETON ISLAND because of their importance to the fishery. This task, undertaken during 1764–5, was carried out in a speedy and comprehensive manner. The Island was divided into three counties, sixty-seven lots or townships, with three areas (George Town, Charlotte Town, and Prince Town) and their accompanying domains or royalties. In addition, Holland completed detailed maps and reports outlining opportunities in the fishery, forestry, the quality and extent of the soil, and the agricultural potential of the Island. He also meticulously assigned names to most of the features surveyed. The survival of so many of these remain as a lasting monument. His career is also commemorated through the name of Holland College in CHARLOTTETOWN.

Holman Island (Prince)   In BEDEQUE BAY. First identified as *Île de Bedec* (de la Roque 1752) and *Indian Island* (Holland 1765). The later ownership is traceable

through a succession of family place names: Flynn's, for an eccentric hermit who once lived there; Pope's, after the Honourable J.C. Pope, merchant and shipbuilder; and finally, Holman's for James Ludlow Holman (1827–1877), a prominent SUMMERSIDE merchant who purchased it from Pope. Holman, literally a man ahead of his time, had an interest in promoting the tourist industry. In the early 1870s he erected the 'magnificent' Island Park Hotel on Holman Island. Unfortunately, the shortness of the season, a mosquito infestation, combined with Holman's sudden death in 1877, rendered the resort a failure.

Howe Bay (Kings)   Fronts on NORTHUMBERLAND STRAIT, between Durell Point and Howe Point. Named by Samuel Holland for Sir William Howe (1729–1814), fifth Viscount Howe, under whom Holland had served during the Seven Years War (1756–63). Howe was later to play a prominent role in the American Revolutionary War, at the Battle of Bunker Hill (1755) and the capture of New York, and in the winning battles of White Plains and Brandywine (1766). He resigned his command in 1778.

Hunter River (Queens)   Flows northeast into RUSTICO BAY. Samuel Holland assigned the name in 1765, for Thomas Orby Hunter, who was stationed at Rotterdam in 1746 as deputy paymaster of the British and Dutch troops. Hunter may well have played a role in Holland's subsequent transfer to the British army. The river was known locally during the nineteenth century as the 'Clyde River,' and later as the 'New Glasgow River'; however, these names did not survive. See also ORBY HEAD.

Huntley River (Prince) Flows northeast into the KILDARE RIVER. Named to mark the career of Sir Henry Vere Huntley (1795–1864), who served as lieutenant-governor from 1841 to 1847. During this period, Henry Wolsey Bayfield (1795–1855) was engaged in a survey of the Island. Huntley and Bayfield became close friends, and the latter's diary is studded with references to the lieutenant-governor. They were frequently in each other's company, and Lady Huntley was given the honour of christening Bayfield's new survey ship, the *Gulnare*, on 18 May 1844, 'with the lieutenant governor and almost everybody [in Charlottetown] attending.' See also GULNARE ISLAND, Newfoundland.

Indian River (Prince) Flows into CHICHESTER COVE, an inden-

tation of MALPEQUE BAY. Alan Rayburn states that it was 'named for the reason that the fishing rights on it were reserved for the Indians.' In addition, the area was the site of a Mi'kmaq settlement as recently as 1935. St. Mary's Roman Catholic Church, the largest wooden church in the province, was built in 1900–2 to a design by noted Island architect William Critchlow Harris (1854–1913). There are numerous items of architectural interest in the exterior, including a cylindrical four-stage tower on the northwest corner. The tower carries above it an octagonal spire that has become a local landmark. The interior, with a seating capacity of 600, is dominated by the east chancel, with its neo-Gothic altar. Harris had a preoccupation 'with acoustical perfection'; the result is a sanctuary that perfectly suits the concerts featuring classical, traditional, and sacred music that are held here each summer.

Inverness (Prince) Northwest of ELLERSLIE, on Highway 2. Named for Inverness, Scotland, the home county of many Scottish emigrants to Prince Edward Island. In addition, the Scottish Inverness has associations with the events of 1745–6 in Scotland. It was near here that the forces of Prince Edward Stuart gathered prior to their defeat at Culloden. The heroine Flora MacDonald is immortalized in a statue on the grounds of Inverness Castle. See also GLENCORRADALE, GLENFINNAN, KILMUIR, and KINGSBORO.

Iona (Queens)   On Highway 206, northeast of BELFAST. This area was first settled by Irish emigrants, a fact that lends appropriateness to the choice of Iona as the community name. In 563, St. Columba sailed from Ireland to a small island off the west coast of Scotland. His objective was to introduce Christianity to the Scots. The mission was successful, and Iona has remained a centre of Celtic Christianity. The word is of Irish derivation; its original form was the Irish for 'island.' Later it was known as 'Ioua Insula,' and the Scottish name originated in a transcribing monk's mistaking the 'u' for an 'n.' In 1907 Iona Station, on the Prince Edward Island Railway, was named Fodhla, after the poetic name for Ireland.

Jacques Cartier Provincial Park (Prince)   On 1 July 1534, after sailing 'in a westerly direction' along the north shore of the Island, Jacques Cartier reported: 'All this coast is low and flat but the finest land one can see, and full of beautiful trees and meadows ... The shore is low and skirted all along with sandbanks. We went ashore in our longboats at several places, and among others at a fine river of little depth [one of the several streams that empty into Cascumpec Bay] we caught sight of some natives in their canoes who were crossing the river. On that account we called this river Canoe River.' More than four centuries later, this section of the coast has changed but little; thus Cartier might well be describing the shoreline of the park that bears his name. It follows a line of sanddunes that parallel the coast for 5 kilometres. The park, south of Cape Kildare (which Cartier called 'cap d'Orléans'), was named in his honour.

Johnny Belinda Pond (Kings)   Near the headwaters of the FORTUNE RIVER, at Dingwells Mills. The name was approved in 1970 as a tribute to the play *Johnny Belinda*, based on the novel *Inner Silence*, written by Elmer Harris in 1934. He made his summer home at Fortune Bridge, where he heard the story of a local deaf and mute girl. This became the basis for his book, later adapted for the stage. It was first produced at the Theatre Royal, Brighton, England, in 1950. The play subsequently became a hit on Broadway, and a movie version starring Jane Wyman was issued. *Johnny Belinda* was also featured at the Charlottetown Festival in 1975.

Johnstons River (Queens) Flows northwest into the HILLS-BOROUGH RIVER. Known as 'Rivière de Brouillan' during the French colonial period. Possibly named for Jacques-François de Monbeton de Brouillan (1651–1705), who served as governor of Acadia from 1702 until his death at Chedabucto (GUYSBOROUGH, Nova Scotia) on 22 September 1705. Renamed by Samuel Holland for Lieutenant William Johnston, commander of HMS *Mermaid*. Mermaid Pond is nearby. See also MERMAID.

Kellys Cross (Queens) Northeast of CRAPAUD. The first settlers were from Ireland, including several families named Kelly, thus giving rise to the name for the crossroads of present-day Highways 13 and 246.

Kelvin Grove (Prince) South of KENSINGTON. Named for Kelvingrove Park, in Glasgow, Scotland. The former railway station was first known as 'Blueshank,' for the Blueshank Road, now Highway 107. It was later changed to Kelvin.

Kensington (Prince) At the junction of Highways 2, 20, 101, and 109. First called Barretts Cross; the site of 'Mrs Barrett's Tavern at the crossroads.' Known as 'Kensington' since 1886, after the royal borough in London, England. Incorporated as a town in 1914.

Keppoch (Queens) Overlooks HILLSBOROUGH BAY, in Lot 48. During the French colonial period, the area was known as 'Anse du Comte de Saint-Pierre' (see MacLEODS ISLAND). Possibly renamed for Keppoch on Loch Duich, or more probably for Back of Keppoch, near Arisaig, South Morar, Scotland. In 1995, Keppoch became part of the town of Stratford. See also STRATFORD, and KEPPOCH MOUNTAIN, Nova Scotia.

Kildare Capes   *See* Cape Kildare.

Kildare Point   *See* Cape Kildare.

Kildare River   *See* Cape Kildare.

Kilmuir (Kings) Southwest of MONTAGUE, on Highway 316. Formerly Whim Road Cross. The school district was renamed in 1911 in memory of pioneer settlers from Kilmuir parish, Isle of Skye, Scotland. Kilmuir is also revered by Scots as the final resting-place of Flora Mac-Donald. See also KINGSBORO.

Kingsboro (Kings) At BASIN HEAD, in Lot 47. Named by James MacDonald for 'Kingsburgh,' estate of Clan MacDonald on the Isle of Skye, one of the hiding-places for Prince Charles Edward Stuart following his defeat at the Battle of Culloden on 16 April 1746. In 1773, while on his tour of the Hebrides, Samuel Johnson visited Kingsburgh and was entertained by Flora MacDonald (1722–1790) who had been largely responsible for the prince's successful escape to France. The event did not go unreported by the faithful scribe James Boswell: 'To see Dr Samuel Johnson, the great champion of the English Tories, salute Flora MacDonald in the isle of Skye was a striking sight; ... for it was very improbable that they should ever meet.' To Johnson fell the honour of sleeping in 'the very bed' used by the prince. Kingsburgh was later spelled 'Kingsborough,' and finally 'Kingsboro.' See also GLEN-CORRADALE, GLENFINNAN, INV-ERNESS, KILMUIR, MILTON, and SCOTCHFORT; and KNOYDART and WINDSOR, Nova Scotia.

Kings County   One of the three counties into which the province was divided by Surveyor General Samuel Holland in 1765. Honours King George III (1738–1820).

Kinkora (Prince)   East of Central Bedeque, on Highway 225. Settled by emigrants from Ireland in the 1840s and named for Kincora ruins, near Killaloe, County Clare, Eire.

Kinloch (Queens); **Kinross** (Queens)   Kinloch is situated in Lot 48, southeast of CHARLOTTE-TOWN. The name may possibly be for Kinlochmoidart, at the head of Loch Moidart, Scotland. Near this location there are commemorative beech trees planted in honour of the seven Moidart men who aided Prince Charles Edward Stuart following his arrival in Scotland in July 1745. In 1995 the PEI Kinloch became part of the newly created town of STRAT-FORD. Kinross is south of UIGG, on Highway 24. This Scottish settlement was probably named for Kinrossie, in Perthshire.

Kinross   *See* Kinloch.

Lady Fane (Queens)   North of CRAPAUD, on the QUEENS–PRINCE county boundary. Named for Lady Cecily Jane Georgina Fane (?–1874), daughter of John Fane, tenth Earl of Westmorland, who inherited a section of Lot 29. The Lady Fane school section was created in 1869.

Lake of Shining Waters (Queens) In PRINCE EDWARD ISLAND NATIONAL PARK. Once known as 'Cavendish Pond.' The lake figures prominently in the fictional works of L.M. Montgomery (see CAVENDISH and GREEN GABLES). Technically, the location may be a case of mistaken identity. Montgomery, writing in 1917, stated:

'The Lake of Shining Waters is generally supposed to be Cavendish Pond. This is not so. The pond I had in mind is the one at Park Corner, below Uncle John Campbell's home.'

Launching Bay; Launching Point; Launching Pond (Prince) The bay is an extension of CARDIGAN BAY, separating BOUGHTON ISLAND from the mainland. The sand bar at the northeast end of the island once reached across the bay, providing an excellent location for the launching of boats. Nearby Launching Point and Launching Pond were also named for the same reason.

Launching Point   *See* Launching Bay.

Launching Pond   *See* Launching Bay.

Lennox Channel; Lennox Island (Prince)   Lennox Channel runs between Lennox Island and the mainland. Both features were named by Samuel Holland in 1765 for Charles, third Duke of Richmond and Lennox (1735–1806). Before the arrival of Europeans, the Mi'kmaq occupied Lennox Island. It was officially designated a reservation in 1840.

Lennox Island   *See* Lennox Channel.

Linkletter (Prince)   West of SUMMERSIDE, on Highway 11. Settled in 1786 by George Linkleighter or Linkletter, a Connecticut Loyalist whose forebears were from Kirkwall, in the Orkney Islands, Scotland. When the Linkletter family arrived, they found evidence of previous French occupation, a house (which provided immediate shelter), apple trees, and an overgrown vegetable garden.

Little Courtin Island   *See* Courtin Island.

Little Pond (Kings)   On Highway 310. Named for an adjacent small pond. In the 1970s this community was selected as the site for an experiment in 'self-sufficient living.' Housed in a futuristic building that soon became known as 'The Ark,' it has now been converted to an inn and restaurant. The resort is operated by a non-profit community-based co-operative.

Little Sands (Kings)   Fronts on NORTHUMBERLAND STRAIT, at the KINGS–QUEENS county boundary. Descriptive for the low sandy shore. The Rossignol Estate Winery, producing fruit and table wines, is located at Little Sands in a panoramic setting overlooking the Northumberland Strait.

Long Creek (Queens)   At the junction of Highways 9 and 19A. Descriptive for the longest branch of the WEST RIVER.

Lord Selkirk Provincial Park (Queens)   On ORWELL BAY, at BELFAST. Commemorates the career of Thomas Douglas, fifth Earl of Selkirk (1771–1820). Following a tour of the Highlands of Scotland in 1792, Selkirk reached the conclusion that emigration was the solution to the economic and social problems then characteristic of the region. In the process of acting on his theories, by 1803 he had bought out several of the Island proprietors in Lots 57 and 58, the Orwell Bay–POINT PRIM area. In July an expedition of three ships, the *Dykes, Polly,* and *Oughton,* arrived, bringing 800 settlers, principally from the Isle of Skye. Others were natives of Ross, Argyll, Inverness, and the Island of Uist. For a time the area at the junction of the north and middle branches of the PINETTE RIVER was known as the 'Selkirk Settlement.'

Lords Pond (Prince)   At North Tryon, Lot 28. A man-made pond which dates from the mid-eighteenth century. The site of an early grist mill, it was named for John Squire Lord, its owner in the 1840s. In 1913 the mill was purchased by Charles Ives, who later added a small electric-power plant. For information on the TRYON RIVER watershed, which drains some of the best agricultural land in the province, see Kate MacQuarrie, *The Tryon River: A Guide to Its Human Resources and Natural History* (Tryon River Watershed Co-operative, 1994).

Lorne Valley (Kings)   North of CARDIGAN HEAD, on Highway 355. Named for the Marquess of Lorne (1845–1914), governor-general of Canada from 1878 to 1883.

Lyndale (Queens)   Northeast of ORWELL CORNER, on Highway 210. First known as 'Orwell Rear.' Use of 'rear' to denote the back portion of a settlement is common in eastern Nova Scotia (see REAR OF ... entry). In the 1880s the residents of Orwell Rear, 'feeling that the name hinted some disparagement, called a public meeting to fix upon a more euphonious name.' Three possibilities were voted upon: Woodville, Valtois, and Lyndale. The last 'captured the almost unanimous vote of the meeting.' It was presented by Ewan Lamont 'in remembrance of his childhood home in the Vale of Lyndale, on the Isle of Skye' (Douglas). Lyndale post office was opened in 1888. The Scots had won another round!

Machon Point (Kings)   Adjacent to GUERNSEY COVE. Daniel Machon from Guernsey settled on the point in 1806. Machon is a common Channel Island surname.

MacLeods Island (Queens) Extends into the HILLSBOROUGH RIVER, north of MERMAID. Known as 'Ilot du Comte-St-Pierre' during the French colonial period, for Louis-Hyacinthe Castel, Comte de Saint-Pierre, who was director-general of the Compagnie de l'Île Saint-Jean, charged with development of the Island. Both Captain Henry Bayfield and J.H. Meacham give the location as McLeods Island, a name that was still in use as late as 1925. Named for James McLeod, who owned land nearby. See also ST. PETERS.

MacPhee Beach (Kings)   Adjacent to GEORGETOWN. MacPhee is a common KINGS COUNTY name; Robert Douglas reported in 1925 'families of this name still live here.'

MacWilliams Cove (Prince) Near WEST CAPE, on the NORTH-UMBERLAND STRAIT, in Lot 7. This area was first settled in the 1830s by members of the MacWilliams family. David MacWilliams operated flour, carding, and sawmills in the area.

Malpeque; Malpeque Bay; Malpeque Peninsula (Prince) The bay is a large indentation in the northwest coast. The name may be traced to a Mi'kmaq settlement known as 'Makpaak,' for 'large bay.' During the course of the 1765 survey, Samuel Holland applied the name Richmond Bay to this feature, for Charles Lennox, third Duke of Richmond (1764–1819), but the name did not survive. During the nineteenth century, it was used as an 'alternative' for Malpeque. Later it was assigned to the the western section of the bay, only to be gradually superseded, through popular usage, by Malpeque. He also designated the peninsula Princetown Royalty, to include 'Prince Town' as the county capital; however, it was destined to exist only as a plan on paper. The internationally famous Malpeque oysters take their name from this bay.

Malpeque Bay   *See* Malpeque.

Malpeque Peninsula   *See* Malpeque.

March Water (Prince)   On the west side of the MALPEQUE PENINSULA, adjacent to Princetown Royalty. While the name Richmond Bay was supplanted by the euphonious Malpeque (see entry above), the Duke of Richmond is still remembered in the area. One of his additional titles was Earl of March, and this inspired a further application by Samuel Holland.

Margate (Prince)   On Highway 6, at the PRINCE–QUEENS county boundary. For Margate, the coastal resort in Kent, England. It was the home of Thomas Smith, the first settler.

Marie River (Kings)   Flows into ST. PETERS BAY, at Marie Provincial Park. The precise origin of the name, which dates from the French colonial period, is unclear. Since Marie Joseph LaGarenne, widow of Jean François Morel (1739–?), was a landowner in the area, it may be assumed that her name was given to the river.

Marshfield (Queens)   Northeast of CHARLOTTETOWN, on Highway 2. In 1751 Louis Franquet (1697–1768), a French military engineer toured, Île Saint-Jean. In his report he refers to La Rivière des Blancs as the name for Marshfield Creek. The latter name originates with that of the farm of Robert Poore Haythorne (1815–1891). Born in England, he served as magistrate in Marshfield, Gloucester, England, prior to emigrating to Prince Edward Island in 1842. Entering provincial politics, he was briefly premier in 1869–70, and again in 1872–3. Haythorne was called to the Senate in 1873.

Maximeville (Prince)   Northwest of CAPE EGMONT. Named for Maxime Arsenault, an early landholder in the district. The post office, established in 1904, is listed as Maximville. The name has been Maximeville since the 1930s.

Mayfield (Queens)   Southeast of CAVENDISH, on Highway 13. Originally known as 'Cavendish Road.' The coined name was selected in 1897 to avoid confusion with nearby Cavendish.

Melville (Queens)   Northeast of the FLAT RIVER, on Highway 207. First settled by Scottish emigrants, and named by them Raasay, for Raasay Island, adjacent to Isle of Skye in the Hebrides. Since this is a Scottish settlement, the new name, dating from the 1860s, may have been inspired by the career of Andrew Melville (1545–1622), famous Presbyterian minister and scholar.

Mermaid (Queens)   On the HILLSBOROUGH RIVER. This community was first known as 'Mermaid Farm,' which, in turn, was named for HMS *Mermaid* in service at Port La Joie in 1764–5. See also JOHNSTONS RIVER.

Middleton; Middleton Pond (Prince)   The midpoint between the NORTHUMBERLAND STRAIT and the PRINCE–QUEENS county boundary. The community name is descriptive of the location. Middleton Pond, on the southwest branch of the DUNK RIVER, was created in the 1830s by John Wright, who once operated grist, shingle, and sawmills there.

Middleton Pond   *See* Middleton.

Midgell River (Kings)   Flows north into ST. PETERS BAY. Name is of uncertain origin. Alan Rayburn suggests that it was 'possibly named for Micael Michell, an Indian chief,' while Robert Douglas notes that 'it may be a corruption of the French Michel.'

Mill River (Prince)   Flows in an easterly direction into CASCUMPEC BAY. A descriptive name indicating the location of a nineteenth-century sawmill. Site of Mill River Provincial Park, the Mill River resort, and a championship eighteen-hole golf course.

Milton (Queens)   West of WINSLOE, on Highway 2. Named for the birthplace of Flora Macdonald (1722–1790): Milton, South Uist, in the Hebrides. She was noted for her assistance to Prince Charles Edward Stuart in his escape to France following the Battle of Culloden in 1746. Later imprisoned in the Tower of London, but released in 1747,

she married Allan MacDonald in 1750. They emigrated, first to North Carolina, then to Nova Scotia, returning to Scotland in 1779. See also GLENFINNAN and KINGSBORO.

Miminegash (Prince)   South of CAPE GAGE, on the NORTHUMBERLAND STRAIT. The name is of Mi'kmaq origin and is translated by Robert Douglas as 'what is carried' or 'portage place.' This is a logical translation, as the location was the site of a Mi'kmaq campground.

Miscouche; Miscouche Cove (Prince)   The community is Northwest of SUMMERSIDE, on Highway 2; Miscouche Cove is on NORTHUMBERLAND STRAIT, east of Ives Point. The name is derived from the Mi'kmaq *Menisgotig*, for 'little marshy place.' It may also be a corruption of the Mi'kmaq *Manuskooch*, 'little grassy island.' The Acadian Museum of Prince Edward Island is located at Miscouche.

Miscouche Cove   *See* Miscouche.

Montague; Montague River (Kings)   One of the three major rivers that empty into CARDIGAN BAY. Name bestowed in 1765 by Samuel Holland for George Brudenell (1712–1790), Earl of

Cardigan, who was later created Duke of Montaqu, or Montagu. The latter spelling, with a 'g,' has always been followed on Prince Edward Island. The town of Montague, located on the river, was incorporated in 1917.

Montague River   *See* Montague.

Montrose (Prince)   North of ALBERTON, on the KILDARE RIVER. Named in 1864 by Donald McIntyre, who noted a local resemblance with Montrose on the east coast of Scotland.

Morel; Morell River (Kings) Southwest of ST. PETERS BAY. Appears as *Morrel* on Holland map of 1765. The name commemorates the family of Jean François Morel, a native of St. Malo, France. Born in 1697, he was married on 4 August 1739 to Marie Joseph La Garenne. See also MARIE RIVER.

Morell River   *See* Morell.

Mount Albion   *See* Albion.

Mount Buchanan (Queens)   On POINT PRIM, in Lot 57. Named for the Buchanan family, who were among the first settlers in the area.

Mount Carmel (Prince)   Fronts on BEDEQUE BAY, in Lot 15. Some-

times called 'Fifteen Point.' The name originates with that of the local parish and is of biblical origin. Mount Carmel, as mentioned in the Old Testament, refers to the location where Elijah summoned Israel to choose between God and Baal. From the Hebrew word for 'garden' or 'fertile ground.'

Mount Mellick (Queens) Northwest of CHERRY VALLEY, on Highway 3. Named for Mountmellick, by settlers who emigrated from that part of Ireland.

Mount Stewart (Queens)   On the south bank of the HILLSBOR-OUGH RIVER. In 1789 a large property was purchased by John Stewart (*ca* 1758–1834). He subsequently built a house 'on a rising stretch of ground overlooking the river ... which he named Mount Stewart.' As a teenage immigrant to the Island, Stewart had earlier earned the nickname 'Hell-fire Jack,' and he did little thereafter to change this reputation. Thus, public harassment of opponents, an occasional duel, and intrigues without number were to characterize his public career. Along the way he was elected to the Assembly and held office as Speaker from 1795 to 1798, and again from 1824 to 1830. Perhaps his most positive contribution, and the one for which he is best remembered, was *An Account of Prince Edward Island*, published in 1806. This work established Stewart as the Island's first historian and promoter of the economic potential of the colony.

Murray Harbour; Murray River (Kings)   Murray River flows east into Murray Harbour. The river was named by Samuel Holland during his 1769 survey. It honours James Murray (1721/22–1794), who served as governor of Québec from 1763 to 1768. The community of Murray Harbour was incorporated as a village in 1953.

Murray River   *See* Murray Harbour.

Nail Head; Nail Pond (Prince) Fronts on NORTHUMBERLAND STRAIT, south of NORTH CAPE. Appears first in Bayfield 1847, and consistently thereafter. The name is probably a corruption of 'Neal,' for an early settler of that surname. On 26 January 1833, a petition was presented to the legislature 'praying aid for putting a road from Neal's Pond to Cascumpeque ...'

Nail Pond   *See* Nail Head.

Naufrage; Naufrage Pond; Naufrage River (Kings)   In Lot 43. The river flows into the GULF OF ST. LAWRENCE. Thomas Pichon, in his *Lettres et Memoires* (1760), records that the name *Etang du Noffrage* was given to the pond following a shipwreck on the coast in 1719. Several of the rescued passengers were among the first residents of ST. PETERS. Shipwreck Point, across the river from Naufrage, is an English translation listed by Samuel Holland in 1765.

Naufrage Pond   *See* Naufrage.

Naufrage River   *See* Naufrage.

Nebraska Creek (Prince)   Flows north into the GRAND RIVER. There does not appear to be any obvious connection between the western American state and the Island. The name was probably selected 'at random' to replace the earlier name, Southwest River.

New Acadia (Kings)   On Highway 8, between NAUFRAGE and ROLLO BAY. The name was suggested by Eusebius Peters, an Acadian settler, as a name for the school district. For derivation of Acadia see chapter 1, page 7.

New Annan (Queens)   Northeast of SUMMERSIDE, on Highway 2. Named by William 'Squire' Jamieson, who emigrated to this area from Annan, Dumfries-shire, Scotland, in the 1820s. See also

ANNANDALE and NEW ANNAN, Nova Scotia.

New Glasgow (Queens)   On the HUNTER RIVER. The settlement was established in 1819 by William Epps Cormack (1796–1868) and named for Glasgow, Scotland. For details of his career see CORMACK and MOUNT CORMACK, Newfoundland.

New Haven (Queens)   Between the CLYDE RIVER and CHURCHILL, on Highway 1. The name, selected when the post office was established in 1872, may be for Newhaven, Edinburgh, Scotland (Rayburn).

New London; New London Bay (Queens)   On the Southwest River, in Lot 21. The bay was known to the French as 'Petit Havre,' and renamed in 1765, by Samuel Holland, Grenville Bay, for George Grenville (1712–1770), then prime minister of Great Britain. This name did not survive. The settlement name New London, for London, England, was in use by 1775. Two contemporary accounts detail the harshness of colonial life in this period. Thomas Curtis's *Voyage to the Island of St John's* is a graphic account of shipwreck and survival during 1775–6. As he wryly commented: 'When we arrived at New London I was much surprised to see what a place it was ... I then began to repent of my voyage and wish myself in old London again.' The second source is the diary of Benjamin Chappell, a carpenter who emigrated to New London in 1775. Both documents form the basis for a play, *The Chappell Diary*, by Harry Baglole and Ron Irving. It depicts, as only drama can, the events of this formative year in the life New London.

New London Bay   *See* New London.

New Zealand (Kings)   Northwest of SOURIS, in Lot 44. Named in 1858 when there was emigration from Prince Edward Island to New Zealand. The brig *Prince Edward* left Charlottetown for New Zealand on 30 November 1858. See also ZEALAND, New Brunswick.

North Cape (Prince)   The northwest extremity of Prince Edward Island. Of this coastline Jacques Cartier wrote: 'On the first day of July [1534] we had sight of *Cape Orléans* [Cape Kildare] and of another cape about seven leagues north ... which we named *Savage Cape* [North Cape].' Because of continuous high winds, North Cape is the location of the Atlantic Wind Test Site, a wind-energy testing laboratory. The 19-metre-high North Cape lighthouse sends its signal over 30 kilometres across the waters of the GULF OF ST. LAWRENCE and the NORTHUMBERLAND STRAIT. It warns mariners of the dangers of the large rock reef formed at the point where the waters of the gulf and strait meet.

North Lake (Kings)   West of Surveyor Point, in Lot 47. An English descriptive. The area was known during the French colonial period as 'Tranche Montagne,' or 'bully,' the nickname of Louis Denys de la Ronde (1675–1741). In the census of 1752, Antoine Dechevery (or Cheverie), a native of Bayonne, France; his wife, Marie Pinet; and their six children were resident there. Later, the Dechevery family moved to become one of the founding families of Souris. Samuel Holland has *Surveyors Inlet* for the location in 1765; it is *North Lake* in the *Meacham Atlas* (1880).

North River (Queens)   Flows south into CHARLOTTETOWN harbour. Known as 'Rivière du Nord' during the French colonial period. Renamed, unsuccessfully, Yorke River by Samuel Holland, for John Yorke (1728–1769), then Lord Commissioner of Trade and Plantations. In the nineteenth century, both names, York and North, were used; however, by 1900 the latter was in common

usage. As of 1 April 1995, North River became part of the town of CORNWALL.

Northumberland Strait   *See* chapter 1, page 21.

Old Ferry Spit (Kings)   In Lot 55, at the mouth of the BOUGHTON RIVER. Named for the ferry that once plied between Launching Place and ANNANDALE, on the opposite side of BOUGHTON BAY.

O'Leary (Prince)   On Highway 142, in Lot 6. Named for Michael O'Leary an early Irish settler in the area. Later, as a very old man, he was accidentally pushed off a wharf, following a return trip to Ireland, and drowned. O'Leary is the location of Canada's only potato museum, housing interpretative displays and artefacts relating to this important Island industry.

Orby Head (Queens)   Extends into the GULF OF ST. LAWRENCE, north of North Rustico. The name was assigned by Samuel Holland for Thomas Orby Hunter. See also HUNTER RIVER.

Orwell Bay; Orwell Corner; Orwell River (Queens)   The bay is an extension of HILLSBOROUGH BAY, into which the river also flows. The bay was known to the French as 'Grande Anse'; it was renamed in 1765 by Samuel Holland, after Francis, Lord Orwell, who served as Lord Commissioner of Trade and Plantations from 1762 to 1768. The river was Rivière de la Grand Ascension to the French. Less than a kilometre off Highway 1, at Orwell Corner, is an example of a nineteenth-century crossroads community. A house, general store, blacksmith shop, post office, community hall, church, and school provide valuable insight on the agricultural heritage of the province. Orwell Corner is part of the PEI Museum and Heritage Foundation.

Orwell Corner   *See* Orwell Bay.

Orwell River   *See* Orwell Bay.

Oultons Island (Prince)   In ALBERTON harbour, an extension of CASCUMPEC BAY. It was first known as 'Cherry Island,' and later renamed for Robert Oulton (1835–1920). The latter, along with his partner Charles Dalton (1850–1933), were pioneers in the establishment of the silver-fox industry on Prince Edward Island. In the mid-1890s, they were able, through selective breeding, to develop the silver-black strain, seldom found in the wild and extremely valuable as fashion fur. With this development, the silver-fox industry was launched. By 1909 there were six fox ranchers (nicknamed the 'Big

Six Combine') in the Alberton–TIGNISH area. However, their monopoly was short-lived; by 1913, there were 277 ranches on the Island. The Oulton–Dalton partnership, which started it all, was dissolved, and Oulton crossed the NORTHUMBERLAND STRAIT to return to his native LITTLE SHEMOGUE, New Brunswick.

Oyster Bed Bridge (Queens)   On the WHEATLEY RIVER, in Lot 23. A descriptive for the abundance of oysters once harvested here.

Panmure Head; Panmure Island (Kings)   Technically not an island, as it is connected to the mainland at Lot 61 by a sand causeway (Panmure Island Provincial Park). Named by Samuel Holland, possibly for William Maule, Earl of Panmure (?–1781), a career soldier who was promoted to the rank of general in 1770. Panmure Head extends into CARDIGAN BAY; the lighthouse, built in 1853, has a 30-kilometre range.

Panmure Island   *See* Panmure Head.

Park Corner (Queens)   West of Cape Tryon. This area was granted in 1775 to James Townshend, for military services. He called his new estate 'Park Corner,' after his former home in Berkshire, England. L.M. Montgomery was a descendant of James Townshend, and a frequent visitor at the Park Corner home of her grandfather Senator Donald Montgomery (1808–1893) and her uncle John Campbell (1833–1917). She named the Campbell homestead 'Silverbush.' The famous Lake of Shining Waters, otherwise known as 'Campbells Pond,' was located here. The Anne of Green Gables Museum, with items of Montgomery memorabilia, is located in the Campbell home.

Percival Bay (Prince)   On the north side of EGMONT BAY. Named Perceval Bay by Samuel Holland in 1765, for John Perceval, second Earl of Egmont and Baron Lovel and Holland (1711–1770). He was first lord of the Admiralty (1763–6). Over time the spelling changed to 'Percival.' See also CAPE EGMONT.

Pinette; Pinette River (Queens) The river flows into Pinette harbour, east of POINT PRIM. The harbour was known as 'Anse à Pinette,' or 'Pinet,' during the French colonial period. On a tour of the Island in 1787, Lieutenant-Governor Edmund Fanning (1739–1818) noted: 'I went around Point Prim and encamped at Primit [Pinette] Village on Lot 58.

Formerly [this was] a considerable French settlement.' The name originated not with *pinette* or *epinette* (fir trees), but with an early resident, Noel Pinet, who was born in Acadia in 1683; married Rose Henry at GRAND PRÉ on 1 September 1710; and then moved to Île Saint-Jean, where he settled at what was to become known as 'Anse à Pinet.'

Pinette River   *See* Pinette.

Pipers Creek (Queens)   Flows into TRACADIE BAY. Settled by members of the McInnes family, one of whom, Michael McInnes, was a noted piper, thus giving rise to the name.

Pisquid; Pisquid River (Queens) On Highway 22, south of MOUNT STEWART; the river flows into the HILLSBOROUGH. Derived from the original Mi'kmaq *Pesigitk*, which has been translated as 'entering at right angles' or 'the forks of a river.' It subsequently was filtered through the French Rivière de Peugiguit or Pegedieg, to the English rendering, Pisquid, common by 1825 and thereafter. Compare with PISIQUID, Nova Scotia. See also WINDSOR.

Pisquid River   *See* Pisquid.

Piusville (Prince)   West of ALBERTON in Lot 4. The name was bestowed by the local parish priest, Father James MacDonald, in honour of Pope Pius IX (1792–1878), pontiff from 1846 to 1878. His reign was noted for the decree of papal infallibility proclaimed at the first Vatican Council (1870).

Platt River (Prince) Flows north into MALPEQUE BAY. The name is a descriptive, after 'La Rivière Platte,' dating from the French colonial period. Robert Douglas suggests that it is derived from 'plat,' or 'a shallow stream.'

Point Deroche (Queens) Extends into the GULF OF ST. LAWRENCE, west of SAVAGE HARBOUR. Named for an early Acadian settler, Etienne Charles Philippe dit La-Roche, who settled here in 1752.

Point Prim (Queens) Extends into NORTHUMBERLAND STRAIT. One of the older names of European origin on Prince Edward Island, the peninsula was known to the French as 'Pte du Sud ou de prime' or 'Pointe à Prime.' The name is a corruption of 'prime,' the first or south point of the compass. The Point Prim lighthouse, the oldest on Prince Edward Island, has been guarding the entrance to HILLSBOROUGH BAY since 1845. The round structure was built to specifications drawn by architect Isaac Smith (1795–

1871). Smith is justly famous as the architect of Province House and of 'Fanning Bank', the residence of the lieutenant-governor, all in CHARLOTTETOWN. However, this utilitarian, though starkly beautiful, building, with its revolving light clearly discernible as far as the Nova Scotia coast, some 40 kilometres away, is also of architectural note.

Portage River (Prince) Flows north into the Trout River, at Lot 10. The name is descriptive and may be traced to a translation of the Mi'kmaq *Onigun*, which meant 'portage.' This is one of the narrowest points on the Island and was the site of a Mi'kmaq portage route from CASCUMPEC BAY to EGMONT BAY.

Port Hill (Prince) East of TYNE VALLEY. On the outskirts of Bideford, in Devonshire, is to be found 'a discreetly proportioned small mansion built by Augustus Saltren Willet ... it was and still is called Porthill' (Greenhill and Giffard). This name was to cross the Atlantic with the West Country emigrants to become Port Hill. Their story is well told in Basil Greenhill and Ann Giffard's *Westcountrymen in Prince Edward's Isle* (1969).

Pownal; Pownal Bay (Queens) The village is east of CHARLOT-

TETOWN; the bay is an extension of HILLSBOROUGH BAY. Named by Samuel Holland for John Pownall, secretary to the Board of Trade and Plantations (1758–61). He was a brother of Thomas Pownall (1722–1805), who served as governor of Massachusetts (1757–9). In 1764 the latter published a treatise, *The Administration of the Colonies*, which advocated the union of all North American colonies in one Dominion. See also PAUL ISLAND, Newfoundland and Labrador. Although in 1925 Robert Douglas maintained that dropping the final 'l' was incorrect, the shortened version has now become accepted. Pownal was the birthplace of the Honourable J. Walter Jones (1878–1954), who served as premier from 1943 to 1953. A colourful and flamboyant individual, Jones is still remembered for his political style and blunt and decisive manner, which made Island politics anything but dull during his decade as premier.

Pownal Bay   *See* Pownal.

Prevost Cove   *See* Augustine Cove.

Prince County; Princetown   The name of the Island's western county was assigned in 1765 by Samuel Holland, for Prince George Augustus Frederick (1762–1830). The eldest son of King George IIII, he became Prince Regent in 1810 because of his father's insanity. On the king's death in 1820, he ascended the throne as King George IV. Princetown was the designated capital of the new county; however, it was to remain 'a plan on paper.' See also MALPEQUE.

Prince Edward Island National Park (Queens)   On 24 April 1937, the act establishing the Prince Edward Island National Park was proclaimed. This legislation succeeded in saving for posterity 40 kilometres of the environmentally fragile coastline of northern QUEENS COUNTY. The park includes red sandstone cliffs, dunes crowned by spiky clumps of marram grass, ponds, woodlands, and salt marshes, along with expansive and secluded beaches without number. Also within the bounds of the park is GREEN GABLES, immortalized by L.M. Montgomery. Some idea of the significance of this national park can be found in the fact that half a million people visit it annually.

Princetown   *See* Prince County.

Queens County   The name, bestowed by Samuel Holland in 1765, was in honour of Queen

Charlotte (1744–1818), wife of King George III. Their marriage and coronation had taken place four years earlier, in September 1761.

Red Head (Prince); **Red Point** (Kings)   Red Head extends into NORTHUMBERLAND STRAIT, at Lot 16; Red Point and Red Point Provincial Park lies southwest of BASIN HEAD, in Lot 46. Red is a dominant colour in the Island landscape. The distinctive brick-red hue is explained by the heavy concentrations of iron oxides in the sandstone and soil. Thus it is not surprising to find the descriptor 'red' incorporated in a number of place names scattered throughout the province. One of the oldest of these, Red Head (Lot 15), may be traced to the French colonial period. It appears as *Cap Rouge* on early maps.

Red House (Kings)   Southwest of FORTUNE BAY. Not named for the landscape, but for a 'red' house built by the notorious land agent Edward Abell. According to local legend, the house was later owned by a coroner named Heal. He once ruled that a man who commited suicide was to be buried at the crossroads immediately in front of the Red House, with a stake driven through his body. See also ABELLS CAPE.

Red Point   *See* Red Head.

Rice Point (Queens)   Projects into NORTHUMBERLAND STRAIT, opposite ST. PETERS ISLAND. Named by Samuel Holland in 1765 for George Rice (1724–1779), Lord Commissioner of Trade and Plantations from 1761 until 1770.

Richard Point   *See* Cumberland Cove.

Richmond Bay   *See* Malpeque Bay.

Rock Barra (Kings)   West of BAYFIELD, on the GULF OF ST. LAWRENCE. Named by settlers from the Hebrides for a rock once located offshore. The original Barra is a hilly and often rocky island in the Outer Hebrides. See also BARRA GLEN, Nova Scotia.

Rocky Point (Queens)   Extends into CHARLOTTETOWN harbour. A descriptive dating from the mid-nineteenth century. Site of the Fort Amherst–Port La Joie National Historic Park. See also FORT AMHERST and HOLLAND COVE.

Rollo Bay (Kings)   On NORTHUMBERLAND STRAIT, southwest of COLVILLE BAY. Commemorates the career of Lieutenant-Colonel Andrew Rollo, fifth Baron Rollo (1703–1765), a British army officer who served at Fortress Louisbourg (1758) and later arranged for the capitulation of Île Saint-Jean and the removal of its inhabitants. See also FORT AMHERST.

Rustico Bay; Rustico Island
(Queens)   The bay is on the GULF OF ST. LAWRENCE and is shielded from the gulf by Rustico Island. The name originates with an early French settler, René Rassicot, who came to Port La Joie in 1724 from Avranches, in Normandy. He later moved to the head of the river (WHEATLEY) that flows into Rustico Bay. Early spellings, 'Racica' and 'Racico' (used by de la Roque in 1752), have gradually evolved into Rustico. This area was once the site of the major Mi'kmaq encampment of Tabooetooetun, a descriptive that has been translated as 'having two outlets.' Writing on 31 December 1846, Abraham Gesner (1797–1864), a prominent nineteenth-century geologist, noted: 'Great collections of oysters and other shells are on the river and the side of the bay. They are only found at the site of ancient [Mi'kmaq] encampments, where they derived a part of their subsistence from the shellfish still abundant upon the shores.'

Rustico Island   *See* Rustico Bay.

Sailors Hope (Kings)   At HOWE BAY, in Lot 56. Named for the residence of William Cooper (*ca*

1786–1867), a one-time land agent who later became a leading figure in the movement for land reform. On 26 February 1820, following the murder of Edward Abell, Cooper was appointed (by Lord Townshend, the proprietor of Lot 56) as Abell's successor. Later, in a dramatic shift of allegiance, Cooper was to change sides and contest a by-election in July 1830. Elected on a platform of 'Our Country's Freedom and Farmers' Rights,' he was denied a seat in the Assembly pending an investigation of a riot on polling day. By a margin of one vote, that of the Speaker, he was allowed to take his seat. For 'the next thirty years Cooper was destined to become *Mr. Escheat* and to be the bane of the proprietary interests' (Bolger). In the election of 1838 the so-called Escheat Party won eighteen of the twenty-four seats in the Assembly, and Cooper became Speaker. Despite electoral success he and his followers were outmanoeuvred by the Executive Council, which had the support of the colonial secretary and the British government. He did not contest the 1846 election but instead built a brig and, with his family of three daughters and six sons, sailed from Fortune Bay on 5 December 1849, bound, via Cape Horn, for the gold fields of California. Soon tiring of life there, he returned to end his days at Sailors Hope, leaving his family behind in California. A controversial and enigmatic figure, Cooper contributed to the gradual improvement in the condition of the tenants by laying the foundation for later political reform. See Harry Baglole, 'William Cooper of Sailors Hope,' *Island Magazine* 7 (Fall–Winter 1979), 3–11.

St. Andrews (Queens)   Northeast of MOUNT STEWART. The community takes its name from St. Andrew, the patron saint of Scotland. On 30 November 1831, St. Andrews College was opened. The founding of this institution was motivated by the need for local clergy and was largely the effort of Right Reverend Angus B. MacEachern (1759–1835), Roman Catholic Bishop of CHARLOTTE-TOWN.

St. Catherines (Queens)   On the WEST RIVER, in Lot 65. The name honours Catherine Livingstone Shaw, wife of Malcolm Shaw, who settled on the West River in 1808. Both were natives of the Isle of Mull; Mrs. Shaw was a cousin of David Livingstone's (1813–1873), famed African explorer. Their grandson, the Honourable Walter Shaw (1881–1981), was to serve as premier of Prince Edward Island from 1959 to 1966.

St. Chrysostome (Prince)   On EGMONT BAY, at the junction of Highways 11 and 135. Originally known as 'Joe League,' an unusual name that may be traced to Captain Joseph Arsenault, a member of the Island militia. Known for his precision in giving distances, 'he earned the nickname Joe League-and-a-half, without act of parliament.' When his family moved to Egmont Bay, 'Joe League' went with them, giving rise to the community name. It was changed in commemoration of the fourth-century Greek patriarch St. Chrysostom in the 1870s. The post office dates from 1893.

St. Eleanors (Prince)   Northwest of Summerside. The precise origin of this name is in dispute. The strongest evidence points to its being named for Eleanor Sanskey, housekeeper of Colonel Henry Compton, an officer in the militia who was posted to this area in 1804. He later moved to Brittany, France, where he died in 1839 (see SUMMERSIDE). William Henry Pope (1825–1879), one of Prince Edward Island's Fathers of Confederation, is buried in St. John's Anglican Churchyard, at St. Eleanors, despite the fact that the Pope family were originally staunch Methodists. According to historian George Leard, 'they lost their Methodism on the way to worldly influence.' In 1967 a memorial lich-gate was unveiled in the churchyard to mark Pope's contribution to the cause of Confederation (see ARDGOWAN NATIONAL HISTORIC PARK). In 1994, St. Eleanors was amalgamated with the city of Summerside.

St. Margarets (Kings)   On Highway 16, southeast of NAUFRAGE. Settled by Scottish emigrants prior to 1800. Named for St. Margaret of Scotland (*ca* 1045–1093), the queen of King Malcolm III. She was canonized in 1251 for her rebuilding of the monastery at Iona and her benefactions to the church.

St. Marys Bay (Kings)   Between PANMURE ISLAND and the mainland. This place name was included in the Holland survey of 1765; however, it may well be the English translation of an earlier French designation.

St. Peters; St. Peters Bay (Kings) On the GULF OF ST. LAWRENCE. It was here, in 1719, that the first unofficial French settlement began with the arrival of two sailors, Francis Douville and Charles Carpentier, from Normandy. They had been shipwrecked farther to the east, at NAUFRAGE. Named Havre St-Pierre in 1721 by Louis Denys de la Ronde (1675–1741), for Louis-Hyacinthe

Castel, Comte de Saint-Pierre, director general of the Compagnie de l'Île Saint-Jean, who was charged with development of the colony from 1719 to 1724. Unfortunately for both the company and France, the Comte de Saint-Pierre 'was a courtier greedy for profit rather than a colonizer,' and eventually the company went bankrupt. Despite these difficulties, the Havre St-Pierre area flourished because of its strategic location as a fishing station. The population in the de la Roque census of 1752 was 63 families, with a total of 353 people. In 1758 all were to suffer deportation, and the village of Havre St-Pierre was destroyed. Prior to the expulsion, the bell of the parish church was buried for safe keeping, only to be rediscovered in 1871 by a farmer ploughing his field. The bell was repaired and now hangs in the church of Saint-Alexis, at ROLLO BAY. The area was resettled in the late eighteenth century by Scottish emigrants and returned Acadians. See *Dictionary of Canadian Biography* III, 176–9.

St. Peters Bay   *See* St. Peters.

St. Peters Island (Queens)   In HILLSBOROUGH BAY. This is one of the oldest place names on the south coast of the province. The name Île St. Pierre was assigned by Robert David Gotteville de Bellisle (fl. 1696–1724) for Louis-Hyacinthe Castel, Comte de Saint Pierre. The name was rendered as 'île du Comte de St. Pierre' by Thomas Pichon in 1760, and later translated into English by Samuel Holland. See KEPPOCH, MacLEODS ISLAND, and ST. PETERS.

Saltgrass Point (Prince)   Extends into Sunbury Cove, an extension of NORTHUMBERLAND STRAIT. A descriptive for the grass known to botanists as *Spartina alterniflora*, which has been identified as the nucleus of the salt marsh. The plant has the ability to surmount the impact of the tide through a complex root system and, over time, has formed the basis for the salt marshes that dot the coastline of the Island. PRINCE COUNTY has a second Saltgrass Point, in Lot 12.

Salutation Cove (Prince) Between MacCallums Point and Graham Head. Named by Samuel Holland for an incident that occurred during the summer of 1765. A member of his survey crew, Lieutenant Peter Frederick Haldimand (1741–1765), ran out of food and supplies, only to be rescued by Holland at 'Salutation Cove.' The cove, in reality a large sandy inlet, is also known locally as 'Big Pond.' See also HALDIMAND RIVER.

Savage Harbour (Queens and Kings)   The village is on the boundary between the two counties; the harbour, as such, largely in KINGS. Known to the French as 'Havre aux Savages' for archaeological evidence of a battle fought prior to the arrival of Europeans. In 1744, Bellin records *Havre à l'Anguille* (Eel Harbour); however, this name did not last. On a tour of the Island in 1786, Lieutenant-Governor Edmund Fanning wrote: 'At St. Peters is a well settled and fine country, where I remained for a few days and then proceeded to Scotch Savage harbour; opposite to which is French Savage harbour, very pleasantly situated villages.'

Scentia Road (Queens)   East of the VERNON RIVER. The French settlement of La Grand Ascension was noted by Samuel Holland as *Great Ascension Village*. The contemporary 'Scentia' Road is a corruption of the latter.

Scotchfort (Queens)   Northeast of TRACADIE, on the HILLSBOROUGH RIVER. Captain John MacDonald (1742–1810), the laird of Glenaladale and Glenfinnan, mortgaged his Scottish property to raise money to purchase lands in Prince Edward Island for the resettlement of needy emigrants. In the late spring of 1772, 210 emigrants, mainly from Uist and the Glenfinnan area, arrived in CHARLOTTETOWN aboard the *Alexander*. They proceeded up the Hillsborough River to the lands purchased by MacDonald. Here they found the ruins of a French fort which was to inspire the new name, 'Scotchfort.' A Celtic cross of Scottish granite stands at Scotchfort in remembrance of these pioneers. See also GLENFINNAN.

Seacow Head; Seacow Pond (Prince)   Seacow Pond is adjacent to the GULF OF ST. LAWRENCE, in Lot 1. The name is descriptive for the seacow or walrus which frequented the Gulf of St. Lawrence and NORTHUMBERLAND STRAIT in the seventeenth and early eighteenth centuries. Now practically extinct, it was described as 'a clumsy animal; with tusks like an elephant sometimes a yard in length. Often measures eighteen feet long and can weigh 2,000 pounds.' Seacow Head, in Lot 26 (sometimes called 'Salutation Point,' for the nearby cove), was so designated because early settlers found tusks of the seacow on the shore. Seacow Head lighthouse, erected in 1864, guards the entrance to BEDEQUE BAY. See also PORTAGE ISLAND, New Brunswick.

Seacow Pond   *See* Seacow Head.

Searletown (Prince)   North of BORDEN. Named for an early settler, James Searle, who was awarded the northern half of Lot 27 in 1767.

Sevenmile Bay (Prince)   An indentation of NORTHUMBERLAND STRAIT, stretching from SEACOW HEAD to BORDEN. The name is descriptive of the approximate distance between these two points.

Shipwreck Point   *See* Naufrage.

Short Point (Kings)   West of SHIPWRECK POINT, on the GULF OF ST. LAWRENCE. The name honours James Short (1710–1768), a famous Scottish optician who provided a telescope used in the 1765 Holland survey.

Sir Andrew Macphail Provincial Park (Queens)   On the ORWELL RIVER, at UIGG. The land was donated in 1961 by descendants of Sir Andrew Macphail (1864–1938) for use as a public park. Macphail was a native of ORWELL and a graduate of McGill University in medicine. He practised in Montreal, lectured at McGill, and was a medical officer during the First World War. He is best remembered as an author and social critic; his classic *The Master's Wife* was first published posthumously in 1939. It is 'a semi-autobiography, a statement of political and social philosophy, and as a document in Canada's social history is a book of rare richness' (Robertson 1977). Unfortunately, by the 1980s, the estate had fallen into disrepair, to be rescued by a group of concerned citizens, known as 'Friends of Macphail,' and later as the Macphail Foundation. This organization completed the restoration in 1993. The estate features a small conference centre, three nature trails, an ecological forestry project, a wildlife nursery, and an interpretation centre. All are projects which enhance the legacy of Sir Andrew Macphail. In 1993 the Institute of Island Studies issued a handsome third edition of *The Master's Wife*. It contains an important essay on Macphail by Dr. Ian Ross Robertson, native Islander and associate professor of history, Scarborough College, University of Toronto.

Skinners Pond (Prince)   In Lot 1, south of NAIL POND. There are two explanations for this name. It may be for a Captain Skinner, whose ship was reputedly wrecked on the coast near here, or a corrupted translation of an early Acadian name, Etang des Peaux, or 'Skin Pond.' Childhood home of singer and song writer 'Stompin'' Tom Connors.

Souris; Souris River (Kings)
The town is on COLVILLE BAY, into which the river flows. Early references to the name include *havre à la Souris* (Bellin 1744) and *Cap à la Soury* (de la Roque 1752). There is no scholarly agreement as to the precise origin of this name. It is known that, in the eighteenth century, the area was periodically infested with mice. This fact has given rise to the 'Mouse River' theory as an explanation for the name. However, Alan Rayburn suggests that it may well be a corruption of 'Havre à l'Echourie,' 'barred harbour,' a descriptive for the entrance to the Souris River. It is from this name that Havre à la Souris, and eventually Souris, may well have evolved. See SOUTH LAKE. There is a ferry service from Souris to the Magdalen Islands.

Souris River   *See* Souris.

South Lake (Kings)   Faces NORTHUMBERLAND STRAIT, Lot 47. Appears as the descriptive *havre de l'Echourie* in de la Roque 1752, and *havre de l'Escoussier* or *Echourie* in Pichon 1760. These are references to the fact that the lake is 'barred' from the ocean by a series of sand dunes. By the time of the *Meacham Atlas* in 1880, the prosaic name South Lake had become fixed.

Southport (Queens)   On the south side of the HILLSBOROUGH RIVER. First known as 'The Ferry,' and later as 'Charlottetown' or 'Hillsborough Ferry.' The descriptive name Southport was in popular usage by 1880. In 1995 it became part of the newly created town of STRATFORD.

Springfield (Queens)   Southeast of KENSINGTON, in Lot 67. A descriptive for the numerous springs on the hillside. Site of the well-known nineteenth-century Haslam's Tavern and Inn. In 1841 the presbytery of the Presbyterian Church of Prince Edward Island met at Haslam's.

Spry Point (Kings)   Adjacent to Durell Point, in Lot 56. Named in 1765 by Samuel Holland for Rear-Admiral Sir Richard Spry (1715–1775), who saw service at the siege and capture of Fortress Louisbourg in 1758. This seems more certain, as nearby Durell Point was named at the same time for Admiral Philip Durell (1706–1766), who was promoted to the rank of rear-admiral for his part in same engagement. Holland frequently juxtaposed related names. In 1766 Admiral Durell succeeded Admiral Colville in command of the North American station at HALIFAX. He died the same year and is buried in St. Paul's Church, Halifax.

Stanchel (Queens)   Southwest of the HUNTER RIVER, in Lot 67. In 1893 a public meeting was held to select a name for the new school section. When unanimity seemed impossible, the oldest resident, Mrs. Allan Nicholson, was asked in Gaelic, 'Will you not give us some name from the old county?' Her immediate reply was: 'I will give you the name of my birthplace, *Stenchol*, on the Isle of Skye' (Douglas). Over the years, there has been a slight lapse from the original Scottish spelling.

Stanhope (Queens)   On Covehead Bay. Named by Samuel Holland in 1765, for William Stanhope (1719–1779), Viscount Petersham and second Earl of Harrington. A cairn at the entrance to the Stanhope Golf Course marks the Scottish migration to Prince Edward Island. It is a smaller version of the monument at Culloden, Scotland. See also CULLODEN.

Stanley River (Queens)   Flows into NEW LONDON BAY. Named by Samuel Holland for Sir Hans Stanley (*ca* 1720–1780), who was serving as first lord of the Admiralty in 1765. Described by the *Dictionary of National Biography* as 'of unquestioned ability, but awkward in appearance, ungracious in manners and eccentric in his habits ... he never laughed ... he never married.' On 13 January 1780, Stanley committed suicide while on a visit to Earl Spencer (1758–1834) at Althorp, Northamptonshire. The latter is an ancestor of the present Princess of Wales. Stanley Bridge, known as 'Fifes Ferry' prior to the construction of the first highway bridge in 1855, takes its name from the river.

Stratford (Queens)   Southeast of CHARLOTTETOWN. Effective 1 April 1995, the communities of Bunbury, Southport, Cross Roads, Keppoch, Kinlock, and Battery Point were amalgamated to form the new town of Stratford. Previously a plebiscite was held to select a name for the new town. On the first ballot, the prosaic Waterview emerged as the winner over Stratford and Belhaven. A citizens' petition forced a second vote between Waterview and Stratford; this time the latter topped the polls. The name may be traced to a school section known as 'Stratford' or 'Stratford Road,' established in 1858.

Strathgartney (Queens)   Overlooks a panoramic view of the WEST RIVER. Robert Bruce Stewart (1813–?) emigrated from Scotland in 1846, settling on a ridge in Lot 30. He named his new home for Strathgartney, a valley in Perthshire, Scotland. The house still stands and is operated as an inn. A section of the original property is part of Strathgartney Provincial Park. The Strathgartney Nature Trail, 1.3 kilometres long, winds through a forested stand of beech, sugar maples, yellow birch, and a variety of softwood trees.

Sturgeon Bay; Sturgeon River (Kings)   East of MONTAGUE, on Highway 17. The name is a translation of the descriptive R. aux Esturgeons from the sturgeon found in the river during the French colonial period. Sturgeon River flows eastward into Sturgeon Bay.

Sturgeon River   *See* Sturgeon Bay.

Summerside (Prince)   On BEDEQUE BAY. Originally 'Green Shores Bedeque,' for the first settler, Daniel Green, a Quaker Loyalist from Pennsylvania. A wayside inn owned by his youngest son, Joseph, was to inspire a new name for the community. Colonel Henry Compton (see ST. ELEANORS) once travelled to Green Shores on a bitterly cold day. 'On approaching his destination, he found himself sheltered from the cruel blast, and as the sun emerged from the clouds he said: "It's like a summer side here."' Green was so captivated with Compton's remark that he placed the name on a sign over the front door. Eventually the postmaster, Patrick Power, suggested to postal authorities that 'Summerside' replace 'Green's Shore.' It was found to be appealing and not duplicated elsewhere, and so has remained (Robert Allan Rankin 1980). Eptek National Exhibition Centre, located on the restored Summerside waterfront, presents a year-round schedule of fine-arts, history, science, and craft exhibits. According to Robert Douglas, the Mi'kmaq *Eptek*, meaning 'the hot place,' was an early descriptive for BEDEQUE BAY. The centre is part of the PEI Museum and Heritage Foundation. The town also played an important role in the development of the silver-fox industry. The International Fox Museum and Hall of Fame traces the evolution of this industry, an important element in the economy of PRINCE COUNTY, from the 1890s through to the 1930s. By 1939 the bottom had fallen out of the market; then the Second World War intervened, and the silver-fox boom was over. Summerside was incorporated as a town in 1877 and achieved the status of a city in 1995. As a result of this legislation which came into effect 1 April 1995, Sherbrooke, St. Eleanors, and WILMOT were amalgamated with Summerside.

Tarantum (Queens)   West of GLENFINNAN, on Highway 215. The area was settled in 1772 by members of clan MacDonald. Earlier, another branch of the family had emigrated to France, where Alexandre MacDonald was born in 1765. He was created Duc de Tarente (for Taranto, in Latin *Tarentum*) in 1806. The place name was suggested by this title.

Tea Hill (Queens)   Southeast of CHARLOTTETOWN, in Lot 48. Variously explained by the presence of the Labrador tea shrub, the spilling of a load of tea, or the two roads that intersect at this point to form a 'T.' In the absence of documentation, the last is the most plausible theory. The hill provides a panoramic view of NORTHUMBERLAND STRAIT. Tea Hill Provincial Park is nearby.

Tenmile House (Queens)   Southeast of TRACADIE, on Highway 1. Named for the wayside inn built by Archibald Ross in 1868. So called because it was located 10 miles from CHARLOTTETOWN.

The Barachois   *See* Barachois Run.

The Fixed Link (Prince)   Upon completion, The Fixed Link between BORDEN POINT, Prince Edward Island, and CAPE JOURMAIN, New Brunswick, will, at

12.9 kilometres, be one of the longest such structures in the world. The bridge portion of the link, connecting two causeways from either side, is to be 40 metres off the water and 60 metres at the navigation span. Scheduled for opening in 1997, and with a reputed design life of a century, it will undoubtedly be formally named upon completion. For the present, the descriptive phrase 'The Fixed Link' has evolved as its unofficial name. To date there have been several facetious suggestions for naming the link: 'The Lucy Maud Montmotorway,' 'The Northumberland Cummerbund,' and 'The Bridge Over Troubled Lobsters' were among the names submitted to the 'Causeway Célèbre' contest conducted by the Toronto *Globe and Mail* in 1994.

Tignish; Tignish River (Prince) The river flows east into the GULF OF ST. LAWRENCE, in Lot 1. The name stems from the Mi'kmaq descriptive *Tedeneche* translated by William Francis Ganong as 'straight across,' a reference to the entrance to the river. Tignish, a largely Acadian town, was the home of Stanislaus Francis Poirier (1823–1898). In 1854 he was the first Acadian to be elected to the House of Assembly. His remarkable political career spanned forty-four years and the contesting of ten provincial elec-

tions, all successfully. He was elected to the House of Commons in 1874; defeated in 1878; re-elected in 1887 and 1891; defeated in 1896, but re-elected in a by-election in 1897. Early in his career he anglicized his name to 'Perry.' Charles Dalton (1850–1933), one of the founders of the silver-fox industry, was also a native of Tignish. A member of the Assembly (1912–19), he was named lieutenant-governor in 1930, serving until his death. In 1917 Dalton was knighted by Pope Benedict xv. See also OULTONS ISLAND.

Tignish River   *See* Tignish.

Tracadie; Tracadie Bay (Queens) Separated from the GULF OF ST. LAWRENCE by BLOOMING POINT, a sandspit 5 kilometres long. The name, common in all three Maritime provinces, is traceable to the Mi'kmaq descriptive *Tulakadik*, for 'camping ground.' It appears as *Tracadie* on the Bellin map of 1744. The Holland 1765 designation was *Bedford Bay* (for the fourth Duke of Bedford); *Tracadi Harbour* was listed as a secondary name. See also Nova Scotia and New Brunswick entries.

Tracadie Bay   *See* Tracadie.

Travellers Rest (Prince)   Northeast of SUMMERSIDE, in Lot 19. In the early nineteenth century, when there was but a bridle path from CHARLOTTETOWN to the west of the Island, the government erected log houses at regular intervals with a fireplace and a supply of dry wood for the convenience of the public. These were called 'traveller's rests.' Others were located on the ST. PETERS and TRYON roads. The PRINCE COUNTY location survives as an interesting place name.

Tryon; Tryon Head; Tryon River (Prince)   Tryon Head extends into NORTHUMBERLAND STRAIT, at Lot 28. The river was known as 'Rivière des Blonds' during the French colonial period (see also LORDS POND). The new name was bestowed by Samuel Holland in 1765, for William Tryon (1725–1788), named governor of North Carolina in 1761, and later, in 1771, to be transferred to the governorship of New York. Holland had served under him prior to 1765. CAPE TRYON, on the GULF OF ST. LAWRENCE, at the entrance to NEW LONDON BAY, was also named by Holland for William Tryon. Tryon in PRINCE COUNTY was the birthplace of Cornelius Howatt (1810–1895). A member of the Assembly from 1859 to 1876, Howatt was an unflinching opponent of the entry of Prince Edward Island into Confederation. On 26 March 1873, along with A.E.C. Holland, another Prince County MLA, he cast one of

the two dissenting votes against union with Canada. In the 1970s the name of Cornelius Howatt was resurrected in an organization dubbed 'The Brothers and Sisters of Cornelius Howatt.' It came into existence 'in reaction to the ostentatious nature of the official celebrations planned ... to mark the centenary of Prince Edward Island's becoming a province of Canada.' Its members felt that 'many of the issues [e.g., Island identity and independence] championed by Howatt were 'still topical in 1973 ... 1974 ... and in ...' The honourable member from Tryon would undoubtedly have been pleased. See Harry Baglole and David Weale, *Cornelius Howatt: Superstar!* (Summerside 1974).

Tryon Head   *See* Tryon.

Tryon River   *See* Tryon.

Tyne Valley (Prince)   On the Trout River, in Lot 13. Earlier names were Trout River and The Landing. The new name was put forward in 1874, for the River Tyne in northeast England.

Uigg (Queens)   Northeast of ORWELL CORNER, in a predominantly Scottish section of the county. Although named for Uig, on the Isle of Skye, it has always been spelled 'Uigg' on Prince

Edward Island. There are three other locations in Scotland named Uig, two in Inverness and one in Argyllshire.

Urbainville (Prince)   Northwest of SUMMERSIDE. Named for an early settler, Urbain Arsenault. Sometimes spelled 'Urbinville' in the nineteenth century but consistently 'Urbainville' since 1901.

Valleyfield (Queens)   On the QUEENS–KINGS county boundary. A descriptive selected by the Reverend Alexander Munroe, who, upon viewing the countryside, reputedly stated: 'It ought to be called Valleyfield.'

Vernon Bridge; Vernon River (Queens)   The river flows southwest into Orwell Bay. The name was assigned by Samuel Holland in 1765, for Admiral Sir Edward Vernon (1723–1794), a relative of Lord Orwell's (see ORWELL BAY). In 1740 Admiral Vernon earned an infamous niche in Royal Navy lore when he substituted watered-down rum for the neat spirit then issued to all ranks. For his efforts, he was nicknamed 'Old Grog,' after his coarse cloth 'grogam' coat. The name was subsequently transferred to the beverage. The tradition lasted until 31 July 1970, when the grog ration to all Royal Navy ratings ended.

Vernon River   *See* Vernon Bridge.

Victoria (Queens)   Southeast of CRAPAUD. The unique quality of this village has been summarized by the Reverend Robert C. Tuck: 'Most Prince Edward Island communities are strung out along roads or radiate like the spokes of a wheel at a crossroads. Victoria is different. It is compact, built on a rectangular grid of short streets ... by design on one family's farm to serve the agricultural communities on the Island's south shore as a seaport.' This 'seaport on a farm' was named for Queen Victoria, to mark her Silver Jubilee in 1862. Victoria Provincial Park is adjacent to the village. Victoria West, Prince County, and Victoria Cross, Kings County, also honour Queen Victoria.

Victoria Cross   *See* Victoria.

Victoria West   *See* Victoria.

Wellington (Prince)   On the GRAND RIVER, west of Highway 2. Named for the Duke of Wellington (1769–1852), hero of the Battle of Waterloo, 18 June 1815. See chapter 1, pages 26–7.

West Cape; West Point (Prince) On NORTHUMBERLAND STRAIT.

Both names are descriptive. West Cape is slightly less than 7 kilometres north of WEST POINT. The latter was named by J.F.W. DesBarres in 1779. The lighthouse was erected in 1875. It was manned until 1963 and is now open to the public as a museum and inn. Nearby is Cedar Dunes Provincial Park, so named because of a stand of eastern white cedar trees. In the winter of 1536–7, following Jacques Cartier's second voyage to the New World, many of his crew fell ill with what he described as 'a Great Sickness and Pestilence [scurvy].' Acting on the advice of the Amerindians, the sick were cured 'by drinking a tea made from twigs and needles of the white cedar tree which was rich in Vitamin C.'

West Point   *See* West Cape.

Westmorland River (Queens) Flows into NORTHUMBERLAND STRAIT, at Lot 29. Named Brocklesby River by Samuel Holland in 1765, for Richard Brocklesby (1722–1797), prominent eighteenth-century English physician. Alan Rayburn notes that it was later renamed 'for the Countess of Westmorland; the mother of Lady Fane who owned property there, which she visited in c1840.' See also LADY FANE.

West River (Queens)   Flows east into CHARLOTTETOWN harbour. The name is a descriptive which dates back to the French Rivière de l'Ouest. It survived an attempt by Samuel Holland to rename the feature after Edward Eliot (1727–1804), Lord Commissioner of Trade and Plantations, in 1760.

West Royalty (Queens)   As a result of legislation passed in 1994, this area is now formally part of the city of CHARLOTTE-TOWN. The name 'Royalty' is traceable to the domain set aside at the time of the founding of the city.

Wheatley River (Queens)   Flows northeast into RUSTICO BAY. First appears as *Whitley* on Samuel Holland's map of 1765, later as *Wheatly*, and finally as *Wheatley*. These changes are undoubtedly attributable to erratic penmanship, since the river was actually named for Thomas Whatley (?– 1772), secretary to the Treasury (1764–5) at the time of the Holland survey. Aside from his political career, Whatley is remembered in the *Dictionary of National Biography* as a 'literary student, and as an authority on Shakespeare and gardening. '

White Sands (Kings)   Between HIGH BANK and GUERNSEY COVE.

Descriptive. According to Captain Henry Bayfield, 'it was named from the sandy beach of a small bay.'

Wilmot; Wilmot River (Prince) The river flows into BEDEQUE BAY, east of SUMMERSIDE. Takes its name from Wilmot Cove, a name assigned by Samuel Holland in 1765. At this time Montagu Wilmot (?–1766) was lieutenant-governor of Nova Scotia and was thus honoured by the survey. In 1994 the village of Wilmot, on the north side of the river, became part of the new city of Summerside.

Wilmot River   *See* Wilmot.

Winsloe (Queens)   Northwest of CHARLOTTETOWN, on Highway 2. It was named for James Hodges Winslow, an early landowner in the area. 'Winslow' was the spelling until 1886. The community was amalgamated with Charlottetown in 1994.

Wood Islands (Kings)   Terminal for the Northumberland Ferry service, linking Prince Edward Island and Nova Scotia. Descriptive; a translation of the French name *I. à Bois*, on Franquet 1751. The Wood Islands Provincial Park is located near the ferry terminal, as is the Wood Island Lighthouse.

Wrights Creek (Queens)   Flows southeast into CHARLOTTETOWN harbour. Named for Thomas Wright (*ca* 1740–1812), who once owned land in the area. On 17 November 1775, two American privateers, the *Hancock* and the *Franklin*, from Marblehead, Massachusetts, raided Charlottetown. The town was ransacked, and several prisoners taken, including Phillips Callbeck (*ca* 1744–1790), administrator of the colony, and Thomas Wright (*ca* 1740–1812), the surveyor general. Wright, released later, was able on another occasion, to take legal revenge on the Americans. In 1797 the United States put forward the claim that the St. Croix River, mapped first by Champlain in 1604, was in reality the Magaguadavic, while Britain insisted that the river then called the Schoodic constituted the boundary. Wright was commissioned to conduct an investigation of the claims. Although Champlain's settlement had been abandoned nearly two centuries earlier, the foundations remained and were excavated by Wright, thus verifying the British claim. See also ST. CROIX RIVER, New Brunswick.

Yankee Hill (Queens)   In Lot 21, at NEW LONDON. According to local sources, 'the first store at the mouth of the harbour, within a stone's throw of the hill, was kept by a Yankee who sold supplies to Yankee fishermen.'

York Point (Queens)   Extends into CHARLOTTETOWN harbour, at the mouth of the NORTH RIVER.

Takes its name from the fact that the river was once named Yorke. The latter name was bestowed by Samuel Holland for John Yorke (1728–1769), Lord Commissioner of Trade and Plantations, in 1765.

Bibliographical Essay

Primary Sources

A complete bibliography for *Place Names of Atlantic Canada* would, of necessity, be unduly long. Therefore, this essay charts for the reader the major sources used in the research for and writing of this book. It will also serve to point the way for those who wish additional detail on the many and varied aspects of toponymy. Place names evolve because of a blend of influences that arise through the interplay of the land and the people. Why do some names survive centuries, while others immediately fall by the wayside? Why do so many campaigns to 'reform' place names fail? While these questions may not have immediate or easy anwers, it becomes clear, as one burrows deeper into the subject, that a complicated network of historical, geographical, and cultural forces are at work. Thus it is that toponymic research must, by its very nature, be interdisciplinary.

By far the largest amount of basic information for this book was gleaned from primary sources such as the official statutes, journals, sessional papers, and proceedings of the four provincial legislatures. Particularly for the period prior to the creation of the Geographic Board of Canada in 1897, these documents are an essential source concerning name changes. An important resource on the early charters and statutes relating to Newfoundland was Keith Matthews, ed., *Collection and Commentary on the Constitutional Laws of the 17th Century* (St. John's: Maritime History Group, Memorial University, 1975). Helpful as well were specialized government reports such as those compiled by provincial geologists and surveyors general. However, these official documents do not tell the whole story. Census reports and gazetteers, local and provincial directories, and publications of the Geographic Board of Canada were all essential tools. The files maintained by the Canadian Permanent Committee on Geographical Names (CPCGN) constituted one of the most important primary sources. I am greatly indebted to Ms Helen Kerfoot, Executive Secretary of the CPCGN, for her assistance and the many courtesies extended to an outside researcher. In addition, her predecessor, Alan Rayburn, was always willing to share his encyclopedic knowledge regarding regional place names. Smaller collections of primary source material in the form of personal papers, diaries, and travel accounts were consulted at the numerous libraries and archives mentioned in the preface to this volume.

Original maps for the earlier centuries are scattered all over western Europe, North America, and beyond. Fortunately there exist reproductions and commentaries relating to many of the most important maps. In attempting to solve the numerous cartographic riddles I relied heavily on William Inglis Morse, *Acadiensia Nova*, 2 vols. (London 1935); T.E. Layng, ed., *Sixteenth Century Maps Relating to Canada* (Ottawa 1956); D.G.G. Kerr, ed., *A Historical Atlas of Canada* (Toronto 1960); Bernard G. Hoffman, *Cabot to Cartier* (Toronto 1961); James A. Williamson, *The Cabot Voyages and Bristol Discovery* (Toronto 1964); W.F. Ganong, *Crucial Maps in the Early Cartography and Place-Nomenclature of the Atlantic Coast of Canada* (Toronto 1964); S.E. Morison, *The European Discovery of America*, 2 vols. (New York 1971); and Joan Dawson, *The Mapmakers' Edge: Nova Scotia through Early Maps* (Halifax 1988). *The Historical Atlas of Canada*: Vol. I *From Beginnings to 1800*; Vol. II *The Land Transformed, 1800–1891*; and Vol. III *Addressing the Twentieth Century*, were all essential aids in research. The Canadian Topographic Map Sheets, historical and contemporary provincial atlases, and CPCGN gazetteers were also used extensively. For coastal communities, editions of the Canadian Hydrographic Service publications such as the *Nova Scotia and Bay of Fundy Pilot* and *Newfoundland Pilot* were extremely helpful in providing information concerning coastal topography and navigational hazards. British Admiralty and Canadian hydrographic charts were also utilized upon occasion.

We are fortunate to have reasonably complete microfilm files of major Atlantic Canadian newspspers. When everything else fails, newspapers are often the answer in tracing name changes. Although they are indispensable, historian Peter Waite has drawn attention to one problem that inevitably ensues: Newspapers 'are a vast ocean of good and ill. In any case one can never be at an end with them. It is a field open to the enter-

prising and the valiant, and it will prove rewarding.' Individual newspapers are not listed here; however, their usage is reflected in many of
the entries scattered throughout the book.

Place-Name Studies

Anyone who delves into the place names of Atlantic Canada must take
into account that which has already been written on the subject. It is
worth recording that many of these specialized works, dating in some
instances from the late nineteenth and early twentieth centuries, are still
definitive. Looming over the research of all others is William Francis
Ganong (1864–1941). A botanist turned historian, Ganong devoted
much of his academic life to the study of the cartography and place
names of what is today Atlantic Canada. More particularly, his *A Monograph of the Place-Nomenclature of the Province of New Brunswick*, read
before the Royal Society of Canada on 19 May 1896, remains a standard
reference, not only on the place names of his native province, but also on
the principles of research in place nomenclature. Because of his overall
contribution to the field, Ganong can be forgiven one 'academic foible' –
namely, his long-standing effort to convince the world that John Cabot's
landfall was on Cape Breton Island.

The first systematic research on Newfoundland place names was
undertaken by the Reverend Michael Howley (1843–1914), who, like
Ganong, was a fellow of the Royal Society of Canada. We are indebted
to him for the preservation of much nineteenth-century information
concerning Newfoundland place names. During the course of his ecclesiastical rounds as Roman Catholic bishop, and later archbishop, Howley was constantly seeking information on place-name lore. Fortunately,
much of this field research was published in a series of articles in the
Newfoundland Quarterly from 1902 to 1914. Other Newfoundland clergy-
men, although not primarily interested in toponymy, made important
contributions to the field. Anglican archdeacon Edward Wix (1802–
1866) and Bishop Edward Feild (1801–1876) left behind fascinating
accounts of their travels which aid greatly in understanding life in
nineteenth-century Newfoundland. On the Methodist side, the Reverend James Lumsden (1854–1915) penned an intimate portrait of life in
the outports during the late nineteenth century. Much the same can be
said for the Reverend Patrick Browne's account of 'coasting' on the
Labrador in the early twentieth century. The voluminous writing of Sir
Wilfred Grenfell (1865–1940), and the work of historians D.W. Prowse

(1834–1913), W.G. Gosling (1863–1930), and H.W. LeMessurier (1848–1931), must also be mentioned in this context. The LeMessurier Papers housed at the Centre for Newfoundland Studies are also of special interest.

For all those who investigate Newfoundland place names, there are two advantages denied researchers in the other provinces. The first is the massive *Encyclopedia of Newfoundland and Labrador,* 5 vols. (St. John's 1981–95), the brain-child of former premier J.R. Smallwood (1900–1991) and the successor, or continuation, of his earlier *Book of Newfoundland,* 5 vols. (St. John's 1937–75). The final two volumes of the encyclopedia were published posthumously, in 1993 and 1995. This work contains a wealth of information concerning communities large and small throughout the province. The two-volume *Bibliography of Newfoundland* (Toronto 1986) begun by Agnes O'Dea (1911–1993) and edited by Anne Alexander is the second essential tool for anyone researching Newfoundlandia. It is to be hoped that one day similar bibliographies will appear for Nova Scotia, Prince Edward Island, and New Brunswick.

Although significant contributions were made by Thomas Chandler Haliburton (1796–1765), Joseph Howe (1804–1873), and the Reverend George Patterson (1824–1897), Nova Scotia had to wait until 1922 for the first formal treatment of its place names. Thomas J. Brown's *Nova Scotia Place Names* (Halifax 1922), while incomplete, remains an informative reference. In 1967 the Public Archives of Nova Scotia published Bruce Fergusson's *Place Names and Places of Nova Scotia.* Some of the toponymic information in this volume is dated, and the work is overshadowed by a pot-pourri of detail on 'places.' A local study by Watson Kirkconnell (1895–1977), *Place Names in Kings County, Nova Scotia* (Wolfville 1971), is a comprehensive guide to the toponymy of a single county. In the absence of other sources during nineteenth- and early-twentieth-century Nova Scotia, one has to turn to the many county and local histories published during this period. Among the most helpful were James F. More, *Queens County* (Halifax 1873); George Patterson, *Pictou County* (Montreal 1877); Israel Longworth, *Colchester County* (Halifax 1886); George S. Brown, *Yarmouth County* (Boston 1888); Mather Byles Des-Brisay, *Lunenburg County* (Halifax 1895); Harriet Cunningham Hart, *Guysborough County* (Windsor 1895); Arthur W.H. Eaton, *Kings County* (Salem 1910); Frank Patterson, *Tatamagouche* (Halifax 1917); and Raymond A. MacLean, ed., *History of Antigonish,* 2 vols. (Antigonish 1976). Two studies that are informative concerning the place names of the New England Planter–Loyalist period are John V. Duncanson's *Falmouth: A*

New England Township in Nova Scotia (Windsor, ON, 1965) and *Rawdon and Douglas: Two Loyalist Townships in Nova Scotia* (Belleville, ON, 1989). In the past, Cape Breton Island has not been covered by specialized toponymic studies. This has now changed with the investigative research being undertaken by historians associated with Fortress Louisbourg and the ground-breaking work of Professor William Davey at the University College of Cape Breton. For an example see his 'European Naming Patterns on Cape Breton Island,' *Omnastica Canadiana* 77/1 (June 1995), 35–59.

   In addition to the contributions of W.F. Ganong already cited, the work of two members of the Place Names Secretariat in Ottawa has served New Brunswick and Prince Edward Island well. Robert Douglas (1881–1930) was for many years secretary of the Geographic Board of Canada. In 1925 he published *Place Names of Prince Edward Island with Meanings*. As was the case with Thomas J. Brown on Nova Scotia, Douglas preserved much toponymic information that would otherwise have been lost. Later, in 1973, his lineal successor at the CPCGN, Alan Rayburn, published *Geographical Names of Prince Edward Island*. Based on careful field and archival research, Rayburn's book will remain, for years to come, a definitive study of the topic. Not content with covering one province, Rayburn went on to publish, in 1975, *Geographical Names of New Brunswick*. As with his previous volume, this work is also authoritative and complete. Equally comprehensive is the scholarly work by E.R. Seary (1908–1984), *Place Names of the Avalon Peninsula of Newfoundland* (Toronto 1971; see SEARY PEAK, Newfoundland). During the course of earlier research on Canadian place names, I had occasion to be in contact with Dr. Seary. In the true 'spirit of academe,' he was always helpful and unfailingly kind in providing assistance and advice. Since Seary's death, Dr. W. Gordon Handcock, of the Department of Geography at Memorial University, has entered the ranks, with several articles and specialized studies on Newfoundland toponymy. See also references cited below.

Historical Geography

There is an obvious linkage between the study of toponymy and historical geography. Since an understanding of settlement patterns is imperative in tracing the evolution of place names, it will come as no surprise that several secondary works in this field have been of considerable assistance. Andrew Hill Clark's *Three Centuries and The Island* (Toronto

1959) and his equally valuable *Acadia: The Geography of Early Nova Scotia* (Madison 1968) were never far from my desk. A select list of other important works includes: Neil MacNeil, *The Highland Heart of Nova Scotia* (London 1948); Charles W. Dunn, *Highland Settler: A Portrait of the Scottish Gael in Nova Scotia* (Toronto 1953); Helen I. Cowan, *British Emigration to British North America* (Toronto 1961); Winthrop Pickard Bell, *The Foreign Protestants and the Settlement of Nova Scotia* (Toronto 1961); Basil Greenhill and Ann Giffard, *Westcountrymen in Prince Edward's Isle* (Toronto 1967); Gillian T. Cell, *English Enterprise in Newfoundland, 1577–1660* (Toronto 1969); D. Campbell and R.A. MacLean, *Beyond the Atlantic Roar* (Toronto 1974); C. Grant Head, *Eighteenth-Century Newfoundland* (Toronto 1978); Graeme Wynn, *Timber Colony: A Historical Geography of Nineteenth-Century New Brunswick* (Toronto 1981); J.M. Bumsted, *The Peoples' Clearances: Highland Emigration to Nova Scotia* (Edinburgh 1982); Peter Thomas, *Strangers from a Secret Land* (Toronto 1986 a study of Welsh migration); Stephen Hornsby, *Nineteenth-Century Cape Breton: A Historical Geography* (Montreal 1993); and Daniel N. Paul, *We Were Not Savages: A Micmac Perspective on the Cultural Collision of European and Micmac Civilization* (Halifax 1993). Material touching upon settlement may also be found in publications of the Prince Edward Island Museum and Heritage Foundation; the Gorsebrook Research Institute, at St. Mary's University; the Centre for Planter Studies, at Acadia University, and the Centre for Canadian Studies, at Mount Allison University. In the same category and not to be overlooked are the numerous books and papers published by the Institute of Social and Economic Research, at Memorial University. John J. Mannion, ed., *The Peopling of Newfoundland: Essays in Historical Geography* (St. John's 1977) was especially useful. Particular attention is directed to essays by W. Gordon Handcock and John J. Mannion. In addition, W. Gordon Handcock's *So Longe as there comes noe women: Origins of English Settlement in Newfoundland* (St. John's 1989) not only effectively chronicles settlement patterns, but is indispensable in understanding the evolution of many Newfoundland communities.

Travel and Exploration

Throughout *Place Names of Atlantic Canada*, the comments of explorers, travellers, surveyors, and regional writers have been woven into the text. Not only do these firsthand accounts reveal significant points concerning place names, but their vivid and sometimes arresting prose lightens what might otherwise be factual but dull. The following examples, evocative of the far horizon of Atlantic Canadian toponymy, are also among the best in this group: Thomas Pichon, *Lettres et Mémoires pour servir à l'histoire naturelle, civile et politique du Cap Breton* (The Hague 1760); Joseph-Octave Plessis, *Journal de deux voyages apostoliques dans le golfe Saint-Laurent et les provinces d'en bas* (Québec 1865); W.F. Ganong, ed., *The Description and Natural History of the Coasts of North America by Nicolas Denys* (Toronto 1908); H.P. Biggar and W.L. Grant, ed., *Lescarbot's History of New France* II, (Toronto 1910); H.P. Biggar, ed., *The Works of Samuel de Champlain* (Toronto 1922); Ramsay Cook, ed., *The Voyages of Jacques Cartier* (Toronto 1993). At the provincial level the following were among the most important works consulted.

NEW BRUNSWICK: Thomas Baillie, *An Account of the Province of New Brunswick* (London 1832); Robert Cooney, *A Compendious History of ... Northern New Brunswick* (Halifax 1832); M.H. Perley, *A Handbook for Emigrants to New Brunswick* (Saint John 1854); W.O. Raymond, *The River St. John* (Sackville 1950); Esther Clark Wright, *The Miramichi* (Sackville 1944); *The Petitcodiac* (Sackville 1945), and *The St. John River and Its Tributaries* (Wolfville 1966); and Michael Collie, *New Brunswick* (Toronto 1974).

NEWFOUNDLAND AND LABRADOR: Charles W. Townsend, ed., *Captain George Cartwright and His Labrador Journal* (Boston 1911); Joseph B. Jukes, *Excursions In and Around Newfoundland, 1839–1840* (London 1842); William Epps Cormack, *Narrative of a Journey across the Island of Newfoundland* (London 1928); Väinö Tanner, *People and Cultures in Labrador*, 2 vols. (Helsinki 1939); Jean M. Murray, ed., *The Newfoundland Journal of Aaron Thomas, 1794–1795* (London 1968); Harold Horwood, *Newfoundland* (Toronto 1969); and Patrick O'Flaherty, *Come Near at Your Peril* (St. John's 1994).

NOVA SCOTIA: John Robinson and Thomas Rispin, *Journey through Nova Scotia* (York 1774); Joshua Marsden, *Narrative of a Mission to Nova Scotia* (Plymouth Dock 1816); Abraham Gesner, *The Industrial Resources of Nova Scotia* (Halifax 1849); Frederic F. Cozzens, *Acadia: A Month with the Bluenoses* (New York); Robert Hale, *Journal of a Voyage to Nova Scotia in 1731* (Essex Institute 1906); Clara Dennis, *Down in Nova Scotia* (Toronto 1934), *More about Nova Scotia* (Toronto 1938), and *Cape Breton Over* (Toronto 1942); Arthur Walworth, *Cape Breton, Isle of Romance* (Toronto 1948); and

M.G. Parks, ed., *Western and Eastern Rambles: Travel Sketches of Nova Scotia by Joseph Howe* (Toronto 1973).

PRINCE EDWARD ISLAND: D.C. Harvey, ed., *Thomas Curtis: A Narrative of a Voyage to the Island of St. Johns; Walter Johnstone: A Series of Letters Descriptive of Prince Edward Island* (Toronto 1955); John Stewart, *An Account of Prince Edward Island* (London 1806); and Helen J. Champion, *Over on The Island* (Toronto 1939).

SURVEYS AND SURVEYORS: The journals and records of the principal surveyors provide a rich source of information concerning the toponymy of Atlantic Canada. Detailed references will be given for the most significant of these. During the summer of 1714, Captain William Taverner (1680–1768), a native Newfoundlander, carried out an important survey of a portion of the colony's south coast. Portions were reprinted in the *Newfoundland Quarterly* 3 (1995). Although the north Atlantic survey of Captain James Cook (1728–1779) has been overshadowed by later exploits in the Pacific, he left a significant imprint on Newfoundland place names. As his chief biographer, R.A. Skelton (1906–1970), suggests: 'Between Cook's practice in bestowing new place names in Newfoundland and the Pacific, there are repeated parallels and echoes.' Many of these are pointed out in the entries for locations named by Cook. The basic reference is J.C. Beaglehole, ed., *Journals of Captain Cook on His Voyage of Discovery*, 4 vols. (Cambridge 1955–74), published for the Hakluyt Society. See also R.A. Skelton, *Captain Cook after 200 Years* [A Commemorative Address before the Hakluyt Society] (London 1969); also his *James Cook: Surveyor of Newfoundland* (San Francisco 1965). The best overview of Cook's Newfoundland surveys is found in W.H. Whiteley, *James Cook in Newfoundland, 1762–1767* (St. John's 1975). In 1764 Samuel Holland completed a survey of St. John's Island (Prince Edward Island) and, in the following year, Cape Breton Island (for highlights of his career see entry for HOLLAND COVE). In addition to Volume V of the *Dictionary of Canadian Biography*, see D.C. Harvey, ed., *Holland's Description of Cape Breton Island and Other Documents* (Halifax 1935). The crowning achievement of J.F.W. DesBarres's (1721?–1824) long career was undoubtedly *The Atlantic Neptune*, published by him, on behalf of the Admiralty, during 1774–84. It contains a collection of charts that covered the eastern seaboard from New England to the Gulf of St. Lawrence. Included within this work is Holland's map of 'The Southeast coast of the Island of St. John.' *The Atlantic Neptune* is important not only for its maps but also for a series of sketches of the coastline. Note also J.F.W. DesBarres, *Nautical Remarks and Observations on the Coasts and Harbours of Nova Scotia* (London 1778). A major biography has been written by G.D.N. Evans: *Uncommon Obdurate: The Several Public Careers of J.F.W. DesBarres* (Toronto 1969). For a more recent assessment, note the DesBarres bicentennial issue of *The Nova Scotia Historical Review* 5/2 (1985). In 1984 and 1986 the Champlain Society published a two-volume edition of the journals of Captain Henry Bayfield (1795–1885). See Ruth Mckenzie, ed., *The Survey Journals of Captain Henry Bayfield*, Vol. II (Toronto 1986). Bayfield was responsible for surveys of the coasts of Labrador, Prince Edward Island, Cape Breton, Sable Island, and the Nova Scotian coastline from Halifax to Canso.

General Studies

PERIODICALS: No attempt is made in this select bibliography to list the hundreds of articles consulted during the writing of *Place Names of Atlantic Canada*. Some of the most important are cited in chapter 1, and others are mentioned throughout the remaining four chapters. The reader is especially directed to the references in the notes to chapter 1, many of which are not repeated here. One example of important information to be found primarily in periodical literature is the reference to the Basque impact on Atlantic Canadian toponymy (see page 36. n.16). For the reader wishing to pursue place-name study and its many related topics, the following list of periodicals may be of assistance. The most important is *Omnastica Canadiana*, the journal of the Canadian Society for the Study of Names. Papers presented at the CSSN conference, held each spring at the Learned Societies, are often printed here. The American equivalent, *Names*, the journal of the American Name Society, occasionally contains articles of direct interest to Canadians. *Canoma*, published by the Secretariat, Canadian Permanent Committee on Geographical Names, features items on all aspects of toponymy. It also keeps readers up to date on CPCGN decisions and developments within the committee and the secretariat. At the national level, the official Canadian journals of all disciplines with a bearing on toponymy – cartography, history, folklore, geography, linguistics, etc. – were consulted. Among the many regional journals that might be cited, the following were the most significant: *Acadiensis*; *Revue de l'Université de Moncton*; *Revue de la Société historique du Madawaska*; *Nova Scotia Historical Review*; *Collections Nova Scotia Historical Society*; *The Cape Breton Magazine*; *Collec-*

tions New Brunswick Historical Society; The Island Magazine; Newfoundland Studies; and *Newfoundland Quarterly.*

LOCAL AND REGIONAL STUDIES: It should be noted that the volumes listed below are but a sampling of the local and regional studies found to be of help in researching Atlantic Canadian toponymy. In 1967 William F.E. Morley published *The Atlantic Provinces: Local Histories to 1950.* It contained 123 tightly packed pages of references to local histories written in the region. If a revised version were to be issued today, the number of listings would easily double. During the research for this book, community histories in the hundreds – good, bad, and indifferent – were consulted. Whatever their merits, they *are* important for the insight they provide on local themes, and for the treasures that are there for the searching. A most encouraging sign is the overall improvement, in recent years, in the writing of such studies. Instead of citing a selection from among the vast number mentioned, I single out the following as worthy exemplars of this genre: Grace Helen Mowat, *The Diverting History of a Loyalist Town: A Portrait of St. Andrews* (Fredericton 1953); Allan Rankin, *Down at the Shore: A History of Summerside* (Summerside 1980); and Marion Robertson, *Kings Bounty: A History of Early Shelburne* (Halifax 1983). The history of the larger cities has not been well covered. There are two exceptions: Paul O'Neil, *The History of St. John's,* 2 vols. (Erin, ON, 1975–6), and T.W. Acheson, *Saint John: The Making of a Colonial Community* (Toronto 1985). Both the expulsion of the Acadians and the coming of the Loyalists have inspired numbers of books. The most balanced interpretation of Acadian history will be found in the work of Naomi E.S. Griffith: *The Acadian Deportation* (Toronto 1969); *The Acadians: Creation of a People* (Toronto 1973); and *Contexts of Acadian History* (Montreal 1991). For an excellent summary account, see Griffith's extended essay in Volume IV of the *Dictionary of Canadian Biography.* Also informative are Jean Daigle, ed., *The Acadians of the Maritimes* (Moncton 1982), and Bona Arsenault, *Histoire des Acadiens* (Montreal 1994). Esther Clark Wright still reigns as the leading authority on New Brunswick Loyalists: see *The Loyalists of New Brunswick* (Wolfville 1973). An important bibliography of Loyalist Nova Scotia, *A Loyalist Guide: Nova Scotia Loyalists and Their Documents,* was published by the Public Archives of Nova Scotia in 1983. Other valuable references of a more general nature are Harold A. Innis, *The Cod Fisheries* (Toronto 1954); J.M. Beck, *The Government of Nova Scotia* (Toronto 1957); A.A. Johnston, *A History of the Catholic Church in Eastern Nova Scotia,* 2 vols. (Antigonish

1960, 1972); Judith Fingard, *The Anglican Design in Nova Scotia, 1783–1816* (London 1972); Brian Cuthbertson, *Johnny Bluenose at the Polls* (Halifax 1994); L.C. Callbeck, *The Cradle of Confederation* (Fredericton 1964); F.W. Bolger, *Canada's Smallest Province: A History of Prince Edward Island* (Charlottetown 1973); W.S. McNutt, *New Brunswick: A History* (Toronto 1963); S.J.R. Noel, *Politics in Newfoundland* (Toronto 1971); Peter Neary, *Newfoundland in the North Atlantic World* (Montreal 1988); and Malcolm MacLeod, *Kindred Countries: Canada and Newfoundland before Confederation* (Ottawa 1994). Panoramic overviews of regional history may be found in W.S. McNutt, *The Atlantic Provinces: The Emergence of a Colonial Society* (Toronto 1965); two co-publications of Acadiensis Press and University of Toronto Press: *The Atlantic Region to Confederation* (1994) and *The Atlantic Provinces in Confederation* (1993); and Peter Neary, ed., *White Tie and Decorations: Sir John and Lady Hope Simpson in Newfoundland, 1934–1936* (Toronto 1996).

DICTIONARIES AND REFERENCE WORKS: Language dictionaries and specialized dictionaries of many kinds were consulted throughout the research and writing of *Place Names of Atlantic Canada*. The most basic and essential was the *Oxford English Dictionary*, 20 vols. (Oxford 1989). Others ranged all the way from *The Oxford Dictionary of Saints* (Oxford 1979) to *A Dictionary of Historical Slang* (London 1972); from *Brewer's Dictionary of Phrase and Fable* (London 1990) to *The Mariner's Dictionary* (New York 1982). Two regional dictionaries became constant companions: G.M. Story, W.J. Kirwin, and J.D.A. Widdowson, eds., *Dictionary of Newfoundland English* (Toronto 1982), and T.K. Pratt, *Dictionary of Prince Edward Island English* (Toronto 1988). These latter volumes are soon to be joined by a dictionary of Cape Breton English, currently under compilation by Professor William Davey and others at the University College of Cape Breton.

Although Alan Rayburn's recent *Naming Canada* (Toronto 1994) takes a popular approach, it is an important resource on regional toponymy. My own *Macmillan Book of Canadian Place Names*, 2d ed. (Toronto 1983) was used, not so much for information, but for the filing cabinet of regional material compiled during its writing. Since many Atlantic Canadian place names may be traced to the United States, George R. Stewart's *American Place Names: A Concise Dictionary* (New York 1970) became another essential reference. Information concerning the meaning of aboriginal names was drawn largely from Silas T. Rand, *Micmac Place Names in the Atlantic Provinces* (Ottawa 1919); E.P. Wheeler, *List of*

Labrador Eskimo Place Names (Ottawa 1953), and F.H. Eckstrom, *Indian Place Names ... of the Maine Coast* (Orono 1974). Other linguistic works cited by Ganong and Rayburn were used for comparative purposes. Occasionally throughout the text mention is made of literature that is evocative of a particular place or time. Two important references were Carl F. Klinck, ed., *Literary History of Canada* (Toronto 1970), and Janice Kulyk Keefer, *Under Eastern Eyes: A Critical Reading of Maritime Fiction* (Toronto 1987). By far the most indispensable reference for checking names, spelling, dates, factual information, and the most up-to-date scholarship was the *Dictionary of Canadian Biography*, 13 vols. (Toronto 1966–95). So essential is this magisterial work that those who write on any Canadian topic cannot afford to be without it.

My final note of acknowledgment does not deal with the printed word. For more than a decade it was my privilege to teach in the Canadian Studies Programme at Mount Allison University. Over the years students from all corners of Atlantic Canada and beyond were enrolled in these interdisciplinary courses. Much that transpired in seminar discussion and debate has found its way into this book, and I extend thanks to all those students who contributed to an understanding of both the commonality and the diversity of Atlantic Canadian history and culture.